Culture and National Identity in Republican Rome

Erich S. Gruen

Cornell University Press

Ithaca, New York

First published 1992 by Cornell University Press.
First printing, Cornell Paperbacks, 1994.

Library of Congress Cataloging-in-Publication Data
Gruen, Erich S.
    Culture and national identity in Republican Rome / Erich S. Gruen.
      p.   cm. — (Cornell studies in classical philology ; v. 52. The Townsend lectures)
    Includes bibliographical references and index.
    ISBN 0-8014-2759-2. — ISBN 0-8014-8041-8 (pbk.)
    1. Rome—Civilization.   2. Rome—Civilization—Greek influences.
I. Title.   II. Series: Cornell studies in classical philology ; v. 52.   III. Series:
Cornell studies in classical philology.   Townsend lectures.
DG77.G78   1992
937—dc20
                                                                    92-52756

Printed in the United States of America

⊗ The paper in this book meets the minimum requirements of
the American National Standard for Information Sciences–
Permanence of Paper for Printed Library Materials, ANSI Z39.48-1984.

Manibus patris

CONTENTS

ILLUSTRATIONS

PREFACE

Writing a preface always brings a sense of relief. The principal labors have been discharged, and it remains only to express gratitude to those who have assisted and encouraged the project. The latter duty, while pleasant and welcome, also carries the burden of inadequacy. A large number of persons have helped to advance or improve this work, often inadvertently and unknowingly; only a portion of them can be registered here.

Stimulus for the book came first from the Classics Department at Cornell University. They paid me the signal honor of an invitation to deliver the Townsend Lectures in the spring semester of 1991, a challenging and exciting opportunity. Happily, they also provided a grace period of a few years. Presentation of ideas and circulation of drafts during the interval brought useful reactions and allowed for intermittent progress. The bracing atmosphere of graduate seminars in Berkeley and Princeton subjected several of the preliminary notions to severe scrutiny. And then the Guggenheim Foundation, through the generous award of a second fellowship, made it possible for me to have a year of uninterrupted research and writing in 1989/1990. Much of the book took shape in the hospitable confines of the American Academy in Rome and the Institute of Classical Studies in London. That invaluable interlude allowed me to arrive in Ithaca with a manuscript in hand. Responses to the lectures from colleagues at Cornell provoked further rethinking and revisions. The final product owes much to many.

Several friends and colleagues commented on draft chapters,

prompting needed improvements. I note with gratitude the generous advice of Timothy Cornell, Arthur Eckstein, Elaine Fantham, Sander Goldberg, Nicholas Horsfall, Jerzy Linderski, Miranda Marvin, Niall Rudd, Andrew Stewart, Peter Wiseman, and Paul Zanker. A special debt is owed to the expertise and searching criticisms of Ann Kuttner. Exchanges with graduate students in seminars sharpened a number of the ideas. I thank, in particular, Anthony Corbeill, Alison Futrell, Christopher Hallett, and Kenneth Lapatin. The Cornell community bestowed warmth and hospitality well beyond the call of duty. It would be quite impossible to name all those who contributed to the pleasures of that semester in Ithaca. Some of them also left their mark on the manuscript (though they might not recognize or acknowledge it): Frederick Ahl, Jacqueline Collins-Clinton, Judith Ginsburg, David Mankin, Pietro Pucci, Jeffrey Rusten, Danuta Shanzer, Barry Strauss, Abby Westerveld, and Jane Whitehead.

Three persons in particular came to my aid in the last stages. Anthony Bulloch provided advice at a crucial time on matters of the computer. Preparation of the final manuscript owes much to the energy and intelligence of Alison Futrell. Peter Wyetzner's proofreading caught numerous errors. And much of the index stands to his credit.

E.S.G.

ABBREVIATIONS

AHB	*Ancient History Bulletin*
AION	*Annali dell' Istituto Universitario Orientale di Napoli*
AJA	*American Journal of Archaeology*
AJP	*American Journal of Philology*
AnnPisa	*Scuola Normale Superiore, Pisa. Annali, Lettere, Storia e Filosofia*
AnnUnivCagliari	*Università di Cagliari, Facoltà di Lettere e Filosofia, Annali*
ANRW	*Aufstieg und Niedergang der römischen Welt*
AntCl	*L'Antiquité Classique*
AR	*Archaeological Reports*
Arch Delt	*Ἀρχαιολογικὸν Δελτίον*
Arch. v. Religionswiss.	*Archiv für Religionswissenschaft*
ArchAnz	*Archäologische Anzeiger*
ArchStorMessinese	*Archivio Storico Messinese*
AthMitt	*Mitteilungen des Deutschen Archäologischen Instituts (Athens)*
AttiAccad d'Italia	*Atti dell'Accademia d'Italia*
AttiAccadTorino	*Atti dell'Accademia delle Scienze di Torino*
BAGB	*Bulletin de l'Association Guillaume Budé*
BCH	*Bulletin de Correspondance Hellénique*
BICS	*Bulletin of the Institute of Classical Studies of the University of London*
BullComm	*Bullettino della Commissione Archeologica Comunale in Roma*
CA	*Classical Antiquity*
CJ	*Classical Journal*
ContrIstStorAnt	*Contributi dell'Istituto di storia antica dell'Università del Sacro Cuore*

ABBREVIATIONS

CP	Classical Philology
CQ	Classical Quarterly
CR	Classical Review
CRAI	Comptes rendus de l'Académie des Inscriptions et Belles-Lettres
CSCA	California Studies in Classical Antiquity
DialArch	Dialoghi di Archeologia
EMC	Échos du Monde Classique
FondHardt	Entretiens Fondation Hardt
HSCP	Harvard Studies in Classical Philology
JbRGZ	Jahrbuch des Römisch-Germanischen Zentralmuseums
JdI	Jahrbuch des Deutschen Archäologischen Instituts
JHS	Journal of Hellenic Studies
JOAI	Jahreshefte des Österreichischen Archäologischen Instituts
JPhilol	Journal of Philology
JRS	Journal of Roman Studies
LCM	Liverpool Classical Monthly
LEC	Les Études Classiques
LIMC	Lexicon Iconographicum Mythologiae Classicae
MdI	Mitteilungen des Deutschen Archäologischen Instituts (Rom)
MEFRA	Mélanges d'Archéologie et d'Histoire de l'École Française de Rome
MemAccadPatav	Memorie dell' Accademia Patavia
MH	Museum Helveticum. Revue suisse pour l'Étude de l'Antiquité classique
NJbb	Neue Jahrbücher für Wissenschaft und Jugendbildung
NotSc	Notizie degli Scavi di Antichità
PBSR	Papers of the British School at Rome
PCPS	Proceedings of the Cambridge Philological Society
Philol	Philologus
PP	La Parola del Passato
Proc. Amer. Philos. Soc.	Proceedings of the American Philosophical Society
QuadStor	Quaderni di Storia
QuadUrb	Quaderni Urbinati di cultura classica
RE	Paulys Realencyclopädie der classischen Altertumswissenschaft
REA	Revue des Études Anciennes
REL	Revue des Études Latines
RendAccadLinc	Rendiconti della Classe di Scienze morali, storiche e filologiche dell'Accademia dei Lincei
RendIstLomb	Rendiconti dell'Istituto Lombardo
RendPontAcc	Rendiconti della Pontificia Accademia di Archeologia
RendPontAccadArch	Rendiconti della Pontificia Accademia di Archeologia
RevBelge	Revue Belge de Philologie et d'Histoire
RhM	Rheinisches Museum
RivCultClassMed	Rivista di Cultura classica e medioevale
RivFilol	Rivista di Filologia e di Istruzione Classica

ABBREVIATIONS

RivIstArch	*Rivista dell'Istituto Nazionale di Archeologia e Storia dell'Arte*
RivStorAnt	*Rivista Storica dell'Antichità*
RSI	*Rivista Storica Italiana*
SCI	*Scripta Classica Israelica*
SitzHeid	*Sitzungsberichte der Heidelberger Akademie der Wissenschaften, Philosophisch-Historische Klasse*
StudItalFilolClass	*Studi Italiani di Filologia Classica*
TAPA	*Transactions of the American Philological Association*
Wiss. Zeitschr. der Humboldt-Universität zu Berlin	*Wissenschaftliche Zeitschrift der Humboldt-Universität zu Berlin, Gesellschafts und Sprachwissenschaftliche Reihe*
WS	*Wiener Studien*
YCS	*Yale Classical Studies*
ZPE	*Zeitschrift für Papyrologie und Epigraphik*

Culture and National Identity
in Republican Rome

INTRODUCTION

The topic embarked upon here is fascinating but formidable. Few experiences in antiquity had more resonant or enduring effects than the encounter of Rome with the legacy of the Greek East. One can trace influence and impact from nearly the beginnings of Roman history. But the pivotal time came when circumstances called forth a form of collective introspection, when the Roman elite felt compelled to articulate national values and to shape a distinctive character for their own corporate persona. The process cannot, of course, be confined to precise chronological limits. It occupied much of the third and second centuries B.C., the period to which this book largely devotes itself, but it could, in certain aspects, be readily extended in either direction. The expansion of Roman authority into the sphere of Hellas prompted a profound reappraisal of national responsibilities—a reappraisal that transcended the bounds of politics, power, and imperial dominion. The Romans strove to establish their place in the cultural world of the Mediterranean.

The lure of Hellenism stirred the consciousness of Rome's leaders in this era, driving them to a new plane of self-awareness. The reaction was complex, enigmatic, and dissonant. Roman *nobiles* projected themselves as custodians of the nation's principles, champions of its characteristic virtues, and guardians of the *mos maiorum*. Yet these very same *nobiles* were the persons most drawn to Greek literary achievements, religion, and visual arts. Hellenic culture challenged and intimidated them—even when it proved irresistible.

This book partly builds upon and extends themes traced in a previous

[1]

work, *Studies in Greek Culture and Roman Policy* (Leiden, 1990). The latter explored some particular episodes that illustrate the transformation of Hellenic cultural traditions on the Roman public scene: for instance, installation of the cult of Magna Mater from Asia Minor at a critical time in the Hannibalic War, persecution of the Bacchic worship to promote the collective ascendancy of the Roman ruling class, government encouragement of early Latin poetry as celebratory of national values, the plays of Plautus as a vehicle for conveying Roman attitudes toward Hellenism, and the simultaneous repression of Greek professors and cultivation of their subjects in the training of the young. A central theme runs through those topics: the intersection of cultural activity and state interest.

The present work endeavors to broaden and deepen the investigation. It pursues its subject beyond manipulation of the Hellenic legacy for the public and political purposes of Rome. The goal is to comprehend Rome's groping toward cultural maturity and self-definition. Each chapter has its own rationale and constitutes an independent entity. All, however, address in some fashion the lengthy and often tortuous process through which Romans gradually came to terms with a culture that both fascinated and deeply troubled them—one that they affected to scorn but in fact assimilated and absorbed.

The relationship between Hellenism and Roman cultural evolution is complex and entangled. Scholarship conventionally concentrates on a familiar issue: the extent to which Roman intellectual achievements depended on Greek models and inspiration rather than on the well-springs of native soil. The pages that follow train their focus elsewhere, on the confrontation itself, its meaning and implications. The phenomenon has received a variety of characterizations: a love-hate relationship, the working out of an inferiority complex, a creative tension. But labels mislead and oversimplify. Collective psychologizing is suspect, and the idea of a tense and anxious association that endured for well over a century strains the imagination. A different approach would be salutary. This book strives to probe past paradox toward some resolution. Its principal aim is to understand the relationship not simply as tense and discordant but as an evolving process through which the Romans shaped their own values and gained a sense of their distinctiveness.

The endeavor begins with a matter of fundamental importance to the Roman image: the development of the legend of Trojan origins. The legend emanated in a bewildering variety of versions, invented by Greek intellectuals, modified by Sicilian historians, and eventually adapted by the Romans themselves. The chapter on this topic explores the vicissitudes the tale underwent at the hands of Hellenic and Roman writers before it took the familiar form canonized by Vergil's *Aeneid*. Inquiry proceeds into when, how, and to what purpose the Romans embraced the story and into the part it played in their own emerging self-consciousness. Acceptance of a Trojan rather than a Greek derivation reveals a sense of special place in the complex of inherited traditions. And manipulation of the legend in international diplomacy allows insight into the image Rome projected in the Mediterranean world.

Cato the Censor holds the next place in the discussion. Traditionally cast as a cranky conservative, he presents, in the general conception, the archetypal paradox. He was a fierce critic of Greek culture and denouncer of Greeks and at the same time widely read in Greek literature and profoundly influenced by Hellenic intellectual traditions. Interpreters have either subordinated one side of Cato to the other or abandoned the matter as irreconcilable contradiction. Yet Cato represents a central figure for understanding Roman attitudes toward Hellenism. To reckon him as a schizophrenic or as tortured by a divided soul has little plausibility and affords little advance. This chapter undertakes to surmount the impasse. Cato's critiques of Greek oratory, philosophy, and institutions were neither random nor irrational. They constituted a deliberate design that drew out the distinctive character and superior strain in the Latin achievement. Cato is here reinterpreted as a subtle and sophisticated thinker who played a pivotal role in elevating the self-esteem of his countrymen.

The reception of Greek art forms the topic of the third chapter. A common misconception brands Romans as boorish louts who indiscriminately snatched Greek masterpieces as spoils to display the might of the conqueror. Ancients lamented the moral decline that came with showy opulence, and moderns rebuke the conqueror for neglect of the aesthetic value and religious character of captured art treasures. The facts are quite different. Roman interest in and appreciation of art had a much more refined edge. The Romans rededicated cult images, acknowledged the separate spheres of public and private art and of sacred and secular representations, promoted sculptors and painters, and encouraged creative work to celebrate achievement or distinction. Artistic treasures from the Hellenic world served to enhance the civic and religious institutions of Roman society and to advertise them as cultural beacons to the Mediterranean.

[3]

Admiration for Greek art and cultivation of Greek artists transformed the appearance of Roman public life. But this development renders more acute the question of where, if anywhere, lay a distinctive Roman contribution in the realm of art. The fourth chapter addresses that question—or, more particularly, the Romans' perception of their distinctive contribution. It concentrates on selective monuments and styles commonly reckoned as conveying a special Roman character, namely, historical reliefs and veristic portraiture. The genres, however, need to be seen in close conjunction with Hellenistic conventions. Insofar as the Romans succeeded in transmitting special qualities it was by directing Greek artists and adapting Greek forms to convey a Roman character within a Hellenistic context.

From visual arts the book moves to dramatic arts. This topic, too, requires selectivity, with no pretense at exhaustive coverage. The chapter treats neither the literary features of the drama nor the architectural features of the theater. Its subject lies at the intersection of political, social, and cultural history, centering upon the era of transition from Plautine to Terentian comedy. Drama gained considerable popularity in this period, becoming a public activity of highly conspicuous form combining entertainment with religious celebration and civic function. A number of controversial and interconnected matters come under scrutiny here: the role of the theater in the promotion of political careers, the relationship of playwright to backers and supporters, the implications of segregated seating arrangements, the tenacious resistance to the building of a stone theater, and the level of taste and understanding that could be expected of a Roman theatergoing audience. Treatment of these ostensibly disparate issues in combination yields the outline of a more general pattern: employment of the drama as part of an aristocratic cultural strategy.

The sixth chapter takes on the broader topic of philhellenism in the circles of the Roman nobility. Attitudes of the leadership seem, on the face of it, riddled with ambiguities and inconsistencies, simultaneously welcoming and resisting the legacy of Hellas. Romans learned Greek, adopted Greek cults, and associated their past with Hellenic traditions, while also frowning on Greek character, expelling Greek intellectuals, and mocking Hellenic pretensions. The phenomenon is not to be explained by postulating party differences or feelings of collective inferiority. Closer study reveals a fundamental consistency and continuity. Roman command of the Greek language and familiarity with Greek conventions and institutions combined with a drive to distinguish Roman from Greek qualities, thereby permitting the westerner both to expropriate and to subordinate the Hellenic heritage.

By the later second century the Roman elite had established its place and asserted its superiority in the sphere of high culture. But a narrow line separated pride from pretentiousness. In the age of the Gracchi and Marius, tensions and upheavals cast a harsher light upon the nobility. Cultivation seemed more like affectation. The circumstances helped to promote an art form that was distinctively Roman: satire. The fiercely independent poet Lucilius, pioneer in the genre, furnishes an appropriate coda to this book. His satires not only illuminate contemporary Roman politics and society; they mock moralism and puncture pomposity. Lucilius incisively penetrated the cultural crusade of the *nobilitas*, ridiculing its excesses and exposing its foibles. A new age had dawned with the coming of the late Republic. The posture of the privileged seemed increasingly anomalous and antique—a suitable stimulus for satire.

[1]

THE MAKING OF THE
TROJAN LEGEND

The canonical tradition on Rome's origins had taken firm root by the age of Augustus. As the orthodox tale had it, the city derived from a settlement of Trojan refugees, adversaries of the Greeks, remnants of a people defeated by the Achaean expedition that sacked Troy. Survivors of that calamity, under the leadership of the intrepid hero Aeneas, made their way west, suffered hardships and detours, and eventually reached the shores of Italy. There they faced still further struggles with the indigenous inhabitants before establishing themselves on a permanent basis. The progeny of Aeneas ultimately effected the founding of Rome—via Lavinium and Alba Longa, and after many generations. That story, at least in essentials, held sway in the Augustan era, enshrined in Vergil's epic and endorsed in Livy's history.

Yet the tale did not commend itself to everyone—even in the *saecula aurea* of Caesar Augustus. Some Greek intellectuals demurred. Eager as they were to assure themselves a place in the larger world of the Roman Empire, they felt discomfort with the idea that Rome owed her beginnings to a people perceived as the preeminent foe of Hellas. The geographer Strabo dissented, citing the authority of Homer to the effect that Aeneas never left the Troad. And he noted other versions, such as the local tale at Skepsis that had Aeneas found a dynasty there or the legends that brought him either to Macedonian Olympus or to Arcadia.[1] Each

1. Strabo, 13.1.53 (C607–608).

of them posed an implicit challenge to the doctrine that made Italy the destination of the Trojans.

But the doctrine dominated. The rhetorician and historian Dionysius of Halicarnassus conceded its validity but reinterpreted its meaning. He took as his mission the demonstration of Rome's Hellenic origins. Indeed, for Dionysius, Rome is a Greek city many times over. Successive bands of Hellenic transplants peopled the peninsula. Aborigines, coming from Arcadia, drove out the Sicels. Then the Pelasgians arrived from Argos via Thessaly.[2] There followed a band of Arcadian colonizers under Evander, sixty years before the Trojan War, who occupied a hill near the Tiber and named it Pallantium, after their own Arcadian home town, thus to account for the later appellation of Palatine.[3] That saga, however, told only part of the tale. The legends of Heracles served Dionysius' purposes as well. The great Greek hero made a detour to Italy on his way home from Spain, fought some successful battles, married the daughter of Evander, and left both offspring and a garrison to help mold the future of the peninsula.[4]

Dionysius could now turn to Aeneas. The Trojan leader's role in Rome's beginnings was too well entrenched to be discarded or ignored. So Dionysius did the next best thing: he made Aeneas a Greek. The Trojans, in his reconstruction, stemmed from the Peloponnesus, from Dardanus, son of Zeus and member of the ruling house of Arcadia. Dardanus led out an expedition after his native land had been devastated by flood and eventually settled in the Troad.[5] That tradition stands in sharp contrast to the account retailed by Vergil, who claimed that Dardanus, ancestor of the Trojans, came from Etruria. The race of Aeneas held Italy as its *patria*. By leading his compatriots to those shores, Aeneas returned to the land of his forefathers.[6] Dionysius rejects

2. Dion. Hal. 1.60.3, 1.89.1–2. On the traditions that brought the Pelasgians to Italy, see now the exhaustive study of D. Briquel, *Les Pélasges en Italie* (Paris, 1984), passim.

3. Dion. Hal. 1.31, 1.60.3, 1.89.2.

4. Dion. Hal. 1.41–44.

5. Dion. Hal. 1.60–61. This version of Dardanus' origin not only circulated among Greek writers but had the authority of Varro; Servius, *Ad Aen.* 3.167, 7.207.

6. Vergil, *Aen.* 1.378–380: *sum pius Aeneas . . . / Italiam quaeso patriam*; 3.94–96, 3.167–168, 7.206–207, 7.240. That Vergil fabricated the idea of Dardanus' Italian heritage was argued by V. Buchheit, *Vergil über die Sendung Roms* (Heidelberg, 1963), 151–166; persuasively questioned by N. Horsfall, *JRS*, 63 (1973), 74–79, now in J. N. Bremmer and N. M. Horsfall, eds., *Roman Myth and Mythography* (London, 1987), 99–104. Note the Etruscan inscription from North Africa in which settlers from Etruria, probably in the early first century B.C., associate themselves with Dardanii; J. Heurgon, *Scripta varia* (Brussels, 1986), 433–447.

the idea altogether. In his text, when Aeneas reaches Italy and confronts Latinus, with both armies drawn up to contest for supremacy in Italy, the Trojan declares unequivocally: "We are Trojans by race, inhabitants of one of the most celebrated cities of the Greeks."[7] Latinus' gracious response duly laid the basis for reconciliation between the forces of the two peoples: "I have a soft spot for the whole Hellenic race."[8] As Dionysius characterized the Trojans, "One would find no people more ancient or more Greek."[9] So Aeneas is a Greek.

Dionysius, as is clear, engaged in Hellenic overkill, swamping Rome with repeated waves of eastern immigrants to confirm its role as torchbearer for Greek civilization. He even goes so far as having Romulus defend the rape of the Sabine women by assuring the victims that this was an ancient Hellenic practice.[10] But then Dionysius was fighting a rearguard action in the age of Augustus—a time when Rome's non-Greek, Trojan origins ranked as orthodoxy.[11]

It had not always been so. Nor was Dionysius by any means the first to insist upon the Hellenic sources of Roman history. Reports of Greek expatriates making their way to Italian shores recur with frequency in Greek literature and historiography, combined in complex and diverse ways with legends on the founding of Rome. The fact deserves emphasis: a strong and tenacious Greek component exists in the fabric of tales surrounding Rome's origins. That component may, in fact, be earlier than the Aeneas story. And it retained vitality well beyond the emergence and development of that story. How did this happen and what does it mean?

An appropriate starting point can be detected: the age of overseas

7. Dion. Hal. 1.58.2: ἡμεῖς γένος μὲν Τρῶές ἐσμεν, πόλεως δὲ οὐ τῆς ἀφανεστάτης ἐν Ἕλλησιν ἐγενόμεθα.

8. Dion. Hal. 1.58.5: ἀλλ' ἔγωγε εὔνοιάν τε πρὸς ἅπαν τὸ Ἑλληνικὸν γένος ἔχω.

9. Dion. Hal. 1.89.2: τούτων γὰρ ἂν οὐδὲν εὕροι τῶν ἐθνῶν οὔτε ἀρχαιότερον οὔτε Ἑλληνικώτερον.

10. Dion. Hal. 2.30.5: Ἑλληνικόν τε καὶ ἀρχαῖον ἀποφαίνων τὸ ἔθος.

11. It does not follow that Dionysius was consciously reacting against anti-Greek prejudice among the Romans, as is inferred by H. Hill, *JRS*, 51 (1961), 88–93; similarly, P. Toohey, *Arethusa*, 17 (1984), 9–12. E. Gabba, *RSI*, 71 (1959), 365–368, believes Dionysius sought to combat a Greek historiographical tradition hostile to Rome and to provide a justification for the Roman empire. P. M. Martin, *MEFRA*, 101 (1989), 113–142, has a similar view. The matter is examined now *in extenso* by Gabba, *Dionysius and the History of Archaic Rome* (Berkeley, Calif., 1991), passim; especially, 1–22, 93–118, 191–200.

colonization. That era naturally sparked an interest in the West. Greeks, in characteristic fashion, inclined to interpret the western past in light of their own national traditions. Ancient tales of voyagers and migrants took on renewed vigor as anticipation of or justification for colonizing activity. The circumstances would naturally call attention to such legends as the western adventures of Heracles or the settler-heroes of the *Nostoi*—most particularly the wanderings of Odysseus. The West was the special sphere of Odysseus. The Homeric *Odyssey* contains several references to Sicily and southern Italy.[12] The hero reappears regularly in stories of western settlement and in connection with Greek colonization.[13] Those traditions eventually connected with legends on the origins of Rome.

An important and intriguing item occurs very early in the record. The concluding lines of Hesiod's *Theogony* register the union of Odysseus and Circe, which produced as offspring Agrius and Latinus, future rulers over the Tyrrhenians.[14] The passage has noteworthy implications. Debate continues on the precise specification of the term "Tyrrhenians," the significance of "Agrius," and the date of the passage. The *Theogony* as such probably dates to the late eighth century, but the concluding appendix most likely represents a later insertion. Etruscans, it has been argued, would hardly have entered Greek consciousness before the sixth century: hence an allusion to that people and to an association with Latium belongs no earlier.[15] But that theory presupposes a strict designation that would be uncharacteristic of early Greek writers on Italy. The Greeks, in fact, used the term "Tyrrhenoi" loosely and broadly, sometimes as equivalent to Pelasgians, sometimes to encompass Latins, Umbrians, and Ausonians.[16] Encounters with Italian peoples, including those of Etruria and Latium, through commercial contact and Greek settlements, extend back to the eighth century and

---

12. Homer, *Odyssey*, 1.182, 20.383, 24.211, 307, 366, 389.

13. See J. Bérard, *La colonisation grecque de l'Italie méridionale et de la Sicile²* (Paris, 1957), 303–322; E. D. Phillips, *JHS*, 73 (1953), 53–55, 64–66; cf. L. Pearson, *YCS*, 24 (1975), 178–180.

14. [Hesiod], *Theog.* 1011–1016: Κίρκη δ' Ἠελίου θυγάτηρ Ὑπεριονίδαο / γείνατ' Ὀδυσσῆος ταλασίφρονος ἐν φιλότητι / Ἄγριον ἠδὲ Λατῖνον ἀμύμονά τε κρατερόν τε. / οἳ δή τοι μάλα τῆλε μυχῷ νήσων ἱεράων / πᾶσιν Τυρσηνοῖσιν ἀγακλειτοῖσιν ἄνασσον.

15. E. Wikén, *Die Kunde der Hellenen von dem Lande und den Völkern der Apenninenhalbinsel bis 300 v. Chr.* (Lund, 1937), 76–77; M. Durante, *PP*, 6 (1951), 216; M. L. West, *Hesiod: Theogony* (Oxford, 1966), 435–436.

16. Dion. Hal. 1.29.1–2.

may find reflection here.[17] The name Agrius remains problematic, possibly an equivalent of Faunus or of Silvius, both figures in the mythical genealogy of ancient Latium.[18] "Latinus," in any case, points to a location with adequate specificity. Whether the Hesiodic lines belong in the seventh or sixth century, they disclose Hellenic interest in central Italy, possibly Etruria and certainly Latium, and the introduction of those lands into the Greek legendary complex. And most significant, Odysseus takes the role of ultimate ancestor to the rulers of those regions. The passage appropriately exemplifies the Greek penchant for reshaping foreign experiences by imposing Hellenic lore.

A long time would pass before Rome itself attracted the attention of Greek intellectuals; just how long no one can specify. Rome captured Veii at the beginning of the fourth century, thus achieving superior power in Latium and Etruria. As Rome entered into relations with the Greek cities of Campania in the mid–fourth century, Hellenic writers took notice of the town previously just on the margins of their consciousness. And when they did, they claimed the site, as so often, for Hellas. Heracleides Ponticus, philosopher, scientist, and pupil of Plato, writing in the mid–fourth century, referred to Rome simply as a "Greek city."[19] The matter seemed straightforward and uncomplicated. Greeks assumed that all cities of stature could be traced to Hellenic roots. Once the assumption is made, invention follows—and an effort to incorporate the origins within the matrix of Greek legend.

The school of Aristotle had a hand in shaping the tales—or rather some of the tales. Aristotle himself endorsed a version that had Achaean, not Trojan, warriors driven by storm to Italy while trying to return home after the fall of Troy. They got no farther. In an act of defiance the Trojan women brought as captives burned the ships. The stranded Achaeans had to remain in Italy and took up permanent residence at a site Aristotle called Latinium.[20] Aristotle's pupil Heracleides Lembos sharpened the identification. He noted that Achaeans returning from Troy were shipwrecked in Italy and made their way to the point on

17. Cf. Phillips, *JHS*, 73 (1953), 55–56; G. Dury-Moyaers, *Énée et Lavinium* (Brussels, 1981), 39–41; T. P. Wiseman, *JRS*, 79 (1989), 131–132. See, in general, the collection of papers, with archaeological testimony, in *PP*, 32 (1977), passim, and *PP*, 36 (1981).

18. See F. Altheim, *A History of Roman Religion* (London, 1938), 214–216; Durante, *PP*, 6 (1951), 216–217; A. Alföldi, *Early Rome and the Latins* (Ann Arbor, Mich., 1965), 238–239; Dury-Moyaers, *Énée et Lavinium*, 43–44.

19. Plut. *Cam*. 22.2: πόλιν Ἑλληνίδα Ῥώμην.

20. Dion. Hal. 1.72.3–4.

the Tiber where now sits Rome, and there they settled when Trojan captives, instigated by a certain Rhome or Rhomes, set their vessels ablaze.[21] So Greek intellectuals stretched the legends attaching to the fall of Troy to extend to the origins of Rome. But this rendition, as is clear, gave Achaeans, not Trojans, credit for settling the site at its beginning.[22]

The notion of Rome as Greek in character and lineage earned widespread credence. Plutarch, in his life of Romulus, conveys a bewildering variety of accounts of how Rome derived its name. One postulated a certain Rhome, daughter of Telephus, the son of Heracles. Another pointed to Rhomanos, son of Odysseus and Circe. Still another suggested Rhomos, sent from Troy by Diomedes. And yet one other named Rhome, granddaughter of Telemachus, and thus descendant of Odysseus.[23] These reconstructions by no means exhaust the extant versions, or even those transmitted by Plutarch, but they indicate both the diversity and the tenacity of tales that presume a Greek derivation. The same holds for the variant retailed by Xenagoras, perhaps in the early third century. He recorded three sons of Odysseus and Circe: Rhomos, Anteias, and Ardeias, the founders, respectively, of the Latin towns, Rome, Antium, and Ardea.[24] Xenagoras' conjecture, however mechanical, suggests a quickened interest among Greeks in the cities of Latium. The fabricated genealogies, despite divergences and inconsistencies, underscore the persistence with which Greek writers ascribed Hellenic descent to Rome. That conviction can be illustrated by a quite different story. Alexander the Great and, after him, Demetrius Poliorcetes, it is reported, remonstrated with the Romans for failure to check Etruscan piracy, which harassed Greek possessions. Demetrius appealed to the Romans for collaboration on the grounds of common kinship with the Greeks.[25]

21. Festus, 329, L. The tale of incendiarism itself had several variants; cf. Dion. Hal. 1.52.4; Plut. *Rom.* 1.2; *Virt. Mul.* 1; Strabo, 6.1.14 (C264); Vergil, *Aen.* 5.613. But Heracleides' text is the first extant one to attach Rhome as chief arsonist to the foundation of the city; see E. J. Bickermann, *CP*, 47 (1952), 78, n. 14; T. J. Cornell, *PCPS*, 201 (1975), 18; N. Horsfall, *CQ*, 29 (1979), 381–382; F. Solmsen, *HSCP*, 90 (1986), 102–107.

22. Still another pupil of Aristotle, the learned Theophrastus, was reportedly the first non-Roman to write with some care about Roman affairs; Pliny, *NH*, 3.57. What he said and how much remain unknown. We cannot be sure even that he dealt with the origins of the city.

23. Plut. *Rom.* 2.1, 2.3.

24. Dion. Hal. 1.72.5. Xenagoras' date is quite uncertain. See F. Gisinger, *RE*, 9A.2 (1967), 1410–1411, n. 1; Cornell, *PCPS*, 201 (1975), 20–21, with good bibliography.

25. Strabo, 5.3.5 (C232): διὰ τὴν πρὸς τοὺς Ἕλληνας συγγένειαν. Cf. L. Braccesi, *Alessandro e i Romani* (Bologna, 1975), 47–72.

None of this, to be sure, shows any deep or abiding curiosity about Rome by Greek intellectuals. The first Greek writer even to provide a sketch of early Roman history, we are told, was Hieronymus of Cardia in the first half of the third century.[26] What it does show is a familiar form of Hellenic intellectual imperialism, a spinning out of tales in accord with Greek legends, and ascription of foreign cities to Greek founders.[27]

Aeneas' part in the legend was, of course, as much a Greek creation as Odysseus', but it may have come later—and been slow to gain ascendancy. A formidable obstacle stood in the way: the authority of Homer. In book 20 of the *Iliad*, Poseidon predicts that "the might of Aeneas and the sons of his sons shall rule over Trojans."[28] Much the same statement recurs in the *Homeric Hymn to Aphrodite*. The goddess here forecasts for Anchises the glorious future of his progeny: his son and descendants will reign among Trojans.[29] That forecast would seem to preclude western migration on the part of Aeneas, or at least to discourage speculation along those lines. The Homeric verses, it may be inferred, represent prevailing opinion on the subject in archaic Greece.[30]

Indeed, they remained a formidable stumbling block for long thereafter. When the link between Aeneas and the origins of Rome had been forged, the Homeric lines became an embarrassment. Greek writers expended considerable energy to reinterpret or to explain them away. Some tried to reconcile the traditions by postulating two men named Aeneas, one of whom went to Italy, while the other remained in the Troad. A different version had Aeneas bring the Trojans to Italy and then return to the Troad to reign there and turn the kingdom over to his son.[31] A third effort sought to evade the implications of the Homeric lines through emendation of the text. By altering Homer's Τρώεσσιν to πάντεσσιν, the emender would have Aeneas and his progeny exercise universal rule, a retrospective anticipation of the Roman Empire.[32] The

26. Dion. Hal. 1.6.1.

27. Cf. Bickermann, *CP*, 47 (1952), 65–81.

28. Homer, *Iliad*, 20.307–308: νῦν δὲ δὴ Αἰνείαο βίη Τρώεσσιν ἀνάξει / καὶ παίδων παῖδες, τοί κεν μετόπισθε γένωνται.

29. Hom. *Hymn Aphr.* 5.196–197: σοὶ δ' ἔσται φίλος υἱὸς ὅς ἐν Τρώεσσιν ἀνάξει / καὶ παῖδες παίδεσσι διαμπερὲς ἐκγεγάονται.

30. Nothing in the epic cycle suggests western movement by Aeneas or his offspring; cf. Horsfall, *CQ*, 29 (1979), 373–375; Dury-Moyaers, *Énée et Lavinium*, 37–38; P. M. Smith, *HSCP*, 85 (1981), 25–28.

31. Dion. Hal. 1.53.4.

32. Strabo, 13.1.53 (C608); cf. Vergil, *Aen.* 3.97–98.

resort to emendation itself implies that the natural reading of the passage interfered with the development of the Trojan legend to explain the origins of Rome. The incongruity continued to trouble writers as late as the end of the Republic and the era of Augustus. Strabo, in fact, appealed to Homer as powerful testimony against those who would have Aeneas reach the land of Italy and perish there.[33] Dionysius of Halicarnassus acknowledged the force of those lines and felt obliged to offer an exegesis: "rule over Trojans" could mean "rule over Trojans in Italy"—hardly what Homer had in mind. Dionysius thus held to the text but also saved the legend.[34] It is plain enough from the refutations and rationalizations that the most obvious reading of the text still caused discomfort several centuries after Homer. At the time of the composition of the *Iliad* and the Homeric hymns, the tale of Aeneas' adventures in Italy had evidently not yet obtained a foothold. And given the authority of Homer, its acceptance would be some time in coming.

A possible fragment of the sixth-century Sicilian poet Stesichorus suggests that the story might be in formation in his day. The evidence comes from the Tabula Iliaca Capitolina, a carved relief of the Augustan period, combining scenes from the *Iliad* and later poems of the epic cycle.[35] The central panel includes a representation of Aeneas carrying Anchises who holds the household gods, leading Ascanius, and being guided by Hermes. The hero is evidently departing from Troy. An inscription, which describes the scene, cites the *Iliupersis* of Stesichorus and reports that Aeneas is heading εἰς τὴν Ἑσπερίαν.[36] Does this constitute evidence that the Trojan legend of Rome's foundation was already circulating in the sixth century?

The authority of this text has more than once been called into question. Discrepancies exist between the scenes depicted on the relief and

33. Strabo, 13.1.53 (C608). Strabo's inference that the Homeric text definitively leaves Aeneas in Troy, however, is inaccurate. A. Momigliano, *Settimo contributo alla storia degli studi classici e del mondo antico* (Rome, 1984), 443, misleadingly suggests that the message of the Homeric poems unambiguously excludes emigration by Aeneas or his descendants.

34. Dion. Hal. 1.53.4–5. That interpretation, of course, may not have been original with Dionysius.

35. See A. Sadurska, *Les Tables Iliaques* (Warsaw, 1964), 24–37. The purpose of those representations has been much debated: as classroom aids for schoolchildren, as votive offerings, or as labeled objets d'art for the newly rich. N. Horsfall, *JHS*, 99 (1979), 31–35, makes a strong case for the last alternative; see also W. McLeod, *TAPA*, 115 (1985), 153–165.

36. Stesichorus, *FGH*, 840 F6b: Ἰλίου Πέρσις κατὰ Στησίχορον . . . Αἰνείας σὺν τοῖς ἰδίοις ἀπαίρων εἰς τὴν Ἑσπερίαν.

the extant fragments of Stesichorus. The term ἑσπερία does not otherwise appear in Greek literature before Apollonius Rhodius. And Dionysius of Halicarnassus, who knew Stesichorus' work well, cited forty-six authors on Aeneas' travels—but never Stesichorus. Hence, it has been maintained, the inscription as well as the pictorial representations reflect knowlege of the *Aeneid*, and cannot convey genuine Stesichorus.[37] The skepticism is salutary but excessive. The relief certainly mirrors the understanding and expectations of the Augustan era, and the wording need not accurately reproduce Stesichorus' lines, but a citation of that poet could hardly have come out of the blue. Some basis for it should exist. The *Iliupersis* of Stesichorus, however garbled and contaminated, gave reason for its use as a caption for the carved relief.[38] But even if the fragment be taken as given, it does not bring Aeneas to Italy, let alone to Rome. That limitation may help to explain why his version is ignored by Dionysius. The most that can be inferred is that the tradition known to Stesichorus had Aeneas migrate westward.

That itself, however, is significant. Stesichorus came from Himera in Sicily. For western Greeks, the stories of heroic wanderers after the Trojan War held special appeal. It would not be unreasonable to suppose that Sicilian writers cultivated the tale of Trojans voyaging west. By the late fifth century Sicilian traditions have Trojans reaching their island.

The fact is attested by the best of authorities. Thucydides reports the tradition that after the fall of Ilium, Trojan fugitives crossed the seas to Sicily, where they settled, took the name of Elymaeans, and founded the cities of Eryx and Segesta.[39] Aeneas receives no mention in this text.

---

37. J. Perret, *Les origines de la légende troyenne de Rome (231–81)* (Paris, 1942), 84–89, 110–115, 306–309; Horsfall, *JHS*, 99 (1979), 35–43; idem, *CQ*, 29 (1979), 375–376; F. Castagnoli, *Studi Romani*, 30 (1982), 7–8.

38. See, *inter alios*, P. Boyancé, *Études sur la religion romaine* (Rome, 1972), 1160; G. K. Galinsky, *Aeneas, Sicily, and Rome* (Princeton, N.J., 1969), 106–113; Dury-Moyaers, *Énée et Lavinium*, 48–53.

39. Thuc. 6.2.3; cf. Paus. 5.25.6. Thucydides' source is generally taken to be Antiochus of Syracuse; K. J. Dover, in A. W. Gomme, A. Andrewes, K. J. Dover, *A Historical Commentary on Thucydides* (Oxford, 1970), IV, 199–202; questioned by Solmsen, *HSCP*, 90 (1986), 97; K. J. Rigsby, *CQ*, 37 (1987), 334. But there is no good reason to doubt that his data ultimately derived from Sicilian traditions. In addition to Trojan migrations Thucydides speaks of "Phocians" sailing from Troy and driven by storm first to Libya, then to Sicily. Rigsby, 332–335, proposes emendation to "Phrygians," thus suggesting that Thucydides followed the Homeric distinction between Trojans and Phrygians from Troy. But that would be at variance with customary fifth-century usage that amalgamated the two terms—and it is hardly an obvious correction.

His entrance into the tale may come later.[40] But there seems little doubt that the inventiveness of Sicilian writers either created or amplified narratives of Trojan travels. They served as pivotal transmitters and formulators.[41]

The Greeks of Sicily, we may safely surmise, maintained contact with fellow nationals in Italy—and with major developments in the peninsula. Those developments increasingly involved Rome. As Romans expanded influence into the Greek-speaking areas of Italy in the fourth century, they thereby provided the impetus for foundation stories fitted into the complex web of Hellenic legend.

Sicilian historians were instrumental in promoting and entangling the tradition. Alcimus composed a work on the antiquities of Sicily and Italy, perhaps in the later fourth century.[42] He provides what may be the earliest extant notice that actually associates Aeneas with the founding of Rome. Alcimus considers Aeneas and Tyrrhenia the parents of Romulus, who then fathered Alba, and she in turn gave birth to Rhomus, who founded the city and gave it his name.[43] It would be faulty to conclude from the non-Greek name Romulus that Alcimus obtained his story from Rome itself, thus reflecting the city's native traditions. Romulus, in his version, is not a twin, or even the city's founder. Alcimus' reconstruction arises from Rome's preeminence in Latium and Etruria, and supplies a Trojan lineage as explanation.[44]

A different and equally involved genealogy comes from another Sicilian author: Callias, historian of Agathocles, the Syracusan ruler, at the beginning of the third century. Callias does not include Aeneas in

40. Certainly he became a central figure in Sicily in subsequent generations. For Cicero, *Verr.* 2.4.33, Aeneas himself was founder of Egesta. A cult of Aphrodite Aeneias at Eryx, and a temple to Aeneas at Egesta existed by the end of the Republic; Dion. Hal. 1.53.1. But no firm evidence allows for a confident dating of their creation. Cf. Galinsky, *Aeneas, Sicily, and Rome*, 63–70.

41. The thesis of J. Perret, in *Mélanges offerts à Jacques Heurgon*, II (Rome, 1976), 791–803, that these tales stem from Athenian justification of imperialist ventures and the rivalries stimulated among Greeks, is farfetched and implausible.

42. The date is, unfortunately, not secure; Perret, *Les origines*, 386–387; Cornell, *PCPS*, 201 (1975), 7, n. 1.

43. Festus, 326, 328, L: *Alcimus ait, Tyrrhenia Aeneae natum filium Romulum fuisse, atque eo ortam Albam Aeneae neptem, cuius filius nomine Rhodius condiderit urbem Romam.* The emendation of Rhomus for Rhodius is plausible and generally acknowledged. On Alcimus' tale, see the contrasting interpretations of Cornell, *PCPS*, 201 (1975), 6; and D. Musti, *Gli Etruschi e Roma* (Rome, 1981), 26–28.

44. Despite Momigliano, *Settimo contributo*, 441, this is not evidence for the way in which Romans expected themselves to be perceived.

the family tree, but he does have a Trojan woman, Rhome, who marries Latinus, and whose sons Romus, Romulus, (and Telegonus) found the city and name it after her.[45] Greek ingenuity played a vital role in the fashioning of Italian legend.

Tales of Trojan origins, however, by no means drove out putative Hellenic ancestors. The traditions overlapped, became amalgamated, and emerged in bewildering blends. The eponymous creations (characteristically invented by Greeks)—Rhome, Rhomos, Romanos—appear in multiple manifestations. Most are undatable either absolutely or relatively. Certain writers, as already noted, gave Rhome solid Greek lineage as daughter or granddaughter of Heracles, Telemachus, or Odysseus. Others made her wife of Aeneas or Ascanius, or granddaughter of Aeneas. Comparable conceptions had Rhomanos as son of Odysseus, Rhomos as son of Aeneas or Ascanius or Emathion or even Zeus. Still others compounded the eponyms: Rhome as wife of Latinus or daughter of Italus, Rhomos as son of Italus and grandson of Latinus.[46] The Hellenic component, however, was rarely absent. Even Latinus had Greek roots: he was son of Telemachus and grandson of Odysseus in one version, son of Odysseus and Circe in another, son of Heracles in a third.[47]

The amalgamation of diverse strands seems especially lively in the late fourth and early third centuries. In that era the school of Aristotle took an interest in the sources of western settlement, and Sicilian writers reinterpreted Hellenic traditions in light of Rome's burgeoning role in Italy. It was probably the period when Xenagoras attached the offspring of Odysseus and Circe to the foundation stories of Rome, Ardea, and Antium.[48] And it may well be the period that produced a

---

45. Dion. Hal. 1.72.5; Festus, 329, L, who gives Caltinus for Callias. C. J. Classen, *Historia*, 12 (1963), 448–463, argues from the names Rhomos and Rhomylos that Alcimus and Callias must have been working with Latin traditions. But the formulation and elaboration are plainly Greek.

46. Plut. *Rom.* 2.1–3; Dion. Hal. 1.72.6; Festus, 326, 328, L; Servius, *Ad Aen.* 1.273; cf. Bickermann, *CP*, 47 (1952), 67; Cornell, *PCPS*, 201 (1975), 17–18. The story of Rhome as Aeneas' granddaughter is ascribed to Agathocles, a Cyzicene historian; Festus, 328, L; cf. Cornell, 19, with bibliography. On Rhome, see R. E. Mitchell, *Illinois Classical Studies*, 1 (1976), 70–82, as against A. Alföldi, *Die trojanischen Urahnen der Römer* (Basel, 1957), 9–34. On subsequent Greek etymological interpretations of the name Roma, see I. Opelt, *Philologus*, 109 (1965), 47–56.

47. Plut. *Rom.* 2.3; Servius, *Ad Aen.* 1.273; Hyginus, 127; Dion. Hal. 1.44.3.

48. See above, n. 24.

particularly bizarre linking of traditions—one that combined the voyages of Odysseus and Aeneas.

The tale requires scrutiny. It has Aeneas come to Italy from Epirus, together with Odysseus, and become founder of the city, which he designated as Rome, taking the name from one of the Trojan women who set fire to the ships.[49] Whence derives this remarkable version that has the old antagonists Aeneas and Odysseus arrive in Italy in tandem as prelude to the founding of Rome? Dionysius assigns it to a treatise titled *The Priestesses of Argos*, and we know from Stephanus of Byzantium that a work by that title was composed by the fifth-century historian Hellanicus of Lesbos. Does the tale, in fact, represent authentic fifth-century Greek opinion on the origins of Rome?

Extended discussion of the fragment would be out of place here. Hellanicus did indeed record traditions about history and events in the West.[50] He calculated, for instance, the dates of migration of Sicels from Italy to Sicily.[51] And he took an interest in the Aeneas story. His *Troika* recorded Aeneas' departure from the Troad across the Hellespont to Pallene in Chalcidice.[52] But arrival in Pallene, apparently as final destination, is hardly compatible with a voyage to Italy.[53] Troubling doubts arise about the antiquity of the tradition in *The Priestesses of Argos*. How likely is it that Hellanicus took any notice of Rome, an insignificant little town in the fifth century? It strains credulity to imagine that any Greek writer at that time would consider it worthwhile to speculate on the origins of Rome. Greeks pursued or elaborated the stories of wanderings after the Trojan War. And they debated the various versions of how and by whom the ships were destroyed.[54] But attachment of these tales to the history of Rome seems premature and anachronistic in fifth-century Greece. If the fragment properly belongs to Hellanicus, it

---

49. Dion. Hal. 1.72.2: Αἰνείαν φησὶν ἐκ Μολοττῶν εἰς Ἰταλίαν ἐλθόντα μετ᾽ Ὀδυσσέως οἰκιστὴν γενέσθαι τῆς πόλεως, ὀνομάσαι δ᾽ αὐτὴν ἀπὸ μιᾶς τῶν Ἰλιάδων Ῥώμης. The reading μετ᾽ Ὀδυσσέως is decidedly preferable to μετ᾽ Ὀδυσσέα; see now Solmsen, *HSCP*, 90 (1986), 94–95.

50. Dion. Hal. 1.28.3.

51. Dion. Hal. 1.22.3.

52. Dion. Hal. 1.47.4–1.48.1.

53. The inconsistency is rightly insisted on by Horsfall, *CQ*, 29 (1979), 377–380. Recognized also by Solmsen, *HSCP*, 90 (1986), 101–102, who, however, supposes that Hellanicus expanded his geographical horizons when he came to write *The Priestesses of Argos*; so also Dury-Moyaers, *Énée et Lavinium*, 53–54.

54. Cf. Strabo, 6.1.14 (C264); Dion. Hal. 1.52.4, 1.72.4; Plut. *Rom.* 1.2; Polyaen. 8.25.2; W. Schur, *Klio*, 17 (1921), 146–148; Solmsen, *HSCP*, 90 (1986), 104–110.

stands quite isolated; no clear evidence of Hellenic speculation on the origins of Rome exists for perhaps another century.[55] Better to suppose that Dionysius erred in ascribing this text to Hellanicus, or that another writer composed a treatise with this title, or that a later scholar interpolated the material.[56] The account, as transmitted, almost certainly represents a patchwork of separate items and independent traditions: the western migration of Odysseus, the flight of Aeneas, the burning of ships after return from Troy, and the foundation story of Rome. That these were assembled by Hellanicus as early as the fifth century is a dubious proposition. A more plausible setting would seem to be the later fourth century when tales of Aeneas and Latium, of Odysseus' western ventures, and of arsonist Trojan women were circulating in the school of Aristotle and elsewhere.

The interweaving of these strands reappears in the infuriatingly obscure *Alexandra* of Lycophron. In that poem, Cassandra, in customary dark and allusive fashion, refers to the meanderings of her kinsman, evidently Aeneas, and has him joined by a former foe in Italy, now bringing a friendly troop: the νάνος, whose own wanderings had carried him over every stretch of land and sea. The reference is clearly to Odysseus, and the verses proceed to recount legends on Aeneas' founding of Lavinium, mother city of Rome.[57] Dispute persists on Lyco-

55. The authenticity of the tradition is usually regarded as settled because Dionysius finds confirmation of it in Damastes of Sigeum; 1.72.2: ὁμολογεῖ δ' αὐτῷ καὶ Δαμαστὴς ὁ Σιγεὺς. Damastes, as we know, was the pupil of Hellanicus, a contemporary of the Peloponnesian War; Dion. Hal. *De Thuc.* 5.330; Suidas, *s.v.* Δαμάστης. But it is unclear just how much of the material cited from *The Priestesses* reappeared in Damastes. The overlap may not have gone beyond the story of the burning of the ships. So Horsfall, *CQ*, 29 (1979), 382; reiterated in Bremmer and Horsfall, *Roman Myth and Mythography*, 15–16.

56. See Perret, *Les origines*, 367–380. His doubts about Hellanican authorship have not met with much favor, and many of his arguments are indeed weak. Some trenchant criticisms were leveled by P. Boyancé, *REA*, 45 (1943) = *Études sur la religion romaine*, 161–170. The case was revived in different form by Horsfall, *CQ*, 29 (1979), 376–383, who, however, places too much weight on ostensible inconsistencies between Hellanicus' *Troika* and *The Priestesses of Argos*. Belief in Hellanican authorship still prevails in the scholarly literature; e.g., Galinsky, *Aeneas, Sicily, and Rome*, 103–106; Dury-Moyaers, *Énée et Lavinium*, 53–56; Momigliano, *Settimo contributo*, 107–109, 444–445; Solmsen, *HSCP*, 90 (1986), 93–110; J. Poucet, *Les origines de Rome* (Brussels, 1985), 185, with further bibliography; Poucet, *LEC*, 57 (1989), 238–240; Gabba, *Dionysius*, 12.

57. Lycophron, 1226–1280. The νάνος is often associated with Nanas, a legendary Etruscan figure noted by Hellanicus, thus a reflection of other tales that link Odysseus to Etruria; Dion. Hal. 1.28.3; Lycophron, 805–806; Theopompus, *FGH*, 115 F354. See the discussions of Schur, *Klio*, 17 (1921), 137–143; Phillips, *JHS*, 73 (1953), 60–61; Dury-

phron's date, and resolution seems remote. No need to enter that controversy.[58] But even if one postulates the earliest possible time, the reign of Ptolemy II, we are no earlier than the first half of the third century. That is an appropriate era. Rome's rising stature on the international stage would give incentive for the patching together of disparate traditions on the city's beginnings.

The tale of collaboration between Aeneas and Odysseus carries special significance. The value lies not in the insight provided into fifth-century Greek opinion of the city's foundation—a problematic and questionable deduction. Rather, it demonstrates the continued claim that Odysseus had upon a place in the story of Rome's origins, a claim still valid well into the third century. That conclusion stands, clear and firm, amidst the shaky hypotheses and the uncertain chronology. The notion of Rome as a Greek foundation or one with a substantial Greek component remained alive and well, even at a time when Aeneas might otherwise have held the field.

Diverse speculations on the origins of Rome proliferated. Tales fitting a postulated Romus or Romulus into traditions of Greek or Trojan migrations took shape.[59] Even Alexandrian scholars contributed to the proliferation: Eratosthenes himself had Romulus as grandson of Aeneas.[60] One need not conclude that Greeks depended on Roman folk tales for these creations. For the most part Hellenic legend makers merely conceived eponyms and attached them to the Aeneas or Odysseus sagas. Few of the reconstructions betray any knowledge of the

---

Moyaers, *Énée et Lavinium*, 65–72—although the near-unanimous assumption that Lycophron's material derives from Timaeus is undemonstrated and undemonstrable. Poucet, *RevBelge*, 61 (1983), 148–149, is properly skeptical. So also L. Pearson, *The Greek Historians of the West: Timaeus and His Predecessors* (Atlanta, 1987), 85. Horsfall, *CQ*, 29 (1979), 381, injects further doubts about the nanos-Nanas equation. These do not, however, affect the conclusion that Lycophron's νάνος is Odysseus. Cf. Homeric references to Odysseus' short stature; *Iliad*, 3.193; *Odyssey*, 6.230.

58. The poem itself, if its author is the court poet of Ptolemy II, will date to the early third century. But the lines in question, implying a preeminence for Rome, may well be a later composition. The early date was ably defended by Momigliano, *JRS*, 32 (1942), 53–64 = *Secondo contributo alla storia degli studi classici* (Rome, 1960), 446–454; followed by P. Lévêque, *REA*, 57 (1955), 36–56. Arguments for a later date, either for the poem as a whole or for the Roman section, can be found in K. Ziegler, *RE*, 13.2 (1927) 2354–2381; S. Josifovic, *RE*, Suppl. 11 (1968) 925–930; P. Fraser, *Ptolemaic Alexandria* (Oxford, 1972), II, 1066–1067, n. 331; S. West, *CQ*, 33 (1983), 122–123, 129–131; *JHS*, 104 (1984), 127–151.

59. Plut. *Rom.* 2.1–3; Dion. Hal. 1.72.1, 1.72.5–6; see above, nn. 43, 45, 46.

60. *FGH*, 241 F45.

twins Romulus and Remus. And those writers who do indicate such knowledge refashioned the story to their own taste. Lycophron, for example, has Odysseus accompany Aeneas to Italy and makes Aeneas the direct ancestor of the twins.[61] This and similar notions eventually raised troubling questions about chronology. The traditional date of Troy's fall, 1184, was not easily reconcilable with that of Rome's foundation, placed by Timaeus in 814/3. The solution, in its essentials, was first adumbrated for the Greek world by Diocles of Peparethus in the middle or late third century: Aeneas' descendants reigned for some generations in Alba Longa, and the last of that line produced a daughter who gave birth to Romulus and Remus. Diocles' version, not any Roman attempt to reconcile the conflicting chronology, paved the way to a solution. Indeed Roman writers such as Naevius and Ennius remained content with the fiction that had Aeneas as maternal grandfather of Romulus. But Diocles' outline was adopted by Fabius Pictor and became the basis for the canonical Roman version.[62] So even the standard and familiar tale, as later consecrated by Livy and Vergil, owed its original form to a Hellenic creation.

Two central points emerge with clarity from all the foregoing, and deserve to be accented. First, the conception and development of traditions that linked the origins of Rome with Troy came from the workshops of Greek historians, writers, and intellectuals. Their initial concerns were not with Rome at all but with spinning tales of migrations to the West in the wake of the Trojan War. The Greeks of Sicily and southern Italy, eager to attach their pedigree to the great legends that derived from the epic tradition, elaborated these tales. Rome came late to Hellenic attention. When it did, in the course of engagement with Italian-Greek cities in the fourth century, Greek writers invented eponymous founders and joined the beginnings of Rome to their own literary traditions—as was their wont.[63] And their formulations in turn served to shape Rome's construction of what became the canonical tale. Second, Greek conceptions by no means concentrated exclusively upon

61. Lycophron, 1232–1233, 1242–1244.

62. Plut. *Rom.* 3.1–3: τὰ μὲν κυριώτατα πρῶτος εἰς τοὺς Ἕλληνας ἐξέδωκε Διοκλῆς Πεπαρήθιος, ᾧ καὶ Φάβιος ὁ Πίκτωρ ἐν τοῖς πλείστοις ἐπηκολούθηκε. It is not clear from this language whether or to what extent Plutarch regarded Diocles as creator of this solution—or in what respects Diocles was followed by Fabius. But Diocles' contribution was plainly pivotal. On Naevius and Ennius, see Servius, *Ad Aen.* 1.273; and the extended discussion of G. d'Anna, *Problemi di letteratura latina arcaica* (Rome, 1976), 43–103. For Timaeus' date, see *FGH*, 566, F60.

63. See, in general, Bickermann, *CP*, 47 (1952), 65–81. Cf. Cornell, *LCM*, 2 (1977), 82–83.

the Aeneas saga, a fact often ignored. Indeed, the initial stories of westward wanderings seem to have featured Greek migrants, notably Odysseus. And even after the Aeneas saga underwent evolution at the hands of Sicilian historians and others, the notion of a basic Hellenic ingredient at the core of Roman history persisted and held its place among the learned reconstructions. It appears, among other sources, in Aristotle and writers of his school, in the third-century historian Xenagoras, and in the hybrid inventions that matched Aeneas and Odysseus as companions in the settlement of the West.[64] Hence, the idea that Roman origins lay in Hellas retained its hold upon many Greek intellectuals. Dionysius of Halicarnassus worked within a long and well-established convention.

These conclusions provoke an even more intriguing question. The discussion hitherto has treated Rome as essentially a passive recipient of Greek legends and fictitious creations. That, of course, tells only part of the story. Rome had its own indigenous traditions to explain the founding of the city, notably those involving the twins Romulus and Remus, which were eventually worked into place with the Hellenic sagas. At the time when Greek versions of the origins of Rome first impinged upon Roman consciousness, however, they came in several varieties. Many of those versions gave a greater role to Achaean than to Trojan heroes, and yet it was the Aeneas tale that eventually prevailed. This outcome could not have been foreseen from the beginning. How to account for it? Why did the Romans adjudge themselves Trojans rather than Greeks? The question goes to the heart of Rome's cultural awakening and sense of identity.

A preliminary issue needs to be confronted. By what route did the Aeneas legend first reach Rome? A common thesis traces transmission through Etruria.[65] Considerable archaeological testimony seems to

64. Even Polybius, who knew the Trojan legend and lived many of his adult years in Rome, endorsed the myth that the Palatine was named after Pallas, son of Heracles and Lavinia, the daughter of Evander; Dion. Hal. 1.32.1. Fabius Pictor too acknowledged the Hellenic elements in prehistoric Italy. He notes Heracles' arrival in the peninsula ; G. Manganaro, *PP*, 29 (1974), 394–397. And he conveys the contribution of Evander; fr. 1, Peter. On the persistence of Odysseus in tales of Rome's origins, see Galinsky, *Latomus*, 28 (1969), 3–18, who goes too far, however, in having Odysseus' part unchallenged before the time of Vergil.

65. E.g., F. Bömer, *Rom und Troia* (Baden-Baden, 1951), 14–39; Alföldi, *Die trojanischen Urahnen*, 14–19; idem, *Early Rome and the Latins*, 278–287; Galinsky, *Aeneas, Sicily, and Rome*, 12–140. Further bibliography in Castagnoli, *Lavinium*, 1: *Topografia generale, fonti, e storia delle ricerche* (Rome, 1972), 98.

stand in support, but as is now increasingly acknowledged, that testimony lends itself to a quite different interpretation. The motif of Aeneas' departure from Troy with Anchises enjoyed relatively high popularity in late sixth-century vase paintings. Approximately seventy vases display that scene, of which at least twenty-one have Etruscan provenance.[66] What does this prove? Another fifteen vases depict scenes of Aeneas as warrior or engaged in other activities.[67] The evidence suggests that Aeneas was a favorite figure in Etruria, not that he was celebrated as a settler in the West. The tastes of the artist rather than the interests of the consumer seem to take precedence. It is noteworthy that almost all these items are clustered in the late sixth century. They suggest an artistic fad, not a foundation myth.[68] A similar conclusion can be drawn from statuettes found at Veii depicting Aeneas carrying Anchises. They exhibit interest in the tale of Aeneas' escape from Troy and perhaps reverence for the qualities of *pietas* displayed in his deed, but they hardly prove that Aeneas was reckoned as a founder hero in Etruria. The terra-cotta statuettes, in any event, previously dated to the sixth or fifth century, may in fact belong to the fourth or even the third century—thus well postdating Rome's dominance of Veii and vitiating any theory that they represent Etruscan transmission of the legend to Rome.[69] Other material is scanty and inconclusive.[70] No substantive evidence buttresses the conclusion that Rome derived the idea of her Trojan origins from Etruria.

Latium is the more logical place to look. Greek writers who speak of western migrations and the founding of cities did not consider Rome the only Latin site worth attention. An early tradition affixed to Hesiod's

66. See the survey of K. Schauenberg, *Gymnasium*, 67 (1960), 176–190; and further W. Fuchs, *ANRW*, I.4 (1973), 615–632; Horsfall, *CQ*, 29 (1979), 386–388; S. Woodford and M. Loudon, *AJA*, 84 (1980), 30–33; F. Calcioni, *LIMC*, I.1 (1981), 386–388, no. 59–91.

67. Galinsky, *Aeneas, Sicily, and Rome*, 125–130.

68. Knowledge of the Aeneas saga is not tantamount to belief in the foundation myth. Cf. J. Perret, *REL*, 49 (1971), 40; Cornell, *LCM*, 2 (1977), 78; Horsfall, *CQ*, 29 (1979), 386–388; Poucet, *AntCl*, 48 (1979), 178–181; Dury-Moyaers, *Énée et Lavinium*, 165–168; Castagnoli, *Studi Romani*, 30 (1982), 3–4.

69. Perret, *REL*, 49 (1971), 41–43; Dury-Moyaers, *Énée et Lavinium*, 169–173; M. Torelli, *Lavinio e Roma* (Rome, 1984), 227–228.

70. See the summaries by Poucet, *AntCl*, 48 (1979), 178–181; and Horsfall, *Roman Myth and Mythography*, 18–19. Cf. F. Zevi, in G. Colonna et al., eds., *Gli Etruschi e Roma* (Rome, 1981), 148–153. Livy, 9.36.3, provides the intriguing notice that, according to some sources, Roman boys in the late fourth century were commonly educated in Etruscan literature. Even if that be true, however, it does not indicate that the Trojan story came via that route.

text, as we have seen, made Odysseus father of Latinus—an evident allusion to Latium rather than to any particular city within it.[71] Aristotle reported that Achaeans whose ships had been burned were forced to settle in "Latinium."[72] Alcimus spoke of Alba, granddaughter of Aeneas who gave birth to Rhomos, founder of Rome.[73] Callias had the Trojan woman Rhome marry Latinus.[74] Xenagoras reported three sons of Odysseus—Rhomos, Anteias, and Ardeias—who were responsible for founding those three Latin cities.[75] Timaeus' researches in the early third century gathered information on the legend of Trojan ancestry that stemmed from both Rome and Lavinium.[76] And Lycophron reports the narrative of the sow with piglets and Aeneas' founding of a city, evidently Lavinium.[77] So the traditions of Trojan or Greek ancestry had encompassed Latium by the early third century. They did not need to reach Rome via Etruria.

The canonical story in its full-blown form associated Rome most closely with two Latin towns: Lavinium and Alba Longa. Aeneas established a Trojan settlement at Lavinium, guided there by a gigantic sow who delivered thirty piglets. The number signified the years to elapse before Aeneas' son Ascanius would in turn depart to found a new city at Alba Longa. Ascanius thereby inaugurated the line of Alban kings which occupied three centuries until the birth of the twins Romulus and Remus who would be the creators of Rome. The roles of Lavinium and Alba Longa had been firmly fixed in the tradition by the end of the Republic.[78] Varro, assiduous researcher into Roman antiquities, reported that Lavinium was the first Trojan settlement in Latium and the repository of the Trojan Penates.[79] The annual ceremony to honor the

71. Hesiod, *Theog.* 1011–1013.

72. Dion. Hal. 1.72.3–4. The word is occasionally emended to "Lavinium," but without good reason. If emendation be resorted to, "Latium" is more plausible.

73. Festus, 326, 328, L.

74. Dion. Hal. 1.72.5; Festus, 329, L.

75. Dion. Hal. 1.72.5.

76. Polyb. 12.4b–4c; Dion. Hal. 1.67.3–4.

77. Lycophron, 1255–1260.

78. E.g., Vergil, *Aen.* 1.267–274; Livy, 1.1–3, 1.23.1; Dion. Hal. 1.52–59, 1.66. Despite common presumption, Sallust, *Cat.* 6.1, does not dispute this tale and present Aeneas as direct founder of Rome. As a careful reading of the passage shows, Sallust only makes the point that a mixture of Trojans and aborigines constituted the early Romans; cf. W. A. Schröder, *M. Porcius Cato: Das erste Buch der "Origines"* (Meisenheim am Glan, 1971), 69.

79. Varro, *LL*, 5.144: *oppidum quod primum conditum in Latio stirpis Romanae, Lavinium; nam ibi dii Penates nostri*; cf. Plut. *Cor.* 29.2; Val. Max. 1.8.8; Servius, *Ad Aen.* 7.661.

cult of Aeneas took place not in Rome but in Lavinium.[80] And Alba Longa had its own special prestige. Late Republican aristocrats traced their lineage back to the legendary rulers of that city.[81] Roman writers embraced the connection and perpetuated it.[82] When and why?

Much speculation surrounds the role of Lavinium in transmission of the Trojan legend, spurred in part by excavations at the site. It is often held that a cult of Aeneas existed in Lavinium from an early stage, thus supplying the intermediate link for adoption of the Trojan lineage in Rome.[83] Literary sources report that Aeneas received worship at Lavinium under the name of Indiges, Pater Indiges, or Jupiter Indiges.[84] An inscription found not far from Lavinium has been read as *Lare Aenia d(ono)*, suggesting a dedication to Lar Aeneas.[85] And the discovery of a seventh-century tomb, restructured as part of a larger monument in the fourth century, when combined with Dionysius' testimony on a hero shrine for Aeneas at Lavinium, seemed to confirm the idea.[86] But the evidence, even in ensemble, is thin, disputed, and untrustworthy. The worship of Aeneas as Indiges implies attachment of the former to a preexisting Laviniate cult that honored a founder-hero. Nothing shows or suggests that the amalgamation of Aeneas and Indiges in Lavinium predated the Roman adaptation of the Trojan legend. Reading of the inscription is highly problematic; clear legibility ends with the *Lare*, and a phrase like Lar Aeneas has no discernible parallel. Hence it gives little

---

80. Serv. Auct. *Ad Aen.* 1.260; Asconius, 21, C; Val. Max. 1.6.7. Other testimony in Alföldi, *Early Rome and the Latins*, 260–261; S. Weinstock, *RE*, 19.1 (1937), 428–440.

81. Livy, 1.30.2. Cf. Alföldi, *Early Rome and the Latins*, 238; T. P. Wiseman, *Greece and Rome*, 21 (1974), 153–154.

82. Cf. Livy, 5.52.8.

83. Alföldi, *Die trojanischen Urahnen*, 19–25; idem, *Early Rome and the Latins*, 250–278; Galinsky, *Aeneas, Sicily, and Rome*, 141–169; G. Moyaers, *RevBelge*, 55 (1977), 43–50; Dury-Moyaers, *Énée et Lavinium*, 173–246. On the excavations, see Castagnoli, *Lavinium, I*; *Lavinium, II: Le Tredici Are* (Rome, 1975); Dury-Moyaers; Torelli, *Lavinio e Roma*. This last needs to be read with great caution; see C. Ampolo, *CR*, 102 (1988), 117–120. Note also Zevi, in *Gli Etruschi e Roma*, 145–148, 153–156. The archaeological data do not suggest chronological priority of Lavinium over Rome, or vice versa; cf. Poucet, *Les origines*, 133–134; idem, *LEC*, 57 (1989), 234–238.

84. Livy, 1.2.6; Festus, 94, L; *Origo gentis Romanae*, 14.4; Vergil, *Aen.* 12.794–795. The information dates back at least to the early second-century historian Cassius Hemina; fr. 7, Peter.

85. M. Guarducci, *BullComm*, 76 (1956–58), 1–13; *ILLRP*, 1271.

86. Dion. Hal. 1.64.5; P. Sommella, *RendPontAcc*, 44 (1971–72), 47–74; idem, *Gymnasium*, 81 (1974), 273–297; Galinsky, *Vergilius*, 20 (1974), 2–11; Castagnoli, *Studi Romani*, 30 (1982), 12–13; Gabba, *Dionysius*, 139.

support to the notion of a shrine for Aeneas. As for the tomb, numerous discrepancies undermine its value as testimony for an antique cult of Aeneas. The mound described by Dionysius has neither the right size nor the right location to correspond with the excavated monument. And an inscription on the shrine attested by Dionysius honors Pater Indiges but makes no mention of Aeneas. So, it predates rather than confirms the identification. The idea of an archaic cult for Aeneas at Lavinium which lay behind Rome's embrace of the legend thus rests on the shakiest foundations and had best be discarded altogether.[87] The cults of Lavinium go well back into antiquity, but the city's adoption of the Aeneas-Troy saga may have awaited Rome's, rather than anticipated it.

The traditions connected with Alba Longa lead to the same conclusion. The Mons Albanus, like Lavinium, served as site for annual Roman rituals recalling its role in Rome's origins. The *feriae Latinae* were celebrated here by Roman officials as reminder and renewal of Rome's ties to its Alban heritage. Alba carried prestige as an ancient religious center for the Latin peoples.[88] The Alban king list spanned the chronological distance required to reconcile the dates of Troy's fall and Rome's foundation. But that artificial creation does not itself undermine the significance of Rome's association with Alba. The fact that Naevius connected Alba with Rome while implicitly denying the chronological gap between the Trojan War and Rome's beginning implies that deeper reasons existed to link the two cities.[89] Tradition had it that Rome had defeated Alba Longa in the seventh century, razed the city, and absorbed its population.[90] This account makes all the more striking Rome's

87. The strongest objections to use of this evidence were leveled by Cornell, *LCM*, 2 (1977), 78–81. See further Poucet, *AntCl*, 48 (1979), 181–183; idem, *RevBelge*, 61 (1983), 153–159; Momigliano, *Settimo contributo*, 446–447; Horsfall, *Roman Myth and Mythography*, 16–17; Poucet, *LEC*, 57 (1989), 231–238. Aeneas' landing place at the port of Lavinium was given the name of Troia; Dion. Hal. 1.53.3. The fact is emphasized by Moyaers, *RevBelge*, 55 (1977), 45–47. But the toponym may be consequence of rather than stimulus for the legend; cf. Castagnoli, *Studi Romani*, 30 (1982), 9. A sixth-century dedication to Castor and Pollux at Lavinium has also been used as evidence for an archaic cult of Aeneas through identification of those deities with the Trojan penates; S. Weinstock, *JRS*, 50 (1960), 112–114; Galinsky, *Aeneas, Sicily, and Rome*, 154–156. But the identification is dubious and the conclusion unwarranted; Castagnoli, *Lavinium, I*, 1909; cf. Dury-Moyaers, *Énée et Lavinium*, 198–205, 211–226.

88. Sources and discussion in Alföldi, *Early Rome and the Latins*, 29–34; Poucet, in F. Decreus and C. Deroux, eds., *Hommages à Josef Veremans* (Brussels, 1986), 239–244.

89. Naevius, *BP*, 1.21–22, W. So, rightly, Cornell, *PCPS*, 201 (1975), 15.

90. Livy, 1.27–30. On this story, see Poucet, in *Hommages Veremans*, 254–258.

willingness to perpetuate and celebrate its ties to Alba as a mother city. The dual ancestry of Lavinium and Alba created some confusion among the early narratives as to priority between them. Fabius Pictor had the pregnant sow lead Aeneas to Alba Longa, where she dropped her litter, whereas Lycophron evidently placed that site at Lavinium.[91] The need to reconcile differences between the two traditions is exemplified by the tale of the Trojan Penates brought from Lavinium to Alba and twice mysteriously vanishing to turn up again in Lavinium. Those episodes produced the compromise which kept the images in Lavinium but gave the task of caring for them to men from Alba.[92] As is clear, the Trojan origins embraced by Rome were embedded in a Latin context and enmeshed with Latin legends.

When did the embrace take place and what was its significance for Rome and the Latins? Greek intellectuals, as we have seen, made reference to Latium or Latin towns, as well as to Rome, in the context of foundation stories. The appendix to Hesiod's *Theogony* shows Hellenic awareness of Latium but alludes neither to Romans nor to Trojans. Aristotle brought Achaeans to Latium; his pupil Heracleides Lembos brought them to Rome. The Sicilian Callias circa 300 had a Trojan woman marry Latinus and their offspring found Rome. None of these alternatives shows close parallel to or direct ancestry of the tales eventually adopted by Latin writers. The reports arose from Greek speculation rather than local tradition.

Alcimus' testimony has more to offer. His may be the first extant text to designate Alba as connecting link between Aeneas and the foundation of Rome.[93] But Alcimus' date is uncertain, and even if one puts him in the later fourth century, it would be prudent to avoid sweeping conclusions. Alcimus' evidence suggests claims by Alba Longa to the ancestry of Rome, but the involvement of Aeneas as grandfather may be the historian's superimposition of Greek legend rather than a sign that Alba acknowledged a Trojan connection.

Greek interest in Rome intensified in the third century. The period brings accumulating testimony that Trojan features of the legend gained ascendancy. Pyrrhus himself signaled their prevalence among the west-

---

91. Fabius Pictor, *FGH*, 809 F2 = Diod. 7.5.4; Lycophron, 1252–1260. On Lycophron's denotation, see d'Anna, *Problemi*, 64–67.
92. Dion. Hal. 1.67.1–3; Val. Max. 1.8.7.
93. Festus, 326, 328, L. See above, n. 43.

ern Greeks. He proclaimed himself in Italy as descendant of Achilles and announced that in that capacity he would duplicate his ancestor's success by bringing a Hellenic war upon the Romans, mere colonists of the Trojans. The taking of Troy provided a talisman that promised similar triumph for the Epirote king.[94] Pyrrhus' declaration does not itself prove that the Romans had already embraced Troy, but it does demonstrate a broad familiarity with the legend in the Greek communities of Sicily and southern Italy by the early third century.[95]

Pyrrhus' failure in Italy further enhanced the reputation of Rome—and the fascination of Greek intellectuals. Hieronymus of Cardia produced the first summary of Rome's early history.[96] And Timaeus, yet another Sicilian historian, pursued a more thorough investigation. He included commentary on Rome in his general history of Sicily, and he composed a separate monograph on the Pyrrhic War.[97] Timaeus' testimony is vital. Most significantly, it indicates that, for him at least, the Trojan origins of Rome were already standard doctrine. The historian's researches aimed at confirmation and demonstration of accepted tenets. He found evidence for Rome's Trojan ancestry in the festival of the October Horse: the sacrifice of the horse on the Campus Martius symbolized the capture of Troy through the ruse of the wooden horse. Polybius took Timaeus to task for that misguided and naive conclusion—rightly so—but Timaeus did not draw it alone and unaided. The belief was widely shared, and the historian obtained it from informants, presumably Roman informants.[98] He acquired corroborative testimony also from Lavinian intermediaries, describing sacred objects in the sanctuary at Lavinium as emblematic of the Trojan Penates. The identification gave evidence of the tradition that Lavinium was the site of a Trojan settlement and a parent city of Rome. Local legends reinforced the

---

94. Paus. 1.12.1: μνήμη τὸν Πύρρον τῆς ἁλώσεως ἐσῆλθε τῆς Ἰλίου καί οἱ κατὰ ταὐτὰ ἤλπιζε χωρήσειν πολεμοῦντι; στρατεύειν γὰρ ἐπὶ Τρώων ἀποίκους Ἀχιλλέως ὢν ἀπόγονος.

95. Perret's bold thesis, Les origines, 409–419, 427–434, and passim, that Pyrrhus' claim created the legend of Rome's Trojan origins, has not found takers. See the decisive refutation by Momigliano, JRS, 35 (1945), 99–104. Further bibliography and discussion in Martin, MEFRA, 101 (1989), 117–118.

96. Dion. Hal. 1.6.1.

97. Polyb. 12.4b.1; Dion. Hal. 1.6.1; Cic. Ad Fam. 5.12.2; Gellius, 11.1.1. See, most recently, F. W. Walbank, SCI, 10 (1989–90), 50–51.

98. Polyb. 12.4b.1–12.4c.1; cf. Festus, 190, L: quem hostiae loco quidam Marti bellico deo sacrari dicunt, non ut vulgus putat, quia velut supplicium de eo sumatur, quod Romani Ilio sunt oriundi.

Sicilian historian's conviction that the legacy of Troy was a prime component in the history of Latium.[99] Although Alba goes unmentioned in the miserably scanty fragments, there is no reason to doubt that it held a place in the narrative by this time. Just when Timaeus penned the relevant passages escapes certainty. Conjectures range from 315 to the 260s.[100] One may tentatively infer that the legend of Rome's Trojan origins as mediated by Lavinium, Alba, or both had taken hold in Latium by the early third century.[101]

A suitable time for Roman adoption and adaptation of the legend now suggests itself. The later fourth century brought a convergence of political and cultural circumstances that made the Trojan connection in a Latin context particularly attractive. This was the era in which Rome defeated the forces of the Latin League and extended military and political control over the cities of Latium. It was also the era in which Rome spread its influence into Campania and entered into diplomatic relations with Greek cities such as Naples. The time proved propitious for embrace of the fables that linked Rome and Latin cities to the heritage of the Hellenic past.

The dissolution of the Latin League after 338 set Roman relations with Latium on a new and different footing. The victor no longer dealt with a federal organization but established separate compacts with the

99. Dion. Hal. 1.67.3–4. Timaeus' language, πυθέσθαι δὲ αὐτὸς ταῦτα παρὰ τῶν ἐπιχωρίων, need not mean that he got the story in Lavinium itself; so Schur, *Klio*, 17 (1921), 142–143. But that seems a preferable surmise to the conjectures that he interviewed Lavinian merchants in Sicily. Perret's effort, *Les origines*, 440–449, to discredit the testimony is unavailing. See d'Anna, *Problemi*, 68–73; Moyaers, *RevBelge*, 55 (1977), 34–35; Castagnoli, *Studi Romani*, 30 (1982), 8–9; Poucet, *LEC*, 57 (1989), 240–242.

100. Alföldi, *Early Rome and the Latins*, 248: ca. 315. Horsfall, *Roman Myth and Mythography*, 19: the 260s. One item inclines to the latter: Dionysius dated Timaeus' treatment of Rome later than that of Hieronymus; 1.6.1.

101. Cornell suggests that the Romans did not become aware of the Trojan legend until the course of the third century but does not discuss Timaeus' evidence; *LCM*, 2 (1977), 82. The assertion of Momigliano, *Settimo contributo*, 448, that the Trojan legend took root in Rome and the rest of Latium by the early fourth century is in no way established by his arguments. The paintings in the Francois tomb at Vulci may be relevant here. If the ingenious reconstruction of F. Coarelli, *DialArch* (1983–84), 43–69, is right, the identification of Romans and Trojans was already accepted fact by the late fourth century, but his conclusions are speculative and undemonstrable. Equally inconclusive are alleged depictions of Aeneas on Praenestine cistae of the third or second century. One depicts a triumphal figure engaged in some religious act, but there is nothing to show that this is Aeneas; G. Bordenache Battaglia, *Le ciste prenestine, I.1: Corpus* (Rome, 1979), 58–60. And another, sometimes regarded as a depiction of Latinus sanctioning the wedding of Aeneas and Lavinia, is of dubious authenticity; Galinsky, *Aeneas, Sicily, and Rome*, 162–164; Bordenache Battaglia, 127–129.

several cities. Rome also extended citizenship to some and framed alliances with others. A complex of arrangements developed which both assured Roman preeminence and maintained the integrity of the Latin communities.[102] The new situation encouraged attention to cultural bonds that tied Latium to Rome, while legitimating the supremacy of the latter.

Whether the legend reached Rome from the Latin towns or vice versa is unanswerable.[103] A different consideration deserves emphasis. The tradition of Trojan origins took shape in the later fourth century because it held advantages both for Rome and for the towns of Latium. It was attractive for Latins to advance the idea that their most ancient and renowned sites had been the mother cities of Rome. The concept offered prestige and priority in the new world of Roman Italy. Alba Longa, no longer extant as a physical site at that time, served as symbolic representative of Latium's antiquity, and Lavinium, seat of religious cults and possessor of a celebrated past, gained revitalized recognition through a formal treaty with Rome that would have ceremonial renewal each year.[104] So the Latin towns had reason to endorse the connection. Rome, for its part, found similarly welcome benefits in the legends. They lent a cultural legitimacy to its position of authority in Latium. Rome was now heir to the region's glorious past; not just conqueror and suzerain but cultural curator. The treaty with Lavinium suited that posture, as did the practice of Roman officials' honoring the cult of the Penates in Lavinium rather than in Rome.[105] And equally important, the assimilation of the legends announced a link with the Hellenic world, thereby to validate Rome's association with the Greek cities of Italy. The political circumstances of the late fourth century provided the proper setting.

The central question now demands response. Why did the Romans choose to consider themselves descendants of Trojans rather than Greeks? It is essential to stress that Greek speculations and creative

102. Cf. H. Galsterer, *Herrschaft und Verwaltung im republikanischen Italien* (Munich, 1976), 87–89; E. T. Salmon, *The Making of Roman Italy* (London, 1982), 40–56; Cornell, in *Cambridge Ancient History*2, VII.2 (Cambridge, 1989), 365–367.

103. Speculation on the matter is pointless and unproductive. A summary of recent contributions to that debate is in Poucet, *AntCl*, 48 (1979), 186–190; cf. idem, *LEC*, 57 (1989), 240–245.

104. Livy, 8.11.15; cf. *ILS*, 5004. See Castagnoli, *Studi Romani*, 30 (1982), 11–12. It is, of course, quite possible that Alba is included in the tale because that city was already tightly associated with Rome's native story of Romulus and Remus.

105. See above, n. 80.

fancies about the remote origins of Latin cities postulated Hellenic roots as often as they imagined Trojan ancestry. The Hellenic versions, as conveyed by writers such as Aristotle, Heracleides Lembos, Callias, and Xenagoras, were still quite current in the late fourth and early third centuries. Furthermore, Trojans had been the losers in the Greek siege and had developed a reputation for effeminacy on top of that.[106] How is it then that the Trojan heritage and not the Greek prevailed in the Roman consciousness?

Did Romans look to Troy as symbol of opposition and resistance to Greece?[107] Such was the construction placed upon the legend by Pyrrhus when he solicited the support of Italian Greeks against the colonists of the Trojans.[108] But the Romans did not conceive the association as an antihellenic gesture. It suffices to cite the dedication made at Delphi in 194 and composed in Greek verse by T. Flamininus, victorious Roman general in the Second Macedonian War. Flamininus proclaimed himself both descendant of Aeneas and champion of Greek freedom.[109] The Romans knew no contradiction between those two postures. Nor did adoption of the Trojan legacy require eradication of Hellenic elements in the Italian past. Heracles and Evander, for instance, both appear in Fabius Pictor's account of early settlers in Italy, and these traditions in no way diluted the Trojan character of the Roman stock.[110] Troy held a meaning quite different from antagonism to Hellas.

Were Romans drawn to Aeneas rather than to Odysseus because the latter had a reputation for sly shrewdness, whereas the former exemplified *pietas*, the preeminent Roman virtue?[111] That interpretation narrows the issue intolerably—as if Romans were merely choosing between heroes, weighing respective qualities, and selecting a favorite.

106. On Trojan effeminacy, see, e.g., Euripides, *Orest.* 1111–1113; Vergil, *Aen.* 4.215–217, 9.614–620, 12.99–100.

107. Perret, *REL*, 49 (1971), 49–50. Cf. Toohey, *Arethusa*, 17 (1984),9–12, who sees Rome's adoption of the Trojan legacy as a sign of Hellenophobia.

108. Paus. 1.12.1.

109. Plut. *Flam.* 12.6–7: Αἰνεάδας Τίτος ὔμμιν ὑπέρτατον ὤπασε δῶρον / Ἑλλήνων τεύξας παισὶν ἐλευθερίαν. There are earlier examples also of the compatibility of Trojan ancestry and collaboration with Greeks; cf. Zon. 8.9.12; Justin, 28.1.5–28.2.14; Suet. *Claud.* 25.3.

110. For Heracles, see the Taormina inscription in Manganaro, *PP*, 29 (1974), 394–397. For Evander, see Fabius, fr. 1, Peter.

111. So Bömer, *Rom und Troia*, 39–49; cf. d'Anna, *Problemi*, 61. Galinsky, *Latomus*, 28 (1969), 6–18, implausibly suggests that the claim on an Odyssean heritage was undisputed until Vergil implicitly denied it.

And if Odysseus were uncongenial to Roman taste, would Livius Andronicus have undertaken a Roman adaptation of the *Odyssey*, the first major literary work in Latin?[112]

The embrace of Troy had subtler and more significant import. It enabled Rome to associate itself with the rich and complex fabric of Hellenic tradition, thus to enter that wider cultural world, just as it had entered the wider political world. But at the same time, it also announced Rome's distinctiveness from that world.[113] The Roman upper classes welcomed incorporation into the cultural legacy of Hellas but preferred to carve out their own niche within it. They sharpened a sense of their identity and laid a foundation for a national character. Troy proved especially serviceable in this quest. Its glorious past lay in remote antiquity, its people no longer extant, its city but a shell of its former self. Troy persisted as a symbol, not a current reality. No risk, then, of identification with contemporary folk whose defects would be all too evident and all too embarrassing. Romans could mold the Trojan image to their own ends. The legacy of Troy gained circulation through the epics of Naevius and Ennius and became the starting point for the historical works of Fabius Pictor and Cato the Elder—all of which celebrated the values of the nation. As in so much else, the Romans astutely converted Hellenic traditions to meet their own political and cultural purposes. The successful and enduring version that made Trojans the forebears of Rome owed its origin to Greek inventiveness and its reformulation to Latin ingenuity. The Greeks imposed the Trojan legend upon the West as a form of Hellenic cultural imperialism, only to see it appropriated by the westerner to define and convey a Roman cultural identity.

The Trojan connection had entrenched itself in Roman consciousness by the early third century. When historiography commenced at Rome, that connection was well established and unquestioned. But unanimity

112. Rightly noted by Poucet, *Les origines*, 285.

113. Cf. G. Colin, *Rome et la Grèce* (Paris, 1905), 147–165; Momigliano, *Settimo contributo*, 109, 447, 459. It might be objected that if Greek intellectuals such as Dionysius of Halicarnassus could identify Trojans with their nation, then the Romans' link with Troy would hardly mark them as distinct from Greeks; cf. Galinsky, *Aeneas, Sicily, and Rome*, 93–96; Gabba, *Dionysius*, 14. But the difference in attitude is, in fact, profound. Dionysius strained to make the Trojans Greek; he did not see the Greeks as Trojans. Rome's acceptance of the Trojan lineage in no way equated Romans with Greeks. One can add further that when Romans first encountered Trojan tales they were not yet conversant with the learned reconstructions represented by Dionysius.

on the fundamental point did not bring uniformity in the tradition—very far from it. The fact is striking and noteworthy. Scholarly efforts to discern a rectilinear progression repeatedly encounter frustration. That should occasion no surprise. Roman writers, well aware that they were working with legendary material and malleable traditions, felt free to redesign and embellish within the general framework. They found no virtue in mere reproduction of predecessors, nor did they regard themselves as promoting a canonical tale. Their presuppositions had little in common with modern expectations.

Historical writing in Rome began perhaps a century after the concept of Trojan origins had taken hold. But the fable stayed fluid. Fabius Pictor, the earliest of Roman historians, composed his narrative toward the end of the third century.[114] The general chronological outline of what became the prevalent tale already found place in his work. Fabius acknowledged a gap of unspecified time between the era of Trojan migration and the founding of Rome, which he set in 748/7, employing the Greek form of reckoning familiar to a readership that commanded the language: the first year of the eighth Olympiad.[115] Just how long a gap he postulated or transmitted eludes certainty. Confident assertions that he accepted Eratosthenes' date for the Trojan War and put Aeneas' peregrinations in the twelfth century go beyond the evidence. But he certainly allotted several generations to the kings of Alba Longa, culminating in the usurpation of Amulius and the birth of the twins. A long time had elapsed.[116] Fabius' conception of the origins of Alba claims still greater interest. The historian had Aeneas led by the great white sow to that site, where she dropped her thirty piglets. An oracle had bidden Aeneas to found a city on the spot to which the sow directed him, but a vision in his dream persuaded him to wait thirty years, as indicated by the number in the litter. Aeneas' death canceled plans, but Ascanius eventually established Alba after the thirty years had elapsed.[117] Lavinium makes no appearance in the skimpy fragments of Fabius Pictor,

---

114. Fabius as earliest historian: Dion. Hal. 1.6.2, 7.71.1; Livy, 1.44.2, 2.40.10. On the date of the work, not susceptible to precise proof, see the discussion of B. Frier, *Libri Annales Pontificum Maximorum: The Origins of the Annalistic Tradition* (Rome, 1979), 227–246.

115. Dion. Hal. 1.74.1; cf. Solin. 1.27.

116. Plut. *Rom.* 3.1–3; Manganaro, *PP*, 29 (1974), 394: πολὶ ὕστερ[ον ἐ]γένοντο Ῥωμύλος [καὶ Ρ]έμος καὶ Ῥώμης [κτίσις ὑ]πὸ Ῥωμύλου. Some have convinced themselves that Fabius invented the Alban king list; Perret, *Les origines*, 491; Alföldi, *Early Rome and the Latins*, 126. The claim is unpersuasive and at odds with Plut. *Rom.* 3.1–2. Cf. Schröder, *Cato: Das erste Buch der "Origines"*, 170–171.

117. Fabius Pictor, *FGH*, 809, F2.

though one cannot rule out the possibility that his text recorded its foundation by Aeneas.[118] What matters, however, is that the sow drew Aeneas to the Alban Mount and not to Lavinium. Fabius' version of the story did not subsequently carry the day.

The broad outlines of the legend in Cato's *Origines* must have had close similarity to the Fabian reconstruction. Roman historians now took as established fact a lengthy divide between the fall of Troy and the beginnings of Rome. Cato, writing in Latin and consequently avoiding certain conventions of Hellenic historiography, abandoned dating by Olympic years. He set Rome's foundation at 432 years after the Trojan War.[119] Cato's starting point remains unclear. Dionysius took it to be the date assigned by Eratosthenes to the fall of Troy, that is, 1184/3 B.C., thus putting Rome's foundation in 752/1 or 751/0, depending on whether Cato did or did not employ inclusive reckoning. But the conclusion of Dionysius, though widely accepted, is only an inference. Eratosthenes' chronology, however influential in Hellas, need not have impressed Cato the Censor. The Alexandrian knew of no long gap between the Trojan War and the origins of Rome, a fundamental fact for Cato. On that matter, Cato and Fabius concurred.[120]

The surviving fragments of *Origines*, book 1, indicate an elaborate tale. The narrative included Aeneas' arrival in Italy with Anchises, his marriage to Lavinia, daughter of the aboriginal king Latinus, the founding of Lavinium, a breakdown of relations between Trojans and Latins, followed by a series of contests that brought about the deaths in turn of Latinus, Turnus, and Aeneas himself, a further war between Ascanius and Mezentius, and then Ascanius' settlement of Alba Longa.[121] How much of his account coincides with Fabius' is a matter for speculation,

---

118. So, rightly, d'Anna, *Problemi*, 93–97, as against Perret, *Les origines*, 325–334.

119. Dion. Hal. 1.74.2: Κάτων δὲ Πόρκιος Ἑλληνικὸν μὲν οὐχ ὁρίζει χρόνον, ἐπιμελὴς δὲ γενόμενος εἰ καί τις ἄλλος περὶ τὴν συναγωγὴν τῆς ἀρχαιολογουμένης ἱστορίας ἔτεσιν ἀποφαίνει δυσὶ καὶ τριάκοντα καὶ τετρακοσίοις ὑστεροῦσαν τῶν Ἰλιακῶν.

120. The reference to Eratosthenes' dating is clearly Dionysius' own, not Cato's; Dion. Hal. 1.74.2: ὁ δὲ χρόνος οὗτος ἀναμετρηθεὶς ταῖς Ἐρατοσθένους χρονογραφίαις κατὰ τὸ πρῶτον ἔτος πίπτει τῆς ἑβδόμης ὀλυμπιάδος. On the whole question, see R. Werner, *Der Beginn der römischen Republik* (Munich, 1963), 113–119, with full bibliography; Schröder, *Cato: Das erste Buch der "Origines"*, 167–170. Roman historians plainly felt no compulsion toward unanimity on the precise date of the city's foundation. L. Cincius Alimentus, a close contemporary of Fabius Pictor, put it "around" the fourth year of the twelfth Olympiad, i.e., 729/8; Dion. Hal. 1.74.1: Λεύκιος δὲ Κίγκιος . . . περὶ τὸ τέταρτον ἔτος τῆς δωδεκάτης ὀλυμπιάδος.

121. Cato, *HRR*, fr. 4–14. See the summary by Schröder, *Cato: Das erste Buch der "Origines"*, 91–92.

not worth pursuing here.[122] But Cato certainly diverged from Fabius in his narrative of the sow prodigy. Whereas the earlier historian had located the event in Alba itself, thus denoting that site as Aeneas' destined foundation from which a vision had to deter him, Cato places it in Lavinium, already the city of Aeneas.[123] The saga lacked uniformity even on so basic a point. The sow's litter, however, carries the same significance for Cato as for Fabius: the thirty piglets presage a thirty-year wait before the foundation of Alba Longa.[124]

Yet even on this matter the Latin historiographic tradition divided. Cassius Hemina, reckoned among Rome's earliest historians, composed his work in the middle or later second century.[125] But Hemina, far from following the versions of his predecessors and contemporaries, put the prodigy of the sow at the time of Romulus and Remus![126] Just what significance the piglets had for Hemina remains obscure, but he evidently felt no obligation to reproduce a canonical tale.[127] Such items as the miracle of the sow, the first designated settlement of Aeneas, and the relationship of Lavinium and Alba were hardly minor details. Roman historians nonetheless felt free to dissent and to refashion the narrative.

That tendency can be discerned in Polybius as well. The Greek historian composed his magnum opus in Rome, had the acquaintance of

122. Perret, *Les origines*, 540–544, ascribed to Cato the idea of Lavinium as Aeneas' initial settlement in Latium, as well as the introduction of such personages as Latinus, Lavinia, Ascanius, Turnus, and Mezentius. Schröder, *Cato: Das erste Buch der "Origines"*, 94, questions some of the conclusions but agrees on Turnus and Mezentius; cf. 118–122; also Horsfall, in Bremmer and Horsfall, *Roman Myth and Mythography*, 23.

123. *Origo gentis Romanae*, 12.5: *Cato in Origine generis Romani ita docet: suem triginta porculos peperisse in eo loco, ubi nunc est Lavinium, cumque Aeneas urbem ibi condere constituisset*, etc. Cf. Perret, *Les origines*, 535–536; W. Ehlers, *MH*, 6 (1949), 168–172; Schröder, *Cato: Das erste Buch der "Origines"*, 141–142. Nor is that the only occasion in which Cato took issue with Fabius on the early history of Rome; cf. Dion. Hal. 4.15.1.

124. Serv. Auct. *Ad Aen.* 1.269: *vel quod Cato ait XXX annis expletis eum [Ascanius] Albam condidisse; Origo gentis Romanae*, 12.5. The first passage is wrongly denied to Cato by Perret, *Les origines*, 524–526, on the basis of Serv. *Ad Aen.* 6.760. In fact, the latter, which suggests that Ascanius did not wait thirty years to found Alba, is more Servius than Cato; cf. d'Anna, *Problemi*, 107–108.

125. Censorinus, *De Die Nat.* 17.11; Pliny, *NH*, 13.84, 28.12. On Hemina's date, see now G. Forsythe, *Phoenix*, 44 (1990), 326–333, with bibliography.

126. Hemina, in Diomed. I.384, K = *HRR*, fr. 11: *Pastorum vulgus sine contentione consentiendo praefecerunt aequaliter imperio Remum et Romulum ita ut de regno pararent inter se. Monstrum fit: sus parit porcos triginta, cuius rei fanum fecerunt Laribus Grundilibus*. Cf. Perret, *Les origines*, 554–555.

127. D'Anna, *Problemi*, 104–113, suggests that Hemina, by divorcing the sow from the Aeneas story, was responsible for the version that has Ascanius found Alba shortly after the death of Aeneas; cf. Serv. *Ad Aen.* 6.760.

Cato, and doubtless knew the *Origines*. But on at least one noteworthy point of early Roman history, Polybius held an opinion at sharp variance with that of the Censor. Cato produced or perpetuated the tradition that Aeneas married Lavinia, daughter of the indigenous king Latinus.[128] That link held a pivotal place in the national past. Polybius, by contrast and quite strikingly, has Lavinia as daughter of Evander and wife of Heracles—a significant chronological distance from the time of Aeneas.[129] Arcadian lore may lurk behind that version. It was surely not Polybius' intent to undermine the Roman self-conception. The presentation of diverse strands and the endorsement of variants had ample precedents; it was accepted practice at a time when traditions were fluid and particulars susceptible to manipulation. What merits notice, however, is that such fluidity continued in the mid–second century, perhaps 150 years after the embrace of the Trojan origins. The connection itself delivered the vital message. All the rest was malleable.

When one moves from historiography, whose practitioners took seriously the duty of recovering the past, to poets, diversity increases. Even the main line of the tradition wavers and fragments.

Naevius' *Bellum punicum* saw the light of day in the late third century.[130] It appeared, therefore, contemporaneously with the history of Fabius Pictor. Our evidence does not permit decision on the priority of one or the other.[131] We do know, however, that Naevius altogether ignored the long chronological span that, for Fabius, separated Aeneas and the foundation of Rome. He had no need for intervening settlements or Alban king lists. The poet simply declared Romulus a grandson of Aeneas through his mother's side.[132] Nothing more can be said with certainty about Naevius' version of this matter.[133] But that is enough. He cared little about perpetuating a canonical tradition on

---

128. Serv. *Ad Aen.* 6.760.

129. Polyb. in Dion. Hal. 1.32.1. By contrast, Polybius' date for the founding of Rome, the second year of the seventh Olympiad, i.e., 751/0, is very close to Fabius', 748/7, and probably to Cato's; see above n. 120.

130. Cicero designates it as a work of Naevius' old age; *De Sen.* 50.

131. Perret, *Les origines*, 477, opts for Naevius. If Fabius' work appeared first, so he postulates, Naevius would never have altered his chronological scheme. That reasoning, as we have seen, is altogether fallacious.

132. Serv. *Ad Aen.* 1.273: *Naevius et Ennius Aeneae ex filia nepotem Romulum conditorem urbis tradunt.*

133. Naevius presumably did know of an Alban connection with Rome's founding, for his text alludes to Amulius; Naevius, *BP*, 24, Morel = 21–22, Warm. Cf. Festus, 370, L, a much disputed fragment; see M. Barchiesi, *Nevio epico* (Padua, 1962), 165–166, 523–526.

Rome's prehistory. Theories about whether he opted for an Eratosthen-
ian or a Timaean date seem singularly misguided.[134] Naevius could
dispense with arcane chronological research.

The great epic of Q. Ennius was produced after publication of Rome's
earliest histories, those of Fabius Pictor and Cincius Alimentus, and
after the chronological studies of Eratosthenes. Yet Ennius simply followed the scheme of his poetic predecessor Naevius: Aeneas' daughter
was mother of Romulus, founder of the city.[135] The discrepancy between the era of Aeneas and the time of Romulus was a matter of
complete indifference. Ennius did have some date in mind for the city's
origins, but he did not press for precision. A speaker in the *Annales*
makes reference to a time "more or less seven hundred years" from the
founding of Rome.[136] That Ennius had recourse to the researches of
Eratosthenes is a common but unverifiable conjecture.[137] There is no
more reason to believe that the poet felt bound by Alexandrian scholarship than by the chronological scheme of Fabius Pictor.[138] Varro, who
had the text of Ennius before him, took the seven hundred years as
reckoned from Ennius' own day.[139] That computation implies a date in
the early ninth century, at odds with all other dates. But why not?
Cincius' date differed from Fabius', both differed from Timaeus', and all
of them from Eratosthenes'. The assumption that Ennius' epic had to
settle upon an established date is fundamentally flawed. The origins of

134. Scholars have devoted much discussion to the date assigned by Naevius to the
city's beginnings. Most put it in 814/3, the Timaean date, on the ground that Naevius
included the Dido-Aeneas tale, thus adopting Timaeus' synchronism of Rome and
Carthage; F. Noack, *Hermes*, 27 (1892), 434–436; Barchiesi, *Nevio epico*, 206, 477–479;
d'Anna, *Problemi*, 79–80. But no Naevian fragment makes explicit reference to the tale.
The nearest we have is Serv. *Ad Aen.* 4.9: *cuius filiae fuerint Anna et Dido Naevius dicit*. The
poet can certainly not have dwelled long over the story; cf. E. V. Marmorale, *Naevius
poeta* (Florence, 1953), 246–247. And no secure inferences can be made about chronology.

135. Serv. *Ad Aen.* 1.273; see above n. 132. The woman's name in this version is Ilia,
probably also the name employed by Naevius; Serv. *Ad Aen.* 6.777. Ennius' version, like
Naevius', included the Alban connection; Ennius, *Annales*, 33, V = 31, Sk.

136. Varro, *RR*, 3.1.2: *septingenti sunt paulo plus vel minus anni / augusto augurio postquam
incluta condita Roma est.*

137. See, e.g., d'Anna, *Problemi*, 80–83; and most recently, O. Skutsch, *The Annals of
Quintus Ennius* (Oxford, 1985), 314–315.

138. The confident assertions of d'Anna, *Problemi*, 83: "per Ennio Eratostene doveva
avere un prestigio superiore a Fabio Pittore," and Skutsch, *Annals*, 314, n. 2: "It is
impossible to surmise that Ennius . . . could have disregarded the chronology of
Eratosthenes," are without foundation.

139. Varro, *RR*, 3.1.2: *nam in hoc nunc denique est ut dici possit, non cum Ennius scripsit,
"septingenti sunt."*

the Roman people in Troy were the paramount point, long since entrenched and firm. All else could fluctuate. The imagination of poets and even the ingenuity of historians had broad leeway.

Roman writers, as is plain, could be quite cavalier about the particulars of their nation's origins. One would, therefore, hardly expect Greek intellectuals to adhere to a standard line of interpretation. Even among those who took the trouble to inform themselves about traditions in Rome and Latium and who regarded the Trojan background as a given, diversity prevailed.

Timaeus subscribed to the legend of Rome's origins in Troy. And he undertook research in Latium to bolster the thesis, finding support both in Lavinian traditions and in Roman institutions.[140] The Sicilian historian's reconstruction also presupposed a stretch of many generations between the fall of Troy and the creation of Rome. He set the former in the distant past, in the twelfth century or possibly even the fourteenth.[141] For the latter he produced a new date: 814/3, to coincide with the founding of Carthage. The symbolism appealed to his imagination, equating the two powers who now dominated the western Mediterranean—or even presaging their coming clash.[142] The date itself stands alone, not elsewhere attested, perhaps drawn from Carthaginian tradition rather than the speculations of Greek or Roman intellectuals. Dionysius of Halicarnassus professed himself baffled: he could not discern the chronological criteria employed by his predecessor.[143] They may owe less to historiographical principles than to contemporary circumstances and ingenious invention. Timaeus certainly felt free to create.

How Timaeus proposed to account for the chronological divide

---

140. See above, nn. 98–99.

141. The date of 1194/3 is indicated by Timaeus, *FGH*, 566, F 125—417 years before the first Olympiad. But a strong case can be made for 1335/4, the date also given by Duris of Samos, *FGH*, 76, F41. See especially Timaeus, *FGH*, 566, F 80—the colonization of Corcyra six hundred years after the Trojan War. See the acute discussion by D. Asheri, *Saggi di letteratura e storiografia antiche* (Como, 1983), 53–67, with good bibliography.

142. Cf. A. Momigliano, *Terzo contributo alla storia degli studi classici e del mondo antico* (Rome, 1966), 46–51.

143. Dion. Hal. 1.74.1: Τίμαιος μὲν ὁ Σικελιώτης οὐκ οἶδ᾽ ὅτῳ κανόνι χρησάμενος ἅμα Καρχηδόνι κτιζομένῃ γενέσθαι φησὶν ὀγδόῳ καὶ τριακοστῷ πρότερον ἔτει τῆς πρώτης ὀλυμπιάδος. D'Anna, *Problemi*, 69–73, implausibly takes this as an example of Dionysius' criticism of Timaean methodology. The view of L. Moretti, *RivFilol*, 80 (1952), 296–298, that Timaeus reconciled the traditions by having Rome founded twice, lacks any basis—though welcomed by d'Anna, 74–75. Cornell, *PCPS*, 201 (1975), 24, rather optimistically, takes the Timaean date as based on solid tradition and buttressed by archaeological data on the Iron Age settlement.

between Aeneas and Rome defies conjecture.[144] The matter may not
have concerned him much. It evidently did concern Diocles of Peparethus, however, a writer of the later third century, whose work, according to Plutarch, was followed in the main by Fabius Pictor. Diocles'
narrative, at least in the view of Plutarch's source, contained reference to
Aeneas' descendants as rulers of Alba, whose last representatives played
out the story that issued in Romulus and the founding of Rome.[145] The
tale of the Alban kings who served to fill the long gap between Aeneas
and Romulus was therefore either invented or first brought to Greek
attention by Diocles.

But not all Greeks by any means chose to adopt that version. Scholars
and writers, even those well acquainted with the tale, could ignore it at
will. The learned Eratosthenes fixed the time of Troy's fall in 1184/3, a
date that held sway among subsequent Greek chronographers; but he
also made Romulus the grandson of Aeneas, thus implicitly discarding
Timaeus' chronology and dismissing the whole saga of the Alban succession.[146] The Alexandrian scholar was plainly familiar with Roman
legends and even, like Timaeus, juxtaposed Rome and Carthage.[147] But
he put the pieces together in his own way.

So also, we may be sure, did another Alexandrian writer, the poet
Lycophron. The problems attaching to Lycophron's difficult text cannot and need not be pursued here. The verses that celebrate an imperial
Rome almost certainly belong to the early second century, at the earliest.[148] The poet therefore would have had access both to Greek reconstructions and to Roman versions of the city's beginnings. His verses, in
fact, show extensive knowledge of various particulars that reflect Hellenic, Latin, and even Etruscan traditions. Lycophron's erudition, however, did not induce him to reproduce the schemata of his predecessors.
There is, for instance, no suggestion that he adopted Timaeus' belief in
an interval of at least three and a half centuries between the Trojan War
and the founding of Rome. Lycophron simply has Aeneas leave two
lion cubs, an obvious allusion to Romulus and Remus.[149] The poet did

144. There is nothing to suggest that his narrative contained the Alban king list;
contra: H. Strasburger, *SitzHeid* (1968), 17.
145. Plut. *Rom.* 3.1–2.
146. Serv. *Ad Aen.* 1.273.
147. Strabo, 1.4.9 = C66.
148. Lycophron, 1226–1230; see above, n. 58.
149. Lycophron, 1232–1233: τοιοῦσδ' ἐμός τις σύγγονος λείψει διπλοῦς / σκύμνους
λέοντας, ἔξοχον ῥώμῃ γένος. The passage can, of course, be interpreted to signify

not have to bother with straightening out chronological inconsistencies. Still more revealing, however, is the legend of the sow and thirty piglets as it appears in the *Alexandra*. Latin writers differed on the story, as we have seen, whether in the location of the prodigy or the era in which it occurred. But Lycophron produced a variant even on the meaning of the omen: it referred not to the years that should pass before the founding of Alba but to the thirty communities that would make up the Latin League.[150] The purpose need not be polemical; Lycophron reflects a patriotic tradition in Lavinium, where a bronze image of the sow and her offspring had been erected to recall the episode.[151] But the poet felt no compulsion to follow an established line. Neither Timaeus nor Diocles set a pattern for the verses of the *Alexandra*.

Hegesianax of Alexandria Troas affords a particularly striking instance. A historian who wrote of Aeneas and the aftermath of the Trojan War, he had the opportunity to obtain firsthand information on Roman attitudes toward the city's origins, for he served as ambassador of Antiochus III to the Roman senate in 193.[152] Yet his version had little in common with anything retailed by Roman writers—or by most of the Greeks for that matter. According to Hegesianax, Aeneas had four sons: Ascanius, Euryleon, Romulus, and Romus, the last of whom founded the city that took his name.[153] If Hegesianax, who surely took the trouble to inform himself, knew of a canonical version, he plainly discounted it.[154] His version is all the more remarkable, for as we now know, the Chians in this very period voted to erect a monument to Romulus and Remus, founders of Rome, prompted by information they had acquired from Rome itself.[155] Hegesianax could treat the legend as he pleased.

It would be superfluous to multiply examples. Further variations could easily be cited long after the time when the idea of a Trojan

---

future rather than immediate descendants—but that reading largely depends on the presupposition that Lycophron followed the Timaean version; cf. d'Anna, *Problemi*, 76.

150. Lycophron, 1253–1260: κτίσει δὲ χώραν ἐν τόποις Βορειγόνων / ὑπὲρ Λατίνους Δαυνίους τ' ᾠκισμένην, / πύργους τριάκοντ', ἐξαριθμήσας γονὰς / συὸς κελαινῆς.

151. Lycophron, 1259–1260.

152. Livy, 34.57–59.

153. Dion. Hal. 1.72.1. Hegesianax wrote under the pseudonym Cephalon of Gergis; Athen. 9.393d.

154. Cf. Perret, *Les origines*, 512–513; Cornell, *PCPS*, 201 (1975), 25.

155. The inscription, with text, Italian translation, and sound commentary, can be found conveniently in Moretti, *RivFilol*, 108 (1980), 33–54.

extraction for Rome had become firm doctrine.[156] As an extreme but illuminating instance, one might note the hopelessly obscure Promathion, who composed a history of Italy perhaps in the first century B.C. He evidently drew on Etruscan memory or fabrication to produce a bizarre tale unparalleled elsewhere in our evidence. The account centers upon an Etruscan king of Alba overthrown by the twins, who were born from the union of a servant girl and a disembodied phallus. That peculiar narrative neatly demonstrates the basic proposition: even in the late Republic, when Greek writers gathered material from Italy on the origins of Rome, they would still encounter a bewildering diversity and inconsistency.[157] The absence of anything resembling a standard line is inescapable.

The fact needed to be established, for it affects an issue often considered and often misconceived: a supposed political dimension to variants on the Trojan legend.

Demetrius of Skepsis, writing in the early second century, composed a learned *Catalogue of the Trojans*. That work contained the claim that Aeneas ruled at Skepsis and the implication that he had never left the Troad to migrate to the West. The sons of Aeneas and Hector then held their royal seat at Skepsis for generations to follow.[158] The thesis of Demetrius, so it has been argued, represents anti-Roman polemic, a denial of Rome's Trojan origins, thus implicitly relegating Romans to the class of barbarians in a Greek intellectual retaliation for Roman imperialism.[159] The omission of reference to Rome's foundation in the *Chronicle* of Apollodorus, composed in the second half of the second century, may, on this theory, indicate disdain for Rome.[160] And further,

---

156. See, e.g., on Agathocles of Cyzicus and Dionysius of Chalcis, Perret, *Les origines*, 380–388, 463–467; Cornell, *PCPS*, 201 (1975), 19–20, n. 3, with further bibliography.

157. Promathion's version is cited by Plut. *Rom.* 2.3–6. The effort of S. Mazzarino, *Il pensiero storico classico*, I (Bari, 1973), 3, 190–199, and II.1 (Bari, 1974), 5, 59–71, to date Promathion to the fifth century, although accepted by d'Anna, *Problemi*, 46–52, was adequately refuted by E. Gabba, *FondHardt*, 13 (1966), 147–149; cf. Cornell, *PCPS*, 201 (1975), 21, n. 4, 25, n. 4, 26.

158. Strabo, 13.1.52–53 = C607.

159. So, most vigorously, E. Gabba, *RSI*, 86 (1974), 630–633; and idem, in M. Sordi, ed., *I canali della propaganda nel mondo antico, ContrIstStorAnt* (Milan, 1976), 85–91. The view is accepted with modifications by Cornell, *PCPS*, 201 (1975), 26–27; Momigliano, *Settimo contributo*, 451–452; Horsfall, in Bremmer and Horsfall, *Roman Myth and Mythography*, 13; and J.-L. Ferrary, *Philhellénisme et impérialisme* (Paris, 1988), 223–229.

160. Gabba, *RSI*, 86 (1974), 630–633; idem, *Dionysius*, 198.

one can cite Menecrates of Xanthos, perhaps a contemporary of Demetrius, who maintained that Aeneas betrayed Troy to the Achaeans
and was welcomed into their ranks, thus suggesting that Rome's ancestor was a despicable traitor, yet another instance of anti-Roman propaganda.[161]

The proposition is dubious and unacceptable. Most fundamentally, it
misconceives a mentality that not only entertained inconsistent versions
but continued to multiply them. The absence of a canonical tale permitted and encouraged variants. If Roman writers could regularly disagree
on key components of the story, Greeks surely encountered no restric-
tions on inventiveness. Readers of Demetrius' work in Skepsis would
find no more animosity to Rome than would readers of Lycophron's
poem in Alexandria. Divergent tales were the very stuff of legend—and
the Trojan tales proved especially prolific.

The thrust of Demetrius' reconstruction is not hard to grasp. Patriotic
motives spurred the scholar who transferred the ancient seat of power
to his own home town, especially as he could contrast Skepsis with
the run-down remains of contemporary Troy. Civic pride and rivalry
among towns in the Troad played a central part.[162] But there is more to
it than that. Squabbles among scholars affected the conclusions. Demetrius' *Catalogue of the Trojans* required him to be steeped in Homer,
and the bard's notorious lines implied that Aeneas and his descendants
never left the Troad.[163] If Demetrius engaged in polemic, he directed
it not against Rome but against those who disputed his reading of
Homer.[164]

A plethora of discrepancies, it might be argued, does not account for
Demetrius. He took the further step of breaking the Roman-Trojan
connection altogether, thus putting his tale in a quite different category.
Is it so? Roman writers, to be sure, held firm to that connection,
whatever their differences on details. But the Greeks went their own

---

161. Gabba, in Sordi, *I canali*, 92–93; cf. Momigliano, *Settimo contributo*, 450–451.

162. Cf. Strabo, 13.1.27 = C594; 13.1.34 = C597. Demetrius visited Ilium around the
time of the Antiochene War; Strabo, 13.1.27 = C594. Gabba, in Sordi, *I canali*, 88, sets
the visit in 190 and suggests that Demetrius may have witnessed L. Scipio's sacrifice at
Troy (Livy, 37.37.1–3)—an altogether speculative proposal.

163. Homer, *Iliad*, 20.307–308. Strabo, 13.1.52–53 = C607, cites the Homeric lines
and discusses the disputes over them in conjunction with the scenario of Demetrius.
There is a full discussion of the Strabo passage, with different objectives, in P. M. Smith,
HSCP, 85 (1981), 34–43.

164. For quarrels among the erudite on this issue, see Dion. Hal. 1.53.4–5.

way, unhindered by cultural motives that prompted the western nation. Legends that ascribed a Hellenic, rather than a Trojan, background to Rome's beginnings continued to circulate in late Hellenistic Greece.[165] Demetrius' version, one among many, might stir civic fever in Skepsis but would hardly stimulate anti-Romanism.

As confirmation one can point to Hegesianax of Alexandria Troas, a close contemporary of Demetrius. Hegesianax composed a *Troika* of his own and, like Demetrius, believed that Aeneas never went to Italy. His rendition has the Trojan hero reach Thrace and perish there. Yet Hegesianax, twice an envoy to the Romans as a courtier of Antiochus III, was surely not producing hostile propaganda.[166] One could go further still. Polybius himself, as we happen to know, subscribed to the tale that Evander brought Arcadians to Italy and was responsible for founding Rome. The Arcadian historian, for intelligible reasons, promoted the story; it was a link between his native land and the conquering power. The Trojan legend does not appear in the extant fragments of Polybius. Yet no one will claim him as an enemy of Rome.[167]

No need to linger over Apollodorus and his failure to record the foundation date of Rome. Any number of reasons can be excogitated for the omission. The bewildering variety and inconsistency of suggested dates prior to Apollodorus might be reason enough. It would take a very so-

165. See above, pp. 16–20.

166. Dion. Hal. 1.49.1. On his service as envoy in 196 and 193, see Polyb. 18.47.4, 18.50.3; Livy, 33.34.1–4, 34.1–4, 34.57–59; Appian, *Syr.* 6. Perret, *Les origines*, 512–513, in fact, takes Hegesianax's story as evidence of scorn and hostility toward Rome. See also P. M. Martin, *MEFRA*, 101 (1989), 119–120. He was, to be sure, a *philos* of Antiochus; Athen. 4.155a–b; cf. 3.80d. And the conference of 193 was a tense affair. But a figure hostile to Rome would not have been chosen as envoy by Antiochus at a time when he sought to maintain cordial relations. Another envoy on that mission, Menippus, was accorded public recognition by Rome; *Syll.*³ 601; see E. S. Gruen, *The Hellenistic World and the Coming of Rome* (Berkeley, Calif., 1984), 626–629. By contrast, Gabba takes Hegesianax as espousing a pro-Roman version: Aeneas died in Thrace but his son founded Rome; Dion. Hal. 1.72.1; Gabba, *RSI*, 86 (1974), 631; idem, in Sordi, *I canali*, 88–89. The whole political dimension, however, is purely hypothetical. If Hegesianax wanted to appease the Romans, why leave Aeneas in Thrace and endorse a tale that coincides with no other known version?

167. For Polybius and the Evander story, see Dion. Hal. 1.32.1. Polybius does refer to the legend of Troy but only to refute Timaeus' faulty inference from the October Horse; Polyb. 12.4.b–c. Bickermann, *CP*, 47 (1952), 67, and Gabba, *RSI*, 86 (1974), 632, take Polybius' version as indicating preference for Greek rather than Trojan origins. But the Evander and the Aeneas tales were by no means incompatible. Fabius Pictor embraced them both; *HRR*, fr. 1. Cf. D. Musti, *FondHardt*, 20 (1974), 129–132; Ferrary, *Philhellénisme et impérialisme*, 226.

phisticated reader indeed to detect propaganda in the silence.[168] Menecrates of Xanthos merits a word or two. He at least endorsed a tradition sharply critical of Aeneas, the tale that he betrayed Troy out of hatred for Paris.[169] Does this then represent negative Hellenic reaction to Rome?[170] The case has nothing to recommend it. For one thing, Menecrates' date is altogether insecure. An anti-Roman objective makes sense only if he is placed in the late third or second century. But the Ionic dialect of the fragments points much more strongly to the late fifth or early fourth century, thus safely removing Menecrates from any debate over Rome's Trojan origins.[171] But even if one postulates a late Hellenistic date, the idea of anti-Romanism has little or no force. The relevant fragment not only records Aeneas' treachery but has him welcomed as "one of the Achaeans."[172] The bland tone suggests a known and acceptable tale, anything but polemic. If Menecrates' story had propaganda value at all, it may have been Lycian propaganda, undermining the Greek tradition of Troy's fall as an Achaean accomplishment.[173] Or perhaps even anti-Persian propaganda, relevant in late fifth- or early fourth-century Hellas, thus equating Asiatic Troy with the realm of Persia.[174] More likely still, Menecrates simply counts among those many writers who addressed conflicting strands of post-Homeric traditions, chose among them, or invented new ones. He may indeed have adopted the line that kept Aeneas in Troy and that knew of no western migration, in which case discrediting Aeneas could not reflect on the repute of Rome.[175] And the transformation of Aeneas into an Achaean would protect his descendants from the charge of barbarism.[176] On any and all counts, Menecrates' treatise stands outside the realm of anti-Romanism. The whole

168. On the silence, see F. Jacoby, *Apollodors Chronik* (Berlin, 1902), 26–28, who, however, shows that Eratosthenes also gave no date for Rome's foundation. Should he too be branded with anti-Romanism? The argument dissolves.

169. Dion. Hal. 1.48.3.

170. Gabba, in Sordi, *I canali*, 92–93; Momigliano, *Settimo contributo*, 450–451.

171. See the careful treatment of Asheri, *Fra Ellenismo e Iranismo* (Bologna, 1983), 127–132, with bibliography.

172. Dion. Hal. 1.48.3: εἰς Ἀχαιῶν ἐγεγόνει.

173. So P. M. Smith, *HSCP*, 85 (1981), 33–34.

174. So Asheri, *Fra Ellenismo e Iranismo*, 151–152. That is a less plausible proposition for a historian who was himself an Asiatic Greek.

175. One need not pause over the suggestion of P. M. Martin, *MEFRA*, 101 (1989), 114–116, that Menecrates' version gives a mythological veneer to hostility between Rome and the tyrants of Syracuse.

176. See the sound remarks of Asheri, *Fra Ellenismo e Iranismo*, 144–153.

concept of the Trojan legend as manipulated by Greeks to avenge themselves on Rome falls to the ground.[177]

Alleged manipulation of the legend for political purposes deserves a closer look. A series of episodes in the third and early second centuries alludes to the link between Troy and Rome in the context of diplomacy and war. The accumulation of instances has fostered a cynical conclusion: that Rome exploited the legend to facilitate intervention and expansionism in the Greek East.[178] That analysis misplaces the emphasis and misconceives the motivation. The episodes themselves, upon further inspection, present a very different picture.

The legend's first appearance as a diplomatic or military instrument lends valuable insight. The device was employed by a Greek, not a Roman. Pyrrhus, the ruler of Epirus, cited the Trojan connection in 281 in order to build support against Rome among the Greeks of the West. He announced to his allies the expectation of a successful outcome: as descendant of Achilles, he would recreate the Achaean victory at Troy by subduing the colonists of Troy.[179] The propaganda may or may not have had effect, but it was Hellenic propaganda. The Romans had no cause to exploit it.[180]

Two decades later appeal to the Trojan story came again in the course of a Roman war, and again from a people other than the Romans. Early in the First Punic War, the city of Segesta expelled its Carthaginian

---

177. A fragment of Naevius is sometimes seen as reflecting knowledge of the story of Aeneas' betrayal; 23, Morel: *blande et docte percontat, Aenea quo pacto / Troiam urbem liquerit*; cf. Gabba, in Sordi, *I canali*, 91–92. But the inference is purely speculative. And even if true, Naevius' *Bellum Punicum* is probably too early to be responding to any anti-Romanism among Greek intellectuals. The composition of A. Postumius Albinus' work, *De adventu Aeneae*, may or may not have been part of the debate. The title hardly proves it; *Origo gentis Romanae*, 15.4; Serv. *Ad Aen.* 9.707. More important, Q. Lutatius Catulus, around the end of the second century, actually endorsed the tale that had Aeneas as betrayer of Troy; *Origo gentis Romanae*, 9.2. One may presume that Catulus did not take that position out of animosity to Rome.

178. So, most recently, Momigliano, *Settimo contributo*, 453: "In general, one can say that Aeneas helped the claims of Rome over Sicily and her interventions in the Greek East"; Horsfall in Bremmer and Horsfall, *Roman Myth and Mythography*, 21: "Trojan kinship would give the Romans a fine pretext . . . for interference in the affairs of Asia Minor."

179. Paus. 1.12.1. See also Pyrrhus' coin issues in southern Italy and Sicily with images of Thetis and Achilles; *BMC, Thessaly*, 111, no. 7–8; 112, no. 9–19.

180. E. Weber, *WS*, 85 (1972), 214, speculates that the Tarentine Greeks suggested this line to Pyrrhus.

garrison and threw in its lot with Rome. The Segestans offered as explanation their consanguinity with Rome: both claimed Aeneas as ancestor.[181] Rome certainly welcomed the defection of Segesta, a major gain in the contest with Carthage. But there is nothing to show that Rome utilized the Trojan connection to advance its own purposes in the island.[182] To this point only the Greeks were playing that game.

A third episode leads to a similar conclusion. War broke out between Acarnania and the Aetolian League in the 230s, inducing the Acarnanians, so the report has it, to seek Roman aid. They reached back to remote antiquity to justify the request: Acarnania had been the only Greek state to refrain from warring on Troy. Roman envoys took up the Acarnanian cause, requesting removal of Aetolian garrisons and autonomy for Acarnania. The Aetolians summarily dismissed the request and treated the legates with scorn. Rome chose not to pursue the matter.[183] The tale's authenticity has long been disputed, and the question need not be decided here.[184] Even if one accepts the events as fact, however, they point clearly to Acarnanian initiative. The Romans were willing to acknowledge the relationship but not to press it on the diplomatic front.

181. Zon. 8.9.12. Allusion to the relationship occurs also in Cic. *Verr.* 2.4.72, 2.5.83, 2.5.125; Diod. 23.5; Plut. *Nic.* 1.3. Cf. the Segestan coins that represent Aeneas and Anchises; *BMC, Sicily,* 59 ff. A relationship was claimed also by Centuripae through Lanuvium; see Manganaro, *PP,* 29 (1974), 396.

182. D. Kienast, *Hermes,* 93 (1965), 478–489, conjectures that Rome seized upon the idea to ingratiate itself with the Greeks of Sicily and to combat Carthaginian influence in the island. But the hypothesis depends on dating Rome's supervision of the Aphrodite cult at Eryx to the immediate aftermath of the First Punic War, a view by no means proved or even suggested by Diod. 4.83.7.

183. Justin, 28.1.5–28.2.14. Other allusions to Roman benefits for Acarnania because of the latter's stance in the Trojan War are given by Strabo, 10.2.25 = C462; Dion. Hal. 1.51.2.

184. M. Holleaux, *Rome, la Grèce, et les monarchies hellénistiques au IIIe siècle avant J.-C. (273–205)* (Paris, 1935), 5–22, made a powerful case against authenticity. The chief exhibit in his presentation is Polyb. 2.12.7, who places Rome's first entrance into diplomatic relations with Greeks in 229/8. The testimony is not necessarily decisive. One can argue that Polybius did not know of the Acarnanian affair—so M. Gelzer, *Hermes,* 68 (1933), 144—or that he did not regard it as a significant diplomatic exchange—so E. Manni, *PP,* 11 (1956), 187; F. P. Rizzo, *Studi ellenistico-romani* (Palermo, 1974), 71–76. The tale can, in any case, not be regarded as a Roman invention, despite Holleaux, for the Romans came off badly in the narrative. S. I. Oost, *Roman Policy in Epirus and Acarnania in the Age of the Roman Conquest of Greece* (Dallas, 1954), 92–97, considered it the product of Aetolian propaganda. Others simply retail it without argument; D. Golan, *RivStorAnt,* 1 (1971), 96–97; Weber, *WS,* 85 (1972), 218–219; Gabba, in Sordi, *I Canali,* 100; Momigliano, *Settimo contributo,* 452; Horsfall, in Bremmer and Horsfall, *Roman Myth and Mythography,* 21.

Their demarche concluded without issue. As before, the Greeks hoped to capitalize on the legend; the Romans merely engaged in response and reaction.

A similar circumstance can be discerned in a Roman reply to diplomatic feelers from the Syrian ruler Seleucus, probably Seleucus II. The king sought *amicitia* and *societas* with the western power, and the Romans replied in positive fashion, with the proviso that Seleucus absolve the Ilians, their *consanguinei*, of liability for tribute. Such, at least, is the information contained in a letter read to the senate by the emperor Claudius three centuries later.[185] The flimsy testimony has given grounds for doubt. Yet no obvious reason for forgery exists.[186] The story itself, in any case, seems consistent with the rest of our information. The initiative again came from the East. Rome did not provoke the diplomatic interchange, but once the proposition was advanced, Roman leaders took the opportunity to reaffirm their association with the legends of Troy. The purpose was hardly imperial expansionism. If anything concrete emerged from this negotiation, we hear nothing of it. The Roman objective was neither protection of Ilium nor interference in the internal affairs of the Seleucid realm. The proposal asserted a cultural connection. Greek initiative enabled the Romans to present that connection in an international context.

The Greek impulse gave rise to Roman policy. By the later third century the Romans themselves promoted the legend in a public and conspicuous manner. Aggrandizement, however, was not the aim. In the dark days of the Hannibalic War, religious consciousness became more intense and more acute. The disaster at Trasimene in 217 called forth urgent advice from the Sibylline Books recommending that a temple be vowed to Venus Erycina. The vow was duly carried out, with Sibylline sanction, by Q. Fabius Maximus two years later. A temple of Venus Erycina rose on the Capitol in 215.[187] The association with Aeneas and Troy plainly provided the central ingredient in this move. The cult had its origin in Sicilian Eryx, a site where, the legend had it,

185. Suet. *Claud.* 25.3: *recitata vetere epistula Graeca senatus populique Romani Seleuco regi amicitiam et societatem ita demum pollicentis, si consanguineos suos Ilienses ab omni onere immunes praestitisset.*

186. Holleaux, *Rome, la Grèce*, 46–60, considered it a Roman invention; D. Magie, *Roman Rule in Asia Minor* (Princeton, N.J., 1950), II, 943–944, n. 40, took it as an Ilian fabrication. But neither offered substantive reasons. For a defense of the story, see Rizzo, *Studi ellenistico-romani*, 83–88.

187. Livy, 22.9.7–10, 22.10.10, 23.30.13–14, 23.31.9.

Aeneas had dedicated a shrine to his mother.[188] Establishment of the cult in Rome was not presented as transfer of a foreign deity. Venus Erycina took her place on the Capitol itself, in the vicinity of Jupiter Maximus Capitolinus, an unmistakeable signal that she represented the national heritage.[189] The principal purpose of the move must have been reassurance and a boost to public morale in the grim circumstances after Trasimene. Homage to the goddess who both promised divine protection and emphasized a link with the ancient past could lend confidence in the endurance of Rome's legacy. Embrace of the Trojan tie now had overt state sanction.[190] It gave public display to Rome's antiquity and the cultural origins that could stimulate patriotic pride.

When military fortunes shifted in the Hannibalic War and Roman success seemed assured, the link with Troy gained still more attention at the state level. In 205, with Rome's forces poised for the invasion of Africa and the conclusion of the conflict, the cult of Magna Mater was transported from Mount Ida to Rome and established on the Palatine. Mount Ida was the birthplace of Aeneas, his refuge, and a place of assemblage before his departure.[191] And Magna Mater was a protective deity of the Trojans.[192] The symbolic features of the move stand out. Rome collaborated here with the kingdom of Pergamum, overlord of the Troad. A striking procession welcomed the goddess who was honored with elaborate rites and a home on the Palatine. The inauguration of the cult and its festival asserted the significance Rome set upon its origins and their links with the antique legends of Hellas.[193] The episode had diplomatic, military, and religious implications. But all were joined by the golden thread of the Trojan legend that announced Rome's cultural credentials to the nations of the Hellenistic world.[194]

---

188. Diod. 4.83.4–7; Vergil, *Aen.* 5.759–760.

189. See, especially, R. Schilling, *La religion romaine de Vénus* (Paris, 1954), 248–254; cf. Galinsky, *Aeneas, Sicily, and Rome*, 173–175; I. Bitto, *ArchStorMessinese*, 28 (1977), 121–133.

190. Cf. also the oracular warning of Cannae by the seer Marcius, a forecast brought to light in 212, which refers to Romans as descendants of Troy; Livy, 25.12.1–10: *amnem, Troiugenam fuge Cannam.* The public identification of Romans and Trojans by this time is quite clear. Perret, *Les origines*, 54–57, wrongly takes this as reflecting hostility between Romans and Greeks. See Galinsky, *Aeneas, Sicily, and Rome*, 177–178.

191. Homer, *Iliad*, 2.820–821; Dion. Hal. 1.46–48.

192. Vergil, *Aen.* 6.784–787, 7.135–140, 9.80–92, 9.617–620, 10.156–158, 10.228–235, 10.250–255; Ovid, *Fasti*, 4.251–254; Paus. 10.26.1.

193. See especially Ovid, *Fasti*, 4.247–272. Other sources, bibliography, and discussion in Gruen, *Studies in Greek Culture and Roman Policy* (Leiden, 1990), 15–21.

194. See the full treatment in Gruen, *Studies*, 5–33.

The conclusion is reinforced by the Peace of Phoenice in 205, which brought a formal terminus to the First Macedonian War. The signatures framed that treaty in the same year as Cybele's cult was transferred to Rome. And there can be no coincidence in the fact that the two states who headed the list of Rome's *adscripti* in the document were Ilium and Pergamum.[195] The war itself had been a rather sorry episode in Rome's history and a stain on its reputation, but Romans could salvage esteem by associating themselves with a proud heritage. Ilium, a small and impotent town in the politics of the Hellenistic titans, had had no part in the war, of course. Rome could satisfy no imperial ambitions by associating her fortunes with that community. The value of Ilium lay on a symbolic plane. It accorded to Rome the cultural stature that could not be won on the battlefield.[196]

Determined and consistent efforts to justify prestige beyond mere military success also accompany Rome's eastern involvement in the early second century. Victory over Philip V and the subsequent "liberation" of the Greeks inspired the Roman commander T. Quinctius Flamininus to wax eloquent in Greek. He dedicated precious objects at Delphi inscribed with his own verses, reminding the Hellenes that their liberation came at the hands of a descendant of Aeneas and a representative of the Aeneiadai.[197] There were no military goals to achieve here; martial supremacy had already been established. The conjunction of Greek freedom and Trojan ancestry tells the tale clearly enough. Flamininus enunciated Rome's claim to a place in the cultivated community of the Mediterranean.

Rome maintained the posture in the course of conflict with Antiochus III. Entrance of Roman forces for the first time into Asia Minor summoned forth an appropriate gesture. The naval commander C. Livius Salinator in 190 made sure to inaugurate the campaign with a sacrifice to Athena at Ilium.[198] And the arrival of the consul, L. Scipio, gave added drama and meaning to the scene. His sacrifices were accompanied by mutual expressions of joy by Romans and Ilians at the common heritage that bound them to one another.[199] Further, the Ilians reaped benefits

195. Livy, 29.12.14.

196. Efforts to deny the authenticity of Ilium's inclusion in the Peace of Phoenice fail to take account of that cultural dimension; see Gruen, *Studies*, 31–33, with references to the literature.

197. Plut. *Flam.* 12.6–7: Αἰνεάδας Τίτος ὕμμιν ὑπέρτατον ὥπασε δῶρον, / Ἑλλήνων τεύξας παισὶν ἐλευθερίαν.

198. Livy, 37.9.7.

199. Livy, 37.37.1–3: *sacrificavit Minervae praesidi arcis et Iliensibus in omni rerum ver-*

from the peace settlement of 188, a tax immunity and the acquisition of two towns. Livy's analysis accurately assesses the meaning: the Ilians obtained favor not so much for any recent services as in acknowledgment of Rome's ancestry.[200] There was little profit in cultivating Ilium for any substantive assistance it might provide, nor is it likely that other Greek states would contribute to a war effort or render postwar allegiance on the basis of a Trojan connection. Rome looked to the symbolic effect. The nation shunned the label of barbarian and struck the pose of heir and standard-bearer of an antique civilization shared by Trojans and Achaeans.

Exploitation for concrete advantage remained a Greek, rather than a Roman, objective in the early second as in the third century. Lampsacus, a city of the Troad, took the Roman pronouncements at face value and staked a claim for privilege and consideration. In the aftermath of the Second Macedonian War, a Lampsacene envoy called attention to the *syngeneia* that held between his city and Rome, hoping for inclusion in the peace treaty and thus protection by the victor.[201] The aim, it appears, went unfulfilled.[202] The Ilians themselves hoped to obtain further stature by championing the causes of allies before the Romans, but their efforts on behalf of the Lycians drew only ambiguous response from the senate and no concrete action.[203] Rome showed little interest in translating cultural propaganda into substantive gains.

---

borumque honore ab se oriundos Romanos praeferentibus et Romanis laetis origine sua; Justin, 31.8.1–4.

200. Livy, 38.39.10: *non tam ob recentia ulla merita quam originum memoria*. Absence of these provisions in Polybius' account of the Peace of Apamea, 21.46, gives no grounds for doubting their genuineness; see Magie, *Roman Rule*, II, 950–951, n. 60; H. H. Schmitt, *Untersuchungen zur Geschichte Antiochos' des Grossen und seiner Zeit* (Wiesbaden, 1964), 292.

201. *Syll.*³ 591, lines 18–19, 21–22, 24–25, 30–31, 54–56, 60–61. Holleaux, *Rome, la Grèce*, 53–56, takes Lampsacus' use of the intermediacy of the Massiliotes rather than the Ilians to mean that the Trojan connection counted for little. Schmitt, *Untersuchungen*, 290–293, by contrast, concludes that Ilium was not free to intervene, a sign that it stood under Seleucid hegemony. But Lampsacus' claim to direct consanguinity with the Romans could only be weakened if it depended on Ilian intermediacy.

202. Cf. Bickermann, *Philologus*, 87 (1932), 277–279; Gruen, *Hellenistic World*, 23, 542–543.

203. Polyb. 22.5.1–7; see H. H. Schmitt, *Rom und Rhodos* (Munich, 1957), 81–128; Gruen, *CQ*, 25 (1975), 64–68; F. W. Walbank, *A Historical Commentary on Polybius* (Oxford, 1979), III, 181–183. Cf. also the Greek oracular pronouncement, perhaps from Delphi, of the early second century, which predicted Rome's victory over Philip and represented the clash between Rome and Carthage as one in which Trojans had overcome Phoenicians; Plut. *Mor.* 399c; cf. Justin, 30.4.1–4. This may represent another instance of Hellenic efforts to curry Roman favor by endorsing the Trojan legend.

Allusions to Troy and the legend in interstate relations cease abruptly after the early second century. They reappear only at the end of the Republic in very different circumstances.[204] Lacunose sources do not account for the absence. We are reasonably well informed on matters of diplomacy and warfare in subsequent years. The change is a real one. An explanation emerges readily and conforms conveniently to the preceding analysis. The Roman conqueror in the late third and early second centuries felt the need to project a different image, to demonstrate roots in distant antiquity, and to claim a share in the common culture of the eastern Mediterranean. Successes on the battlefield were accompanied by insistence upon the civilized qualities of the victors, who revived the distinctions of their Trojan forebears. With the conclusion of the eastern wars, that insistence lost its urgency. The Trojan connection had been recognized and acknowledged across the Mediterranean. Roman arms had vindicated Troy. And the nation's spokesmen had established its cultural credentials. There was no further need to reproduce the message.

Greek intellectuals created the myth of Troy. And Greek intellectuals molded it to help explain and justify the colonization of the West. The story evolved in multiple forms. Greek pioneers held prime place at the outset, then were paralleled or overlaid in importance by Trojan refugees and by Troy's principal survivor, Aeneas. The fables expanded and diversified, shaped by Sicilian historians and combined with the indigenous traditions of Etruria and Latium. Rome's increasing power and authority in the peninsula soon demanded its inclusion in the complex fabric of developing legend. Greeks invented Hellenic forebears, eponymous founders, and Trojan intermediaries. By the time such creations reached the level of public consciousness in Rome, a bewildering variety of versions entangled the tradition.

The matter of articulating its origins took on importance for Rome in the late fourth century. The aftermath of the Latin War and expanded contacts with Hellenic Italy provided the impetus. Political and cultural motives combined to develop a narrative that would bring mutual esteem to Romans and Latins and establish a pedigree that connected Rome to the Hellenic world. The idea of a Trojan rather than a Greek derivation proved especially appealing. It fitted the Romans within the matrix of Greek legend that stretched back to remote antiquity while

204. For references, see Weber, *WS*, 85 (1972), 221–225.

marking a differentiation and projecting a separate identity. The absence of contemporary Trojans enhanced the appeal; the tale was malleable and adjustable to national needs.

The adoption of Trojan roots, however, did not entail coalescence of the tradition. A wide range of versions still circulated in the third and second centuries. Greek intellectuals, even those conversant with Roman accounts, had no reason to hew to a Roman line and continued to produce variants that contrasted in character, chronology, and narrative. Hence, those who altered the Aeneas tale in discrepant and ostensibly unflattering ways engaged not in political propaganda but in conventional scholarly wrangling. The notion of a canonical story remained remote. That conclusion is more strikingly confirmed by Roman writers themselves. While unanimous on the Trojan connection, they coincided on little else. Historians and poets felt free to improvise, extract, conflate, and diverge. The multifarious strands of the tradition, long after the embrace of Troy, give insight into a mentality that prized inventiveness over consistency.

Advertisement of the Trojan association had cultural rather than political or diplomatic ends in view. Allusions to the legend in interstate relations of the third and early second centuries represent either Greek initiative or Roman posturing and did not issue in concrete benefits. But in a broader sense the distinctions dissolve and the objectives are mutually reinforcing. The circumstances attendant upon Rome's new status in late fourth-century Latium and Magna Graecia gave incentive for adoption of the Trojan heritage, and the parading of that heritage a century later closely accompanied the display of Roman might in the Mediterranean. The attachment of Troy and Rome carried a comparable symbolism in each case. Preeminence in the peninsula went hand in hand with embrace of traditions that gave the suzerain a cultural legitimacy. And demonstration of military power abroad prompted insistence on the antiquity and the refined credentials of the conqueror.

[2]

CATO AND HELLENISM

M. Porcius Cato has earned a memorable and enduring reputation. He is the Roman curmudgeon par excellence. The stern censor and gruff champion of native values gained repute as arch-critic of Hellas and Hellenism. The culture of the Greek world, its practitioners, and its admirers came in for sharp rebuke. Cato's statements, actions, and postures created an image that persists and prevails. He became an emblem of resistance to the alien intrusion.

Yet that is but part of the story. As is well known, the Censor was no stranger to things Hellenic. He gained considerable familiarity with the language, literature, and learning of the Greek world. The paradox is stark, and efforts to resolve it remain inadequate. But a resolution must be sought. Cato's character and attitudes stand at the heart of any inquiry into the reaction to Hellenism. Wherein lies the significance of his demeanor?

Ostensible hostility pervades the record, manifested in a variety of contexts. Greek oratory, for instance, incurred the scorn of Cato. He denounced the insincerity and empty rhetoric associated with the Hellenic race: the words of Greeks issue from their lips, those of Romans from the heart.[1] He took special aim at the training purportedly provided by Isocrates and his followers: apprentice orators in his system were still studying in old age, and by the time they had met requirements, they were fit to ply their trade only in Hades.[2] Those quips

1. Plut. *Cato*, 12.5; cf. 22.4.
2. Plut. *Cato*, 23.2.

appropriately suit the man who advocated directness and simplicity in public speech. For Cato, the proper orator is defined as a good man— who also happens to be skilled in speaking.[3] And his celebrated advice sums up the position pungently: stick to the facts and the words will come.[4] Greek garrulity discredits the enterprise.

Poetry suffers comparable criticism. The *ars poetica*, so Cato claims, lacked honor. Those who were especially zealous for it or devoted themselves to it at banquets acquired the insulting label of *grassatores*.[5] The Censor singled out a certain tribune, M. Caelius, whom he stigmatized for, among other things, the recitation of Greek verses.[6]

Cato leveled still more stinging abuse at Greek philosophy. In the formulation of Plutarch, he was totally at odds with philosophy.[7] He branded Socrates a raging babbler whose ideas aimed at undermining traditions, drawing disciples away from the laws, and preparing the ground for his own tyranny.[8] Philosophers are mere graveclothes or funeral dirges for the dead.[9] Most notorious, of course, was Cato's reaction to the philosophic embassy in 155. A trio of Athenian thinkers, a Stoic, a Peripatetic, and an Academic, represented their city's interests in Rome. They came on a mission to enlist Roman favor in a diplomatic wrangle, but they took the occasion to deliver lectures and introduce their teachings to eager Roman audiences. Special popularity attached to Carneades, whose spellbinding eloquence dazzled listeners and won converts to philosophy. Cato, disturbed by their methods and their success, sprang into action, speeding completion of their diplomatic business and thus hastening their departure from Rome. He expressed deep concern that Roman youth might abandon allegiance to laws and magistrates, lured by the siren song of philosophy, by verbal conjuring, and by thinkers who pay no regard to the truth.[10] The Censor's intervention cut short that mission, thereby terminating its intellectual side effects.

Education of the young held a high priority for Cato. His household included a gifted Greek slave who served as tutor for many of the

---

3. Seneca, *Contr.* 1, pr. 9: *vir bonus dicendi peritus.*
4. Victor, 374, H: *rem tene, verba sequentur.*
5. Gellius, 11.2.5; cf. Cic. *Tusc. Disp.* 1.3.
6. *ORF*, fr. 115 = Cugusi, *OR*, fr. 85.
7. Plut. *Cato*, 23.1: ὅλως φιλοσοφίᾳ προσκεκρουκώς.
8. Plut. *Cato*, 23.1.
9. Gellius, 18.7.3.
10. Plut. *Cato*, 22.1–5; Pliny, *NH*, 7.112; Cic. *De Rep.* 3.9.

children in that extended *familia*. But Cato would not expose his own son to such teachings. The doting father took personal charge of his education, stressing fundamental training in the ancient traditions of his own people.[11]

Further, Cato projected himself as a sharp critic of luxurious habits and lax moral discipline, characteristics conventionally associated with the Greeks—at least by Romans. The Censor conspicuously and continually denounced luxury and its insidious effects upon Roman character. He frequently concerned himself with sumptuary laws. Livy accords him a powerful speech resisting repeal of the *lex Oppia* in 195, including a passage that links the arrival of debilitating luxury to Roman expansion into Greece and Asia.[12] A *lex Porcia de sumptu provinciali* stood on the books, evidently restricting acquisitions by provincial governors.[13] And Cato rose to defend the *lex Orchia* when its repeal was under consideration.[14] The luxury theme recurs regularly in Cato's speeches. He harshly criticized the Roman practice of lavish private building.[15] He castigated those who expropriated public booty for private purposes.[16] A censorial speech, or at least the title thereof, reflects persistent concern with the display of art objects for personal advantage: *de signis et tabulis*.[17] Cato lost no opportunity to reiterate his stance. He blasted Lepidus for erecting statues to two Greek cooks.[18] And in a speech *ad populum*, he lamented that extravagant spending and moral slackness had reached a point where one paid a higher price for male prostitutes than for farmlands, for table delicacies than for farm workers.[19]

Cato directed his most virulent attacks against a particular branch of Greek learning: the profession of medicine. Antipathy to Greek doctors reached a shrill pitch of intensity. Cato retailed the story of the physician Hippocrates who declined a handsome cash offer from the king of Persia, declaring that he would never cater to barbarians, the enemies of Greece. From that tale Cato extrapolated a much broader conclusion:

11. Plut. *Cato*, 20.3–5.
12. Livy, 34.4.1–4.
13. *ILS*, 38, lines 15–17.
14. *ORF*, fr. 139–146 = Cugusi, *OR*, fr. 128–132, 210, 235, 238.
15. *ORF*, fr. 133, 174, 185 = Cugusi, *OR*, fr. 97, 218, 139.
16. *ORF*, fr. 98 = Cugusi, *OR*, fr. 72.
17. *ORF*, fr. 94; cf. 185 = Cugusi, *OR*, fr. 52; cf. 139.
18. *ORF*, fr. 96; cf. 95 = Cugusi, *OR*, fr. 178; cf. 53.
19. Polyb. 31.25.5a; cf. Gellius, 11.2.5.

that all Greek physicians had sworn an oath to poison barbarians, among whom they reckoned the Romans. He issued grave warning to his son to steer clear of Greek medicine and to shun its practitioners.[20]

Cato also delivered more sweeping pronouncements on Greek culture and character. He declared to his son that the Greeks were a thoroughly wicked and obtuse race.[21] He uttered a dire prediction that the absorption of Greek learning would corrupt all and would cause Romans to lose control of affairs.[22] As a preventive, he repeatedly called for expulsion of all Greeks from Italy.[23] The blanket condemnation is also reflected in the claim noted earlier: that Greeks speak from the lips, Romans from the heart.[24] Cato dwelled on the negative whenever occasion permitted. He is associated with the complaint that Romans acquired from Greeks the deplorable habit of appearing in the nude.[25] And he heaped scorn on Greek kings: Antiochus III was dismissed as a warrior who waged war with pen and ink, and Eumenes II as a carnivorous animal.[26]

The Censor was equally harsh on Romans who professed admiration for and seemed absorbed with Greek culture. He evinced displeasure with C. Acilius, who showed too much eagerness in translating and advancing the cause of Athens' philosophic embassy before the senate in 155.[27] And he expressed sharp hostility toward the arch-philhellene A. Postumius Albinus, who had composed a history in Greek and then apologized to readers for his less-than-flawless command of the language. Cato ripped him for his self-disparagement: if he had to ask for indulgence, he ought not to have written Greek in the first place; who asked him to? Polybius adds the comment that men like Postumius gave philhellenism a bad name among the older and most esteemed Romans.[28]

It causes no surprise then that M. Cato earned notoriety as a fierce foe of Hellas and a stalwart opponent of infection by Greek culture. That image of Cato holds sway through much of the modern scholarship.

---

20. Plut. *Cato*, 23.3–4; Pliny, *NH*, 29.14.
21. Pliny, *NH*, 29.14: *nequissimum et indocile genus*.
22. Pliny, *NH*, 29.14; Plut. *Cato*, 23.2.
23. Pliny, *NH*, 7.113.
24. Plut. *Cato*, 12.5.
25. Plut. *Cato*, 20.6.
26. *ORF*, fr. 20 = Cugusi, *OR*, fr. 4; Plut. *Cato*, 20.7–8.
27. Plut. *Cato*, 22.4–5.
28. Polyb. 39.1.1–9; Plut. *Cato*, 12.5.

Interpreters see him as fighting a rearguard battle for antique virtue against Hellenic infiltration, as prime representative of the authentic rural Roman mentality and old-fashioned Italian values, as advocate of a narrow traditionalism resistant to alien intrusion, even as head of a political movement featuring anti-hellenism.[29]

That thesis, however, requires modification and reconsideration, as has been increasingly recognized in recent years.[30] Cato by no means resisted the allure of Greek learning.

The Censor, so report has it, applied himself to the study of *Graecae litterae* only in old age.[31] That phrase signifies "Greek literature," not the Greek language.[32] Indeed, it presupposes knowledge of the latter. Cato evidently acquired facility with Greek much earlier. As military tribune during the Syrian War, he delivered an address to the Athenian assembly in 191, electing to give it in Latin and have it translated—rather than use Greek, which, according to Plutarch, he could just as easily have done.[33] The biographer did not invent or presume that conclusion. It came directly from Cato, whom Plutarch cites on the speech at Athens.[34] Nor would that be especially surprising. Cato had spent time in Greek-speaking areas, two tours of duty in Sicily, and perhaps a stint at Tarentum, during the Hannibalic War before taking service in Greece itself during the campaign of 191.[35] The accuracy of the report, however,

29. See, e.g., A. Besançon, *Les adversaires de l'hellénisme à Rome pendant la période républicaine* (Paris, 1910), 83–151; O. Rossi, *Athenaeum*, o.s. 10 (1922), 263–273; F. Klingner, *Die Antike*, 10 (1934), 239–263 = *Römische Geisteswelt*[5] (Munich, 1965), 34–65; R. E. Smith, *Greece and Rome*, 9 (1940), 153–165; F. Della Corte, *Catone Censore*[2] (Florence, 1969), 108–122; H. H. Scullard, *Roman Politics, 220–150 B.C.*[2] (Oxford, 1973), 113–114, 132–133, 222–224; M. Gelzer, *RE*, 31 (1953), 108–145; L. Alfonsi, *PP*, 9 (1954), 168–176; K. Jax, *Serta Philologica Aeniponta*, 7–8 (1962), 291–298; N. Petrochilos, *Roman Attitudes to the Greeks* (Athens, 1974), 70–75, 164–170; E. Flores, *Letteratura latina e ideologia del III–II a.C.* (Naples, 1974), 116–124; C. Letta, *Athenaeum*, 62 (1984), 4–23; Ferrary, *Philhellénisme et impérialisme*, 531–539; R. MacMullen, *Historia*, 40 (1991), 430–436.

30. See, especially, D. Kienast, *Cato der Zensor* (Heidelberg, 1954), 101–116; H. Haffter, *Römische Politik und römische Politiker* (Heidelberg, 1967), 158–192; A. E. Astin, *Cato the Censor* (Oxford, 1978), 157–181.

31. Cic. *De Rep.* 5.2; *Acad.* 2.5; *De Sen.* 3, 26; Nepos, *Cato*, 3.2; Val. Max. 8.7.1; Quint. 12.11.23; Plut. *Cato*, 2.4.

32. That is clear from Val. Max. 8.7.1; so rightly, Astin, *Cato the Censor*, 159.

33. Plut. *Cato*, 12.4.

34. Plut. *Cato*, 12.5; Astin, *Cato the Censor*, 160.

35. Nepos, *Cato*, 1.2; Cic. *De Sen.* 10, 39, 41; Plut. *Cato*, 2.3, 3.5–7; Livy, 29.25.10; *Vir. Ill.* 47.1.

is less important than the fact that Cato retailed it. He had no qualms about declaring a fluent command of Greek when he was in his forties.

When did this facility in the language translate itself into immersion in the literature and learning of the land? The tradition that serious study came only late in life has been properly called into question.[36] Other evidence suggests a longer and fuller engagement. Cato advised his son to scan Greek literature but not to bother to acquire a thorough knowledge of it.[37] That advice implies more than a nodding acquaintance with Hellenic letters. One need not credit the tale that Cato learned *Graecae litterae* at the feet of Ennius.[38] But the fact that Cato brought Ennius to Rome in 204 demonstrates an interest in Hellenic learning already in Cato's younger years.[39] So also does the presence of the learned Greek slave Chilon in Cato's household.[40]

More telling are allusions in Cato's own writings or in remarks attributed to him that require familiarity with Greek legends, learning, and tradition. Perhaps as early as 202 a speech of Cato made use of a Greek proverb.[41] His quip about Antiochus waging war with pen and ink seems an echo of Demosthenes' similar mocking of Philip II.[42] As censor in 184, he directed the construction of a basilica, obviously patterned on Greek models, the first of its kind in Rome.[43] Cato's knowledge of Homer is plain from quotations of the *Odyssey* made late in life.[44] The proem to his great historical work, the *Origines*, imitates the opening of Xenophon's *Symposium*.[45] He paraphrased Demosthenes once again in a speech on Carthage circa 150.[46] According to Plutarch, Cato's oratory gained much from Demosthenes and profited also from Thucydides.[47] Scattered comments ascribed to the Censor show his

36. E. V. Marmorale, *Cato Maior*[2] (Bari, 1949), 147–155; Astin, *Cato the Censor*, 159–165.

37. Pliny, *NH*, 29.14: *illorum litteras inspicere, non perdiscere.*

38. *Vir. Ill.* 47.1.

39. Nepos, *Cato*, 1.4.

40. Plut. *Cato*, 20.3.

41. Gellius, 13.18.3 = *ORF*, fr. 217 = Cugusi, *OR*, fr. 196; see Cugusi's commentary, 459; on the date, see Kienast, *Cato der Zensor*, 39–42.

42. *ORF*, fr. 20 = Cugusi, *OR*, fr. 4; Demosth. *Phil.* 1.30.

43. Livy, 39.44.6–7; Plut. *Cato*, 19.2; *Vir. Ill.* 47.5; cf. *ORF*, fr. 87 = Cugusi, *OR*, fr. 70.

44. Polyb. 35.6.3–4, 36.8.7; Plut. *Cato*, 9.3, 27.4.

45. *HRR*, fr. 2 = Cic. *Pro Planc.* 66; Xen. *Symp.* 1.1; cf. M. Chassignet, *Caton: Les Origines* (Paris, 1986), 57.

46. *ORF*, fr. 195; Demosth. *Phil.* 3.8, 3.17.

47. Plut. *Cato*, 2.4.

acquaintance with various personages from Greek history: Lycurgus, Solon, Cleisthenes, Leonidas, Themistocles, Pericles, Epaminondas, Socrates, and Isocrates.[48] He was knowledgeable enough to make an offhand allusion to the Delphic Amphictyony.[49] He even enriched the Latin language by adding words of Greek derivation.[50] And he went so far as to make a collection of apothegms and adages drawn from the learning and lore of the Greeks.[51] As these and other examples indicate, Cato could hardly have acquired his knowledge of Hellenic culture only in his declining years.[52]

Such testimony makes all the more puzzling the tradition that Cato refrained from serious Greek studies until late in life. The tradition was fixed by the era of Cicero, who refers to it unquestioningly more than once. And it reappears in several other sources, which may or may not be dependent on the orator.[53] But Cicero's witness is itself significant. One might wish to explain it away as mere supposition based on a preponderance of Greek allusions in Cato's later works. Or perhaps Cicero judged Cato's Hellenism by the more refined standards of his own intellectual circles.[54] Yet it must be borne in mind that Cicero, in general, strained to emphasize rather than to diminish Cato's familiarity with Greek culture. In the De senectute, he repeatedly puts into Cato's mouth references to Greek figures such as Homer, Hesiod, Semonides, Sophocles, Themistocles, Stesichorus, Solon, Peisistratus, Lysander, Gorgias, Pythagoras, and Plato.[55] If anything, Cicero might lean in the direction of enhancing and embellishing the Censor's Hellenism. The preface to the De senectute indeed concedes that the dialogue will have

---

48. Lycurgus, Solon, and Cleisthenes: Cic. De Rep. 2.2, 2.37; Leonidas: HRR, fr. 83 = Gellius, 3.7.19; Themistocles, Pericles, and Epaminondas: Plut. Cato, 8.8; Socrates: Plut. Cato, 20.2, 23.1; Isocrates: Plut. Cato, 23.2.

49. Polyb. 39.1.6; Plut. Cato, 12.5.

50. Horace, Ars poetica, 52–58.

51. Plut. Cato, 2.4; Cic. De Off. 1.104.

52. See further discussion and references in Astin, Cato the Censor, 160–169; Letta, Athenaeum, 62 (1984), 8–14. It would be out of place here to go further and speculate about Greek influences in Cato's own published works. See, e.g., S. Boscherini, Lingua e scienza greca nel "De agri cultura" di Catone (Rome, 1970), 23–91.

53. See sources cited in n. 31.

54. Cf. Marmorale, Cato Maior, 148–150; Astin, Cato the Censor, 161.

55. Cic. De Sen. 8, 22–23, 63, 72–73. On the Ciceronian portrait of Cato, see F. Padberg, "Cicero und Cato Censorius: Ein Beitrag zu Ciceros Bildungsgang" (Diss., Münster, 1933), passim, especially 46–62; Della Corte, Catone Censore, 174–184; Haffter, Römische Politik, 165–180; U. Kammer, "Untersuchungen zu Ciceros Bild von Cato Censorinus" (Diss., Frankfort, 1964), passim; especially, 118–125; G. Garbarino, Roma e la filosofia greca dalle origini alla fine del II secolo a.C. (Turin, 1973), 324–330.

Cato discourse in rather more erudite fashion than he displayed in his own works.[56] Elsewhere, Cicero delivers high praise of Cato's juridical, oratorical, and political skills, attributing to him command of everything except the most sophisticated *doctrina* imported from abroad.[57] That Cicero nonetheless regards Cato's interest in things Hellenic as an afterthought, following a lengthy career of public service, shows that the idea had already taken firm hold by the late Republic. The truth or falsity of that idea is less important than the fact of its existence. It must have had strong authority—perhaps from Cato himself. The stance would be consonant with other declarations on his part. It forms a piece with the broader image of Cato's association with Hellenism.

That image did not require the denial of all Greek elements in the story of Rome. On the contrary, Cato acknowledged and reaffirmed them in his pathbreaking historical work, the *Origines*. The study itself depended on Greek models and looked to Greek predecessors. A branch of Hellenic historiography issued in *ktisis* literature, a blending of local history and legend regarding the foundation of cities. Practitioners included Antiochus of Syracuse, Dionysius of Chalcis, Alcimus, Hippias of Rhegium, and Cato's contemporary Polemon of Ilium.[58] The *Origines*, of course, went well beyond the limited scope of mere foundation stories, but Cato was certainly familiar with the *ktisis* genre.[59] Further, he can hardly have been ignorant of the great Greek historian of the West, Timaeus, who, among other things, discussed κτίσεις of cities.[60] The Hellenic background plays a critical role.

More striking, Cato conveyed and endorsed traditions that inserted Greek components into Italic prehistory. The shadowy aborigines whom legend placed in Italy prior to the Trojan arrival were identified by Cato as Greeks who had migrated many generations prior to the fall of Troy.[61] Whether Cato advanced this theory in polemical fashion against

---

56. Cic. *De Sen.* 3: *eruditius videbitur disputare quam consuevit ipse in suis libris.*

57. Cic. *De Orat.* 3.135: *quid enim M. Catoni praeter hanc politissimam doctrinam transmarinam atque adventiciam defuit?* Cf. Nepos, *Cato,* 3 (on the *Origines*): *in quibus multa industria et diligentia comparet, nulla doctrina.*

58. References and discussion in D. Timpe, *MemAccadPatav,* 83 (1970–71), 16–18.

59. Skepticism on this point by Astin, *Cato the Censor,* 227–228, and W. Kierdorf, *Chiron,* 10 (1980), 210, partly on the grounds that κτίσις is not the proper equivalent of *origo*; cf. Dion. Hal. 1.11.1. But see Letta, *Athenaeum,* 62 (1984), 25, n. 125.

60. Polyb. 12.26d.2. In general, on this genre, see B. Schmid, "Studien zu griechischen Ktesissagen" (Diss., Freiburg, Switzerland, 1947).

61. *HRR,* fr. 61; Dion. Hal. 1.11.1, 1.13.2. Sallust followed Cato in seeing the aborigines as the first inhabitants of Italy; Serv. *Ad Aen.* 1.6. That need not mean that Sallust's rather negative characterization of the aborigines also derived from Cato;

earlier accounts of aborigines as primitive savages or drew upon prior Hellenic reconstructions makes little difference. He plainly adopted the idea that Italic peoples had their roots in Hellas.[62] And he went further. A fragment of the *Origines* shows that Cato believed in the subsequent migration of Arcadians under Evander, who spread the Aeolic dialect among Italians, and even claimed that Romulus spoke Aeolic![63] The tale that the Sabines owed their origins to a Spartan settler named Sabus also appeared in Cato's work.[64] And he did not hesitate to record fables that linked figures from Greek tradition—Philoctetes, Orestes, Iphigenia— to Italian sites.[65] The historical fragments demonstrate not only Cato's familiarity with Hellenic legends but his readiness to accept Hellenic ingredients in the making of early Italy.[66]

Cato was, first and foremost, a man of the nation's affairs, committed to the public scene, but not one to disdain the virtues of a contemplative life. The preface to the *Origines* expressed the Censor's advocacy of the proper balance: men of renown and greatness should place as high a value on their *otium* as on their *negotium*.[67] The passage itself looks to a

---

Sallust, *Cat.* 6.1. On the Catonian fragment, see Schröder, *M. Porcius Cato*, 102–108, 126, 179; Chassignet, *Caton: les Origines* , 3.

62. Letta, *Athenaeum*, 62 (1984), 424–428, speculates at length about possible sources for Cato's notion, notably Fabius Pictor—an unverifiable conjecture. Nor does it dilute the importance of Cato's view to point out that he has the aborigines defeated by Trojans or subjected by Sabines; *HRR*, fr. 9–11, 50. On these fragments, see J.-C. Richard, in *Hommages à Robert Schilling* (Paris, 1983), 403–412. And Letta's claim (425) that, for Cato, the aborigines spoke no Greek, is quite unfounded. Appeal to the authority of R. M. Ogilvie, *CR*, 88 (1974), 64, does not help the claim.

63. *HRR*, fr. 19 = Lydus, *De Mag.* 1.5; E. Gabba, *Miscellenea di studi alessandrini in memoria di A. Rostagni* (Turin, 1963), 188–194; Schröder, *Cato: Das erste Buch der "Origines,"* 176–178. The conclusion is doubted unpersuasively by Letta, *Athenaeum*, 62 (1984), 428–429. Note also that Cato has Tibur founded by an officer of Evander; *HRR*, fr. 56 = Solinus, 2.7.

64. *HRR*, fr. 51 = Serv. *Ad Aen.* 8.638. Whether he went further and took the view that Sabine toughness in character and war stemmed from Spartan forebears is more controversial. Dionysius appears to deny it; 2.49.2–4. But Letta goes too far in arguing that Cato actually polemicized against that version; *Athenaeum*, 62 (1984), 432–438. See also Chassignet, *Cato: les Origines*, 76–78.

65. *HRR*, fr. 70–71; Chassignet, *Cato: les Origines*, 81–83.

66. For Astin, *Cato the Censor*, 223–225, Cato simply followed accepted convention in retailing stories of Greek elements in Rome's past. But the very fact that he chose to perpetuate rather than to alter those traditions carries real significance. Cato certainly did not regard himself as bound by convention. The decision to write a history in Latin was itself a conscious innovation. So also was Cato's departure from Greek practice in abandoning Olympiads as a dating device; Dion. Hal. 1.74.2.

67. *HRR*, fr. 2 = Cic. *Pro Planc.* 66: *clarorum virorum atque magnorum non minus otii quam*

Greek source, the opening of Xenophon's *Symposium*, which it clearly and consciously echoes.[68] But even more significant implications lie therein. Cato here juxtaposes the *vita contemplativa* with the *vita activa*, according comparable weight to each. The Censor thereby explicitly endorses the life of the mind as emblematic of the aspirations of Rome's most eminent statesmen and most influential figures.[69] That was an appropriate and undoubtedly a genuine position for Cato the Elder. He earned his reputation as a man of high culture as well as a leader in matters of state. He fell short in no sphere of public or private activity.[70] He could exhibit his remarkable skills as farmer, jurist, military commander, orator—or man of letters.[71] That last distinction required an intensive engagement with the culture of the Greeks.

So Cato presents a puzzling enigma. He emerges both as fierce foe of Hellenism and as learned disciple of Hellenic culture. How to account for the patent paradox? The question is no idle one. Cato stands as the pivotal figure for understanding Rome's sense of its relationship to the cultural world of the Greeks. His character and attitudes hold a key for any inquiry into the Roman reaction to Hellenism—and for the de-

---

negotii rationem exstare oportere. Cato elsewhere put somewhat comparable sentiments into the mouth of Scipio Africanus; Cic. *De Rep.* 1.27; *De Off.* 3.1: *numquam se minus otiosum esse, quam cum otiosus, nec minus solum, quam cum solus esset.* The statement is glossed as meaning that Scipio, even when not occupied with public duties, was thinking about them; *De Off.* 3.1, 3.4. But that is Cicero's interpretation, not necessarily Scipio's meaning—let alone Cato's intent.

68. Xen. *Symp.* 1.1: ἀλλ' ἐμοὶ δοκεῖ τῶν καλῶν κἀγαθῶν ἀνδρῶν ἔργα οὐ μόνον τὰ μετὰ σπουδῆς πραττόμενα ἀξιομνημόνευτα εἶναι, ἀλλὰ καὶ τὰ ἐν ταῖς παιδιαῖς. The connection has long been recognized; see bibliography in Letta, *Athenaeum*, 62 (1984), 12, n. 53. Garbarino, *Roma e la filosofia greca*, 340–342, rightly points out that Cato's passage implies a deeper meaning than is contained in Xenophon's mere introduction to a dialogue, but she does not disprove a deliberate imitation of the phraseology.

69. Cf. Alfonsi, *PP*, 9 (1954), 163–168; J.-M. André, *L'otium dans la vie morale et intellectuelle romaine* (Paris, 1966), 45–49. For a different and provocative interpretation, see Letta, *Athenaeum*, 62 (1984), 25–30. Letta cites *HRR*, fr. 118 (*clarorum virorum laudes atque virtutes*) and Tac. *Agr.* 1.1 (*clarorum virorum facta moresque*) to argue that Cato's *otium* refers not to intellectual activity but to moral qualities as distinct from public deeds. But his effort to equate the connotations of *virtutes* and *mores* with *otium* and to see the *otium/negotium* contrast as parallel in meaning to *mores/facta*, let alone *virtutes/laudes*, uncomfortably stretches the point. As Plutarch noted, Cato's notion of leisure was to write books and to farm; *Cato*, 24.8: ἀναπαύσεσιν ἐχρῆτο καὶ παιδιαῖς, ὁπότε σχολάζοι, τῷ συντάττεσθαι βιβλία καὶ τῷ γεωργεῖν.

70. Livy, 39.40.4: *nulla ars neque privatae neque publicae rei gerendae ei defuit.* Here the private sphere plainly alludes to intellectual and literary achievement; Livy, 39.40.5–8.

71. Nepos, *Cato*, 3.1: *et agricola sollers et peritus iuris consultus et magnus imperator et probabilis orator et cupidissimus litterarum fuit.*

velopment of a Roman cultural identity. The paradox needs to be resolved.

Of course, suggestions already exist in number and variety. It can be argued that Cato's attitude changed over time, that a narrow-minded antipathy toward Hellenism in his youth gradually ripened into a broader sympathy as he gained maturity.[72] Or one can take the reverse line that Cato's outlook hardened with time and his personality became increasingly crotchety with old age.[73] Those who prefer a more consistent Cato offer a range of interpretations. Perhaps he distinguished among Greeks, reserving his fire for some but not others, displaying a preference for the ancients but scorn for his Greek contemporaries.[74] In a similar formulation, it has been supposed that Cato maintained a serious respect for Hellenic culture, while having contempt for the Greeks themselves, their morals, opinions, and behavior.[75] Cato's antihellenism, therefore, was selective and circumspect, choosing from the Greek experience those aspects that would advance Roman values and denouncing those that might undermine native principles, a selectivity sometimes viewed as a predilection for the Spartan rather than the Athenian features of Hellenism.[76] The education of Roman youth took precedence in the mentality of the Censor; he intended to safeguard them from the ill effects of certain Greek doctrines.[77] Cato's motives were patriotic: Hellenic culture could become an instrument whereby to combat the Greeks and to liberate Romans from their cultural dependency and inferiority.[78] Along such lines scholars have sought to reconcile the ostensible contradictions. The efforts, however, plainly create their own strains and tensions. Others abandon the attempt for a different approach. Some hold that the sources are at fault: Catonian antihellenism does not appear in the testimony of Republican writers but surfaces only much later, in Pliny and Plutarch, and is therefore suspect.[79] Or else, the antihellenism is a deep-seated emotion and preju-

72. Cf. Della Corte, *Catone Censore*, 89–111.

73. Cf. Garbarino, *Roma e la filosofia greca*, 320, 375.

74. Cf. Timpe, *MemAccadPatav*, 83 (1970–71), 29–30; Astin, *Cato the Censor*, 172–173.

75. Cf. Marmorale, *Cato Maior*, 147–155.

76. Cf. Alfonsi, *PP*, 9 (1954), 163–164; Kienast, *Cato der Zensor*, 103–105; Astin, *Cato the Censor*, 176–178; Petrochilos, *Roman Attitudes to the Greeks*, 166–169.

77. Cf. Della Corte, *Catone Censore*, 59–66.

78. Cf. Letta, *Athenaeum*, 62 (1984), 22–23; Ferrary, *Philhellénisme et impérialisme*, 537–539.

79. Cf. Haffter, *Römische Politik*, 190–191.

dice, not to be explained in rational terms, and coexisting with a respect for Greek learning and tradition.[80] In this formulation, the inner contradiction prevails and resists resolution.[81]

The divergent analyses are rich in ingenuity but fall short in persuasiveness. Grave problems attach to each. The notion that Cato altered his outlook, whether narrowing or broadening it, runs afoul of the evidence. Sources attest his exposure to things Hellenic at early stages of his career: the promotion of Ennius' migration to Rome, instruction by the Pythagorean Nearchus at Tarentum, the speech at Athens which he refrained from delivering in Greek, and the presence of Chilon as tutor in the Catonian household.[82] As for the latter part of his career, that was marked, among other things, by his association with Polybius and was identified in the tradition as the time of his serious study of Greek literature.[83] Hence the later years do not appear to have brought notable change in his attitude toward Greek learning. Did Cato elevate ancient Greeks while disparaging their corrupt descendants? He did indeed praise some great figures of the past: Leonidas, Epaminondas, Pericles, Themistocles.[84] But he heaped criticism upon Socrates and Isocrates.[85] And he evidently enjoyed rapport with Polybius.[86] Any interpretation that relies on a division between "good old Greeks" and "bad new Greeks" is clearly simplistic.

That Cato found some aspects of Hellenism more appealing than others may well be true, but one would be hard pressed to discern any systematic principles of selectivity. Cato advises his son to sample Greek literature without becoming engrossed in it, and in the same passage proceeds to denounce the whole Hellenic race.[87] That hardly lays down guidelines for discrimination. The theory that later sources fabricated Cato's antihellenism does not hold up. Granted that neither

---

80. Cf. Astin, *Cato the Censor*, 178–180.

81. Cf. Klingner, *Römische Geisteswelt*, 45–47, 64–65; Timpe, *MemAccadPatav*, 83 (1970–71), 6–7.

82. Plut. *Cato*, 12.4, 20.3; Nepos, *Cato*, 1.4. For Cato and Nearchus, see Cic. *De Sen.* 39, 41; Plut. *Cato*, 2.3. The notice may not be authentic, but it indicates, at least, what could be believed about Cato in the late Republic.

83. For Polybius and Cato, see Polyb. 31.25.5a, 35.6.1–4; Plut. *Cato*, 9.2–3. A close intellectual relationship is postulated by C. Nicolet, *FondHardt*, 20 (1974), 243–255. Cf. Walbank, *Historical Commentary on Polybius*, III, 649–650.

84. Plut. *Cato*, 8.8; *HRR*, fr. 83 = Gellius, 3.7.

85. Plut. *Cato*, 20.2, 23.1–2.

86. See above, n. 83.

87. Pliny, *NH*, 29.14.

Cicero nor Nepos indicates such leanings and that Cicero indeed underscores Cato's cultivation in the *De senectute*. But one need not await
Pliny and Plutarch. The most intemperate statements about Greek
character and designs stem from Cato's own treatise to his son.[88] To
label the Censor's antipathy toward Hellenes and Hellenism irrational
or to judge his ambivalence as irreconcilable inconsistency is a counsel
of despair and abandons the quest prematurely. That Cato approached
Greek culture with Roman values in mind is doubtless true, but it
misses the mark to characterize his purpose as overcoming an inferiority
complex. And the interpretation fails to grasp a central fact: that the
encounter with Hellenism was itself a critical ingredient in the shaping
of Roman values.

A fresh investigation is warranted. The query has as objective an
understanding not only of Cato's paradoxical posture but of the broader
implications for the cultural confrontation of Hellas and Rome. To that
end the evidence previously set out requires closer scrutiny and more
probing attention.

Cato's remarks on oratory, a sphere of special competence, provide an
appropriate starting point. Plutarch credits him with the sentiment that
Greek speeches come from the lips, Roman speeches from the heart.[89]
The context of that observation is significant and revealing. It applied to
the address that Cato himself made to the Athenian assembly in 191
while serving as Roman officer in the war against Antiochus. He delivered a brief and pointed speech in Latin, leaving to an interpreter the task
of reproducing it in Greek. The latter's rendition used much more
verbiage and occupied much more time, thus causing the Athenians to
marvel at Cato's economy of language and the forceful brevity of his
native tongue.[90] The report itself comes from Cato, who plainly orchestrated the whole event—with the precise objective of drawing
the contrast that he desired. Whether the Athenians did, in fact, look
with admiring awe upon the military tribune's demonstration may be
doubted. That is irrelevant. What matters is Cato's report and the
message it delivered. The purpose was not so much to denounce Hel-

88. Pliny, *NH*, 29.14; Plut. *Cato*, 23.
89. Plut. *Cato*, 12.5: τὸ δ'ὅλον οἴεσθαι τὰ ῥήματα τοῖς μὲν Ἕλλησιν ἀπὸ χειλέων,
τοῖς δὲ Ῥωμαίοις ἀπὸ καρδίας φέρεσθαι.
90. Plut. *Cato*, 12.5: θαυμάσαι δέ φησι τοὺς Ἀθηναίους τὸ τάχος αὐτοῦ καὶ τὴν
ὀξύτητα τῆς φράσεως; ἃ γὰρ αὐτὸς ἐξέφερε βραχέως, τὸν ἑρμηνέα μακρῶς καὶ διὰ
πολλῶν ἀπαγγέλλειν.

lenic oratory as to exhibit its inferiority to Roman practice. The contrast closely parallels his mockery of the school of Isocrates, which trains students only in long-windedness.[91] Roman rhetoric, as Cato emphasized, has the advantage over Greek, for it rivets attention upon substance, not verbiage: *rem tene, verba sequentur*.[92] The episode at Athens had another feature of central importance. Cato let it be known that he could have delivered the speech in Greek had he wished.[93] Whatever the truth of that claim, it reaffirmed that the Roman holds the upper hand. Unlike his audience, he had the option of employing either tongue—and he chose the superior one.

The matter of philosophy is more complex and entangled. Plutarch concluded that Cato was altogether hostile to that branch of learning.[94] Is that a valid inference? How thorough a censure did he, in fact, deliver, and what meaning did it have? The criticism of Socrates contains an interesting implication. Cato did not fault the famous Athenian on grounds of the perniciousness of philosophy. Rather he censured Socrates for despotic ambitions that, if fulfilled, would undermine institutions and induce his fellow citizens to embrace views contrary to their own laws.[95] The censure is far from blanket condemnation. Indeed Cato presents an arresting formulation. By branding Socrates as a subversive, he implies approval of established Hellenic institutions and traditions. That implication, obvious though rarely noticed, sets matters in a different light. The criticism leveled at Socrates bears close similarity to that rendered by the Censor against Carneades and the Athenian philosophic embassy of 155. Cato objected to Carneades' playing fast and loose with the truth: the verbal pyrotechnics of the philosopher who could advocate both sides of an issue placed a premium on words rather than deeds, suited to the classrooms of Greece but not for Roman youth, who pay heed to laws and magistrates.[96] The parallel is instructive. In both instances Cato counterposes philosophic chicanery to adherence to legal and social conventions. The criticisms do not stigmatize philosophy—let alone Hellenism—as unmitigated

91. Plut. *Cato*, 23.2.
92. Seneca, *Contr.* 1, pr. 9; Victor, 374, H.
93. Plut. *Cato*, 12.4.
94. Plut. *Cato*, 23.1: ὅλως φιλοσοφίᾳ προσκεκρουκώς.
95. Plut. *Cato*, 23.1: καταλύοντα τὰ ἔθη καὶ πρὸς ἐναντίας τοῖς νόμοις δόξας ἕλκοντα καὶ μεθιστάντα τοὺς πολίτας.
96. Plut. *Cato*, 22.3–5: οἱ δὲ Ῥωμαίων νέοι τῶν νόμων καὶ τῶν ἀρχόντων ὡς πρότερον ἀκούωσι; Pliny, *NH*, 7.112; Cic. *De Rep.* 3.9; Quint. 12.1.35.

evil. Nor is it likely that Cato genuinely feared the ability of Greek philosophers to erode Roman morals.[97] A different motive prompted his strictures. Cato contrasted the Greeks' fondness for self-indulgent ratiocination, even at the cost of their own traditions, with the Roman attachment to the *mos maiorum*. The contrast, to be sure, can be dismissed as a stereotype, distorted and dubious. Stereotypes, however, have a hold on the imagination. And Cato played an important role in the manufacture or at least the dissemination of that stereotype.

The comments hardly constitute a crusade against philosophy. Plutarch exaggerated and misconstrued their intent. His assertion that Cato was thoroughly at odds with philosophy seems to be little more than an inference from the Carneades episode to which it is attached.[98] Nor should one inflate the importance of Cato's snide remark comparing philosophers with funeral garb or funeral dirges.[99] At most, it represents mockery of vacuous verbiage, a parallel to the point made about Carneades' rhetoric, and it may indeed have been made in that very context.

The thesis of tenacious malice toward philosophy has little basis. In fact, a tradition recorded by Cicero placed Cato in Tarentum as a young officer of Fabius Maximus in 209, where he encountered, conversed with, and was hosted by the philosopher Nearchus.[100] The tale itself is generally discounted by moderns as Ciceronian fiction, designed to fashion an idealized portrait of Cato.[101] But to question its historicity

97. As is believed by most scholars; e.g. Garbarino, *Roma e la filosofia greca*, 313–315, 362–370; Petrochilos, *Roman Attitudes to the Greeks*, 167–169; Astin, *Cato the Censor*, 175–177. The idea that Carneades castigated Roman imperialism has been effectively questioned by J.-L. Ferrary, *REL*, 55 (1977), 152–156; idem, *Philhellénisme et impérialisme*, 351–363; cf. Gruen, *The Hellenistic World and the Coming of Rome*, 341–342.

98. Plut. *Cato*, 22.5–23.1. The biographer proceeds to buttress his point by reference to the Catonian comment on Socrates—which by no means supports the conclusion. Pliny attaches to the tale of the Athenian embassy a different and equally dubious comment: that Cato incessantly urged expulsion of all Greeks from Italy; *NH*, 7.113. No other evidence supports that assertion—which is not true even of the Carneades episode. Fanciful hyperbole is transparent in Pliny's immediately subsequent statement that Cato drove away the Greek language itself.

99. Gellius, 18.7.3: *vos philosophi mera estis, ut M. Cato ait, mortualia*. The quip, of whose context we are entirely ignorant, is given too much weight by Garbarino, *Roma e la filosofia greca*, 333–334; similarly, Astin, *Cato the Censor*, 177.

100. Cic. *De Sen.* 39, 41. Plutarch adds that Nearchus was a Pythagorean; *Cato*, 2.3. That notice does not appear in Cicero, although he elsewhere has Cato express agreement with certain Pythagorean doctrines; *De Sen.* 78.

101. E.g., Della Corte, *Catone Censore*, 178–179; Garbarino, *Roma e la filosofia greca*, 325–329; Astin, *Cato the Censor*, 160, n. 7. For a defense of the tradition, see A. Mele,

does not deprive the story of value. Its appearance in the *De senectute* shows that the portrait of Cato as dogged enemy of philosophers did not prevail in the late Republic. What did prevail was the image of a broadly learned and multifaceted man whose one deficiency lay in the area of *doctrina transmarina*.[102] That image may well have been cultivated by the Censor himself. *Doctrina transmarina* almost certainly refers to Greek philosophy.[103] Cato presented himself as one who had exposure to it but found it wanting. Overrefined philosophic study leads to self-absorption and empty phrase-mongering that distract one from more productive pursuits, namely, commitment to established norms, institutions, and traditions. His purpose was not to deliver wholesale censure of philosophy but to set up that discipline as a foil in order better to express the distinctiveness of Roman values.

In this connection, the presence of Chilon as tutor in the *familia* of Cato makes sense. Chilon was a skilled *grammatistes* who, as Plutarch informs us, taught many youths in the Catonian establishment. The Censor evidently had no reservations on that score. He made it a point only to undertake personal supervision of his son's elementary education. The explanation he offered, however, did not focus on Chilon's nationality. Cato reckoned it as unseemly that his heir, if slow in his lessons, should be cuffed about by a slave—or, even if a good student, should owe his education to a slave.[104] Status, rather than Chilon's national origins, determined the decision. But the origins were not altogether irrelevant. A vital part of the young man's training involved exposure to the ancient traditions native to his land.[105] No Greek could supply that training. Chilon could have a free hand with others in the household—the Censor here indirectly *promoted* Hellenic education—but the aspirant to Cato's position of leadership in the state required something more: grounding in just those principles that distinguished Roman experience from Greek. Once again, Cato's main message stressed the superiority of Rome's practices and traditions.

AION, 3 (1981), 69–77. And see further Letta, *Athenaeum*, 62 (1984), 14, with bibliography.

102. Cic. *De Orat.* 3.135; Nepos, *Cato*, 3.4. See above, n. 57.

103. Cf. the usage in Cic. *De Rep.* 3.5 and Nepos, *Atticus*, 17.3. See Marmorale, *Cato Maior*, 148–150; Della Corte, *Catone Censore*, 196–197; and especially, Garbarino, *Roma e la filosofia greca*, 321–323.

104. Plut. *Cato*, 20.4: οὐκ ἠξίου δὲ τὸν υἱόν, ὥς φησιν αὐτός, ὑπὸ δούλου κακῶς ἀκούειν ἢ τοῦ ὠτὸς ἀνατείνεσθαι μανθάνοντα βράδιον, οὐδέ γε μαθήματος τηλικούτου τῷ δούλῳ χάριν ὀφείλειν.

105. Plut. *Cato*, 20.5: πρὸς ἐμπειρίαν τῶν παλαιῶν καὶ πατρίων.

The claim that Cato gave serious attention to Greek literature only in old age may, as previously suggested, derive from his own statements.[106] If so, the assertion would fit suitably with the actions elsewhere indicated. Cato did not disguise his familiarity with Hellenic culture. He sprinkled his orations and writings with allusions to Greek legends, literature, and history. Did that practice involve him in a fundamental inconsistency? Quite the contrary. Cato's posture here was deliberate, calculating, and of central importance. He let it be known that, even in the course of an active political and military life at the center of public affairs, he had the *otium* to profit, so far as was useful, from the Hellenic experience. But concentrated study of Greek letters should await the fulfillment of national duties. That was time enough to gain adequate expertise.[107] As ever, the obligations of the Roman statesman take priority. Cato did not deny the benefits of Hellenism—but he put them in their place.

An interpretation along such lines illuminates Cato's celebrated counsel to his son: looking through Greek literature has its value, but not poring over it.[108] That passage not only declares that Cato had a thorough enough acquaintance with *Graecae litterae* to render an informed judgment but also coheres with the other evidence on Cato's attitude. He acknowledged the merits of Hellenic learning, while keeping it secondary and in the service of Roman statesmen and intellectuals. Cato's purpose here was not to advocate selectivity along any systematic lines.[109] That would be overinterpretation. He implied simply that, while Greeks might immerse themselves in literary pursuits, Romans would find adequate advantage in perusing the classics as adjunct to their own fuller and more comprehensive existence.[110]

In this light too Cato's conduct in Athens in 191 takes on greater meaning. Delivery of the speech in Latin, followed by an interpreter's translation, conveyed a clear message.[111] As noted already, it signified

---

106. See above, pp. 58–59.

107. Cf. Cic. *De Sen.* 26: *et ego feci, qui litteras Graecas senex dedici . . . ut ea ipsa mihi nota essent, quibus me nunc exemplis uti videtis;* Nepos, *Cato*, 3.2: *quarum studium etsi senior adripuerat, tamen tantum progressum fecit, ut non facile reperiri possit neque de Graecis neque de Italicis rebus quod ei fuerit incognitum.*

108. Pliny, *NH*, 29.14: *quod bonum sit illorum litteras inspicere, non perdiscere;* cf. 29.27.

109. As, e.g., Marmorale, *Cato Maior*, 155.

110. Letta, *Athenaeum*, 62 (1984), 22–23, offers the best analysis but goes too far in viewing this as an open invitation for Romans to exploit Greek learning and liberate themselves from subjection to Greek culture.

111. Plut. *Cato*, 12.4.

the superior economy and directness of Cato's native tongue, as against the overblown wordiness of Greek. But Cato's act also carried a further implication. By asserting command of both languages and choosing the better, he announced superiority at yet another level. The Athenian audience knew no Latin and had to receive a translation. Cato had the advantage of them also in this regard. In effect, he declared that Roman ascendancy carried over from the military sphere to the realm of high culture.

Other pronouncements by Cato, customarily taken as attacks on Greeks or Greek practices, may be quite irrelevant to the issue. Cato's strictures on luxury, for instance, seem, on the face of it, to be directed against the insidious effects of Hellenic imports on the Roman character.[112] A closer look, however, casts serious doubt on that proposition.

Cato stood forth as champion of sumptuary legislation. In this he was far from alone. The Roman assembly regularly passed *leges sumptuariae* in the second century, announcing their resistance to excessive opulence among the upper classes. The measures were generally ineffective, loosely enforced, and designed more as advertisement of aristocratic conscience than as authentic reform.[113] They need not, however, signal discontent with specifically Hellenic features of Roman luxury. Extant texts on sumptuary laws are silent on Greek culture. Certainly nothing in the fragments from Cato's speech on the *lex Orchia* suggests Hellenism as the villain.[114] The *lex Porcia de sumptu provinciali* may or may not have been sponsored by Cato. There is, in any case, no reason to interpret it as directed against Greek habits.[115]

Only a single passage suggests that Cato's stance on sumptuary laws associated Roman luxury with Hellenism. Livy's reconstruction of the debate on repeal of the *lex Oppia* in 195 ascribes a lengthy and famous speech to Cato, consul in that year. The measure, passed originally in 215, restricted the amount of gold women could own, the garments

---

112. So, in general, Petrochilos, *Roman Attitudes to the Greeks*, 69–87; and in particular, Letta, *Athenaeum*, 72 (1984), 19–22.

113. For discussions of the *leges sumptuariae*, see D. Daube, *Aspects of Roman Law* (Edinburgh, 1969), 117–128; I. Sauerwein, *Die leges sumptuariae als römische Massnahme gegen den Sittenverfall* (Hamburg, 1970), passim; G. Clemente, in A. Giardina and A. Schiavone, eds., *Società romana e produzione schiavistica* (Bari, 1981), III, 1–14, 301–304; M. Bonamente, *Tra Grecia e Roma* (1980), 67–91; Gruen, *Studies in Greek Culture and Roman Policy*, 170–174, 178–179.

114. *ORF*, fr. 139–146 = Cugusi, *OR*, fr. 128–132, 210, 235, 238. On the *lex Orchia*, see Macrob. *Sat.* 3.17.2–3; Sauerwein, *Die leges sumptuariae*, 70–76.

115. *ILS*, 38, lines 15–17.

they could wear, and the vehicles in which they could ride.[116] Its promulgation doubtless served to demonstrate state solidarity in the darker days of the Hannibalic War. In the aftermath of that conflict, its continuance seemed superfluous and a repeal effort was mounted. Cato resisted that effort. In the course of his speech, he denounced the extravagance into which Romans, both men and women, had fallen and connected that vice with the expansion of empire into the Greek East. In particular, he singled out statues brought to Rome from Syracuse and the trinkets from Corinth and Athens that Romans now prized above the images of their own gods.[117] That outburst, however, does not qualify as authentic Cato. Livy composed the speech, utilizing the clichés of the Augustan era. No fragment of such a speech survives, and if Livy had had one before him, he would not have composed his own.[118] The anachronism of the reconstructed oration is plain enough. Rome did not possess marble statues in numbers sufficient to provoke this complaint in 195. Pliny, in fact, indicates that Roman shrines lacked marble statues before the conquest of Asia.[119] And more damning still is the reference to imports from Athens and Corinth—forty years in anticipation! The speech is invention, and the crucial passage dissolves upon inspection. Cato's attitude toward sumptuary laws was not tantamount to antihellenism.

The assault on ostentatious wealth and luxurious life-style runs as a constant theme through Cato's career. He adopted a self-conscious pose as defender of old-fashioned austerity. But the stinging rebuke of fellow Romans on this score possessed adequate force without attributing to them the taint of Hellenism. The censorial speech, *de signis et tabulis*, evidently protested against the display of ill-gotten gains in quest of public office.[120] He finds fault with those who spend extravagantly for private dwellings and boasts of his own restraint on that score.[121] And

116. Livy, 34.1.3.

117. Livy, 34.1–4.

118. See Livy, 45.25.2–4, where the historian declines to put a speech on the Rhodians in Cato's mouth, since the real thing was extant. The argument of Kienast, *Cato der Zensor*, 21–22, that Cato's speech on the Oppian law was published for the first time by Livy, is hard to take seriously. And Letta's claim, *Athenaeum*, 62 (1984), 21, n. 110, that the speech in Livy, though not authentic, was composed out of authentic Catonian material is pure speculation. See the bibliography assembled there. Doubts about the speech's genuineness have often been voiced. See Astin, *Cato the Censor*, 25–26, with references.

119. Pliny, *NH*, 34.34.

120. *ORF*, fr. 94 = Cugusi, *OR*, 52: *honorem [t]emp[ta]tavere, [ma]lefacta benefactis non redemptitavere.*

121. *ORF*, fr. 133, 174, 185 = Cugusi, *OR*, fr. 97, 218, 139.

criticism extends to malefactors who convert what should be state property to personal use, including statues and paintings for domestic adornment.[122] None of these reproaches links the offenses with Hellenic contamination. Cato mentioned a Babylonian coverlet and Punic pavements, but surviving fragments leave out the Greeks.[123] To be sure, he castigates Lepidus, in a speech of unknown date and context, for erecting statues to two effeminate cooks, both of whom have Greek names.[124] Lepidus' offense, however, was not Hellenism but the demeaning act (in Cato's eyes) of a Roman *nobilis'* paying honor to lower-class Greeks. Perhaps the Censor's most celebrated slur denounced Roman deterioration as exemplified by the higher value placed on smoked fish and handsome boys than on farms and farmhands.[125] That sally fits Cato's consistent presentation as pillar of antique resistance to contemporary self-indulgence.[126] It does not indict the Greeks.[127]

Nor did Cato's comments on poetry direct themselves against Greeks. His *Carmen de moribus* contains an intriguing statement on the subject. Cato, as so often, looked to the Roman past to supply a standard whereby contemporary society could be judged—usually for the worse. People clothed themselves in seemly fashion in the old days, he affirmed. Horses cost more than cooks. And the *ars poetica* was not held in esteem. Those who showed zeal for it and practiced their trade at banquets were reckoned as *grassatores*.[128] The statement is arresting and peculiar. Did Cato here reach back to the authority of earlier generations to condemn contemporaries who pursued poetry to the detriment of character and *Romanitas*? That conclusion is hard to credit. The *Origines* made reference to songs performed at banquets praising the virtues of famous men. The practice was common long before his own day, and the Censor obviously looked on it with favor.[129] Indeed, he endeavored to continue the practice at his own dinner table, encouraging guests to hail the deeds

---

122. *ORF*, fr. 98 = Cugusi, *OR*, fr. 72.

123. Plut. *Cato*, 4.4: ἐπίβλημα δὲ τῶν ποικίλων Βαβυλώνιον—Cato refused to accept it; *ORF*, fr. 185 = Cugusi, *OR*, fr. 139: *pavimenti Poenicis*.

124. *ORF*, fr. 95 = Cugusi, *OR*, fr. 178.

125. Polyb. 31.25.5a; cf. Gellius, 11.2.5.

126. Cf. *ORF*, fr. 144, 174 = Cugusi, *OR*, fr. 132, 218; Plut. *Cato*, 4.3–4.

127. The absence of direct connection between Greek influence and Roman luxury is rightly noted by Astin, *Cato the Censor*, 173–174.

128. Gellius, 11.2.5: *Poeticae artis honos non erat. Si quis in ea re studebat aut sese ad convivia adplicabat "grassator" vocabatur.*

129. Cic. *Brutus*, 75: *illa carmina, quae multis saeculis ante suam aetatem in epulis esse cantitata a singulis convivis de clarorum virorum laudibus in Originibus scriptum reliquit Cato*; similarly, Cic. *Tusc. Disp.* 1.3, 4.3.

of Rome's distinguished and accomplished citizens.[130] What then to make of the negative characterization in the *Carmen de moribus*? Enlightenment comes from a fragment of Cato's speech against M. Fulvius Nobilior. The Censor took sharp issue with Fulvius' decision to have the poet Ennius accompany him to his overseas assignment in the Antiochene War—evidently with an eye to the composition of a laudatory poem. Cicero, who preserves the fragment, understood its import: although Cato's *Origines* spoke of banquet verses that sang the praises of famous men, his speech against Fulvius pointed out that this form of praise—that is, the type Fulvius was presently encouraging—had not been welcomed.[131] The sentiment in the *Carmen de moribus* no longer seems anomalous. Cato's ancestors did not frown upon all poets but only those whom they labeled *grassatores*, a term conveniently defined by Festus as "flatterers."[132] The pieces fall into place. Cato's strictures aimed only at a certain genre of poetry, which had been scorned in better days and which Fulvius Nobilior now sought to revive.[133] The Censor had no brief against poetry in general—let alone against Greek poetry, which is nowhere singled out for opprobrium.[134] Cato, after all, had been responsible for the transport of the great Ennius from Sardinia to Rome, an event pregnant with consequences for Latin poetry and Roman culture.[135] The deep-rooted Hellenism of Ennius was a recommendation rather than a disadvantage.

Cato had a strong sense of propriety. He gave paramount importance to the maintenance of Roman dignity and the assertion of Roman superiority—very different matters from antihellenism. So, for instance, Cato's speech against the tribune M. Caelius blasts him for

130. Plut. *Cato*, 25.3: πολλὴ μὲν εὐφημία τῶν καλῶν καὶ ἀγαθῶν πολιτῶν ἐπεισῄγετο.

131. Cic. *Tusc. Disp.* 1.3: *quamquam est in Originibus solitos esse in epulis canere convivas ad tibicinem de clarorum hominum virtutibus, honorem tamen huic generi non fuisse declarat oratio Catonis, in qua obiecit ut probrum M. Nobiliori, quod is in provinciam poetas duxisset.*

132. Festus, 86, L: *grassari antiqui ponebant pro adulari.* For discussion, see R. Till, *Neue Jahrbücher*, 115 (1940), 165–166; J. Préaux, *Latomus*, 25 (1966), 710–725; M. Martina, *Labeo*, 26 (1980), 161–164.

133. The particular target is signaled by Cicero's *huic generi* in *Tusc. Disp.* 1.3, rightly observed by L. Ferrero, *Mondo Classico*, 11 (1941), 208–209.

134. Alfonsi, *PP*, 9 (1954), 169, simply assumes without argument that the criticism of poetry was directed against Hellenism, an assumption repeated by Letta, *Athenaeum*, 72 (1984), 10, 19.

135. Nepos, *Cato*, 1.4. One need not, however, credit the further inference that Cato was trained in Greek letters by Ennius; *Vir. Ill.* 47.1.

singing whenever the spirit moves him, telling jokes, using false voices, dancing, and reciting Greek verses.[136] The combination of reproaches shows that the Hellenic character of the poems was not the issue.[137] Cato simply complained about the unseemly behavior of a Roman official who demeaned his office. His famous criticism of Scipio Africanus had the same import. Cato castigated the general for extravagant behavior in Sicily, including a frivolous frequenting of palaestras and theaters.[138] Once again, stress fell on the impropriety of a Roman commander in public service yielding to trivial pleasures rather than on the deficiencies of Hellenic institutions.[139] Magistrates of the Roman Republic should conduct themselves with *gravitas* and exhibit their ascendancy abroad in matters political and cultural. Cato himself made the exemplary demonstration to that effect in his address to the Athenians in 191.[140] And not only abroad. Cato showed impatience with the prominent senator C. Acilius for his excessive zeal in offering himself as interpreter for the Athenian philosophic mission.[141] The annoyance had nothing to do with Acilius' cultural leanings, as is sometimes thought. It fits rather with the other examples noted. Roman senators should hold the whip hand in diplomatic dealings, not put themselves at the service of foreign delegations.

The conviction emerges with greatest clarity in a well-known episode that is regularly misconstrued: Cato's caustic attack on the "philhellene" A. Postumius Albinus. Postumius, characterized by Polybius as excessively devoted to Hellenic matters, composed a history in Greek and asked his readers' indulgence for any errors and infelicities in his use of that language. His disclaimer, not the book, drew the withering scorn of Cato: if Postumius had been commissioned to write the work, he might legitimately offer an apology for his flaws, but since the decision had been his own, such an apology is preposterous, akin to a

---

136. *ORF*, fr. 115 = Cugusi, *OR*, fr. 85: *praeterea cantat, ubi collibuit, interdum Graecos versus agit, iocos dicit, voces demutat, staticulos dat.*

137. Despite Cugusi, *OR*, 268; Letta, *Athenaeum*, 62 (1984), 19. Cf. Polybius' strictures against undignified dancing by persons of rank; 30.26.7–8.

138. Plut. *Cato*, 3.7.

139. That is clear from Plutarch's language; *Cato*, 3.7: διατριβὰς αὐτοῦ μειρακιώδεις ἐν παλαίστραις καὶ θεάτροις, ὥσπερ οὐ στρατηγοῦντος, ἀλλὰ πανηγυρίζοντος. For the occasion of Cato's speech, a disputed matter, see Della Corte, *Catone Censore*, 252; Astin, *Cato the Censor*, 13–15.

140. Plut. *Cato*, 12.4–5.

141. Plut. *Cato*, 22.4: ἀνὴρ ἐπιφανὴς σπουδάσας αὐτὸς καὶ δεηθεὶς ἡρμήνευσε Γαίος Ἀκίλιος.

boxer asking spectators to forgive him if he failed to parry blows.[142] Cato's irritation is appropriate and intelligible, but its import needs to be underlined. To regard Cato's mockery as directed against Postumius' philhellenism misses the point. The problem was not that he wrote in Greek but that his Greek was not good enough! The request that readers make allowance for his failings was, in Cato's view, undignified and humiliating. That a Roman senator would ask the indulgence of Greeks reversed the proper power relationship. If Postumius chose to write in Greek, he had better show command of the language and thereby reiterate the cultural accomplishment of Rome. In that central regard, the criticism of Postumius accords perfectly with other opinions and acts ascribed to Cato the Elder. The Censor took as his task not the repression of Hellenism but the assertion of its inferiority to national values.[143]

Recapitulation to this point would be salutary. The ostensible paradox perceived by most may be more appearance than reality. Cato's knowledge of Greek and Greek culture, on the one hand, and his disparaging attitude, on the other, were mutually reinforcing. It is unnecessary to conjure up theories about a change of heart in later years; a distinction between old and new, good and bad Greeks; a detaching of the culture from the ministers of that culture; a selective antihellenism; or occasional eruptions of irrational prejudice that marred an otherwise temperate outlook. In fact, a strong line of consistency underlies the comments and conduct. Cato's belittlement of windy rhetoric and philosophical artifice aimed at accentuating Hellenic flaws, thereby to promote a sharper awareness of distinctive Roman characteristics. The point receives greater force from Cato's claim that he had command of Greek but deliberately eschewed use of it, or that he had been taught by a Pythagorean and had a Greek intellectual on his estate but preferred to praise native virtues and values. The latter increase in stature through the contrast, and Cato augments his credibility through his credentials. The tale that he explored Greek literature only late in life and the recommendation to his son that it needs only perusal rather than immersion fortified the sense of superiority for the Roman who was conversant with both cultures.

142. Polyb. 39.1.1–9; Plut. Cato, 12.5
143. Postumius' apologetic preface may, in fact, have been no more than a literary convention blown out of proportion by Cato; see Walbank, Historical Commentary on Polybius, III, 727. And Polybius doubtless exaggerated Postumius' failings still further. He had personal reasons to despise the man who helped block the release of Achaean hostages; Polyb. 33.1.3–8; cf. 39.1.10–12.

The drive to establish a distinctive national character that would be widely hailed as estimable explains Cato's flailing of contemporaries for extravagance and self-indulgence. It is not the Greeks themselves who are villains but Roman leaders who fail to play the part their nation's preeminence had thrust upon them. So, for example, a passage of Plutarch, recounting Cato's attitude, expressed distress that Romans had adopted the Hellenic habit of bathing in the nude. Worse still, they had aggravated the practice by introducing mixed nude bathing—in which offense they had schooled the Greeks! Cato, if the sentiment is his, aimed his vitriol, as is clear, primarily at his lapsed fellow countrymen.[144] Rome's international stature brought with it the obligation of deportment that commands respect. Hence, Cato naturally showed scorn for Greek rulers such as Antiochus III and Eumenes II, whose nations had forfeited the right to leadership in the Mediterranean world.[145] But he felt still more passionate about Roman aristocrats whose conduct compromised the leadership their nation had earned. Postumius Albinus' self-deprecation before Greeks therefore merited deep contempt. The reproaches logically extended to Roman magistrates who cheapened their offices through unseemly behavior and to those individuals who engaged poets to sing their praises, damaging the collective character of the Roman achievement. Cato's stance was firmly consistent, neither paradoxical nor schizophrenic. A man of high culture himself, he readily endorsed the value of a reflective *otium* in conjunction with active public service. Cato does not dismiss the Hellenic achievement. On the contrary, it can serve to set off the preeminence of the Romans who had commandeered that achievement to their own ends.

A preponderance of evidence converges to show consistent design and deliberate purpose in Cato's posture toward Hellenism. He emerges as a subtle and sophisticated leader rather than a blunderbuss antihellenist. What then is to be made of the few savagely hostile outbursts attributed to him, the vicious condemnation of Greek physicians, the sweeping denunciation of the entire Hellenic race, and the dire warning that its culture will bring corruption and even terminate Roman control? A methodological point needs to be insisted upon. The few drastic assertions ought not to dissolve the rest of the record. To count the most

---

144. Plut. *Cato*, 20.5–6: εἶτα μέντοι παρ᾽ Ἑλλήνων τὸ γυμνοῦσθαι μαθόντες, αὐτοὶ πάλιν τοῦ καὶ μετὰ γυναικῶν τοῦτο πράσσειν ἀναπεπλήκασι τοὺς Ἕλληνας. The statement may, however, be Plutarch's rather than Cato's.
145. *ORF*, fr. 20 = Cugusi, *OR*, fr. 4; Plut. *Cato*, 20.7–8.

extreme declarations as the touchstone of Cato's entire career and interpret all else in their light is unsound procedure. Better to reexamine
those texts with an eye to that broader pattern of actions and attitudes
already discerned.

What, in fact, do the texts say? Greek medicine comes in for the
severest abuse. Cato alleged that Greek physicians had sworn a collective oath to poison all *barbari*—and to pocket a fee while doing it.[146]
From that category of despicable types Cato proceeds to excoriate the
entire Hellenic stock: an altogether villainous and incorrigible lot.[147]
The coming of Greek letters to Italian shores will ruin everything, and
Romans, once imbued with them, will lose control of affairs.[148] Far
from being central to and exemplary of Catonian philosophy, these
exclamations deviate sharply from all else in the testimony. How should
they be construed?

A point of high importance has gone unrecognized by modern scholarship. All the most immoderate expressions appear to derive from the
same work—namely, a tract addressed to and containing advice for
Cato's son. The citations make this clear beyond a reasonable doubt.
The denunciation of Greek doctors takes the form of a warning to the
younger Cato: he is prohibited from consorting with them.[149] The
Censor's flat condemnation of the whole Hellenic race also occurs as
counsel to his son, as does the admonition that Greek culture will be a
corrupting force in Roman society.[150] The extremist statements, therefore, may all stem from a single segment of a single work.

What was the nature of this volume? Most previous treatments have
imagined an elaborate production, even a multivolume study, the so-
called *Libri ad filium*, a veritable Roman encyclopedia, encompassing at
least the subjects of agriculture, medicine, and rhetoric.[151] The re-

146. Pliny, *NH*, 29.14: *iurarunt inter se barbaros necare omnes medicina, et hoc ipsum
mercede faciunt ut fides is sit et facile disperdant*; Plut. *Cato*, 23.3: ἔλεγε κοινὸν ὅρκον εἶναι
τοῦτον ἰατρῶν ἁπάντων.

147. Pliny, *NH*, 29.14: *nequissimum et indocile genus*.

148. Pliny, *NH*, 29.14: *quandoque ista gens suas litteras dabit, omnia conrumpet*; Plut.
Cato, 23.2: ὡς ἀπολοῦσι Ῥωμαῖοι τὰ πράγματα γραμμάτων Ἑλληνικῶν ἀναπλησθ-
έντες.

149. Pliny, *NH*, 29.14: *interdixi tibi de medicis*; Plut. *Cato*, 23.4: παρεκελεύετο φυλά-
ττεσθαι τῷ παιδὶ πάντας.

150. Pliny, *NH*, 29.14: *dicam de istis Graecis suo loco, M. fili*; Plut. *Cato*, 23.2: τὸν δὲ
παῖδα διαβάλλων πρὸς τὰ Ἑλληνικά.

151. See, especially, M. Gerosa, *La prima enciclopedia romana, I "libri ad Marcum filium"
di Catone Censore* (Pavia, 1910); F. Della Corte, *RivFilol*, 69 (1941), 81–96. An extensive
bibliography can be found in Astin, *Cato the Censor*, 332.

construction has, in more recent years, received vigorous and convincing challenge. References to the work or works take various forms, whether as *libri, oratio, epistula*, or simply *praecepta*. Nothing suggests an encyclopedia or even a systematic compendium. A study in agriculture in addition to Cato's extant *De agri cultura* would be an anomaly, a treatise on oratory could hardly have escaped the notice of Cicero, and Cato did produce a handbook on medicine but plainly separate from the work addressed to his son. So, it is argued, the *ad filium*, if that be its title, can be conceived as a collection of axioms, pieces of advice, exhortations, and admonitions rather than a carefully composed didactic work.[152] The precise form is probably irrecoverable. Cato did compose a letter or letters to his son which were subsequently published, but those for which we have evidence treated rather different subjects.[153] Catonian *orationes*, so far as they can be reconstructed, have little in common with the *ad filium* fragments. The search for form and genre encounters frustration.

All discussions of the subject share a common assumption: that Cato's tract, whatever its nature, had a serious didactic purpose in the education of his son. That assumption might benefit from reconsideration. When would the tract have been composed? Cato had two sons, one born circa 192, the second in Cato's old age after a second marriage circa 154.[154] That Cato embarked upon an educational treatise in his final years to instruct an infant son not yet capable of comprehension has little likelihood.[155] Yet the usual answer, that Cato produced the

152. A. Mazzarino, *Introduzione al "De agri cultura" di Catone* (Rome, 1952), 19–29, issued cogent criticisms of the *communis opinio*, and the thesis was demolished by Astin's excellent discussion; *Cato the Censor*, 332–340. The fragments are collected in H. Jordan, *M. Catonis praeter librum de re rustica quae extant* (Leipzig, 1860), 77–80, although he includes under the rubric *Libri ad Marcum filium* some fragments not so labeled in the sources.

153. I.e., a congratulatory letter on his valor while in military service and another (or the same?) reminding him that a soldier could not reenter battle after discharge by his commander; Plut. *Cato*, 20.7–8; *Quaest. Rom.* 39; Cic. *De Off.* 1.36–37. Two other fragments survive, without context; see P. Cugusi, *Epistolographi latini minores*, I (Turin, 1970), 67–69, fr. 6–9. See discussions by Cugusi, *AnnUnivCagliari*, 33.1 (1970), 46–54; P. L. Schmidt, *Hermes*, 100 (1972), 568–576; Cugusi, *Evoluzione e forme dell' epistolografia latina* (Rome, 1983), 152.

154. The elder, M. Porcius Cato Licinianus, gained election to the praetorship in 152, probably *suo anno* or not much later; Cic. *Tusc. Disp.* 3.70; Gellius, 13.20.9; Livy, *Per.* 48; Plut. *Cato*, 24.6. The younger, M. Porcius Cato Salonianus, was born when his father had reached his eightieth year; *Vir. Ill.* 47.9; Plut. *Cato*, 24.3–6; Gellius, 13.20.7–8; Pliny, *NH*, 7.61–62; Solinus, 1.59.

155. That view was held by Gerosa, *La prima enciclopedia*, 36. It is summarily dis-

work for his first son, has grave problems of its own. A didactic volume composed to school his son in moral, political, cultural, and practical matters ought to have come at an early, formative stage of the young man's life. Yet Cato, as Plutarch informs us, was an old man when he wrote his intemperate words to Marcus Junior about the Greeks.[156] The idea that this composition was intended as a bona fide handbook for the tuition of his son becomes the less plausible. Cato had a wider audience in view. Publication itself suggests more than a mere private communication. Cato used the *ad filium* form for a larger purpose.[157]

The work, it may be postulated, had a public intent and thus a somewhat stylized character. That postulate is buttressed by a closer look at the "anti-Greek" dicta. The claim that all Greek physicians formed a sworn conspiracy to poison Romans is plain hyperbole, designed to arrest readers' attention. That does not mean that the outburst was mere irrational ejaculation—or indeed that it can be discarded as senseless. The rhetoric itself served a serious interest. Cato placed emphasis, as in most of his comparable statements, upon contrast between Greek practice and Roman values. Pliny, who claims to reproduce his very words, juxtaposes the sentence about murderous Greek physicians to one in which the Censor complains about Greek disparagement of Romans: they repeatedly call us *barbari* and bespatter us in more obscene fashion than others with the name of *opici*.[158] The juxtaposition tempts an inference that ill temper and retaliation motivated Cato's attack on the doctors.[159] But that conclusion is narrow and reductive. The extravagant stigmatization of Greek medicine as a homicidal conspiracy provided a mirror image of the Greek denunciation of Roman barbarism, thus exposing both as caricatures. The assertion suits Cato's general

---

missed by Astin, *Cato the Censor*, 332. Della Corte, *RivFilol*, 69 (1941), 81, seeks to strike a balance, seeing the work as written originally for Licinianus, then, after Licinianus' death, employed for Salonianus.

156. Plut. *Cato*, 23.2: φωνῇ κέχρηται θρασυτέρᾳ τοῦ γήρως.

157. The notion of a broadly aimed didactic work has been argued even for the *epistula* or *epistulae* to his son; cf. J. Carcopino, *Les secrets de la correspondance de Cicéron* (Paris, 1947), 17–18; Schmidt, *Hermes*, 100 (1972), 568–576. Others see the *ad filium*, whether letter or extended treatise, as private advice, only subsequently published; e.g., Della Corte, *RivFilol*, 69 (1941), 81–96; Cugusi, *AnnUnivCagliari*, 33.1 (1970), 46–51.

158. Pliny, *NH*, 29.14: *nos quoque dictitant barbaros et spurcius nos quam alios opicon appellatione foedant*. On the term *opici*, see the full and careful treatment by M. Dubuisson, *Latomus*, 42 (1983), 522–545. The word's especially offensive character may be more in the Roman perception than in the Greek intention; Dubuisson, 543–545.

159. Cf. Marmorale, *Cato Maior*, 154; Astin, *Cato the Censor*, 173.

drive to elevate the stature of Roman culture.[160] Pliny himself indicates that he did not, in fact, condemn the entire medical profession outright. The ancient Romans, so he pointed out, arraigned not medicine itself but the practice that expected them to purchase their lives for a fee.[161] Cato indeed made a show of outstripping Hellenic skill in this area, as in others. He worked up his own annotated collection of home remedies, whereby he could minister to his son, slaves, and extended household. And he could claim the superior efficacy of his method by pointing to his own longevity and to that of his wife.[162] Once more the Censor strove to bolster Roman pride and to reassert the special qualities of Roman culture. Greek medicine supplied a useful foil, as did Greek philosophy and Greek oratory. The *ad filium*, produced in the form of a didactic treatise for a young son, could put the contrast in stark terms, thus to assure attention: *interdixi tibi de medicis*. Later sources, with considerable naiveté, took it as sheer hatred of Hellenism.

The contrived mode of discourse employed in the *ad filium* can be further illustrated. Cato, at least when he delivered his heaviest broadside against the Greeks, adopted the posture of a prophet. He specifically announced as much to young Marcus in connection with his slur on the entire Hellenic race and in offering the prediction that Greek literature would corrupt everything in Rome. So Pliny reports.[163] Plutarch confirms it, declaring that Cato took on an oracular and prophetic tone when impressing upon his son that Greek letters will ruin Roman ascendancy.[164] The deliberate posturing signals a literary artifice. So indeed does the content. By the time of Cato's old age, Greek literature had long since entered the mainstream of Roman high culture, had been an integral part of it for two generations. To forecast in the mid–second

160. It is perhaps noteworthy that Pliny prefaced this passage with reference to the first Greek physician to practice in Rome—a man who acquired the name and reputation of *carnifex*; *NH*, 29.12–13.

161. Pliny, *NH*, 29.16: *non rem antiqui damnabant, sed artem, maxime vero quaestum esse manipretio vitae recusabant*.

162. Pliny, *NH*, 29.15: *subicit enim qua medicina se et coniugem usque ad longam senectam perduxerit . . . profitaturque esse commentarium sibi quo medeatur filio, servis, familiaribus*.

163. Pliny, *NH*, 29.14: *et hoc puta vatem dixisse: quandoque ista gens suas litteras dabit, omnia conrumpet*; cf. 29.27: *vatem prorsus cottidie facit Catonem et oraculum*. Another fragment of the *ad filium*, also in oracular form, does not appear to involve Greeks; Pliny, *NH*, 7.171: *quippe cum censorius Cato ad filium de validis quoque observationem ut ex oraculo aliquo prodiderit senilem iuventam praematurae mortis esse signum*.

164. Plut. *Cato*, 23.2: οἷον ἀποθεσπίζων καὶ προμαντεύων. On the association of Cato with an oracular pose, see also Seneca, *Contr.* 1, praef. 9; Pliny, *NH*, 18.174, 18.200.

century the future influence of Hellenism would be absurdly anachronistic. Plutarch understandably takes Cato to task for this remark, castigating him for statements too foolhardy for a man of his years and pointing out that Rome, far from losing control, reached the peak of her authority at the time when she embraced Greek learning and culture.[165] But Plutarch, it appears, took Cato too literally. This can hardly have been genuine prognostication and serious warning. Cato struck a retrospective pose as seer to reiterate the need for Romans to take pride in their own cultural achievement, distinct from and not subordinate to the Hellenic contribution. What motivated the Censor was neither blind prejudice nor anxiety for Rome's future. When he belittled Greek culture it was in a spirit of rivalry and contention for supremacy: φιλοτιμία.[166]

In every regard, therefore, the anti-Greek pronouncements of the *ad filium* stand apart. Cato fashioned them intentionally as dramatic exaggerations in an artificial construct. The pretense of advice to a young son helps explain the stark terms in which Cato couched these assertions, thereby alerting his readers to consider them in context.[167] That does not authorize their dismissal or reduction to narrow prejudice.[168] But it should warn against employing them as the core of Catonian thought and the basis on which all else must be interpreted. Cato's attitude was more nuanced and more calculated.

Cato the Censor approached Greek culture not as an enemy of Hellas but as an advocate of Rome. He gained appreciation of the language and

---

165. Plut. *Cato*, 23.2–3: φωνῇ κέχρηται θρασυτέρᾳ τοῦ γήρως . . . ἐν ᾧ τοῖς τε πράγμασιν ἡ πόλις ἤρθη μεγίστη καὶ πρὸς Ἑλληνικὰ μαθήματα καὶ παιδείαν ἅπασαν ἔσχεν οἰκείως.

166. Plut. *Cato*, 23.1: πᾶσαν Ἑλληνικὴν μοῦσαν καὶ παιδείαν ὑπὸ φιλοτιμίας προπηλακίζων.

167. Note, for example, Cato's pronouncement to his son that he will convince him that Greeks are a most wicked and incorrigible people, thus implying that this is a novel and singular position for him; Pliny, *NH*, 29,14: *Vincam nequissimum et indocile genus illorum.* The *vincam* belongs more naturally with this clause than with the preceding, which is governed by *dicam*—despite the punctuation favored by many editors.

168. Haffter, *Römische Politik*, 190–192, regards the broad condemnation as applying only to Greek medicine. For Astin, *Cato the Censor*, 177–178, Plutarch wrongly extrapolated in general terms what Cato intended to be directed only against Greek philosophy. Kienast, *Cato der Zensor*, 104–105, reduces the application of the pronouncements to both medicine and philosophy. This view is rightly criticized by Letta, *Athenaeum*, 62 (1984), 18, who, however, takes the statements as authentic Catonian distaste for the effects of Greek culture in general. So also Garbarino, *Roma e la filosofia greca*, 314–317.

learning of Greece at a time when his own nation was groping to define its relationship to that older and far more celebrated civilization. Cato perceived the risk of being engulfed by its attractive traditions and established patterns more acutely than most of his contemporaries. And he undertook a lifelong campaign not to repress Greek culture but to employ it as a means to mark off the distinctiveness of the Roman character.

Insistence on Roman dignity in the presence of Greeks was a repeated refrain. Hence, Cato made a display of addressing Athenians in Latin, while giving the job of translation to an interpreter. Those who demeaned themselves before Greeks he affected to despise—notably Acilius, who showed unseemly eagerness in serving the interests of Athenian envoys, and Postumius who humbled himself before a Greek readership. Romans needed to maintain their bearing and to give reminders of their privileged position. Cato accordingly rebuked public officials who donned Greek garb, honored Greek cooks, or danced Greek dances. The magistrates of the Republic had an obligation to affirm national values to the international community.

Cato's familiarity with Hellenism, far from paradoxical or problematic, formed an integral part of his cultural strategy. He openly effected the migration of Ennius to Rome, and employed a Greek tutor in his household. Others found nothing incongruous in spreading tales that he discussed philosophy with a Pythagorean or studied Greek literature with Ennius. The message delivered in Latin to the Athenians had the greater force because Cato could have used Greek, whereas his audience was monolingual. He professed a close study of Greek literature only in his later years, indicating its subordination to the responsibilities of a Roman statesman. And his recommendation that perusal was preferable to immersion in that literature aimed not only to indicate his own acquaintance with it but to assign it a secondary status. Roman superiority could best be asserted by a man who commanded Greek language and literature—and found them wanting.

The Censor cultivated a sense of pride in Roman values and qualities. But more than that. His actions and writings endeavored to give definition to those values. For such an objective, confrontation with Hellenic practices proved to be eminently serviceable, a means whereby to sharpen perception of national principles. The critique of Greek oratory suited that purpose. By fostering the stereotype of loquaciousness and windy rhetoric, Cato could mark off Roman virtues by contrast: *rem tene, verba sequentur*. He found fault with Greek philosophy on precisely those points that allowed him to promote Roman distinctiveness. He singled out Hellenic thinkers who could be censured for abstract speculation, subversion of institutions and traditions, and reckless disregard of the truth. Focus on those flaws encouraged Romans to vaunt (or invent) their special intellectual and moral attributes: practicality, respect for ancestral laws and practices, and adherence to principle. The *Origines* contributed significantly to the campaign. Not that Cato employed the document to denigrate Greeks. Indeed, he conveyed with approval those traditions that claimed Greek origins for early inhabitants and settlers of Italy.[169] But there can be no doubt that the work served as vehicle to advertise the national character. The fact that it was composed in Latin sent its own message. The first full-scale history in that language announced the maturity of Roman culture.[170] Greek comparisons, as so often, could draw attention to Roman accomplishments. Cato reminded readers of the celebrated tale of Leonidas and the three hundred Spartans at Thermopylae, a signal instance of heroism. But he did so in order to bring to light a far less celebrated but equally heroic deed by a Roman military tribune in the First Punic War. Cato's point was not to detract in any way from the glory of Leonidas' name but rather to underscore the contrast with the absence of publicity accorded the Roman. The historian indeed reckoned such anonymity as a proud characteristic of his nation. He made it a point even to omit the names of Roman *imperatores* in his work. Unlike the Greek, the Roman achievement was a national, not an individual, one.[171] Cato celebrated the learning and life of Italy.[172]

---

169. That Cato chose to abandon Olympic years as a means of dating Rome's foundation ought not to be considered an anti-Greek gesture, as does, e.g., Letta, *Athenaeum*, 62 (1984), 24. The decision may reflect only the convenience of his readers. In fact, Cato reckoned the date from the time of the Trojan War—thereby endorsing a tradition that also stemmed from the Greeks; Dion. Hal. 1.74.2

170. The choice to write in Latin does not imply scorn for Greek historiography—or even for the writing of Roman history in Greek. Cato's work drew heavily and unmistakably upon Fabius Pictor; see, e.g., Kierdorf, *Chiron*, 10 (1980), 205–224, with bibliographic references.

171. The story of the military tribune is given in *HRR*, fr. 83 = Gellius, 3.7. See, especially, 3.7.19: *Leonides Laco, qui simile apud Thermopylas fecit, propter eius virtutes omnis Graecia gloriam atque gratiam praecipuam claritudinis inclitissimae decoravere monumentis: signis, statuis, elogiis, historiis aliisque rebus gratissimum id eius factum habuere; at tribuno militum parva laus pro factis relicta, qui idem fecerat atque rem servaverat.* See commentary by Chassignet, *Cato: Les Origines*, 87–89. The practice of omitting commanders' names is recorded in *HRR*, fr. 88 = Pliny, *NH*, 8.11; Nepos, *Cato*, 3.4. R. E. Smith, in A. J. Dunston, ed., *Essays in Roman Culture: The Todd Memorial Lectures* (Toronto, 1976), 214,

The Censor made a closely parallel comparison in one other realm as well: that of the constitution. He pointed to the most renowned political systems of Hellas and the changes they had undergone—all ascribed by Greek tradition to the genius of individual lawgivers: Minos, Lycurgus, Theseus, Draco, Solon, Cleisthenes, Demetrius of Phalerum. Not so in Rome, whose constitution, according to Cato, did not derive from a single conception at a specific time but owed its evolution to multiple contributors over a span of generations and centuries.[173] Once more, the Greek experience served to throw Roman distinctiveness into high relief. Cato's fellow citizens paraded a collective success.

Cato the Elder could boast of accomplishments in a remarkable variety of spheres, public and private, military, political, and literary, but none perhaps more important than his contribution to the self-consciousness of a Roman national character. His expressed attitudes and actions toward the Greeks must be interpreted in that context. Cato's mission was neither to resist Hellenism nor to liberate Rome from its influence but to highlight its features, both admirable and objectionable, in order to give clearer definition to the qualities and values that set Rome apart. Mastery achieved in the world of politics and war should now be matched by a comparable sense of esteem in the cultural world. Cato prodded his countrymen toward an articulation of their own national character.

---

implausibly sees the omission of names as a snub to senatorial historians who glorified their ancestors. Cf. Flores, *Letteratura latina e ideologia*, 124–125.

172. *HRR*, fr. 76 = Serv. *Ad Aen.* 9.600: *Italiae disciplina et vita laudatur.*

173. Cic. *De Rep.* 2.1–2: *nostra autem res publica non unius esset ingenio, sed multorum, nec una hominis vita, sed aliquot constituta saeculis et aetatibus.* The analysis was adopted by Polybius as well; 6.10.13–14; Nicolet, *FondHardt*, 20 (1974), 248–249—thus obviously not a matter of hostility to Greeks.

[3]

ART AND CIVIC LIFE

Roman moralists deplored the effects of alien art upon the national character. The complaint became a *topos*, repeated in various forms and at various times. Hellenic art, of course, was a prime culprit. Its allurements eroded Roman morals, corrupted attitudes, and weakened the fiber of the nation. Ancient writers acknowledged the attractiveness but lamented the corrosive consequences of Greek art. The censure plainly exaggerates and misrepresents. Yet the misrepresentation itself has had a potent impact, affecting interpretation of the relationship between Rome and the arts of Hellas down to the present day. The subject calls for more probing inquiry.

The infiltration of Greek art, as our sources present it, meant luxury, softness, and a compromise of Roman traditional values. On that presentation, Marcellus' sack of Syracuse in 211 triggered the process. The artistic treasures carted home after his victory began to wean Romans away from sturdy simplicity to an appetite for wealth—and generated jealousies to boot. Marcellus delivered huge numbers of paintings and statues, indiscriminately looting sacred and profane objects, stimulating a taste for art while inuring the Romans to sacrilege. Critics bemoaned the fact that gods as well as men were dragged around in triumphal processions and that Romans neglected civic duties while idly chattering about the merits of art and artists.[1]

1. Polyb. 9.10.1–12; Livy, 25.40.1–3; Plut. *Marc.* 21.1–5. Cf. G. Becatti, *Arte e gusto negli scrittori latini* (Florence, 1951), 9–12.

Matters became worse still with expansion to the east and the consequent influx of Hellenic creations. *Triumphatores* scrambled to outdo one another in the quality and quantity of objects seized and transported to Rome. L. Scipio even brought Greek craftsmen and artists back with him to continue producing in Italy. The treasures from Greek Asia that accompanied his return gave him the reputation of introducing luxury to his countrymen. The spoils of Cn. Manlius Vulso aggravated the situation further. His loot included bronze couches and elegant furniture. And his homecoming was reckoned as the advent of *luxuria* in Rome.[2]

Roman generals, so the moralists claimed, not only transmitted opulent art that undermined national character but showed neither aesthetic sensibility nor religious scruples. The victims of M. Fulvius Nobilior charged him with stripping the temples of Ambracia of every sacred image, thereby, in effect, depriving worshipers of their gods. The redoubtable Cato the Elder supposedly branded the statuary from Syracuse a menace to the state and lamented that the lavish decorations from Athens and Corinth caused Romans to scorn the terra-cotta images of their own deities. And the prime *exemplum* of boorishness was the notorious L. Mummius whose soldiers converted precious paintings into gaming tables and who, it was alleged, had no feel for artistic quality and lacked all discrimination in the aesthetic realm.[3]

Modern scholarship, while eschewing the moralism, paints a series of portraits hardly any more edifying. Greek art captured by Roman conquerors in the second century represented booty rather than connoisseurship, tokens of power and dominance. Genuine appreciation of Hellenic artistry did not run deep.[4] Statues, paintings, and decorative objects came to Rome as showpieces. Economic value counted for more than aesthetic quality.[5] And political advantage held a central place: *imperatores* put their accomplishments on display not only through parade of captured art in triumphs, but through dedication of statues,

2. Pliny, *NH*, 34.14, 34.34, 37.12; Livy, 39.6.7; Aug. *CD*, 3.21.

3. Nobilior and Ambracia: Livy, 38.43.5; cf. Pliny, *NH*, 35.66. Cato: Livy, 34.4.4. Mummius: Polyb. 39.2.1–2; Strabo, 8.6.23 (C381); Vell. Pat. 1.13.4; Pliny, *NH*, 35.24; Dio Chrys. 37.42.

4. So, e.g., F. Poulsen, *Die Antike*, 13 (1937), 125–140; M. Pape, *Griechische Kunstwerke aus Kriegsbeute und ihre öffentliche Aufstellung in Rom* (Hamburg, 1975), 58–65; E. Künzl, *Der römische Triumph* (Munich, 1988), 109–113; R. MacMullen, *Historia*, 40 (1991), 425–426.

5. Cf. H. Jucker, *Vom Verhältnis der Römer zur bildenden Kunst der Griechen* (Frankfurt, 1950), 58–62; Pape, *Griechische Kunstwerke*, 56–58, 95–96, 99.

commission of paintings, and erection of monuments.[6] Insofar as appreciation of artistic creativity existed, that was limited to a circle of "philhellenes" who struggled against a nativist reaction.[7] Such are the principal interpretations and broad analyses offered by moderns on Roman attitudes toward Greek art in the mid-Republic. They all contain truth, without doubt. The acquisition of artistic products from the Greek East had political and economic significance, both for individual members of the elite and for the nation as a whole. The imports graced the city, elevated the reputations of returning conquerors, and increased the economic power of the state. But concentration on Marcellus and then the eastern wars obscures significant precedents and postulates an artificial turning point. Polarization of Romans between connoisseurs and philistines oversimplifies complex attitudes. And emphasis on the political and economic elements omits what may be more important: the cultural context and implications.

The acquisition of art works from the defeated enemy and their installation as tokens of victory in Rome did not await the intiative of M. Marcellus. The practice had a long and honored history in the Roman experience. Religious overtones are discernible from the start. So are individual ambitions—and national interest.

An event of high notoriety occurred very early. At the siege of Veii in 396, Rome's commander, M. Furius Camillus, called upon Juno, divine protectress of the city, to abandon it and take up residence in Rome. There she would obtain due reverence, including a temple worthy of her greatness. The *evocatio* came to fruition after the Roman victory at Veii, when Roman soldiers were assigned the job of transporting the goddess' cult statue to Rome. The duty was performed with scrupulous care and sensitivity. Report had it that the young soldiers approached their task with trepidation and awe, hesitating to act until the goddess herself signified acquiescence. The statue then proved to be of miraculous portability. It soon found its permanent resting place on the Aventine Hill, where, four years later, Camillus dedicated the temple he

6. Pape, *Griechische Kunstwerke*, 41–47, 53–54, 97–98; G. Waurick, *JbRGZ*, 22 (1975), 1–46; T. Hölscher, *MdI*, 85 (1978), 315–357; L. Pietilä-Castrén, *Arctos*, 16 (1982), 121–143; idem, *Magnificentia Publica: The Victory Monuments of the Roman Generals in the Era of the Punic Wars* (Helsinki, 1987), 24–27.

7. Cf. Poulsen, *Die Antike*, 13 (1937), 137–140; Jucker, *Vom Verhältnis der Römer*, 102–117; Becatti, *Arte e gusto*, 13–18; J. J. Pollitt, *TAPA*, 108 (1978), 155–164; idem, *Art in the Hellenistic Age* (Cambridge, 1986), 159–160.

had vowed to Juno during the war.[8] It is unnecessary either to defend or to dispute the particulars of the story. Its tenor carries more importance. The Romans showed proper deference to the deity of an enemy state but carried off her image anyway, consecrating it afresh and providing a new sanctuary. The Veientane work of art would now signal a great Roman victory, enhance and expand the national religion, and provide a reminder of Camillus' achievement. The tale, not incidentally, stressed the voluntary character of the goddess' migration to Rome. This was not booty but absorption of the enemy's cult into the state religion.

A not dissimilar outcome featured the Roman contest with Praeneste in 380. T. Quinctius Cincinnatus led Roman forces to victory in that struggle and then carried off the statue of Jupiter Imperator to the Capitol, dedicating it at a site between the shrines of two other deities. Cincinnatus attached an inscribed plaque commemorating his accomplishments and giving credit to Jupiter and his fellow gods for their support.[9] Display of the trophy thus affirmed divine favor for the Roman cause while underscoring the exploits of the leader. Once again, stress fell not on seizure of enemy goods but on the deity's new stance as a defender of Rome.

The Tuscan god Vortumnus from Volsinii undertook a parallel pilgrimage. In the course of his city's war with Rome, so Propertius has him say, Vortumnus deserted his former seat to take up a new locus in Rome.[10] The transferral presumably occurred in 264, as consequence of Roman victories in Etruria and the reduction of Volsinii by the consul M. Fulvius Flaccus, who earned a triumph for his successes. Vortumnus obtained his own temple on the Aventine.[11] Hostile critics later blamed Rome for taking Volsinii only to confiscate two thousand statues.[12] But the cult images, at least, received respect and new honors.

Falerii fell to the Romans in 241. The city yielded up at least two divinities whose images and cults subsequently found place in Rome. A statue of Janus with four faces was discovered after the capture of

8. Livy, 5.21.3, 5.22.3–7, 5.31.3; cf. R. M. Ogilvie, *A Commentary on Livy, Books 1–5* (Oxford, 1965), 673–675.

9. Livy, 6.29.8–9.

10. Prop. 4.2.3–6.

11. *Fasti triumph.* on 264; Festus, 228, L; cf. Varro, *LL*, 5.46. On the campaign, see W. V. Harris, *Rome in Etruria and Umbria* (Oxford, 1971), 83–84, 115–118.

12. Pliny, *NH*, 34.34. Some of the statue bases, with inscriptions recording Fulvius' dedication, have been recovered; M. Torelli, *Studi di topographia romana*, 5 (1968), 71–75; cf. Hölscher, *MdI*, 85 (1978), 320–322.

Falerii, thus inducing the Romans to build a new temple with four doors to honor the god.[13] And the shrine of Minerva Capta near the foot of the Caelian Hill provoked Ovid to conjecture that her name derived from her arrival as a captive after the conquest of Falerii.[14] The phraseology employed here would seem to set Minerva's migration into a category rather different from that of Juno's voluntary move from Veii. True enough. But a more fundamental parallel takes precedence. In each instance the divinities received Roman embrace, and the images that were brought to Rome entered new houses of worship.

The purloining of art objects from defeated foes, however, by no means confined itself to images of gods. Victorious generals found other means to bring their deeds before the public and to keep their memories fresh. C. Maenius led Romans to success against Antium in the Great Latin War in 338 and had suitable souvenirs installed in Rome: the prows of surrendered Antiate ships were fixed as decorative items upon a platform in the Forum, the area thenceforth to be called the Rostra.[15] Similarly, L. Papirius Cursor commemorated his defeat of the Samnites in 309 by setting up gleaming captured shields with gold inlay to adorn the Forum.[16] Sp. Carvilius employed an even more ingenious means of self-promotion which combined both religion and art. From the captured military spoils of the Samnites—breastplates, greaves, and helmets—he had a colossal bronze statue of Jupiter made on the Capitol, one so large that it could be seen from the temple of Jupiter Latiaris in Alba. And the leftover scraps of metal provided enough material to fashion another, smaller statue, this one of Carvilius himself, placed at the foot of the new Jupiter figure.[17] In this instance, then, surrendered enemy goods produced works of art rather than constituted them. The event discloses a complex intertwining of self-display, national triumph, religious devotion, and artistic creativity. The massive Jupiter beamed its multiple message throughout the city and its environs.[18]

13. Servius, Ad Aen. 7.607.

14. Ovid, Fasti, 3.835–844: an quia perdomitis ad nos captiva Faliscis venit? Cf. R. E. A. Palmer, Roman Religion and Roman Empire (Philadelphia, 1974), 42–43; J.-L. Girard, REL, 67 (1989), 163–169.

15. Livy, 8.14.12; Pliny, NH, 34.20; Hölscher, MdI, 85 (1978), 318–319.

16. Livy, 9.40.16, 10.39.13–14, 10.46.4.

17. Pliny, NH, 34.43. On the Capitol as locus for statues, see G. Lahusen, Untersuchungen zur Ehrenstatue in Rom (Rome, 1983), 7–12.

18. The Samnite triumph of Sp. Carvilius came in 293 and included huge spoils, most of which were deposited in the treasury and the rest spent on the construction of a temple

The accumulation of art taken from Italian cities that fell under Roman power proceeded apace. M'. Curius Dentatus' defeat of Pyrrhus and his allies at Malventum—soon to be renamed Beneventum—resulted in a resplendent triumph that included, we are told, precious statuary, paintings, and other luxuries from Tarentum.[19] Still another haul came in the next decade. A late Republican foe of Rome, Metrodorus of Skepsis, as previously noted, charged the Romans with having sacked Volsinii in 264 for the sake of two thousand statues.[20] One may doubt the alleged motivation and question the exaggerated figure, but the bringing of statuary to Rome in substantial numbers is not likely to have been invented.[21]

The exploitation of art to exhibit Roman martial achievements thus had clear precedents in the fourth and third centuries, had indeed established itself as a form of institution. The practice cannot be dismissed as a series of treasure hunts. Statues of the gods were accorded honor in Rome, reconsecrated, or located in new temples not only out of piety but to broadcast the transfer of divine favor. Handsome trophies became permanent fixtures in the Forum for the admiration and delectation of observers. Captured material was refashioned into new creations, whether sacred images or statuary, to advertise individual exploits and provide reminders of the state's growing dominance in the peninsula. The increasing quantity of art objects brought into Rome betokens a

---

to Fors Fortuna. Livy, 10.46.13–15, describes the triumph but makes no mention of the statue of Jupiter or of Carvilius' own statue. This omission may mean that the latter belong to Carvilius' second consulship in 272 when he celebrated another triumph in the Pyrrhic War—which did involve Samnites; Hölscher, *MdI*, 85 (1978), 323; E. T. Salmon, *Samnium and the Samnites* (Cambridge, 1967), 272, prefers the date of 293.

19. Florus, 1.13.26–27: *pompam, aurum, purpura, signa, tabulae Tarentinaeque deliciae.* Dentatus' triumph was celebrated in 275; T. R. S. Broughton, *Magistrates of the Roman Republic* (Cleveland, Ohio, 1951), I, 195. The fall of Tarentum, however, did not come until 272. Thus, Florus' account may contain some confusion. Perhaps, it has been suggested, the Tarentine objects were captured in the camp of Pyrrhus; O. Vessberg, *Studien zur Kunstgeschichte der römischen Republik* (Lund, 1941), 21; Pape, *Griechische Kunstwerke*, 89; Waurick, *JbRGZ*, 22 (1975), 6–9. But that would be difficult to extract from Florus' text, 1.13.25. In any case, there is no reason to doubt that Tarentine art was brought to Rome after the Pyrrhic War.

20. Pliny, *NH*, 34.34: *propter MM statuarum Volsinios expugnatos obiceret.* This testimony seriously undermines the thesis of Waurick, *JbRGZ*, 22 (1975), 6–12, that Romans had no interest in art as booty before the late third century.

21. If the number even approximates the truth, most of the objects must have been statuettes, perhaps terra-cotta votives. But such spoil is hardly likely to have provoked the ire of Metrodorus. Better to assume that the number is inflated.

more intense public awareness, and the diversity of ends they served sets them firmly apart from mere war spoil.

Commissions for artists to celebrate the deeds or character of eminent Romans also gained in frequency during the century and more before the Hannibalic conflict. The consuls of 338 who commanded Roman forces in the Great Latin War, L. Furius Camillus and C. Maenius, were honored by statues set up on columns in the Forum.[22] Q. Marcius Tremulus, consul in 306, earned the distinction of an equestrian statue placed outside the temple of Castor for his victory over the Hernici.[23] The First Punic War gave occasion for more commemorative columns. C. Duillius obtained Rome's first naval triumph for his defeat of the Carthaginians in 260, a memorable event that warranted a column on the Forum.[24] And M. Aemilius Paullus received a similar column, decorated with ships' prows, on the Capitol, for another naval success in 255.[25] Paintings could provide even more graphic depictions of Roman military conquests. L. Papirius Cursor had his victories over Samnites and Tarentines in 272 memorialized on a painting that went into the temple of Connus. Eight years later M. Fulvius Flaccus followed suit with a painting of his success at Volsinii installed in the temple of Vortumnus.[26] Housing the art works in places of worship reinforced the symbolism of divine favor for the national cause and for its leaders. But paintings that honored generals by portraying their victories could also find place in a secular context. M. Valerius Messalla's defeat of Carthaginians and Syracusans in 263, for instance, was painted on wood and set up on the side of the Curia Hostilia.[27]

The initiative need not always come from Rome. Citizens of Thurii honored the Roman tribune C. Aelius, who had protected them against a hostile magistrate in 285, by presenting him with a statue and a golden crown to be displayed in Rome. Three years later they financed a statue

22. Pliny, NH, 34.20; Livy, 8.13.9; Eutrop. 2.7; cf. Pliny, NH, 7.212, 34.23. Livy calls them equestrian statues—items not readily set atop columns. Cf. Hölscher, MdI, 85 (1978), 338; Lahusen, Ehrenstatue, 56–59.

23. Cic. Phil. 6.13; Livy, 9.43.22; Pliny, NH, 34.23; Hölscher, MdI, 85 (1978), 339. The practice of erecting equestrian statues is ascribed by Pliny to Greek influence; NH, 34.19. But it is unclear whether such influence might have come as early as the mid–fourth century.

24. Pliny, NH, 34.20; Serv. Ad Georg. 3.29; Quint. 1.7.12; Sil. Ital. 6.663–666; Pietilä-Castrén, Magnificentia Publica, 30.

25. Livy, 42.20.1; cf. Lahusen, Ehrenstatue, 82–84.

26. Festus, 228, L.

27. Pliny, NH, 35.22.

for C. Fabricius Luscinus, the Roman consul who had relieved them of a siege.[28] That the Thurians chose to pay homage to Roman benefactors in this fashion suggests that the practice had become entrenched by the early third century.

The statue of a Roman tribune presented by Thurii shows that such distinctions were not confined to military heroes. Other instances confirm the fact. The courageous deed of L. Caecilius Metellus who burst through the flames to rescue the Palladion from the burning temple of Vesta in 241 earned him a statue on the Capitol.[29] And state policy authorized statues for envoys who perished in the line of duty, such as the two men who had conducted an abortive mission to the court of the Illyrian queen Teuta in 230/29.[30] That public art had now become a regular means of marking distinguished deeds or notable state service indicates that the medium itself was held in high esteem.[31]

Artistic creations for public purposes extended beyond honors for Roman leaders or heroes. A variety of circumstances could call them forth. Tradition had it that in the course of the Samnite Wars Pythian Apollo advised the Romans to produce statues of the wisest and the bravest of the Greeks. In consequence, two portraits were set up in the corners of the Comitium, one of Pythagoras, the other of Alcibiades.[32] The tale itself raises doubts and suspicions. Did Rome really consult the Delphic Oracle this early in its history? What relevance would such statues have to the Samnite Wars? Were they not, in fact, confiscated goods taken from some Greek city in southern Italy, such as Tarentum in 272?[33] Whatever skepticism one applies to the story, however, there are no grounds to question the fact of the two statues on prominent display. Sulla had to remove them in order to build his new curia there.[34] A colossal representation of Hercules was dedicated on the

28. Pliny, *NH*, 34.22.
29. Dion. Hal. 2.66.3–4.
30. Pliny, *NH*, 34.24.
31. The assemblage of instances undermines the view of A. Wallace-Hadrill, *PCPS*, 36 (1990), 150–166, 170–173, that statuary as public honor, rather than on private initiative, awaited Roman experience with Greek practice. If Pliny, *NH*, 34.21, be believed, the populace awarded its first honorific statue in 439—and the senate had commonly bestowed them before that time! Notice also Cic. *Phil.* 9.14: *maiores quidem nostri statuas multis decreverunt.*
32. Pliny, *NH*, 34.26; Plut. *Numa*, 8.10.
33. Cf. Jucker, *Vom Verhältnis der Römer*, 53; R. W. Wallace, in W. Eder, ed., *Staat und Staatlichkeit in der frühen römischen Republik* (Stuttgart, 1990), 289.
34. Pliny, *NH*, 34.26.

Capitol in 305. The context and occasion for that event go unrecorded, but it bespeaks heightened public interest in conspicuous statuary.[35] Heightened interest is evident also in the realm of painting. Even Roman aristocrats tried their hand at it. C. Fabius Pictor acquired his cognomen by painting murals in the temple of Salus in 303. Although the profession of painting later fell in esteem, becoming an occupation reserved for men of lesser social standing, Fabius had no hesitation in advertising his own wares, even making it a point to inscribe his name on his compositions.[36] The curule aediles of 296, Cn. and Q. Ogulnius, using cash gleaned from the confiscated property of convicted usurers, put up a statue of Jupiter in a *quadriga* on the roof of his Capitoline temple and another of the twins Romulus and Remus being suckled by the she-wolf at the site of the *ficus Ruminalis*.[37] So, Rome's own national mythology now gained full exposure through public art.

The collection of examples amounts to an impressive array. The Romans placed considerable value upon artistic creations and reckoned them from the start as closely bound up with a variety of public purposes. Art treasures captured from vanquished foes in Italy regularly found display in Rome during the fourth and third centuries. The practice had aims that went well beyond political publicity for conquering generals or economic benefits from confiscated booty.[38] Images of the gods were frequently rededicated in Rome and set in shrines or temples constructed to house them. Those ceremonies attest to Roman reverence for sacred representations, even in the enemy camp, representations that were obviously considered more than mere victors' loot. The conduct of the ceremony and construction of the shrines might redound to the advantage of individual *nobiles* or *gentes*, but they also gave notice of divine backing for the national cause. To what extent the works brought to Rome were sought out for their aesthetic value rather than their religious implications is quite impossible to determine. The two features, of course, are not at cross-purposes. Other testimony allows inferences about Roman taste for art in the period prior to the

---

35. Livy, 9.44.16. The work may have been fashioned in consequence of a religious vow or perhaps came to Rome as an acquisition during the Samnite Wars.

36. Pliny, *NH*, 35.19; Val. Max. 8.14.6; Cic. *Tusc. Disp.* 1.4; cf. Dion. Hal. 16.3. Vessberg, *Studien zur Kunstgeschichte*, 25, rightly defends the authenticity of the tradition. Pliny, in fact, attests to the endurance of Fabius' paintings—and presumably his signature—down to his own day.

37. Livy, 10.23.11–12.

38. Hölscher's analysis, *MdI*, 85 (1978), 350–357, is excessively political.

Hannibalic War. Repeated use of statuary as mark of distinction for generals or outstanding public servants implies public approbation of art as a suitable vehicle for such honors. When captured prows are transformed into a permanent monument, the item takes on a character different from that of temporary display of spoils. Commissioning of statues and paintings to enshrine memorable deeds further underscores Roman respect for these media. The state would hardly authorize expensive creations, nor would individuals promote their own advantage, except on the assumption that Romans prized the products of artistic talent. Pictor's zeal for painting and the erection of a monument to symbolize Rome's own legendary origins suffice to establish that.

Further, and no less important, Rome did not await Marcellus' depredations to become acquainted with Greek art. The statues cast and shipped to Rome by Thurii to honor its Roman benefactors provided examples. So also, in all probability, did the images of Pythagoras and Alcibiades, set up in the Comitium. Pliny traced Greek influence in the equestrian statues that began to make their appearance in the late fourth century. And the Tarentine treasures that reached Rome in the wake of the Pyrrhic War must have substantially advanced public familiarity with Hellenic art. Marcellus' spoils created no revolution.

These developments gathered greater momentum during the Second Punic War. Ominous portents in 218 called for expiation. Among the steps taken was the dedication of a bronze statue to Juno and its emplacement on the Aventine.[39] Works of art thus continued to serve as expressions of Roman religiosity. Among the portents recorded by Livy under the year 217 was the report that Mars's statue on the Appian Way and images of wolves had burst into perspiration.[40] That incidental notice discloses what might have been surmised anyway: that sculptures had become quite ubiquitous in Rome and its environs. In 216, after the disaster at Trasimene, Hiero of Syracuse sent supplies, reinforcements, and weaponry to his Roman allies—and, in order to bolster confidence in divine aid, he dispatched a very large image of the goddess Victory as a permanent gift.[41] Hiero knew what he was doing. Romans had enjoyed increasing exposure to Greek art. The gift by the Sicilian ruler acknowledged Roman interest in art objects as expressions of

---

39. Livy, 21.62.8.
40. Livy, 22.1.12.
41. Livy, 22.37.2–5: *omnium primum ominis causa Victoriam auream pondo ducentum et viginti adferre sese.*

relationship to the gods and symbols of national goals. It also gave the recipients a taste of the craftsmanship of Sicilian Greeks.

One other episode illustrates the continuity of past practices with those of the Hannibalic War. Ti. Sempronius Gracchus as proconsul in 214 secured a victory over Carthaginian forces at Beneventum, for which he and his troops were lavishly hosted and banqueted by the grateful citizens of that town. The event left a powerful impression, one that Gracchus wished to preserve for posterity. Upon his return to Rome, the proconsul instructed artists to produce a painting of the banquet scene for the temple of Liberty on the Aventine, which had been dedicated by his father a generation earlier.[42] The Sempronian gens thereby took credit for being prime champions of *libertas* while celebrating the state's success and doing so through the means of artistic representation. By commissioning a painting that recorded his martial success and its reception and housing it in a temple, Gracchus followed precedents set long before by L. Papirius Cursor, M. Fulvius Flaccus, and M. Valerius Messalla.[43]

When Rome concluded a treaty of alliance with Aetolia in 212 or 211, a treaty designed to keep Philip V of Macedon occupied while Rome concentrated on Hannibal, the pact contained a revealing clause. It provided that victories by the partners would bring a share of acquisitions: all land, farms, buildings, and walls would go to the Aetolians; the Romans would have free disposal of all movable booty.[44] As they well knew, that could include art objects of every variety.[45]

The foregoing examples provide pertinent context for the event much trumpeted in the sources: Marcellus' sack of Syracuse. The great commander, M. Claudius Marcellus, already three times consul and now proconsul in Sicily, recaptured the powerful city of Syracuse in 211, a major turning point in the Hannibalic War.[46] Later writers looked back and saw it also as a major turning point in Roman behavior, attitudes, and moral character. Marcellus, it was alleged, seized a treasure trove of Hellenic art objects and carted them off to Rome, where

42. Livy, 24.16.16–19.
43. Festus, 228, L; Pliny, *NH*, 35.22.
44. *SEG*, XIII, 32; Livy, 26.24.11.
45. Pape, *Griechische Kunstwerke*, 92.
46. For Marcellus' actions in Sicily, see A. M. Eckstein, *Senate and General: Individual Decision Making and Roman Foreign Relations, 264–194 B.C.* (Berkeley, Calif., 1987), 157–169.

the public became beguiled and seduced by them, abandoning the austere life of the ancient Roman. In view of the preceding discussion, that assessment needs substantial modification.

Polybius, who passed judgment on Marcellus' deed two generations later, found it objectionable and disadvantageous to Rome. The seizure of booty, he maintained, is perfectly acceptable when it advances the interests of the conqueror, especially one who aspires to world dominion. But when the spoils comprise superfluous luxury items, a people whose devotion to austerity had made it a conqueror then adopts the fashions of the conquered. Confiscation of gold and silver made sense, but the Romans did not add luster to their nation by decorating it with paintings and images instead of dignity and grandeur.[47]

Livy conveys a comparable indictment. The rights of war justify the acquisition of booty, but the removal to Rome of Syracuse's abundant store of statues and paintings for the first time stimulated Roman zeal for Greek art. Worse still, it generated that indiscriminate appetite for despoiling all things, sacred and profane, which would eventually be turned against the dwellings of the Roman gods themselves.[48]

Plutarch's version carries a similar tone, at least when representing criticism of Marcellus. The general encountered harsh reproof for hauling gods as well as men around in his triumphal procession and, further, for introducing opulence and idleness to a people hitherto devoted to war and the hardy agricultural life.[49] Romans had previously displayed only war trophies consisting of captured barbarian weapons and bloodstained spoils and had no prior exposure to the elegant and sophisticated arts of the Greeks.[50]

47. Polyb. 9.10.1–12. Note especially, 9.10.5: εἰ δ᾽ ἁπλουστάτοις χρώμενοι βίοις καὶ πορρωτάτω τῆς ἐν τούτοις περιττότητος καὶ πολυτελείας ἀφεστῶτες ὅμως ἐπεκράτουν τούτων αἰεὶ παρ᾽ οἷς ὑπῆρχε πλεῖστα καὶ κάλλιστα τὰ τοιαῦτα, πῶς οὐ νομιστέον εἶναι τὸ γινόμενον ὑπ᾽ αὐτῶν ἁμάρτημα; 9.10.12: ἐνδοξοτέραν ποιεῖν τὴν σφετέραν πατρίδα μὴ γραφαῖς καὶ τύποις, ἀλλὰ σεμνότητι καὶ μεγαλοψυχίᾳ κοσμοῦντας αὐτήν.

48. Livy, 25.40.1–3: *ceterum inde primum initium mirandi Graecarum artium opera licentiaeque hinc sacra profanaque omnia volgo spoliandi factum est, quae postremo in Romanos deos . . . vertit.*

49. Plut. *Marc.* 21.4–5: Μάρκελλον δ᾽ ᾐτιῶντο πρῶτον μὲν ὡς ἐπίφθονον ποιοῦντα τὴν πόλιν, οὐ μόνον ἀνθρώπων, ἀλλὰ καὶ Θεῶν οἷον αἰχμαλώτων ἀγομένων ἐν αὐτῇ καὶ πομπευομένων, ἔπειτα ὅτι τὸν δῆμον εἰθισμένον πολεμεῖν ἢ γεωργεῖν, τρυφῆς δὲ καὶ ῥαθυμίας ἄπειρον . . . σχολῆς ἐνέπλησε.

50. Plut. *Marc.* 21.2. On the basis of this passage and others, P. Gros, *REL*, 57 (1979), 85–114, argues that Plutarch's account derives from a Greek source favorable to Marcellus, stressing his philhellenism and thus providing a sharp contrast with the rest of the

Cicero offers a rather different vantage point on the episode—but he has a particular axe to grind. The evidence derives primarily from the speeches against Verres, in which the orator strains to excoriate Verres' purported plunder of art objects from Sicily by contrasting it with the restraint of his predecessors, notably Marcellus. Hence, Cicero proclaims at one point that men marveled at the Sicilian treasures Marcellus had left untouched.[51] That is transparent exaggeration and distortion. Elsewhere in the *Verrines* themselves, Cicero acknowledges that the general brought large quantities of Sicilian art to Rome, though only to adorn the city and without stripping Syracuse bare. The orator, in fact, stresses the civic-mindedness of Marcellus, whose acquisitions decorated the temples and public sites in Rome and Italy. None of them found its way into his private possession.[52] Or almost none. Marcellus retained, according to Cicero, only the impressive globe of the heavens that had been made by the great Archimedes.[53] But the orator could not deny that the spoils of Syracuse added a substantial quantity of Hellenic art to the city of Rome.

As the texts indicate, critics of Marcellus held him to account on two major charges. First, his reckless plundering had eradicated distinctions between the sacred and the profane, demeaning the gods as well as men. And second, he injected for the first time a taste for expensive art and other accouterments of affluence, which lured his countrymen away from their simple, rugged rural past. Did the spoils of Syracuse in fact mark a new departure in Roman attitudes and the inception of a shift in Roman aesthetic and moral sensibilities?

The previous discussion has already cast the more sweeping statements into serious doubt. Long before the sack of Syracuse, Romans had become accustomed to the erection of art objects captured from the vanquished foe, the transfer of images of the gods from defeated communities to Rome, and the construction of monuments and memorials to honor civic leaders. Marcellus followed well-established traditions. The *populus Romanus* was hardly getting its first glimpse of statues and paintings—even of Greek statues and paintings. Perhaps the scale of Syracuse's artistic booty made it especially memorable to the ancients.

---

tradition. J.-L. Ferrary, *Philhellénisme et impérialisme*, 573–575, expresses skepticism on this point. Be that as it may, the negative criticism reproduced by Plutarch closely coincides with statements in Polybius and Livy.

51. Cic. *Verr.* 2.2.4.
52. Cic. *Verr.* 2.1.55, 2.4.120–121.
53. Cic. *De Rep.* 1.21.

The amount taken, so it was reported, would have exceeded that available in Carthage itself, had that city fallen. The Syracusan accusers of Marcellus claimed that he had left nothing portable in the city.[54] But difference in scale cannot be the principal explanation. Half a century earlier Rome had allegedly taken two thousand statues from Volsinii alone, also a point of subsequent reproach.[55] But there is no suggestion of contemporary criticism. Nor, one might emphasize, is there evidence for contemporary criticism of Marcellus on this score.[56]

The texts themselves, on more careful inspection, can yield different results. Polybius' complaint does not dwell on moral considerations. Indeed, he asks whether Marcellus, in transporting Sicilian art treasures to Rome, had acted both correctly *and* advantageously for Rome—or the reverse. Advantage and propriety are thus conjoined rather than contrasted.[57] Morality is not the issue, nor is aesthetics, about which Polybius has nothing to say. His criticism has a fundamentally pragmatic basis. The expropriation of items useless to the establishment of power or to its expansion can do nothing but excite resentment among victims and hatred among others. It constitutes an act of folly and an obvious transgression against self-interest.[58] The historian exploits the episode to read a lesson to imperial powers: they should not despoil cities under the mistaken impression that others' misfortunes bring

54. Livy, 25.31.11, 26.30.9; Plut. *Marc.* 19.3; cf. Livy, 25.40.1; Pliny, *NH,* 24.13.

55. Pliny, *NH,* 34.34.

56. Cf. Pape, *Griechische Kunstwerke,* 81–86. To be sure, Marcellus' political foes denied him a triumph in 211 on the grounds that the Sicilian War had not been completed and the army could not be withdrawn; Livy, 26.21.1–6; Plut. *Marc.* 22.1; *Vir. Ill.* 45.6. And in the following year, when Sicily was again assigned to Marcellus, this time as a consul, his *inimici* brought Sicilians to Rome to complain of his excesses. *Invidia* prompted the attacks; Livy, 26.26.6–8, 26.29.5, 26.32.1–5; Plut. *Marc.* 23.1. This is not the place to explore the political machinations in this affair. See A. Lippold, *Consules* (Bonn, 1963), 265–270; F. Cassola, *I gruppi politici romani nel III secolo a.C.* (Trieste, 1962), 320–330; R. Develin, *The Practice of Politics at Rome, 366–167 B.C.* (Brussels, 1985), 195–198; Eckstein, *Senate and General,* 169–177. The Sicilian accusations, if Livy's paraphrase is trustworthy, did mention Marcellus' ruthless looting; Livy, 26.30.9. But the senate exonerated Marcellus and a *senatus consultum* sanctioned his actions in Sicily; Livy, 26.32.6; Plut. *Marc.* 23.5; Val. Max. 4.1.7; Zon. 9.6. A subsequent decree provided for some inquiry into recovering property for Syracusans who had lost it; Livy, 26.32.6. But there is no hint that art treasures might be restored—or indeed that anyone objected to their seizure at the time.

57. Polyb. 9.10.3: πότερα δ' ὀρθῶς τοῦτο καὶ συμφερόντως αὐτοῖς ἔπραξαν ἢ τἀναντία; cf. Walbank, *Historical Commentary on Polybius,* II, 135; Gros, *REL,* 57 (1979), 90.

58. Polyb. 9.10.6–10.

credit to their own nation.[59] The sack of Syracuse was a tactical error rather than a moral failure.[60] Only one item in the Polybian text seems discordant: the allusion to ancient Romans who had led simple lives and had conquered those with vast and beautiful possessions but who were now adopting the characteristics of the vanquished.[61] In this, the historian may be reflecting contemporary Roman protests against undue luxury, as expressed in Catonian speeches or in mid–second-century sumptuary laws. They do not mirror circumstances at the time of Marcellus' sack of Syracuse.[62]

The strictures contained in Livy's account suffer from even greater anachronism. He laments that Marcellus' indiscriminate looting of sacred and profane objects generated a disrespect for the gods that would eventually express itself even against Roman deities.[63] The passage clearly refers to neglect of temples and shrines in Livy's own day, in the turbulence of civil war.[64] No one laid such a charge against Marcellus at the time. And the practice of transferring sacred images from conquered foes to Rome had been entrenched long before Marcellus.

Plutarch paints a stark contrast between the city's appearance before and after the treasures from Syracuse. Before Marcellus' booty, Rome knew nothing of refined art, restricted displays to barbaric weaponry and bloody spoils, and set up trophies of victory fit to be seen only by the brave and the hardy.[65] How seriously should one take that observation? It is instructive to compare Florus' description of M'. Curius Dentatus' triumph after the Pyrrhic War. Prior to that glorious event, so

---

59. Polyb. 9.10.13: οὐ μὴν ἀλλὰ ταῦτα μὲν εἰρήσθω μοι χάριν τῶν μεταλαμβανόντων ἀεὶ τὰς δυναστείας, ἵνα μὴ σκυλεύοντες τὰς πόλεις κόσμον ὑπολαμβάνωσιν εἶναι ταῖς ἑαυτῶν πατρίσι τὰς ἀλλοτρίας συμφοράς.

60. It is quite unnecessary to ascribe Polybius' view to hostility toward Marcellus, stemming from the historian's association with the Scipiones, as do D. Musti, *Polibio e l'imperialismo romano* (Naples, 1978), 91–92; and Gros, *REL*, 57 (1979), 92. Indeed the extant fragment on the spoils of Syracuse does not even contain the name of Marcellus.

61. Polyb. 9.10.5–6.

62. Ferrary, *Philhellénisme et impérialisme*, 576–578, acknowledges the parallel with Catonian rhetoric but sees as principal influence on Polybius the resentment of Greek communities toward Roman pillaging of art. But such resentment would not likely be formulated in terms of a Roman descent from austerity to affluence.

63. Livy, 25.40.2, quoted above, n. 48.

64. So, rightly, Gros, *REL*, 57 (1979), 88. Cf. Lippold, *Consules*, 264.

65. Plut. *Marc.* 21.1–2: οὐδὲν γὰρ εἶχεν οὐδ' ἐγίνωσκε πρότερον τῶν κομψῶν καὶ περιττῶν, οὐδὲ ἦν ἐν αὐτῇ τὸ χάριεν τοῦτο καὶ γλαφυρὸν ἀγαπώμενον, ὅπλων δὲ βαρβαρικῶν καὶ λαφύρων ἐναίμων ἀνάπλεως οὖσα καὶ περιεστεφανωμένη θριάμβων ὑπομνήμασι καὶ τροπαίοις οὐχ ἱλαρὸν οὐδ' ἄφοβον οὐδὲ δειλῶν ἦν θέαμα καὶ τρυφώντων θεατῶν.

Florus remarks, one would have seen as trophies of victory nothing but cattle seized from the Volscians, herds from the Sabines, Gallic wagons, and broken arms of the Samnites. But Curius' triumphal procession changed everything: gold, purple, statues, paintings, and Tarentine luxuries.[66] The two passages, concerning two episodes more than sixty years apart, show unmistakable similarity. Plutarch, it appears, conveyed a cliché. Certainly the description could bear little resemblance to the appearance of Rome at the time of Marcellus' return.

The biographer adds that Marcellus' critics accused him of dragging images of gods as well as men around in his procession.[67] The charge, if made at all, was altogether devoid of substance. Quite apart from the fact that the capture and transport of sacred images had a long history prior to Marcellus, the implication of insensitivity is readily refutable. Polybius observes that the Sicilian art that had been in private homes at Syracuse went into private possession in Rome, whereas the public ornaments became state property.[68] Marcellus evidently drew distinctions and distributed the art work to appropriate destinations. Further, as Plutarch reports, Marcellus made dedications to the gods in Rome, and Syracusan statues and paintings became offerings at temples in Samothrace and in Rhodes.[69] An extant inscription records Marcellus' dedication to Mars.[70] The *imperator* evidently took his relationship to the gods seriously.[71]

He also, it appears, took Greek art seriously. A story conveyed by Plutarch even has Marcellus boast to the Greeks that he had introduced his rude countrymen to the wonders and beauty of Hellenic masterpieces. That tale is imbedded in a tradition plainly hostile to Marcellus: critics blamed him also for inducing Romans to while away their days in idleness and chatter about arts and crafts.[72] The tendentious treatment

---

66. Florus, 1.13.27: *ante hunc diem nihil praeter pecora Vulscorum, greges Sabinorum, carpenta Gallorum, fracta Samnitium arma vidisses; tum si . . . pompam [vidisses], aurum, purpura, signa, tabulae Tarentinaeque deliciae.*

67. Plut. *Marc.* 21.4.

68. Polyb. 9.10.13: ταῖς μὲν ἰδιωτικαῖς κατασκευαῖς τοὺς αὑτῶν ἐκόσμησαν βίους, ταῖς δὲ δημοσίαις τὰ κοινὰ τῆς πόλεως.

69. Plut. *Marc.* 30.4.

70. *ILS*, 3139: *Martei M. Claudius M.f. consol dedit.* Cf. *ILLRP*, 295.

71. The Rhodians even erected a statue to Marcellus, with a flattering inscription; Plut. *Marc.* 30.5. That may not have been produced in his lifetime, but it signifies Hellenic attachment to Marcellus; cf. Pape, *Griechische Kunstwerke*, 7; Gros, *REL*, 57 (1979), 111–112. On Marcellus' piety, see Val. Max. 1.1.8.

72. Plut. *Marc.* 21.5: σχολῆς ἐνέπλησε καὶ λαλιᾶς περὶ τεχνῶν καὶ τεχνιτῶν ἀστεϊζόμενον καὶ διατρίβοντα πρὸς τούτῳ πολὺ μέρος τῆς ἡμέρας. οὐ μὴν ἀλλὰ

can be discounted. Marcellus surely did not insult his fellow citizens by contrasting their barbaric ignorance to the refinement of Greek artistry. But the very existence of such a tradition implies that the general had advocated or was associated with a taste for high culture. Sicilian art works were no mere loot.[73]

Not that Marcellus conducted a crusade to educate contemporary Romans in the creative subtleties of Hellenic art.[74] The general had rather different aims. The statuary and paintings brought from Syracuse would decorate the city of Rome, thereby enhancing its international image.[75] But this was more than a beautification project. Marcellus tied the display of Greek art to the civic and religious interests of Rome. He had vowed to build a temple to Honos and Virtus after the battle of Clastidium in 222.[76] The Hannibalic War and absence of funds dictated postponement of that project. Marcellus was nevertheless determined to fulfill the vow. The sack of Syracuse provided the needed wherewithal to undertake construction.[77] The pontifices intervened, however, when Marcellus hoped to dedicate such a temple in his fifth consulship of 208. They pointed to the impropriety of a single shrine to two deities. Marcellus resolved instead to construct a temple to Virtus alone and to set it beside an earlier structure to Honos outside the Porta Capena. The great *imperator* did not live to see its dedication, which was accomplished by his son in 205.[78] But he lived long enough to supply

---

τούτοις ἐσεμνύνετο καὶ πρὸς τοὺς Ἕλληνας, ὡς τὰ καλὰ καὶ θαυμαστὰ τῆς Ἑλλάδος οὐκ ἐπισταμένους τιμᾶν καὶ θαυμάζειν Ῥωμαίους διδάξας. Gros, *REL*, 57 (1979), 101–102, oddly sees the passage as supporting a positive judgment of Marcellus.

73. Cf. Plut. *Marc.* 1.2, 30.4; Pape, *Griechische Kunstwerke*, 93–100, rather myopically allows for no aesthetic sensibilities on the part of the Romans here. For her, the capture of art objects derived from motives of revenge against rebellious Syracusans and desire for economic benefits. She makes no serious effort to analyze the evidence of Plutarch.

74. Gros, *REL*, 57 (1979), 102–105, 112–114, believes Marcellus spearheaded a form of philhellenic party, at odds with more conservative Romans such as Fabius Maximus, and endeavored to raise Roman consciousness about a more cultivated artistic tradition.

75. Cic. *Verr.* 2.4.120: *victoriae putabat esse multa Romam deportare quae ornamento urbi esse possent*; Plut. *Marc.* 21.1; Livy, 25.40.1.

76. Livy, 27.25.7, 29.11.13; Plut. *Marc.* 28.1; Val. Max. 1.1.8.

77. Plut. *Marc.* 28.1: ναὸν ἐκ τῶν Σικελικῶν λαφύρων.

78. Livy, 27.25.7–9, 29.11.13; Plut. *Marc.* 28.1; Val. Max. 1.1.8; cf. Vessberg, *Studien zur Kunstgeschichte*, 27; Lippold, *Consules*, 356–357; Gros, *REL*, 57 (1979), 105–108; Pietilä-Castrén, *Magnificentia Publica*, 56–58. The earlier temple to Honos had been sponsored by Q. Fabius Maximus in 233; Cic. *De Nat. Deor.* 2.61; Pietilä-Castrén, 49–51.

the edifice with art works drawn from the treasures of Syracuse.[79] The fact is significant. Marcellus paid special homage to abstract divinities that represented the soul of Roman character—at least as Roman leaders sought to project it. Honos and Virtus took prime place in this projection. Nor is it coincidence that their shrines stood with the temple of Mars, also outside the Porta Capena, the site of a dedicatory offering by Marcellus.[80] By associating the captured art of Sicily with cults that exemplified Roman qualities, Marcellus delivered a message to the Mediterranean world: Hellenic culture would serve to highlight the character, religion, and power of Rome.[81]

Such a message took effect at more than one level. The broader objective could coexist with the aim of self-advertisement. Adornment of the city coincided with augmentation of Marcellus' glory.[82] The general, it was said, won the favor of the populace by enriching the city's sights through the graceful, charming, and lifelike art of Hellas.[83] The idea of adverse moral consequences is plainly *post eventum*.

Marcellus' contemporary and great rival Q. Fabius Maximus similarly elevated national pride and individual fame through the confiscation of art treasures. Fabius' recapture of Tarentum in 209 marked one of the pivotal events of the war. The conqueror celebrated a lavish triumph embellished not only by large quantities of captured wealth but also by Tarentine paintings and statuary—on a scale to rival the haul from Syracuse.[84] The comparison was clearly deliberate and pointed. Fabius' friends added another feature to his reputation: whereas Marcellus plundered images of gods and men alike, the more sensitive and restrained Fabius left the divine figures in place. The allegation included Fabius'

79. Livy, 25.40.3: *dedicata a M. Marcello templa propter excellentia eius generis ornamenta*; Cic. *Verr.* 2.4.121: *Romam quae adportata sunt, ad aedem Honoris et Virtutis itemque aliis in locis videmus*; *De Rep.* 1.21.

80. *ILS*, 3139; see above, n. 70.

81. Cf. the somewhat different formulation by Gros, *REL*, 57 (1979), 107–108.

82. Plut. *Marc.* 21.1: ἐπανερχόμενος τὰ πλεῖστα καὶ κάλλιστα τῶν ἐν Συρακού-σαις ἐκίνησεν ἀναθημάτων, ὡς αὐτῷ τε πρὸς τὸν θρίαμβον ὄψις εἴη καὶ τῇ πόλει κόσμος; Livy, 25.40.1: *ut non modo suam gloriam sed etiam maiestatem populi Romani augeret, ornamenta urbis, signa tabulasque quibus abundabant Syracusae, Romam devexit.*

83. Plut. *Marc.* 21.3: διὸ καὶ μᾶλλον εὐδοκίμησε παρὰ μὲν τῷ δήμῳ Μάρκελλος ἡδονὴν ἐχούσαις καὶ χάριν Ἑλληνικὴν καὶ πιθανότητα διαποικίλας ὄψεσι τὴν πό-λιν. Gros, *REL*, 57 (1979), 104, needlessly strains to interpret the δῆμος as the young sons of Rome's cultivated aristocracy—a quite unparalleled and altogether implausible use of the term.

84. Livy, 27.16.7: *signa tabulae, prope ut Syracusarum ornamenta aequaverint.*

celebrated retort to his inquiring assistant: "Leave to the Tarentines their angry gods."[85] A neat justification. In fact, Fabius simply made a virtue of necessity. As Pliny points out, the colossal statues were too heavy for transport.[86] Or else Fabius deliberately abstained from statues of the gods in order to score a point against Marcellus. He had no qualms about bringing back a colossal statue of Heracles, a creation of Lysippus, and stationing it on the Capitol.[87] Further, he erected a bronze statue of himself, probably through proceeds from the Tarentine spoils, and set it next to the figure of Heracles.[88] Such use of monumental art for self-display had at least one respectable model: Sp. Carvilius, victor in the Samnite Wars more than two generations earlier.[89] The effort to outshine Marcellus' achievement produced a backlash. Advocates of Marcellus reinterpreted Fabius' actions as unseemly and labeled their hero gentle and magnanimous.[90] The political maneuvering is plain enough, but the differences between those two potentates did not rest on the propriety of transferring and appropriating Hellenic art. Fabius, at most, sought to claim the advantage of superior piety—a posture that may have appealed to some of Rome's more senior leaders.[91] As for attitudes toward representational art and its contribution to Roman public and private interests, Fabius and Marcellus were on common ground.

No dissent on that issue surfaced in the Hannibalic War. The fall of Capua in 210 brought images and bronze statues to Rome.[92] Scipio Africanus' climactic triumph in 201 included representations of the captured cities and depictions of the war's events, doubtless commis-

---

85. Livy, 27.16.8: *maiore animo generis eius praeda abstinuit Fabius quam Marcellus . . . deos iratos Tarentinis relinqui iussit*; Plut. *Marc.* 21.3–4; *Fab.* 22.6.

86. Pliny, *NH*, 34.40.

87. Pliny, *NH*, 34.40; Strabo, 6.3.1 (C278); Plut. *Fab.* 22.6; *Vir. Ill.* 43.6. Lippold, *Consules*, 273, 351–353, suggests that Fabius was calling attention to his family's association with the cult of Heracles; cf. Plut. *Fab.* 1.1; Pape, *Griechische Kunstwerke*, 104–105, n. 36.

88. Plut. *Fab.* 22.6.

89. Pliny, *NH*, 34.43.

90. Plut. *Fab.* 22.6: πολὺ Μαρκέλλου φανεὶς ἀτοπώτερος περὶ ταῦτα, μᾶλλον δ᾽ ὅλως ἐκεῖνον ἄνδρα πρᾳότητι καὶ φιλανθρωπίᾳ θαυμαστὸν ἀποδείξας. Cf. Gros, *REL*, 57 (1979), 92–97, who, however, sees the rivalry between Marcellus and Fabius as a cultural clash between philhellenists and conservatives (101–105, 112–114). Similarly, Pollitt, *TAPA*, 108 (1978), 160.

91. Plut. *Marc.* 21.3: εὐδοκίμησε παρὰ μὲν τῷ δήμῳ Μάρκελλος . . . παρὰ δὲ τοῖς πρεσβυτέροις Φάβιος Μάξιμος.

92. Livy, 26.34.12.

sioned by Scipio for the occasion.[93] The concept of artistic creations as a means to promote Roman values and to broadcast both individual and national achievements was well entrenched and undisputed. The development cannot be reduced just to pragmatism or cynicism. Political, religious, and aesthetic elements all played a part, overlapping and entwined. Art objects as religious dedications by public figures or as representations of the divine were now ubiquitous in Rome.[94] And Roman public policy, far from sanctioning reckless plunder and indiscriminate disposal, took care to demonstrate responsibility and to draw proper distinctions. As we have seen, when the Sicilian treasures reached Rome, they had already been suitably earmarked. Those that had graced public places in Syracuse would do so again in Rome; privately owned objects would enter private collections.[95] And when the Capuan booty arrived in 210, the authorities immediately requested pontifical scrutiny. The *collegium pontificum* had the task of determining which paintings and statues were sacred and which profane before any subsequent distribution would take place.[96] Objects certified as sacred, it can be assumed, would be reconsecrated in Roman temples and shrines. The differentiation of public from private and of religious from secular gives important insight into Rome's outlook. It shows a genuine regard for foreign art— and for its value in promoting Roman religious sensibilities and national pride.[97]

Attitudes and actions during the third century provide a vital perspective for understanding the experience of the eastern wars. Rome expanded its power eastward with dramatic strides during the early years of the second century. Its generals established the Republic's superiority over Hellenistic monarchies and returned laden with lavish plunder. The goods paraded in triumphs, distributed to the victors, or displayed

93. Appian, *Pun.* 66: μιμήματα τῶν εἰλημμένων πόλεων, καὶ γραφαὶ καὶ σχήματα τῶν γεγονότων. The μιμήματα may have been female personifications of the cities.

94. Cf. Livy, 26.23.4, 27.11.2–3, 27.36.9, 27.37.11–15, 31.50.2.

95. Polyb. 9.10.13, quoted above n. 68.

96. Livy, 26.34.12: *signa statuas aeneas quae capta de hostibus dicerentur, quae eorum sacra ac profana essent ad pontificum collegium reiecerunt.* A. Wardman, *Rome's Debt to Greece* (London, 1976), 54–58, oddly suggests that Greek art was admissible in Rome only as religious objects.

97. Waurick, *JbRGZ*, 22 (1975), 36–40, argues unconvincingly that artistic booty brought to Rome became increasingly earmarked for secular rather than for religious purposes. The argument requires a devaluation of the literary sources, whom he charges with excessively concentrating on the latter.

in the city gained notoriety and drew criticism as the advent of eastern luxury and the breakdown of Roman austerity. Works of art were conspicuous among the acquisitions—and in the indictment. In fact, however, these actions followed solid precedents and fit into a familiar pattern. And the criticisms, again, are not contemporary.

L. Quinctius Flamininus commanded the Roman fleet in Greece in 198 during the course of the war on Philip V. The campaign included capture of the chief cities of Euboea. At Eretria, Flamininus breached the walls, forced the enemy to surrender, and then collected the spoils. Livy adds the note that although cash and uncoined gold and silver proved sparse, statues, paintings of antique craftsmanship, and decorative items of that sort were discovered in greater quantities than would have been expected in a city of Eretria's size.[98] The historian says no more. But that is enough. The offhand remark reveals that a search for art objects in a captured city, far from marking a new departure, had become routine.

Proceeds from booty could also serve to create new art. L. Stertinius, proconsul in Spain, returned to Rome in 196 and used part of his spoil to erect two *fornices* in the Forum Boarium which would hold sculptures fashioned of gold.[99] The idea of a *fornix*, a monument designed to carry a statue and commemorate a victory, may have been novel. But use of booty to finance art as a celebration of military success certainly was not. On this matter Stertinius had ample precedent.[100]

The celebrated T. Quinctius Flamininus, victor in the Second Macedonian War, exhibited vast treasures in his triumph in 194. They included bronze and marble statuary and bronze and silver embossed vases. Livy offers no particulars. The display of captured art by returning *triumphatores* had become a conventional practice that did not call for special comment.[101] We do, however, know of one particular. Flamininus, a man familiar with things Hellenic, did not simply sweep up all art objects undiscerningly for transport to Rome. He made special point of taking from its site in Macedon the renowned statue of Jupiter Imperator, a statue that Cicero ranked among the three finest works on that subject in the world. Flamininus in a separate ceremony placed the

---

98. Livy, 32.16.17: *signa tabulae priscae artis ornamentaque eius generis plura quam pro urbis magnitudine aut opibus ceteris inventa.* Cf. *ILLRP*, 321.

99. Livy, 33.27.3–4.

100. On Stertinius' *fornices*, see I. Calabi Limentani, *ContrIstStorAnt*, 8 (1982), 123–135; Pietilä-Castrén, *Magnificentia Publica*, 71–74.

101. Livy, 34.52.4–5.

image on the Capitol, where it received homage and reverence from the citizenry.[102] The episode not only speaks to Flamininus' aesthetic taste but illustrates again Roman respect for sacred images from abroad. They were reconsecrated and honored anew. The symbolism of transferring the protection of Jupiter Imperator from Macedon to Rome would be obvious to any Roman. And the precedents can be traced all the way back to the migration of Juno from Veii.

Something comparable may have followed the triumph of M'. Acilius Glabrio, victor at Thermopylae, in 190. Livy's account of the items carried in the triumph mentions no *tabulae* or *signa*, although the procession did include large numbers of embossed silver vessels and the royal silver furniture.[103] But a stray item in Festus offers intriguing information. The text records three statues of divinities set up on the Capitol in front of Minerva's shrine. Festus' sources gave conflicting versions: they were either dedicated by Glabrio or they reached Rome after the fall of Corinth.[104] No decisive reason dictates choice of the former, but association of dedicated statues with the booty from Corinth was common, an easy assumption to make when evidence was inadequate. Hence, the connection with Glabrio may have a more substantive basis.[105] The proconsul would, not surprisingly, maintain the tradition of transplanting images of foreign deities to places of honor where they could be brought within the embrace of Rome.

The triumph of L. Cornelius Scipio Asiagenus in 189 had a bigger impact. His campaigns had extended to Greek Asia, a land emblematic of luxury—at least in the eyes of classical writers. Pliny delivers the expected verdict: the conquest of Asia first introduced luxury into Italy, and he cites Asiagenus' triumph as evidence of the fact.[106] The fascination with turning points is a literary phenomenon, not to be confused with historical data. Pliny credits the victories of L. Scipio and Cn.

---

102. Cic. *Verr.* 2.4.129: *Iovem autem Imperatorem quanto honore in suo templo fuisse arbitramini? Conicere potestis, si recordari volueritis quanta religione fuerit eadem specie ac forma signum illud quod ex Macedonia captum in Capitolio posuerat T. Flamininus.*

103. Livy, 37.46.3–4. Economic value probably counted for more than aesthetic quality in this instance.

104. Festus, 182, L.

105. So Pape, *Griechische Kunstwerke*, 10. Livy's failure to mention the statues in discussing Glabrio's return need not be significant. He also omitted Flamininus' dedication of the image of Jupiter Imperator. Note the statue base at Luna recording Glabrio's victory in Greece; *ILLRP*, 321a.

106. Pliny, *NH*, 33.148: *Asia primum devicta luxuriam misit in Italiam, siquidem L. Scipio in triumpho transtulit argenti caelati*, etc.

Manlius with introducing embossed silver vases to Rome.[107] In fact, as Livy's testimony makes clear, such items had already formed part of the haul brought in by T. Flamininus and again by M'. Glabrio. By the time of Asiagenus' triumph, they were conventional merchandise.[108] Did Asiagenus indeed introduce any novelty at all? After returning to Rome, he exhibited on the Capitol a painting that recorded his victory over Antiochus III.[109] That form of presentation, as we have seen, had sound and venerable precedent.[110] Livy adds, on the authority of Valerius Antias, that Asiagenus gathered *artifices* in Asia and brought them to Rome.[111] The historian does not specify that that action was the first of its kind, nor is it likely to have been. The fashioning of statues and other objects from booty or from its sale and the painting of scenes to repre-sent recent victories and accomplishments were surely not all the work of homegrown artists. L. Scipio, as in his other actions, followed a worn path. The idea that the accouterments of his triumph set Rome on the road to perdition is inventive fantasy. The episode provoked no Roman resistance to Hellenic art.

The same can be said of another triumph that became even more proverbial as precipitating the onset of decline. Cn. Manlius Vulso's celebration of his Asian victories in 187 left a memorable imprint. His procession not only included precious metals and objects of fabulous wealth but novel items that excited interest and admiration: bronze couches, costly garments, woven drapes, and luxurious furniture of all varieties.[112] The late second-century historian L. Calpurnius Piso made mention of the unusual items delivered from Asia through Manlius' conquests. But despite common misconception, Piso did not identify the event as inaugurating moral decline in Rome.[113] The idea turns up

---

107. Pliny, *NH*, 37.12.

108. Livy, 34.52.5, 37.46.3, 37.59.4–5.

109. Pliny, *NH*, 35.22.

110. L. Papirius Cursor in 272 and M. Fulvius Flaccus in 264: Festus, 228, L; M. Valerius Messalla in 263: Pliny, *NH*, 35.22; Ti. Gracchus in 214: Livy, 24.16.16–19.

111. Livy, 39.22.10: *congregatosque per Asiam artifices*. The term here almost certainly means artists or artisans, not dramatic actors. There were ample numbers of the latter already in Italy. Contra: J. C. Balty, *MEFRA*, 90 (1978), 683–684.

112. Livy, 39.6.7–39.7.2.

113. The citation of Piso gives only a factual report of objects in Manlius' triumph; Pliny, *NH*, 34.14: *nam triclinia aerata abacosque et monopodia Cn. Manlium Asia devicta primum invexisse triumpho suo, quem duxit anno urbis DLXVII, L. Piso auctor est.* Piso, in fact, set the beginning of Rome's decline in 154, with no allusion to luxury or art; Pliny, *NH*, 17.244.

only later, repeated by Livy, Pliny, and even Saint Augustine.[114] It is plainly a red herring. Manlius did come under heavy fire from critics and political rivals who sought to block his triumph and derail his career, but none of the allegations faulted him for introducing luxury or softness into Roman life—let alone for adding to the stockpile of Hellenic art.[115] Indeed, although many diverse items are recorded in Manlius' triumphal train, there is no mention of sculptures or paintings.

The effort to pinpoint the inception of Rome's surrender to self-indulgence became a literary *topos*. As noted, various writers in various forms ascribed it to the treasures transported by Marcellus, by Scipio Asiagenus, or by Manlius Vulso. None of that speculation can be traced back to contemporaries. And more important, none of it indicates a contemporary indictment of Hellenic art. Confusion and error stem from the determined quest to identify the origins of luxury. Pliny illustrates it pointedly by a statement too often swallowed whole by moderns: images of the gods dedicated in shrines were made of wood or terra-cotta until the conquest of Asia introduced luxury to Rome.[116] The assertion is readily rebutted. Examples of dedicated or rededicated statues, most of them doubtless bronze, from the fourth and third centuries have already been registered. In addition, expiation of prodigies in 218 involved a bronze statue consigned by Roman *matronae* to Juno on the Aventine. And the aediles in 200 used money realized from fines to set up five bronze statues to Ceres, Libera, and Liber.[117] Pliny's source, striving to find turning points, delivered a simplistic and refutable judgment. A continuity in attitudes toward foreign art runs through Roman experience from the fourth to the second centuries, and the eastern wars of the early second century show no interruption in those attitudes. The art of Greece and Hellenic Asia found welcome as tokens of Roman supremacy, enhancements of religious devotion, and stimuli to cultural enrichment.

Those developments gained clear expression when M. Fulvius Nobilior returned to Rome after his successful completion of the Aetolian War in 187. Fulvius' chief accomplishment was the taking of Ambracia,

---

114. Pliny, *NH*, 34.34: *ad devictam Asiam, unde luxuria*; 37.12; Livy, 39.6.7: *luxuriae enim peregrinae origo ab exercitu Asiatico invecta in urbem est*; Aug. *CD*, 3.21: *tunc primum . . . Asiatica luxuria Romam omni hoste peior inrepsit.*

115. For the political attacks on Manlius, see Livy, 38.44.9–38.50.3.

116. Pliny, *NH*, 34.34: *lignea potius aut fictilia deorum simulacra in delubris dicata usque ad devictam Asiam, unde luxuria.*

117. Livy, 21.62.8 (218); 31.50.2 (200); 33.25.2–3 (197).

once the seat of Pyrrhus' kingdom. The *imperator* refrained from sacking the city but did make it a point to carry off art objects. He took dedicatory offerings, sculptures, and paintings.[118] The triumph itself exhibited them in striking quantities: 785 bronze statues and 230 marble statues.[119] Fulvius, like other returning generals in these years, faced prosecution by *inimici* who hoped to prevent his triumph and tarnish his reputation. In his case, however, the confiscation of art treasures did become part of the accusation. Ambraciote witnesses who had been summoned to Rome delivered damaging testimony. Fulvius, so it was claimed, had despoiled every temple in the city, snatching all images of the gods, in an act tantamount to sacrilege, and had left the bereaved Ambraciotes with nothing but bare walls and doorposts to pray to.[120] Fulvius had scorned items made of terra-cotta but taken everything else.[121] Does Fulvius then qualify as the quintessential looter, irreverent toward divine images and indiscriminate in amassing art objects in order to pile up the numbers for a triumph?

In fact, the reverse is true. M. Fulvius Nobilior was a man of high cultivation and religious sensibilities. Among other things, he composed a learned work on the religious calendar of Rome.[122] The accusation and its outcome deserve a closer look. The very fact that Nobilior's political rivals prompted the Ambraciotes to protest the seizure of sacred images implies that Rome's official policy frowned upon sacrilegious plunder. That policy had been exemplified in 210 when the college of pontiffs decided which items from the spoils of Capua were to be certified as sacred and which as profane.[123] Precisely the same process recurred in 187. The senate decreed that all the artistic works in question would be submitted to the pontifices to determine the category to which they belonged.[124] The resolution speaks to Rome's con-

---

118. Polyb. 21.30.9: τὰ δ' ἀγάλματα καὶ τοὺς ἀνδριάντας καὶ τὰς γραφὰς ἀπήγαγεν ἐκ τῆς πόλεως; Livy, 38.9.13: *signa aenea marmoreaque et tabulae pictae*; *Vir. Ill.* 52.2; cf. Walbank, *Historical Commentary on Polybius*, III, 129.

119. Livy, 39.5.15.

120. Livy, 38.43.5: *templa tota urbe spoliata ornamentis; simulacra deum, deos immo ipsos, convulsos ex sedibus suis ablatos esse; parietes postesque nudatos quos adorent, ad quos precentur et supplicent, Ambraciensibus superesse.*

121. Pliny, *NH*, 35.66: *figlina opera, quae sola in Ambracia relicta sunt.* The hyperbolic statement doubtless derives from charges hurled during the trial.

122. Macrob. *Sat.* 1.2.16.

123. Livy, 26.24.12.

124. Livy, 38.44.5. Pape, *Griechische Kunstwerke*, 43, wrongly sees this as a purely political move against Fulvius.

tinued scrupulousness in the proper disposition of sacred images. Fulvius would have no complaint on that matter. His interest in art went
well beyond mere accumulation of numbers to embellish the triumph.
Like Scipio Asiagenus, he brought many artists from Greece in his
train, artists who arrived to do him honor.[125] They would doubtless
stay to swell the artistic community in Italy and to contribute to its
traditions.

Fulvius' sentiments emerge most clearly from a particular set of
objects brought to Rome from Ambracia: images of the nine Muses,
which he placed in the newly built or refurbished temple of Hercules of
the Muses.[126] That did not end the matter. Fulvius transferred the small
aedicula Camenarum, which had been in the shrine of Honos and Virtus,
into the temple of Hercules Musarum as well.[127] The symbolism is clear
enough. This was a blending of Greek and Latin deities of song, of
religion and literature, of Hellenic art and native imagery. The aedes
Herculis Musarum would contain representations of the Muses and the
Camenae, it would house an annotated copy of Fulvius' Fasti, and it
would serve as the seat of Rome's collegium poetarum.[128] And it is not
irrelevant that Nobilior dedicated the spoils of war to the Muses themselves.[129] The symbolism carries significance. It put the fruits of war in
the service of the advancement of culture.

The example of M. Fulvius Nobilior sheds important light on the

125. Livy, 39.22.2: multi artifices ex Graecia venerunt honoris eius causa.

126. Pliny, NH, 35.66; Eumenius, Pan. Lat. 9.7.3. Eumenius wrongly states that
Fulvius actually built the temple in his censorship of 179. This is confusion with the
portico Fulvius added to Hercules' shrine in his censorship; Livy, 40.51.6.

127. Servius, Ad Aen. 1.8.

128. The Fasti of Fulvius: Macrob. Sat. 1.2.16; the collegium poetarum: Val. Max.
3.7.11; Pliny, NH, 34.19; Porphyrio on Horace, Sat. 1.10.38 and Horace, Epist. 2.2.91;
Juvenal, Sat. 7.38; see B. Tamm, Opuscula Romana, 3 (1961), 157–161; N. Horsfall,
BICS, 23 (1976), 82–86. The temple of Hercules of the Muses has received much recent
attention; see Tamm, 157–167; E. Badian, FondHardt, 17 (1972), 187–191; M. Martina,
DialArch, 3 (1981), 62–68; M. T. Marabini–Moevs, Bolletino d'Arte, 66.12 (1981), 1–58;
Pietilä-Castrén, Magnificentia Publica, 97–103; Ferrary, Philhellénisme et impérialisme, 566–
572; Gruen, Studies in Greek Culture, 117–118. The temple appears on the Severan
Marble Plan of Rome; see E. Nash, Pictorial Dictionary of Ancient Rome, I (London, 1961),
471. And the images of the Muses might have been recorded on the coins of Q.
Pomponius Musa; M. H. Crawford, Roman Republican Coinage (Cambridge, 1974), 410,
437–439. B. S. Ridgway, Roman Copies of Greek Sculpture: The Problem of the Originals
(Ann Arbor, 1984), 18, implausibly suggests that Fulvius disregarded the theatrical
associations of the statue group.

129. Cic. Pro Arch. 27: Fulvius non dubitavit Martis manubias Musis consecrare.

intellectual atmosphere of the early second century. A scholar, writer, and general who brought the poet Ennius with him on the Ambraciote campaign, Fulvius also had a lively interest in the fine arts. Although charges of a thorough sweep through all the art collections and public monuments of Ambracia are plainly tendentious, he certainly gathered bronze and marble statuary and paintings in substantial quantities for shipment to Rome. Numerous precedents had marked out the path before him. Fulvius could anticipate a positive reception for new creative work to grace the city and add to its temples and shrines. The attacks on Nobilior by political foes alleged ruthless plundering but did not object to Hellenic art as such. And the senate's decree restored property to aggrieved Ambraciotes but did not propose restoration of the statues and paintings.[130] For the latter, procedures were already in place. The pontiffs would decide which items held sacral significance and which were secular. The divine images would be reconsecrated; the others would presumably find themselves either on public display or in private possession.[131] Fulvius' temple of Hercules of the Muses, which contained both Greek and Latin, human and divine representatives of the literary arts, presented a subtle and complex symbolism. Fulvius, like victorious commanders before him, sought to identify the personal with the national accomplishment, but he did so through an interweaving of artistic, literary, religious, and political elements. The achievement is impressive. And its very undertaking implies an enlightened constituency in Rome.[132]

Is there, in fact, any evidence for Roman objection to the influx of art objects and the increasing zeal for sculptures, painting, and metalwork which marked this era? One turns naturally and immediately to M. Porcius Cato the Elder. Cato, notorious as stern critic of luxurious living and heedless extravagance, fulminated against such dissipation more than once in published speeches, and works of art play a repeated role in his denunciations. What is that role? Did Cato serve as spokes-

---

130. A clear distinction is made by Livy, 38.44.4–5: *ut Ambraciensibus suae res omnes redderentur . . . signa aliaque ornamenta . . . placere ad collegium pontificum referri.* Statue bases with inscriptions were found in Rome and Tusculum; *ILLRP*, 124, 322.

131. Cf. Arnob. *Adv. Nat.* 3.38 (from Cincius Alimentus): *solere Romanos religiones urbium superatarum partim privatim per familias spargere, partim publice consecrare.*

132. A. Stewart, *Attika: Studies in Athenian Sculpture of the Hellenistic Age* (London, 1979), 43, speculates that Nobilior might have promoted the work of the Athenian sculptor Polycles, whose son Timarchides was subsequently engaged by Roman *nobiles* to decorate temples; Pliny, *NH*, 36.35.

man for traditionalist sentiment that sought to reduce or curtail Roman exposure to the attraction and distraction of creative art? The matter merits close attention.

The speeches of Cato, of course, exist only in fragments, usually of the scantiest and most frustrating variety. But adequate hints survive to allow for suggestive reconstruction. An oration of uncertain date bore as title *uti praeda in publicum referatur*. We possess a single fragment of it, but a significant one. Cato expresses dismay that men dare to ignore religious precepts, setting up statues of the gods, creative representations, and sculptures at home like household furniture.[133] The complaint reinforces what we have seen as official policy: a distinction between sacred objects and other art works. It points also to an additional and overlapping distinction, that between public and private usage of the spoils of war. Cato insists upon the maintenance of proper boundaries and denounces the appropriation of divine images to decorate personal dwellings. As the title of the speech indicates, the orator targets in particular the misuse of public booty for private purposes. Nothing here implies or suggests an antipathy toward the fine arts. Cato protests against those who, in effect, confiscate property belonging to the state or the gods and employ it for self-advancement. The thrust of the speech, in fact, may well be to underscore the value of captured art for public purposes and national interest.[134]

Cato's concern about the correct use of booty emerges again in a speech devoted to that topic: *de praeda militibus dividenda*. A memorable fragment from the work compares thieves of private property with those who pocket public moneys: the former spend their lives in fetters and shackles, the latter in gold and purple.[135] The scathing comment evidently reasserts sentiments expressed in the previous speech. Cato once more takes aim at expropriation by individuals of *praeda* that belongs in the public coffers. It was from that high moral ground that he delivered testimony against M'. Acilius Glabrio in 190. He had seen captured items in Glabrio's camp in Greece which never turned up in his triumph or in the treasury.[136] The orator maintained the firm line

---

133. *ORF*, fr. 98 = Cugusi, *OR*, fr. 72: *miror audere atque religione non teneri, statuas deorum, exempla earum facierum, signa domi pro supellectile statuere.*
134. Cf. Pape, *Griechische Kunstwerke*, 74.
135. *ORF*, fr. 224 = Cugusi, *OR*, fr. 172: *fures privatorum furtorum in nervo atque in compedibus aetatem agunt, fures publici in auro atque purpura.*
136. Livy, 37.57.13–14; cf. *ORF*, fr. 66 = Cugusi, *OR*, fr. 48.

between public and private gain. But that scruple suggests no misgivings about imported art.

Cato pursues the topic in yet another speech and from another angle. The sole fragment is unhelpful, but the title affords a clue: *ne spolia figerentur nisi de hoste capta*. The Censor directs his fire at *imperatores* who set up captured objects without having captured the enemy.[137] The charge closely parallels allegations made against Fulvius Nobilior in 187, claiming that he had carried off plunder from a state that he had not taken in war.[138] Once more the issue is not the art itself but the legitimacy of its acquisition. Cato objects to the display of items wrongfully obtained, rather than to display as such.

One Catonian oration, to judge from the title, concerned itself directly with art objects: *de signis et tabulis*. The single preserved fragment, however, leaves all in the dark. It appears to attack those who have purchased *honor*, distinction of some kind, possibly public office, and whose benefactions have failed to compensate for their crimes.[139] One might conjecture that Cato protests against questionable donations, including statues and paintings, to advance political careers.[140] The speculation, however, is not worth pursuit. Available testimony, in any case, affords no support to the idea that Cato found works of art themselves in any way objectionable.[141]

A solitary reference might give comfort to that idea, but it dissolves upon inspection. The speech on the *lex Oppia* which Livy puts into Cato's mouth bemoans the damaging consequences of the statues from Syracuse and the insidious effects of *ornamenta* from Corinth and Athens,

---

137. *ORF*, fr. 97 = Cugusi, *OR*, fr. 71. The fragment itself brings more confusion than enlightenment. See Cugusi's note, 247–248.

138. Livy, 38.43.2–5, 38.44.6.

139. *ORF*, fr. 94 = Cugusi, *OR*, fr. 52: *honorem emptitavere, malefacta benefactis non redemptitavere*. The text is by no means certain; see Cugusi, 223–224, with references.

140. Cf. Cato's strictures against those who live luxuriously in a speech with the notable title, *ne quis iterum consul fieret*; *ORF*, fr. 185 = Cugusi, *OR*, fr. 139.

141. A fragment often assigned to the *de signis et tabulis* expresses Cato's indignation that statues were erected to women in the provinces; *ORF*, fr. 95 = Cugusi, *OR*, fr. 53. That too, of course, is an objection not to the statues but the use to which they were put. It is sometimes claimed that Cato's objection to public nudity reflected Roman attitudes toward unclad Greek statues; Plut. *Cato*, 20.5–6; cf. Jucker, *Vom Verhältnis der Römer*, 57; Becatti, *Arte e gusto*, 19–21. But allusions in Ennius and Cicero to Roman scorn for public nudity refer to the real thing, not to statues; Cic. *Tusc. Disp.* 4.70; *De Rep.* 4.4. And Pliny's remark contrasting Greek and Roman practices on this matter does not state that Romans disapproved of nudity in Greek art and, indeed, seems to imply the reverse; *NH*, 34.18.

which cause Romans to sneer at their own modest terra-cotta images.[142]
But the speech, as we have seen, is a fiction, invented by Livy, shot
through with anachronisms, and expressive of late Republican biases.[143]
It offers no glimpse into the mentality of Cato the Censor. The whole
concept of a resistance movement to the arts of Hellas lacks foundation
and is best discarded. Political squabbles generated criticism of those
whose art works were wrongfully acquired, inappropriately displayed,
or generally misused for private advantage. But no one challenged the
practice, now long since established, that welcomed art from abroad to
promote the cultural and religious ends of Rome and to elevate its
international stature.

The application of art to public purposes had become a standard
feature of Roman civic life. Illustrations can be provided in plenty from
the first half of the second century. And they imply the existence of
many others that our sources did not have occasion or reason to record.
The convention was altogether noncontroversial.[144]

Statuary and other artistic creations commonly served religious ends
in this period. So, for example, two praetors in 197 exhibited their piety
by having bronze statues cast and dedicated to Ceres, Liber, and Libera.
Funds for the purpose came from fines levied upon offenders.[145] The
temple of Hercules in the Forum Boarium received a new painting in
the early second century, the work of the multitalented poet-artist
Pacuvius.[146] From this same period came a figure of the god Veiovis
made of cypress wood, of whose remarkable endurance Pliny makes
note.[147] P. Scipio, possibly Nasica, the consul of 191, on the advice of
the *decemviri sacris faciundis*, placed a statue of Hercules in the temple of

142. Livy, 34.4.4: *Infesta, mihi credite, signa ab Syracusis inlata sunt huic urbi. Iam nimis
multos audio Corinthi et Athenarum ornamenta laudantes mirantesque et antefixa fictilia deorum
Romanorum ridentes.*

143. See above, pp. 69–70; note also Pape, *Griechische Kunstwerke*, 83–85.

144. One might note, for instance, two examples mentioned in passing by Livy who
did not feel the need even to explain their purpose or significance. Scipio Africanus
installed seven bronze statues and two equestrian representations to decorate an arch he
had just had built on the Capitol. The event occurred in 190, prior to Scipio's departure
to the Asian war; Livy, 37.3.7. In the following year, the aedile Q. Fulvius Flaccus
financed two golden statues from the monies realized out of fines; Livy, 38.35.6. Whatever the motives, it is plain that Roman leaders gained credit for promotion of artistic
creativity.

145. Livy, 33.25.2–3.

146. Pliny, *NH*, 35.19.

147. Pliny, *NH*, 16.216.

that divinity and a gilded chariot on the Capitol in 189.[148] The sources do not disclose occasions or motives for these acts. Expiation may have prompted some of them. Such was the case in 187 when an accident felled the statue of Pollentia, bringing a vote of the senate to erect two statues in its place in the Circus.[149] Again in 180, in response to a plague, religious officials directed the dedication of gold statues to Apollo, Aesculapius, and Salus.[150] Or else the divine representations simply gave expression to national reverence. In any case, they were conspicuous and numerous, as incidental references in the testimony make clear.[151] The close association of artistic creativity and public piety remained intact.

The same continuity held for display of art works as signs of Roman conquests and the extension of national power. Ti. Sempronius Gracchus in 174 commissioned a huge painting to memorialize his victory in Sardinia, including a map of the island depicting the successful battles and an inscription recording his accomplishment. The work was lodged in the temple of Mater Matuta and dedicated to Jupiter.[152] That gesture had several notable models, as we have seen, and was by no means an innovation. It does provide a marked example of the multiple purposes to which a Roman leader could apply a single work of art. The great painting authorized by Ti. Gracchus combined individual publicity with observance of a national military success, the conquest of a province, and an expression of gratitude for divine favor.

The end of the Third Macedonian War produced a triumph that could rival those of two decades earlier. And captured art, then as before, played a prominent role in the display. L. Aemilius Paullus, victor at Pydna and a man with a keen eye for the fine arts, brought home a dazzling assortment that excited the admiration of his countrymen. It comprised, among other things, sculpture, paintings, textiles, vases of gold, silver, bronze, and ivory, beautifully embossed and studded with gems, golden shields, dedicatory plaques, and colossal statues.[153] The accumulation awed bystanders and impressed later writers. Yet Paullus had not simply snatched everything in sight. The cultivated *imperator* had made a tour of cultural and religious sites in Greece.[154] And af-

---

148. Livy, 38.35.4.
149. Livy, 39.7.8–9.
150. Livy, 40.36.14–40.37.2.
151. E.g., Livy, 40.2.1–3, 40.51.3.
152. Livy, 41.28.8–10; Plut. *Aem. Paull.* 32.2, 32.5, 33.2; Diod. 31.8.11.
153. Livy, 45.33.5–6, 45.39.5.
154. Livy, 45.27.5–45.28.5.

ter return to Rome, he made a point of dedicating at the temple of Fortuna a statue of Athena executed by Phidias himself.[155] The gesture implies comprehension and receptivity on the part of the Roman public. Paullus, like others before him, transported an artist, the Athenian Metrodorus, to decorate his triumph. This would be no temporary employment. Metrodorus was to stay as instructor for Paullus' children. Paullus, indeed, like L. Scipio and M. Fulvius Nobilior twenty years earlier, brought a number of Greek sculptors and painters in his train to bolster and expand the Roman artistic community.[156] That decision should not be ascribed to ardent philhellenism, nor was Paullus spearhead of a philhellenic party contending with defiant nativists and traditionalists. His activities show more reduplication than innovation. Objections to Paullus' triumph, a familiar maneuver in Roman politics, focused upon the purported harshness of his discipline and the limits set on distribution of booty to his troops—not on his tastes for Hellenic art.[157] On that matter there was no dissent.

Paullus' subordinate officer, the praetor Cn. Octavius, commanded Rome's fleet in the war against Perseus. His victories, of course, earned fewer accolades than those of his superior, and did not justify a comparably glittering triumph. But Octavius did leave a lasting reminder of his military achievement by financing construction of a double portico near the Circus Flaminius, very probably designed to display works of art and decorative items.[158] The structure may have been funded through sale of booty from the Macedonian War.[159] That would provide yet another instance of the conversion of war spoils into fine art.

A most prominent example of that practice occurred twenty years later, after the crushing of Andriscus and the subjugation of Macedon.

155. Pliny, *NH*, 34.54.

156. Pliny, *NH*, 35.135; Plut. *Aem. Paull.* 6.5.

157. Livy, 45.35.5–6; Plut. *Aem. Paull.* 30.2–4. More successful attacks were launched against C. Lucretius Gallus who commanded the fleet and fought in Greece as praetor in 171. His depredations at Chalcis included stripping the temples of adornments, and he brought back paintings with which he decorated the shrine of Aesculapius in Antium; Livy, 43.4.5–7, 43.7.10, 43.8.4–5. Lucretius was then convicted for maltreating an ally of Rome and sentenced to a heavy fine by an assembly of the people; Livy, 43.8.7–10. But although the senate demanded certain reparations for Chalcis, there is no mention of the return of art works. Aesculapius would keep his decorations. Cf. the similar decision in the case of Fulvius Nobilior; Livy, 38.44.4–5.

158. Pliny, *NH*, 34.13; Aug. *RG*, 19.1; Festus, 188, L. See the discussion by Pietilä-Castrén, *Magnificentia Publica*, 118–123, with references to the modern literature. The later portico of Metellus Macedonicus did contain exhibits of Hellenic art; Cic. *Verr.* 2.4.126; Vell. Pat. 1.11.3.

159. Pliny, *NH*, 34.13, puts the construction in the context of Octavius' triumph.

Q. Metellus Macedonicus, victor in the so-called Fourth Macedonian War, celebrated a triumph in 146 and chose to invest a substantial sum, doubtless derived from the *manubiae*, in a major building project. The venture included a portico that enclosed two temples, at least one of which was built or rebuilt on the instructions of Metellus, who engaged the Greek architect Hermodorus for the purpose.[160] Metellus further received credit for providing Rome with its first marble temple—if credit it was. Some regarded this too as the commencement of luxury, that hackneyed phrase, overused and devoid of historical value. Classical authors plainly persisted in seeking that elusive pivotal event that triggered decline.[161] It applies no more to Metellus Macedonicus than to Marcellus, L. Scipio, or Manlius Vulso.

Macedonicus, in fact, showed an appreciation of Hellenic art which joined him firmly to a lengthy list of predecessors. He had the knowledge (or the right advice) to seek out the celebrated statue group of Alexander and the Companions who fell at the Granicus, sculpted by the great Lysippus. The monument soon became the prime exhibit at Macedonicus' Porticus Metelli.[162] His portico indeed housed a number of artistic masterpieces put on public show.[163] Metellus obviously gained no financial benefit from works he chose to exhibit rather than to sell, nor do the sculptures located at the portico appear to have had religious significance.[164] They carry a different and perhaps even more weighty implication. Their display attests to the value placed upon

160. Vell. Pat. 1.11.3–5; Pliny, *NH*, 34.31; Vitr. 3.2.5; Festus, 496, L. Two Spartan architects are mentioned by Pliny, *NH*, 36.42. Controversy surrounds the question of whether Metellus had one or two temples built. The matter need not be decided here. See, especially, the discussions of M. G. Morgan, *Hermes*, 99 (1971), 480–505 and Pietilä-Castrén, *Magnificentia Publica*, 129–134, with relevant bibliography.

161. Vell. Pat. 1.11.5: *hic idem primus omnium Romae aedem ex marmore in iis ipsis monumentis molitus huius vel magnificentiae vel luxuriae princeps fuit.*

162. Vell. Pat. 1.11.3–4: *quique hanc turmam statuarum equestrium, quae frontem aedium spectant, hodieque maximum ornamentum eius loci, ex Macedonia detulit;* Pliny, *NH*, 34.64. It is unnecessary and inadequate to argue that Metellus chose the statue group because the Romans, by annexing Macedon, now considered themselves Alexander's heirs; as Pape, *Griechische Kunstwerke*, 66; Pietilä-Castrén, *Magnificentia Publica*, 133. The Granicus group did not carry such a message, nor did the Romans reckon themselves as monarchs of Macedon; cf. Gruen, *The Hellenistic World and the Coming of Rome*, 433–435.

163. Cic. *Verr.* 2.4.126.

164. Statues to Artemis and Aesculapius, produced by Greek sculptors, did stand in the temple of Juno inside the *Porticus Octaviae*, which succeeded the *Porticus Metelli*; Pliny, *NH*, 36.24; cf. 34.31; Vell.Pat. 1.11.3. They may originally have come with Metellus' booty. The cult statue of Juno herself was also carved by Greek sculptors; Pliny, *NH*, 36.35. But there is no reason to believe that the colonnade contained images of deities.

high-quality art by the Roman public—and to the prestige that promotion of such art could bring to Roman leaders.

Comparable or greater *gloria* was sought by P. Scipio Aemilianus, the conqueror of Carthage, whose victories and triumph closely coincided with those of Macedonicus. Art treasures played a pivotal part in that quest as well. Scipio, however, found an intriguingly different way to publicize his virtues. Most of the art works he gathered from Carthage after the fall of the city had originally come from elsewhere, the result of Carthaginian plunder over the years. The vast bulk of that purloined loot, naturally enough, had once sat in the cities of Greek Sicily. Scipio seized the occasion to restore to the Sicilians all those precious items that could be identified as taken from their shrines and cities. This was, of course, no mere selfless generosity on the part of the *imperator*. Scipio made certain to advertise his magnanimity by having his name inscribed on the bases of restored statues as permanent reminder of his benefactions. He could anticipate enduring gratitude on the part of the Sicilians and a rise in his international esteem.[165] But restoration of the artistic booty to its original owners does not mean indifference to the aesthetic quality of the works. Although the donations to Sicily receive most attention from the sources, Scipio Aemilianus also brought an appreciable number of art objects back to Rome. Appian reports a triumph that eclipsed all previous ones in splendor and that included statues and votive offerings the Carthaginians had accumulated through many years and many victories.[166] One of them was evidently a colossal Apollo set up opposite the Circus.[167] And another, in all probability, was the image of Hercules that later stood in front of the Porticus ad Nationes.[168] Scipio Aemilianus, in short, gained credit not only for

165. The inscriptions on statue bases are noted by Cic. *Verr.* 2.4.74, 2.4.78, 2.4.97, 2.5.186; two examples from Himera: *ILS*, 8769; E. Stefani, *NotSc* (1935), 201. Other references to Scipio's restoration of art works to Sicily: Cic. *Verr.* 2.2.3, 2.2.86, 2.4.73, 2.4.84, 2.4.93, 2.5.185; Appian, *Pun.* 133; Diod. 13.90.4–5, 32.25. Cf. A. E. Astin, *Scipio Aemilianus* (Oxford, 1967), 76–77.

166. Appian, *Pun.* 135: ἐπιφανέστατα δὴ πάντων διεθριάμβευε πολύχρυσον θρίαμβον, ἀγαλμάτων τε γέμοντα καὶ ἀναθημάτων ὅσα Καρχηδόνιοι χρόνῳ πολλῷ καὶ συνεχέσι νίκαις ἐκ πάσης γῆς συνενηνόχεσαν ἐς Λιβύην. Note the statue base that he dedicated at Marruvium Marsorum; *ILLRP*, 326.

167. Plutarch, *Flam.* 1.1, makes reference to the statue in passing and notes that it came from Carthage. That almost certainly places it as part of Scipio's haul; cf. Pape, *Griechische Kunstwerke*, 21.

168. Pliny, *NH*, 36.39, observes that the statue had once been at Carthage, presumably a Carthaginian creation. Cf. Vessberg, *Studien zur Kunstgeschichte*, 36.

magnanimity in restoring lost statuary to Sicily but for accomplishment and taste in adding to Rome's religious and cultural life. Clearly, he cultivated his image as promoter of the fine arts.[169]

Scipio's claim on *gloria* for the conquest of Carthage did not go altogether unchallenged, and the challenger also employed the medium of art to publicize his role. L. Hostilius Mancinus, legate and commander of the fleet in the Third Punic War, insisted on his pivotal part in the campaign. He maintained that he had been the first to breach the walls of Carthage, and he used pictorial representation to advance his case. Mancinus set up in the Forum a painting that depicted assaults on the city, with himself in prominence—and, in the event that anyone should miss the point, Mancinus stood with the *tabula* prepared to narrate the details to passersby. The blatant self-promotion, not surprisingly, offended and angered Scipio Aemilianus. But Mancinus profited. The publicity helped him win a consulship and some favorable attention in the subsequent tradition on the war.[170] The use of representational art to dramatize military accomplishments in the service of the state thus persisted without interruption or objection. Mancinus' maneuver repeated the practice made familiar by *imperatores* from L. Papirius Cursor in 272 through Ti. Gracchus in 174. There are no sharp turning points to be found here, rather, an extended continuity in utilization of the arts to further the ends of Roman leaders and the *res publica*. And as exemplified by Marcellus, Flamininus, Paullus, Macedonicus, and Aemilianus, there was continuity too in appreciation of artistic merit.

Statues to honor prominent Romans, even outside the context of military achievement, became increasingly common in the second century, an ever more conspicuous part of the political landscape and a further boost for the arts. A variety of occasions or motives could prompt the erection of an honorific statue in Rome. So, for example, the figure of Claudia Quinta graced the vestibule of the temple of Magna Mater, set there perhaps at the dedication of the temple in 191. That sculpture honored the woman who had been chosen to receive

---

169. Whether Scipio was also responsible for a temple of Hercules in the Forum Boarium is quite uncertain; Pietilä-Castrén, *Magnificentia Publica*, 136–137; and A. Ziolkowski, *Phoenix*, 42 (1988), 313, are too confident. Cf. also F. Coarelli, *PBSR*, 45 (1977), 5–6. But see Astin, *Scipio Aemilianus*, 121.

170. Pliny, *NH*, 35.23. The Livian tradition gives credit to Mancinus' successes; Livy, *Per.* 51; Florus, 1.31.10; Ampelius, 32.1. A less favorable version is in Appian, *Pun.* 113–114. Cf. Astin, *Scipio Aemilianus*, 71.

Magna Mater when she first reached Italian shores.[171] L. Scipio Asiagenus erected a statue of himself, wearing Greek cloak and slippers, on the Capitol.[172] Our sources provide no information on date or purpose. Asiagenus called attention, in some fashion, to his exposure to Hellenism, perhaps even to his experiences in Greece and Greek Asia in 190, but this was certainly no ordinary triumphal monument. Statuary could serve a multitude of ends. A bronze image of T. Flamininus stood outside the Circus, inscribed in Greek letters, another token of its subject's engagement with the Hellenic world.[173] The first golden statue in Rome took its place in the temple of Pietas in 181 when that edifice was dedicated by young M'. Acilius Glabrio, appointed duumvir for the occasion. The piece honored Glabrio's father, consul in 191 and victor over Antiochus III at Thermopylae, who had originally vowed to construct the building. This was not a victory monument, strictly speaking, but a memorial to his career, a genuine act of *pietas* by his son.[174] Glabrio's filial devotion was outdone, however, by M. Claudius Marcellus, the three-time consul of 166, 155, and 152. In the temple of Honos and Virtus he placed statues not only of his father but of his grandfather as well. The latter had initially vowed to build the temple and his son had dedicated it.[175] This use of portraits to underscore a whole family's service to the state was a natural and uncontested development. In yet a different category was the statue set on the Rostra to honor Cn. Octavius, who was killed in the line of duty as envoy to Syria in 162. That form of commemoration dates back at least to 229, when the same distinction had been accorded to two envoys allegedly slain while on a mission to the Illyrian coast.[176]

A diverse range of reasons could be produced to justify statues for individuals. Perhaps the most remarkable instance was that of C. Hostilius Mancinus, consul in 137. Mancinus had suffered a crushing defeat in Spain, fled the field, and, after falling into a trap, negotiated an ignominious peace. The senate subsequently renounced the treaty and, in order to salvage its *fides* and relations with the gods, turned Man-

171. Val. Max. 1.8.11. On Claudia Quinta, see Gruen, *Studies*, 26, with references.
172. Cic. *Pro Rab. Perd.* 27; Val. Max. 3.6.2.
173. Plut. *Flam.* 1.1. Balty, *MEFRA*, 90 (1978), 669–686, seeks to identify this with the statue of the so-called "Hellenistic ruler" in the Terme Museum.
174. Livy, 40.34.4–5; Val. Max. 2.5.1.
175. Ascon. 12, C. On the earlier Marcelli and the temple of Honos and Virtus, see above, n. 78.
176. Cic. *Phil.* 9.4; Pliny, *NH*, 34.24.

cinus, naked and in chains, over to the Numantines as requital. The Spaniards, however, declined to impose punishment and restored the former consul to Rome. In a surprising turn of events the ostensibly disgraced Mancinus resumed his place in the senate, obtained election to a second praetorship, and most striking, commissioned a statue that would depict him in the garb—or lack thereof—that had marked his delivery to the Numantines.[177] The statue set that extraordinary episode in a very different light. Mancinus evidently took pride in the event, portraying it as a personal decision for self-sacrifice to rescue the *fides* of his nation and to restore the *pax deorum*.[178]

The erection of statues to prominent individuals for services to the state or personal distinction had, by the mid–second century, become a firm convention. Q. Marcius Rex took responsibility in 144 for the building of the Aqua Marcia and received a statue on the Capitol behind the temple of Jupiter.[179] Another sculpture on the Capitol, decreed by the senate, honored a certain Aemilius Lepidus, perhaps the consul of 187, who, while still a callow youth, won distinction in battle by personally slaying a foe and saving a citizen.[180] The assassination of C. Gracchus provoked his followers to plant statues of him and his brother on a permanent site where obeisance and sacrifices could be made, thus treating them almost as if they were shrines of gods.[181] The purpose here was plainly political: to keep green the memory of the Gracchi and to defy the opponents of their policies. A similar motive may have produced the statue of Cornelia, mother of the Gracchi, placed in the Porticus Metelli probably after her death and some time in the later second century.[182] Hers was not the first statue to a woman set up in the Roman Republic. Cato had complained a half century earlier about statues to women in the provinces.[183] But in the volatile circumstances of the later second century, a monument to the mother of the Gracchi was bound to have political resonance.

As is plain, the honorific statue held a notable place in the public life

177. Pliny, *NH*, 34.18: *Mancinus eo habitu sibi statuit, quo deditus fuerat*. On the events, see O. Wikander, *Opuscula Romana*, 11 (1976), 85–104.

178. A convincing interpretation of this episode has at last been provided by N. Rosenstein, *CA*, 5 (1986), 230–252, with references to scholarship.

179. *CIL*, 3, 846.

180. Val. Max. 3.1.1. The date and circumstances are unknown. Lepidus' bravery is commemorated by a descendant's coinage in the late Republic; Crawford, *Roman Republican Coinage*, 443–444, no. 419.

181. Plut. *C. Gr.* 18.2.

182. Pliny, *NH*, 34.31; Plut. *C. Gr.* 4.3.

183. Pliny, *NH*, 34.31.

of midrepublican Rome. It could commemorate military accomplishments, advertise civic services, display personal virtues, or promote political objectives.[184] The numbers accumulated, even to the point of crowding public places. The censors of 179 actually removed some statues from the columns of Jupiter's temple on the Capitol, which were encumbering the structure.[185] The Forum had become still more crammed. In 158 the censors took steps to deal with the situation, clearing out all statues of officials which had not been authorized by senate or people.[186] The move did not, of course, signal any discontent with public art itself, nor was it simply a housekeeping measure to reduce clutter in the Forum. The distinction drawn by the censors enunciated an important principle: that statuary should memorialize national achievements and serve the collective interest rather than private ambitions. Not that the edict had any lasting effect. Mancinus' statue and the monuments to the Gracchi were hardly sanctioned by senate or assembly. But the fundamental principle had gained articulation or reaffirmation. Creative art on the public scene had as prime objective the display of those qualities that characterized the nation.

Prevalence of the practice even brought about a form of reverse snobbery among some prominent individuals. Scipio Africanus evidently felt that it would be more distinctive to decline statues than to encourage them. The hero of Zama and Magnesia made a point of forbidding any representations of himself in the Comitium, the Rostra, the Curia, the Capitol, or the Cella of Jupiter.[187] The ostensibly self-effacing gesture, of course, had its own publicity value. Africanus called attention to his restraint by contrast with others' excesses. In fact, however, he could not—or perhaps simply did not—prevent an image of himself from being lodged in the temple of Jupiter Optimus Maximus.[188] Cato the Elder adopted a kindred posture. He expressed contempt for those whose self-esteem depended on the craft of sculptors

---

184. The origins of honorary portraits in Rome remain obscure. Stewart, *Attika*, 115–132, offers some incisive suggestions on the motives and meaning of honorific statues in Hellenistic Athens. But the Hellenistic influence was secondary at best; statuary for Roman leaders goes back at least to the fourth century.

185. Livy, 40.51.3.

186. Pliny, *NH*, 34.30: *statuas circa forum eorum qui magistratum gesserant sublatas omnes praeter eas quae populi aut senatus sententia statutae essent.* Cf. Lahusen, *Ehrenstatue*, 18–19. Wallace-Hadrill, *PCPS*, 36 (1990), 163–165, sees the edict as a censorial effort to curry popular favor against the ostentation of the nobility—an interpretation altogether at variance with Pliny's language and meaning.

187. Livy, 38.56.12.

188. Livy, 38.56.13; Val. Max. 8.15.1; Appian, *Iber.* 23.

and painters. His fellow citizens, he claimed, carried his fairest images in their mind's eye. In a typically Catonian anecdote, when asked why lesser men had statues and he had none, Cato responded that he would rather be questioned about the absence of a statue than asked about the presence of one.[189] Yet he too relented, or at least ceased to object. The *populus* commissioned a portrait of Cato after his censorship, installing it in the temple of Salus and attaching an inscription that praised his civic rather than his military accomplishments: the censor who, when the state was slipping into decline, set it right again.[190] The posturing of Africanus and Cato demonstrates that the award of honorific statues had already become habitual by the early second century.[191] Their affectation of modesty had obvious political benefits—especially since they got the statues anyway.

One can confidently put to rest any notion of a split in Roman ruling circles over attitudes toward the fine arts. The welcome for Hellenic art works and the creation of statuary in Rome persisted through the period. No resistance surfaced, and no objections were voiced to the art or artists. Scipio Africanus and Cato Censorinus, often depicted as heading philhellenic and antihellenic movements, respectively, in fact comported themselves in identical fashion on this front. Both affected disdain for personal honors in portrait form, and both, after feigned reluctance, somehow endured them. Another pair of political antagonists from the next generation offers a similar illustration. Metellus Macedonicus and Scipio Aemilianus had sharp differences on the public scene.[192] Yet in their eagerness to demonstrate appreciation and cultivation of the arts after victories in Macedon and Carthage their attitudes are indistinguishable. The nearest that the officialdom came to an expression of displeasure was the censorial edict of 158, which removed from the Forum statues unauthorized by senate or people. That gesture,

189. Plut. *Cato*, 19.4.

190. Plut. *Cato*, 19.3. Val. Max. 8.15.2 speaks of a statue, presumably a second one, in the Curia. It is not impossible that the monuments to Africanus and Cato were erected after their deaths, but the sources imply that they existed during their lifetimes. Cf. Val. Max. 8.15.1: *imaginem in cella Iovis Optimi Maximi* [Scipio] *positam habet*; Plut. *Cato*, 19.3–4: ἀνδριάντα γοῦν ἀναθεὶς ἐν τῷ ναῷ τῆς Ὑγιείας [ὁ δῆμος] ἐπέγραψεν κτλ . . . καίτοι πρότερον αὐτὸς [Cato] κατεγέλα τῶν ἀγαπώντων τὰ τοιαῦτα.

191. Note also the allusion by Ennius to a potential statue or column that the *populus Romanus* might erect for Scipio Africanus; Ennius, *Varia*, 2, Vahlen = *SHA* "Claudius" 7.6; cf. Wallace-Hadrill, *PCPS*, 36 (1990), 161–162. It was an expected gesture.

192. Cf. Cic. *De Off.* 1.87; *De Amicit.* 77; *De Rep.* 1.31; Pliny, *NH*, 7.144; Plut. *Apophth. Caes.* 3.

however, only articulated the acknowledged premise that state interest takes precedence over individual distinction. And the gesture did not, in any case, prevent subsequent monuments to individuals on political or partisan grounds. Nevertheless, there was no partisan issue over the acquisition, creation, or exhibition of art itself. The practice of self-advertisement, posthumous honors, or display of national achievements through artistic media had been embraced thoroughly and eagerly. By the later second century, as Cicero notes, Italy was full of Hellenic art and learning.[193]

If all this be true, what then is to be made of the notorious L. Mummius, victor at Corinth in 146, who acquired the reputation of dullness and insensitivity to the fine arts? Was Mummius an aberration to be dismissed as exceptional, or was he, in fact, representative of the authentic Roman indifference to and scorn for things Hellenic, a more characteristic figure than a Fulvius Nobilior or a Scipio Aemilianus?[194] Neither conclusion is defensible. The truth lies elsewhere.

The negative verdict on Mummius has ostensible support in the evidence—or some of the evidence. An episode graphically familiar to almost all students of antiquity forms the most damning indictment. Polybius, an eyewitness of the events, reports that Mummius' soldiers at the sack of Corinth showed so much contempt for works of art and religious dedications that they employed Corinthian masterpieces as dice boards.[195] Velleius Paterculus gives the hostile judgment sharp focus: Mummius was such a bumpkin that, when arranging for the shipment of captured art treasures to Italy, he instructed the agents to replace any lost works with new ones.[196] That judgment became harsher still over the years, as reflected in a speech of Favorinus, included in the corpus of Dio Chrysostom. His version brands Mummius as unschooled, ignorant, and without appreciation of beauty: he mis-

---

193. Cic. *Pro Arch.* 5: *erat Italia tum plena Graecarum artium ac disciplinarum.*

194. The tradition on Mummius' boorishness is accepted unquestioningly in Pollitt, *Art in the Hellenistic Age,* 158–159; cf. also MacMullen, *Historia,* 40 (1991), 425.

195. Polyb. 39.2.1–2 (from Strabo): Πολύβιος . . . προστίθησι καὶ τὴν στρατιω-τικὴν ὀλιγωρίαν τὴν περὶ τὰ τῶν τεχνῶν ἔργα καὶ τὰ ἀναθήματα; φησὶ γὰρ ἰδεῖν παρὼν ἐρριμμένους πίνακας ἐπ' ἐδάφους, πεττεύοντας δὲ τοὺς στρατιώτας ἐπὶ τούτων.

196. Vell. Pat. 1.13.4: *Mummius tam rudis fuit, ut capta Corintho cum maximorum artificum perfectas manibus tabulas ac statuas in Italiam portandas locaret, iuberat praedici conducentibus, si eas perdidissent, novas eos reddituros.*

took a portrait of Zeus for one of Poseidon, inscribed the name of Philip on a bust of Zeus, and labeled the statues of two youths Nestor and Priam![197] Pliny has Mummius hold an auction of the captured paintings and withdraw one only when King Attalus of Pergamum offered an exorbitant sum for it—maybe there was some merit in the picture after all.[198] Even his generosity with art works could be interpreted to his discredit. In Strabo's view, Mummius gave away items readily to all who asked more out of high-mindedness than any understanding of art.[199] Such is the familiar portrait of L. Mummius, and the one that endured.[200]

In fact, it is a distortion and a caricature. Mummius' soldiers, in all probability, played their games on Corinthian paintings without the *imperator*'s consent or knowledge. This could easily have happened at a preliminary stage before he began to collect the booty. Certainly Polybius did not record the item with intent to embarrass L. Mummius, a man whom he otherwise treats in a most positive fashion.[201] The general's instructions to contractors to replace any lost paintings with others need not be a sign of philistinism. The arrangement reflects a standard business contract.[202] That Mummius mistook a statue of Poseidon for one of Zeus causes no surprise. Modern art historians have been guilty of the same confusion. A comparable error might have been made in substituting Zeus's name for that of Philip II on a bust from Thespiae if the Thespians had flattered the Macedonian king by giving him the likeness of the god.[203] More likely, the charge served the purposes of Favorinus' biting wit, as surely did the statement that Mummius chose the names of Nestor and Priam for two portraits of youths. The acid comments are not to be taken as serious history. Pliny's

197. Dio Chrys. 37.42: φεῦ τῆς ἀμαθίας . . . ἄνθρωπος ἀπαίδευτος καὶ μηδενὸς τῶν καλῶν πεπειραμένος.

198. Pliny, *NH*, 35.24: *pretium miratus suspicatusque aliquid in ea virtutis, quod ipse nesciret.*

199. Strabo, 8.6.23 (C381): μεγαλόφρων γὰρ ὢν μᾶλλον ἢ φιλότεχνος ὁ Μόμμιος, ὥς φασι, μετεδίδου ῥᾳδίως τοῖς δεηθεῖσι.

200. G. Nenci, *AnnPisa*, 8 (1978), 1007–1023, even argues that the *ferus victor* of Horace's famous line, *Epist.* 2.1.156, refers not to Romans generally but to Mummius in particular.

201. Cf. Polyb. 39.3.3, 39.3.10, 39.6.1–4.

202. This was seen long ago by F. Münzer, *RE*, 16.1 (1933), 1199–2000. Walbank, *Commentary*, III, 729, objects to Münzer's defense of Mummius but offers no reasons.

203. See the elaborate and highly speculative arguments of A. M. Prestianni Giallombardo, *AnnPisa*, 12 (1982), 513–532, who even postulates that Mummius changed the inscription in order to have a statue of Zeus to dedicate at Olympia!

tale of the auction and the withdrawal of a painting after Attalus' handsome bid is demonstrably false. Attalus, in fact, was not even in Greece. Pausanias' fuller account reports that Mummius retained the most attractive and most admired works of art, consigning to Attalus' representative Philopoemen those of lesser value.[204] The painting that Attalus desired, Aristides' portrait of Dionysus, went instead to the temple of Ceres in Rome. Pliny asserts that it was the first picture from abroad to become Roman property—a statement flatly contradicted by substantial testimony on *tabulae* brought to Rome from the time of Marcellus' sack of Syracuse through Aemilius Paullus' triumph. The error further undermines Pliny's credibility here.[205] Strabo's story about Mummius' liberality with art objects actually stands to the general's credit. L. Lucullus had borrowed some of the statues in Mummius' haul to enhance the inauguration of his temple of Felicitas, and then dedicated them to the goddess, offering Mummius the option of taking them back. The latter declined, thereby gaining more in reputation than did Lucullus. The comment of Strabo that Mummius' action showed magnanimity rather than art appreciation is gratuitous and uncomprehending. The dedication put those objects out of reach, and Mummius evinced his respect for the religious context into which they had been placed.[206] The negative tradition on L. Mummius Achaicus thus disintegrates.[207]

Literary and epigraphic texts in abundance attest to Mummius' active concern for works of art in the service of religion. The general was assiduous in leaving dedications not only in Greece's holiest shrines of Delphi and Olympia, but in many sites across the land, receiving in return honorific decrees and public distinctions. The *imperator* either visited, gave donations to, or obtained honors from Isthmus, Sicyon, Nemea, Pheneus, Tegea, Epidaurus, Sparta, Messenia, Olympia, Del-

---

204. Paus. 7.16.8: ἀναθημάτων δὲ καὶ τοῦ ἄλλου κόσμου τὰ μὲν μάλιστα ἀνήκοντα ἐς θαῦμα ἀνήγετο, τὰ δὲ ἐκείνοις οὐχ ὁμοίου λόγου Φιλοποίμενι ὁ Μόμμιος τῷ παρ' Ἀττάλου στρατηγῷ δίδωσι. Cf. Jucker, *Vom Verhältnis der Römer*, 115–116.

205. Cf. Vessberg, *Studien zur Kunstgeschichte*, 39. On the dedication of the painting, see Pliny, *NH*, 35.24, 35.99. It is mentioned also by Polyb. 39.2.3 as among those damaged by Mummius' soldiers.

206. Strabo, 8.6.23 (C381).

207. Mummius has had few modern defenders. But see, among earlier works, Colin, *Rome et la Grèce*, 628–638; Münzer, *RE*, 16 (1933), 1195–1206. More recently, see the brief remarks of Ridgway, *Roman Copies*, 17; E. Rawson, in *Cambridge Ancient History*[2], VIII (Cambridge, 1989), 474.

phi, Thebes, Thespiae, Aulis, and Chalcis.[208] The considerable expenditure of time and energy can doubtless be explained in part by desire to emulate and eclipse Aemilius Paullus, but it would be myopic to ascribe it all to politics. Mummius' special attention to religious dedications suggests a sensitivity to Hellenic concerns—or at least the desire to project such a sensitivity. Cicero offers a concrete example to bolster the case. Mummius removed all the unconsecrated statues from Thespiae but left intact the marble Cupid of Praxiteles because it had been consecrated.[209] One may note further the instances, probably numerous instances, in which Mummius' inscribed dedications left intact the earlier Greek inscriptions. He thus linked himself directly to Hellenic predecessors.[210] The victor's claim on art objects as booty had long since been institutionalized; it was deplorable and unwelcome but expected. Acknowledgment of Greek religious sensibilities, however, would leave a better impression and earn more esteem. And Mummius was by no means impervious to distinctions in the quality of creative art. As we have seen, he chose the handsomer and more admirable works for shipment to Italy, leaving the less desirable to the representatives of Attalus of Pergamum.[211] His actions in Achaea are equally revealing; Mummius resisted the demand of at least one Roman that he destroy all the statues to the Achaean statesman Philopoemen on the grounds of his alleged hostility to Rome. The general, responsive to Achaean opinion, permitted the statues to stand. And on the urging of Polybius, he ordered the reinstatement of monuments to Achaeus, Aratus, and Philopoemen which had already been sent to Acarnania for dispatch to Rome.[212] A concession to Achaean feelings in the matter generally corresponds with the commander's actions in Greece. Mummius was no unlettered ignoramus trampling thoughtlessly on Greek sentiments and heedless of the value and quality of Greek art.

The *imperator*'s return to Rome fills out the picture. His actions fall

208. Polyb. 39.6.1–2; Paus. 5.10.5, 5.24.4; *IvOlympia*, 278–281, 320–324; *IG*, V, 2, 77; *IG*, VII, 433, 1808, 2478, 2478a. Further references and discussion in H. Philipp and W. Koenigs, *AthMitt*, 94 (1979), 193–216. Cf. Walbank, *Commentary*, III, 735–736; Gruen, *The Hellenistic World and the Coming of Rome*, 171. The donations of Mummius followed in a tradition well established by Roman commanders in Greece; M. Guarducci, *RendPontAccadArch*, 13 (1937), 41–58.

209. Cic. *Verr.* 2.4.4: *ceteraque profana ex illo oppido signa tolleret, hunc marmoreum Cupidinem, quod erat consecratus, non attigit.*

210. *IG*, IV², 306D; *IG*, VII, 1808; *IG*, V,2,77; G. Daux, *BCH*, 83 (1959), 683; A. D. Keramopoullou, *Arch Delt*, 13 (1930–31), 105–118; Waurick, *JbRGZ*, 22 (1975), 31–35.

211. Paus. 7.16.8.

212. Polyb. 39.3.2–3, 39.3.10.

predictably within the lines established by earlier victorious generals. The triumph itself paraded statues of gold and marble, as well as paintings.[213] Mummius then prolonged the publicity of his achievements and provided tangible evidence of his piety. He disclaimed personal proprietorship of any of the art objects, distributing them instead to temples, shrines, and sites of civic significance all over Rome and various parts of Italy. Only his own home remained conspicuously free of spoils that belonged to the public at large and to the gods. The ghost of Cato the Elder could rest in peace.[214] Extant inscriptions from towns in Italy and from Italica in Spain confirm how widespread were Mummius' donations.[215] All this munificence constituted showmanship, of course. Mummius attended to his reputation and his image. The statues and dedications in temples and other places bore the inscribed name of the donor and reminded the citizenry of his deeds. What matter, however, are not the private motives of Mummius but the medium through which they were implemented. The pride in displaying Hellenic art works, including those of especially high quality, won Mummius favor both as a successful conqueror and as a man of cultivation. He appears indeed to have made a particular effort to raise public consciousness about Greek painting. Mummius' victory became associated in the Roman mind with *tabulae pictae*.[216] The placement of Aristides' Dionysus in the temple of Ceres was doubtless only one of many such permanent exhibits.[217] It illustrates also the continuing connection, emphasized by Roman leaders, between art and religion. This was no hypocrisy on Mummius' part. In the fashion of Rome's great *imperatores* of the past, he fulfilled a vow by constructing a new temple, this one to Hercules Victor, as attested by the dedicatory inscription on the Caelian Hill.[218]

213. Livy, *Per.* 52.

214. Cic. *De Off.* 2.76; *Verr.* 2.1.55, 2.3.9; Livy, *Per.* 52; *Oxyr. Per.* 53; Pliny, *NH*, 34.36; Frontin. *Strat.* 4.3.15; *Vir. Ill.* 60; Vitr. 5.5.8; cf. Strabo, 8.6.23 (C381).

215. *ILLRP*, 327–331. Further examples in Pape, *Griechische Kunstwerke*, 17–18; Waurick, *JbRGZ*, 22 (1975), 23–25, 28. These, of course, are only a fraction of the number that must have originally been set up. Hence, it is hazardous to conclude with Pietilä-Castrén, *Arctos*, 12 (1978), 120–122, that Mummius concentrated attention on places where his family or allies had local connections. Mummius' embellishments of buildings became proverbial; Festus, 125, L: *Mummiana aedificia a Mummio dicta*.

216. Pliny, *NH*, 37.12. Pliny's statement in *NH*, 35.24, that Mummius was responsible for the first foreign painting to become Roman property is false, as we have seen, but may reflect Mummius' keen interest in this form of art.

217. Pliny, *NH*, 35.24.

218. *ILLRP*, 122. See the discussion by Pietilä-Castrén, *Magnificentia Publica*, 140–144. Ziolkowski, *Phoenix*, 42 (1988), 309–333, makes a strong case for identifying

The accumulation of evidence is overwhelming. L. Mummius Achaicus reproduced and expanded the practices of his predecessors. He manifested high regard for Greek art, promoted its display in Rome and Italy, and reinforced its association with the Roman state and Roman religion.[219]

How then to explain the tradition that presents Mummius as a reckless plunderer and boorish bumpkin? It will not do to suggest that Mummius, as a *novus homo*, lacked the refined education of a Scipio Aemilianus.[220] In fact, his brother, Sp. Mummius, was a man of considerable learning and a member of Aemilianus' intellectual circle.[221] The solution offered recently, that Mummius deliberately affected indifference or ignorance in order to cater to Roman prejudice, founders on the absence of any hard evidence for such prejudice in this period.[222] The negative portrait is sometimes ascribed to a putative Greek tradition, seeking posthumous revenge for the theft of art treasures.[223] But Mummius' acts of plunder hardly set him apart. There were precedents aplenty. And much of the hostile commentary is conveyed by Latin writers anyway. More probably, the adverse treatment of Mummius stems from the attempt of political *inimici* to taint his reputation and reduce his influence—an echo of the parallel efforts mounted a generation earlier against Manlius Vulso and Fulvius Nobilior. What requires emphasis, however, is the form of attack. The very attempt to brand Mummius as a dense and uncultured personage disdainful of Hellenic art carries an interesting implication. Roman public opinion evidently considered such an attitude to be unworthy and unwelcome. The attack itself failed to impede his advance. Mummius reached the censorship in 142, together with Scipio Aemilianus, whose policies he boldly challenged.[224] He obviously gained in stature. The nature of the criticism and its miscarriage reinforce the picture drawn here. The Roman citi-

Mummius' temple with the extant round temple on the Tiber, but his interpretation dwells almost exclusively on Mummius' political motives.

219. On Mummius' acquaintance with Greek traditions, see also Plut. *Quaest. Conv.* 9.737a; Tac. *Ann.* 14.21.

220. So, e.g., Pape, *Griechische Kunstwerke*, 19; Philipp, *AthMitt*, 94 (1979), 195, 204; Pietilä-Castrén, *Arctos*, 12 (1978), 123. The contrast is made by the hostile tradition as reproduced by Vell. Pat. 1.13.2–4.

221. Cic. *De Rep.* 1.18; *De Amicit.* 69, 101.

222. Gruen, *Hellenistic World*, 266.

223. Cf. Jucker, *Vom Verhältnis der Römer*, 114; Prestianni Giallombardo, *AnnPisa*, 12 (1982), 516–518.

224. Sources in Broughton, *Magistrates of the Roman Republic*, I, 474–475.

zenry valued Hellenic art on the public scene and indeed recognized Corinth's conqueror as a principal promoter of it. The case of L. Mummius Achaicus therefore requires neither reversal of the general argument nor dismissal as an anomaly. Indeed, it bolsters and confirms the argument.

Roman attitudes and reactions to the development of the arts show a striking consistency from the fourth through the second century. Late Republican moralism fastened on the sack of Syracuse and the early eastern wars as marking a pivotal change in character, a succumbing to Hellenic luxury, and the inception of decline. Modern interpretations have often drawn a comparably critical portrait: the Romans hauled off art as booty, looked to political and economic gain, and remained indifferent to aesthetic quality or religious sanctity. A review of the evidence allows for a very different and more plausible assessment.

Art objects as the fruits of war became increasingly familiar in Rome during the fourth and third centuries. The reconsecration of sacred images in Roman shrines and temples bespeaks not only regard for their significance but recognition of their value for Roman public purposes. At the same time, the encouragement of sculptors and painters to reproduce the scenes of Roman success gave official blessing and a major boost to the arts in Italy. The arrival of Sicilian masterpieces through the triumph of Marcellus added further impetus to those developments instead of creating new ones. Marcellus stimulated the tastes of his countrymen for Hellenic art while bringing that art into association with traditional Roman civic and military virtues. Romans understood creative work as more than mere war spoils. Even with the great influx of Greek sculptures and paintings through the wars of the early second century, Romans showed discrimination, differentiating public from private art, sacred from profane art. The treasures brought by Fulvius Nobilior and the uses to which they were put exemplify the combination of art, literature, religion, and nationalism that could bring prestige to the commander and elevate the self-image of the community.

No voices were raised in opposition to Hellenic art and artists or to artistic activity in Italy. Cato's thunderings on this subject had different targets, namely, those who would distort the civic and religious value of the art by exploiting it for private enhancement or enrichment. Attitudes toward the creative work of the Greek world did not issue in partisan strife. Artistic representations multiplied in the second century, honoring individuals for services to the state or its religion. The censorial decree that temporarily checked them did so only to restate a basic principle: the precedence of public interest over private ambition. That principle held true throughout. Indeed private ambition was best advanced in this area through the encouragement of artistic developments that raised the cultural stature of the nation. L. Mummius, far from breaking the mold, fitted it perfectly. The new haul of statuary and, particularly, pictorial masterpieces after the fall of Corinth held a broad significance. Rome would henceforth be not only the military and diplomatic center of the Mediterranean but the custodian of its cultural heritage.

[4]

ART AND IDEOLOGY

The Romans' high regard for Greek art should admit of no doubt. Statuary from Magna Graecia, Sicily, and the Greek East graced temples, enhanced monuments, and gained prominent display in civic buildings and public spaces. In the late Republic sculpture and paintings multiplied as decorative items in private villas, estates, and gardens, available for more restricted viewing but by no means concealed or disclaimed. Romans took pride in the quality, significance, and implications of the art.

Yet contemporary artists themselves did not enjoy commensurate distinction. Far from it. Vergil's celebrated lines constitute the *locus classicus*: others will breathe life into bronze and bring living features out of marble; Roman *artes* excel in governance and empire.[1] Romans of status, for the most part, shunned the profession of artist. The large majority of known artists working in Italy during the Republic were Greek or of Greek extraction. That fact carries meaning and provokes questions. If Romans held artistic creativity in esteem, why so heavy a reliance upon Hellenic craftsmen? Did they in truth resign this realm to others and disdain to express a distinct artistic character of their own?

Artists and artisans from the Greek-speaking world predominate in our testimony on Republican Rome. The significance of that testimony requires closer attention than it has received. A relative paucity of

---

1. Verg. *Aen.* 6.847–853.

Roman names need not signify absence of Roman interest or lack of Italian talent. The matter is more complex—and more intriguing.

Painting at the outset claimed a respectability denied to other crafts. In the early period even Roman aristocrats did not scorn the metier. C. Fabius obtained the cognomen Pictor through his famed frescoes in the temple of Salus in 303, to which he proudly affixed his signature.[2] To be sure, the acquisition of the cognomen suggests that such talents were not common, or at least not much exploited, in upper-class Roman society. But it plainly served as a mark of distinction rather than a source of embarrassment.[3] The same held for the multitalented Pacuvius, a major dramatist of the early and middle second century, who also contributed a painting for the temple of Hercules in the Forum Boarium.[4] There may have been a few others in that period, unknown or unrecorded, but none thereafter. A shift in attitude took hold. According to Pliny, the profession of painting was not subsequently regarded as suitable for men of rank and station.[5] Later artists in the medium were Greeks, Italians of lesser status, or even women.[6]

Few Roman names surface in the genre of architecture. But building activity was heavy in second-century Rome, with multiple influences at work. Flourishing architectural traditions already existed in Etruria, Latium, Campania, and elsewhere.[7] Native talent certainly played a part, although no tabulations can be made of proportions or extent. Vitruvius speaks generally of great architects in the Roman past, *antiqui nostri*, and even an adequate number *nostra memoria*.[8] But he provides only two examples. The celebrated Roman architect of the second century, a certain D. Cossutius, entered the employ of Antiochus IV of Syria to give final form to the Olympieion at Athens. Vitruvius describes him as a *civis Romanus*, a man of great skill and mastery of his craft.[9] He may have worked for Antiochus also on an aqueduct near

2. Pliny, *NH*, 35.19; Val. Max. 8.14.6; cf. Cic. *Tusc. Disp.* 1.4; Dion. Hal. 16.3.

3. The attitude can be paralleled among the Greeks, for whom painting formed part of a liberal education for freeborn youth; Aristotle, *Pol.* 8.1338a.13–1338b.2; Pliny, *NH*, 35.77.

4. Pliny, *NH*, 35.19.

5. Pliny, *NH*, 35.20: *postea non est spectata honestis manibus.*

6. Pliny, *NH*, 35.115–116, 35.120, 35.147–148.

7. See, e.g., the survey by A. Boethius and J. B. Ward-Perkins, *Etruscan and Roman Architecture* (London, 1970), 96–180.

8. Vitr. 7, praef. 15, 18.

9. Vitr. 7, praef. 15: *magna sollertia scientiaque summa civis Romanus Cossutius nobiliter est architectatus*; cf. 7, praef. 17; *IG*, II–III², 4099.

Antioch.[10] Cossutius' experience, however, gives no direct access to practice at Rome. The Cossutii, in fact, were a Campanian family. Their architectural training may well have stemmed from the Greek-speaking areas of that region, thereby recommending Cossutius to the Hellenic king of Syria who had spent time as a hostage in Rome.[11] This was a Greek, not a Roman enterprise. The same applies to the Stalii a century later, hired by King Ariobarzanes of Cappadocia to help restore the Odeion in Athens. They too were Campanian.[12] The other Roman architect named by Vitruvius for this period, C. Mucius, a highly accomplished professional, did work in Rome; he completed the temple of Honos and Virtus circa 100 B.C.[13] Mucius enjoyed the patronage of C. Marius, and the building had its propaganda value in the politics of the late second century. Given the image that Marius sought to project, a native artist would serve his purposes more pointedly than an imported Greek.[14] Other Roman architects can be discovered in the last generation of the Republic. A certain L. Cornelius is described as *praefectus fabrum* of Q. Catulus during his consulship and as his architect during the censorship. This notice presumably signifies that he was employed by Catulus to oversee work on reconstructing the temple of Jupiter Capitolinus and building the Tabularium in 65.[15] And the Ostian architect Valerius provided a cover for the theater in which L. Scribonius Libo, probably the consul of 34 B.C., presented his games.[16] It would be prudent to refrain from drawing sweeping conclusions from these instances. Cornelius, who had been *praefectus fabrum* as well as *architectus*, may have served more as supervisor than as practicing architect, and the attested work of Valerius hardly suggests major significance. The known examples do not authorize any secure assessment of numbers and importance of Roman architects in the Republic.[17]

10. *IGLS*, 825; E. Rawson, *PBSR*, 43 (1975), 37.

11. See the brief discussion by J. M. C. Toynbee, *Some Notes on Artists in the Roman World* (Brussels, 1951), 9, and the fuller treatment by Rawson, *PBSR*, 43 (1975), 36–38.

12. *IG*, II–III², 3426; Rawson, *PBSR*, 43 (1975), 37.

13. Vitr. 3.2.5, 7, praef. 17.

14. Cf. P. Gros, *L'Italie préromaine et la Rome républicaine: Mélanges offerts à Jacques Heurgon* (Rome, 1976), II, 407–408.

15. The inscription giving the information is published and discussed by G. Molisani, *RendAccadLinc*, 26 (1971), 41–49; cf. Gros, *Architecture et société à Rome et en Italie centro-méridionale aux deux derniers siècles de la République* (Brussels, 1978), 60–63.

16. Pliny, *NH*, 36.102.

17. Note Vitruvius' complaint that Romans, unlike Greeks, rarely wrote on architecture; 7, praef. 14–15, 17–18.

Roman sculptors constituted an even rarer breed, if extant evidence be any guide. Not a one is known for the third and second centuries, and quite possibly none even for the first. The solitary sculptor with a Latin name, Coponius, dates to the end of the Republic, for he created the fourteen statues of the *nationes* which were set in the theater of Pompey.[18] And even he may be a Greek freedman who took on the Latin nomenclature upon manumission and whose Greek name Pliny did not know or did not care to record. Similarly, no Roman names turn up among gem engravers, metalworkers, or mosaicists. By contrast, Greek signatures on works of art appear with some frequency and consistency.[19] The argument from silence looms large. Our surviving record knows little or nothing of Roman artists.

The reverse holds with regard to Greek artists in Rome. They began to come across the sea in significant numbers from the early second century. L. Scipio Asiagenus capped his victory over Antiochus III of Syria in 190 by collecting cash contributions from kings and cities to help finance the games he had vowed in the event of success. In addition, or perhaps with help of the cash, Scipio gathered artists from various parts of Greek Asia to bring to Rome.[20] M. Fulvius Nobilior, not to be outdone, organized votive games to celebrate his completion of the Aetolian War in 188. And, so we are told, many *artifices* arrived from Greece to do him honor. The building projects of Nobilior and his keen interest in Hellenic culture no doubt provided inducement for migration of the artists.[21] Such are the first explicit attestations, but the new migrants were hardly the first Greek artists in Rome. Paintings, statuary, and other monuments had been accumulating for years in religious shrines and public places, many of them new creations, and we may be certain that Greek artists, whether from south Italy or elsewhere, contributed mightily to that development. A fragment of Nae-

18. Pliny, *NH*, 36.41.
19. Evidence is conveniently gathered by G. M. A. Richter, *Three Critical Periods in Greek Sculpture* (Oxford, 1951), 45–57; Toynbee, *Some Notes*, 18–28, 35–40, 43–46. I. Calabi Limentani, *Studi sulla società romana: Il lavoro artistico* (Milan, 1958), 153–180, supplies a valuable collection of epigraphical attestations of artists. On gem engravers, the exhaustive and definitive work is M.-L. Vollenweider, *Die Porträtgemmen der römischen Republik* (Mainz, 1974), 2 vols. See also the list of artists' signatures in Vollenweider, *Die Steinschneiderkunst und ihre Künstler in spätrepublikanischer und augusteischer Zeit* (Baden-Baden, 1966), 139–141.
20. Livy, 39.22.10: *tum collatas ei pecunias congregatosque per Asiam artifices.*
21. Livy, 39.22.2: *multi artifices ex Graecia venerunt honoris eius causa.*

vius fortuitously discloses the name of one of them: the painter The-
odotus.[22] The number of those from abroad jumped after the Third
Macedonian War. L. Aemilius Paullus, conqueror of Macedon and
agent for the destruction of the monarchy, pulled a host of Greek
intellectuals with him when he returned to Rome, including painters
and sculptors. Prominent among them was the Athenian Metrodorus
who could provide both instruction in philosophy and a painting to
commemorate the triumph of Paullus.[23] Marcus Plautius, an Asian by
birth who later obtained Roman citizenship, painter of the temple of
Juno at Ardea, may have been part of this migration.[24] The Alexandrian
landscape painter Demetrius was certainly part of it. A man often
entertained by Ptolemaic royalty, he had acquired high repute in Alexandria. The move to Rome perhaps brought greater stimulus and patronage for his work, but high rents in the city meant a sharp reduction
in his standard of living. Demetrius had to ply his trade in a run-down
tenement.[25] Rome evidently held a strong attraction.

Greek sculptors of renown worked in Rome or for Rome. Timarchides executed the cult statue for the temple of Apollo perhaps in the
early second century. A generation later, his sons Polycles and Dionysius gained further commissions for the image of Juno in her temple
and Jupiter in his, plus another statue of Juno.[26] Polycles also received an
assignment to produce a statue of Hercules.[27] The family continued its
artistic activity, so it appears, for at least another generation. Polycles
had two sons, Timarchides and Timocles, the former of whom signed a
portrait of a Roman at Delos in the late second century, as did Di-

22. Festus, 260, L.
23. Pliny, *NH*, 35.135; Plut. *Aem. Paull.* 6.5.
24. Pliny, *NH*, 35.115.
25. Diod. 31.18.2; Val. Max. 5.1.1f.
26. Pliny, *NH*, 36.35: *eum qui citharam in eodem templo tenet Timarchides fecit, intra
Octaviae vero porticus in aede Iunonis ipsam deam Dionysius et Polycles aliam . . . iidem Polycles
et Dionysius Timarchidis filii Iovem qui est in proxima aede fecerunt.* F. Coarelli, *DialArch*, 2
(1968), 334, places a comma after *ipsam deam*, thus making Timarchides also the sculptor
of Juno's cult image for the temple of Juno Regina in 179. So also Stewart, *Attika*, 43, 58,
n. 45. The temple of Juno was dedicated in 179; Livy, 40.52.1–3. But despite Coarelli,
there is no evidence for a restoration of Apollo's temple in that year. Cf. T. P. Wiseman,
PBSR, 42 (1974), 12. Even if the hypothesis were valid, however, the further conjectures
about Timarchides as employed in the political rivalries of M. Fulvius Nobilior and M.
Aemilius Lepidus are sheer speculation; as in Coarelli, *Studi Miscellanei*, 15 (1969–70),
77–89; Stewart, *Attika*, 43.
27. Cic. *Ad Att.* 6.1.17; Coarelli, *MEFRA*, 81 (1969), 148–154.

onysius, perhaps his uncle.[28] Other Greek artists too are associated with important public statuary in Rome. The Rhodian sculptor Philiscus, perhaps in the later second century, created statues of Apollo, Venus, Artemis, Leto, and the nine Muses, which by Pliny's day stood near the Porticus Octaviae.[29] Athenian sculptors in Delos, such as Myron and Graphicus, carried out commissions for Romans or Italians in the later second century.[30] The gifted south Italian Greek Pasiteles, both sculptor and art historian, produced an ivory statue of Jupiter for a temple in the Campus Martius, probably in the late second century. Pasiteles earned high honors, including the award of Roman citizenship after the Social War, and spawned a school of Greek artists in Rome.[31] Additional names are known, though dates are uncertain. Heliodorus, for example, perhaps circa 100 B.C., depicted a contest between Pan and Olympos in the Porticus Octaviae which Pliny characterized as a *symplegma nobile*, and Apollonius fashioned a chryselephantine statue for the temple of Jupiter Capitolinus, probably in the mid–first century.[32] And a case can be made for a certain Scopas, namesake of the more celebrated artist of the fourth century, who was active in Rome in the later second century, contributing statuary to, among other places, the temple of Mars built by Dec. Brutus Callaicus.[33] Sculptors' signatures, almost

28. The signatures are given in *IDelos*, 1688. The sons of Polycles: Paus. 6.12.9, 10.34.6, 10.34.8. The family's stemma is much disputed. Among various reconstructions, see G. Becatti, *RivIstArch*, 7 (1940), 18; Coarelli, *DialArch*, 2 (1968), 331–333; J. Marcadé, *Receuil de signatures de sculpteurs grecs* (Paris, 1957), II, 731; Stewart, *Attika*, 42–45; C. Habicht, *AthMitt*, 97 (1982), 178–180.

29. Pliny, *NH*, 36.34, 36.35. The approximate date derives from letter forms of a statue base signed by Philiscus. But the identification of this Philiscus with the sculptor of the Apollo group is uncertain; cf. M. Bieber, *The Sculpture of the Hellenistic Age*² (New York, 1961), 130.

30. *IDelos*, 1750. Myron too was part of a family of sculptors, which included Hephaistion and Eutychides, artists whose signatures appear on many portrait bases in Delos; see references to the inscriptions in Stewart, *Attika*, 165. Cf. Toynbee, *Some Notes*, 19–20.

31. Pliny, *NH*, 33.156, 35.156, 36.39–40; Cic. *De Div.* 1.79. See M. Borda, *La scuola di Pasiteles* (Bari, 1953).

32. Heliodorus: Pliny, *NH*, 36.35; cf. Bieber, *Sculpture*, 147. Apollonius: Chalcid. on Plato, *Timaeus*, p. 440 (Meurs.).

33. On that theory, Pliny, *NH*, 36.25–26, confused the younger Scopas with his more illustrious predecessor; see P. Mingazzini, *Arti figurative*, 2 (1946), 137–148; Coarelli, *DialArch*, 2 (1968), 325–327, 336–337; idem, *DialArch*, 4–5 (1970–71), 247–252. Doubts are expressed but not argued by Wiseman, *PBSR*, 42 (1974), 13. The existence of a Scopas *minor* is attested by an inscribed statue base; *CIL*, VI, 33936: *o Olivarius opus Scopae minoris*. Note also the Aristander, son of Scopas, who restored statues at Delos; O. Rubensohn, *JdI*, 50 (1935), 51.

without exception, designate Greeks.[34] To what extent the statues produced for civic purposes in Rome were actually carved in the city by
imported artists or their successors or simply commissioned from
workshops in Greece and then transported to Italy cannot be known.
But the attested creators were almost exclusively Greek and the profession remained thoroughly Hellenic.

Evidence on the minor arts is slim but consistent. Signatures of gem
cutters exist in some quantities for the later Republic and early Empire.
The names that can be assembled are overwhelmingly Greek.[35]

Architecture too felt the lure of Hellenism. In this realm, of course,
Roman names do occur, and Italian traditions played a large role, but
where testimony exists for buildings of major public import, the ruling
class turned again to Greeks. Q. Metellus Macedonicus commemorated
his decisive victory in the "Fourth Macedonian War" by directing the
construction of Rome's first marble temple, a shrine to Jupiter Stator,
circa 143, and he entrusted the plans and execution of that work to the
Greek architect Hermodorus of Cypriote Salamis.[36] That same master
builder was called upon a decade later by Dec. Brutus Callaicus, who had
him design the new temple of Mars in the Circus Flaminius.[37] Such
major assignments attest to the high repute of Hermodorus, and the
conspicuous structures doubtless influenced building activity more
widely in Rome during Hermodorus' generation and later.[38] For other
buildings in the second century architects' names fail us. One may note,
however, the double portico near the Circus Flaminius constructed by
Cn. Octavius as a memorial to his naval triumph in the Macedonian War

34. Cf. Richter, *Three Critical Periods*, 45–47; Toynbee, *Some Notes*, 23–26.

35. See the evidence and discussion in Vollenweider, *Die Steinschneiderkunst*, 23–80.
She finds only three Latin names out of twenty-three—and one or two of them may
conceal Greek origins.

36. Vitr. 3.2.5. According to Pliny, *NH*, 36.42, two Spartan architects worked on the
temples within the Porticus Octaviae, thus presumably including the temple of Jupiter
Stator. The story has been dismissed by many, but ably defended by Morgan, *Hermes*, 99
(1971), 491–499. They may have assisted Hermodorus.

37. Nepos, *apud* Priscian, 8.17; cf. Pliny, *NH*, 36.26. On the temple, see F. Zevi, in
L'Italie préromaine et la Rome républicaine: Mélanges offerts à Jacques Heurgon (Rome, 1976),
II, 1047–1064.

38. See, especially, Gros, in *Mélanges Heurgon*, I, 393–409. On the temple of Jupiter
Stator, see further M. J. Boyd, *PBSR*, 21 (1953), 152–159; Morgan, *Hermes*, 99 (1971),
480–505; P. Gros, *MEFRA*, 85 (1973), 137–161. Note also Hermodorus' work on the
Roman boatyards; Cic. *De Orat.* 1.62. The speculations of Coarelli, *DialArch*, 2 (1968),
340–341, are excessive; cf. Morgan, *Hermes*, 99 (1971), 503; Wiseman, *PBSR*, 42 (1974),
13.

of 167 and designated as *Corinthia*. The appellation, according to Pliny, derived from the bronze capitals of the columns, but it could also attest to the Hellenic character of the structure generally. A Greek architect was very likely responsible for the design.[39] The same may be true of many of the second-century buildings for which no architects' names are preserved.[40] When names do surface in the Ciceronian age, they are all Greek.[41]

A vital point must here be registered. None of the preceding implies the impoverishment of native artistic traditions or the absence of homegrown talent. Architectural activity on several fronts thrived in central Italy during the middle Republic: forums, basilicas, temples, theaters, domestic structures all grew up on native soil. The impressive productivity issued in at least one later Republican treatise on the topic, the *De modo aedificorum* of Rutilius.[42] The Italian contribution to painting requires no rehearsal. Even some eminent Romans, as we have seen, took to the profession. Etruscan sepulchral paintings speak eloquently for themselves. And as for Rome, the celebrated frescoes from the Esquiline tombs suffice as evidence.[43] Bronze work perishes all too easily, thus preventing any real insight into this craft for the era under consideration, but one need only contemplate the famed Capitoline *Brutus*—which may or may not date to this period—or the *Arringatore* from Perugia to gain a sense of the Italian artistic tradition in bronze.[44] Clay modeling was firmly rooted in Italian soil. Varro affirmed that this art form developed in Italy, especially in Etruria, and Pliny adds that Republican terra-cotta temple sculptures of splendid quality survived in Rome and the Italian *municipia* of his own day.[45] Nor should one neglect coin dies. Greek models from Magna Graecia and Campania served as initial impetus, but Roman engravers at mints in Rome and cities under Roman control developed styles of their own in the third and second

39. Pliny, *NH*, 34.13: *a Cn. Octavio, qui de Perseo rege navalem triumphum egit, factam porticum duplicem ad circum Flaminium, quae Corinthia sit appellata a capitulis aereis columnarum.* See the discussion of Gros, in *Mélanges Heurgon*, I, 388–392.

40. See the summary of building activity in Gros, *Mélanges Heurgon* (1976), I, 389; Coarelli, *PBSR*, 45 (1977), 4–6, 20–22.

41. References in Toynbee, *Some Notes*, 10.

42. Suet. *Aug.* 89.2. On building in the middle Republic, see above nn. 7, 40.

43. Its date, unfortunately, is much in dispute. See, most recently, E. La Rocca, in *Ricerche di pittura ellenistica* (Rome, 1985), 169–191, with references to earlier scholarship.

44. Cf., e.g., D. Strong, *Roman Art*[2] (London, 1988), 32–34.

45. Pliny, *NH*, 35.154–158.

centuries.[46] Works in marble owed less to Italian craftsmanship—for readily discernible reasons. No marble quarries of significance functioned in the Republic, a fact that helps to explain the preponderance of Greek sculptors in Italy and the employment of Greek architects in the construction of marble temples. Where the materials existed, as with bronze, clay, and silver, native skills came to the fore.

Other factors, too, complicate the record and demand its modification. The preserved names of artists, as we have noted, are overwhelmingly Greek, but the testimony itself contains inherent imbalance. A heavy proportion of names appears in Pliny's chapters on art history, material that may ultimately derive from Greek treatises such as the five volumes on *opera nobilia* by the Italian Greek Pasiteles.[47] The preponderance of Greek signatures on works of art may be equally misleading, reflecting Hellenic inclination to sign rather than a true ratio. The artists themselves must in some instances have been second- or third-generation immigrants, as with the families of Timarchides or Myron, not recent arrivals or imports for the occasion. In that event, the Hellenic roots would be less important than the Roman context. Artists' workshops installed on Italian soil for two or more generations would owe relatively little to the experience of their ancestral home.

The existence of artistic traditions and artists in Italy intensifies the problem posed at the outset. If creative productivity prospered in the peninsula, why did Romans seek out the talents of Hellas? For seek them out they did, as we have seen, in abundance. Greek artists in substantial numbers either migrated to Rome in the second century or carried out commissions allotted to them by Romans. Public buildings, temples, statuary, paintings, and decorations contracted for by members of the nobility were executed by men from the Hellenic world.[48] Romans of rank and stature shunned such an occupation or profession. A few, at an early stage, found painting attractive, but only as an

46. Cf. M. H. Crawford, *Coinage and Money under the Roman Republic* (Berkeley, Calif., 1985), 25–74.

47. Pliny, *NH*, 36.39–40.

48. R. R. R. Smith, *JRS*, 71 (1981), 28, claims that "there is something of a conspiracy of silence . . . about this." In fact, it is widely recognized; cf., e.g., Richter, *Proc. Amer. Philos. Soc.*, 95 (1951), 184–191; idem, *Three Critical Periods*, 37–64; Toynbee, *Some Notes*, 9–56; Coarelli, *DialArch*, 2 (1968), 328–337; idem, *DialArch*, 4–5 (1970–71), 249–260; idem, *Caratteri dell' ellenismo nelle urne etrusche* (Florence, 1977), 36–38. For a more skeptical view, see N. Horsfall, *Prudentia*, 20 (1988), 12–14.

avocation—and even that soon became reckoned as unsuitable.[49] The attested Roman architects are not men of social significance. Vitruvius indicates that architects were expected to be of good birth, training, and ethics, but he ascribes those criteria to the Romans of old, the *maiores*; they no longer apply in his own day.[50] The number of *ingenui* attested for any of the arts is revealingly small.[51] The ruling class, on the whole, had determined to consign these callings to others—and very often to Greeks.

Why? Why not promote and develop native talents that could rival Hellenic achievements and express national values? Why summon alien craftsmen, modes, and traditions? It will not do to assert that works of art were matters of secondary or tertiary interest to aristocratic Romans or that artists themselves were of a status held in low esteem. The keen attention paid to art, the conspicuous places occupied by civic and religious monuments, and the public significance borne by artistic creations decisively refute the idea of indifference. And the social status of artists is a fact that needs explanation; it does not itself provide explanation. Nor, on the other hand, should one resort to the reverse interpretation: that Romans held the Hellenic accomplishment in awe and judged their own competence as inferior, thus cultivating the masters of the craft and resigning themselves to the role of beneficiaries. Such an attitude would be entirely out of character for Roman *nobiles* and the molders of public opinion. If the ruling class had chosen to sponsor and subsidize the training of Roman artists, they could certainly have done so.

The decision to encourage Hellenic craftsmen was deliberate and meaningful. Emphasis needs to be placed on the broad connotations conveyed by that decision. Romans showed respect for Greek artists and Greek art. Their consistent and conspicuous promotion of them could carry no other meaning. The importation of painters, sculptors, and architects, the commissioning of their work, and the employment of Hellenic talent to enhance the appearance and advance the purposes of Rome held a significance of wide import. Far from betraying a sense of inferiority, that policy announced that the refinements of Greek art were now put to the service of Roman ends. Hellenic skills would serve

49. See above, nn. 2–6.
50. Vitr. 6, praef. 6; cf. E. Rawson, *Intellectual Life in the Late Roman Republic* (London, 1985), 86–88.
51. Cf. Calabi Limentani, *Studi sulla società romana*, 19–42; Horsfall, *Prudentia*, 20 (1988), 16–17.

to decorate the city, provide structures for its public activities, commemorate its accomplishments, and solidify its relations with the gods. The Romans put on display not only their taste in Greek art but their management of that art.

If Republican Rome employed the skills, talent, and traditions of Hellenic craftsmen, where does one find the articulation of Roman distinctiveness? The problem is vast in scope and multiple in possibilities. A full study would encompass, among other things, tomb paintings, terra-cotta reliefs, architectural forms, and numismatic engravings—an impractical proposition in this context. Two genres, however, conventionally count as central expressions of *Romanitas*: the historical relief and veristic portraiture. Concentration on these media will focus the inquiry and sharpen the issue.

First the historical relief. Sculptured documentation of events, accomplishments, or institutions seems peculiarly Roman, a means whereby to announce individual achievements or expound national values.[52] Impressive and imposing monuments exemplify the genre: the Ara Pacis, the Arch of Titus, the Column of Marcus Aurelius. What were its roots, and how distinctively Roman?

The earliest surviving example holds special interest. L. Aemilius Paullus, victor at Pydna, undertook a tour of the sights and monuments of Greece in 167. In the holy city of Delphi, where he made sacrifice at the temple of Apollo, Paullus discovered a large quadrangular pillar (or pillars) in process of erection for a statue of Perseus of Macedon. The Roman *imperator* directed that the work be completed but that his own statue be installed: the conquered must yield to the conqueror.[53] An extant inscription asserts the conqueror's prerogatives and marks the significance of the dedication: *L. Aimilius L.f inperator de rege Perse Macedonibusque cepet.*[54] The use of Latin alone delivered a pointed message. Of Paullus' equestrian statue, which stood atop the monument, little trace survives, but fragments of the tall pedestal on which it rested do exist, as do substantial portions of the decorative frieze about thirty

---

52. So, most recently, A. Stewart, *Greek Sculpture* (New Haven, Conn., 1990), 220: "that quintessentially Roman genre, the historical relief." For a full bibliography and discussion of the genre as later developed, see G. Koeppel, *ANRW*, 2.12.1 (1982), 477–506 (bibliography) and 507–535 (discussion).

53. Polyb. 30.10.2; Plut. *Aem. Paull.* 28.2; Livy, 45.27.7. Plutarch refers to just one pillar, Polybius, followed by Livy, to more than one.

54. *ILLRP*, 323.

centimeters high which formed the top of the pillar beneath the statue (see Plate 1).[55] That frieze seems to represent, so far as extant material allows for judgment, a watershed, fountainhead of the great tradition of Roman historical reliefs that would stretch through the period of the Empire.

The scenes pointedly record an event of major international import: the battle of Pydna. No allegory here, no indirect allusion to historical occasions, as in the contest of gods and giants in the Great Altar of Pergamum. The Paullus monument, it appears, provides explicit details of the battle itself, an idea suggested by depiction of a horse without rider or trappings. The battle, as we happen to know, was touched off when a horse (or beast of burden) escaped its handlers (or was deliberately loosed by Paullus as a stratagem), thereby provoking a clash between the Romans who chased it and Macedonian auxiliaries who encountered them.[56] The four sides of the frieze ostensibly portray individual, perhaps successive, episodes in the battle. Particulars cannot be reconstructed from the literary texts—if indeed the reliefs aimed at depicting recognizable particulars—but the objective of evoking the contest at Pydna is plain and unequivocal.[57]

Is it new? Paullus may have directed the enterprise in outline but would hardly have supervised the specifics. He pursued his lengthy tourist trip in Greece after leaving Delphi, conferred with Perseus at Apollonia, arranged the Macedonian settlement with the *decem legati*, administered affairs in Greece, put on a grand festival at Amphipolis, conducted the devastation of Epirus, and then returned to Rome. The monument was obviously carved in his absence. And one may be certain that a Greek artist undertook the commission. Paullus did not take Italian sculptors with him to Greece.[58] The work, in fact, is thoroughly Greek. The pillar that carried Paullus' statue stood alongside two others, similar marks of honor, gifts of the Aetolians to pay respects to Eumenes II of Pergamum and to Prusias II of Bithynia.[59] The monu-

55. See the valuable publication, with excellent photographs, by H. Kähler, *Der Fries vom Reiterdenkmal des Aemilius Paullus in Delphi* (Berlin, 1965).

56. Different versions of the tale appear in Livy, 44.40.4–10 and Plutarch, *Aem. Paull.* 18.1—who knows the other version.

57. Commentary on the frieze by Kähler, *Der Fries*, 7–23, is essential reading—ably recapitulated by Pollitt, *Art in the Hellenistic Age*, 155–158.

58. On Paullus' movements, see Livy, 45.27–34. The suggestion that a south Italian artist was responsible for the monument was effectively refuted by Kähler, *Der Fries*, 19–20.

59. *Syll.*[3] 628, 632.

ment for Perseus would have had a comparable form and purpose. The practice goes well back into Greek history and by the second century had become commonplace.[60] Paullus' objective was not to replace a Hellenistic institution with a Roman one. On the contrary, it suited his ends far better to substitute himself for Perseus, thereby to appropriate the Hellenistic institution.

To be sure, the frieze depicted a Roman victory, a specific event, and perhaps even particulars of the battle. The four sides of the pillar, it can be argued, represented separate episodes at Pydna, to be read by the viewer in sequence as a narrative account of the contest.[61] That inference is attractive but unverifiable, a heavy burden to be carried by the riderless horse alone. No other scene can be matched with the literary evidence. Nor should one expect it. The smallish frieze could do little more than evoke the sense of the battle, mark its result, and underscore its significance. For an enterprise of that nature, Hellenistic models were by no means lacking. The bronze statue group executed by Lysippus for Alexander memorialized the fallen heroes of the battle of the Granicus.[62] Since the group included Alexander himself, it was plainly designed to call forth the battle itself, not just to honor the dead. Lysippus' son Euthycrates, as Pliny mentions in passing, also produced a sculptural depiction of a cavalry battle.[63] Such scenes were evidently not rare in Hellenistic art. An extant example supplies the best testimony—and an appropriate precursor for the Paullus monument. The so-called Alexander Sarcophagus, dating probably to the late fourth century, was carved on all four sides and two pediments on the ends. Four of the six panels (including the two gables) present battle scenes that include both mounted warriors and infantrymen, both clothed and unclothed figures, combinations analogous to those on the Paullus relief. The particular scenes depicted and the identity of the persons are

60. Cf. Pliny, NH, 34.27: *columnarum ratio erat attolli super ceteros mortales quod et arcus significant novicio invento; primus tamen honos coepit a Graecis*; Kähler, *Der Fries*, 8–10. Note the recently discovered base of a monument with quadriga probably dedicated by a Pergamene ruler at the northeast corner of the Parthenon; G. Touchais, *BCH*, 110 (1986), 675; A. W. Catling, *AR*, 35 (1988–89), 8–9. For illustrations of Hellenistic pillar monuments, see R. Ling, in *Cambridge Ancient History*², Plates to vol. VII.1 (Cambridge, 1984), 65.

61. Kähler, *Der Fries*, 12–15; L. Budde, *ANRW*, I.4 (1973), 801–802; Pollitt, *Art in the Hellenistic Age*, 157.

62. Arrian, *Anab*. 1.16.4; Plut. *Alex*. 16.7–8; Vell.Pat. 1.11.3–4. On this, see now the full study by G. Calcani, *Cavalieri di bronzo* (Rome, 1989).

63. Pliny, *NH*, 34.66.

items of dispute but do not matter for our purposes.[64] The work itself provides graphic proof that Hellenistic artists worked in this medium well before Aemilius Paullus commissioned the creator of his frieze.[65]

Paullus' monument, so it is often said, inaugurated the tradition of Roman historical reliefs. That proposition may contain some meaning in art-historical retrospective, but so stated, it misleads and deceives. The structure, after all, stood in Delphi, not in Italy. The holy city was, of course, well known to Rome's leadership, but it did not draw a steady stream of Roman visitors. Nor is it likely that any *nobiles*, inspired by the Delphic frieze, produced comparable historical reliefs in Rome. The idea is unnecessary and implausible. There is little, if anything, in Paullus' monument that can be claimed as innovative. But innovation is not the point.[66] The work fits comfortably within the traditions of Hellenistic art. Aemilius Paullus, it appears, gave general guidelines but left the execution of the monument to a Greek workshop. The Hellenistic form and content held symbolic meaning of real importance. Not that Paullus conceived of himself as heir to the Hellenistic monarchs.[67] A different aim took precedence. As reminder of Rome's triumphant

---

64. See the treatments of K. Schefold, *Der Alexander-Sarkophag* (Berlin, 1968); and V. von Graeve, *Der Alexandersarkophag von Sidon und seine Werkstatt*, Istambuler Forschungen, 28 (Berlin, 1970).

65. On a grander scale one can, of course, reach back to the classical era, as with the historical frieze on the temple of Athena Nike in Athens from the late fifth century, depicting battle scenes that pit Greeks against Persians and even Greeks against Greeks; cf. T. Hölscher, *Griechische Historienbilder des 5. und 4. Jahrhunderts v. Chr.* (Würzburg, 1973), 91–98.

66. To be sure, placement of the scene at the top of the pillar, just below the statue, may be an innovation by Paullus, but this hardly proclaims any special Roman quality. Kähler, *Der Fries*, 15–17, strains to set the concept of the Paullus frieze somewhere between the concentrated recapitulation of several events in one, as with the Alexander mosaic, and the episodic depiction apparent in the wall painting found in an Esquiline tomb. But not only may one question the value of comparing a sculptured relief with examples from different genres, the conclusion is itself somewhat forced. We cannot be sure that the Alexander mosaic did combine the three great battles into one. Nor, in fact, is it clear that the Delphic frieze depicts specific episodes at Pydna. If so, it leaves much out or, more probably, alludes in general fashion to what could not be depicted—as indeed does the Alexander mosaic. Such comparisons do not advance the argument much. Still less does the Esquiline tomb painting, for its function and purpose, whatever they might be, were quite different from those of the Paullus monument. On the Alexander mosaic, see B. Andreae, *Das Alexandermosaik aus Pompeji* (Recklinghausen, 1977), with bibliography. On the Esquiline tomb painting, see Kähler, *Rom und seine Will: Erläuterungen* (Munich, 1960), 69–70, and now E. La Rocca, in *Ricerche di pittura ellenistica* (Rome, 1985), 169–191, with bibliography.

67. So J.-L. Ferrary, *Philhellénisme et impérialisme*, 554–565.

smashing of Macedonian power, a Hellenic monument of familiar genre and style would have the greater impact upon visitors to Delphi. Greeks would instantly recognize that the Roman success was immortalized by their own crafts and craftsmen, and that the Roman victor was set within their own cultural traditions. Hence, to view the Delphic frieze as the first of Rome's historical reliefs stands the matter on its head. It was directed at a Greek audience, employed a Greek medium, and chose Greek conventions to dramatize a Roman achievement. The Paullus monument aimed to display both Rome's participation in and its control of the cultural world of the eastern Mediterranean.

The introduction of historical reliefs into Rome itself defies dating. But when the genre surfaces, the Greek component is central and critical. A monument of high importance and high controversy provides the chief exhibit: the so-called Altar of Domitius Ahenobarbus (see Plates 2 and 3). The work has generated a long and growing body of literature, and most of the vital questions are still unsettled: date, purpose, artist, and patron. With such facts in dispute, it might be prudent to limit discussion. Emphasis here dwells on the blend of Hellenic medium and Roman message. The *Ara*—as it might conveniently be called for the sake of convention—has a striking character that defies easy categorization. In fact, it consists of two separate sculptured friezes, with two independent and quite different scenes. The one, with three sides, now in Munich, portrays the wedding of Poseidon and Amphitrite, the other, now in Paris, constitutes the fourth side and depicts the closing of a censorial *lustrum* in Rome. The combination is unique and baffling. What meaning does it possess? And what part does it play in the development of monumental art for Roman national purposes?

Discovery of the marine relief that celebrated the marriage of Poseidon and Amphitrite immediately called to mind a pertinent passage of Pliny. The text records a statue group by Scopas that included Neptune, Thetis, Achilles, Nereids, Tritons, and various sea creatures set up in a temple constructed by Cn. Domitius in the Circus Flaminius.[68] The temple of Neptune *in Circo Flaminio* is attested on an imperial inscription and its reconstruction by Cn. Domitius Ahenobarbus is alluded to on a coin issued by the consul of 32 B.C.[69] It seemed logical to suppose that Ahenobarbus, a legate of M. Antony in the early 30s,

68. Pliny, *NH*, 30.26.
69. *CIL*, VI, 8423; Crawford, *Roman Republican Coinage*, no. 519.1.

brought Scopas' sculpture back from the East and that the statuary must have had some connection with the thiasos frieze. Demonstration that the census scene formed part of the same monument complicated the argument and multiplied the hypotheses. It appeared certain that a censor commissioned the work to call attention to his year in office and presumably that he had a naval victory to his credit, thus making appropriate the combination of *lustrum* and marine frieze. Domitius Ahenobarbus was the favored candidate, hence the conventional label for the structure. The consul of 32 never attained the censorship, but his ancestor Cn. Domitius Ahenobarbus had held one in 115 and may even have had some exploits by sea. That reconstruction, however, did not become canonical. Other names have won adherents, notably M. Antonius, censor in 97, and the two censors of 70.[70] There is little consensus in sight. No less controversial is the function of the monument. The reliefs derive from the vicinity of the church of San Salvatore in Campo, beneath which lie the remains of a Roman temple. That structure has been identified with the temple of Neptune that dates back to the third century and was restored by Domitius Ahenobarbus, or with the temple of Mars built by D. Brutus Callaicus in 132.[71] The *Ara* accordingly may be the base for a cult statue of Neptune or of Mars. Alternatively, it could be a freestanding monument constructed to hold the marine statuary of Scopas or another statue group, perhaps serving as a votive and calling attention to the patron of the monument.[72] Certainty seems quite impossible on these matters in the present state of

70. The older literature is usefully summarized by Zevi, in *Mélanges Heurgon*, II, 1055–1058. Photographs, with commentary, are best consulted in Kähler, *Seethiasos und Census: Die Reliefs aus dem Palazzo Santa Croce in Rom* (Berlin, 1966). Kähler opted for the censors of 70 as sponsors of the monument (30–36). Wiseman, *Greece and Rome*, 21 (1974), 160–164 = *Roman Studies, Literary and Historical* (Liverpool, 1987), 214–218, fastens on one of those censors, L. Gellius Publicola. A case is made for M. Antonius by Coarelli, *DialArch*, 2 (1968), 338–343; so also T. Hölscher, *ArchAnz*, 94 (1979), 337–342; and most forcefully, A. Kuttner, in P. Holliday, ed., *Narrative and Event in Ancient Art* (Cambridge, forthcoming). M. Torelli, *Typology and Structure of Roman Historical Reliefs* (Ann Arbor, Mich., 1982), 14–16, returns to the suggestion of Ahenobarbus, the censor of 115. S. Lattimore, *The Marine Thiasos in Greek Sculpture* (Los Angeles, 1976), 17–18, sees M. Antony behind it, with allusions both to his censorial ancestor and to that of his follower Domitius Ahenobarbus.

71. For the former, see Coarelli, *DialArch*, 2 (1968), 302–325; for the latter, Zevi, in *Mélanges Heurgon*, II, 1055–1064.

72. For various suggestions, see Coarelli, *DialArch*, 2 (1968), 325–327; idem, *DialArch*, 4–5 (1970–71), 248; Lattimore, *Marine Thiasos*, 18; Torelli, *Typology and Structure*, 8–9; Wiseman, *Roman Studies*, 215, 381; Kuttner, in *Narrative and Event*.

the evidence, but the subject might perhaps benefit from a fresh perspective.

On one matter consensus has been firm, consistent, and nearly unanimous. The monument, so it is regularly asserted or implied, represented the political interests of a particular Roman *nobilis*. That fundamental assumption has provoked the search for an appropriate sponsor, whether Antonius, Gellius, or one of the Domitii, for whom the *lustrum* scene would advertise his censorship and the sea-thiasos would commemorate a naval victory.[73] Yet that conclusion is neither necessary nor obvious.

Maritime mastery may be the message of the Neptune relief. Nothing requires us to believe that it has reference to a specific naval triumph, and there is little to suggest it.[74]

The census relief creates even greater difficulties for the conventional thesis, difficulties generally unacknowledged or unnoticed. The scene quite plainly portrays the closing of the *lustrum*, that is, the purification ceremony that formally concluded the census and the censors' duties, climaxed by the *suovetaurilia*, the sacrifice of a bull, ram, and pig.[75] Chief argument for the relief as political advertisement for a particular *nobilis* lies in the composition of the work. The central figure in the panel is the censor himself, on the point of conducting the lustral sacrifice, and holding a slightly more prominent position than the god Mars to whom the ceremony is dedicated.[76] Does that prominence in fact show that a specific historical occasion is carved on the relief? It

---

73. F. Castagnoli, *Arti Figurative*, 1 (1945), 181–196, stands as a solitary exception to this consensus, reckoning the *lustrum* scene to be a general representation of the censorship as an institution. But his view has been repeatedly and summarily dismissed. See, e.g., Kähler, *Seethiasos*, 10, 33; Coarelli, *DialArch*, 2 (1968), 338; Lattimore, *Marine Thiasos*, 17.

74. Cf. Zevi, in *Mélanges Heurgon*, II, 1062–1063. Hölscher, *ArchAnz*, 94 (1979), 338–339, reaffirms that a specific occasion is here commemorated, pointing to earlier Hellenistic examples. So also H. Meyer, *Kunst und Geschichte* (Munich, 1983), 88. But depictions of a sea-*thiasos* go well back into Greek history, occur in a variety of contexts and media, and few, if any, can be associated with any victories at sea; cf. Lattimore, *Marine Thiasos*, 28–49.

75. On the ceremony, with collection of evidence, see T. Mommsen, *Römisches Staatsrecht*³ (Leipzig, 1887), II.1, 412–413; H. Berve, *RE*, 13.2 (1927), 2046–2048; cf. R. M. Ogilvie, *JRS*, 51 (1961), 31–39. That this does constitute the central scene of the Paris frieze was established long ago by A. von Domaszewski, *Arch. v. Religionswiss.*, 12 (1909), 67–82.

76. The point is stressed by Kähler, *Seethiasos*, 28, 33, and followed consistently by others, e.g., Coarelli, *DialArch*, 2 (1968), 338; Wiseman, *Roman Studies*, 215.

does not seem immediately obvious that a Roman aristocrat would give himself priority over the god, thereby risking offense. A slight change in composition could have avoided the risk while still displaying the eminence of the man. Far better to suppose that the act receives top billing.

The case can be further strengthened. Although the *lustrum* ceremony forms the centerpiece of the Paris frieze, it is not the only event depicted. The figures on the left clearly represent the registration of citizens and the recording of property, a censorial act of vital importance for the enrollment of men in their military ranks or *classes*. Individuals in military attire on the relief call attention to that fact. The impressive seated figure with registration books on the extreme left may well be the censor himself.[77] Certainly the veiled individual carrying the *vexillum* on the right side of the frieze must be the censor. As Varro states explicitly, only one censor conducted the *lustrum* and the same man carried the *vexillum* to complete the ceremony.[78] A conclusion suggests itself: the frieze represents not a single event or moment but a selection of the principal functions attaching to the office of censorship. The institution here takes central place.[79]

It may not be too bold to propose that the same analysis be applied to the *thiasos* reliefs. The wedding of Poseidon and Amphitrite suggests not so much naval victory or personal triumph as a secure and tranquil control of the seas. Such an approach offers a different and broader but perhaps more illuminating perspective.

Too much ink has been spilled on identifying individual political

77. Kähler, *Seethiasos*, 27, prefers to see him as a *scriba*. For Torelli, *Typology and Structure*, 9–11, he is a *iurator*, and the third figure from the left is the censor. In view of his relatively inconspicuous position, that seems unlikely. Cf. the procedure in the *lex Iulia municipalis*, according to which the censor himself receives information from citizens and has it inscribed in the public records; *FIRA*, I, 13, lines 144–149.

78. Varro, *LL*, 6.87: *censores inter se sortiuntur uter lustrum faciat*; 6.93: *quod censorem exercitum centuriato constituit quinquennalem, cum lustraret et in urbem ad vexillum ducere debet.* Cf. Castagnoli, *Arti Figurative*, 1 (1945), 184. Torelli, *Typology and Structure*, 11–12, wrongly calls the bearer of the *vexillum* an *accensus velatus*. Kähler, *Seethiasos*, 28, realizes that it must be the censor, but makes him the second censor, lamely suggesting that the first might have temporarily handed him the *vexillum*.

79. To be sure, narrative art could depict a single individual at different times, as, e.g., Aeneas in the Tabula Iliaca Capitolina or Trajan on his column. But the *Ara* seems not so much a narrative in time as the portrayal of functions attaching to an office. Note, e.g., the absence of distinct facial features on the censor with the *vexillum*. No conclusions can be drawn from the face of the central censor, for that has been largely restored.

profit. And perhaps too much ink also in seeking a precise function for the *Ara*. The environs of the find and the representations of Mars and Neptune prompted suggestions that the monument might carry a cult image for one deity or the other or serve as a votive offering erected in front of one or another of their temples.[80] The matter does not admit of definitive solution. Since three sides of the structure contain reliefs of the Neptune-Amphitrite wedding, with accompanying figures and creatures of the sea, thereby framing and surrounding the *lustrum* scene, it appears that the latter is the *Ara*'s primary face. Hence it would seem inappropriate as a dedication for Neptune. The censorial ceremony involves a sacrifice to Mars, and the god, so it is generally asserted, appears on the relief. But the figure, if indeed it is Mars, does not hold central place in the scene. Censorship and censorial duties comprise the principal message of the panel. Homage to Mars is unlikely to have been the prime objective.

The religious context may be the wrong one. And the combination of two altogether different depictions remains unexplained. A more abstract symbolism may be at work here. The primary face calls attention to the censorship as an institution, the enrollment of citizens, the proper registration of men in their census classes, which lay at the basis of both political and military organization of the citizenry, and, above all, the closing of the *lustrum*, which signified successful completion of the task and a stable order in the state. The marine *thiasos*, by celebrating the nuptials of Neptune, expressed the joy that accompanied safe and secure control of the seas. When would such a double message have special meaning? The period of the *lustrum* was generally quite consistent from the mid–fourth century on. Censors almost always took office every five years, and even the occasional exceptions departed from the norm by only a year or two.[81] But a long gap did open up in the age of Sulla: no censors were elected between 86 and 70. The reasons for that anomaly need not here be pursued, but anomaly it was. The censors of 70/69, for the first time in over a decade and a half, performed all the censorial duties, conducted a vigorous tenure of office that included expulsion of

80. See above, n. 72. Kuttner, *Narrative and Event*, makes the intriguing suggestion that the monument honored both Mars and Neptune, and stood in a spot where all four sides could be seen, within range of both the temple of Neptune and the temple of Mars erected by D. Brutus.

81. See the list in J. Suohlati, *The Roman Censors: A Study on Social Structure* (Helsinki, 1963), 692–698; and cf. A. E. Astin, *Historia*, 31 (1982), 174–187.

unsavory members from the Roman senate, and solemnly closed the *lustrum* that betokened the return of traditional practice and system.[82] Two years after the closing of that *lustrum*, the Romans at last cleared the seas of piracy under the effective organization and skillful leadership of Cn. Pompeius Magnus.[83] The two former censors of 70/69, L. Gellius Publicola and Cn. Lentulus Clodianus, played a role in that campaign, perhaps more symbolic than real, but no less important for that. They had responsibility for protecting the Italian coastlines as legates of Pompey while he eliminated the pirate lairs elsewhere.[84] It does not follow that the monument was a personal tribute to Gellius and Lentulus who, so far as we know, had no direct naval encounters or victories, or indeed for Pompey, who had never held the censorship. A turn in the fortunes of the nation gains expression here. The censorial *lustrum* signified a revival of traditional procedures and internal order, the nuptial celebrations of Neptune represented the return of stability and control to the Mediterranean.[85]

The monument, in short, expressed sentiments and illustrated achievements that belonged to the nation as a whole. But a further question, more directly pertinent to this investigation, must be posed.

---

82. For sources on the censorship of 70/69, see Broughton, *Magistrates of the Roman Republic*, II, 126–127. It is doubtful whether the censors of 86 even completed the *lustrum*, in which case it had been twenty years since that ceremony was performed.

83. Sources in Broughton, *Magistrates of the Roman Republic*, II, 146.

84. Appian, *Mithr.* 95; Florus, 1.41.9.

85. Castagnoli, *Arti Figurative*, 1 (1945), 181–196, recognizes that the representation of the censorship alludes to the institution. But he identifies the Nereids in the marine *thiasos* as Nymphs and links the monument with the temple of Nymphs wherein censorial records were kept, a shrine burned down by Clodius in 58 and presumably restored thereafter, thus leading to the erection of the *Ara*. The conjecture fails to convince, both on grounds of a dubious identification of the Nereids and Nymphs and the absence of any completed *lustrum* between 69 and 28; see Augustus, *RG*, 8.2. A *terminus ante quem* for the census relief has often been found in 107, with the claim that the Marian army reforms rendered the military census obsolete; e.g., Torelli, *Typology and Structure*, 14. But Marius' reforms extended the range of volunteers without affecting the structure of the census; cf. E. Gabba, *Republican Rome: The Army and the Allies* (Berkeley, Calif., 1976), 13–15; P. A. Brunt, *Italian Manpower, 225 B.C.–A.D. 14* (Oxford, 1971), 406–410. Efforts to find a *terminus ante* or *post* on the basis of the military uniforms has brought widely divergent opinions and thus cannot serve as a reliable criterion; cf. the contrasting conclusions of Zevi, in *Mélanges Heurgon*, II, 1063–1065; and Hölscher, *ArchAnz*, 94 (1979), 340–341. Stylistic criteria generally, despite the confidence of some, can hardly provide distinctions between the later second and middle first centuries B.C. For an attempt along these lines, see Kähler, *Seethiasos*, 30–32.

How does the structure illuminate Roman attitudes toward Hellenic creative activity?

The two reliefs, on initial inspection, leave very different impressions. The marine *thiasos* is thoroughly Hellenistic in theme, conception, and execution. The flow and movement of the overlapping figures—gods, Nereids, Tritons, and imaginative sea creatures—recreate the vibrant marriage procession of Poseidon and Amphitrite so familiar to the Greeks. By contrast, the census scene appears stiff and stylized, with figures taking formal roles and performing ritual acts. The refined skill of the carver, so evident in the Neptune relief, seems quite distinct from the ostensibly more rudimentary product of the *lustrum* relief. One might be tempted to infer that the one set of reliefs emerged from a Greek workshop long experienced in the practice of Hellenistic sculpture, the other from a less capable artist trained in Italy or from a Greek master unfamiliar with the institutions of Rome.[86] Neither inference would be valid. In fact, there are close correspondences in composition and treatment between the two friezes, parallels and echoes not only in placement of figures but even in depiction of faces. There can be no question that the census relief and the thiasos scene belong together as a unified idea.[87] Why then the different feelings evoked by the two segments? It will not do to speak of inferior craftsmanship or Italian as against Greek training. No evidence attests even the existence of Roman sculptors, and by the late Republic, Greek artists were thick on the ground in Rome. The notion of apprenticeship in Italian workshops is pure fantasy. The links between the two parts of the monument demand a different thesis: the one was molded to set off the other.[88] The differences between them represent a conscious decision.

---

86. So, for instance, among standard works, Strong, *Roman Art*², 52.

87. See now the sensitive treatment by Kuttner, in *Narrative and Event*. Kähler, *Seethiasos*, 29–30, unduly stresses the contrast between the two parts. P. Zanker, *The Power of Images in the Age of Augustus* (Ann Arbor, Mich., 1988), 12–14, pronounces unconvincingly that this "must have had a disturbing effect."

88. The two friezes, as it now appears, were carved from two different types of marble, the Neptune scene evidently from the East, whether Greece or Asia Minor; Meyer, *Kunst und Geschichte*, 87–88; Kuttner, in *Narrative and Event*, consequently sees the marine *thiasos* reliefs as war booty taken by M. Antonius in the course of his pirate campaigns, to which the *lustrum* relief was added as a subsequent composition to harmonize with it and to publicize the feats of the sponsor. The latter hypothesis does not require the former. It is unlikely that Antonius, whose campaigns confined themselves to chasing pirates in Cilicia, would have had occasion to acquire this monument as booty.

The figures on the census relief may be somewhat awkward in posture, rigid in stance, and stilted in appearance, but the institution in which they took part was recognizably Roman. And the rigidity itself evoked participation in a time-honored tradition, passed on unchanged by the *maiores* and now resumed in faithful and precise fashion. The very archaic feel of the relief, accentuated by contrast with the dynamic *thiasos*, gave the sense of a ceremony continuous with the antique past.[89]

Those who commissioned the monument sent off signals of subtle but significant import. Greek artists produced the work, as was clear to anyone who viewed the *thiasos* scene. But the association of that scene with the *lustrum* frieze made a more telling point. The two reliefs are very different in conception, appearance, and subject matter, yet plainly linked in structure and purpose. The contrast is important. The festive gaiety of the one plays off against the solemnity and formalism of the other. The Romans here gave voice to what, in their perception at least, expressed distinctive characteristics of the nation: *gravitas* of demeanor and adherence to tradition. That expression did not, in any sense, involve disparagement of the Greeks. The magnificent marine *thiasos* demonstrated Rome's adaptation of a purely Hellenic subject and composition to enunciate its own achievement. And the census frieze had employed Hellenic artists to produce a purely Roman scene that conveyed the values of the *mos maiorum*. The combination gave real force to the monument, a creation of exceptional imagination and intelligence.

Republican portraiture stands next in the investigation, a genre regularly reckoned as exemplifying the peculiarly Roman character. Numerous busts convey representations of the rugged, grim, and even ravaged faces of Romans, suggesting in many cases a lifetime of toilsome service to the state, selfless devotion, and hard-earned experience. They summon up the *mos maiorum*, the endurance of tradition through the labors of its champions. Those values are appropriately displayed in the tough and uncompromising visages that glare at the viewer of Republican busts.

The genre is striking and memorable, though an appropriate term for it has eluded scholars and students. "Realism" gives only a faint sense, and a misleading one at that. To describe the objective as accurate rendering of physiognomic detail is quite inadequate. The particulars

89. For a similar view, see the excellent and incisive comments of Kuttner, *Narrative and Event*.

often seem more than "realistic." Wrinkled, creased, haggard countenances, blemishes and disfigurement, protruding ears, and toothless
gazes characterize many of the busts. The "warts-and-all" treatment has
demanded another term, now accepted as conventional: "verism." The
style would appear to set off Romans in a separate category, insisting
upon their individuality through physical distinctiveness.

A fundamental question arises. Is "verism," in fact, the manifestation
of a peculiarly Roman spirit? The question needs to be faced before
larger inferences are drawn. It plunges one inescapably into a tangled
issue on which so much has been written: the roots of this artistic mode.
Some derive it from Italian sources and judge it an authentically native
product; others stress external influences, thereby diluting its force as
reflection of Roman values. In view of the extensive scholarship, the
issue can be treated with some brevity—but it must be confronted.

One can assign the origins of veristic portraiture to a solidly Roman
institution: the practice of bearing masks of one's ancestors in the
funeral processions of Roman *nobiles*.[90] Some celebrated literary texts
provide impetus for the reconstruction. Polybius reports that images of
ancestors were set up in a conspicuous place in the home, encased in a
wooden structure, and then brought out at funeral ceremonies, where
they were decorated and borne by family members who most closely
resembled the originals. The image itself was a mask, *prosopon*, with as
near a likeness as possible to the deceased.[91] The information is reinforced by Pliny, writing two centuries later but alluding to a time long
before his own day. He laments that *imagines*, which had once most
accurately conveyed the features of their subjects, were now obsolete.
In the age of the *maiores*, wax models of faces were set up in cupboards

---

90. For discussions of the evidence, see G. Kaschnitz von Weinberg, *Ausgewählte
Schriften*, II (1965), 43–47; A. N. Zadoks-Josephus Jitta, *Ancestral Portraiture in Rome and
the Art of the Last Century of the Republic* (Amsterdam, 1932), 22–88; O. Vessberg, *Studien
zur Kunstgeschichte der römischen Republik* (Lund, 1941), 97–108; B. Schweitzer, *Die
Bildniskunst der römischen Republik* (Weimar, 1948), 19–33. The strongest case for the
influence of funerary masks upon Republican portraiture was made by H. Drerup, *MdI*,
87 (1980), 81–129. See also, more recently and more briefly, D. Jackson, *Greece and Rome*,
34 (1987), 32–47.

91. Polyb. 6.53.4–6: τιθέασι τὴν εἰκόνα τοῦ μεταλλάξαντος εἰς τὸν ἐπιφανέστατον
τόπον τῆς οἰκίας, ξύλινα ναΐδια περιτιθέντες. ἡ δ᾽εἰκών ἐστι πρόσωπον εἰς ὁμοιό-
τητα διφερόντως ἐξειργασμένον καὶ κατὰ τὴν πλάσιν καὶ κατὰ τὴν ὑπογραφήν . . .
ἐπάν τε τῶν οἰκείων μεταλλάξῃ τις ἐπιφανής, ἄγουσιν εἰς τὴν ἐκφοράν, περιτιθέντες ὡς ὁμοιοτάτοις εἶναι δοκοῦσι κατά τε τὸ μέγεθος καὶ τὴν ἄλλην περι-
κοπήν.

and paraded at funerals, when the deceased would be accompanied by the *imagines* of his entire clan.[92] Ancestral images held a place of high prominence in the political ideology of the Republic. Sallust adverts to Rome's heroes of the Hannibalic War, asserting that Fabius, Scipio, and other worthies declared themselves inspired to feats of virtue by gazing upon *maiorum imagines*.[93] The idea that public figures were held to account by the *imagines* of their forefathers, who stared at them with approval or reproach, recurs repeatedly in texts of the late Republic and after.[94] The representations of distinguished ancestors who had held high office, so it could be claimed, were almost enough in themselves to promote undeserving descendants to positions of authority.[95] Individuals might even appropriate images from related families or feel embarrassment at those that seemed not to correspond to the dignity of the *gens*.[96] *Novi homines* labored under a severe handicap when they could not boast a string of *imagines* that attested to their predecessors' public service. Some, of course, made a virtue of necessity, affirming that their personal qualities outstripped the *imagines* of those unworthy of their distinguished forebears.[97]

The institution is clear and significant, but no text informs us of what these *imagines* looked like. Polybius' evident allusion to a mask, *prosopon*, with his emphasis on the close likeness to the features of the deceased, and Pliny's reference to wax images have given rise to the theory that death masks were employed to commemorate the departed and that such masks, providing an accurate reproduction of grim physiognomic features, served as models for veristic portraiture.[98] The physical evidence does little to advance the hypothesis. A few extant

92. Pliny, *NH*, 35.4–7: *Imaginum quidem pictura, qua maxime similes in aevum propagabantur figurae, in totum exolevit . . . aliter apud maiores in atriis haec erant, quae spectarentur . . . expressi cera vultus singulis disponebantur armariis, ut essent imagines, quae comitarentur gentilicia funera, semperque defuncto aliquo totus aderat familiae eius qui umquam fuerat populus.*

93. Sallust, *Iug.* 4.5: *quom maiorum imagines intuerentur, vehementissume sibi animum ad virtutem accendi.*

94. E.g., Cic. *Pro Mur.* 88; *Pro Sulla*, 88; *Pro Planc.* 51; *Pro Caelio*, 33–34; *De Orat.* 2.225–226; Livy, 30.45.7; Pliny, *Epist.* 5.17.6, 8.10.3. Other references in G. Lahusen, *MdI*, 92 (1985), 265–274.

95. Cf. Cic. *In Pis.* 1.1: *obrepsisti ad honores errore hominum, commendatione fumosarum imaginum*; *Pro Planc.* 18; Horace, *Sat.* 1.6.15–17.

96. Pliny, *NH*, 35.8.

97. E.g., Cic. *De Leg. Agrar.* 2.100; Val. Max. 2.10.8; Sallust, *Iug.* 85.25, 85.29, 85.38; Plut. *Mar.* 9.2. This contrast becomes a commonplace later; cf. Seneca, *Epist.* 44.5; *De Ben.* 3.28.2; Martial, 2.90.5–8, 4.40.1–4, 5.20.5–7; Juvenal, 8.1–32.

98. See works cited above, n. 90.

masks and half masks, mostly of plaster, with one or two in stucco or wax, attest to the casting of masks, some, but by no means all, of which are death masks.[99] An isolated example of a terra-cotta bust, now in the Louvre, evidently employed a death mask as model (Plate 4).[100] One can point to a number of heads whose features have some of the characteristics of death masks, notably sunken temples and cheeks, with protruding cheekbones and sharply defined jaw lines that almost give the impression of a skull.[101] But nothing shows or suggests that death masks served as *imagines* of ancestors proudly installed in the home and paraded at funerals. Certain of them were cast from the faces of children or quite young persons who would not readily do the job as ancestors.[102] Some grave reliefs do depict busts set in cupboards, which evidently represent ancestral *imagines*, none of which is an obvious reworking of a death mask.[103] The celebrated Barberini statue portrays a Roman *nobilis* holding two busts, doubtless ancestral *imagines* and probably his father and grandfather. Neither has the least resemblance to a death mask (Plate 5).[104] Indeed it is not easy to imagine that anyone would wish to place in the atrium of the house such grisly and forbidding objects—more likely to repel than to inspire the young. An anecdote in Quintilian makes the point with clarity: a wax mask taken from the corpse of an old man, when brought into the courtroom to assist the case of his widow, produced instead mirth and ridicule, undermining the advocate's eloquence with its unsightliness.[105] The connection between death masks and ancestral portraits is quite tenuous.

More tenuous still is the putative association between death masks and veristic portraiture. Fundamental differences stand in the way. *Rigor mortis* sets in rapidly after death, causing cheeks to sag and giving prominence to the bone structure of the skull but also smoothing away wrinkles, lines, and blemishes in the face. This effect hardly corresponds to the obsession with such defects and signs of age evident in

99. See Drerup, *MdI*, 87 (1980), 85–95, with plates 34–42, 44–49.

100. Zadoks, *Ancestral Portraiture*, 48–49; Drerup, *MdI*, 87 (1980), 99 and plate 50.2. Drerup, 98, plate 50.1, also puts some small busts from the "House of Menander" in Pompeii in this category, without clear justification.

101. So Zadoks, *Ancestral Portraiture*, 49–57, with plates VIII–XIV; Schweitzer, *Die Bildniskunst*, plates 11–14; Drerup, *MdI*, 87 (1980), 126–127, with plates 53–54. Some of them, in fact, bear little resemblance to death masks.

102. Drerup, *MdI*, 87 (1980), plates 34, 36–37.

103. Zadoks, *Ancestral Portraiture*, plates IV–V.

104. Drerup, *MdI*, 87 (1980), plate 51; Lahusen, *MdI*, 92 (1985), plate 106.

105. Quint. 6.1.40.

many veristic busts.[106] Further, the casting of death masks and the creation of portraits in bronze or marble were very different matters. Even the sculptor who reportedly invented the process of making plaster casts from actual faces and employing them as models for bronze statuary did not produce anything like veristic portraits.[107] The plaster masks and half masks that have survived do not much bolster the case. None stems from the Republic; almost all belong to the second or third century A.D. Very few, in fact, come from Italy at all; North Africa and Egypt supplied the greater part. Hence any conclusions about artistic developments in Republican Rome or Italy on the basis of this testimony is fragile in the extreme. Further, all the masks come from graves. Whether they possessed any function outside that context or in any realm beyond the private one remains entirely unknown.[108] The hypothesis provides no secure basis from which to operate. That the death masks furnished inspiration for verism, thereby stamping it with a native character remains in the sphere of sheer speculation.

An indigenous source for the style can be sought also among the Etruscans. Heads on Etruscan sarcophagi and on cinerary urns offer parallels for some late Republican portraits, especially on funerary reliefs.[109] The resemblances seem evident enough and are hardly coincidental. One may compare for instance the Etruscan head of Lars Pulena on a sarcophagus from Tarquinia with the male figure on a Roman funerary relief now in the Museo Nuovo of the Capitoline Museum (Plate 6). The similarities in conception and technique are demonstrable.[110] What is not demonstrable, however, is that Etruscan workshops supplied the prototypes and stimulus that translated into the late Republican sculpture of Rome.

A number of caveats need to be issued. The relative dates of Etruscan

---

106. As is acknowledged by Zadoks, *Ancestral Portraiture*, 47–48, 83–84.

107. Pliny, *NH*, 35.153. So, rightly, R. R. R. Smith, *JRS*, 71 (1981), 32.

108. Doubts about an association between masks and veristic portraiture have often been expressed. See Vessberg, *Studien zur Kunstgeschichte*, 97–108; A. Boethius, *Acta Archaeologica*, 13 (1942), 226–235; G. M. A. Richter, *JRS*, 45 (1955), 40; J. D. Breckenridge, *Likeness: A Conceptual History of Ancient Portraiture* (Evanston, Ill., 1968), 146–152; U. W. Hiesinger, *ANRW*, I.4 (1973), 814–818; Smith, *JRS*, 71 (1981), 31–32; Lahusen, *MdI*, 92 (1985), 262–265.

109. Discussion in Vessberg, *Studien zur Kunstgeschichte*, 175–208; Kaschnitz, *Ausgewählte Schriften*, II, 28–54; E. K. Gazda, *ANRW*, I.4 (1973), 855–870. An extensive collection of grave reliefs from various Italian sites can now be consulted in H. G. Frenz, *Römische Grabreliefs in Mittel- und Süditalien* (Rome, 1985).

110. See Gazda, *ANRW*, I.4 (1973), 866–867, with plates 6, 8, 10.

funerary figures and Roman veristic representations cannot be fixed with certainty. The tombs of Chiusi, Perugia, and Volterra, whence come many of the relevant carvings, are dated generally to the second and first centuries.[111] The extant Roman busts probably belong, in almost all cases, to the first century B.C. But survival of the busts alone is relevant. The Romans did not turn to portraits in marble, the durable material that has allowed examples to survive in significant numbers, until the late Republic. We know that Rome housed a substantial amount of statuary in the second century which has not endured and whose character can only be guessed at, leaving open the question of whether style and technique traveled from Etruria to Rome or vice versa. Etruscan workshops may have been the recipients rather than the creators of this form of portraiture.[112] More significant, however, is the fact that late Etruscan art had come heavily under the influence of Hellenistic portraiture and can hardly be reckoned as an independent and distinctive source of inspiration.[113]

Recourse has sometimes been had to terra-cotta heads of Etruscan and central Italian provenance which were employed as votive offerings. Ostensibly the case has some force. The very practice of offering votive busts seems peculiarly Italian. Isolated heads have no parallel in the Greek world. Do such objects then, some of which are of fine craftsmanship, lie behind Roman portraiture?[114] The testimony allows for no such conclusion. Dating of the votive heads has divided scholars. A broad survey finds them to range all the way from the fifth century to the end of the first century B.C.[115] And they exhibit considerable variety rather than a homogeneous tradition that could mold or stimulate a style. Very few of them, in fact, show anything resembling realistic

111. See Smith, *JRS*, 71 (1981), 30–31, with bibliography.

112. Cf. Richter, *JRS*, 45 (1955), 40; Smith, *JRS*, 71 (1981), 31.

113. Breckenridge, *Likeness*, 160–161; idem, *ANRW*, I.4 (1973), 848–849; P. Zanker, in Zanker, ed., *Hellenismus in Mittelitalien*, (Göttingen, 1976), II, 594. This is not to deny the force of Gazda's arguments, *ANRW*, I.4 (1973), 855–870, on the parallels in design and carving techniques between Roman and Etruscan examples. But these do not prove that Etruscan artists took the lead. And even Gazda concedes the strongly Hellenistic elements in the heads she discusses.

114. See Kaschnitz, *Ausgewählte Schriften*, II, 5–19. The extensive collection of such heads in the Museo Gregoriana Etrusco in Rome is thoroughly treated by G. Hafner, *MdI*, 72 (1965), 41–61, with plates 14–25; and idem, *MdI*, 73–74 (1966–67), 29–52, with plates 5–18. A fuller survey of the votive heads in Italy by S. Steingräber, *MdI*, 87 (1980), 215–253, with plates 69–80.

115. Steingräber, *MdI*, 87 (1980), 222–227.

portraiture that could serve as a model for Republican verism. It is, indeed, easy to detect Hellenistic influence in many of the later ones, thereby vitiating any notion of an undiluted native tradition. Few, if any, suggest actual portraits of individuals; their purpose was to propitiate or give thanks to divinities through an offering that substituted for rather than depicted an individual.[116] The small minority that evoke some "veristic" suggestions are probably contemporary with late Republican portraiture and cannot be cited as its forerunners.[117] Votive busts may themselves be inherently Italian, but that does not account for the peculiar character of veristic portraits.

In consequence, some have postulated an external source, namely the kingdom of Egypt. No small number of Egyptian portrait busts exist, carved from native materials—basalt, granite, or other hard stone—displaying characteristics that approximate the late Republican veristic style. Hence a case can be made for the influence of Egypt, fostered by commercial and diplomatic contacts between that land and Rome, accompanied perhaps by the migration of Egyptian artists to the western power.[118] Resemblances and parallels can hardly be gainsaid. Any selection of examples will make them clear enough (see Plate 7).[119]

Yet the inference that Egyptian art served as forerunner for Roman verism runs into difficulties and ambiguities. For one thing, the art in question is late Egyptian sculpture, developed in the Ptolemaic era and hence thoroughly permeated by Greek influence. Native traditions endured, of course, as in the rigorous frontality and conventional posturing of the bodies. But Hellenistic features in rendering of the heads are plain. It would be misleading to call it an Egyptian style; better to reckon it as Greco-Egyptian.[120] The proper context, therefore, is that of the Mediterranean world in the late Hellenistic period and not an exclusively Egyptian one. Indeed, systematic, consistent, and significant

116. Steingräber, *MdI*, 87 (1980), 234–236, 246–253. See, e.g., plates 71.3–4, 72.1–2, 73.2, 77.3; Kaschnitz, *Ausgewählte Schriften*, II, plates 7.1–2, 8.1–2.

117. See, e.g., Kaschnitz, *Ausgewählte Schriften*, II, plates 9.1, 11, 15, 17.

118. A brief discussion, with illustrations, appears in Drerup, *Ägyptische Bildnisköpfe griechischer und römischer Zeit* (Münster, 1950). A fuller collection may be found in B. von Bothmer, *Egyptian Sculpture of the Late Period, 700 B.C.–A.D. 100* (Brooklyn, N.Y., 1960). The best case is made by A. Adriani, *MdI*, 77 (1970), 72–109, with plates 32–51.

119. See, e.g., von Bothmer, *Egyptian Sculpture*, plates 94–95, 97, 99–100, 104, 109–110, 117–119; Adriani, *MdI*, 77 (1970), plates 33.1–2, 36.1–4, 38, 39, 46.1–4.

120. Cf. the summary in Richter, *JRS*, 45 (1955), 40–44; Breckenridge, *Likeness*, 165–178; idem, *ANRW*, I.4 (1973), 849–851.

contact between Rome and Egypt comes only at the very end of the Republic. Hence, Egyptian influence upon Roman portraiture is an unlikely proposition—as is the reverse proposition.[121] Egyptian artists, working within a long-established indigenous tradition, with the super-imposition of Hellenism in the ruling circles and elite of Alexandria, had no need of Roman guidance on this score. Nor do we have record of Egyptian artists among the mainland and eastern Greek migrants who worked in Rome. Moreover, the chronology is controversial. The Egyptian heads that possess some "veristic" qualities have generated varied datings that range from the fourth century B.C. to the first century A.D. or even later. There is nothing to show that any of them preceded the emergence of this style in Rome.[122] And there is little likelihood that Rome looked for inspiration to Egypt.

The style of radical realism in Rome did not emerge *de novo*. Antecedents may be difficult to identify in Italy, but they abound in the Greek world. Late Hellenistic portraiture, as is widely recognized, possesses characteristics strongly analogous to and sometimes indistinguishable from the products of Republican Rome.

Gems and coins offer testimony in the first instance. A number of gem portraits, some signed by Greek artists and datable to the third and second centuries, show realistic and unflattering features. So also do several coin portraits in that period, depicting eastern rulers for whom the artists produced lifelike and homely representations.[123] Something like the veristic style, therefore, was practiced by Greek artists outside the context of and prior to the extant series of late Republican Roman busts. The same phenomenon may be observed in marble portraits. Naturalistic representations of middle-aged and elderly men have turned up in various sites in mainland Greece, the islands, Asia Minor, and Egypt.[124] A notable example is provided by the bust of an Athenian priest from the agora, presenting an aspect quite evocative of Republican

121. For a roster of scholars who held one or the other of these positions, see Adriani, *MdI*, 77 (1970), 98.

122. Cf. Breckenridge, *Likeness*, 167–176; Smith, *JRS*, 71 (1981), 32–33.

123. See examples and illustrations in Richter, *JRS*, 45 (1955), 44–45. For R. R. R. Smith, *Hellenistic Royal Portraits* (Oxford, 1988), 113–114, the realistic individualization of Pontic and Bactrian kings represents an effort to distinguish themselves from Greek monarchs.

124. See, e.g., G. Hafner, *Späthellenistische Bildnisplastik* (Berlin, 1954), plates 25–26, 28. Cf. Richter, *JRS*, 45 (1955), 45; S. Howard, *CSCA*, 3 (1970), 106–112; Zanker, *Hellenismus in Mittelitalien*, II, 582–584.

representations (Plate 8). To reckon this famous piece as itself influenced by Roman sculptural practice is circular and implausible.[125] Further, one may cite a series of heads from Delos, certainly carved before 88 B.C. when the island was devastated by Mithridates, which approximate or foreshadow the style of Republican verism.[126] To be sure, most of the Delian busts, and indeed many of those from elsewhere in the eastern Mediterranean, were portraits of Romans and Italians, and presumably in a style chosen by the patron. But they were fashioned by Greek artists working with Hellenic traditions, conventions, and experience.

None of this evidence should be taken to imply that late Republican sculpture was simply a branch of Hellenistic art. Analogies, parallels, and similarities can be discerned without difficulty. Yet the "veristic" visages of Roman senior citizens, weathered and wrinkled, bearing the facial folds in which one can read long years of experience, possess a consistency and identity that set them—or most of them—apart. A range and variety of artistic styles characterize late Hellenistic portraiture; an uncompromising realism predominates among the Romans.[127] It is, however, essential to emphasize that late Republican portraiture sits in a Mediterranean-wide context and that Greek modes and conventions defined that context. Greek artists set the patterns and indeed produced the works that we label Roman portraits. But the matter does not end there. The familiar features that denote Roman "verism" were no more dictated by Hellenic practices than by death masks, terra-cotta votives, or Egyptian statuary.[128] A central question needs to be asked:

125. See E. Harrison, *The Athenian Agora, I: Portrait Sculpture* (Princeton, N.J., 1953), 84–85, with plate 3: "In the Agora priest we have before us Roman realism in a Greek translation." Followed, e.g., by Breckenridge, *ANRW*, I.4 (1973), 853. Rightly countered by Stewart, *Attika*, 80–84, and 96, n. 75: "Republican verism must be Greek realism in Roman translation."

126. The Delian heads are treated in detail by C. Michalowski, *Delos XIII: Les portraits hellénistiques et rómaines* (Paris, 1932), passim; J. Marcadé, *Au Musée de Delos* (Paris, 1969), 308–354; and see Stewart, *Attika*, 65–78, with plates 18–20d.

127. This is not to suggest that Romans were unaffected by other late Hellenistic influences, e.g. "Neoclassicism"; cf. Stewart, *Greek Sculpture*, 94–96, 229–232, 303–306. But discussion here concentrates on those aspects in which the Romans endeavored to express their own distinctiveness. On late Hellenistic portrait heads, see the valuable collection of photographs, with description and analysis, in Hafner, *Bildnisplastik*, passim. A comparable assemblage is in E. Buschor, *Das hellenistische Bildnis* (Munich, 1949). Roman busts can be conveniently consulted in Schweitzer, *Bildniskunst*, passim. Cf. the general remarks of A. Stewart, in E. D. Reeder, ed., *Hellenistic Art in the Walters Art Gallery* (Baltimore, 1988), 35–38.

128. Cf. Breckenridge, *Likeness*, 178–180. Zanker, *Hellenismus in Mittelitalien*, II, 581–584, may go too far in assimilating the Roman style to Hellenistic forebears. Cf. also

what induced Republican Romans to accentuate this particular aspect of Hellenistic art and thereby to make it emblematic of their own self-representation?

A matter of chronology intrudes before one can proceed. When did the Romans adopt or adapt that harshly naturalistic style known as "verism"? None of the surviving busts can be placed with certainty prior to the first century B.C., and many scholars therefore date the inception to the last generation of the Republic. But caution must be exercised. Judgment depends upon surviving examples, and survival in turn largely corresponds to the material in which the objects were worked. The durability of marble portraits gives them a decided advantage, and Romans evidently turned to that medium in consistent fashion only in the late Republic. Yet we know that they produced statuary (or had statuary produced) in substantial numbers during the middle Republic and particularly in the second century B.C.[129] No sound reason requires us to believe that the sculptured heads of second-century Romans possessed countenances altogether different from those in the age of Cicero.

Statuary, in any case, does not constitute the only evidence. Coin portraits offer some tempting items for reconstruction and speculation. The earliest known Roman represented on a coin is T. Quinctius Flamininus on a series of gold staters circa 196 B.C. (Plate 9).[130] The issue is unparalleled, lacking clear and helpful Roman comparanda. Since the coins were minted in the Greek world and the portrait was plainly engraved by a Greek artist, they are generally dismissed as irrelevant for our knowledge of Roman portraiture.[131] Hellenic parallels, such as the numismatic portrayals of Macedonian monarchs, notably Philip V and Perseus, have seemed more appropriate.[132] Yet the dismissal may be hasty. The staters were produced in the immediate aftermath of the Second Macedonian War, in which Flamininus had led Roman forces to victory over Philip V. It does not seem the most obvious proposition that Greek craftsmen, celebrating the victory and cultivating the favor

---

E. Berger, *Eikones: Studien zum griechischen und römischen Bildnis, Antike Kunst,* 12 (1980), 67. See the corrections by Smith, *JRS,* 71 (1981), 33–34; idem, *Hellenistic Royal Portraits,* 115–116, 125–128—who, however, tends to dilute the association to an unnecessary and misleading degree.

129. See above, Chapter 3, passim.

130. Crawford, *Roman Republican Coinage* I, 544. Reproductions in Breckenridge, *ANRW,* I.4 (1973), 175, fig. 1; Vollenweider, *Porträtgemmen,* plate 45.2–3.

131. E.g., Breckenridge, *ANRW,* I.4 (1973), 835: "outside the field either of Roman numismatics or Republican art." Cf. Crawford, *Roman Republican Coinage,* I, 548.

132. Cf. Breckenridge, *Likeness,* 153; F. Felten, *JOAI,* 56 (1985), 109–110.

of the Roman, would present him in the likeness of his defeated foe. The images show some similarities but greater differences. Flamininus, indeed, though not in the "veristic" mode of the late Republic, has features, at least in some of the staters, that are quite different from the conventionally heroic and idealized depictions of the early Hellenistic kings. The unkempt hair and haphazard growth of beard, the pointed nose and weak chin present a posture rather less than entirely flattering.[133] It is perhaps noteworthy that the inscription on the reverse of the coins, *T. Quincti*, has Latin rather than Greek lettering. Flamininus may have played some role in the direction of the portrait. The Greek engraver, at the least, had an impression of how Romans expected to be represented. The image was not altogether dictated by Hellenistic models.

Coin portraits produced in Rome, by contrast, do not begin to appear until the late second century, and then they do not represent contemporary personages. Depiction by moneyers of semilegendary ancestors naturally produced idealized images, such as the heads of Kings Titus Tatius Sabinus, Numa Pompilius, and Ancus Marcius on the coins of their putative descendants in the early first century.[134] In similar fashion, M. Brutus, a generation later, called attention to his forebears, L. Junius Brutus and C. Servilius Ahala, the celebrated tyrannicides of the early Republic, by setting them respectively on obverse and reverse of his coins—with no trace of realistic countenances.[135] That practice would be expected, even inevitable, in the depiction of storied ancestors from the distant past. When coin portraits of more recent predecessors enter the scene, however, in the mid–first century, the difference is notable and noteworthy. Realistic features become common, and unflattering types more frequent.[136] Q. Pompeius Rufus, probably the tribune of 52, put on his coins his maternal and paternal grandfathers, the two consuls of 83, one of whom was the future

133. So, rightly, Smith, *Hellenistic Royal Portraits*, 126.

134. Crawford, *Roman Republican Coinage*, no. 344.1–3, 346.1, 346.3–4, 404.1. A later representation of Numa is no. 446.1.

135. Crawford, *Roman Republican Coinage*, no. 433.

136. One must exclude from consideration the coins of Cn. Cornelius Blasio in the late second century (Crawford, *Roman Republican Coinage*, no. 296), whose obverses present an idealized figure, with universal features, often taken as Scipio Africanus; so, e.g., M. Bieber, *ANRW*, I.4 (1973), 878–879. If the later Scipiones themselves did not put Africanus on their coins, there is no reason to suppose that Blasio did. The image more likely represents a god; Breckenridge, *ANRW*, I.4 (1973), 836; Crawford, 310–311. See the photograph in Vollenweider, *Porträtgemmen*, plate 10.9.

dictator Sulla. Their visages show a tendency to greater naturalism, although they are hardly unflattering.[137] At about the same time, however, the moneyer C. Coelius Caldus, probably quaestor in 50, represented his ancestor, the consul of 94, with a variety of appearances on his coins, all of them quite individualistic, and several of them rather homely.[138] The great hero M. Claudius Marcellus, consul in 222, appears on coins of P. Lentulus Marcellinus in 50 as a gaunt figure with receding hairline (Plate 10).[139] More "veristic" still are the depictions of A. Postumius Albinus, consul in 99, by his descendant, the consul designate of 42. Postumius' lined face and stern expression closely approximate those on the marble busts of this period.[140] Similarly, the moneyer L. Livineius Regulus in 42 showed two ancestors on his coins sporting furrowed brows and long noses.[141] Most striking are the issues of C. Antius Restio, moneyer in 47, who depicted his father in uncompromising ugliness (Plate 11).[142] One may observe with some interest that that harsh style in the mid–first century extended even to representations of mythical ancestors, as with the head of Ancus Marcius on the coinage of L. Philippus, moneyer in 56.[143]

The initial appearance of veristic portraiture on coins in the last generation of the Republic is not itself decisive for chronology. The fact is that no coin portraits of any real person appeared prior to that time. Hence no conclusion can legitimately be drawn about the inception of the style. Die engravers doubtless employed portrait busts as models whenever they were available. There is nothing to indicate that the manner of depiction would have been significantly different had they portrayed real personages in the second century.

Engraved gem stones provide a large corpus of evidence. The heads

---

137. Crawford, *Roman Republican Coinage*, no. 434.1; Vollenweider, *Porträtgemmen*, plate 36.7–10.

138. Crawford, *Roman Republican Coinage*, no. 437.1–4; Vollenweider, *Porträtgemmen*, plates 22.4–8, 23.1–12, 24.1–8.

139. Crawford, *Roman Republican Coinage*, no. 439.1; Vollenweider, *Porträtgemmen*, plates 78.5–6, 83.4–6.

140. Crawford, *Roman Republican Coinage*, no. 450.3; Vollenweider, *Porträtgemmen*, plates 33.67, 34.5–12.

141. Crawford, *Roman Republican Coinage*, no. 494.26–31; Vollenweider, *Porträtgemmen*, plates 56.4, 57.1–15.

142. Crawford, *Roman Republican Coinage*, no. 455.1; Vollenweider, *Porträtgemmen*, plates 16.1–6, 24.10–11, 89.3; cf. Smith, *Hellenistic Royal Portraits*, 116–117.

143. Crawford, *Roman Republican Coinage*, no. 425.1; Vollenweider, *Porträtgemmen*, plates 63.3–6, 78.7.

on Republican gems, often of excellent quality, constitute a range of styles and modes. Some are clearly conventional, highly stylized, or idealized, but a remarkable proportion present unattractive countenances, sharp, exaggerated features, hooked noses, cropped hair or bald heads, folds, and wrinkles.[144] The absence of inscriptions renders dating impossible. The similarity of depictions on these stones to those on late Republican busts and coins has placed them generally in the first century B.C. But the reasoning is circular and unconvincing. One cannot rule out the possibility that some of these gems, perhaps many of them, belong to the previous century.

The earlier date can only be hypothesized, not proved.[145] But a combination of items inclines in that direction. Honorific statues had a long history in Rome, with a markedly increasing number during the first part of the second century.[146] The sculptors were in all known cases Greek, and the Hellenic experience dominated that craft. Greek artists had an established tradition of realistic portraiture, already entrenched by the second century and especially prevalent in late Hellenistic art. The fact (if it is a fact) that extant Roman realistic portraiture begins only with the the first century may be due in the first instance to the use of marble, in the second to numismatic convention. Neither implies a change in aesthetic style or sensibility. Verism may very well have its roots in the encounter of Roman and Greek culture that played so vital a role in the second century.[147]

That conclusion adds still greater significance to the question of central concern here. What disposed the Romans to fasten upon that intense form of realism to transmit their own image? And what implica-

144. Vollenweider, *Porträtgemmen*, passim, e.g., plates 18.1, 18.5, 19.1–4, 20.2, 20.5, 22.1–3.

145. So, for instance, the attempt of Hafner, *Das Bildnis des Q. Ennius: Studien zur römischen Porträtskunst des 2. Jahrhunderts v. Chr.* (Baden-Baden, 1968), 22–28, to place the so-called Postumius Albinus head from the Louvre in the mid–second century is entirely speculative. The identification of the head itself, from which the argument proceeds, depends upon resemblance to a coin portrait of A. Postumius Albinus; Crawford, *Roman Republican Coinage*, no. 450.3. But the resemblance itself is not strong, and the rest of the argument has little force. The contention that this bust represents Cato the Censor is equally speculative; so, most recently, L. Giuliani, *Bildnis und Botschaft: Hermeneutische Untersuchungen zur Bildniskunst der römischen Republik* (Frankfurt, 1986), 190–199, with bibliography. A good photograph of the bust is in Hiesinger, *ANRW*, I.4 (1973), 163, fig. 3.

146. See above, Chapter 3, passim, and, in general, Lahusen, *Untersuchungen zur Ehrenstatue in Rom*, passim.

147. See Smith, *JRS*, 71 (1981), 29–30.

tions did this choice have for the relationship of Rome to the culture of Hellas?

A number of suggestive proposals have emanated from various vantage points. Some can be disposed of swiftly, others warrant closer attention. One aberrant notion has found no takers and need not detain us. An eminent art historian found the explanation for verism in the faces of the Romans themselves. Greek artists, long accustomed to producing naturalistic portraits, found the physiognomy of the Romans ideally suited to their training and experience. The "veristic faces" of the Romans inspired Hellenic sculptors to create the new genre.[148] The thesis, of course, requires no refutation. One will hardly imagine that Romans conveniently and consistently supplied homely visages that had no counterparts in the Mediterranean—and did so only in the late Republic! That solution is quite unthinkable.

Or did Greek carvers make the Romans uglier than they were in reality? Did the spread of Roman power over the East, accompanied by wholesale expropriation of art works, occasional destructiveness, arrogance, condescension, and general offensiveness induce the Greeks, whether consciously or unconsciously, to produce portraits of an unusually harsh character? "Realism," on that interpretation, became caricature.[149] The suggestion is as ingenious as it is implausible, and illustrations to support the argument are highly selective. One can easily find stark contrasts to exemplify the idealized Greek and the unattractive Roman.[150] But the contrast blurs when the net is cast more widely. Some late Hellenistic Athenian busts could just as readily be interpreted as harsh and unsympathetic (Plate 12).[151] And a number of Republican heads give a rather handsome appearance, for example, the famous bronze bust of Cato Uticensis from Volubilis (Plate 13).[152] Further, can one really imagine Greek artists rendering their Roman

148. So Richter, *JRS*, 45 (1955), 45–46.

149. The idea is advocated by Smith, *JRS*, 71 (1981), 34–38; for a similar analysis of the Delian portraits of Romans, see Stewart, *Greek Sculpture*, 228.

150. Smith's prime exhibit is a generalized portrait of Mithridates VI and the famous Copenhagen head of Pompey; *JRS*, 71 (1981), 35, with plate V.1–2.

151. E.g., Hafner, *Späthellenistische Bildnisplastik*, plates 25.A3–4, 26.A8, 28.13.

152. J. M. C. Toynbee, *Roman Historical Portraits* (London, 1978), 40, fig. 38. On the "Republican general" from Tivoli, see Vessberg, *Studien zur Kunstgeschichte*, plates XLVIII–XLIX. See further H. Weber, *Ktema*, 1 (1976), 113–127; and Berger, *Eikones*, 64–75, on a Republican head in Basel. Cf. the criticisms of Smith by Zanker, in *Les "bourgeoisies" municipales italiennes aux IIe et Ier siècles av. J.C.*, Coll. Intern. Inst. Franc. de Naples (Paris, 1983), 256, n. 26.

sitters (and patrons) unattractive to the point of caricature without either sculptor or subject noticing it? The thesis demands both an unconscious subtlety on the part of the Greeks and a myopic obtuseness on the part of the Romans.[153] It would be better to abandon that line of approach.

The choice lay with Romans, not Greeks. They elected to have themselves represented as tough and hardened, aging or aged, marked by the wrinkles and lines acquired through many years of burdensome responsibilities. The reasons for that choice remain debatable. A recent study offers a tempting suggestion: Roman leaders endeavored to point a contrast with the imagery of Hellenistic kings. On that interpretation, repeated success by Romans in the eastern wars promoted aggressive diplomacy and severe treatment, reinforcing Roman ascendancy and confirming the sense of superiority. The conqueror toppled Hellenistic rulers, installed client kings, and demanded subservience from princes and dynasts. Popillius Laenas' brusque handling of Antiochus IV after Pydna serves as the paradigmatic example. Arrogance and disdain for the political world of the Greeks then translated itself into sharply differentiated public images. Hellenistic royal style featured idealized portraiture, youthful, godlike faces repeating and building upon Alexander imagery. The Romans thus made a point of presenting the opposite type of physiognomy. The very homeliness of their appearance represented the characteristics of virility, power, and earned authority that put to shame the effeminate softness and mocked the unreality and empty aspirations contained in Hellenistic royal portraits. That imagery underscored the antithesis between Republican ideals and monarchic rule.[154] The dichotomy, on the face of it, seems neat and reasonable—but too neat. It reduces to simplicity what was, in fact, a highly complex, diverse, often delicate, and ever-changing political and diplomatic relationship between Rome and the states of the Greek East. Romans dealt as much with republics, cities, and federations as with kings. They could be harsh with republics or supportive of kings, and through much of the second century their prevailing mood was, in fact, indifference.[155] The Popillius paradigm is unrepresentative and indeed misrepresented.[156] Romans neither needed nor wanted to propagate the

153. Cf. Jackson, *Greece and Rome*, 34 (1987), 43–44.

154. See the well-formulated presentation of Smith, *Hellenistic Royal Portraits*, 128–130, who proceeds to interpret the few "veristic" portraits of late Hellenistic princes as imitation of Roman style by royal clients (130–132).

155. See the evidence collected and examined in Gruen, *Hellenistic World*, passim.

156. Cf. Gruen, *Chiron*, 6 (1976), 76–79; idem, *Hellenistic World*, 657–663.

virtues of their political system in the East. Nor did they feel a monolithic disdain for Hellenic character, values, and institutions.[157] The affinities of Republican verism to portrait styles developed by artists in Greece and the East would make it difficult to discern such a message in any case. And the Romans never paid so much heed to the issue of Hellenistic monarchy as to require creation of a portraiture to express their distinctiveness from it.

Perhaps the push for distinctiveness went in another direction. Several interpretations hold that the array of Republican heads, reminding observers of arduous labors in service of the state, represent a collective solidarity. The aristocracy here sought to revive the principles of the past, to reassert the joint enterprise of the noble houses against challenges by popular agitators, charismatic leaders, ambitious and egotistical individuals. The affirmation of oligarchic governance, exemplified by a realistic portrait style, on this view, came in reaction to the deeds of the Gracchi and the rise of Marius and represented resistance to the personal power wielded by a Sulla, a Pompey, or a Caesar, and later by an Antony or an Octavian.[158] The hypothesis is attractive but unpersuasive. For a start, it presupposes inception of the style in the last generation of the Republic. As we have seen, that is mere assumption based on faulty premises. Portraiture of a veristic sort may go back well into the second century and thus have no connection whatever with political developments of the post-Gracchan period. Further, the notion that realistic portraits presented a united front against individual personalities who burst the confines of aristocratic conventions implies a very different mode of portraiture for the latter, readily distinguishable from verism. Is it so? The supposed bust of Marius now in the Munich Glyptothek shows features quite consonant with the veristic style: the knitted brow, the grave expression, the bald forehead, and close-cropped hair (Plate 14).[159] Of course, one can dismiss the item as of uncertain identification, or even uncertain authenticity.[160] But a piece of literary testimony has relevance here. Plutarch reports personal inspection of a marble statue of Marius in Ravenna: it displayed the roughness

157. See below, Chapter 6, passim.
158. See the insightful comments of S. Nodelman, *Art in America*, 63 (1975), 27–28; also Lahusen, *MdI*, 92 (1985), 276–281. In the formulation of R. Bianchi Bandinelli, *Roma: L'arte romana nel centro del potere* (Milan, 1969), 75–86, the style was born in the Sullan era, a time of sharp oligarchic reaction against the tendencies of the Gracchan and Marian eras.
159. See Schweitzer, *Bildniskunst*, plate 170.
160. On the "Marius," see, most recently, Giuliani, *Bildnis und Botschaft*, 175–182.

and harshness of the man, his virile character and warlike nature.[161] That description would certainly not be at variance with veristic statuary. The busts of Pompey, while clearly identifiable and not characteristic of standard veristic representations, could hardly be regarded as flattering glorifications.[162] A variety confronts us in the portraits of Caesar, but some at least, both sculpture in the round and coin depictions, fall readily within the category of veristic representation.[163] And one can go further. Gem portraits of Roman *principes*, individuals of distinction and power whose faces would be stamped on all personal and business correspondence, include numerous hyper-realistic depictions of homely, aged men.[164] The cumulative evidence suffices to undermine the idea that verism signified an aristocratic class solidarity against the excesses of the individual.

Is the style then characteristic of a different class? It can be urged that the most representative veristic portraits derive from funerary monuments and individual busts depicting members of the "middle class," that is, merchants, tradesmen, artisans, and laborers, most of them freedmen, who did not need to maintain an official posture and could forgo public visibility (Plate 15). They opted for a rigorous realism, thus to present themselves as individuals and to leave an accurate physiognomic record for friends and relatives. The "bourgeois" mentality of such persons inclined them also toward portraiture that emphasized the arduous path they had traversed in reaching a modicum of social and economic success.[165] One can argue even that the crude features of some of the more extreme naturalistic reliefs and busts reflect the lesser skills of those artists hired by a humbler clientele.[166] But concentration

161. Plut. *Mar.* 2.1.

162. Schweitzer, *Bildniskunst*, plates 123–125; Vollenweider, *Porträtgemmen*, plates 72–73.

163. E.g., Vollenweider, *Porträtgemmen*, plates 75, 77, 80; F. S. Johansen, in A. A. Houghton, M. True, and J. Frell, eds., *Ancient Portraits in the J. Paul Getty Museum*, 1 (Occasional Papers on Antiquities, 4) (Malibu, Calif., 1987), 17–40.

164. E.g., Vollenweider, *Porträtgemmen*, plates 42.1–2, 45.4–6, 49.1, 49.4, 50.1, 50.4, 52.6–7, 53.1, 54.1–2.

165. See, especially, Zanker, *Hellenismus in Mittelitalien*, 592–596; Stewart, *Attika*, 142–148; Lahusen, *MdI*, 92 (1985), 282–283. Grave reliefs provide the most extensive testimony. See the data assembled by Zanker, *JdI*, 90 (1975), 267–315, with plates 1–53; D. E. E. Kleiner, *Roman Group Portraiture* (New York, 1977); Frenz, *Römische Grabreliefs*, passim.

166. Hiesinger, *ANRW*, I.4 (1973), 812–813; Zanker, *Hellenismus in Mittelitalien*, 594–595, with plates 7–8.

on that level of society fails to explain the phenomenon. Veristic portraiture certainly did not confine itself to the "Mittelschicht." The ruling class employed it with frequency as a mode of representation. The testimony of coins and gems, of course, applies only to men of rank and status, and there is no reason to doubt that a substantial portion of extant sculptures in the round portray members of that class as well.[167] Can one really conclude that Roman *nobiles* looked to the funerary reliefs of *liberti* and the busts of tradesmen and entrepreneurs for the examples on which to pattern their own self-image? Surely the reverse holds. Portraits of Rome's statesmen, generals, and preeminent figures set the style imitated by those outside the elite, whether on a lesser rung of Roman society or from the local leadership of municipal communities.[168] The matter therefore boils down to a fundamental question: what attraction did the veristic style have for the Roman aristocracy?

Verism possesses a character rather different from straightforward

167. To be sure, they did not confine themselves to that style in the late Republic. The era accommodated a wide diversity. Zanker, *Hellenismus in Mittelitalien*, 587–592, finds a tendency among Roman *principes* to imitate the "Pathosformels" of Hellenistic rulers, a tendency that distinguished them sharply from the ultrarealism sought by their social inferiors. But the dichotomy is overdrawn. Similarities with portraits of Hellenistic dynasts are relatively superficial and can easily be accounted for by the traditions of Hellenic portraiture. If heads like the Tivoli general or the so-called Postumius Albinus share some features with those of Hellenistic rulers, the explanation surely lies more with the Greek artist than with the Roman sitter. It is difficult to imagine that Republican leaders looked to deposed Hellenistic monarchs as models for their own self-image. Still less likely is the notion that insofar as the portraits took on a more individualistic character, they express the subject's desire to appear as a member of a Hellenistic world-citizenry. Such an analysis pays little heed to the Romans' drive to announce their distinctiveness. The so-called "Terme ruler" has often been identified as a Roman general in Hellenistic guise; see, most recently, S. Nodelman, in A. A. Houghton, M. True, and J. Frell, eds., *Ancient Portraits in the J. Paul Getty Museum, I* (Occasional Papers on Antiquities, 4) (Malibu, 1981), 68–69; Zanker, *Power of Images*, 5. But he is more probably a Greco-Macedonian prince; see Smith, *Hellenistic Royal Portraits,* 84–85; N. Himmelman, *Herrscher und Athlet: Die Bronzen von Quirinal* (Milan, 1989), 126–142.

168. Cf. Lahusen, *MdI,* 92 (1985), 283–286, who rightly compares the Barberini *togatus,* holding the busts of two ancestors, with certain funerary reliefs of the lesser orders; plate 107.1–2. Cf. also Giuliani, *Bildnis und Botschaft,* 231–233. J. C. Balty, *Wiss. Zeitschr. der Humboldt-Universität zu Berlin,* 31 (1982), 139–142, recognizes the priority of aristocratic portraits, but postulates a threefold division, "patrician-type," "ruler-type," and "bourgeois-type," thus combining and compounding the speculations of Bianchi-Bandinelli and Zanker. On the portraiture of municipal leaders, see Zanker, *Hellenismus in Mittelitalien,* 597–605, who acknowledges the influence wielded by portraits of Roman *nobiles.* Cf. also Zanker, *Les 'bourgeoisies' municipales,* 257–260, 263–264.

realism or naturalism. It has too often been interpreted as aiming to reproduce with detailed accuracy the physiognomy of the sitter.[169] In fact, the style calls for a heightened and exaggerated realism that focuses attention on wrinkles, lines, and folds, grim expressions, and unattractive features. The initial impression is one of candor, a commitment to honest representation with no flattery or disguise, but repetition of that pattern alters the impression. Excessive candor compromises the candor itself and, indeed, invites a different perspective. The consistency and frequency with which middle-aged or elderly men receive homely countenances produce an air of artificiality. Ostensibly individualized portraits become part of a collectivity. The objective of veristic portraiture was not to reproduce a particular face accurately but to convey a stylized image.[170] Of course, the artist would incorporate personal features of the individual, but the larger context requires emphasis.[171] The stern and severe visage, in which every crease proclaimed hardships endured for the state, reinforced principles that the Roman aristocracy displayed to the public. Perusing the portraits gives a sense of sameness, a sense that the Romans doubtless cultivated with deliberation. The leadership of the state presented itself with unified purpose. Verism dwells on particulars but expresses the general. The *res publica* held primacy, maintained by men of grim resolve and unflagging patriotism who subordinated individuality to the collective interest.

The style suited the political and cultural circumstances of the second century. At a time when Rome obtained a dramatically more conspicuous place in the larger Mediterranean world and the opportunity for individual aggrandizement increased exponentially, the *nobiles* strove to articulate broader values and common principles. Veristic portraiture had its part in that process. Emphasis upon the shared objectives of the ruling class reaffirmed the *mos maiorum* in a period when external temptations might diminish its force. Such a signal was appropriate in the second century and became all the more urgent in the first. And the medium chosen has still wider implications. Rome employed Greek artists and had recourse to the artistic traditions of Hellas. In characteristic fashion, the Romans adapted the naturalistic conventions of late Hellenistic art to their own purposes. The exaggerated realism of veris-

169. Cf. Zanker, *Hellenismus in Mittelitalien*, 596; Lahusen, *MdI*, 92 (1985), 282–283; Zanker, *Power of Images*, 9.
170. Cf. Nodelman, *Art in America*, 63 (1975), 27–28.
171. Cf. Giuliani, *Bildnis und Botschaft*, 225–233.

elphi Museum. Photo courtesy *Fouilles de Delphes,* 4 (1927), plate 78

Plate 1. Frieze, column of Aemilius Paullus

Munich Glyptothek

Plate 2. Thiasos frieze, "Altar of Ahenobarbus"

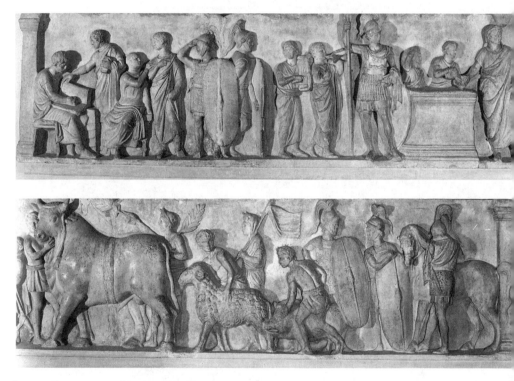

Louvre. Photo courtesy Photographie Giraudon

Plate 3. Census frieze, "Altar of Ahenobarbus"

Louvre

Plate 4. Terra-cotta death mask

[173]

Capitoline Museum. Photo courtesy Alinari/Art Resource

Plate 5. Barberini *"Imagines"* statue

Capitoline Museum.
Photo courtesy DAI, Rome

Lars Pulena, Tarquinia Museum.
Photo courtesy DAI, Rome

Plate 6. Funerary busts

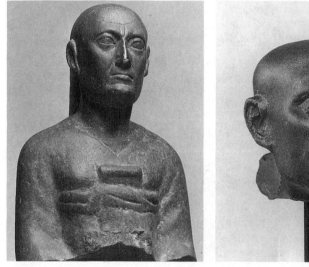

Walters Art Gallery, Baltimore

Museu Calouste Gulbenkian

Plate 7. Egyptian portrait busts

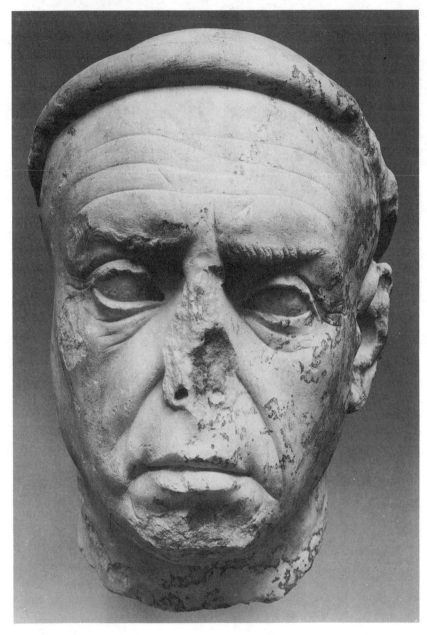

Agora Museum

Plate 8. Agora priest

Berlin Museum.
Photo courtesy Hirmer Verlag

Plate 9. Gold stater of
T. Quinctius Flamininus

Trustees of the British Museum

Plate 10. Denarius of Marcellus

Trustees of the British Museum

Plate 11. Denarius of Restio

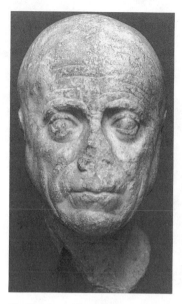

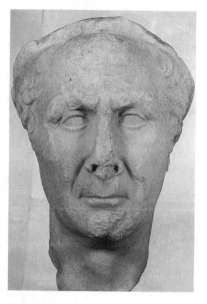

Ny Carlsberg Glyptothek.
Photo courtesy A. Stewart

National Museum, Athens

Ny Carlsberg Glyptothek.
Photo courtesy DAI, Rome

Plate 12. Hellenistic portrait heads

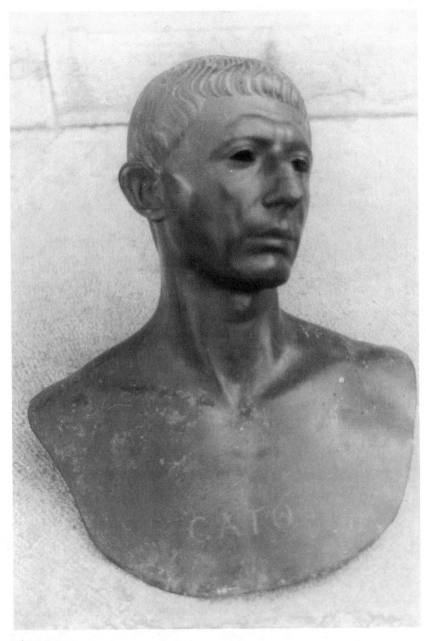

Rabat Museum

Plate 13. Bust of Cato from Volubilis

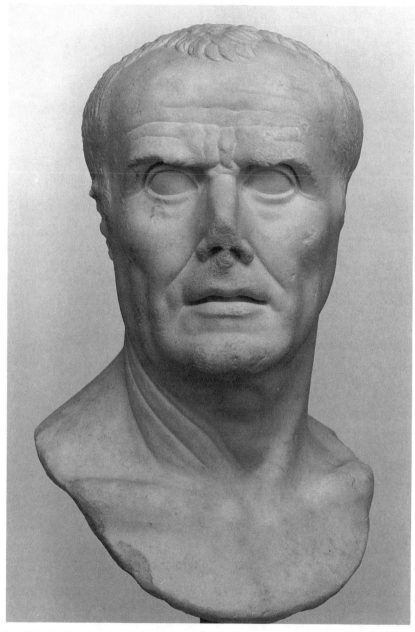

Staatliche Antikensammlungen and Munich Glyptothek

Plate 14. Bust of "Marius"

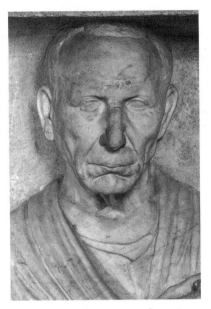

Vatican Museum.
Photo courtesy DAI, Rome

Berlin Museum

Villa Wolkonsky.
Photo courtesy DAI, Rome

Plate 15. Portraits from Roman funerary reliefs

[181]

tic heads both set the portraiture within a Hellenistic context and served
to define those features of Roman society that kept it distinct.

The attitudes of Rome toward Hellenic art were complex and subtle
rather than single-minded or simplistic. Admiration for it stands out
with clarity. The collection of Greek statuary and paintings, the importation and subsidization of Greek artists, and the deployment of their
creations in the most prominent civic and religious sites put that admiration beyond doubt. But this was not merely a matter of veneration.
The ruling class commissioned Greek artists and channeled their art to
display Roman achievements and to enhance Roman public life. Greek
signatures on works of art only underscored the relationship: the artists
exhibited their skills but occupied a subordinate post. Republican historical reliefs serve as illustration. The monument of Aemilius Paullus in Delphi demonstrated Roman triumphal achievement through a
Greek medium and for a Greek audience. The "*Ara* of Domitius Ahenobarbus," in more intricate manner, combined a Hellenic mythological
theme with a venerable Roman institution to express both military
accomplishment and civic continuity. And the conventions of Hellenic
art proved especially serviceable in communicating the character and
values of Rome's leadership. The realistic portraiture developed by late
Hellenistic sculptors provided the impetus. Roman aristocrats adapted
and transformed that genre to express resolute commitment to the *mos
maiorum*, the rigors of public service, and the solidarity of the ruling
class.

[5]

THE THEATER AND
ARISTOCRATIC CULTURE

Roman drama was as much a social as a literary phenomenon. From the late third century B.C. crowds flocked to the theater, occasions for plays multiplied, the popularity of the genre soared. Public opinion held playwrights, producers, and performers to account. The institution carried significance that went well beyond mere entertainment. Dramatic art impinged upon the public scene at various levels: plays became an integral part of religious celebrations; magistrates of the Republic took responsibility for supervising the shows that recurred at regular intervals; individual aristocrats sponsored them on ad hoc occasions to advance particular purposes; funeral games presented by the families of prominent public figures could include theatrical productions. Playwrights—or at least some of them—hobnobbed with the mighty, and links were forged between artists and the leaders of state. Public debate engaged Romans over seating arrangements in the theater and over the question of erecting a permanent structure for the performance of dramas. Sources allude to disruptions at the plays, and on one occasion at least unruly behavior extended to the stage itself. Dramatic productions could provide a medium for public posturing, stir civic passions, or serve as forum for popular outbursts.

The impact of the theater on the broader public scene needs attention. Assumptions and presuppositions plague the subject. The issues go well beyond narrow political interpretations and spill over the bounds of literary history. Latin drama, especially comic drama, enjoyed great success in the second century. It provokes inquiry on several fronts: the role of the theater in the political ambitions and careers of aspiring Roman leaders; the relations between artists and public figures and the mutual benefits thereby generated; the import of contention over seating privileges and of resistance to the construction of a permanent edifice for theatrical productions; the theater as arena for the expression of public opinion; and, most important, the part played by the drama in expressing the values of the Roman elite. The plays of Terence hold center stage in the mid–second century. They appear to move in a markedly different intellectual world from those of his great predecessor Plautus, although only a generation separated them. The change betokens more than literary evolution. It lies at the intersection of political, social, and cultural history.

The notion of the theater as setting for political demonstrations has a strong hold on the imagination. Certain familiar episodes reinforce the impression. A speech of Cicero maintains that authentic expression of popular sentiment is heard only occasionally in formal assemblies and meetings but regularly in the theater and the arena.[1] The orator cites instances in which actors emphasized lines with contemporary resonance, confounding Cicero's enemies and elevating his reputation, while the audience reacted with thunderous enthusiasm, responding not to the play but to current political conditions.[2] The outspoken young politician C. Curio became a vociferous opponent of Julius Caesar in 59 and received a grand ovation in the theater, whereas Caesar's own arrival was greeted by stony silence. The play itself featured lines that, spoken in that year, unmistakably alluded to Pompey the Great and stimulated a noisy response from spectators.[3] A few years later, the aged orator, Q. Hortensius, who had escaped public criticism throughout his career, faced a hostile crowd in the theater who vented their rage at his recent stance in a criminal trial.[4] In a letter to Atticus, Cicero, avid for political news in the aftermath of Caesar's assassination, asked for reports of popular demonstrations in the theater.[5] Selected lines from Roman tragedies stirred emotions among the people at Caesar's funeral games, thereby turning sentiments against his slayers.[6] Drama, as is clear, could

1. Cic. *Pro Sestio*, 115; cf. 106.
2. Cic. *Pro Sestio*, 118–123.
3. Cic. *Ad Att.* 2.19.3; cf. 2.18.1.
4. Cic. *Ad Fam.* 8.2.1.
5. Cic. *Ad Att.* 14.3.2.
6. Suet. *Iul.* 84.2. Among other examples, see Cic. *Phil.* 1.36; Macrob. *Sat.* 2.7.2–3. A fuller collection appears in F. W. Wright, *Cicero and the Theater*, Smith College Class. Stud. 11 (Northampton, Mass., 1931), 4–9.

furnish a vehicle for comments on current affairs and could display either hostility toward or zeal for prominent contemporaries. But practices of the Ciceronian age can distort and mislead. The turbulent politics of that era found expression through various media, and it causes little surprise to see the fierce contentions reflected in the theater. Extrapolation from that testimony to the circumstances of the early and middle second century, however, is hazardous. The political scene was markedly different, and no comparable episodes stand on record. The earlier period of Latin drama needs to be viewed in its own terms.

Dramatic productions under public auspices date back to the fourth century B.C. Livy places the introduction of *ludi scaenici* in the year 364, possibly—but by no means certainly—in connection with the venerable *ludi Romani*.[7] Performances at that time were rudimentary playlets, mimes, and Atellane farces. The *ludi Romani* did, in any case, supply the setting for the first full-fledged drama, by Livius Andronicus, staged in 240.[8] The momentum of the genre built rapidly thereafter. In 214 four days were reserved for scenic performances, evidently at the *ludi Romani*, for they were in the charge of the curule aediles.[9] Creation of new public games further increased the occasions. The *ludi plebei* had been installed by 216 under the supervision of the plebeian aediles.[10] Scenic games may have been part of their offerings from the start, and such games were certainly in place by 200 when Plautus' *Stichus* had its presentation.[11] The Hannibalic War, with its stepped-up propitiation of the gods, proved a fruitful time for the installation of new festivals. The *ludi Apollinares* made their first appearance in 212 and may have featured

---

7. Livy, 7.2.1–3, gives the year, but he does not specify the *ludi Romani* and may indeed imply that these were ad hoc games designed to appease the gods in face of a plague. Similarly, Val. Max. 2.4.4. The testimony is generally combined with Livy's notice under the year 366 on reorganization of the *ludi maximi*—an additional day was prescribed for the games—and the newly created curule aediles who would evidently take them as part of their responsibilities. A connection with *ludi scaenici* may be indicated by a fragmentary passage of Festus, 436, L, whose surviving text speaks of aediles and, apparently, of inauguration of *ludi scaenici*. See reconstructions by Mommsen, *Römisches Staatsrecht*, II³, 482; C. Saunders, *TAPA*, 44 (1913), 89; L. R. Taylor, *TAPA*, 68 (1937), 287; J. A. Hanson, *Roman Theater Temples* (Princeton, N.J., 1959), 10–11. The evidence is shaky and inadequate.

8. Cic. *Brutus*, 72–73; *De Sen.* 50; *Tusc. Disp.* 1.3. The *ludi Romani* are specified by Cassiodorus, 239. On the form of early drama or predrama, all is obscure; see G. E. Duckworth, *The Nature of Roman Comedy* (Princeton, N.J., 1952), 4–17.

9. Livy, 24.43.7.

10. Livy, 23.30.17. It is customary to date their inception in 220, when the Circus Flaminius was built, or earlier. There is no explicit evidence; Habel, *RE*, Suppl. 5 (1931), 620–621.

11. Didasc. Plautus, *Stichus*.

dramatic productions from the beginning or shortly thereafter.[12] The festival became a permanent annual event in 208 and thus generated additional days each year for the production of plays.[13] It would soon be an event of high importance for Roman drama, for which the censors of 179 would let contracts for a theater and stage and where Ennius' *Thyestes* would premier in 169.[14] The government added yet another national celebration to the roster in 204: the first *ludi Megalenses*, established to commemorate transferral of the Magna Mater to Rome.[15] A decade later, in 194, that festival incorporated *ludi scaenici*, supplying as many as six days annually for dramatic productions. An impressive setting existed for those *ludi*, the Palatine Hill in full view of the goddess, who was enshrined in the temple constructed for her in 191. The production of Plautus' *Pseudolus* marked the occasion of the temple's dedication, and four of Terence's plays graced the Megalesia thirty years later.[16] The *ludi Cereales* are first attested under the year 201; by then they were apparently an established event, perhaps also created during the intensified religiosity of the Second Punic War. Those games included *ludi scaenici* that extended over a seven-day period during the Roman Empire and whose origins doubtless derive from this same period.[17] In a somewhat separate category, the *ludi Florales*, instituted circa 240 and made annual in 173, featured mimes and erotic skits rather than full-scale plays.[18]

---

12. The institution of the games in 212 is recorded by Livy, 25.12.12–15. And the celebrated tale of a mime who continued his performance uninterrupted lest he offend the gods, despite the departure of his audience, who were called to arms, is placed by Festus in 211; 436–438, L.

13. A *senatus consultum* to this effect was passed in 211; Livy, 26.23.3. But the *lex* that fixed permanency, for some reason, awaited the year 208; Livy, 27.23.5–7.

14. The contract: Livy, 40.51.3; the *Thyestes*: Cic. *Brutus*, 78.

15. Livy, 29.14.13–14.

16. Livy sets the inauguration of *ludi scaenici* at the Megalesia in 194; 34.34.3. The alternative date of 191 favored by Valerius Antias may be a confusion with the dedication of the temple; Livy, 36.36.3–5; cf. J. Briscoe, *A Commentary on Livy, Books XXXIV–XXXVII* (Oxford, 1981), 134, 276. On the number of days for scenic games, see Habel, *RE*, Suppl. 5 (1931), 626–628; Taylor, *TAPA*, 68 (1937), 290. On the site, see Cic. *Har. Resp.* 24; Hanson, *Roman Theater Temples*, 13–16; P. Pensabene, *Archeologia Laziale*, 2.3 (1979), 67–74. The didascalic notices for *Pseudolus*, *Andria*, *Hecyra*, *Heauton timorumenos*, and *Eunuchus* place them all at the Megalesia.

17. The games in 201: Livy, 30.39.8. In general, Habel, *RE*, Suppl. 5 (1931), 624–625.

18. Ovid, *Fasti*, 5.347–348: *scaena levis decet hanc; non est, mihi credite, non est / illa [Flora] conturnatas inter habenda deas.* Ovid places the inception of the *ludi* in 240 and their establishment on a permanent basis in 173; *Fasti*, 5.287–296, 5.327–330. Slightly different dates for the beginning are given by Vell. Pat. 1.14.8; Pliny, *NH*, 18.286. On the

Religious ceremonies that encompassed scenic games had thus firmly entrenched themselves in the later third and early second centuries. The number of days devoted to dramatic productions of one form or another markedly expanded as well. A scholarly estimate reckons that *ludi scaenici* occupied eleven days annually by 200 B.C., and perhaps as many as twenty by the mid–second century.[19] And this estimate accounts only for the regularly scheduled *ludi*, fixed on the annual calendar. Extra days could be added, and very frequently were added, whenever improprieties, disturbances, or *prodigia* occurred in the course of the ceremonies, thus obliging the authorities to repeat the *ludi*, together with the dramas attendant upon them. Such *instaurationes* took place with particular frequency in the late third and early second centuries, and some required as many as seven repetitions before they were done properly. On a conservative calculation, the practice could add an average of five or six days a year for the witnessing of dramas.[20] A variety of occasional and irregular *ludi* increased the number still further, although defensible totals cannot be ascertained. Votive games, held on the initiative of a magistrate and fulfilling vows made on behalf of the state's welfare, may or may not have included stage performances. But theatrical performances did form part of at least some ceremonies that accompanied the dedication of temples.[21] Triumphal celebrations gained in frequency and splendor during the early second century, tributes to the nation's, as well as to an individual's accomplishments. Whether returning *triumphatores* incorporated *ludi scaenici* as part of their commemoration must be reserved for subsequent discussion. But the funeral games of prominent public figures certainly could provide occasion for *ludi scaenici*.[22] The

character of the presentations, see also Val. Max. 2.10.8; Seneca, *Epist.* 97.8; Lactantius, *Inst.* 1.20; Augustine, *CD*, 2.26; Arnobius, *Adv. Nat.* 7.33.

19. Taylor, *TAPA*, 68 (1937), 284–291.

20. On *instaurationes* generally, see Cic. *Har. Resp.* 23; cf. Festus, 438, L. The Livian references are conveniently tabulated and the subject discussed by Taylor, *TAPA*, 68 (1937), 291–296. Her inference, shared by many (e.g., Duckworth, *Nature of Roman Comedy*, 77–78), that the popularity of Plautus helps to account for the increase of *instaurationes*, is mere guesswork—and presupposes a cynical manipulation of the institution. Reasons for repetition, when Livy provides them, are religious rather than theatrical; e.g., Livy, 39.7.8–10, 40.59.6–8.

21. As at the dedication of Magna Mater's temple in 191; Livy, 36.36.3–5; Didasc. Plautus, *Pseudolus*; similarly, the temples of Juno Regina and Diana in 179; Livy, 40.52.1–3; and that of Fortuna Equestris in 173; Livy, 42.10.5.

22. Four days of dramatic productions at T. Flamininus' funeral games in 174: Livy, 41.28.11. Performances of Terence's *Hecyra* and *Adelphoe* at the elaborate festivities for L. Paullus in 160 are attested by the didascalic notices. Taylor, *TAPA*, 68 (1937), 299–300, goes too far, however, in claiming that we can assume *ludi scaenici* at all funeral games.

accumulation of religious festivals and celebratory events, augmented by frequent *instaurationes*, reached impressive figures by the mid–second century. Their significance for Roman public life could be quite telling. Wherein lay that significance?

Standard opinion has it that *ludi scaenici* played a key role in the working of Roman politics. Aediles, both curule and plebeian, held responsibility for the organization and supervision of the games, including the dramatic performances that became an increasingly important part of them. Aspiring politicians, so it is argued, could capitalize upon the aedileship, a notable station on the *cursus honorum*. Fame and popularity accruing from sponsorship of shows that stimulated the *populus* could boost a senatorial career and facilitate movement to the higher magistracies.[23] A general picture emerges: competition among young politicians to gain the services of the most talented dramatists, a scramble to secure control of promising scripts, a premium placed upon attractive productions to win popular backing, patronage links between playwrights and members of the nobility; in short, a tight interconnection between drama and politics.

The presumption could benefit from closer analysis. Did promotion of the games, in fact, constitute a major stepping stone for aediles en route to higher office? One might note, to begin, that not all dramatic festivals lay in the charge of aediles. Curule aediles did have supervision of the *ludi Romani*, a task of high visibility.[24] Whether they reaped full political advantage from it, however, or even expected to do so is not so obvious as it might seem. The most conspicuous figure at the *ludi Romani*, in fact, was the consul or the urban praetor who gave the signal that started the chariot races. On one occasion when the praetor fell ill, the job went to a dictator, an unmistakable sign of that function's importance.[25] What role magistrates played at the production of plays

23. See, among recent works, P. Veyne, *Bread and Circuses: Historical Sociology and Political Pluralism*, trans. B. Pearce (London, 1990 [French ed., 1976]), 212–213; A. S. Gratwick, in E. J. Kenney and W. V. Clausen, eds., *The Cambridge History of Classical Literature, II: Latin Literature* (Cambridge, 1982), 82; G. Williams, in B. Gold, ed., *Literary and Artistic Patronage in Ancient Rome* (Austin, Tex., 1982), 6; J. Barsby, *Plautus: Bacchides* (Warminster, Eng., 1986), 7; B. Gold, *Literary Patronage in Greece and Rome* (Chapel Hill, N.C., 1987), 41.

24. Livy, 6.42.12–13, 24.43.7.

25. Livy, 8.40.2. Ennius, 84–86, V = 79–81, Sk, has the consul give the signal for chariot races, presumably at the *ludi Romani*; cf. Skutsch, *Annals of Q. Ennius*, 228–230. The fact that Ennius uses the races, rather than plays, as his image for what generates audience attention is itself significant.

remains obscure. That they came forth to claim credit at the time of performance is nowhere attested in the evidence—and ought not to be assumed. Curule aediles generally had responsibility for the *ludi Megalenses* as well.[26] Yet the didascalic notice on Plautus' *Pseudolus*, which was performed at the Megalesia of 191, specifies only the urban praetor of that year in connection with the play.[27] Plebeian aediles, as might be expected, were the authorizing officials for the *ludi plebeii*.[28] But the presiding magistrate for the *ludi Apollinares* was the *praetor urbanus*.[29] As for the *Floralia*, plebeian aediles inaugurated the festival circa 240, but when it became an annual event in 173, the consuls of that year sponsored the games.[30] Divided responsibilities and shared functions, it appears, characterized the supervision of the games.

How far, then, did these activities promote movement up the political ladder? In the case of urban praetors, hardly or not at all. Men who reached that office had a range of responsibilities to discharge. They certainly did not need to rely on presidency of the games to enhance their chances for consular rank. The *fasti*, in fact, show little correlation between the urban praetorship and success in later elections: only two-fifths of the known urban praetors between 220 and 150 proceeded to the consulship.[31] The promotion of shows was obviously quite irrelevant.

Matters are more complicated for the aediles. In the late Republic one could assume a connection between sponsorship of handsome spectacles as aedile and subsequent attainment of the highest offices. Cicero even reports that one aspirant failed to reach the consulship because he had decided to forgo the aedileship. But he could also name others who went unhindered to the summit of the magisterial career without offering any entertainment in previous offices. He himself admitted to a modest outlay during his own aedileship—too little, of course, to account for his meteoric rise to the top, or so he claimed.[32] The connection, therefore, was not clear or consistent even in the Ciceronian age.

26. Livy, 34.54.3.

27. By contrast, the curule aediles are mentioned by name in the *didascalia* to Terence's dramas at the Megalesia: *Andria, Heauton timorumenos, Eunuchus,* and *Hecyra*. The reliability of the *didascaliae* on individual names, of course, is a different matter; see, most recently, J. Linderski, *AHB,* 1 (1987), 83–88.

28. Livy, 23.30.17.

29. Livy, 25.12.12, 27.23.5; Cic. *Brutus,* 78; Festus, 436–438, L.

30. Ovid, *Fasti,* 5.287–292, 5.327–330.

31. See Broughton, *Magistrates of the Roman Republic,* on the relevant years.

32. Cic. *De Off.* 2.58–59.

And the expectations of the second century may, in any case, have been quite different. To be sure, the vast majority of curule aediles in the period 220 to 150 went on to hold the consulship, but half of them were patricians, and the office tended to draw on Rome's noblest houses. Their names and families would suffice to explain the success.[33] There is nothing to show that the games helped. As example, take the curule aediles of 194 who introduced scenic games into the Megalesia. One of them waited twenty four years for the consulship, the other never got there.

Plebeian aediles had a still harder time of it. Of the two who sponsored Plautus' *Stichus* in 200, one reached the consulship eighteen years later, the other got only so far as the praetorship thirteen years later. And little more than a quarter of the known plebeian aediles between 220 and 150 attained the consulship anyway.[34]

The link between aedilician entertainment and subsequent political success is threadbare. And not surprisingly. How many voters in a consular election would recall which aediles sponsored which shows several years before they stood for the chief magistracy?[35] And how many cared? A critical fact, easily forgotten but vital, needs to be underscored. Election to the highest magistracies took place in the *comitia centuriata*, an institution structured to assure a preponderance of weight for voters of means and standing. Such voters would constitute only a small portion of the attendance at aedilician games. The bulk of the audience carried little clout in the elections for the top offices. The notion that candidates capitalized on their earlier, often much earlier, *ludi* to reach consular rank stretches the imagination.[36]

Attention to the prologues of Terence undermines the *communis opinio*. They imply that the playwright's reputation—not the indirect advantage of a Roman magistrate—was on the line with every perfor-

33. Cf. Plut. *Aem. Paull.* 3.1. And see M. G. Morgan, *Philologus*, 134 (1990), 28–29.

34. See Broughton, *Magistrates*, under relevant years. On the aedileship and advancement to higher office, see Develin, *Practice of Politics at Rome*, 92–96, 98–99, 139–140.

35. A closer correlation holds between aedileship, whether curule or plebeian, and acquisition of the praetorship; see the tables of I. Shatzman, *Senatorial Wealth and Roman Politics* (Brussels, 1975), 159–161, calculated for the years 217–182. It does not, however, follow that the sponsorship of entertainments as aedile was the decisive criterion. Whatever force it might have had was weakened by passage of the *lex Villia* in 180, which required a two-year interval between offices.

36. The giving of games in the actual canvassing for election is, of course, a different matter; cf. Cic. *Pro Mur.* 76–77; Shatzman, *Senatorial Wealth*, 164, with references. But even in this practice, none of the evidence specifies dramatic productions.

mance. The prologue of the *Andria* asserts that the poet always sought audience approval and that he now courts the favor of his listeners in order to cultivate attendance for his future comedies.[37] A comparable sentiment occurs at the beginning of the *Eunuchus*: the poet professes desire to please the tastes of as many worthy spectators as possible, while giving least offense to the majority.[38] The presumed spokesman in the *Hecyra* prologue, L. Ambivius Turpio, reinforces that message. He takes credit for salvaging the repute of the dramatist Caecilius through his own production skills, restoring his popularity, livelihood, and zeal for a return to his profession. Success of the plays, or lack thereof, reflected directly upon the poet himself.[39] And the prologue to the *Adelphoe* declares that the author, stung by harsh criticism of his script by an adversary, submits his play to the judgment of spectators, who will administer praise or blame.[40] That testimony, however contrived and calculated, indicates that the reception of the drama determines the dramatist's fame, not the politician's career.

Aediles, to be sure, had a hand in the financing of *ludi*. The precise function, however, remains tantalizingly elusive. Terence, as we happen to know, sold at least two plays to the aediles on separate occasions: the *Andria* and the *Eunuchus*.[41] But we do not know that this was standard procedure. A line in Terence's *Hecyra* suggests that the producer or impresario could also purchase the script.[42] The latter has, therefore, been considered a middleman between the state and the

---

37. Ter. *Andr.* 2–3: *id sibi negoti credidit solum dari, / populo ut placerent quas fecisset fabulas*; 24–27: *favete, adeste aequo animo et rem cognoscite, / ut pernoscatis ecquid spei, sit relicuom, / posthac quas faciet de integro comoedias, / spectandae an exigendae sint vobis prius.*

38. Ter. *Eun.* 1–3: *si quisquamst qui placere se studeat bonis / quam plurimis et minime multos laedere, / in is poeta hic nomen profitetur suom.*

39. Ter. *Hec.* 14–27.

40. Ter. *Adelph.* 1–5: *postquam poeta sensit scripturam suam / ab iniquis observari, et advorsarios / rapere in peiorem partem quam acturi sumus, / indicio de se ipse erit, vos eritis iudices, / laudin an vitio duci id factum oporteat.*

41. *Andria*: Suet. *Vita Ter.* 1, 3: *qui primam Andriam antequam aedilibus venderet; Eunuchus*: Ter. *Eun.* 20: *Menandri Eunuchum, postquam aediles emerunt.* The latter fetched a handsome price; Suet. *Vita Ter.* 3. H. B. Mattingly's efforts to discredit this testimony are tortured; *Athenaeum*, 37 (1959), 168–169; idem, *RivCultClassMed*, 5 (1963), 45–46.

42. Ter. *Hec.* 56–57: *mihique ut discere / novas expediat posthac pretio emptas meo.* Donatus' commentary on these lines, however, interprets the *meum pretium* as simply the *actor*'s estimated price—which was then paid by the aediles: *pretio emptas meo: aestimatione a me facta, quantum aediles darent, et proinde me periclitante, si reiecta fabula a me ipso aediles quod poetae numeraverint repetant.* Cf. T. F. Carney, *P. Terenti Afri: Hecyra* (Pretoria, 1963), 35.

author.[43] No firm conclusions seem possible on that score. The dramatist's rights themselves are unclear. Plautus indicates that his *Epidicus*
was being produced by the actor-impresario Pellio, to his own displeasure, thus suggesting that the playwright had sold away his proprie-
tary privileges. Yet Terence asserted that his second production of the
Hecyra was not motivated by desire to profit from it again, thus implying that he had not yielded up legal possession.[44] It is illusory to imagine
that we can reconstruct a regular pattern for these transactions—if
indeed there was such a thing. That the aediles did play a prominent
role, however, is incontrovertible. In addition to the purchase of plays,
aediles let contracts for production and staging.[45] And their names
found place in the didascalic notices for performances, evidently as
presiders or presenters. Those responsibilities could involve a substantial outlay of cash.

But none of this involvement entails personal aggrandizement or
exploitation of the theater to advance political ambition. Aediles were
magistrates of the Roman Republic. Their participation signaled state
interest in the encouragement and subsidy of dramatic performances.
Who paid the expenses? A basic allocation surely came from the public
coffers. How then would aediles benefit? General presumption has it
that Republican aediles supplemented the outlays from their own poc-
kets.[46] The matter could use closer attention. Evidence for personal
expenditure and self-promotion again derives from the late Republic or
after. Cicero affirms that lavish entertainments had come to be expected

---

43. See, e.g., W. Beare, *The Roman Stage*[3] (London, 1965), 164–165; Duckworth,
Nature of Roman Comedy, 74; Gratwick, *Cambridge Hist. of Class. Lit.*, II, 82; Barsby,
Plautus: Bacchides, 7–8.

44. On Pellio, Plautus, *Bacch.* 214–215: *etiam Epidicum, quam ego fabulam aeque ac me
ipsum amo, / nullam aeque invitus specto, si agit Pellio*. Pellio was also producer of Plautus'
Stichus, as the didascalic notice to that play reports. He had evidently established a
reputation as an entrepreneur; cf. Plautus, *Men.* 404. Terence's assertion is in *Hec.* 5–7:
*nunc haec planest pro nova, / et is qui scripsit hanc ob eam rem noluit / iterum referre, ut iterum
posset vendere.*

45. Plautus, *Pers.* 159–160.

46. Hypothesis to this effect by Beare, *Roman Stage*[3], 164; Duckworth, *Nature of
Roman Comedy*, 74; Gratwick, *Cambridge Hist. of Class. Lit.*, II, 82; F. Dupont, *Le théâtre
latin* (Paris, 1988), 29, and S. Ireland, *Terence: The Mother in Law* (Warminster, Eng.,
1990), 101, none of whom provides any testimony. In the view of Veyne, *Bread and
Circuses*, 208–212, the state initially provided adequate funding, but the magistrates
gradually supplied more and more of it themselves. That progression is possible but
hypothetical. His argument that officials took personal responsibility for financing
instaurationes lacks foundation.

of aediles as a sign of their wealth, magnanimity, and status. The orator cites a number of examples from his own day and the previous generation of *optimi viri* who felt the pressure to conform to this practice.[47] But the practice may not have held in the second century, when far fewer Romans could command the private resources needed to finance elaborate public entertainments.[48] Upon inauguration of the *ludi Apollinares* in 212, for instance, the senate authorized a sum of twelve thousand *asses* for the praetor to organize festivities. If more should be needed, so it was proposed, a public subscription would make up the difference.[49] And a further distinction must be drawn. Reference to the *ludi* and to heavy expenditures need not apply to the dramatic productions.[50] Other spectacles claimed the high costs.

No reason indeed exists to believe that aediles purchased plays for their own advancement. What gain could accrue from personal proprietorship of a script? It must be stressed that aediles held that office for just one year and lacked subsequent occasion to sponsor a production. By the same token, individual promotion and patronage of a dramatist offered little advantage to an ambitious young *nobilis*.[51] Hence the absence of explicit testimony for association between aediles and playwrights is unsurprising. The magistrate did not reap personal benefit from the successes of Roman drama.

In fact, we possess information on the principal beneficiaries. The

---

47. Cic. *De Off.* 2.57; *Pro Mur.* 40; cf. *Verr.* 2.4.133; *Q. Fr.* 3.8.6.

48. Ti. Gracchus' unusually heavy outlays for *ludi* as aedile led to a *senatus consultum* in 179, putting a ceiling on such expenditures; Livy, 40.44.12. But as Livy's account shows, Gracchus used revenues from Latins, *socii*, and provincials, not personal funds; cf. Develin, *Practice of Politics*, 139–140. See further E. J. Jory, *Studies in Honour of T. B. L. Webster* (Bristol, Eng., 1986), 146–147, with references. Nor is there reason to believe that *ludi scaenici* were involved anyway.

49. Livy, 25.12.9–12.

50. The most spectacular display, the theater created by M. Scaurus in 58, decorated with 360 marble columns, each of them 38 feet high, rising to three stories, with 3,000 bronze statues in the interstices and an auditorium that accommodated 80,000 spectators, was plainly exceptional and hence memorable; Pliny, *NH*, 36.5–6, 36.113–115; further references in Broughton, *Magistrates*, II, 195. On other occasions, so it is reported, aediles would provide silver, gold, or ivory decorations for the stage, or supply paintings as ornaments; Val. Max. 2.4.6; Morgan, *Philologus*, 134 (1990), 29. The evidence is rightly branded as exaggerated and dubious by M. Bieber, *The History of the Greek and Roman Theater*[2] (Princeton, N.J., 1961), 168.

51. In the age of Augustus, praetors rather than aediles purchased scripts, again no doubt with public funds; Ovid, *Trist.* 2.507–508. At a later date, poets evidently sold their plays to actors; Juvenal, 7.87.

spokesman in Plautus' prologue to the *Asinaria* addresses spectators with the hope that his play will be of advantage to the audience and to himself, as well as to the *grex*, the *domini*, and the *conductores*.[52] The meaning of *grex* in this context is clear enough and uncontested. It appears consistently in comic drama with the connotation of actors' company or actors' troupe.[53] The term *dominus* is more problematical. The producers of plays often cited in the *didascaliae* regularly carry the designation of *actor*, never of *dominus*. Nor would it be prudent to see in the word an allusion to a master of slaves. Performers in the dramas were by no means all slaves, and even if some of them were, it would make little sense to single out their masters as prime beneficiaries of a play's success. Better to take the word as denoting the stars of the company, its principals or its most celebrated members—a meaning suggested by two extant inscriptions.[54] What of *conductores*? Might they, in fact, be the aediles?[55] If so, one would have expected explicit reference, or at least the term *magistratus*. The proposition that aediles who presided over the event were placed last in the roster and given a vague designation strains credulity. More probably, *conductores* denoted the contractors or subcontractors, such as the *choragi*, who had responsibility for the particulars of the production.[56] Only one of the beneficiaries in the passage remains to be identified: the speaker himself. He can hardly be any other than the producer or, conceivably, the poet. Any advantage accruing to political figures or magistrates on the climb is passed over in silence. The participation of magistrates in the process has a significance rather different from personal or political benefit. It

---

52. Plautus, *Asin.* 1–3: *hoc agite sultis, spectatores, nunciam, / quae quidem mihi atque vobis res vortat bene / gregique huic et dominis atque conductoribus.* The passage offers no support whatever to the once-prevalent notion of a *dominus gregis* as controlling manager of an actors' troupe or overseer of production. The idea was decisively exploded by E. J. Jory, *CP*, 61 (1966), 102–105. That phrase, unfortunately, reappears in Gold, *Literary Patronage*, 42; and E. Rawson, in *Cambridge Ancient History²*, VIII (Cambridge, 1989), 437.

53. Cf. Plautus, *Cas.* 22; *Pseud.* 1334; Ter. *Heaut.* 45; *Phorm.* 32. See Jory, *CP*, 61 (1966), 102–103.

54. *CIL*, 4, 3877: *[s]caen[ae] domine v[a]le*; 4, 5399: *acti dominus scaenicorum v[ale]*. The items are rightly cited and understood by Jory, *CP*, 61 (1966), 103. But he oddly proceeds to consider the *domini* of the *Asinaria* prologue as "masters of those individuals in the company who happen to be slaves" (104). That conclusion has nothing to recommend it.

55. So Jory, *CP*, 61 (1966), 104. But he operates on the common assumptions that aediles financed the games privately and utilized them for personal advantage, both, as we have seen, very shaky foundations.

56. Cf. Plautus, *Curc.* 464; *Persa*, 159; *Trin.* 858.

represents a commitment on the part of the government to give prominence to the dramatic arts.

Personal and political advertisement, it could be argued, might apply
to scenic performances produced outside the annual and official *ludi*.
Votive games, triumphal celebrations, and funeral ceremonies could, in
theory, provide occasion for *ludi scaenici* to be used as more pointed
publicity for an individual. How commonly, in fact, did such institutions include dramatic presentations? The evidence is surprisingly
flimsy—and that flimsiness is itself revealing.

Votive games came at the behest of particular Roman generals in
fulfillment of vows made when seeking divine assistance in battles or
wars. Insofar as such games included *ludi scaenici*, they would presumably involve exploitation of the dramatic medium to advance private
goals.[57] The idea existed at least in principle. A tradition associated new
seating arrangements in the theater with votive games sponsored in
194.[58] Even if that information is itself erroneous and invalid, it implies
that votive games could encompass theatrical shows. But how many
concrete examples can one point to? Two are customarily cited. M.
Fulvius Nobilior had vowed *ludi magni* for Jupiter upon the capture of
Ambracia in 187, and he redeemed the promise with games in the
following year. The participants included many *artifices* from Greece
who arrived to do Fulvius honor.[59] L. Scipio actively sought and gathered *artifices* from Asia who would grace the *ludi* he had vowed during
the Antiochene War, which eventually took place in 186.[60] In neither
case, however, is there explicit mention of *ludi scaenici*. The presumption that the term *artifices* must mean Greek actors and performers, the
Dionysiac *technitai* who would stage and staff the play, may be questioned. Livy can employ the term to mean something rather different:
artisans or artists.[61] If Fulvius and Scipio needed actors, there were
plenty in Italy to do the job. Plautine dramas had called upon them for
more than two decades. Indeed, the Dionysiac *technitai* had been active
in Italy long before the spectacles sponsored by the victors of the
Antiochene and Aetolian wars.[62] Hence, the evidence for *ludi scaenici* as

57. Cf. Taylor, *TAPA*, 68 (1937), 297–298.
58. Asconius, 70, C.
59. Livy, 39.5.7, 39.22.2: *multi artifices ex Graecia venerunt honoris eius causa.*
60. Livy, 39.22.8–10: *collatas ei pecunias congregatosque per Asiam artifices.*
61. Cf. Livy, 42.3.11.
62. See E. J. Jory, *Hermes*, 98 (1970), 228–233; B. Gentili, *Theatrical Performances in the*

personal promotion for the careers of Fulvius and L. Scipio evapo-rates.[63] This does not rule out the possibility that others employed that medium. But the absence of testimony suggests that it was hardly standard procedure.

Spectacles that accompanied triumphs might seem a logical vehicle for scenic performances. In fact, the first recorded instance came only in 145, as part of the celebration sponsored by L. Mummius to commem-orate his victory in the Achaean War. And the single tortured passage conveying the information indicates that Mummius produced an un-precedented form of spectacle.[64] Wherein lay the novelty remains a matter for dispute, but it seems plain that dramatic shows of Greek origin had not been a regular feature of the Roman triumph.[65] And Mummius' own recourse to that form of entertainment, it can be surmised, went beyond mere self-aggrandizement. There were, after all, other means available—and utilized—to publicize his exploits. The sponsorship of *theatrales artes* at Mummius' triumph after the conquest of Greece had symbolic connotations. It signified Roman expropriation of Hellenic artistry to serve national ends.

Evidence does exist for dramas at funeral games for prominent aristo-crats, but not much. Livy's extant text provides just one instance: the gladiatorial show presented by the younger T. Flamininus for his de-ceased father in 174, a show accompanied by *ludi scaenici*.[66] Apart from that report, we know that the funeral obsequies of L. Paullus in 160 gave occasion for two plays of Terence—and that only from the didascalic notices for *Hecyra* and *Adelphoe*. It does not follow that the practice was

---

Ancient World: Hellenistic and Early Roman Theater (Amsterdam, 1979), 15–41; P. Grimal, in *IXe Congrès Int. de Rome de l'Assoc. Budé* (1973), I, 252–255.

63. Votive games themselves, in fact, would normally draw upon the state treasury. The senate declined to supply funds only when the *imperator* had vowed the games without seeking a *senatus consultum*; Livy, 36.36.1–2.

64. Tac. *Ann.* 14.21.2: *et possessa Achaia Asiaque ludos curatius editos, nec quemquam Romae honesto loco ortum ad theatralis artes degeneravisse, ducentis iam annis a L. Mummii triumpho qui primus id genus spectaculi in urbe praebuerit.* A confused interpretation by H. Hill, *CR*, 46 (1932), 152–153.

65. The one ostensible exception, the games of L. Anicius in 167, stands apart in every regard and can hardly be considered representative; Polyb. 30.22. It requires separate treatment; see below pp. 215–218. The games of Scipio Africanus in 205 and 200 are not described as *ludi scaenici*; Livy, 28.38.14, 28.45.12, 31.49.4. Contra: Walbank, *Historical Commentary on Polybius*, III, 446. There is nothing to show that Naevius' *Clastidium* or Ennius' *Ambracia* were performed at triumphal games sponsored respectively by M. Marcellus and Fulvius Nobilior.

66. Livy, 41.28.11.

rare and exceptional, but we may infer that it carried too little significance to warrant comment by the sources. Gladiatorial contests were the main events at elaborate funeral ceremonies; plays were mere sideshows.[67] They would do little to advance the political interests of the deceased's clan. As with votive games and triumphal festivities, the drama at a funeral was never a centerpiece, only an occasional adjunct.

A brief recapitulation is in order. To reckon the involvement of public officials or individual *nobiles* in the production of dramas as pure political ambition both demeans and distorts the enterprise. Success of the plays redounded to the credit of the playwright and exhibited the skill of the impresario.[68] Praetors and aediles oversaw the *ludi* as representatives of the state, not as promoters of personal careers. The *res publica* extended its favor to the guild of writers and actors about 206, granting them official status, a site in the Aventine temple of Minerva, and the right to assemble and make offerings. That striking gesture, a tribute to Rome's poet-laureate Livius Andronicus, signaled public sanction for the dramatic arts and its linkage to the national religion.[69] Annual presidency of the games by magistrates of the Republic reinforced the message. They provided recurrent reminders of state support for the theater. A cultural rather than a political significance held primacy.

Politics in the theater has often been inferred from a celebrated relationship: the supposed collaboration between Terence and his noble *patroni* in the circle of Scipio Aemilianus. Scipio and his friends, on the usual view, actively encouraged the work of the playwright, perhaps even aided in the composition, and employed the medium of the drama to promote Hellenism and humanism against hidebound conservatives and nativists.[70] Does the evidence justify such inferences?

---

67. Cf. Livy, 23.30.15, 28.21.10, 31.50.4, 39.46.2. Taylor, *TAPA*, 68 (1937), 299–300, cites Plautus, *Most.* 427–428 as evidence for the regularity of scenic games at funerals. But Plautus refers only to *ludi*, not to *ludi scaenici*.

68. The central role of the *actor*, i.e., the actor-manager-impresario, such as Pellio and Turpio, is clear from Ter. *Hec.* 12–27, 55–57; *Phormio*, 10, 33–34; *Heaut.* 12–13. See the treatment of C. Garton, *Personal Aspects of the Roman Theater* (Toronto, 1972), 60–64, and app. 1, no. 4, 125.

69. Festus, 446, L. See Gruen, *Studies in Greek Culture and Roman Policy*, 87–91, with references to modern literature.

70. The fullest statement of the position is by I. Lana, *RivFilol*, 75 (1947), 44–80, 155–175. See also Smith, in *Essays in Roman Culture*, 210–211; P. MacKendrick, *RivFilol*, 82 (1954), 30–35; L. Cicu, *Sandalion*, 1 (1978), 100–121. L. Perelli, *Il teatro rivoluzionario di Terenzio* (Florence, 1973), 5–13, 146–155, accepts the basic thesis but argues that Terence

Two statements in Terentian prologues stand at the heart of this reconstruction. The prologue to the *Heauton timorumenos* declares that a malevolent old poet repeatedly calls attention to Terence's sudden arrival on the artistic scene, claiming that it depended upon the talent of his friends rather than any ability of his own.[71] The accusation recurs in more pointed form in the *Adelphoe*. Certain malicious persons allege that *homines nobiles* provide Terence with assistance and constantly share in his writing.[72] The playwright's spokesman responds to the latter charge with a proud boast: his detractors might regard this as a reproach, but not he. In fact, he considers it praise of the highest order to be held as favored by those who have themselves earned universal favor. They achieved success, without arrogance, in war, peace, and commerce, from which all have benefited.[73] Those statements constitute the sum of contemporary testimony. All else is interpretation— and perhaps speculation.

To be sure, some of the interpretation is learned and ancient. Porcius Licinus, writing in the late second or early first century, identified the powerful backers of Terence as P. Scipio Aemilianus, C. Laelius, and Furius Philus. And he proceeded to add some scurrilous gossip: Terence's relationship with these men was not only literary or political but homosexual; worse still, the three *nobiles* exploited the young artist, deceived him, and discarded him. Porcius Licinus skewered the Scipionic trio in venomous verses.[74] By the age of Cicero, the association of Terence with Aemilianus and Laelius had become received wisdom. Cicero in the *De amicitia* has Laelius refer to the poet as his *familiaris*.[75] The collaborative relationship redounded to Terence's discredit. Nepos, who considered Scipio, Laelius, and Terence coevals, reports an anecdote that has Laelius as author of some verses in the *Heauton timorumenos*—and, by implication, much else besides in the Terentian corpus.[76]

---

added dimensions that did not simply derive from Greek teachings in order to challenge traditionalist Roman thinking. Cf. also Flores, *Letteratura latina*, 137–148; R. H. Martin, *Terence: Adelphoe* (Cambridge, 1976), 6–10.

71. Ter. *Heaut*. 22–24: *tum quod malevolus vetus poeta dictitat / repente ad studium hunc se adplicasse musicum, / amicum ingenio fretum, haud natura sua.*

72. Ter. *Adelph*. 15–16: *nam quod isti dicunt malevoli, homines nobilis / hunc adiutare adsidueque una scribere.*

73. Ter. *Adelph*. 17–21: *quod illi maledictum vehemens esse existumant, / eam laudem hic ducit maxumam, quom illis placet, / qui vobis univorsis et populo placent, / quorum opera in bello in otio in negotio / suo quisque tempore usust sine superbia.*

74. Suet. *Vita Ter*. 2, 6. On Porcius Licinus, see H. Gundel, *RE*, 22.1 (1953), 232–233.

75. Cic. *De Amicit*. 89.

76. Suet. *Vita Ter*. 2, 4.

Cicero puts the matter more guardedly: the elegance of language in Terence's plays gave rise to the belief that they were actually written by Laelius.[77] The poet-politician C. Memmius, in a speech in his own defense, ascribed authorship of the comedies to Scipio Aemilianus.[78] The consensus held in the late Republic and was evidently adopted by Suetonius in his *Life of Terence*—at least with regard to the dramatist's close association with Scipio and Laelius.[79] And that consensus still prevails in modern scholarship.[80]

Yet the tradition came under challenge already in the generation after Cicero. Fenestella asserted that the chronology would not work: Terence was older than both Scipio and Laelius, and thus had no need of whatever literary skills they might possess.[81] The grammarian Santra pressed the contention and expanded the argument. In Santra's view, Scipio and Laelius were too young to have provided assistance to the

---

77. Cic. *Ad Att.* 7.3.10: *cuius fabellae propter elegantiam sermonis putabantur a C. Laelio scribi.*

78. Suet. *Vita Ter.* 4. The allegation is picked up again later by Quintilian, 10.1.99: *licet Terenti scripta ad Scipionem Africanum referantur.* An allusion to this belief seems to have been made by a certain Vallegius, as reported in Donatus' commentary on Terence; *Vita Ter.* 9: *Scipionis fabulas edidisse Terentium Vallegius in actione ait.* W. M. Lindsay, *CQ*, 22 (1928), 119, surmises that Vallegius made the claim in a prologue for reproduction of Terence's plays at Scipio's funeral in 129. The conjecture is accepted by Carney, *P. Terenti Afri: Hecyra*, 11; and K. A. Garbrah, *Athenaeum*, 59 (1981), 189. But none presents evidence or argument. C. Memmius is most likely the praetor of 58, the patron of Lucretius and would-be poet, who was prosecuted in 54, as generally recognized. M. Drury's assertion, in E. J. Kenney and W. V. Clausen, eds., *Cambridge History of Classical Literature, II: Latin Literature* (Cambridge, 1982), 815, that he was the orator C. Memmius of the later second century, is less probable.

79. Suet. *Vita Ter.* 2: *hic cum multis nobilibus familiariter vixit, sed maxime cum Scipione Africano et C. Laelio.* Cf. 4.

80. So even Mattingly, who is skeptical about so much else in the tradition, clings to the association of Terence with Scipio and Laelius as incontrovertible; *Athenaeum*, 37 (1959), 164; idem, *RivCultClassMed*, 5 (1963), 36–38. Among others, see also Carney, *P. Terenti Afri: Hecyra*, 6–7; Perelli, *Il teatro rivoluzionario*, 146–151; Flores, *Letteratura latina*, 138–142; Martin, *Terence: Adelphoe*, 6–9; E. Segal and C. Moulton, *RhM*, 121 (1978), 287; Garbrah, *Athenaeum*, 59 (1981), 188–191; Williams, in *Literary and Artistic Patronage*, 6; Gold, *Literary Patronage*, 41, 46; A. J. Brothers, *Terence: The Self-Tormentor* (Warminster, Eng., 1988), 11. The most vigorous criticism of the whole tradition on Terence's life was delivered by W. Beare, *Hermathena*, 59 (1942), 20–29; somewhat softened in *Roman Stage*[3], 91–94. Others offer cautious and noncommittal assessments; Duckworth, *Nature of Roman Comedy*, 57–58; Drury, in *Cambridge Hist. of Class. Lit.*, II, 815; W. E. Forehand, *Terence* (Boston, 1985), 6–7; S. M. Goldberg, *Understanding Terence* (Princeton, N.J., 1986), 8–9.

81. Suet. *Vita Ter.* 2: *Fenestella arguit, contendens utroque maiorem natu fuisse.* Fenestella wrote in the age of Augustus and Tiberius; Pliny, *NH*, 8.195, 33.146; Jerome, *Chron.* ad ann. 19.

playwright. He proposed instead three other *nobiles*: the learned C. Sulpicius Gallus, consul in 166 and a man of the highest intellectual distinction, Q. Fabius Labeo, consul in 183, and M. Popilius Laenas, consul in 173, both poets.[82] Those were not bad suggestions if one had to guess, and Santra was plainly guessing, as he himself concedes.[83] In fact, he had nothing more to go on than Terence's own prologue to the *Adelphoe*. Santra merely offered an interpretation of the poet's lines on *homines nobiles* who had excelled in *bello*, *otio*, and *negotio*. Neither Scipio nor Laelius had earned such a reputation in Terence's lifetime.[84] Santra's conjecture carries no weight, but the fact that he had to conjecture is telling. If Santra had no testimony beyond the Terentian prologues, we may be confident that Cicero, Memmius, and Nepos labored under the same handicap. The ostensibly impressive consensus of the Ciceronian era dissolves into mere transmission of gossip—gossip that goes back to the vitriolic poem of Porcius Licinus. And his slanders, delivered two generations after the death of Terence, aimed not so much at the dramatist as at wealthy Roman *nobiles* who indulged themselves in *la dolce vita* and left impoverished artists in the lurch.[85] That is far from unimpeachable testimony.[86]

In fact, a chronological problem does exist. Scipio reached the consulship in 147, Laelius in 140, and Furius in 136. It strains credulity beyond the breaking point to imagine that Terence's lines about men who had won universal acclaim for accomplishments in war and peace could possibly have applied to those striplings in the 160s.[87] Terence

82. Suet. *Vita Ter.* 4. Santra's dates are uncertain. Jerome puts him between Varro and Nepos, but that placing may not reflect chronological order. A time under Augustus and Tiberius is postulated by Mattingly, *RivCultClassMed*, 5 (1963), 35–36.

83. Suet. *Vita Ter.* 4: *Santra Terentium existimat, si modo in scribendo adiutoribus indiguerit, non tam Scipione et Laelio uti potuisse, qui tunc adulescentuli fuerunt.*

84. Suet. *Vita Ter.* 4: *ideo ipsum non iuvenes designare, qui se adiuvare dicantur, sed viros, quorum operam et in bello et in otio et in negotio populus sit expertus.*

85. Suet. *Vita Ter.* 2: *nil Publius Scipio profuit, nil illi Laelius, nil Furius, tres per id tempus qui agitabant nobiles facillime.*

86. The actual state of Terence's finances remains in dispute. Porcius Licinus' claim that Terence could not even afford to rent a house is rejected by Suetonius who reports that the poet left an estate of twenty *iugera* on the Appian Way and that his daughter married a Roman *eques*; *Vita Ter.* 6. He earned a handsome sum for sale of the *Eunuchus*; Suet. *Vita Ter.* 3. The tradition on his affluence is doubted by Mattingly, *Athenaeum*, 37 (1959), 167–169; cf. Carney, *P. Terenti Afri: Hecyra*, 9—and most recently defended by D. Gilula, *SCI*, 8–9 (1989), 74–78.

87. The effort of Perelli, *Il teatro rivoluzionario*, 146–150, to get around these facts by pointing to Scipio's service at Pydna (when he was seventeen!) is quite unconvincing. Nothing comparable can be unearthed for Laelius—let alone Furius. Polybius' flattery of

was their contemporary or perhaps even a decade older.[88] The poet did not rely upon the "Scipionic circle" for the success of his career.

How then to account for the tradition on this alleged relationship? Porcius Licinus may have had it in for Scipio and his friends, but he hardly plucked their names out of thin air. An obvious answer lies to hand. The *didascaliae* inform us that both the *Adelphoe* and the second production of the *Hecyra* took place at the funeral games of L. Aemilius Paullus, natural father of Aemilianus, in 160. Whether or not these notices derive from contemporary testimony, there is no obvious reason for invention here.[89] It seemed plausible to infer from the games a connection between the artist and the house of Aemilius Paullus. Porcius Licinus or a predecessor simply applied that inference to an interpretation of Terence's lines on the *homines nobiles*. It was a classic case of adding two and two to reach five. That same arithmetic, unfortunately, reappears in modern textboooks.[90] In fact, the usual deduction should be turned on its head. Selection of Terentian plays to grace the games of Aemilius Paullus reflects the reputation of the poet, not the patronage of the family. The house of Scipio was the beneficiary, rather than the benefactor.

---

the young Scipio does not overcome the obstacle. Mattingly, *RivCultClassMed*, 5 (1963), 36–48, proposes to solve the problem by redating Terence's *floruit* to the 150s rather than the 160s. That is characteristically ingenious but most implausible. Even if one were to scrap the only testimony on Terence's dates, ca. 184–159 (Suet. *Vita Ter.* 5; Jerome, *Chron.* ad ann. 158)—a highly dubious methodology—relocating the plays to the 150s does not help much. Scipio Aemilianus' public activities in that decade were limited to service as a military tribune in Spain—and that only in 151; Polyb. 35.4–5. Equally desperate is the attempt of Cicu, *Sandalion*, 1 (1978), 112–120, to see in the *amici* of *Heaut.* 24 and the *homines nobiles* of *Adelph.* 15 two separate groups of Terence's backers.

88. Ancient tradition set his death in 159; Suet. *Vita Ter.* 5. Jerome, *Chron.* ad ann. 158, put it a year later. In Suetonius' text, Terence died at the age of twenty-five, thus supplying a date of birth in 185. This would mean that his first play, the *Andria*, produced in 166, was composed at the age of eighteen; Didasc. Ter. *Andr.*; cf. Suet. *Vita Ter.* 1, 3. It might be preferable to accept the variant manuscript reading of "thirty-five" rather than "twenty-five" and put the poet's birth in 195. That would concur with Fenestella's statement that Terence *utroque maiorem natu fuisse*; Suet. *Vita Ter.* 2. Both Scipio and Laelius were born ca. 185.

89. Mattingly, *Athenaeum*, 37 (1959), 148–173, seeks to impugn the reliability of the *didascaliae* generally. In this particular instance, however, he has to resort to the desperate hypothesis that the *ludi scaenici* at Aemilius Paullus' funeral games of 160 were confused with the (unattested) *ludi scaenici* at Aemilius Lepidus' funeral games a decade later!

90. See, most recently, Brothers, *Terence: The Self-Tormenter*, 11. Garbrah, *Athenaeum*, 59 (1981), 190–191, professes to find an echo of Ter. *Adelph.* 19–21 in an oratorical fragment of Scipio; *ORF*, n. 21, fr. 16. Even if it were conscious imitation, however, this hardly "confirms the close connection of Terence with the Scipios."

The whole notion of Terence as a showpiece for the "Scipionic circle" or a purveyor of their principles and ideals can happily be allowed to vanish.[91] The poet's plays did not advance the interests of a coterie. Nor did he employ the medium, as Plautus had, to comment wryly on contemporary social, political, and institutional developments.[92]

The accusation leveled against Terence bears a closer look. Hasty reading or common misperceptions consider it a complaint about powerful backers exercising influence on his behalf. Not so. The criticism has nothing to do with patronage or promotion. It concentrates entirely upon assistance in composition, the lending of talent rather than wealth or authority. Terence's adversary sought to impugn his artistry, not his connections.[93] It was the playwright, in his retort, who boasted of association with those whose accomplishments in all spheres of life have won them admiration throughout the citizenry.

Who were the *homines nobiles*? An altogether new proposition might be considered. Perhaps the phrase refers not to a senatorial faction or a philhellenic party but, in a broader sense, to Rome's aristocratic leadership. Terentian drama provided an outlet for the expression of an upper-class culture in second-century Rome. That proposition suggests a different line of inquiry: the theater as setting for the articulation and propagation of aristocratic values.

An innovation of conspicuous public import takes on meaning in this light. The censors of 194, Sex. Aelius Paetus and C. Cornelius Cethegus, instructed the curule aediles to set aside special seats for members of the senatorial order, thus segregating them from the populace as a whole—the first time such a distinction had been enacted.[94] The occa-

91. Even the idea of a "Scipionic circle" in the sense of a political or ideological group with common goals and policies has little to recommend it; see, especially, H. Strasburger, *Hermes*, 94 (1966), 60–72; Astin, *Scipio Aemilianus*, 294–296; J. E. G. Zetzel, *HSCP*, 76 (1972), 173–179. And see the sensible remarks of Goldberg, *Understanding Terence*, 8–15.

92. On Plautus' practice, see Gruen, *Studies*, 124–157. The general absence of Roman political or legal terminology in Terence is noted by D. C. Earl, *Historia*, 11 (1962), 469–477, who, however, accepts the notion that Terence wrote under Scipionic patronage. The effort of M. F. Callier, *IXe Congrès Int. de l'Assoc. Budé* (1973), I, 412–423, to find political significance in the second act of *Adelphoe* is strained and unconvincing.

93. Cf. Ter. *Heaut.* 24: *amicum ingenio fretum, haud natura sua*; *Adelph.* 15–16: *homines nobilis / hunc adiutare adsidueque una scribere*.

94. Livy, 34.44.4–5: *aedilibus curulibus imperarunt, ut loca senatoria secernerent a populo; nam antea in promiscuo spectabant*; 34.54.4: *primum senatus a populo secretus spectavit*; Ascon. 69, C; Val. Max. 2.4.3, 4.5.1: *usque ad Africanum et Ti. Longum consules promiscuus senatui et populo spectandorum ludorum locus erat*.

sion for the change, it appears, came at the *ludi Romani*, most ancient of Roman festivals. Institution of the new practice at that ceremony would carry the weightiest significance—and presumably serve as model for other *ludi*.[95] What was its import?

Our sources report that the man who instigated the move was P. Scipio Africanus.[96] Scipio, consul in 194, had been named *princeps senatus* by the censors of that year.[97] Hence, temptation arises to see cooperation between Scipio and the censors who ordered the change in seating as part of a political maneuver. The temptation should be resisted. The censors of 194 did not appoint Scipio as *princeps senatus* but simply renewed the appointment made five years earlier under the previous censors—of whom Scipio himself was one. That was routine procedure, not a political act.[98] Yet it can hardly be accident that Africanus publicly advocated or endorsed the innovation, perhaps even proposing a formal motion in his capacity as consul.[99] The new seating

95. That the innovation took place at the *ludi Romani* was reported by Valerius Antias; Ascon. 69, C; followed by Livy, 34.44.5, 34.54.4. Cicero put the occasion at the *ludi Megalenses*; *Har. Resp.* 24; Ascon. 70, C. So also Val. Max. 2.4.3, whose information may be drawn from Cicero. One can dismiss that information as erroneous, perhaps a confusion with the fact that the *ludi Megalenses* first acquired theatrical shows in 194; Livy, 34.54.3. And Cicero had a point to make about the Megalensian games anyway: he wished to contrast their normal solemnity with the disruptions created by Clodius. For J. O. Lenaghan, *A Commentary on Cicero's Oration "De Haruspicum Responso"* (The Hague, 1969), 123, Cicero made an honest mistake, for curule aediles preside over both *ludi Romani* and *ludi Megalenses*. The statement, however, may inadvertently suggest that the new system, once established, spread to other *ludi*. Still another tradition associated the initial change with votive games sponsored by the consuls of 194; Ascon. 70, C— perhaps from Fenestella; cf. B. A. Marshall, *A Historical Commentary on Asconius* (Columbia, Mo., 1985), 248.

96. Livy, 34.54.8; Cic. *Har. Resp.* 24; Val. Max. 2.4.3—with confusion of Africanus and Aemilianus.

97. Livy, 34.4.4.

98. Livy, 34.4.4.

99. Cf. Livy, 34.54.8: *quod consul auctor eius rei fuisset*; Cic. *Har. Resp.* 24: *senatui locum P. Africanus iterum consul ille maior dedit*; Ascon. 70, C: *auctore Scipione consule*. In an earlier speech, the fragmentary *Pro Cornelio*, Cicero expressed himself more guardedly, saying only that Scipio permitted the change to occur. Asconius takes him to task for that inconsistency, alleging that Cicero altered his emphasis to suit his audience: the orator shielded Scipio when speaking to the populace in the *Pro Cornelio*; Ascon. 69–70, C. But the commentator's nit-picking misses the point. Cicero calls attention to Scipio's role in both passages, even omitting to mention censors and aediles; so, rightly, Marshall, *Commentary on Asconius*, 247–248. Asconius is similarly wrong to infer that Cicero follows Valerius Antias in giving Scipio a passive role; 69, C. If Cicero were following Antias, he would hardly have placed the innovation at the *ludi Megalenses*, for Antias (erroneously) dated the first *ludi scaenici* at the Megalesia to 191; Livy, 36.36.4. U. Schlag, *Historia*, 17 (1968), 509–512, pins too much faith on Asconius' interpretation and even

arrangement came with immense *auctoritas*. Its champion was hero of the Hannibalic War, consul, *princeps senatus*, and Rome's most prestigious figure. The symbolic character of the move stands forth. The theater would reassert the preeminence of the *nobiles*.

The aftermath of the event provokes further interest. Livy's account suggests second thoughts and controversy, sharp differences of opinion among the citizenry. Some applauded the change as a deserved honor, long overdue, for the senatorial order; others complained that it was a gratuitous blow to the esteem of the commons and that any augmentation of senatorial authority diminished the worth of the *populus*. The latter could point to five and a half centuries of undifferentiated seating, now broken by arrogant senatorial self-indulgence.[100] Scipio Africanus, the man most closely identified with the change, also became a target of criticism. Acccording to Cicero, some of Rome's wisest men rebuked him. Valerius Maximus adds that popular favor toward Scipio was severely shaken. The great general, we are told, had misgivings and engaged in self-reproach.[101] Was this, then, a hotly debated issue, dividing Rome along political lines and creating class dissension?

That would be a hasty and erroneous conclusion. Livy's account gives a stylized polarization, akin to obsolete narratives on the patrician-plebeian struggles.[102] Even if one takes the presentation as given, however, it breathes no hint of senatorial debate or dispute over policy. Livy professedly provides only talk and rumor, *sermones*—and that after the fact.[103] These cannot derive from official records or hard data. At best the account is speculation, perhaps invention, by Valerius Antias or another of Livy's sources. The historian had no better testimony on Scipio's alleged subsequent repentance; he presents it as hearsay: *ferunt*.[104] If Africanus lost any credit with the *populus* over this matter, it left his career unaffected. The glory of the Antiochene War still awaited

---

hypothesizes that the two divergent Ciceronian passages were both incorporated in Livy's account, an altogether fanciful hypothesis. See the criticisms of J. von Ungern-Sternberg, *Chiron*, 5 (1975), 157–163.

100. Livy, 34.54.4–7.

101. Cic. *Pro Corn. apud* Ascon. 69, C: *non solum a sapientissimis hominibus qui tum erant verum etiam a se ipso saepe accusatus est*; Val. Max. 2.4.3: *eaque res avertit vulgi animum et favorem Scipionis magnopere quassavit*; Livy, 34.54.8: *postremo ipsum quoque Africanum, quod consul auctor eius rei fuisset, paenituisse, ferunt*.

102. Cf. Livy, 34.54.5: *demptum ex dignitate populi, quidquid maiestati patrum adiectum esset*.

103. Livy, 34.54.4: *praebuitque sermones, sicut omnis novitas solet*.

104. Livy, 34.54.8: *postremo ipsum quoque Africanum . . . paenituisse ferunt*.

him. But whatever truth clings to the tale of criticism and self-reproach, the new seating arrangements remained in effect and unchallenged.

The change, in fact, brought innovation more in principle than in practice. Valerius Maximus reports that the practice of deference to senators in the theater long preceded the censorial edict of 194: no member of the *plebs* would seat himself ahead of a senator. Nor were they bound by technicalities thereafter. L. Flamininus, stripped of senatorial rank by the censors of 184, dutifully chose a seat at the rear of the theater, but the spectators would not permit it and insisted that he occupy a place consonant with his senatorial background.[105] The anecdote offers welcome illumination on two counts. First, despite stories of rebuke and remorse, senatorial privileges in the theater endured, consistently sustained by the *plebs* themselves. Second, and perhaps more revealing, the pattern of de facto segregation held long before its de jure declaration. Senators, in short, did not require a new edict to maintain preferred seating in the theater.

Why then do it? The enactment of 194 may not have had a practical goal, but it did have symbolic significance. Scipio Africanus' prestige underscored its importance. The measure made public pronouncement that drama was no mere popular entertainment but a highbrow institution claimed as part of the cultural milieu of the upper classes. The theater would be a visible reminder of the ascendancy of the *nobiles*.

Rome possessed no permanent stone theater in this period. Instead, wooden structures were erected annually or for each of the scenic games, with temporary stage and benches that would be demolished after the performances.[106] Deliberate choice dictated that policy. The government could surely have constructed a durable edifice to house dramatic presentations, had it desired. Whatever the initial cost, it was bound to be less than the repeated creation and demolition of improvised arrangements every year.[107] Yet the ruling class— or at least the dominant portion thereof—insisted upon makeshift rather than continuing structures. The purpose and implications of that policy have

105. Val. Max. 4.5.1. Cf. Plut. *Flam.* 19.4: ὥσπερ εἴωθε. Justin, 43.5.10, even has special seats for senators as early as the fourth century.
106. Cf. Tac. *Ann.* 14.20: *nam antea subitariis gradibus et scaena in tempus structa ludos edi solitos.*
107. Cf. Tac. *Ann.* 14.21: *sed et consultum parsimoniae quod perpetua sedes theatro locata sit potius quam immenso sumptu singulos per annos consurgeret ac destrueretur.*

never received serious attention. They can shed needed light upon the attitudes of the Roman aristocracy.

The policy, to be sure, encountered occasional challenges. The censors of 179, M. Aemilius Lepidus and M. Fulvius Nobilior, let contracts for an auditorium and a stage to be built near the temple of Apollo.[108] Plainly they intended a permanent structure. A censorial *locatio* would hardly have been required for the annual improvisation, nor would Livy have bothered to record the fact. But what became of the effort? The sources fall silent. That a theater arose and subsequently collapsed or was destroyed seems quite improbable without any notice in the evidence. More likely, the project never got off the ground. A consensus among the *nobiles* still resisted the idea of long-term theatrical structures. The next pair of censors, in 174, Q. Fulvius Flaccus and A. Postumius Albinus, made a more modest attempt to circumvent that consensus. They let a contract for a stage to be provided for aediles and praetors—evidently as a permanent structure for all the *ludi* for which those magistrates were responsible.[109] This too is never heard about again. The *locatio* may have been blocked or the enterprise aborted. At most, this was a *scaena*, not a theater, and the annual construction process would continue.

A more serious challenge came in the mid 150s. The censors of 154, C. Cassius Longinus and M. Valerius Messalla, went beyond the letting of a contract. They pressed ahead with the construction of a stone theater, to the point where the edifice was nearly complete, an impressive structure located at the Lupercal in the direction of the Palatine. The project, however, did not come to fruition, thwarted at the eleventh hour, perhaps as late as 151. A senior statesman, P. Scipio Nasica, who had the distinction of twice holding the consulship, spoke out vigorously against the undertaking, construction ceased, and the theater was demolished by senatorial directive.[110] The event must have left a

---

108. Livy, 40.51.3: *theatrum et proscaenium ad Apollinis . . . locavit*. Livy specifies Lepidus as taking the initiative for this *locatio*. On the location, see Hanson, *Roman Theater Temples*, 18–24.

109. Livy, 41.27.5: *et scaenam aedilibus praetoribusque praebendam*.

110. Some nagging discrepancies exist in the sources, but the basic picture is clear enough. Valerius Maximus gives the names of the censors, thus fixing the year of 154 for the beginning of the project; 2.4.2: *quae inchoata quidem sunt a Messala et Cassio*. The year of Nasica's intervention remains uncertain. Considerable time must have passed, for the building was nearly finished when the senate called a halt; Appian, *BC*, 1.28: καὶ ἤδη που τέλος ἐλάμβανεν. Orosius, 4.21.4, alone gives a date, 151 B.C., but since he places

powerful impression. Dismantling a large stone theater on the brink of completion, one that would have accommodated a good portion of Rome's citizenry, could hardly go unnoticed. The episode, in fact, gained considerable notoriety and was frequently mentioned in subsequent literature. It demands explanation.

Scipio Nasica and those for whom he spoke offered reasons. It was a matter of national character: a theater would not only be valueless, it would do damage to public morals.[111] Resistance to this construction expressed the *severitas* of the state, the clearest sign of Rome's true values.[112] Demolition of the theater would prevent it from being a staging ground for dissension and upheaval. And it was, in any case, not beneficial for Romans to accustom themselves to Greek pleasures.[113] Such, in brief, are the purposes ascribed by our sources to Nasica and like-minded allies in their campaign to block a permanent theater. Protection of the national character rings true—at least as a posture struck by Nasica.[114] That advocates did employ such sloganeering is confirmed by another step taken in close conjunction with this one. A *senatus consultum* banned seating altogether at the *ludi* in Rome and for a mile outside the city.[115] However makeshift the previous arrangements

---

the censors themselves in that year, confidence in his accuracy is diminished. That date, nevertheless, is not far wrong. The Livian *Periocha*, 48, puts the destruction some time in the years 154 to 150—and also reports that it was done on senatorial orders. An aberrant notice appears in Saint Augustine, *CD*, 2.5, who puts the whole affair a generation earlier, but he has simply confused Nasica, the consul of 155, with his father, consul in 191. A different sort of confusion lurks in the accounts of Velleius Paterculus, 1.15.3, and Appian, *BC*, 1.28, who ascribe the building to the censor Cassius and its cancellation to a consul Caepio. Cassius can stand, but there is no consul Caepio who fits the bill in these years. The usual emendation of "Caepio" to "Scipio" is no help, for Nasica's consulship came in 155. A variant tradition obviously existed, perhaps based on the conflict between Q. Caepio and L. Cassius at the end of the second century. See the cogent analysis by E. T. Salmon, *Athenaeum*, 41 (1963), 5–9. Cf. Hanson, *Roman Theater Temples*, 24–25. Orosius, 4.21.4, specifies what might have been guessed anyway, that the theater was made of stone.

111. Livy, *Per.* 48: *inutile et nociturum publicis moribus*.

112. Vell. Pat. 1.15.3: *eximia civitatis severitas . . . inter clarissima publicae voluntatis argumenta*.

113. Appian, *BC*, 1.28: τόδε στάσεων ἄρξον ἑτέρων ἢ οὐ χρήσιμον ὅλως Ἑλληνικαῖς ἡδυπαθείαις Ῥωμαίους ἐθίζεσθαι.

114. M. G. Morgan, *Historia*, 39 (1990), 72–74, suggests that Nasica's posturing would be especially appropriate in 151, when he advocated the value of *metus hostilis* in opposing war with Carthage. Cf. Rawson, *Cambridge Ancient History*², VIII, 470.

115. Val. Max. 2.4.2; Livy, *Per.* 48; Tac. *Ann.* 14.20.

had been, they had always provided seats for the audience, as many allusions in the Plautine plays testify.[116] After the *senatus consultum* of circa 151, however, spectators would have to stand. The rationale that was offered once again took the high moral ground: standing on one's feet built character. To sit in the theater was tantamount to wasting days in idleness; to stand would demonstrate the characteristic *virilitas* of the Roman people.[117] How long this measure remained on the books or was actively enforced eludes discovery.[118] No matter. The message delivered by the *senatus consultum* underscored the propagation of Roman values and their manifestation in the context of the theater.

The public pronouncements, however, do not disclose genuine motivation. The measures of circa 151 might display a commitment to Roman *severitas* and *virilitas*, but that commitment seems quite inadequate to account for the demolition of a stone theater. The authorities, after all, only removed the structure; they did not abolish the institution. Plays would continue to be produced; audiences would still attend the theater; *ludi scaenici* remained a fixture on the Roman cultural scene. Scipio Nasica made no move to reverse those developments. How then should one understand the opposition to a *theatrum lapideum*? Appian offers two alternatives: Scipio sought either to avoid *stasis* in the theater or to shield the people from "Greek pleasures."[119] Neither of these reasons will do. Both represent mere conjectures by the Alexandrian historian three hundred years after the fact. It was natural enough for him to imagine concern about political tumult as a motive for dismantling the theater. But the concern is anachronistic. Nothing in the previous history of the institution suggests that it had served as outlet for popular discontent or sedition.[120] And, in any case, if dissidents wished

116. E.g., Plautus, *Amph.* 65–66; *Aul.* 718–719; *Capt.* 12; *Curc.* 646–647; *Epid.* 733; *Merc.* 160; *Miles,* 81–82; *Poen.* 17–20, 224; *Pseud.* 1–2; *Truc.* 968. See discussions by A. Rumpf, *MdI,* 3 (1950), 42–43; Beare, *Roman Stage*[3], 241–247; and Duckworth, *Nature of Roman Comedy,* 80–81.

117. Val. Max. 2.4.2: *standi virilitas propria Romanae gentis nota esset*; Tac. *Ann.* 14.20: *stantem populum spectavisse, ne, si consideret theatro, dies totos ignavia continuaret.*

118. Duckworth, *Nature of Roman Comedy,* 80–81, asserts that seats were restored by L. Mummius for the plays produced at his triumphal games in 145. So also E. Frézouls, in *Théâtre et spectacles dans l'antiquité* (Actes du colloque de Strasbourg, 1981), 195. We know only that they had been reintroduced by the time of Marius; Plut. *Mar.* 2.2; cf. Tac. *Ann.* 14.20.

119. Appian, *BC,* 1.28; quoted above, n. 113.

120. Frézouls's political interpretation along these lines is strictly based on late Republican evidence; *Théâtre et spectacles,* 195–196; idem, *ANRW,* II.12.1 (1982), 353–356. Similarly, Rumpf, *MdI,* 3 (1950), 41–45; Dupont, *Le théâtre latin,* 17. The earliest period

to demonstrate their feelings, they could do so as well from wooden as from stone seats. The supposed anxiety over attachment to Greek pleasures cannot be taken seriously either as motive or pretext. Roman audiences had been witnessing *fabulae palliatae* for three-quarters of a century and would continue to do so long after the 150s. Although the creative energies invested in that genre may have waned in the late second century, demand for the revival of comedies by Plautus, Terence, and Turpilius attests to the continued popularity of the form, still a worthy rival to the *togata*.[121] Tragedy gained yet greater success, and the production of tragic plays proceeded apace.[122] Toppling the stone theater in no way cleared the stage of Hellenic drama, nor would Nasica have claimed to do so.

A very different solution recommends itself, especially in light of other developments discerned in this period. Eliminating the stone structure struck a blow at the idea of permanence in the Roman theater. In an important sense, this represents reassertion of aristocratic privilege and control in that realm of cultural activity. Under the system then in force, decisions on dramatic performances rested with public officials each year. Praetors or aediles, with the guidance of the senate, determined which scripts would be bought, which performances would be financed, which *ludi* would include plays, and perhaps whether productions would be mounted at all. Such decisions, even if reached with expected consistency, provided a repeated reminder that the leadership of the state oversaw the course of Latin drama—and did so afresh each year. The ritual of erecting and then dismantling temporary structures gave annual notice that the ruling class held decisive authority in the artistic sphere. A permanent theater, whatever its advantages in cost and convenience, would represent a symbolic relaxation of that authority. The vast edifice, exhibiting solidity and endurance, would enshrine

---

in which reference is made to popular feelings expressed in the theater is the age of the Gracchi and Saturninus. And that is alluded to in general terms, without specifics, by Cic. *Pro Sest.* 105. L. R. Taylor, *Roman Voting Assemblies* (Ann Arbor, Mich., 1966), 30–31, offers the ingenious but unsupported suggestion that Romans resisted the stone theater lest it be used for popular assemblies in which voters would sit like the Greeks rather than stand like the Romans. For C. Nicolet, *The World of the Citizen in Republican Rome* (Berkeley, Calif., 1980), 363, a stone theater might tempt the masses to political gatherings of their own—a most unlikely proposition. Stone seats were not indispensable for such assemblages.

121. Cf. Beare, *Roman Stage*[3], 128–129; Duckworth, *Nature of Roman Comedy*, 68–69.

122. See Beare, *Roman Stage*[3], 70–84, 119–127; Gratwick, in *Cambridge Hist. Class. Lit.*, II, 128–137.

the drama as an unshakable institution, no longer dependent upon the resolve of magistrates and the verdict of the aristocracy. Resistance was inevitable. The stone theater crumbled under senatorial directive, and none other arose for a century thereafter. The nobility preferred the traditional system, which manifested their own cultural control.

The preceding interpretations run into an ostensible obstacle. A basic objection might counter that the theater seems an unlikely locus for a cultural statement by the Roman elite. The tastes of the populace, so we are usually told, ran away from serious drama or genteel comedy. Their attention was easily distracted, especially when more popular forms of entertainment such as gladiatorial shows or boxing exhibitions were available.[123] On this view, the successful playwright and impresario would have to tailor productions to appeal to a mass audience and could not hope to lift the genre to a level of discriminating refinement. Is it so? What evidence do we have for the allegedly vulgar tastes of Roman spectators?

The prime exhibit for this assessment—indeed, nearly the only one— is the double flop of Terence's *Hecyra*. Twice, it is reported, the play failed to gain audience favor, outstripped by other attractions and abandoned in midperformance, until a third attempt finally gained acceptance. The testimony, which derives exclusively from the prologues to the comedy, has gone almost entirely unchallenged, giving rise to sweeping statements about the tastes of Roman spectators and the fate of Roman drama. Terence's lines will repay a closer look.

The *Hecyra* first hit the stage, so the didascalic notice informs us, at the *ludi Megalenses* of 165. It was produced again five years later at the funeral games of Aemilius Paullus and performed once more in that same year of 160.[124] The comedy did not fare very well in its first two presentations. If

---

123. Cf. Beare, *Roman Stage*³, 161; Duckworth, *Nature of Roman Comedy*, 81–82; Garton, *Personal Aspects*, 52–53; Martin, *Terence: Adelphoe*, 6; Forehand, *Terence*, 22; Jory, *Studies in Honour of Webster*, I, 145–146.

124. This is not the place for discussion of Terentian chronology, and it does not affect the issues here under discussion. The authority of the *didascaliae* was challenged by L. Gestri, *StudItalFilolClass*, 13 (1936), 61–105, who also revised the order of the plays, based in part on the prologues to *Hecyra*'s performances, which he saw as following one another in fairly rapid succession. His views, in modified form, won the adherence of Mattingly, *Athenaeum*, 37 (1959), 148–173; idem, *RivCultClassMed*, 5 (1963), 12–61. They have found little favor elsewhere. See objections raised by M. R. Posani, *AttiAccad d'Italia*, 7 (1942), 247–280, with Gestri's reply, *StudItalFilolClass*, 20 (1943), 3–58. A more sweeping attack on Gestri's methodology is in D. Klose, *Die Didaskalien und*

the prologue be believed, the initial occasion in 165 turned into a fiasco. A peculiar misfortune and calamity intervened to disrupt proceedings, says Terence: the audience, struck senseless by anticipation, fixed their minds upon the coming of a tightrope dancer.[125] So much appears in the "first prologue," purportedly delivered prior to the play's second production. But that was not the end of the matter. The "second prologue," attached to the third and successful production, describes the abortive initial effort in fuller detail. The *calamitas* involved more than excitement over a prospective tightrope walker. Word arrived of boxers with an illustrious reputation, their entourage assembled, followed by a great hubbub, shouts by women, and general melee that drove the actors' troupe out of the theater and rang down the curtain on whatever remained of the performance.[126] The second attempt had no better luck. This time the company got through the beginning of the play with some success, but when report reached the spectators that a gladiatorial show was in the offing, people crowded in from all sides, shouting tumultuously, fighting for seats, and once again ousting the ill-starred drama.[127] No wonder, then, that modern scholars disparage the tastes of Roman audiences.

The matter, however, is not so simple. How should one interpret these episodes? And how far can one generalize from them about the attitudes and actions of the theatergoing public?

The failure of the *Hecyra*, it can be argued, stemmed from the short-comings of the audience. Roman spectators were unprepared for a quiet, sophisticated comedy that made undue demands upon their intel-

---

Prologe des Terenz (Bamberg, 1966), passim, especially 51–80, with further bibliographic references. Klose, among other things, effectively refutes Gestri's effort to deny the authenticity of the second *Hecyra* prologue.

125. Ter. *Hec.* 1–5: *haec quom datast / nova, novom intervenit vitium et calamitas / ut neque spectari neque cognosci potuerit, / ita populus studio stupidus in funambulo / animum occuparat.*

126. Ter. *Hec.* 33–36: *quom primum eam agere coepi, pugilum gloria, / [funambuli eodem accessit exspectatio], / comitum conventus, strepitus, clamor mulierum / fecere ut ante tempus exirem foras.* The second of these four lines is often excised as an interpolation. The older view that Terence's audience deserted the theater to attend other entertainments elsewhere rests on a hasty reading of these verses. They show plainly enough that the *Hecyra* company was driven out of the theater while the audience remained to welcome the substitute shows. Cf. *Phormio*, 32: *quom per tumultum noster grex motus locost.* The fact was established independently and decisively by Gilula, *SCI* 4 (1978), 45–49; and F. H. Sandbach, *CQ*, 32 (1982), 134–135.

127. Ter. *Hec.* 39–42: *primo actu placeo, quom interea rumor venit / datum iri gladiatores, populus convolat, / tumultuantur, clamant, pugnant de loco; / ego interea meum non potui tutari locum.*

lects. Better to turn to lighter fare such as gladiators, boxers, or acrobats. The first two versions of the play, on this analysis, exceeded the grasp of the audience or attempted subtleties that they found uncongenial.[128] That analysis, however, lacks force and cogency. The subtle techniques, novelties, or unconventional sophistication that scholars have discerned in the play all derive from the extant version—the successful version! Hence they can hardly account for earlier misfirings. Further, if the prologues' information be relied upon, neither of the first two productions got very far before distraction, disruption, and tumult terminated the performance. The first barely got off the ground, the second lasted only through the opening portion. So, the audience had little time to pass judgment on the quality of the piece.[129] The verdict on the *Hecyra* was not an aesthetic one.[130]

Did the disruptions then represent deliberate sabotage? Terence had his enemies, and the prologue hints that they had a hand in manufacturing the disturbances that twice sank the *Hecyra*. The prologue's spokesman appeals to citizens attending the third production, injects a *captatio benevolentiae*, and requests that they prevent the dramatic art from falling into the control of a few.[131] And he proceeds to exhort them not to permit the "unjust" to mock the playwright and cheat him of his due.[132] It would seem logical to deduce that Terence's rivals organized boxers, gladiators, and other entertainers with the express purpose of wreaking havoc upon the *Hecyra*. And if it could be done on those occasions, it might well have been a regular occurrence on the Roman stage, "a rough and tumble place."[133] That thesis now commands a

128. Cf. Duckworth, *Nature of Roman Comedy*, 149; Mattingly, *Athenaeum*, 37 (1959), 167: "He had tried comedy too subtle and quiet for Roman taste"; Carney, *P. Terenti Afri: Hecyra*, 9: "the novelty of the *Hecyra* . . . seems to have taken it beyond the tastes of Roman theatergoers." T. Frank, *AJP*, 49 (1928), 309–322, especially 319–320, offered a more elaborate argument: Terence abandoned Plautus' expository prologues, thus leaving spectators in suspense and forgoing the conventional technique of dramatic irony: "Not surprising, therefore that this play . . . failed twice." The idea was revived most recently by Ireland, *Terence: The Mother in Law*, 9. Cf. Goldberg, *Understanding Terence*, 159–169.

129. See the telling arguments of Gilula, *Athenaeum*, 59 (1981), 29–37. On the meaning of *primo actu* (Ter. *Hec.* 39), see Carney, *P. Terenti Afri: Hecyra*, 32; Ireland, *Terence: The Mother-in-Law*, 108.

130. For a sympathetic treatment of the play, see the fine analysis by D. Konstan, *Roman Comedy* (Ithaca, N.Y., 1983), 130–141, with bibliography.

131. Ter. *Hec.* 46–47: *nolite sinere per vos artem musicam recidere ad paucos.*

132. Ter. *Hec.* 52–54: *ne eum circumventum inique iniqui inrideant.*

133. So Forehand, *Terence*, 22; similarly, Dupont, *Le théâtre latin*, 19. The notion that Terence's enemies purposely drove the play off the boards is widespread; e.g., Mattingly,

consensus, but it contains serious flaws that have gone largely unrecognized. Reference to the *pauci* and the *iniqui* may correspond to similar complaints elsewhere about critics who charged Terence with everything from *contaminatio* to plagiarism.[134] All those accusations, however, concern the character or quality of the plays. They are aesthetic disagreements or captious backbiting. None of them has anything in common with organizing lowbrow troupes of entertainers and loosing them upon the stage—an altogether different category of activity. Further, if Terence's envious rivals arranged the fiasco to embarrass him, why use the ploy only with the *Hecyra*, and why use it twice with a five-year interval while Terence enjoyed success with five other dramas?

A radical proposition merits consideration. Perhaps the prologue to the *Hecyra* did not describe a historical situation at all. The idea, heretical though it might appear, bears pursuing. Terentian prologues generally possess a stylized character, heavily and consciously influenced by contemporary rhetoric. Their principal objective was to catch the attention of the house, rouse expectations, and win favor.[135] Historicity was not required—or perhaps desirable.[136] How plausible is the material in the *Hecyra* prologue?

An item of importance needs attention here. The production of games in Rome took place in accord with a fixed internal schedule. *Ludi circenses* were held on days different from *ludi scaenici*. And when *munera* (gladiatorial contests) had a part in the festival, they too occurred on days kept separate from the dramatic shows. Hence, the conjunction of plays with other forms of entertainment would normally not even arise.[137]

Athenaeum, 37 (1959), 166–167; Carney, *P. Terenti Afri: Hecyra*, 33–34; Martin, *Terence: Adelphoe*, 5; Gilula, *Athenaeum*, 59 (1981), 30.

134. Cf. Ter. *Andria*, 1–7; *Heauton*, 16–26; *Phormio*, 1–8, 18; *Adelph*. 1–3, 15–17.

135. See the perceptive and persuasive discussion by Goldberg, *Understanding Terence*, 31–60; cf. idem, *CP*, 78 (1983), 198–211. He rightly reckons Terence's quarrel with Luscius Lanuvinus as more a dramaturgical device than a historical record. The most recent essay on Terence's prologues, Gilula, *QuadUrb*, 33 (1989), 95–106, does not pronounce on this matter. On Luscius, see the inventive reconstruction by Garton, *Personal Aspects*, 41–139.

136. Note, for example, that the prologue to the *Andria* indicates criticism and objections to Terence's earlier plays; Terence, *Andria*, 1–7. Yet the *Andria*, as the didascalic notice affirms and is generally recognized, was Terence's first drama.

137. The separation is clearly alluded to by Cicero, *De Leg.* 2.38: *iam ludi publici quoniam sunt cavea circoque divisi*. The practice seems to have held from the start. Note, e.g., the four days devoted to scenic games at the *ludi Romani* in 214; Livy, 24.43.7. T. Flamininus' funerary games for his father in 174 had four days for the *ludi scaenici* and

One most serious obstacle to the *communis opinio* has been entirely overlooked. The second showing of the *Hecyra* took place at the funeral games of L. Aemilius Paullus. The celebration was elaborate, financed and organized by the great statesman's sons, Scipio Aemilianus and Fabius Maximus. They took responsibility not only for the *ludi scaenici* but for the gladiatorial games.[138] Did the brothers have gladiators descend upon their own *ludi*, thereby not only discomfiting Terence but compromising their father's memorial ceremony? Or did those eminent patricians lose control of their festivities, allowing others to exploit their negligence, confound their arrangements, and humiliate their chosen poet and producer?[139] The improbabilities mount.

The reliability of the prologue founders on other counts. For one thing, the *Hecyra* may not, in fact, have done so badly. Suetonius informs us in the *Life of Terence* that all the poet's six plays enjoyed popular success.[140] Second, if the difficulties encountered by the *Hecyra* were at all representative of what might happen in the theater, why do we have no parallel instances elsewhere?[141] Further, a discrepancy exists between the purported prologue to the second performance and that to the third, both supposedly describing the failure of the first. In the one instance, an anticipated rope walker broke up proceedings; in the other

---

three for the *munera*; Livy, 41.28.11. And the games of Q. Fulvius Flaccus in 172 included a four-day segment for dramas and one day *in circo*; Livy, 42.10.5.

138. Polyb. 31.28.5–6.

139. Scipio, to be sure, was only nineteen years old at the time, but friends and retainers of that powerful family would surely have seen to the arrangements and assured a smooth operation. Nor would Polybius have called attention to the event if proceedings had dissolved in tumult and demonstrated Scipio's ineptitude.

140. Suet. *Vita Ter.* 3. To be sure, the critic Volcacius Sedigitus, who composed his *De poetis* around the end of the second century, ranked the *Hecyra* last among Terence's comedies. But Volcacius' views were notoriously unorthodox; cf. Gellius, 15.24.1; Gilula, *Athenaeum*, 59 (1981), 30–31. And his opinion does not, in any case, speak to the success of the play.

141. Caecilius, it might be thought, suffered similar misfortune, but the relevant remarks in the *Hecyra* prologue suggest a figurative rather than a literal driving off of the production; Ter. *Hec.* 14–15: *partim sum earum exactus partim vix steti*; cf. *Andria*, 27. Certainly the comparable remarks made a few verses later fall in that category; *Hec.* 21–23: *ita poetam restitui in locum, / prope iam remmotum iniuria advorsarium / ab studio atque ab labore atque arte musica.* At most, the *exactus* implies a barrage of hoots and catcalls—but nothing parallel to an audience's turning its attention to a different medium of entertainment. The evidence of Horace, *Epist.* 2.1.182–186, on the preference of the *plebicula* for low-grade entertainment rather than drama, plainly draws on the *Hecyra* prologues and does not represent independent testimony; cf. C. O. Brink, *Horace on Poetry: Epistles, Book II* (Cambridge, 1982), 219.

news of a boxing match turned the production into a shambles.[142] The credibility of the play's prologue wanes still further. At the very least, we can no longer cite it as exemplary of crowd behavior or popular tastes in outdoor entertainment. The text contains more creativity than fidelity to fact.

A problem remains. One might not demand accuracy from Terence, but should expect at least plausibility. The prologue, even if unhistorical, would have to portray a scenario that listeners could reckon as realistic. If the stage never encountered invasion by pugilists, acrobats, or other lowbrow entertainment, such an invention would be unintelligible, and hence pointless. In fact, however, a precedent did exist—and a very recent one.

In 167 the propraetor L. Anicius Gallus returned to Rome, fresh from a smashing victory over the Illyrians, allies of Perseus of Macedon. Conquest of Illyrians did not have quite the glamor of Aemilius Paullus' success against Perseus, but Anicius was determined to leave a memorable mark on the public scene. Paullus' triumph was a spectacular affair, incomparable and unmatchable. Anicius' attempt at imitation fell short. Observers made an overt comparison: the celebrations had many similarities, but were unequal in every way; Anicius was inferior in rank as in family to Paullus, just as the Illyrian king was inferior to Perseus and his people to the Macedonians; Paullus' triumph outstripped Anicius' in booty, treasure, and gifts.[143] But Anicius had an additional design, and a most striking one. Whereas Paullus had greatly impressed Greeks abroad by staging elaborate games at Amphipolis, Anicius organized a dramatic performance in Rome itself, with imported artists and entertainers.[144] The result was an event unique and bizarre. For unfathomable reasons, it has never provoked scholarly analysis. The episode will repay attention.

Our information derives from a lengthy fragment of Polybius transmitted in the *Deipnosophistai* of Athenaeus. The narrative is intriguing

---

142. Terence, *Hec.* 1–5, 33–36.

143. Livy, 45.43.1–2; cf. Vell. Pat. 1.9.5.

144. There was nothing comparable in Paullus' triumph. Despite Garton, *Personal Aspects*, 55, we have no evidence that Pacuvius' *Paulus* was presented at the triumph, or that there were *ludi scaenici* of any sort; cf. Flores, *Letteratura latina*, 154, with bibliography. Nor is it likely that Anicius' show formed part of his own triumph. Descriptions of that triumph omit any notice of dramatic entertainment; Livy, 45.43.5–8; Vell. Pat. 1.9.5; Appian, *Ill.* 9. Walbank, *Commentary on Polybius*, III, 446, suggests that these were votive games; cf. Walbank, 32.

but also bewildering. Anicius summoned from Greece the most celebrated dramatic artists and built a gargantuan structure in the Circus Maximus to house their performance.[145] To open the proceedings, he brought on pipers, four of them, advertised as the most illustrious of their day. Having set them upon the stage, Anicius instructed them to play in unison, together with a chorus. The musicians dutifully performed their pieces with suitable movement, but they soon received new instructions, demanding that they engage in a contest. When the performers expressed puzzlement, they were told to confront one another as if doing battle.[146] The whole affair issued in a mighty confusion, with dancers divided into groups and squaring off against one another, pipers blowing vehemently and discordantly, chorus members mounting the stage and alternately rushing upon and retreating from those opposite them.[147] Still more bedlam ensued when one of the dancers struck up the pose of a boxer prepared to take on the piper who approached him, amidst a crescendo of audience applause and shouts. They were soon joined in combat by a motley array of pugilists, dancers, buglers, and trumpeters, bringing about a veritable pandemonium.[148] The entire event, says Polybius, was beyond description.[149]

Can any explanation account for that anarchic fracas? Polybius found it indigestible. He stigmatized Anicius' behavior as ludicrous, and forbore even to write about the tragic actors lest his readers conclude that he was pulling their leg.[150] On the face of it, Polybius' verdict seems reasonable. Anicius can be dismissed as an archetypically blundering Roman, insensitive to Greek artistic traditions, the barbarous *imperator* who could not distinguish a musical performance from a prizefight.[151] Or else one might conclude that Anicius was too inept to maintain control of the situation; the crowd created a melee and converted the dramatic production into an all-out brawl.[152] Such assessments, however, run afoul of both evidence and plausibility. The course of the

145. Polyb. 30.22.2.

146. Polyb. 30.22.3–6.

147. Polyb. 30.22.7–9.

148. Polyb. 30.22.10–12.

149. Polyb. 30.22.12: ἄλεκτον ἦν τὸ συμβαῖον.

150. Polyb. 30.22.1: παντὸς γέλωτος ἄξια πράγματα ἐποίησεν; 30.22.12: περὶ δὲ τῶν τραγῳδῶν . . . ὅ, τι ἂν ἐπιβάλωμαι λέγειν, δόξω τισὶ διαχλευάζειν.

151. See, most recently, N. B. Crowther, *AntCl*, 52 (1983), 270: "Roman vulgarity is here apparent"; cf. Gilula, in H. Scolnicov and P. Holland, *The Play out of Context* (Cambridge, 1989), 106–107; MacMullen, *Historia*, 40 (1991), 425.

152. Cf. Garton, *Personal Aspects*, 65.

proceedings suggests neither ignorance nor ineptitude on the part of Anicius Gallus. Far from letting matters slip out of his hands, Anicius dictated them from start to finish. The Roman issued orders to the performers, instructing the pipers to play in unison and then to enter combat.[153] When the musicians professed themselves at a loss to understand his meaning, one of the lictors spelled it out explicitly.[154] Lictors, as minions of the *imperator*, do not take independent action. Anicius was calling the shots. Dancers, instrumentalists, and pugilists were waiting on cue. The *imperator* plainly orchestrated events with design and purpose. But that premeditation complicates the problem still further. For Anicius to reduce the event to a shambles would only demean his own victory celebration. So the mystery deepens.

The affair must be considered from a different angle. Anicius did indeed have his victory celebration very much in view.[155] Whereas Aemilius Paullus displayed Roman superiority in Greece by producing Greek games with a finesse that showed his command of the Hellenic institution, Anicius could deliver a comparable message in contrasting form at home.[156] The *triumphator* made a point of gathering the most renowned entertainers in the Greek world.[157] And he announced that the pipers whom he provided were the premier virtuosi of that profession.[158] The objective, of course, was not to mount a sterling performance but to demonstrate that Hellas' frontline performers now worked at the behest of the Roman commander—and he could manipulate them at will. Polybius' pique is readily intelligible.

The affair, however, involved more than self-aggrandizement on Anicius' part. Choice of this particular medium had cultural implications that went beyond power relationships. The *imperator* organized an event that was billed as Greek in character and personnel, indeed repre-

---

153. Polyb. 30.22.4–5: αὐλεῖν ἐκέλευσεν ἅμα πάντας . . . ἀλλ᾽ ἀγωνίζεσθαι μᾶλλον ἐκέλευσεν.

154. Polyb. 30.22.6: τῶν δὲ διαπορούντων ὑπέδειξέν τις τῶν ῥαβδούχων ἐπιστρέψαντας ἐπαγαγεῖν ἐφ᾽ αὑτοὺς καὶ ποιεῖν ὡσανεὶ μάχην.

155. Polyb. 30.22.1: ἀγῶνας ἐπιτελῶν τοὺς ἐπινικίους. The phrase need not mean "triumphal games" strictly speaking; Walbank, *Commentary on Polybius*, III, 446. There is no clear evidence that *ludi scaenici* had a place in any formal triumph prior to Mummius' games in 145; Tac. *Ann.* 14.21. Cf. H. Versnel, *Triumphus* (Leiden, 1970), 101–115. But the phrase obviously refers to festivities calling attention to Anicius' military successes.

156. On Paullus' games, see Polyb. 30.14; Livy, 45.32.8–11; Diod. 31.8.13; Plut. *Aem. Paull.* 28.3–4.

157. Polyb. 30.22.2: τοὺς ἐκ τῆς Ἑλλάδος ἐπιφανεστάτους τεχνίτας.

158. Polyb. 30.22.3: οἵτινες ἐπιφανέστατοι ἦσαν.

senting the finest that Hellas had to offer. By turning it into a fiasco and inviting a Roman audience to egg on the entertainers in activities that discredited their talents, he braced the spectators' sense of their own cultural superiority. It was conscious parody, doubtless recognized as such and intended to be so recognized.[159] The audience was not meant to mistake this for an authentic representation of Greek theater. Anicius supplied an occasion for mockery, even playful mockery, which could advance the cultural self-esteem that *nobiles* promoted in the society of second-century Rome.

One might take the analysis one step further to a still bolder hypothesis. The parody perhaps struck not only at Greek amusements but indirectly at lowbrow Roman diversions. Insofar as the latter approximated slapstick, fisticuffs, or farce, they could be subject to the same derision. Not that Anicius or any Roman aristocrat campaigned for stamping out popular entertainments. The message was subtle but not opaque. It promoted a more elevated taste in the theater.

On this score the endeavors of Anicius and of Terence converge. The prologue to the *Hecyra* could touch responsive chords. Anicius' striking spectacle in 167/6 had left a strong impression. Allusions to tumult on the stage and in the audience, discordant combinations of entertainers, and performances that give way to physical confrontation would have a familiar sound—not because such incidents were common, but because a singular episode had made them memorable. Terence's lines, therefore, held particularly pointed meaning: failure on the part of the audience to discern the merits of his tasteful comedies would be akin to storming the stage with pugilists, acrobats, and trained swordsmen. *Imperator* and playwright thus delivered comparable messages, each from his own angle. Anicius manipulated and distorted a Hellenic performance to demonstrate Roman control of the dramatic genre, and Terence adapted the Hellenic form to advance the genre itself. Both endeavors brought Greek scenic entertainment under more intense scrutiny by the Roman public. And both, by disparaging or caricaturing vulgar tastes, aimed to cultivate a more discriminating constituency.

That Terentian comedy differed markedly from that of Plautus is no secret. Differences stand out in language, style, tone, technique, characterization, and purpose. The younger dramatist, for the most part,

---

159. It is noteworthy that Athenaeus includes the incident in a collection of stories about jokesters and jests; 14.613d–615e.

eschewed clownish antics, broad caricature, fantasy, or gross exaggerations. He preferred a quieter humor, credible characters, restrained language, subtle and thoughtful delineation of persons and situations.[160] As a result, the poet suffered criticism in some quarters for lack of exuberance, a thin style, and shallow compositions.[161] Terence struck back: he would not indulge in overstated and fanciful dramatizations, or in the caricatures of conventional comic stereotypes.[162] He opted for placid plays, more talk than action.[163] The shift in emphasis and temperament is often ascribed to the growth of Hellenism in second-century Rome, to Terence's greater fidelity to Greek models, to a philhellenic turn away from conservatism and nativism.[164] Or the contrast can be put differently: Terence had a broader sympathy for mankind, a deeper sensitivity to persons, a commitment to *paideia*, a belief in the capacities of human nature and individual reason as against the bonds of social convention; in short, *humanitas*.[165] The analyses contain truth but do not get to the heart of the matter. "Philhellenism" was no more a motivation for Terence than "antihellenism" was for Plautus. The dichotomy is superficial and misconceived. In fact, the younger poet encountered criticism for *inadequate* fidelity to his Greek models.[166] And the celebrated passage often taken as emblematic of Terence's *humanitas—homo sum, humani nil a me alienum puto*—is no more than a character's justification for failing to mind his own business.[167] Another route should be pursued.

160. See, e.g., J. Wright, *Dancing in Chains: The Stylistic Unity of the Commoedia Palliata* (Rome, 1974), 127–151.

161. Ter. *Phorm.* 4–5: *qui ita dictitat, quas ante hic fecit fabulas / tenui esse oratione et scriptura levi.* Cf. P. Grimal, *CRAI* (1970), 281–288.

162. Ter. *Phorm.* 6–8; *Heaut.* 30–40.

163. Ter. *Heaut.* 35–36: *adeste aequo animo, date potestatem mihi / statariam agere ut liceat per silentium;* cf. Brothers, *Terence: The Self-Tormentor*, 164–165.

164. So, e.g., Lana, *RivFilol*, 75 (1947), 44–80, 155–175; MacKendrick, *RivFilol*, 82 (1954), 30–35; Flores, *Letteratura latina*, 137–153; R. L. Hunter, *The New Comedy of Greece and Rome* (Cambridge, 1985), 21–23.

165. See Beare, *Roman Stage*³, 108–112; M. R. Posani, *StudItalFilolClass*, 37 (1965), 85–113; Grimal, *IXe Congrès*, I, 299–305; Perelli, *Il teatro rivoluzionario*, passim, especially 5–13, 151–155.

166. Ter. *Andr.* 8–16; *Heaut.* 16–18. On the meaning of *contaminare*, a much-vexed question, see Beare, *Roman Stage*³, 96–108, 310–313; idem, *CR*, 9 (1959), 7–11; Duckworth, *Nature of Roman Comedy*, 202–208; Goldberg, *Understanding Terence*, 91–122. Further bibliography in H. Marti, *Lustrum*, 8 (1963), 23–27.

167. Ter. *Heaut.* 77; see Duckworth, *Nature of Roman Comedy*, 303–304; H. D. Jocelyn, *Antichthon*, 7 (1973), 14–46. Cf. also the sensible and cautious statement by Gratwick, in *Cambridge Hist. Class. Lit.*, II, 122–123.

All readers of Terence can agree on certain basics—and they are vital. His comedies, by comparison with Plautine plays, have more elevated language, subtler characterizations, more nuanced relationships, more insightful judgments—and less amusing or entertaining content. Did Terence then aim his sights at an elite audience, a more sophisticated and urbane constituency, thereby effectively to restrict the theater to those who could appreciate the higher art? The playwright announces explicitly in the prologue to the *Eunuchus* his commitment to please as many *boni* as possible. But that end does not exclude appreciation by the general public. The same verse promises to offend the *multi* as little as possible.[168] Elsewhere, Terence declares that his sole intention from the time he first composed plays was to please the *populus*.[169] The objectives were entirely compatible. Terence looked to the standards set by the *boni* and endeavored to elevate the tastes of the *populus*. His repeated requests for calmness, attention, and reflection in the audience suggest that goal.[170] That the effort fell short of success, perhaps far short, is another story.[171] The playwright had a cultural mission: to set an aristocratic tone in his comedies and to educate the public to an appreciation of that art form at a higher level.[172] He was no creature of the Scipios, nor perhaps a protégé of any segment of the ruling classes. A reverse image might be closer to the truth. The elegance and refinement of Terence's comedies made them congenial to the *nobiles* who became promoters and backers. And the reputation of Terence made him the most suitable poet to grace the memorial celebration for L. Aemilius Paullus. The shift in direction of Roman comedy in the mid–second century illustrates still again the broader cultural developments of that

---

168. Ter. *Eun.* 1–3: *si quisquamst qui placere se studeat bonis / quam plurimis et minime multos laedere, / in is poeta hic nomen profitetur suom.* The interpretation given in the text is surely preferable to taking *placere se studeat bonis quam plurimis* as "eager to please the *boni* rather than the masses," as does M. Martina, *QuadStor,* 17 (1983), 161–165. The latter rendering requires identifying the *plurimis* with the *multos,* a most awkward construction. To see *multos* as *multos [bonos]* is worse still, for it makes the first two lines redundant. The Loeb translation simply omits *multos*!

169. Ter. *Andr.* 1–3: *Poeta quom primum ad scribendum adpulit, / id sibi negoti credidit solum dari, / populo ut placerent quas fecisset fabulas.*

170. Terence, *Andr.* 24–27; *Heauton,* 35–40; *Phormio,* 30–32; *Hecyra,* 31–32, 43–45, 55–57.

171. See on this now Goldberg, *Understanding Terence,* 203–220.

172. For a comparable move to distinguish popular diversions from elite cultural taste in late nineteenth-century America, see L. W. Levine, *High Brow / Low Brow* (Cambridge, Mass., 1988), passim, especially 33–34, 56–81, 132–146, 165–168, 179–195, 206–207, 215–219, 226–231.

era: propagation of aristocratic ideals as a means of defining standards of the society as a whole.[173]

The upper classes who benefited from the expansion of Roman authority abroad were determined to reshape Rome's image at home. The success of Terentian drama, however short-lived, exemplifies critical trends in the intellectual atmosphere of mid-Republican Rome. Study of the theater not as a political arena or as a vehicle of literary evolution but as a feature of cultural history provides the needed perspective.

The pronounced expansion in quantity and extent of state-sponsored *ludi* in this period supplied the setting. The games blended religion and entertainment, linking gratitude to the divine with festive celebrations for the community. Scenic performances fitted perfectly into that blend, beginning with plays that commemorated national triumphs and continuing as adjunct to ceremonies that honored the gods and expressed communal solidarity and elation. Playwrights, actors, and producers all profited from the swelling public interest. Ministers of the state, praetors and aediles, took responsibility for organizing the games and displaying government support for theatrical production. Individual *nobiles* might occasionally obtain personal advantage through dramas presented at funeral ceremonies and rarely, if at all, at votive games or triumphal celebrations. But the politics of the theater had a broader significance: a locus for national observances and an advertisement of national values. When L. Mummius first introduced Greek scenic games in a triumph, they marked the Roman achievement of mastery in Greece.

The ruling class that guided Rome to dominance in the Mediterranean strove to put its stamp on Roman culture as well. The stage offered a convenient medium whereby to assert aristocratic ascendancy in the arts. Establishment of preferred seating for senators delivered a conspicuous reminder of the *nobiles*' leadership and a message that the theater

173. Flores, *Letteratura latina*, 140–148, recognizes the aristocratic spirit in the plays and the advancement of an elite culture, but he sees it as directed only at an elite audience. H. Kindermann, *Das Theaterpublikum der Antike* (Salzburg, 1979), 164–168, rightly proposes that Terence hoped to educate, not to neglect, the theatergoing public; cf. also Beare, *Roman Stage*[3], 109. Spectators, even in Plautus' day, were no mere bumpkins baffled by anything but simplistic slapstick; see J.-P. Cebe, *REL*, 38 (1960), 101–106; W. R. Chalmers, in T. A. Dorey and D. R. Dudley, eds., *Roman Drama* (New York, 1965), 121–150; E. W. Handley, *Dioniso*, 46 (1975), 117–132; Rawson, in *Cambridge Ancient History*[2], VIII, 439.

should reflect upper-class tastes. The opposition to a stone structure for *ludi scaenici* carried similar import. Retention of the old system entailed annual decisions to purchase plays, mount productions, and construct makeshift stages and accouterments that reaffirmed senatorial control of popular entertainment.

That control encouraged a trend toward more highbrow drama that would put a suitable aristocratic imprint upon the art form. Among other things it promoted a move away from Plautine buffoonery and broad slapstick. L. Anicius' games, coming on the heels of Roman victory in the East, both mocked Greek scenic amusements and caricatured popular diversions generally. The same distinction between elevated and vulgar entertainment reappears in the famous prologues to the *Hecyra*, less a narrative of events than a statement of principle. Terence's preference for more reflective comedy and nuanced characterizations suited the temper of the times. He did not require Scipionic patronage or a philhellenic movement. The *nobiles* who applauded his efforts saw refined drama as a showcase for their own cultural crusade. The theater provided a channel through which the ruling class could propagate aristocratic values by shaping the direction of popular culture.

[6]

THE APPEAL OF HELLAS

Diplomacy and war thrust together the lands on both sides of the Adriatic. The period that commenced in the late third century brought increasing intensity to political and military interchange between Rome and the Hellenistic world. And with it came an ever more urgent drive on Rome's part to come to grips with the meaning and relevance of Greek culture. The effort to define a place in the larger cultural world of the Mediterranean took on special significance in an era when Roman power and authority expanded in the East. Rome strained both to participate in that cultural world and to exhibit its own primacy within it. Not surprisingly, that effort engendered some baffling complexities. Ambiguity and ambivalence appear as the principal characteristics of Rome's attitude toward Hellas.

The strains surface repeatedly in our texts. Many public figures at Rome expressed familiarity, admiration, and close involvement with Greek culture. M. Marcellus took pride in introducing his fellow countrymen to Sicilian art treasures and even boasted of this accomplishment to the Greeks themselves. Q. Fabius Pictor paid homage to Greek historiography in his written work and to Greek religion in his mission to Delphi. T. Flamininus displayed his fluency in Greek both orally and in writing. L. Aemilius Paullus undertook an extensive tour of shrines and sites in Greece which declared his deep respect for Hellenic traditions. Paullus' son, Scipio Aemilianus, obtained instruction from the historian Polybius and welcomed to his home the philosopher Panaetius. Roman aristocrats carried on intellectual exchanges with Greek thinkers, both at home and abroad, exhibited their ease with the language, and promoted the advance of Greek learning. Philhellenism, it would appear, became pervasive in the cultivated circles of second-century Rome.

Yet one can as readily multiply examples of ostensible hostility, repugnance, and alienation. The authorities repressed the Bacchanalian cult and burned Pythagorean books in dramatic public fashion. Greek rhetors and philosophers found themselves expelled from the city on more than one occasion in the second century. Negative stereotypes of Greeks recur with regularity in the Latin literature of the period. Formidable political figures such as Cato, Mummius, and Marius, who collectively spanned the century, developed reputations as antagonists of Greece and Greek culture. And even the refined and highly learned L. Crassus seemed to squirm with discomfort at too close an identification with Hellenism.

Scholars have struggled mightily to account for the paradox and make sense of the ambivalence. A once-favored solution divided Rome's leadership into groups partially defined by their attitudes toward Hellas. In this view, a philhellenic movement, spearheaded by Flamininus or Scipio Africanus or both of them struggled against Cato and others who resisted influences from the Greek East.[1] That approach, in a different form, can be carried to the next generation and framed as a contest that pitted those with a foreign policy favorable to Greeks against those who represented a "hard-line" attitude.[2] The analysis can be shorn of its political implications and still be seen as a cultural battle. The "Scipionic circle" emerges as the prime modern construct, a group of public figures and intellectuals who most actively promoted and cultivated the spread of Greek learning in Rome, often against the opposition of detractors and conservatives, champions of native traditions.[3] Through such anal-

---

1. Cf. Besançon, *Les adversaires*, 8–32, 83–151; T. Frank, *Roman Imperialism* (New York, 1914), 163–195; R. M. Haywood, *Studies on Scipio Africanus* (Baltimore, 1933), 59–85; R. M. Brown, *A Study of the Scipionic Circle* (Scottdale, Pa., 1934), 20–44; T. J. Haarhoff, *The Stranger at the Gate* (London, 1938), 203–215; H. H. Scullard, *Roman Politics, 220–150 B.C.*[2] (Oxford, 1973), 97–102, 119–121, 131–152.

2. Cf. Scullard, *Roman Politics*, 194–219; J. Briscoe, *JRS*, 54 (1964), 73–77; idem, *Historia*, 18 (1969), 60–70. In the earlier formulation by Colin, *Rome et la Grèce*, 130–136, 242–257, 269–310, a philhellenic attitude among the Roman nobility in the later third century gave way to an increasingly negative outlook and harsher actions as the Romans got to know the deficiencies of the Greeks, provoking an antihellenic reaction in Rome (349–372).

3. See Colin, *Rome et la Grèce*, 555–562; Besançon, *Les adversaires*, 158–172. Brown, *Scipionic Circle*, especially 13–19, with references to earlier scholarship and the origins of

yses, the apparent inconsistencies in our texts lend themselves to explanation: two separate tendencies, philhellene and antihellene, each inspired by influential leaders, contended in Rome.[4]

Other interpretations account for the phenomenon in a variety of ways. The Romans perhaps drew finer distinctions than a simple dichotomy of sympathy and antipathy toward Hellenism might suggest. One can find evidence for their distinguishing between Greek culture, a desirable heritage, and the Greeks themselves, an unworthy race; or between admirable Greeks of the past and their degenerate contemporary descendants; or between those Greeks who espoused proper values and those with unacceptable characteristics.[5] On a different thesis, it has been argued that the Romans sharply compartmentalized their public posture and their private predilections, simultaneously welcoming Hellenism in the coteries of the cultivated while disparaging it at an official level and as a matter of state policy.[6] For some, the Romans' drive to familiarize themselves with Greek culture had pragmatic purposes or at least consequences: the advance and success of Roman imperialism in the East.[7] To others, the combination of conspicuous Hellenism and raw exercise of power signaled a desire on the part of Roman *principes* to emulate Hellenistic princes.[8] Or else both the admiration and the scorn for the Greek achievement derive from the same psychology, a deepseated sense of cultural inferiority on the part of the Romans. The feeling of inadequacy would naturally manifest itself not only in emulation but in resistance.[9]

---

the concept; C. Saunders, *CP*, 39 (1944), 209–217; K Jax, *Serta Philologica Aenipontana*, 7–8 (1962), 291–298. The Scipionic circle is treated as a political rather than a cultural group in E. S. Gruen, *Roman Politics and the Criminal Courts, 149–78 B.C.* (Cambridge, Mass., 1968), 16–44. The cultural interpretation is revived, in modified form, by Ferrary, *Philhellénisme et impérialisme*, 531–539, 589–602.

4. Note also the cultural conflict postulated by Zanker, *Power of Images*, 5–25.

5. Cf. Petrochilos, *Roman Attitudes to the Greeks*, 35–53, 63–67, 141–162; J. P. V. D. Balsdon, *Romans and Aliens* (London, 1979), 30–40; MacMullen, *Historia*, 40 (1991), 419–438.

6. Earl, *Historia*, 11 (1962), 477–485; Gruen, *Hellenistic World*, 250–272. Cf. Zanker, *Power of Images*, 25–31.

7. Momigliano, *Alien Wisdom* (Cambridge, 1975), 16–21; M. H. Crawford, in P. D. A. Garnsey and C. R. Whittaker, eds., *Imperialism in the Ancient World* (Cambridge, 1978), 193–207.

8. Ferrary, *Philhellénisme et impérialisme*, 554–565, 578–588, 602–615; Zanker, *Power of Images*, 5–11.

9. Cf. Crawford, in *Imperialism in the Ancient World*, 202; I. Opelt, *Atene e Roma*, 14. 2–3 (1969), 21; M. Dubuisson, *LEC*, 49 (1981), 27–45; idem, *AntCl*, 50 (1981), 283–285; idem, *Ktema*, 9 (1984), 67–68.

Explanations thus range from the political to the psychological. But problems adhere to each, and a genuine resolution remains elusive. The conventional political interpretations leave much to be desired. Few will now buy the notion that Scipionic and Catonian parties possessed cultural platforms and wrangled over relations with Greeks. The simplistic reconstructions of political alignments in the early second century have undergone searching criticisms in more recent years and need no longer be revived or refuted.[10] The thesis that groups would form on the basis of "hard" or "soft" attitudes toward the Greeks collapses in the face of the ancient evidence. Numerous examples can be cited from the mid-second century alone to demonstrate that no consistent divisions along these lines either existed or would be expected to exist.[11] The whole idea of a "Scipionic circle," whether cultural or political, has little to recommend it. Alleged members of the group by no means saw eye to eye on public issues; many individuals who were associated with learning and culture clashed with Scipio Aemilianus or his friends; and many artists and writers stood outside that clique. The dialogues of Cicero, on which rests the reconstruction, offer little to justify it.[12] Analysis of philhellenism as a matter of politics reaches a dead end.

Other approaches have been similarly unproductive or inadequate. Scattered texts imply that certain Romans, when the occasion suited, might draw distinctions between "good Greeks" and "bad Greeks," between contemporary Greeks and their predecessors, or even between the culture and its representatives. But the fragmentary instances do not amount to a consistent, let alone a widespread, attitude that could characterize Roman opinion. Public posture and private sentiment might indeed differ, but to leave the matter at that fails to probe the significance or implications of that bifurcation. The hypothesis that Roman behavior that both cultivated and patronized Hellenism modeled itself upon Hellenistic monarchy applies at best only to a few *imperatores*, and strains the evidence even there. It cannot qualify as a general solution

10. Cf., e.g., Develin, *Practice of Politics*, passim; especially 43–57, 231–252; A. E. Astin, *Politics and Policies in the Roman Republic* (Belfast, 1968), 3–18.

11. For some examples, see Gruen, *Hellenistic World*, 245–247.

12. See Strasburger, *Hermes*, 94 (1966), 60–72; Astin, *Scipio Aemilianus*, 294–299; J. E. G. Zetzel, *HSCP*, 76 (1972), 173–179. Efforts to rehabilitate the "circle" largely confine themselves to the association between Panaetius and the friends of Scipio; K. Abel, *Antike und Abendland*, 17 (1971), 119–143; Garbarino, *Roma e la filosofia greca*, 15–21, 380–445; Ferrary, *Philhellénisme et impérialisme*, 589–608. They do not establish a philhellenic orientation for the Scipionic group which carried impact upon the public scene.

to the problem of ambivalence and paradox in Roman comportment. That intensive involvement with Greek culture went hand in hand with the spread of Roman power to the East is manifestly true. The connection of those parallel developments, however, needs exploration, not mere assertion. And the hypothesis of an inferiority complex resorts to simplistic psychologizing that both disparages and trivializes a complicated phenomenon. We need a deeper understanding.

The attraction of Hellenism for the Roman aristocracy long predated overseas expansion to the lands of the Greek world. Evidence for early inclinations is fragmentary and problematic, allowing for few secure conclusions.[13] But certain items offer hints and prompt consideration.

From the late fourth century a few Roman *nobiles* elected to attach Greek cognomens to their family names. Even some consular houses took them on. Roman chief magistrates appear on the *fasti* with the cognomens Philo (consul 339), Sophus (consul 304), Philippus (consul 281), and Philus (consul 223). What meaning one should apply to this choice is unclear. The fashion did not catch on as a general phenomenon. Only a few families adopted it in the middle Republic and not many more in the late Republic. The cognomen often did not go beyond a single generation, thus suggesting that a peculiar occasion called it forth, without expectation of continuance. But the practice followed no single path. P. Sempronius Sophus, consul 304, had a like-named son who reached that office in 268, and the Marcii Philippi retained their cognomen for generations.[14] It would be prudent to avoid sweeping inferences from what seems to have been a limited usage. It hardly counts as rampant philhellenism. What matters, however, is that some Roman aristocrats in the late fourth and the third centuries chose to add Greek names to their inherited ones quite voluntarily and without any sense of stigma. Acquaintance with Greeks in this period must have come through encounters in Campania and Magna Graecia. Such encounters may also have prompted interest in Greek statuary, an inter-

13. The extent to which "Hellenization" had affected Roman culture and society by the late fourth century remains in dispute. For a good survey of scholarly opinions, with perhaps unduly skeptical conclusions, see Wallace, in *Staat und Staatlichkeit*, 278–291.

14. The examples of Republican *nobiles* are summarized by H. Solin, *Beiträge zum Kenntnis der griechischen Personennamen in Rom* (Helsinki, 1971), 86–91. The cognomen Philo attached to the consular tribunes of 400 and 399 is probably a later and erroneous insertion; Solin, 87–88. See further J. Kaimio, *The Romans and the Greek Language* (Helsinki, 1979), 182–183.

est that resulted in setting up portraits of Alcibiades and Pythagoras in the Comitium some time during the Samnite Wars.[15] The south Italian sage Pythagoras seems to have held some fascination for the Romans, who wove tales about an association between the philosopher and Rome's second king, Numa Pompilius.[16] This interest did not, of course, require any deep understanding of Pythagoreanism or any desire to obtain it.[17] But it does at least imply, as do the other scraps of evidence discussed, a positive and welcoming attitude toward things Hellenic.

More important and more telling is the receptivity of Rome to Hellenic cults. The fact is well known and often remarked upon but rarely emphasized adequately in this context.[18] Tradition dated the acquisition of the Sibylline Books to the reign of Tarquinius Superbus and reported regular consultation of the books in the fifth and fourth centuries.[19] Whatever stock one puts in those tales, it is clear that the books ranked as an established institution by the third century.[20] Roman *decemviri* supervised the consultation, but the Books were written in Greek and the whole process was conducted *Graeco ritu*.[21] Sibylline pronouncements, of course, were linked with the origins of Apollo's cult in Rome. The sources put its installation in 431, a very early manifestation of Hellenism in Rome.[22] A temple to Demeter allegedly arose even earlier, in 493. If so, that will have been in her Italian guise. But in the late fourth and early third centuries the cult became transformed: Greek

15. Pliny, *NH*, 34.26; Plut. *Num.* 8.10.

16. See discussion, with references, in Gruen, *Studies in Greek Culture and Roman Policy*, 158–162.

17. Cicero's allusion to the "Pythagorean" quality of a poem by Ap. Claudius Caecus, censor of 312, is problematic; *Tusc. Disp.* 4.4; see Garbarino, *Roma e la filiosofia greca*, 224–226. Certainly one cannot infer a thorough familiarity with the philosophy.

18. See, in general, G. Wissowa, *Religion und Kultus der Römer* (Munich, 1902), 42–46, 239–271; W. Warde Fowler, *The Religious Experience of the Roman People* (London, 1911), 223–269; K. Latte, *Römische Religionsgeschichte* (Munich, 1960), 148–194, 213–263; G. Dumézil, *Archaic Roman Religion* (Chicago, 1970), II, 407–431, 446–456.

19. The origins: Gellius, 1.19.1; Dion. Hal. 4.62; Lactantius, *Div. Inst.* 1.6.10–11; Zonaras, 7.11.1; Servius, *Ad Aen.* 6.72; Tzetzes on Lycophron, 1279. Early consultations: Dion. Hal. 4.62, 6.17, 10.2; Zonaras, 7.11.1; Livy, 3.10.7, 4.25.3, 5.13.5, 5.50.2; Pliny, *NH*, 13.88.

20. Lycophron, 1278–1279.

21. Varro, *LL*, 7.88: *et nos dicimus XV viros Graeco ritu sacra non Romano facere*. The classic study is still H. Diels, *Sibyllinische Blätter* (Berlin, 1890), passim. Other bibliography in Gruen, *Studies*, 7–8, n. 11.

22. Livy, 4.25.3, 4.29.7; cf. J. Gagé, *Apollon romain* (Paris, 1955), 19–113.

priestesses from Naples and Velia took charge of it, and the Hellenic features predominated.[23] Overt public transfer of a Greek cult came in 293. A fearsome epidemic prompted the state, again on the recommendation of the Sibylline Books, to send an official delegation to Epidaurus, whence to fetch the healing god Aesculapius. And a temple to the god, symbolized by the Epidaurian serpent, was erected on the Tiber Island in 291, no doubt served by Greek priests.[24] The readiness to turn to Hellenic deities for assistance and support manifested itself again in the First Punic War. The *libri Sibyllini* in 249 sanctioned celebration of the Secular Games with ceremonies that called upon Greek divinities of the underworld, Dis Pater and Proserpina, in a renewal of national traditions with Hellenic overtones.[25] The pace picked up in the Hannibalic conflict. Venus Erycina, a Sicilian-Greek goddess who could also serve as emblem of Rome's Trojan origins, came to Rome from Eryx in 217. She received a shrine on the Capitoline itself.[26] And in 205, once more on recommendation of the Sibylline Books, Roman authorities transported the Hellenized cult of Magna Mater from Asia Minor to a place on the Palatine in an act replete with religious, political, and cultural implications.[27] Other instances could be cited.[28] But the facts are abundantly clear. Not only did Hellenic elements permeate Roman religion from a quite early stage, but the Romans reached out deliberately and repeatedly to import Greek deities, incorporate Greek cults, and employ Greek rites. The Roman officialdom, of course, was in charge, but there is no sign of ambivalence toward Hellenism.

A parallel development reinforces the picture: more and more Romans learned the Greek language. The first recorded instance enjoys special notoriety. L. Postumius Megellus, Roman ambassador to Taren-

---

23. Dion. Hal. 6.17.2; Cic. *Pro Balbo*, 55; Pliny, *NH*, 35.154; Festus, 86, 268, L; cf. Cic. *Verr.* 2.4.115; Val. Max. 1.1.1; H. Le Bonniec, *Le culte de Cérès à Rome* (Paris, 1958), 379–400.

24. Livy, 10.47.6–7; *Per.* 11; Val. Max. 1.8.2; *Vir. Ill.* 22.1–3; cf. Ovid, *Met.* 15.626–744; Wissowa, *Religion und Kultus*, 253–255; Latte, *Römische Religionsgeschichte*, 225–227.

25. Varro, in Censorinus, 17.8–10; cf. Val. Max. 2.4.5; Livy, *Per.* 49; Wissowa, *Religion und Kultus*, 255–259; Latte, *Römische Religionsgeschichte*, 246–248.

26. Livy, 22.9.7–10, 22.10.10, 23.20.13–14, 23.31.9. See I. Bitto, *ArchStorMessinese*, 28 (1977), 121–133.

27. Full discussion, with references, in Gruen, *Studies*, 5–33.

28. Note, e.g., the Roman association with Delphi in the later third century; Plut. *Marc.* 8.6; *Fab.* 18.3; Livy, 22.57.4–5, 23.11.1–6; Appian, *Hann.* 27; also the conversion of the *ludi Apollinares* in 212 into an annual festival to be celebrated *Graeco ritu*; Livy, 25.12.10; Gagé, *Apollon romaine*, 270–279.

tum in 282, conducted negotiations in Greek, a language whose finer points unfortunately escaped him. His slips in that tongue called forth jeers and insults from the Tarentines, one of whose members, to show his contempt, even defecated on Postumius' toga. The confrontation served to justify Rome's war on Tarentum.[29] Whatever trust one puts in the details of the story, Postumius' use of Greek at an early stage of Roman interstate diplomacy remains striking. The envoy's command of the language may have been less than perfect, but his willingness to address the Tarentines in their own tongue demands notice. Nor did he exhibit gross ineptitude. Our texts suggest that the audience waited to pounce upon anything that fell short of precision.[30] So, Postumius' knowledge of Greek must have attained a reasonable level of competence, and he is unlikely to have been the only Roman *nobilis* to reach that level. An incentive to learn Greek was presumably spawned by contact with the western Greeks. Diplomatic relations with the cities of Magna Graecia in the late fourth and early third centuries already had cultural consequences.

Interest and competence in Greek expanded dramatically during the course of the third century. Only bits of information survive, but they are indicative and adequate. Livius Andronicus, a Greek from Tarentum, came to Rome some time in the mid–third century, taught there in Greek and Latin, on both public and private commissions, lectured on Greek authors, and read aloud from his own Latin texts.[31] Obviously the Roman elite produced eager listeners and students.[32] The fruits of that zeal became increasingly evident. Epigrams on the tombs of the Scipios, beginning with the *elogium* of L. Scipio (consul 259), show clear signs of a Hellenic education.[33] And the distinguished consul of 244 and 241, A. Manlius Torquatus, proudly adopted the cognomen Atticus.

Still deeper learning is evident in Q. Fabius Pictor, who inaugurated

29. Dion. Hal. 19.5; Appian, *Samn.* 7.2. An alternative tradition does not mention the use of Greek; Val. Max. 2.2.5; Florus, 1.13.4; Orosius, 4.1.1; Dio, fr. 39.5–6. But there is no good reason to question that item; cf. Kaimio, *Romans and the Greek Language*, 96–97.

30. Dion. Hal. 19.5: εἰ τι μὴ κατὰ τὸν ἀκριβέστατον τῆς Ἑλληνικῆς διαλέκτου χαρακτῆρα ὑπ' αὐτοῦ λέγοιτο; cf. Appian, *Samn.* 7.2: εἴ τι μὴ καλῶς ἑλληνίσειαν.

31. Suet. *De Gramm.* 1: *Livium et Ennium dico, quos utraque lingua domi forisque docuisse adnotatum est, nihil amplius quam Graecos interpretabantur, aut si quid ipsi Latine composuissent praelegebant.*

32. Cf. Plut. *Mor.* 278e: the first primary school in Rome was opened by the freedman Sp. Carvilius ca. 230.

33. *ILLRP*, I, 310; cf. 309, 311–312, 316; discussion and bibliography in M. Martina, *QuadStor*, 12 (1980), 149–170; J. Van Sickle, *AJP*, 108 (1987), 41–55.

the genre of Roman historiography in Greek. Pictor served as the senate's emissary to Delphi in the dark days after Cannae in 216, on the instructions of the Sibylline Books. The pronouncements at Delphi were uttered in Greek verse, then rendered into Latin by Pictor, who was fluent in both languages.[34] He subsequently turned to the writing of history, recreating his nation's past in the language of Hellas.[35] The designated audience, so it is usually said, was Greek, the work a means whereby to justify Roman encroachment upon the Greek world. But that motive, if it played any part at all, does not suffice. Nothing suggests that Fabius' work circulated across the Adriatic or was ever intended to. Greeks would read their own historians of the West, and there is little in the fragments that seems designed for that readership. Fabius followed a tradition of Greek historiography, as did other Roman historians for the next generation and more. They certainly did not need to explain the ways of Rome to Greece repeatedly. The history of Fabius Pictor must have been intended primarily for Romans.[36] The same holds for his successors who wrote Roman histories in Greek: L. Cincius Alimentus, a close contemporary of Pictor; P. Scipio, son of Africanus, in the next generation; and C. Acilius and A. Postumius Albinus, who belong to the mid–second century.[37] That genre not only implies the existence of a cultured elite of Romans who could read Greek. It also shows that both authors and readers found it entirely acceptable that the records and traditions of their nation should be composed in Greek. The fact bears stress. It belies any notion of an inferiority complex, and it reveals a mentality that welcomed the transmission of Rome's own heritage in the language of another culture.

That feature cannot be paralleled in other genres of early Latin literature. Drama was composed from the outset in Latin, for obvious reasons: the production of plays depended on reaching a wider audience. Legal writing had no body of Greek treatises on which to draw.

34. Livy, 22.57.4–5, 23.11.1–6; Plut. *Fab.* 18.3; Appian, *Hann.* 27; especially Livy, 23.11.4: *ex Graeco carmine interpretata recitavit.*

35. Dion. Hal. 1.6.2; Cic. *De Domo*, 1.43.

36. The conclusion was reached independently and on different grounds by Kaimio, *Romans and the Greek Language*, 224–228, and Gruen, *Hellenistic World*, 253–255, with references to sources and literature. And see now A. Momigliano, *The Classical Foundations of Modern Historiography* (Berkeley, Calif., 1990), 88–102, who argues that Fabius wrote in Greek because he found the Roman historiographical tradition unsatisfactory.

37. For Cincius, see F. Münzer and C. Cichorius, *RE*, 3.2 (1899), 2556–2557; for Scipio, Cic. *Brutus*, 77; for Acilius, Cic. *De Off.* 3.115; Dion. Hal. 3.67; Livy, *Per.* 53; for Postumius, Cic. *Brutus*, 81; *Acad. Prior.* 2.137; Polyb. 39.1; Gellius, 11.8.

The composition of epic poetry in Greek was perhaps too daunting a proposition. And lyric or elegiac poetry would wait several generations before circumstances were ripe for their flourishing. But none of this implies any resistance to the language or literature of Hellas. Greek models, of course, served for almost every genre developed by Romans, and translations from the Greek stand at the very inception of the high literary arts in Rome. There was no embarrassment or hesitation, and no sense that the emulation of Hellas demeaned or diminished the native product.[38]

One can go further. Plautus composed his plays in Latin for spectators who represented a reasonable cross section of Roman society. Yet the comedies, as is well known, contain a fair number of Greek phrases or Latinized Greek words. This is not the place to explore the possible meaning and intention of that usage, but the fact itself carries significance. Plautus could expect recognition and comprehension on the part of his audience. It does not, to be sure, follow that all onlookers would catch the Greek or discern its significance. In some cases just the apprehension of an alien tongue would suffice to make the point. But elsewhere the pun or the sense requires a grasp of the language.[39] Some acquaintance with Greek had evidently seeped beyond the confines of the cultural elite.

Training in Greek expanded notably in the second century. Ennius, like Livius Andronicus before him, taught at Rome in both languages, gave private lessons, and also lectured in public.[40] Cato the Elder employed a skilled Greek intellectual to tutor members of his house-

---

38. Kaimio, *Romans and the Greek Language*, 209–215, stresses the social distinction between those who composed history in Greek and those who used Latin in other literary genres. But that distinction does not explain juridical writings, the province of the upper classes, nor is it easy to see what connection holds between drama or poetry and the lower social standing of its practitioners. Kaimio's formulation, 266, of a "competitive spirit" between Latin and Greek literature makes little sense for this period.

39. E.g., *Capt.* 880–882; *Casina*, 728–732; *Pseud.* 653–654, 700–712. On the use of Greek words by Plautus, see Colin, *Rome et la Grèce*, 143–147; J. N. Hough, *AJP*, 55 (1934), 346–364; G. B. Shipp, *WS*, 66 (1953), 105–112; R. Perna, *L'originalità di Plauto* (Bari, 1955), 230–235; Chalmers, in *Roman Drama*, 39–41. Understanding would demand more than just the odd phrase that a Roman soldier might have picked up on service in southern Italy.

40. Suet. *De Gramm.* 1. S. F. Bonner, *Education in Ancient Rome* (London, 1977), 21–22, interprets *domi forisque* not as "in private and in public" but as teaching "in residence and as a visitor [in other residences]." That interpretation is possible but strained.

hold.[41] The association of Roman aristocrats and erudite Greeks proceeded apace thereafter.[42] Greek rhetors and philosophers plied their
trade in Rome in sufficient numbers to prompt a senatorial decree in 161
authorizing their removal if that seemed in the state interest.[43] The
numbers had swelled after the Third Macedonian War when Greek
intellectuals migrated to Rome as a place for support and advancement.[44] Two celebrated anecdotes buttress the argument. The Stoic
grammarian and philologist Crates of Mallos arrived in the city as envoy
from the court of Pergamum probably in the early 160s. He had the
misfortune to break his leg, but employed the forced period of recupera-
tion to offer lectures on textual criticism and grammatical cruxes. His
audiences obviously had an advanced command of Greek.[45] The same
conclusion can be drawn from Carneades' experience at Rome. The
Academic philosopher also came on a diplomatic mission, and the delay
before its senatorial hearing afforded him the occasion to lecture in
public to Roman audiences. Listeners were enthralled, young men and
their fathers alike. Carneades had them under his spell, so it was said,
until Cato hastened the senatorial meeting and terminated the business
of the embassy.[46] As is clear, the fascination exercised by Carneades
depended upon a relatively sophisticated knowledge of Greek among
those who flocked to hear him.[47]

Roman engagement with Hellenic culture can be illustrated in a quite
different way. The activities of Romans abroad in the third and second
centuries went beyond military conquest, diplomatic exchange, and

41. Plut. *Cato*, 20.3–5. Other references to schools in the third and early second
centuries make no specific mention of the teaching of Greek. But the availability, at least
in some circles, of primary education could lay a basis for higher training in matters
Hellenic. See Plut. *Mor.* 277a; Cato, *ORF*, fr. 205; Plautus, *Asin.* 226–228; *Bacch.* 129,
427–448; *Curc.* 258; *Merc.* 303–304; *Most.* 125–126; *Pers.* 173; *Truc.* 735–736. Of course,
the Plautine passages may not all refer to Roman circumstances.

42. See the list of examples collected by Balsdon, *Romans and Aliens*, 54–58.

43. Suet. *De Rhet.* 1.2; Gellius, 15.11.1.

44. Polyb. 31.24.6–7; Plut. *Aem. Paull.* 6.4–5; Cic. *De Orat.* 1.14; cf. Pliny, *NH*,
35.135.

45. Suet. *De Gramm.* 2; cf. della Corte, *RivFilol*, 12 (1934), 388–389; Garbarino, *Roma
e la filosofia greca*, 356–362.

46. Cic. *De Orat.* 2.155; Plut. *Cato*, 22.2–3; cf. Cic. *Acad. Prior.* 2.137; *Tusc. Disp.* 4.5;
Ad Att. 12.23.2; Gellius, 17.21.48.

47. The depth of Roman familiarity with Greek is questioned by N. Horsfall, *EMC*,
23 (1979), 84–87, with some justice. But knowledge of the language did not have to
reach the level of Alexandrian scholars to meet the needs of Rome.

economic investment. And the activities did not confine themselves to members of the highest orders. *Rhomaioi* begin to turn up in Greek inscriptions in the third century; that is Romans or Italians who visited or elected to reside in the Greek East. Some were given proxeny honors by Hellenic states, and one even took service with the Ptolemaic monarchy for which he financed and dedicated a Nymphaeum.[48] Proxeny decrees for *Rhomaioi* multiply in the second century, attesting to generous benefactions to the civic life of Greek communities.[49] Romans evinced increasing interest in the religious and cultural activities of those communities. A diplomatic mission to Greece after the First Illyrian War in 228 gained admittance to the Isthmian Games and initiation into the Eleusinian Mysteries. The accompanying tale of the Roman who won the stadion at the Isthmian Games is somewhat less credible for the third century.[50] But there is no question that Romans or Italians participated in Greek athletic contests and religious festivals in growing numbers during the second century.[51] Those Italians who migrated abroad might form associations of their own modeled directly upon parallel Greek institutions, and their sons would obtain citizenship, membership in the city's ephebate, and thorough absorption in its civic and cultural life.[52] The behavior of Romans abroad, of course, need not reflect attitudes at home, but it indicates at least that they did not carry with them ethnic stereotypes and prejudicial intellectual baggage that would discourage entrance into an alien culture.

The willingness of Romans to associate themselves with Hellenism has perhaps its most striking manifestation in a theory on the origins of the Latin language. By the late Republic erudite researchers propounded the idea that Latin had its roots in Greek, more specifically in Aeolic. The eminent scholar and philologist L. Aelius Stilo Praeconinus discovered etymological connections between Greek and Latin words.[53] The still more learned Varro pointed to a host of parallels.[54] And he

48. Proxeny decrees: *IG*, XII, 3, Suppl. 127; IX, 1², 117. The Nymphaeum: *IC*, III, 115, 18.

49. E.g., *IG*, IX, 1², 208; XII, 5, 917; other examples collected by R. M. Errington, in P. Kneissel, ed., *Alte Geschichte und Wissenschaftsgeschichte, Festschrift für K. Christ* (Darmstadt, 1988), 151–152.

50. Polyb. 2.12.8; Zonaras, 8.19.

51. *IG*, II², 960, lines 32–33; *IG*, XII, 9, 952; *SEG*, 29 (1979), 806; Errington, in *Alte Geschichte* 105–107.

52. References in Errington, *Alte Geschichte*, 144–145, 148–150.

53. Festus, 180, L. On Praeconinus, see Cic. *Brutus*, 205; Suet. *De Gramm.* 13.

54. E.g., Varro, *LL*, 5.25–26, 5.96, 5.101–102; *De Re Rust.* 3.12.6.

devoted an entire treatise to the theory of Aeolic origins for Latin.[55] The idea had surfaced earlier, in the works of Greek grammarians such as Hypsicrates of Amisos and Philoxenos of Alexandria in the early first century B.C. Hence, it has been dismissed as the artificial construct of Greeks who sought to legitimize Roman rule by granting the "barbarian" a Hellenic linguistic pedigree.[56] But that conclusion overlooks a critical text: Cato's *Origines*. The Censor endorsed the tradition that had Evander and his Arcadians bring the Aeolic dialect to Italy and even asserted that Romulus himself spoke that dialect.[57] The thesis, therefore, had solid Roman support by the mid–second century, and by no less an authority than Cato the Elder. In sum, an impressive and consistent array of testimony affirms Roman readiness to embrace the legacy of Hellas.

The embrace, however, was neither simplistic nor one-dimensional. The matter is generally put too schematically: Romans, so it is claimed, were embarrassed or ambivalent about their attitudes toward Hellas and struggled with an unresolved tension between admiration and animosity. In fact, the response to Greek culture was consistent, sophisticated, and purposeful. The posture of Cato proves neither unique nor aberrant. Instead, it illuminates and exemplifies national sensibilities. The subject will benefit from more extended scrutiny.

The imperfect Greek of L. Postumius Megellus had caused difficulties. Jeering and insults by Tarentines in 281 provoked Rome to fearsome retaliation—or so at least the tradition has it.[58] There is some truth at least in that tale, a fundamental truth: the Romans needed only one lesson of this sort. They soon made certain not to find themselves in a similar situation again, establishing a practice that would hold until the late Republic and, for the most part, well beyond. Representatives of the Roman state employed only Latin in all official exchanges with foreign peoples and their spokesmen. The principle applied to magistrates abroad in Greece and Asia, as well as in Rome itself.[59] Further, the

55. Varro, fr. 295–296, 383, 417F; see J. Collart, *Varron, grammarien latin* (Paris, 1954), 205–228.

56. So Dubuission, *Ktema*, 9 (1984), 59–67, and on Hypsicrates and Philoxenos, see references, 60.

57. Cato, *HRR*, fr. 19 = Lydus, *De Mag.* 1.5.

58. See above, nn. 29–30.

59. Val. Max. 2.2.2: *magna cum perseverantia custodiebant, ne Graecis umquam nisi Latine responsa darent . . . non in urbe tantum nostra, sed etiam in Graecia et Asia.*

patres observed a convention not violated until the age of Sulla whereby foreign embassies were prohibited from addressing the senate in their native tongue. They had to speak in Latin or employ an interpreter.[60] Valerius Maximus, who conveys this vital information, also provides a perceptive analysis: the convention underscored the *maiestas* of the Roman people. The Romans lacked no zeal for learning, he asserts, but believed firmly that the *pallium* should yield to the toga. It was unthinkable to place the charms and delights of culture ahead of the weight and authority of empire.[61]

The principle, one may imagine, was put into operation not long after Postumius' fiasco at Tarentum. Henceforth, the Romans would insist on the upper hand in matters of diplomacy: Latin would be the language of negotiation. The record preserves no further instance of blunder or timidity on the part of the Romans. If the language barrier constituted a burden, the Greeks would have to adjust to it. Pyrrhus' chief counselor and emissary Cineas bargained for peace in Rome in 280 or 279, making private representations to individual *nobiles* and a formal presentation to the Roman senate. The private parleys may well have been in Greek with those aristocrats who commanded the language, but a speech to the *curia*, perhaps through translation or an interpreter, must have been delivered in Latin.[62] Use of interpreters may well have

---

60. Val. Max. 2.2.3.

61. Val. Max. 2.2.2: *magistratus vero prisci quantopere suam populique Romani maiestatem retinentes se gesserint hinc cognosci potest . . . nec illis deerant studia doctrinae, sed nulla non in re pallium togae subici debere arbitrabantur, indignum esse existimantes inlecebris et suavitati litterarum imperii pondus et auctoritatem donari.* Kaimio, *Romans and the Greek Language*, 94–96, wrongly regards Valerius' text as propounding propaganda of the age of Tiberius and not applicable to the middle Republic; so also Horsfall, *EMC*, 23 (1979), 86; C. Montella, *AION*, 4 (1982), 201. The evidence of individual episodes, in fact, bears out Valerius' point. A much more cogent analysis is delivered by Dubuisson, *Ktema*, 7 (1982), 192–210, who usefully points to the comparable text by John Lydus, *De Mag.* 3.27. But Dubuisson, like others, retains the idea that Rome's attitude was scornful and hostile to Hellas (193–194).

62. Plut. *Pyrrh.* 18.2–3; cf. Pliny, *NH*, 7.188; Solin. 1.109. P. Boyancé, *REL*, 34 (1956), 113–114, finds Cineas' address to the senate to be at odds with the evidence of Valerius Maximus. But that is on the unlikely assumption that he spoke in Greek. Dubuisson, *LEC*, 49 (1981), 38–39, and *Ktema*, 7 (1982), 197–198, argues that the rule requiring Latin was not yet in effect and that the majority of the *patres* understood Greek perfectly well—an implausible proposition for the early third century. Ferrary, *Philhellénisme et impérialisme*, 559–560, n. 45, points out quite rightly that Val. Max. 2.2.3 refers not to a regulation but to a convention: *huic consuetudini.* It does not follow, however, that Cineas could make himself understood or was permitted to address the *curia* in Greek. Kaimio, *Romans and the Greek Language*, 103–104, makes the proper inference: Cineas employed an interpreter.

become standard procedure when Romans multiplied missions to Hellas after the Illyrian Wars, expanding still further in interchanges during the First Macedonian War and preliminaries that led to the Second. A Greek freedman, Cn. Publilius Menander, served in that capacity at a time *apud maiores* of Cicero.[63] He was surely not alone. Greek would have to be rendered into Latin for diplomatic discourse with Romans in the East and for formal appearances before the *patres*—a sign of the superior partner.

The institution took on significance in itself. It served as vehicle whereby *imperatores* and *legati* who knew the language and experienced the culture could reaffirm the Roman upper hand in matters of international import. When Scipio Africanus and Hannibal entered into a parley on the eve of Zama, each brought along an interpreter.[64] The item is worth notice, for both men spoke Greek and could have dispensed with intermediaries.[65] But Scipio, we may readily surmise, would not countenance an exchange at that level of authority in Greek—let alone in Punic. The Roman commander must have insisted on Latin.[66] Cato the Elder, as we have seen, made the point with unmistakeable clarity at Athens in 191. He addressed the crowd in Latin, leaving to a subordinate the task of rendering the thoughts into Greek. Cato let it be known both that he controlled Greek but chose not to use it and that a Greek translation of his speech was inferior and overblown.[67] That device of putting the Greeks in their place would be activated more than once by subsequent *imperatores*.[68] And Greek missions to the Roman senate were obliged to employ interpreters, for the *patres* would conduct the business

---

63. Cic. *Pro Balbo*, 28; *Dig.* 49.15.5.3.
64. Polyb. 15.6.3; Livy, 30.30.1.
65. Cf. Nepos, *Hann.* 13.3; Livy, 29.19.11–13.
66. Cf. Dubuisson, *Ktema*, 7 (1982), 198–199.
67. Plut. *Cato*, 12.4–5.
68. See below pp. 243–252. Flamininus' ability in Greek was well known; Plut. *Flam.* 5.5. He may have used it in private parleys with Philip V during the Second Macedonian War; cf. Polyb. 18.8.4–7; Livy, 32.35.5–8. But he doubtless employed Latin in formal interchanges; cf. Polyb. 18.1–7; Livy, 32.32–34, 34.30.6–34.32.20. Decisive evidence comes in Flamininus' celebrated Isthmian proclamation of 194; it was read out to the Greeks by a herald; Polyb. 18.46.4–9; Livy, 33.32.4–8; Plut. *Flam.* 10.3–5; Val. Max. 4.8.5. Similarly, at the Nemean Games at Argos; Plut. *Flam.* 12.2. Dubuisson, *Ktema*, 7 (1982), 199–200, gives a perceptive discussion. In the encounter between M'. Acilius Glabrio and Aetolian spokesmen in 191, the consul obviously spoke in Latin, thereby perhaps contributing to Greek confusion; Polyb. 20.9.5, 20.10.12; Livy, 36.27.4–36.28.9. On the vexed question of this supposed misunderstanding, see Gruen, *Athenaeum*, 60 (1982), 50–68; G. Freyburger, *Ktema*, 7 (1982), 177–185; Dubuisson, *Le latin de Polybe: Les implications historiques d'un cas de bilinguisme* (Paris, 1985), 100–112.

of state only in the language of their forefathers.[69] As Valerius Maximus aptly put it, the Romans lacked nothing in appreciation for learning, but the insistence on Latin in official transactions served to demonstrate the subordination of letters to the *maiestas* of the Roman people.[70]

Epigraphical testimony stands in support. Official communications from senate or magistrate to eastern cities and principalities supply the evidence. The vast bulk of extant material is in Greek, but a Roman mentality pervades the texts and the authoritative documents were composed in Latin. A number of *senatus consulta* survive, attesting to formal relations between Rome and Hellenistic communities and referring to treaties, arbitration, grants of privileges, postwar settlements, or property distributions. The Greek texts, naturally, were designed for a Greek readership, but the documents have a decided Roman stamp. A uniformity of style, method of composition, technical terminology, and format in decrees scattered over the Greek world and ranging over a considerable span of time make it clear that they are the product of the Roman officialdom working within an established tradition. The texts contain numerous Latinisms, infelicities or awkwardness in the Greek, and the repetition of Roman formulaic expressions in Greek vocabulary. The originals, of course, were in Latin, deposited in the *aerarium* or the temple of Ceres. And the translations must have been official ones, turned out by professionals whose concern was not to produce elegant Greek but to convey the intentions of Rome.[71]

An interesting parallel holds in the matter of treaties between Rome and Greek states. The surviving epigraphical documents show a stan-

---

69. The principle is illustrated by the famous philosophic embassy from Athens to Rome in 155. Carneades could enjoy a private conversation in Greek with A. Postumius Albinus; Cic. *Acad. Prior.* 2.137. But when the envoys were heard before the senate, the occasion required the intermediacy of a Roman senator, C. Acilius, who addressed the house in Latin; Plut. *Cato,* 22.4; Gellius, 6.14.9; cf. Macrobius, 1.5.16. Plutarch's remark that Acilius translated τοὺς πρώτους λόγους suggests that more professional interpreters were employed for the rest. The first Greek permitted to address the senate in his native tongue was the Rhodian rhetor Apollonius Molo, a teacher of Cicero, who visited Rome in the 80s; Val. Max. 2.2.3; cf. Cic. *Brutus,* 307, 312. The *patres* made an exception for Molo, who had trained more than one Roman orator; Val. Max. 2.2.3. But it remained open for any senator to request a translator; Cic. *De Fin.* 5.89. And interpreters continued to stand by; Cic. *De Div.* 2.131. Cf. Kaimio, *Romans and the Greek Language,* 105–106; Montella, *AION,* 4 (1982), 201–202.

70. Val. Max. 2.2.2; see above, n. 61.

71. The *senatus consulta* in Greek are conveniently collected by R. K. Sherk, *Roman Documents from the Greek East* (Baltimore, 1969), 20–184, drawing on the assemblage by P. Viereck, *Sermo graecus* (Göttingen, 1888).

dard form, heavily influenced by the conventions of the Hellenistic world. In this case, they disclose a serious investigation of Greek usage and a willingness on the part of Rome to fit into diplomatic patterns familiar to the Greek East. Most of them date to the later second century and beyond, a time when Roman ascendancy was clear and unquestioned, so that the treaties, framed in bilateral form and denoting equal obligations, constituted mere gestures of beneficence by the superpower and a token whereby Rome signified its place within long-standing Hellenistic traditions.[72] At the same time, however, the document itself, in original form, would be composed in Latin and lodged on the Capitoline. A copy would go to the Greek ally, whether translated in Rome or left to local scribes to render into Greek. The Roman version was the authoritative one, the other an *antigraphon*, using the dating by Roman consuls and citing the authorization by the Roman senate—including instructions for the display of the treaty.[73] Rome could thereby express its concordance with Greek traditions and its reciprocal relationship with Greek states, and at the same time reassert its ascendant role as benefactor and as director of the accord.

The letters of Roman magistrates to the East also closely followed the format and style long familiar to the Greeks from the chanceries of Hellenistic monarchs. The courtesies, formulas, and language of the epistles show that Roman officials had taken the trouble to adopt practices with which their addressees would feel comfort and security. It was yet another signal that the western power fitted neatly into the political culture of the East. The extant letters are almost all in Greek, and where we once have a Latin copy for comparison, it is plain that precise rendering was not a chief desideratum. Latinisms abound in some letters but are nearly absent in others. The surviving examples range from elegant Greek to sloppy and awkward prose punctuated by errors. But the aggregate demands the conclusion that Romans themselves composed the letters, with or without occasional assistance. Magistrates and *imperatores* framed the missives, awarding privileges, judging disputes, and announcing settlements. They placed their own stamp

---

72. See Gruen, *Hellenistic World*, 46–51, 731–744, with references and bibliography.
73. So, e.g., the treaty with Cibyra: *OGIS*, 762, lines 12–15; with Maronea: *BCH*, 102 (1978), 724–726, lines 41–43; with an Attalid city: *Syll.*³ 694, lines 23–31; with Epidaurus: *IG*, IV²,11, 63, lines 5–9; with Astypalaea: Sherk, *Roman Documents*, no. 16B, lines 48–50. Note also the literary references to a treaty with Jews: I Macc. 8.22; Jos. *Ant.* 12.416; and one with Heraclea Pontica; Memnon, *FGH* 3B, 434F, 18.10. On the publication of Roman-Greek treaties, see A. Heuss, *Klio*, 27 (1934), 244–250.

upon communications as representatives of the *res publica*. The epistles served as vehicles to demonstrate familiarity with Hellenistic conventions, competence in and often sophisticated control of the language, and the magnanimity of the superior power.[74] In such matters, the dichotomy of philhellenism and animosity toward the Greeks has no place and makes no sense. Romans claimed participation in a shared culture of which they were both the heirs and the custodians.

To what extent the generals, legates, and envoys who served on Roman missions to the East spoke Greek is beyond our grasp. Capacity in the language could have its uses, if only to underline the Roman advantage. And the numbers in the Roman elite who enjoyed that capacity doubtless grew as the second century progressed. But there is no reason to believe that the state chose its representatives to the East on the basis of experience and familiarity with the area or competence in the language. That practice would go against the grain of Rome's political leadership, which assumed versatility in its members and frowned on the promotion of "experts".[75] Official intercourse would be conducted in Latin anyway. The Roman would not find himself at a disadvantage. By the late Republic, it could be taken for granted that members of the Roman elite knew Greek and could use it whenever appropriate. Cicero's limitless list of charges against Verres included the allegation that he knew not a word of Greek. The very fact of the reproach presupposes that knowledge of Greek was expected—and desirable.[76] Cicero himself then came under attack by Verres' successor in Sicily, L. Caecilius Metellus, for indiscretions of the opposite sort. Metellus censured the orator for appearing before a Greek senate in Syracuse and, worse still, for addressing that body in Greek.[77] The complaint was legitimate;

---

74. See the texts gathered in Sherk, *Roman Documents*, 211–264, with Sherk's analysis, 186–209. As an example of impressive familiarity with *koine* Greek, note the letter of Flamininus to Chyretiae; Sherk, no. 33, and the careful discussion of D. Armstrong and J. J. Walsh, *CP*, 81 (1986), 32–46. Roman composition of the Greek version could also forestall possible misunderstanding of the magistrate's intent; cf. Sherk, no. 52, lines 54–57.

75. Kaimio's efforts, *Romans and the Greek Language*, 101–102, to show the development of "eastern experts" are refuted by the very statistics he employs. The only ancient texts he cites are Livy, 33.24, 34.59, and Paus. 7.9.5—all of which plainly refer to exceptional decisions, thereby accounting for their special mention. For full discussion, with sources and bibliography, see Gruen, *Hellenistic World*, 203–249.

76. Cic. *Verr.* 2.4.127; cf. 2.3.84.

77. Cic. *Verr.* 2.4.147: *ait indignum facinus esse, quod ego in senatu Graeco verba fecissem; quod quidem apud Graecos Graece locutus essem, id ferri nullo modo posse.*

Cicero, in any case, offered no cogent response.[78] But it had nothing to do with hostility toward Greeks or Hellenism. Cicero's imprudence consisted in delivering a speech to a political assemblage of Greeks in their own tongue, a demeaning act for a representative of the Roman government. That fundamental mode of thinking had held firm for two centuries.

An impressive array of Roman leaders in this period felt attraction to and even enthusiasm for the culture of Greece. As individuals or as a collectivity they have served scholarship as symbols of "philhellenism" or a "philhellenic movement," thus to be contrasted to those who resisted and sought to curb those inclinations. The simplistic character of that formulation has been noted more than once in general terms. Greater value may derive from examination of the more conspicuous examples. They disclose thoughtful and purposeful attitudes that go beyond naive admiration to a level of cultural policy.

M. Claudius Marcellus, conqueror of Syracuse, returned to Rome in 211 with spectacular spoils of war, notably a great haul of Sicily's choicest art treasures. The subsequent moral judgments passed on this act need not concern us here.[79] More striking is Marcellus' own posture, a quite deliberate one. He did not place emphasis on mere conquest and acquisition. Marcellus presented himself as a man of culture and discernment, obviously without the slightest embarrassment. The proconsul transferred art objects from private dwellings in Syracuse to similar abodes in Rome, reserving public monuments for public display. This was not an indiscriminate distribution.[80] Moreover, he put his religious sensibilities on show through dedicatory offerings in Rome and at selected Hellenic sites, drawn from captured Syracusan art.[81] The gestures had larger ends in view. Marcellus professed to stimulate Romans to an appreciation and admiration of Hellenic creativity.[82] The general gained reputation as a devotee of Greek education and letters and an admirer of those who excelled at them.[83] His objective, however,

78. The orator simply engaged in an irrelevant counterattack.
79. An extended discussion above, pp. 94–101.
80. Polyb. 9.10.13.
81. Plut. *Marc.* 30.4. See further P. Gros, *REL*, 57 (1979), 111–112.
82. Plut. *Marc.* 21.5. The language employed here is negative, deriving from a hostile tradition. But that does not cast doubt on the posture of Marcellus himself.
83. Plut. *Marc.* 1.2: Ἑλληνικῆς παιδείας καὶ λόγων ἄχρι τοῦ τιμᾶν καὶ θαυμάζειν τοὺς κατορθοῦντας ἐραστής.

was not so much to spread the Hellenic gospel as to draw Hellenism into the service of the Roman civic structure. The treasures from Syracuse helped to finance the new temple to Virtus, and the art works from that city served to decorate the building. It would highlight a whole array of public decorations provided by the Sicilian art works.[84] To see Marcellus as vanguard of a philhellenic group, engaged in a political struggle with more conservative senators from older families, misses the point altogether.[85] The general earned plaudits and popularity, for he had raised the level of Roman cultural consciousness and had appropriated Hellenic art to enhance Roman civic and religious life. At the same time, he presented a model that would be imitated and repeated again and again by later Roman leaders: the statesman who familiarized himself with Greek education and learning only so far as national duties permitted.[86] Marcellus advanced the proper order of priorities.

Q. Fabius Pictor, as already observed, had a deep knowledge of Greek, the language in which he composed Rome's first historical annals.[87] His appointment to Delphi after Cannae on a mission to obtain oracular advice on appeasing the gods plainly presupposed his fluency and skill. The accomplished Hellenist brought back the Delphic instructions duly inscribed in Greek verse. His report to the senate on the Pythian pronouncements, however, was delivered in Latin, no doubt his own translation from the original.[88] That rendering did not simply serve the pragmatic purpose of intelligibility. Fabius' mission and its conclusion symbolized the application of Greek religious authority to the needs of the Roman nation.

The most celebrated hero of the period, P. Scipio Africanus, made no secret of the high esteem in which he held Greek culture. He even employed part of his time in Syracuse enjoying walks in the gymnasium, dressed in Greek cloak and sandals, reading Greek books, and exercising in Greek fashion. That form of indulgence exceeded customary proprieties and provoked some pointed criticism.[89] The critics,

---

84. Cic. *Verr.* 2.4.120–121; *De Rep.* 1.21; Livy, 25.40.1–3; Plut. *Marc.* 28.1; Val. Max. 1.1.8.

85. As does Gros, *REL*, 57 (1979), 102–105, 112–114. Plutarch's formulation, *Marc.* 21.3, is schematic and based on partisan sources.

86. Plut. *Marc.* 1.2: αὐτὸς δὲ ὑπ' ἀσχολιῶν ἐφ' ὅσον ἦν πρόθυμος ἀσκῆσαι καὶ μαθεῖν οὐκ ἐξικόμενος.

87. Dion. Hal. 1.6.2; Cic. *De Div.* 1.43.

88. Livy, 23.11.1–6.

89. Livy, 29.19.11–12; Val. Max. 3.6.1; Plut. *Cato*, 3.7.

however, directed their reproaches not at the Hellenism as such but at the unseemliness of a Roman commander and representative of the *res publica* behaving in an undignified and inappropriate fashion.[90] Admiration for Greek culture was a different matter—and unaffected. Africanus had no inhibitions on that score. He left dedications at Delphi and Delos, composed letters in Greek to Colophon, Heraclea, and Philip of Macedon, and enjoyed honors from Greek communities.[91] His son received a thorough Hellenic training, which issued in a work of Roman history composed in Greek.[92] And most striking, Africanus' brother L. Scipio Asiagenus even had a statue of himself set up on the Capitol in full Greek regalia—cloak, sandals, and all.[93] That monument left a clear statement: Asiagenus took pride in associating himself with the traditions and practices of the Greeks. Testimony on the Scipios in general does not warrant the conclusion that they represented a philhellenic wing of the Roman senate. Rather, it firmly buttresses the notion that serious engagement with Hellenic culture and the traditional aspirations of Rome's ruling class were reckoned as entirely compatible.

The experience of T. Quinctius Flamininus reconfirms that notion. A long register of scholarly contributions has treated the cultural predilections of Flamininus, and the pendulum has swung back and forth between those who stress his authentic philhellenism and those for whom his cynical manipulation of Greeks reveals the essential character of the man.[94] The controversy, however, bogs down in misconception, as if cultural leanings and political realities stood in conflict. Genuine appreciation for Hellenism, it has been assumed, should preclude diplomatic bullying or chicanery.[95] The duality needs to be overcome. Fla-

90. See, especially, Plut. *Cato*, 3.7.

91. Delphi: *SEG*, I, 144. Delos: *I de Délos*, 427, lines 12–13; 428, lines 13–14; 439A, line 81, etc.; cf. Zonaras, 9.18. Colophon: Sherk, *Roman Documents*, no. 36. Heraclea: Sherk, no. 35. Philip V: Polyb. 10.9.3. Honors from Delos: *Syll.*³ 617.

92. Cic. *Brutus*, 77.

93. Val. Max. 3.6.2.

94. See the fascinating survey of opinions by E. Badian, *Titus Quinctius Flamininus: Philhellenism and Realpolitik* (Cincinnati, 1970), 3–27.

95. For an eloquent defense of Flamininus' philhellenism, see J. P. V. D. Balsdon, *Phoenix*, 21 (1967), 177–190. Badian, *Flamininus*, 28–57, sees him as given to shiftiness and trickery, with but a veneer of Greek learning. Flamininus' behavior has also been explained by compartmentalizing his cultural inclinations and his political attitudes; see Gruen, *Hellenistic World*, 267–272. Most recently, Armstrong and Walsh, *CP*, 81 (1986), 32–37, defend Flamininus' Greek prose style but insist that he learned Greek only to conduct political parleys and to negotiate policy, thus implicitly endorsing the conventional bifurcation.

mininus, it is reported, was fluent in Greek, his voice and diction thoroughly Hellenic. And we have no grounds to deny that report.[96] To his dedications of spoils at Delphi, Flamininus attached Greek verses of his own composition.[97] His statue installed at Rome bore a Greek inscription, thus showing, if nothing else, that he preferred to be presented to the public as a man closely associated with Hellenism.[98] How deep and how learned was his Hellenism we cannot know. It was, however, eminently serviceable. Flamininus could engage in private discussions with Philip V, doubtless in Greek, and even exchange banter with him in public, although he surely insisted on conducting negotiations in Latin.[99] His familiarity with the language also permitted him to speak freely with leaders of allied communities and contingents, while keeping the upper hand for himself. Flamininus' command of Greek facilitated his intrigues in Boeotia, his intimidation at Demetrias, and his directives to Greek commanders and cities.[100] None of this implies inconsistency and tension. Fluency in the tongue that could allow either informal interchange or the firm delivery of Roman instructions, while reserving official communications for Latin, gave Flamininus the advantage and assured his centrality in all diplomatic dealings.

C. Sulpicius Gallus, the consul of 166, deservedly gained reputation as a scholar of high distinction. This was no mere dabbler in things Hellenic. Gallus was the most accomplished of all Roman *nobiles* in Greek letters, a scientist as well as humanist, whose learned explanation of lunar eclipses relieved the anxieties of a Roman army in Macedon.[101] His cultivated tastes, however, could also lead to arrogance and officiousness when he was in the East as representative of the *res publica*. He disdained to arbitrate a territorial dispute between Sparta and Argos or to rule on a secessionist request by Aetolians in Achaea.[102] At Sardis he invited complaints against the Pergamene monarch, allegedly out of

96. Plut. *Flam.* 5.5: φωνήν τε καὶ διάλεκτον Ἕλληνι.

97. Plut. *Flam.* 12.6–7: ἀνατιθεὶς γὰρ εἰς Δελφοὺς ἀσπίδας ἀργυρᾶς καὶ τὸν ἑαυτοῦ θυρεὸν ἐπέγραψε; denied without argument by Badian, *Flamininus*, 54.

98. Plut. *Flam.* 1.1.

99. Polyb. 18.7.3–6, 18.8.4–7; Livy, 32.35.5–8; Plut. *Flam.* 17.2.

100. Boeotia: Polyb. 18.43; Livy, 33.27.5–33.29.1. Demetrias: Livy, 35.31.13–16. Directives: Livy, 35.39.1–4, 35.39.8, 35.50.3, 36.31.8–10.

101. Cic. *Brutus*, 78: *maxume omnium nobilium Graecis litteris studuit . . . et fuit reliquis rebus ornatus atque elegans*; *De Rep.* 1.21: *doctissimus homo*; 1.23–24, 1.30; *Pro Mur.* 66; *De Sen.* 49; *De Off.* 1.9; Livy, 44.37.5–9; Pliny, *NH*, 2.53; Quint. 1.10.47; Val. Max. 8.11.1: *maximum in omni genere litterarum percipiendo studium*.

102. Paus. 7.11.1–3.

personal hostility.[103] Polybius' negative characterization is biased and suspect, but there is no reason to doubt that Gallus behaved imperiously and insolently, a prime example of the cultivated Roman driven to demonstrate that he was the equal of Greeks in erudition and their superior in authority. Sulpicius Gallus simply took to undue lengths a characteristic form of Roman deportment.

That deportment is no better exemplified than by L. Aemilius Paullus, victor at Pydna and celebrated devotee of Hellenism. The information on Paullus' activities after Pydna is especially rich—and especially revealing. His fluent Greek was put on display shortly after the surrender of Macedon to Roman power in 168. The defeated and humbled Macedonian monarch, Perseus, was ushered into the presence of the consul, prepared for self-abasement. Paullus, however, treated his prisoner with respect and consideration, extracted still more tears from him, and promised him the traditional clemency of the *populus Romanus*. The conversation, of course, was conducted in Greek, in a show both of magnanimity and of cultivation on Paullus' part. Having completed the discourse, Paullus then turned to his own staff and summarized in Latin the gist of the interview.[104] The *imperator* had, therefore, not only reminded the deposed Macedonian of Roman cultural and political superiority, he also engaged in a bit of cultural snobbery toward his own subordinates.

Those, of course, were informal proceedings. When formalities commenced, Paullus reverted to standard official demeanor. The postwar settlement had been dictated in general terms by the senate and then worked out in detail by the commander and the *decem legati*. Paullus announced the results at Amphipolis before an assembled throng of Macedonians in an impressive ceremony that emphasized the *maiestas* of Rome. The commander naturally delivered the peace terms in the language of the conqueror. Having done so, he turned proceedings over to his subordinate, the praetor Cn. Octavius, who produced a translation in Greek for the awestruck audience.[105] The whole affair had been carefully orchestrated so as to assert Roman ascendancy in the cultural as in the military sphere. On a lesser scale, Cato had done the same in his address to the Athenians, with its appended translation, in 191. Aemilius Paullus moved in an established tradition.

103. Polyb. 31.6.1–5.
104. Livy, 45.7.4–45.8.8; cf. Val. Max. 5.1.8.
105. Livy, 45.29.1–3.

In another matter, however, Paullus went beyond convention to an even more dramatic exhibit of his refined tastes and sensibilities. The proconsul took his son Scipio Aemilianus and the brother of the Pergamene king on an extended tour of the major historical and religious sites in mainland Greece. At every step Paullus showed respect, appreciation, and piety for the heritage of Hellas. Among other things, Paullus performed sacrifice at holy shrines and celebrated sanctuaries in Delphi, Athens, and Olympia, visited Aulis where was launched the Trojan expedition, paid homage to the wealth of Athenian monuments, gazed upon the lofty citadel of Corinth and the austere aspect of Sparta, and paid respects to the temple of Aesculapius at Epidaurus whence the Romans once fetched the symbol of the god to cure a plague.[106] The trip also enhanced Paullus' admiration for Greek art, most especially for Phidias' masterpiece, the statue of Olympian Zeus, which he subsequently brought to Rome for dedication in the temple of Fortuna.[107] Paullus had organized a careful and comprehensive excursion. There is no reason to doubt that he was both knowledgable about and respectful of Greek traditions, religion, and art.

At the same time, this was more than a mere tourist trip. When Paullus reached Delphi he saw a column or columns erected to hold the sculptured image of Perseus. The Roman might have ordered them destroyed or even left incomplete in order to symbolize the Macedonian defeat. Instead, he took a further and significant step, ordering that his own statue be carved and stationed on top of the column meant for Perseus.[108] The symbolic import would, of course, be unmistakable. And lest anyone miss it, Paullus, philhellene though he was, had the monument inscribed with the notice of its capture—in Latin.[109] Paullus' conspicuous admiration for the Hellenic achievement went hand in hand with the message of Roman appropriation.

That message came through again in Paullus' lavish games at Amphipolis in 167. The Roman commander made preparations with scrupulous care and attention to detail. The events would be magnificent, impressive—and precisely in accord with Greek practice. During his tour Paullus himself had alerted the *principes* of various Greek states to the coming celebration and had sent notices to communities and kings

106. Livy, 45.27.5–45.28.5; Polyb. 30.10.3–6; Plut. *Aem. Paull.* 28.1–2.
107. Polyb. 30.10.6; Pliny, *NH*, 34.54.
108. Polyb. 30.10.2; Livy, 45.27.7; Plut. *Aem. Paull.* 28.2.
109. *ILLRP*, 323: *L. Aimilius L.f. inperator de rege Perse Macedonibusque cepet*. See the perceptive discussion by Ferrary, *Philhellénisme et impérialisme*, 556–558.

in Greek Asia. He gathered artists of all kinds, as well as athletes, skilled professionals, and entertainers. The show itself, preceded by sacrifices and including generous banquets as well as performances, followed a procedure thoroughly researched to reproduce Greek practice in every particular.[110] Paullus had a clear and well-thought-out purpose. The Greek spectators, invited in large numbers, greeted and arranged according to proper Greek etiquette, were mightily impressed. Their astonishment, however, stemmed not so much from the splendor and lavishness of the show as from the remarkable precision with which it duplicated the best Hellenistic traditions.[111] Paullus' own comments expressed the objective as clearly as could be wished. He observed that a commander who could marshal troops and draw up a battle line for victory could also order and administer a public festival.[112] Aemilius Paullus had driven his point home quite decisively: he had outstripped Macedonians in war and Greeks in peace. The Roman commander could produce Greek games better than any Greek.[113]

Paullus' active interest in Greek culture extended well beyond the aftermath of Pydna. He looked ahead to the next generation, notably the Hellenic education of his sons. He had had them surrounded from an early age with Greek intellectuals and professionals of all sorts: not only philologists, philosophers, and rhetors, but sculptors, painters, even animal trainers and hunting instructors.[114] The young men were both with him on the Macedonian campaign. At its conclusion, Paullus made a show of declining to profit personally from any of the wealth and spoils collected from the defeat of Perseus—with one exception. He allowed his sons, eager to advance their education, to select whatever volumes they wished from the library of the Macedonian kings.[115] He

---

110. Polyb. 30.14; Livy, 45.32.8–11; Plut. *Aem. Paull.* 28.3–5.

111. Livy, 45.32.10: *ut non magnificentiam tantum, sed prudentiam in dandis spectaculis, ad quae rudes tum Romani erant, admirarentur*; Plut. *Aem. Paull.* 28.4: αἴσθησιν οὕτως ἀκριβῆ καὶ πεφροντισμένην ἐνδεικνύμενος ὥστε θαυμάζειν τοὺς Ἕλληνας, εἰ μηδὲ τὴν παιδιὰν ἄμοιρον ἀπολείπει σπουδῆς, ἀλλὰ τηλικαῦτα πράττων ἀνὴρ πράγματα καὶ τοῖς μικροῖς τὸ πρέπον ἀποδίδωσιν.

112. Polyb. 30.14; Livy, 45.32.11: *vulgo dictum ipsius ferebant et convivium instruere ut ludos parare eiusdem esse, qui vincere bello sciret*; Plut. *Aem. Paull.* 28.5: καὶ πρὸς τοὺς θαυμάζοντας τὴν ἐπιμέλειαν ἔλεγε τῆς αὐτῆς εἶναι ψυχῆς παρατάξεώς τε προστῆναι καλῶς καὶ συμποσίου.

113. Ferrary, *Philhellénisme et impérialisme*, 560–565, misses this point and chooses, quite unconvincingly, to see Paullus as imitating a Hellenistic ruler.

114. Plut. *Aem. Paull.* 6.4–5. This list does not even include Polybius or the category of historians.

115. Plut. *Aem. Paull.* 28.6.

encouraged Scipio Aemilianus to take up the Greek sport of hunting, at which the rulers of Macedon had traditionally excelled.[116] Moreover, he asked the Athenians to supply their most experienced philosopher to supervise the higher education of his sons, which they proceeded to do.[117] All these actions further substantiate Paullus' authentic commitment to Hellenism. But there is more to it than that. They demonstrated not only enthusiasm for Greek culture but confiscation of it. By inviting his sons to choose books from Perseus' collection, Paullus concretely signified that the intellectual possessions of Macedon were now at the disposal of Rome. That same message accompanied the introduction of young Scipio to the pleasures of hunting. Paullus had him learn that sport on the estates of Perseus and with the king's huntsmen as his tutors. Once again Macedonian possessions served to facilitate the cultural development of the Roman conqueror. It need hardly be said that the transport of an Athenian philosopher to advance Scipio's higher education, like the transport of art treasures to enhance the city of Rome, neatly symbolized the summoning of Greek culture for the edification of Romans.[118] The education of Scipio, like that of his father, would be zealously Greek at its upper reaches but solidly Roman at its core.[119]

Comparable demonstrations, though in a strikingly different form, featured the games sponsored by L. Anicius who earned his own triumph in the Third Macedonian War for victories over Illyrians. It was a lesser foe and also lesser glory than that gained by Aemilius Paullus.[120] So the games too would be less resplendent—but also designedly novel. Whereas Paullus had gathered skilled performers for an impressive show at Amphipolis, Anicius would bring professional troupes and the most gifted artists to Rome itself. There they would not only exhibit their wares to a Roman audience but would be conspicuously manipulated by the *imperator* in a stunning display of Roman power to exploit Hellenic culture.[121]

A host of Roman *nobiles* in the middle and late second century can claim substantial philhellenic credentials.[122] But their demonstration of

---

116. Polyb. 31.29.5–7.

117. Pliny, *NH*, 35.135.

118. On Paullus and Greek art, see above, pp. 114–115.

119. Plut. *Aem. Paull.* 6.4: τοὺς παῖδας ἀσκῶν τὴν μὲν ἐπιχώριον παιδείαν καὶ πάτριον ὥσπερ αὐτὸς ἤσκητο, τὴν δ' Ἑλληνικὴν φιλοτιμότερον.

120. Livy, 45.43.1–3.

121. Polyb. 30.22. The episode is discussed more fully above, pp. 215–218.

122. See, in general, Colin, *Rome et la Grèce*, 562–591.

those credentials very often served, as in the instances previously noted, to reinforce the sense of Roman control and superiority. The eminent and erudite Ti. Gracchus, son-in-law of Scipio Africanus and father of the Gracchi, headed an extended mission to the Greek East in 165, which included a stay in Rhodes. There he delivered a speech subsequently published, and admired by Cicero—in Greek.[123] The performance no doubt gave proof of Gracchus' fluency in the tongue, but that will not have been its sole purpose. The context, unmentioned by Cicero, needs to be taken into account. Rhodes had undergone severe reprimand at the hands of Rome as consequence of its behavior during the Third Macedonian War. The island had been stripped of key territorial possessions and confronted with harsh demands, including execution of certain leaders who had pursued a policy that now appeared foolish or possibly criminal. There were even elements in Rome who threatened to make war on Rhodes. The Rhodians did all they could to make amends, fulfilled the demands of *senatus consulta*, prosecuted, expelled or executed former leaders, and asserted their contrition. Ti. Gracchus' mission, at least insofar as it concerned Rhodes, was to check up on compliance with demands. And his return to the senate certified that the Rhodians had, in fact, carried out all the instructions delivered by Rome. The islanders, duly humiliated and impotent, would now get their wish: a protective alliance with Rome.[124] The setting for Gracchus' speech in Rhodes thus gains some welcome clarity. Gracchus used Greek as a gesture of good will, an expression of the graciousness of the superior. Rhodes had already been humbled. The Roman envoy came to grant clemency and exhibit generosity. Gracchus' elegant oration showed that the Roman *nobiles* controlled the native tongue of Rhodes, just as they controlled the island's destiny.

Still more accomplished in the nuances of Greek was P. Crassus Mucianus, consul in 131, whose skill extended to knowledge of five separate Hellenic dialects. He had plainly immersed himself in linguistic study with an enthusiasm inexplicable by external motivation alone. But the application of his skill abroad fits into the pattern already discerned. Mucianus' consular year found him in Asia with the task of suppressing Aristonicus' rebellion. The job included the conduct of hearings on various appeals brought before his tribunal in Asia. Mucianus took great

123. Cic. *Brutus*, 79.

124. See, especially, Polyb. 30.31. For treatment of Roman-Rhodian relations and the relevant references, see Gruen, *CQ*, 25 (1975), 58–81; idem, *Hellenistic World*, 39–42, 569–572.

pride in rendering judgment in precisely the dialect and shade of language employed by each plaintiff.[125] He had not schooled himself with this objective in mind, nor was such sophisticated knowledge required for the purpose, but once he occupied the role of *imperator*, it proved eminently useful. Mucianus demonstrated, as Aemilius Paullus had in a different way, that a Roman could attain a level of mastery in matters Greek that even few Greeks could aspire to. And the point was doubly underscored, for Mucianus exhibited that mastery while passing judgment on the Greeks themselves. Here too the combination of cultural and political supremacy was the principal point. Mucianus prized his *dignitas* and that of the *res publica*.[126]

A younger relative of Mucianus, L. Licinius Crassus, offers a similar example. Crassus eventually became a man of considerable and diverse learning. Already at an early stage of his career, as a quaestor in the Greek East about 109, he sat at the feet of the most distinguished philosophers and rhetors in Asia and in Athens.[127] Equally eager to familiarize himself with Hellenic religious ritual, Crassus soundly rebuked Athenian officials for failing to reschedule the Mysteries so as to coincide with his visit.[128] This was not merely the impetuosity of youth, nor is there any inconsistency between Crassus' zeal for Athenian learning and arrogance toward Athenian officials. He considered it legitimate for a magistrate of the Roman Republic to commandeer Greek cultural events for his own edification.

L. Gellius Publicola, proconsul in the East in 93, took the matter to its logical conclusion—or at least expressed himself in that fashion. While at Athens, he assembled the Greek philosophers who were present and announced that, since they could not resolve their intellectual differences, he would step in to settle their controversies and bring harmony to philosophic discourse.[129] The proposition was intended as a joke, and doubtless understood as such. But the jest itself had point only because it exposed a fundamental fact: the intellectual heritage of Greece was now at the disposal of Rome. That fact was reaffirmed by the high

---

125. Quint. 11.2.50; Val. Max. 8.7.6.

126. Dubuisson, *Ktema*, 7 (1982), 204–205, misplaces the emphasis in interpreting Mucianus' actions primarily as an effort to win Greek favor. When Mucianus felt that his position was compromised, he had no hesitation in ordering a Greek official to be stripped and beaten; Gellius, 1.13.9–13.

127. Cic. *De Orat.* 1.45–47; cf. 1.82, 1.92, 2.365.

128. Cic. *De Orat.* 3.75.

129. Cic. *De Leg.* 1.53.

sums an erudite Greek, even a slave could fetch. Some Roman aristocrats were willing to invest substantial amounts for such an educator.[130] For those who could afford it, Greek learning presented itself to Roman purchasers.

The list of Roman aristocrats with sincere interest in Hellenism and notable accomplishments in that sphere attained impressive numbers in the later second century. A representative sample will suffice. L. Marcius Censorinus, the consul of 149, reached a level of sophistication that allowed him to carry on a philosophic correspondence with the noted Academic Clitomachus.[131] Q. Lutatius Catulus, consul in 102, had a command of the finer points of the Greek language which even native speakers found striking.[132] Q. Aelius Tubero, nephew of Scipio Aemilianus, worked laboriously at his studies and enjoyed the tutelage of the great Panaetius.[133] The polish and artistry of M. Aemilius Lepidus' oratorical style were due to his mastery of Greek models.[134] Q. Mucius Scaevola, another pupil of Panaetius, spent part of his praetorship circa 120 in Rhodes, where he debated the erudite Apollonius on Panaetius' teachings.[135] Scaevola had also been present as a young man when Carneades lectured at Rome in 155. The fame of those performances reechoed years later when young Q. Metellus, the future Numidicus, spent time in Athens in order to hear the now elderly Carneades on a more continuous basis.[136] In similar fashion, the youthful M. Claudius Marcellus, a zealous student, engaged in vigorous discussions with philosophers in Athens.[137] Nor were such studies confined to the senatorial elite. The gifted scholar L. Aelius Stilo Praeconinus was an eques but also trained in philology and most accomplished in Greek and Latin letters, hence much admired as a speech writer for Roman *nobiles*.[138] And M. Vigellius, a friend of L. Crassus, became an expert in Stoicism and even lived with Panaetius.[139] Other instances could readily be cited.[140] The testimony is extensive and incontrovertible. Roman aristocrats and,

---

130. Cf. Suet. *De Gramm.* 3.
131. Cic. *Acad. Prior.* 2.102.
132. Cic. *De Orat.* 2.28.
133. Cic. *Acad. Prior.* 2.135; cf. *De Orat.* 3.87; *De Rep.* 1.14.
134. Cic. *Brutus*, 95–96—the consul of 137.
135. Cic. *De Orat.* 1.75.
136. Cic. *De Orat.* 3.68.
137. Cic. *De Orat.* 1.57.
138. Cic. *Brutus*, 205; Suet. *De Gramm.* 3.
139. Cic. *De Orat.* 3.78.
140. See, on the period of Cicero's youth, Rawson, *Intellectual Life*, 3–7.

to some extent, men of means outside aristocratic circles sought instruction in Greek learning, immersed themselves in studies, and often became quite proficient and adept. There is nothing to show that any stigma was attached to that pursuit prior to the late Republic or that practitioners felt the slightest embarrassment about it. The reasons are clear enough. Young Romans schooled themselves in the Hellenic legacy partly, of course, for intellectual enrichment—and partly to demonstrate that that legacy was theirs to command.

One figure stands out in the literature as prime *exemplum* of philhellenism. P. Scipio Aemilianus, much celebrated by Cicero two generations later for both intellectual and political leadership, represents for many moderns the emblem of Rome's successful assimilation of Greek culture.[141] The idea of a "Scipionic circle," the center of Roman Hellenism, encompassing the nation's cultivated elite and the source of intellectual activity in the city, no longer carries conviction. Too many men of letters in Rome show no connection with Scipio, and for many of his *amici* there is no record of intellectual achievement. Scipio himself, it can be argued, gives little sign of philosophic teaching or of *humanitas* in the harshness of his actions abroad, and even his attachment to Hellenism has been seen as mere shallow exposure.[142] The reaction may have gone too far. Cicero's relevant dialogues, the *De Republica* and the *De Amicitia*, are certainly inventive and idealized but hardly without any foundation. The orator could draw on the recollections of Q. Mucius Scaevola and P. Rutilius Rufus, who had known Scipio and could testify to his interests.[143] Evidence on the relations between the eminent Stoic Panaetius and Scipio, as well as the number of Panaetius' Roman pupils who had demonstrable connections with Scipio suggests more

141. See above, nn. 3–4.

142. The study of Brown, *Scipionic Circle*, passim, reckons as a member of the "Scipionic circle" every Roman for whom the sources register any intellectual aspirations at all, both well before Scipio's *floruit* and after his death! Cf. Saunders, *CP*, 39 (1944), 209–217. See the trenchant criticisms of Strasburger, *Hermes*, 94 (1966), 60–72, who considers the group a fiction of Cicero's based on his youthful experience with the circle of Crassus, Antonius, and Scaevola. Strasburger doubts several of the alleged associations with Scipio and also questions the depth of his attachment to Hellenism. Astin, *Scipio Aemilianus*, 294–299, points to a number of individuals with demonstrable Hellenic interests but no connection with and occasionally even antagonism toward Scipio, and denies any influence by Panaetius on Scipio's political or ethical views. Similarly, Earl, *Historia*, 11 (1962), 477–483. Zetzel, *HSCP*, 76 (1972), 173–179, sees a literary circle invented by Cicero for the *De Republica*. On the political associates of Scipio, see Astin, *Scipio*, 80–96; Gruen, *Roman Politics*, 16–44.

143. Cic. *De Amicit*. 1; *Brutus*, 85.

than a casual flirtation with Hellenism.[144] What needs investigation is not the depth of Aemilianus' Hellenic immersion, which one can debate endlessly to little purpose, but the light that his intellectual interests shed upon the cultural attitudes of the Roman nobility.

Scipio Aemilianus, we are told, together with his intimate friends C. Laelius and L. Furius Philus, men of refined tastes and serious weight in the *res publica*, always kept public company with the most learned men of Greece.[145] Laelius, in the *De Amicitia*, is even made to refer to the ascendancy Scipio enjoyed in "our, so to speak, circle."[146] The evidence does not establish a tightly knit political or intellectual coterie, but it suggests at least a community of interests. More important, however, is the free and open association between Roman *nobiles* and Greek intellectuals. Cicero had no reason to invent that feature. The public character of the relationship, however profound or shallow, carries significance.[147]

Of one particular relationship between Aemilianus and a Greek intellectual we have firsthand information: the tutelage of the young Roman by the historian and statesman Polybius. And testimony on that association gives the clearest insight into aristocratic cultural aspirations. A famous and extensive passage of Polybius describes the origin and character of his connection with Scipio. The latter's father, Aemilius Paullus, had been responsible not only for making the library of Macedon available to his sons but also for bringing Polybius back to Rome as a valued hostage. The brothers, Scipio and Fabius Maximus, found Polybius' company most advantageous and successfully urged that he be kept in Rome rather than sent off to some Italian municipality. There commenced a teacher-pupil relationship in which each party took pride. When Scipio lamented that he was not taken seriously by his fellow citizens because of a predilection for intellectual matters rather than the vigorous combat of the law courts, Polybius promised to pro-

144. See Garbarino, *Roma e la filosofia greca*, 380–445; Ferrary, *Philhellénisme et impérialisme*, 589–602; K. Abel, *Antike und Abendland*, 17 (1971), 119–143, goes too far in the other direction, overemphasizing the influence of Panaetius on the "Scipionic circle."

145. Cic. *De Orat.* 2.154: *et certe non tulit ullos haec civitas aut gloria clariores aut auctoritate graviores aut humanitate politiores P. Africano, C. Laelio, L. Furio, qui secum eruditissimos homines ex Graecia palam semper habuerunt.*

146. Cic. *De Amicit.* 69: *saepe enim excellentiae quaedam sunt, qualis erat, Scipionis in nostro, ut ita dicam, grege.* Cf. 101, wherein Laelius refers to himself, Scipio, Furius, P. Rupilius, and Sp. Mummius as friends and contemporaries.

147. Cf. Cic. *Pro Mur.* 66: *Scipio ille fuit quem non paenitebat . . . habere eruditissimum hominem Panaetium domi.*

vide instruction in those areas that would win the esteem of Romans. Thenceforth, according to Polybius, the two were inseparable, and mutual bonds developed that were akin to filial affection.[148] The historian may, for his own purposes, have exaggerated the depth and intimacy of the *amicitia*, and the extent to which Scipio's ideas were shaped under the influence of Polybius is a subject for speculation. What catches interest is the type of instruction and the objectives as the historian depicts them. Polybius observed to Scipio that any number of Greeks now arriving in Rome from their homeland could further his current interests in intellectual matters.[149] But he, Polybius, would take charge of Scipio's training in statesmanship and political leadership, the disciplines through which he would regain the respect of his countrymen. No better illustration could be wanted for the theme that underlies the attraction of Hellenic teachings for Rome. Polybius offered precisely what the young man desired: a Greek education, primarily in political theory and practice, which would serve to make Scipio a better Roman. The historian promised to hone his student's speech and behavior so as to make him worthy of his ancestors.[150] The one specific piece of Polybian advice to Scipio of which we have record tells the tale clearly enough. The teacher recommends that his pupil never leave the Forum without first securing the friendship of at least one person encountered there.[151] Polybius' point, we may be sure, was not to enlarge Scipio's circle of intellectual acquaintances. The suggestion addressed itself to Roman practice and pragmatic ends: the accumulation of *clientelae* in the interests of political advancement.

Scipio Aemilianus, it has been observed, held to traditional aristocratic goals, the ambitions and aspirations that drove *nobiles* to seek *honores* and *gloria*. Indeed. But it misconceives the point to regard this attitude as inconsistent with or compartmentalized from an enthusiasm

---

148. Polyb. 31.23.1–31.25.1; cf. Diod. 31.26.5.

149. Polyb. 31.24.6–7: περὶ μὲν γὰρ τὰ μαθήματα, περὶ ἃ νῦν ὁρῶ σπουδάζοντας ὑμᾶς καὶ φιλοτιμουμένους, οὐκ ἀπορήσετε τῶν συνεργησόντων ὑμῖν ἑτοίμως, καὶ σοὶ κἀκείνῳ.

150. Polyb. 31.24.5: ἐγὼ δὲ κἂν αὐτὸς ἡδέως σοι συνεπιδοίην ἐμαυτὸν καὶ συνεργὸς γενοίμην εἰς τὸ καὶ λέγειν τι καὶ πράττειν ἄξιον τῶν προγόνων. And note Scipio's response, 31.24.10: δόξω γὰρ αὐτόθεν εὐθέως ἐμαυτῷ καὶ τῆς οἰκίας ἄξιος εἶναι καὶ τῶν προγόνων.

151. Plut. *Mor.* 199F: τὸ δὲ Πολυβίου παράγγελμα διαφυλάττων ἐπειρᾶτο μὴ πρότερον ἐξ ἀγορᾶς ἀπελθεῖν ἢ ποιήσασθαί τινα συνήθη καὶ φίλον ἁμωσγέπως τῶν ἐντυγχανόντων; cf. 659E–660A.

for Hellenism.[152] The two marched together, or better, the one was pressed into service for the other. Aemilius Paullus, as we have seen, ardently urged a Hellenic education upon his sons—but only with the understanding that it was founded on established Roman principles.[153] Scipio always had to hand a copy of Xenophon's *Cyropaedia*, a valuable pragmatic guide for the political and military leader.[154] Once again Hellenic learning would serve the ends of a Roman aristocrat. On this central matter, the comments of Cicero on Aemilianus, although exaggeratedly favorable, ring true. Like M. Cato, his *adfinis*, Scipio left the deliberate impression that he could devote time to intellectual pursuits because he also carried out the duties owed to his nation's service. His nephew Q. Aelius Tubero might labor at his studies endlessly, but Aemilianus acquired his learning with apparent effortlessness.[155] His education, or so he professed, derived more from experience and home-grown precepts than from Greek literature—though he was conversant with the latter from childhood.[156] Scipio, like Laelius and Furius, added the teachings of Greek philosophy to the native foundations of the *mos maiorum*.[157] In learned debates with Panaetius and Polybius, he would advocate the superiority of Rome's inherited institutions to the constructs of political philosophers.[158] The pursuit of national values as embodied by individual virtue justified the zeal for intellectual matters. That principle held for Cato as for Aemilianus, Laelius, and Furius.[159] A consistency runs through all the evidence. The legacy of Hellas neither supplants nor conflicts with the ancestral precepts of Rome; rather, it enhances and enriches them. Far from downgrading that legacy, Scipio and his like-minded associates took pride in their dedication to it.[160] Such is the Ciceronian portrait, and one that endured. Velleius Paterculus echoed it accurately: Aemilianus was the most outstanding man of

152. As, e.g., Earl, *Historia*, 11 (1962), 477–484; Strasburger, *Hermes*, 94 (1966), 69–72; Gruen, *Hellenistic World*, 268–269.

153. Plut. *Aem. Paull.* 6.4.

154. Cic. *Tusc. Disp.* 2.62; *Ad Q. Fr.* 1.1.23.

155. Cic. *De Orat.* 3.87; cf. *De Rep.* 1.14–15.

156. Cic. *De Rep.* 1.36.

157. Cic. *De Rep.* 3.5: *quod ad summam laudem clarorum virorum pertineret, ad domesticum maiorumque morem etiam hanc a Socrate adventiciam doctrinam adhibuerunt.*

158. Cic. *De Rep.* 1.34.

159. Cic. *Pro Arch.* 16; *Top.* 78.

160. Cf. Cic. *De Amicit.* 104: *nam quid ego de studiis dicam cognoscendi semper aliquid atque discendi, in quibus remoti ab oculis populi omne otiosum tempus contrivimus?*

his day not only in the qualities of military leadership and statesmanship but in native talent and acquired learning.[161] Of course, that portrait amplifies and embellishes the character of a man otherwise flawed and imperfect—like all men. But the principles that he is made to represent are what count, and there is no reason to reckon them as sheer inventions of the Ciceronian age. The actions and attitudes of Scipio cohere closely to those of other second-century Romans prominent both in public life and in letters. Their interest in the latter gave further distinction to the former.

One fact stands out here and bears repeating. The philhellenic inclinations and intellectual aspirations of Roman *nobiles*, far from being suppressed or concealed, gave stature and prestige. We may revert again to the notice that the most honored and influential men of the state openly paraded their friendship with Greek scholars.[162] The distinguished Stoic philosopher from Rhodes, Panaetius, furnishes the best illustration. He was on close terms with Scipio Aemilianus, even lived for a time at his home, and accompanied him on a celebrated public commission to the East.[163] During the time he spent in Rome on one or more extended visits, Panaetius acquired a considerable number of pupils from the Roman ruling class, some of whom not only profited from his tutelage at home but also sought him out in Rhodes. The students of Panaetius included C. Laelius, P. Rutilius Rufus, Q. Aelius Tubero, Q. Mucius Scaevola, C. Fannius, and M. Vigellius.[164] How enduring an effect he had upon them remains a matter for speculation. Three of them, in any case—Rutilius, Scaevola, and Tubero—became devotees of Stoicism, doubtless under his influence.[165] Beyond that we need not go. What matters is the open and frequent intercourse between the

---

161. Vell. Pat. 1.12.3: *omnibus belli ac togae dotibus ingenique ac studiorum eminentissimus saeculi sui.*

162. Cic. De Orat. 2.154.

163. Cic. Tusc. Disp. 1.81: *vixit cum Africano; Pro Mur.* 66; *De Fin.* 4.23: *dignus illa familiaritati Scipionis et Laeli; De Off.* 1.90; *De Rep.* 1.15, 1.34; *Ad Att.* 9.12.2. On the eastern embassy, see Cic. *Acad. Prior.* 2.5; Athen. 12.549d; Plut. *Mor.* 777a; other references in Broughton, *Magistrates of the Roman Republic,* I, 418. Ferrary, *Philhellénisme et impérialisme,* 608–615, sees a connection with the behavior of Hellenistic monarchs. But Panaetius' accompaniment of Scipio has no more in common with Hellenistic monarchy than does Ennius' accompaniment of Fulvius Nobilior to the East a half century earlier.

164. Cic. *Brutus,* 101, 114; *De Off.* 3.10, 3.63; *De Orat.* 1.75, 3.78; *De Fin.* 4.23; *Acad. Prior.* 2.135; *Tusc. Disp.* 4.4.

165. Athen. 6.274 c–e.

Greek intellectual and Romans of the highest social rank. No stigma or taint attached to philhellenism. It was not only acceptable but laudable.

Exceptions have been found to this pattern. Two Roman philhellenes, A. Postumius Albinus and T. Albucius, came under fire for their cultural enthusiasm. In fact, those cases confirm rather than undermine the rule. Postumius claimed repute for erudition and scholarship. With the history he composed in Greek, he also included a preface that requested the indulgence of his readership for any errors in that language. For that disclaimer he received sharp rebuke from Cato.[166] The Censor's reproach, however, directed itself not against Postumius' philhellenism as such but against his apology for failings in the language. From Cato's vantage point, Romans who try their hand at writing Greek should do so at least as well as the Greeks themselves—and should certainly not ask their forbearance. The attitude corresponds closely to that of another philhellene, L. Aemilius Paullus.[167] The Catonian strictures by no means imply that Hellenic leanings were discredited, or even that writing history in Greek had become suspect. Rutilius Rufus composed a history in that language in the next generation and provoked no criticism.[168] Postumius was censured for demeaning a Roman's capacity to command Greek.

The example of T. Albucius carries similar overtones. Albucius, a student of Epicureanism and well schooled in Greek matters, flaunted his Hellenism in an offensive manner—or at least offensive to some. Q. Scaevola mocked him for his affectation, thus generating *inimicitia* and later a prosecution. The poet Lucilius plainly had no use for Albucius and skewered him in a satire, also for excessive Hellenic ostentation. And Cicero himelf gives Albucius the label "perfect Epicurean"—a phrase loaded with irony.[169] Does this disapproval suggest that Hellenic leanings had lost respectability? Hardly. The critics of Albucius were all men steeped in Greek culture. Albucius had discredited himself in their eyes

---

166. Polyb. 39.1; cf. Cic. *Brutus*, 81; *Acad. Prior.* 2.137; Gellius, 11.8; Plut. *Cato*, 12.5; Macrob. *Sat.* 1, praef. 13–16.

167. Polyb. 39.1.3 does speak of Postumius' behavior as making τὴν αἵρεσιν τὴν Ἑλληνικὴν offensive to older and most distinguished Romans, but he refers to Postumius' peculiarities, not to any general disapprobation of philhellenism.

168. Athen. 4.168 c.

169. Cic. *Brutus*, 131: *perfectus Epicurius*. Cicero's negative view of Albucius as Epicurean is further indicated at *Tusc. Disp.* 5.108; cf. *Prov. Cons.* 15: *Graecum hominem ac levem*. On the attitudes of Scaevola and Lucilius, see Cic. *De Fin.* 1.8–9; *De Orat.* 3.171; *Orat.* 149.

because he, like Postumius Albinus, pandered to Greeks. Proper Romans harnessed Hellenism to their nation's cause. Albucius paraded about as a veritable Greek: *plane Graecus*.[170] Once again the critics aimed their reproaches not at the commitment to Greek culture but at the compromise of Roman *dignitas*. The cases of Postumius and Albucius reinforce the fundamental principle that has here been traced throughout: acquisition of Hellenic learning should augment the Roman achievement.

Serious objections, however, challenge that proposition. Did not the Romans in the second century endeavor to curb or even repress certain aspects of Hellenism? Did they not take measures to stamp out Bacchanalian worship, burn the books of Pythagoras, and expel Greek rhetors and philosophers from the city? Did they not associate Greek behavior with luxury and effeminacy? Were there not Romans openly hostile to or harshly scornful of Greeks and Greek practice? The objections are ostensibly weighty, but response can be relatively brief. The issues have already been treated in this work or an earlier one and require only a short summary here. They do not, in fact, pose a grave obstacle.

The Bacchanalian affair held important symbolic significance. Rome took steps against the cult of Dionysus in 186, hunting down, arresting, and, in some instances, executing its adherents. Magistrates received orders to dismantle Bacchic cells and a *senatus consultum* prohibited future observances of the religion. The severity of the action constituted high drama, but the long-term results may not have been so devastating. Exceptions were allowed for individuals and small groups of worshipers, so long as they obtained permission from Roman magistrates and from the senate itself. That feature merits emphasis. The affair was manipulated by the *patres* to reaffirm and entrench public control of religion. Forceful action, accompanied by widespread advertisement of senatorial authority in Italy delivered the principal message. The purpose was not to resist Hellenism or a form thereof but to assert the subordination of an alien cult to the needs of the state. At a time when the eastern wars had just concluded, when the cultural products of that region were streaming into Rome, and when the intoxication of Hellenism gripped individual leaders, the government felt a need to establish

---

170. Cic. *De Fin.* 1.8; *Brutus*, 131.

responsibility for regulation and a collective ascendancy in the peninsula.[171]

Five years later the senate orchestrated yet another dramatic episode of similar character and with similar motivation. A coffin or coffins were exhumed in 181 which purported to contain volumes on Greek philosophy by Pythagoras and material on pontifical law by the ancient Roman king Numa Pompilius. Inquiry by magistrates and *patres* concluded with a condemnation of the books as subversive of Roman religion and a directive to burn them in a public bonfire. The spectacular event was plainly contrived to capture the attention of the citizenry. To what end? The motive could hardly be to stamp out Pythagoreanism, a generally harmless philosophic creed, or indeed to purge Roman religion of Hellenic elements, an impossible and altogether undesirable task. Indeed, the supposed writings of Numa, Rome's legendary and venerated ruler, went up in flames together with the Pythagorean teachings. As with the Bacchanalian episode, the symbolic rather than the pragmatic character of the event stands out. While individual Romans were becoming increasingly enamored of Hellenic culture, the state found it the more important to enunciate community values that transcended the influence of the East. A public exorcism of material that allegedly linked the beginnings of Roman religion to Greek philosophy would provide a clean slate. With that symbolic act, the senate reclaimed the primacy of the *mos maiorum* for which Hellenism would henceforth be an adjunct rather than a core element.[172]

Two *senatus consulta* in the mid–second century ordered the expulsion of Greek intellectuals from Rome. One, in 161, authorized the praetor to remove philosophers and rhetors from the city; the other, either in 173 or in 154, banished two Epicureans. On the face of it these might seem an indication of official animosity toward Hellenic teachings, but the conclusion would be simplistic. How would Rome enforce the enactments? The idea of sweeping through the city to collect all the practitioners of rhetoric and philosophy in 161 is transparently absurd. Most plied their trade in the private households of the *principes*, who would surely not discharge and dismiss them en masse. And one will hardly imagine house-to-house searches. Indeed, we know that such professors continued to lecture and offer instruction in Rome. Here

171. See the extended treatment, with sources and literature, in Gruen, *Studies*, 34–78.

172. The matter is explored in some detail in Gruen, *Studies*, 158–170.

again the effect was plainly symbolic. The number of Greek academics moving to Italy jumped noticeably after the Third Macedonian War. An expulsion order that came on the heels of that influx gave notice that the state maintained responsibility for articulating and overseeing communal values. The task had not been consigned to individuals who encouraged and gained intellectual profit from the migration of Hellenic teachers. The symbolic character of such a step becomes clearer still in the second *senatus consultum*, which singled out only two Epicureans— plainly a token act. Their creed could conveniently be branded as ethically dubious and devoted to hedonism. The state thereby identified as pernicious a philosophy that was made to represent principles at furthest remove from the *mos maiorum*. It may be no coincidence that the same year in which the senate made an example of two Epicureans also witnessed its resistance to a stone theater that was in process of construction. In both instances the *patres* affirmed collective control of cultural institutions.[173]

Romans, it is customarily asserted, held negative stereotypes of Greeks as luxury-ridden, effeminate, shifty, untrustworthy, and given to empty rhetoric and intellectualizing. The existence of such conceptions or misconceptions at some level and to some degree is undeniable. But that does not itself speak to the central question. Did the conventional disparagement entail resistance to Hellenism or a deprecation of philhellenic tendencies among Roman *nobiles*?

The connection, in the Roman mind, between luxury and Hellenism is itself far thinner than is normally assumed. Lamentations by Latin writers about the insidious effects of luxury items on Roman character, in fact, almost never indict the Greeks as culprits. Captured art objects as a source of moral decline becomes a *topos* in the later Republic. The origins are attached to M. Marcellus, or to L. Scipio, or to Manlius Vulso, or even to Metellus Macedonicus; thus they are transparent inventions after the fact, none of them ascribable to contemporaries.[174]

---

173. On the expulsion of rhetors and philosophers, see Gruen, *Studies*, 171–178, with references. A. Wallace-Hadrill, *CP*, 83 (1988), 225, recently and implausibly refers to Roman "hysteria" in expelling intellectuals, an attitude indiscernible in the texts. On the demolition of the theater, see above, pp. 205–210. One might note also the removal of astrologers and adherents of Sabazius in 139; Val. Max. 1.3.3. The persons involved are not Greek and hence, strictly speaking, fall outside the subject of antihellenism. But the action reveals a continued determination to demonstrate state authority over alien practices.

174. See above, pp. 94–99, 105–107, 116.

Other versions place the onset of degeneracy at the end of the Second Punic War and the defeat of Philip V, or else at the year 154, with no connection to Hellenism or Greek imports.[175] Cato's strictures against luxury were numerous and vehement, but remarkably and significantly, none of his extant complaints links that vice with the Greeks. Nor does the series of second-century sumptuary laws designed to curb luxury—or at least to make a show of doing so—include any mention of Hellenic habits.[176] In fact, the only unequivocal association of moral decline with the effects of Hellenism in this period was made by a Greek! Polybius dates the time of Roman moral failure to the aftermath of the Third Macedonian War and assigns it to the infection of the Romans by Greek lack of discipline.[177] The comment reflects both a sadness and a bitterness on the part of Polybius: a sadness about the change in Roman character and behavior in the years after Pydna and a bitterness about the failure of his own countrymen. It is the latter whom that passage most pointedly indicts.[178] Polybius' disappointment with his own contemporaries need not mirror the attitude of Romans.

The alleged hostility, indifference, or disdain for Hellenism turns out to be more a modern construct than an ancient fact. The two most notorious figures in this category, Cato and Mummius, prove upon inspection to have been miscast. As we have seen, Cato's criticisms of Greeks did not signal a rearguard conservative assault on Hellenism, a contempt for Greeks and a deep suspicion of their culture, a blind and irrational prejudice, or an internal division that produced ambiguity or even schizophrenia. In fact, a more subtle design runs through the comments and actions of Cato. His censure of supposed Greek deficiencies aimed to throw Roman values into clearer focus, to augment national pride, and to sharpen a sense of cultural identity. Cato's own engagement with Hellenism was no mere shallow encounter but a fairly extensive exploration. Insofar as he slighted that engagement, his posture underscored a Roman's facility with and manipulation of the Greek

175. Val. Max. 9.3.1; Pliny, *NH*, 17.244; cf. Cic. *Ad Fam.* 9.22.2.

176. On Cato and luxury, see above, pp. 69–71.

177. Polyb. 31.25.4–6: ταχέως ἡρπακότες ἐν τῷ Περσικῷ πολέμῳ τὴν τῶν Ἑλλήνων εἰς τοῦτο τὸ μέρος εὐχέρειαν; Diod. 31.26.7, 37.3.1–6. Polybius proceeds to cite Cato on luxury and the signs of decline in Roman character, but there is nothing to show that the association with Greek laxity comes from Cato. Cf. also Polyb. 6.56.13–15.

178. Cf. Dubuisson, *Le Latin de Polybe*, 282–283, who rightly sees that Greeks are the principal targets of the passage but, more questionably, regards this attitude as reflecting a Roman vantage point.

achievement.[179] In all of this Cato's attitudes and opinions closely parallel those of T. Flamininus or L. Aemilius Paullus or others like them. The dichotomy of philhellene and antihellene dissolves. It was a mere matter of style.

The reputation of L. Mummius as blundering ignoramus, unknowing or insensitive to Greek art and religion is similarly misconceived. The record shows a discrimination in works of art, attention to Greek religious sensibilities, and generosity in gifts and dedications to Hellenic shrines. The display of statuary and the advocacy of painting in Rome further attest to Mummius' authentic interest in the culture of Greece. At the same time, his appropriation of art treasures from the East and his distribution of them to civic and religious sites throughout the peninsula adhere to an established tradition of Roman commanders who combined appreciation of Greek art with self-advertisement through the adornment of Italy.[180]

None of this evidence, of course, denies that negative stereotypes of Greeks existed in the Roman consciousness and received expression by Latin writers. The fact is well known and often noted. But the connotation is not so simple, and understanding requires some care.

The plays of Plautus exhibit ostensible prejudice. His unflattering verses on Greeks ought, on the face of it, to reflect not only the dramatist's bias but the preconceptions of a popular audience. Plautus' barbs at Greeks come in various forms. He employs the terms *pergraecari* and *congraecari* as synonyms for intemperance and debauchery.[181] He holds a very dim view of Bacchic rites and their effects.[182] He jibes at Greek philosophers and intellectuals generally.[183] And other miscellaneous disparaging remarks about Greeks can be found in his pages.[184] What exactly do they amount to? To conclude that they represent antipathy to Hellenism would be rash and simplistic. The Plautine plays were all, or almost all, based on Greek models, as everyone in the audience knew and as prologues repeatedly reminded them. The disparaging remarks about Greeks are, of course, delivered by Greek characters, usually slaves. The device may suggest that the dramatist, far from endorsing

179. See above, Chapter 2, passim.
180. See above, pp. 123–129.
181. Plautus, *Bacch.* 742–743, 812–813; *Most.* 20–24, 64–65, 958–960; *Poen.* 600–603; *Truc.* 86–87; cf. Macrob. *Sat.* 3.14.9.
182. Plautus, *Amph.* 703–704; *Aul.* 408–409; *Bacch.* 53, 56, 371–372; *Cas.* 980; *Men.* 828–841; *Miles,* 856–858, 1016.
183. Plautus, *Capt.* 284; *Curc.* 288–291; *Merc.* 147; *Pseud.* 687, 974; *Rudens,* 986.
184. Plautus, *Cas.* 67–72; *Miles,* 641–648; *Stich.* 226–227, 446–448; *Truc.* 1–3.

the stereotypes, was lampooning them. Further, Plautine characters could also make anti-Roman remarks, branding the westerners as barbarians—as indeed could the playwright himself.[185] The comic manipulation plainly has a character quite different from mere animosity toward Greeks. Nor does it cater to anti-Greek feelings in the audience. Plautus mocks Roman disparagement of Greek behavior, a far cry from hostility to Hellenism. Plautine jokes are witty but not bitter. The playwright also offers indirect criticism of Roman intellectual snobbishness, a feature perhaps indicated by the frequency with which the speech of servile characters slips into Greek.[186] If so, this would form a neat parallel to the criticisms leveled at self-demeaning philhellenes such as Postumius Albinus and T. Albucius. In short, Plautus is parodying Roman misapprehensions of Greeks rather than expressing hostility to Hellenism.[187]

The stereotypes, to be sure, persisted. Negative depictions of Greeks or Greek character can be found scattered in various texts that date to or harken back to the second century. Dramatists continued to find place for them. Pacuvius, we are told, reproached false philosophers who rely on verbal chicanery; and Afranius contrasted Roman practical wisdom to Greek abstract theorizing.[188] An exemplary instance of the latter was the ludicrous Greek academic Phormio, who, so it was alleged, delivered a learned disquisition on military strategy without ever having been on a battlefield, thereby drawing the contempt of Hannibal.[189] The poet Ennius puts into the mouth of a Greek character the oft-quoted phrase that philosophizing is acceptable up to a point, so long as one is not altogether devoted to it.[190] M'. Acilius Glabrio, in a sharp exchange with Aetolians in 191, rebuked them for "acting in a Greek manner."[191] Roman senators in 172 spoke of *calliditas Graeca*, so Livy reports in a passage derived from Polybius.[192] Cato's sneer about Greeks speaking with their tongues and Romans from the heart was surely not a senti-

---

185. Plautus. *Asin.* 11; *Bacch.* 121–124; *Capt.* 492, 884; *Cas.* 748; *Poen.* 598, 1313–1314; *Trin.* 19. Rightly recognized as parody by A. D. Leeman, in H. Zehnacker and G. Hentz, eds., *Hommages à Robert Schilling* (Paris, 1983), 350–352.

186. Plautus, *Bacch.* 1162; *Capt.* 880–882; *Cas.* 728–732; etc.

187. See Gruen, *Studies*, 148–157.

188. Gellius, 13.8.1–5.

189. Cic. *De Orat.* 2.75–76.

190. Cic. *Tusc. Disp.* 2.1.1; *De Rep.* 1.30; *De Orat.* 2.156; Gellius, 5.15.9; and cf. Gellius' paraphrase, 2.16.5.

191. Polyb. 20.10.6–7: ἔτι γὰρ ὑμεῖς ἑλληνοκοπεῖτε; cf. Livy, 36.28.4–5.

192. Livy, 42.47.7.

ment unique to him. It is echoed elsewhere.[193] Cicero's grandfather went further still, alleging that greater familiarity with Greek makes one increasingly wicked.[194] And the learned L. Crassus called attention to Greek *ineptia*, a penchant for tactlessness and inappropriateness that characterizes the whole race.[195] Similar jibes and disapproving remarks recur with frequency in the Ciceronian age.[196] But their significance ought not to be exaggerated or misconstrued. They repeat stereotypes and conventions, superficial *topoi* that allowed Romans to smile knowingly and enjoy their own superiority. It is essential to note, however, that the derisive comments are all aimed at supposed personal characteristics of Greeks—not at Roman taste and interest in Hellenism. The distinction needs to be insisted upon. Romans strove to differentiate their values from those of the Greeks, an effort quite consonant with the exploration, absorption, and manipulation of Greek culture.

Attitudes at the turn of the century show continuity and consistency. Cicero's *De Oratore*, set in 91, furnishes a document of high importance. The dialogue, to be sure, is a creation, inventive and imaginative, not a work of history. But as Cicero knew, and as he explicitly stated, there were limits on how inventive he could be. When dealing with persons whose speeches and public acts were known by many in his readership, he could hardly fabricate opinions or personality. Cicero composed the arguments and interchange, but he strove to reproduce the tone and sentiments of the speaker.[197] The matter has special significance for the two principal interlocutors of the *De Oratore*, L. Licinius Crassus and M. Antonius. The two men stood at the head of the oratorical profession at the beginning of the first century and therefore offer a precious glimpse into the intellectual response to Hellenism on the eve of the Ciceronian age.

L. Crassus merits special attention in this regard. On the face of it, his attitude is riddled with ambiguity and inconsistency. Crassus had a wide familiarity with the learning of Greece, yet took some pains in the *De Oratore* to distance himself from it. He repeats certain stereotypes:

193. Plut. *Cato*, 12.5; cf. Livy, 8.22.8: *a Graecis, gente lingua magis strenua quam factis.*
194. Cic. *De Orat.* 2.265: *ut quisque optime Graece sciret, ita esse nequissimum.*
195. Cic. *De Orat.* 2.17–18; cf. 1.221; *Tusc. Disp.* 1.86.
196. See Petrochilos, *Roman Attitudes*, 35–53; Balsdon, *Romans and Aliens*, 30–40.
197. Cic. *De Orat.* 2.7–9. On the general question of Cicero's reliability in the *De Oratore*, see R. D. Meyer, *Literarische Fiktion und historischer Gehalt in Ciceros "De Oratore"* (Stuttgart, 1970), 24–96. A. D. Leeman and H. Pinkster, *M. Tullius Cicero: De oratore, Libri III* (Heidelberg, 1981), I, 90–96, II, 186–188, are unduly skeptical. Cicero asserts his aim for accuracy in characterizations elsewhere as well; *Ad Att.* 12.20.2; *Brutus*, 218–219.

Greeks as idle and loquacious, more desirous of argument than of truth.[198] They may be educated and erudite, but the learning is compromised by arrogance and pomposity.[199] Crassus went further to claim that the value of the Twelve Tables alone exceeds the libraries of all the philosophers.[200] He sought the reputation of one who scorned erudition and preferred the astuteness of his own countrymen to the Greeks in all matters.[201] Crassus, in fact, made a point of asserting that he had had little time for formal education and, moreover, little need of what is contained in *Graecae litterae*.[202] The cumulative remarks would seem to add up to a disdain for Hellenic learning.

Yet the facts are quite different. Crassus was a man of high culture and considerable intellectual attainments. Nor did he miss an opportunity for exposure to Greek educators. He seized the occasion of his quaestorship in the East to seek out the leaders of the Academy in Athens for philosophic encounters, and he discussed Plato with them, being already quite conversant with that form of discourse.[203] Some years later, as proconsul in Cilicia, he returned to Athens, once more to engage in learned debates with intellectuals.[204] Crassus' Greek was so expert that listeners concluded it was his native tongue.[205] Some regarded him as more the instructor than the instructed in his interchange with Greeks.[206] His justification for a censorial edict of 92 that banned Latin rhetors included ringing praise for the ancient and excellent wisdom of the Greeks.[207] And he looks forward unabashedly to the *otium* that will facilitate his absorption in philosophy.[208]

The impasse seems rigid. Yet it is more apparent than real. Cicero lets it slip that Crassus' disclaimers about his education constituted posturing.[209] An irony and even self-parody pervades Crassus' disclaimers.[210]

198. Cic. *De Orat.* 1.47: *Graeculos homines, contentionis cupidiores quam veritatis*; 1.102: *tamquam alicui Graeculo otioso et loquaci.*

199. Cic. *De Orat.* 1.102–103.

200. Cic. *De Orat.* 1.195.

201. Cic. *De Orat.* 2.4: *ut Crassus non tam existimari vellet non dicidisse, quam illa despicere et nostrorum hominum in omni genere prudentiam Graecis anteferre.*

202. Cic. *De Orat.* 1.82.

203. Cic. *De Orat.* 1.45–47, 1.57, 1.93, 2.2, 2.365, 3.75.

204. Cic. *De Orat.* 1.82, 2.365.

205. Cic. *De Orat.* 2.2; cf. 1.155.

206. Cic. *De Orat.* 3.228: *ut non a Graecis didicisse sed eos ipsos haec docere posse videare.*

207. Cic. *De Orat.* 3.95: *veterem illam excellentemque prudentiam Graecorum.*

208. Cic. *De Orat.* 2.145.

209. Cic. *De Orat.* 2.4; see above n. 201.

210. See Leeman, in *Hommages R. Schilling* 352–355.

But why? The reason may not be, as is often thought, an embarrassment about Hellenic leanings corresponding to a general distrust of Hellenism. Crassus insists on more than one occasion that public service occupied him from an early age, that affairs of state left few opportunities to indulge in intellectual matters. His instruction came from the laws, the institutions, and the *mos maiorum* of the Roman people.[211] He could take only the odd moment for study when the duties of the nation permitted.[212] The pose was not unique or novel but indeed quite familiar. Cato the Elder had made a similar point of stressing the primacy of public service and national traditions, with attention to Greek *litterae* coming only if time allowed. The underlying implication has nothing to do with antihellenism. Rather, a more telling point, an intelligent Roman who has his priorities straight can master what he needs of Greek learning in his spare time.[213] Crassus could make that case effectively precisely because his intellectual credentials were impeccable. The reprise of Cato's stance is umistakeable.

L. Crassus, like Cato and like a host of learned Roman *nobiles*, presented his involvement with Hellenism as a means to demonstrate the superiority of Roman values. That is clear enough in the rhetorical assertion that the Twelve Tables had greater authority and utility than all the libraries of Greek philosophers.[214] The same message adheres to Crassus' claim that public service was his education and the *mos maiorum* the basis of his learning.[215] Crassus, more explicitly than most of his predecessors, enunciated the proposition fundamental to his cultivated fellow citizens: the venerable and valuable wisdom of the Greeks is transmitted for Roman use and practice.[216] It is no coincidence that he juxtaposes Greek erudition to Roman virtue. They are not at odds or in conflict. The one serves as buttress for the other.[217] Crassus thus stands in complete accord with a long tradition.

---

211. Cic. *De Orat.* 2.365, 3.74: *cui disciplina fuerit forum, magister usus et leges et instituta populi Romani mosque maiorum*; 3.85; cf. 1.82, 1.99, 1.111.

212. Cic. *De Orat.* 3.85: *nec vero . . . ullum umquam habuisse sepositum tempus ad discendum, ac tantum tribuisse doctrinae temporis quantum mihi puerilis aetas, forenses feriae concesserint.*

213. See above, pp. 65–68.

214. Cic. *De Orat.* 1.195: *bibliothecas mehercule omnium philosophorum unus mihi videtur XII tabularum libellus, si qui legum fontis et capita viderit, et auctoritatis pondere et utilitatis ubertate superare.*

215. Cic. *De Orat.* 3.74; see above n. 211.

216. Cic. *De Orat.* 3.95: *veterem illam excellentemque prudentiam Graecorum ad nostrum usum moremque transferri.*

217. Cic. *De Orat.* 3.137: *nam ut virtutis a nostris, sic doctrinae sunt ab illis exempla repetenda.*

THE APPEAL OF HELLAS

M. Antonius' rhetorical posture is more pointed and more exaggerated. He repeatedly asserts that he had received no advanced education, that he understands no more of Greek literature than the average man in the street, that he has grasp neither of *Graecae litterae* nor of oratorical theory.[218] Some concluded that Antonius was altogether unlettered and uneducated.[219]

The truth, however, seeps through in this case as well. As proconsul of Cilicia about 101, Antonius found time to spend in Athens and Rhodes and used that time to surround himself with the most learned men of the city, from whose conversations he took profit.[220] He was by no means unacquainted with a range of Greek historians, rhetoricians, and philosophers, whose work he notes and acknowledges.[221] He even composed a pamphlet on rhetoric, and then claimed—in order to maintain a consistent posture—that it inadvertently reached public attention without his knowledge or consent![222] The writing alone, however, implies familiarity with Greek rhetorical treatises.

Once more, ostensible paradox dissolves into consistent posturing. That Antonius' self-projection as unlettered autodidact is a pose cannot be doubted. Cicero makes that clear enough.[223] The context helps to explain it. Antonius' chief concern is to ensure oratorical success. Speakers who engage in the rough and tumble of the law courts need to play to the crowd. The image of the self-made, artless orator plays better than that of the cultivated intellectual.[224] Antonius does not, in fact, disparage Hellenism but discourages its display in forensic battles, a pragmatic consideration.[225] Indeed, he goes so far as to recommend eavesdropping upon Greek conversations on topics of profound interest, so long as one does not openly admit to the practice. To do so would

218. Cic. *De Orat.* 1.91, 2.28–29, 2.60–61: *haec dumtaxat in Graecis intellego, quae ipsi, qui scripserunt, voluerunt vulgo intellegi; in philosophos vestros, si quando incidi . . . verbum prorsus nullum intellego.*

219. Cic. *De Orat.* 2.1: *M. autem Antonium omnino omnis eruditionis expertem atque ignarum fuisse.*

220. Cic. *De Orat.* 1.82, 2.3: *ille vel Athenis vel Rhodi se doctissimorum hominum sermonibus dedisset.* See also 2.95, evidently an earlier trip to Asia, in which Antonius heard some leading rhetors.

221. Cic. *De Orat.* 2.55–59, 2.152.

222. Cic. *De Orat.* 1.94; cf. Quint. 3.1.19, 3.6.45, 12.9.5.

223. Cic. *De Orat.* 2.4, 2.350: *libenter enim te cognitum iam artificem aliquandoque evolutum illis integumentis dissimulationis tuae nudatumque perspicio* [Crassus speaking].

224. Cic. *De Orat.* 2.4, 2.72.

225. Cic. *De Orat.* 2.156: *ego ista studia non improbo, moderata modo sint; opinionem istorum studiorum et suspicionem artifici apud eos, qui res iudicent, oratori adversariam esse arbitror, imminuit enim et oratoris auctoritatem et orationis fidem;* Quint. 12.9.5.

risk loss of credibility with the public.[226] The advice may well be tongue-in-cheek, but it underlines the difference between the pursuit of Hellenic learning and the avoidance of that reputation in the setting of the law courts. Antonius advocates the latter but does not discourage the former.

In the end, the position of M. Antonius, as portrayed in the *De Oratore*, is not so different from that of the roster of Roman *nobiles* who both familiarized themselves with Greek culture and kept it in its place. One contrived disclaimer by Antonius is especially striking. He maintains that his acquaintance with *Graecae litterae* came only late in life— and then was just superficial.[227] Once again the echoes of Cato can hardly be missed. The Hellenism of a Roman aristocrat needs to be worn lightly. Its value rests in the advance of traditional interests.

A final—and notorious—example serves to confirm the argument. The impression of C. Marius, fostered by himself, his supporters, his opponents, or some combination thereof, is that of the rugged, rural nationalist untutored by and uninterested in higher learning. Sallust ascribes to Marius a speech in which he denies any exposure to Greek literature, adding that he had rejected such learning because it had brought no virtue to those who professed it.[228] The story that he was uneducated in Greek and deliberately scorned such education plainly circulated in his own day and after.[229]

The truth lies elsewhere. The pose of Marius is closely akin to that of several Roman *nobiles* of the previous three generations. He put weight on native *virtus* as opposed to Hellenic rhetorical overrefinement—long since a standard line. Political and pragmatic purposes dictated such a stance on appropriate occasions.[230] In fact, Marius was not ignorant of Hellenic matters. Plutarch at one point has him make reference to a line of Pindar.[231] And after his victories in the German wars, it was said, Marius took to drinking from a Bacchic vessel in deliberate imitation of Dionysus' practice after his Indian triumph.[232] Hence, Marius did not

---

226. Cic. *De Orat.* 2.153.

227. Cic. *De Orat.* 1.82: *sero ac leviter Graecas litteras attigissem.*

228. Sallust, *Iug.* 85.32: *neque litteras Graecas didici; parum placebat eas discere, quippe quae ad virtutem doctoribus nihil profuerant.*

229. Cf. Plut. *Mar.* 2.2: λέγεται δὲ μήτε γράμματα μαθεῖν Ἑλληνικὰ; Sallust, *Iug.* 63.3, 85.12–13; Cic. *Pro Arch.* 19; Val. Max. 2.2.3; Schol. Bob. 176, St.

230. Cf. T. F. Carney, *A Biography of C. Marius*[2] (Chicago, 1970), 13–14.

231. Plut. *Mar.* 29.3.

232. Val. Max. 6.3.6; Pliny, *NH*, 33.150.

shrink from overt allusion to Hellenic myth and tradition. Plutarch offers the best insight into Marius' public attitude: he never used the Greek language for serious matters.[233] The statement implies that he knew Greek but would not employ it in an official capacity or in situations of public import. That stance, as we have seen, has a host of precedents. The purpose, it need hardly be said, was to reaffirm Roman mastery and superiority. Marius delivered the point by explaining that it would be absurd to take instruction from those who are the slaves of others.[234]

A particular episode exemplifies Marius' attitude. The great general, after his second triumph, sponsored a public show in Greek style. When the performance took place, Marius sat down in the theater, took one look, and then exited.[235] It would seem natural to infer that he arranged the incident in order to exhibit contempt for Greek plays and, by extension, for Greek culture generally. That would be a rash conclusion. If Marius' conspicuous entrance and departure expressed disdain, they would surely reflect disdain for the populace who attended—not a polite or politic act. A more plausible motive suggests itself. Marius financed and produced the show for the edification of the public, attended its opening, and then withdrew. Like L. Anicius in 167, the Roman *imperator* demonstrated that his nation controlled the cultural products of Greece and could employ them for the advantage of its own citizens.

The response of Roman *nobiles* to Hellenism exhibits a surprising consistency through the third and second centuries. The supposed ambiguities and inconsistencies turn out upon scrutiny to form a discernible pattern. One need not resort to hypotheses about political divisions or a national schizophrenia. The leadership of Rome found Greek culture both welcome and serviceable.

The attraction of Hellas lay deep and started early. Romans blended Greek cults, deities, and religious practices with indigenous beliefs from the beginning decades of the Republic and continued that adaptation

233. Plut. *Mar.* 2.2: μήτε γλώττῃ πρὸς μηδὲν Ἑλληνίδι χρῆσθαι τῶν σπουδῆς ἐχομένων.

234. Plut. *Mar.* 2.2. The best discussion of Marius' education and exposure to Hellenism is Carney, *Biography of Marius²*, 9–14; see also G. M. Paul, *A Historical Commentary on Sallust's "Bellum Jugurthinum"* (Trowbridge, Eng., 1984), 168, 212.

235. Plut. *Mar.* 2.2: θέας Ἑλληνικὰς παρέχων, εἰς τὸ θέατρον ἐλθὼν καὶ μόνον καθίσας εὐθὺς ἀπαλλαγῆναι.

through the third and second centuries. In the latter period knowledge of Greek noticeably expanded among the upper classes, as did active engagement in Hellenic institutions abroad even by those below the top social rungs. The fact that some sought to establish Greek origins for the Latin language itself makes clear the overwhelmingly positive image of Hellenism in the Roman perception.

The attitude, however, was not simply one of respectful awe. Romans took care from the outset to project the primacy of their own interests and the subordination of Hellenism to national goals. That tendency is illustrated by insistence upon Latin in official intercourse and in the appearance of foreign legations before the Roman senate. And it is reemphasized by senatorial decrees, epistles by magistrates, and interstate treaties that exhibited Roman familiarity with Hellenic conventions and magnanimity toward Hellas—pointed reminders of Rome's control and ascendancy.

Numerous Romans of stature and influence became open devotees of Hellenism. Close examination of the more conspicuous examples from Marcellus' distribution of art objects to Scipio Aemilianus' relations with Polybius and Panaetius reveals a clear and repeated pattern. There was no "philhellenic party" or "philhellenic movement" in Rome, for there was no need for one. A widespread consensus held that command of Greek learning was not only respectable but fundamental in projecting Rome's own cultural ascendancy. The fact can be illustrated by a variety of instances, including Flamininus' diplomatic dexterity, Paullus' appropriation of Hellenic institutions, and Mucianus' linguistic mastery, which underlined the dependency of the Greeks. For such objectives an authentic involvement with Hellenism was indispensable. The interests of the nation would encourage rather than discourage it.

Episodes of ostensible resistance to Hellenism take on different coloration in light of the general picture. The Bacchanalian affair and the burning of Pythagorean books constituted symbolic acts that proclaimed collective control of religion by the Roman ruling class and the subordination of Hellenic elements to national values. Symbolism played a central part in enunciation of those values. Token expulsion of philosophers and rhetors took place at a time when their disciples in fact became increasingly important and popular in Rome. The expulsion orders did not curb and were not meant to curb those disciples; they were intended to assure the community's role as custodian of Roman traditions.

Negative stereotypes of Greeks carried a similar connotation. To take them as condemnation of Hellas or Hellenism misses the point. They served to shed a brighter light upon those qualities that set Romans apart. The exaggerated posturing of a Cato or a Marius had the same ends in view: the manipulation of Greek *topoi* to accentuate Roman qualities. The stereotypes would be taken seriously only by the literal-minded. Plautine comedies, in more appropriate fashion, treated them with levity and parody. The only ones to encounter harsh criticism were those like Postumius and Albucius who carried Hellenic enthusiasm to excess and diminished the *dignitas* of Rome. The cultural claims of the nation would not countenance that behavior. The attitudes of L. Crassus and M. Antonius in the early first century, at least as conveyed by Cicero, supply a neat coda. In denying what all knew to be true, they gently mocked their own Hellenic pretensions, thereby reinforcing the proper order of values: the priority of the *mos maiorum*. Hellenism held great advantage for the Romans. It served both to enrich their heritage and to highlight the special merits of their nation.

[7]

LUCILIUS AND THE
CONTEMPORARY SCENE

The Roman elite by the later second century had confirmed its cultural credentials. The legend of Trojan origins, now widely circulated and generally acknowledged, set Rome within the antique traditions of the Mediterranean world. The acquisition and encouragement of Hellenic art and artists added distinction to the city and exhibited the discernment of the aristocracy. The ruling classes promoted literature to express national values and employed the theater as a medium to refine the tastes of the populace. The advance of cultural aims had two significant corollaries. It gave testimony to Roman power through the commandeering of Greek art and literature for purposes of the nation, and it provided a medium whereby the elite controlled the shape and evolution of Latin culture.

Those developments, however, also had a negative side. They engendered some unattractive qualities: pomposity and pretentiousness, arrogance and condescension. Examples abound from the moralism of Cato to the expropriations of Mummius. But the patronizing attitudes of a cultivated oligarchy became increasingly anomalous in the age of the Gracchi and Marius, when turbulence invaded the domestic scene and much of the Greek East rose in resistance to Rome. In such circumstances, the posturing of the upper classes appeared less impressive and more unseemly—an incentive to ridicule. It may be no coincidence that this period witnessed the birth of satire.

One will not, of course, claim that the developments examined in this book supplied either a necessary or a sufficient condition for satirical writing. But they revealingly elucidate the circumstances in which that genre could flourish and they provide a setting for its pioneer practitioner.

Lucilius earned high repute in antiquity. His death even occasioned a public funeral, a rare honor indeed for a literary figure.[1] The reputation grew apace in subsequent generations. Later satirists looked back to Lucilius as exemplar of the genre, according him kudos for a fierce and fearless cast of mind. For Horace, he picked up where Old Comedy left off, becoming a scourge to the wicked and immoral who were freely flayed in his verses. Lucilius' poetry tore away the facade behind which the corrupt concealed their shamelessness.[2] Persius perceived him as slicing through the city and cracking his jaw upon victims.[3] As Juvenal put it, Lucilius drove his steeds through the field and raged with righteous ardor, brandishing his sword to intimidate miscreants.[4] The portrait of the savage satirist prevailed among the ancients.

Yet modern scholarship often presents a very different portrait. Lucilius has been reckoned either as adherent of a political faction or as expounder of a particular political and social ideology. In most analyses, the writer was friend and adherent of Scipio Aemilianus, his verses advanced the interests of the Scipionic circle and regularly attacked the foes of his patron.[5] One scholar even maintained that Lucilius' *saeva indignatio* was unleashed only when his political supporters held sway and their enemies were vulnerable.[6] Or else the satirist wrote with a special partisan bias. That interpretation, however, has led to strikingly

---

1. Jerome, *Chron.* Ol.169.3.

2. Horace, *Sat.* 1.4.1–7, 2.1.62–70.

3. Persius, 1.114–115.

4. Juvenal, 1.19–21, 1.165–166. Cf. also Cic. *Ad Fam.* 12.16.3, who cites Lucilius as a standard for *libertas* in lacerating verses.

5. Note the formulation in C. Cichorius, *Untersuchungen zu Lucilius* (Berlin, 1908), 56: "Er ist der Feind von Scipios Feinden gewesen, wie er der Freund von dessen Freunden war." That approach, explicit or implicit, recurs with regularity. See, e.g., F. Marx, *Lucilii carminum reliquiae* (Leipzig, 1904), xxv–xxvi; A. Kappelmacher, *RE*, 13.2 (1927), 1623–1624; N. Terzaghi, *Lucilio* (Turin, 1934), 11–17; Gruen, *Roman Politics*, 22, 40, 54, 114, 117; W. Krenkel, *Lucilius: Satiren* (Leiden, 1970), I, 21–22; E. S. Ramage, D. L. Sigsbee, and S. C. Fredericks, *Roman Satirists and Their Satire* (Park Ridge, N.J., 1974), 33; W. J. Raschke, *JRS*, 69 (1979), 83–87. More qualified views are in M. Coffey, *Roman Satire* (London, 1976), 38, and N. Rudd, *Themes in Roman Satire* (London, 1986), 44–51, who, however, accord significance to Lucilius' praise of Scipio and vilification of his enemies. Most recently, Raschke, *Hermes*, 115 (1987), 299–318, questions the idea of patronage but reiterates belief in Lucilius' Scipionic partisanship.

6. L. A. Robinson, *CJ*, 49 (1953), 31–35.

dissonant conclusions. Some see Lucilius as champion of popular causes and sympathizer with the Gracchan movement. Others regard him as a "conservative" and defender of the *mos maiorum*.[7]

A different approach may bring rewards.[8] The fragmentary character of what survives frustrates investigation and imperils any confident conclusions.[9] But enough remains to elevate the satirist beyond the realm of political infighting or special ideological pleading.

Lucilius stood apart. He turned a sharp eye on several of the developments traced in earlier chapters. That is, he had particular sensitivity to the interaction of social, cultural, and intellectual currents. He was attuned to the rhetoric of the upper classes and pierced through its facade. He had an acute feel for the elite's grappling with Hellenism—and the excesses that confrontation could engender. And he recognized the tortuous reappraisals of attitude that had been forced upon the Romans by the upheavals of the Gracchan era. Lucilius' evaluation of some of these larger issues offers the perception of an especially incisive contemporary thinker and provides an invaluable resource for social and cultural history.

The biography of Lucilius remains elusive. Few facts can be established with certainty regarding his lifespan, family, social status, and economic circumstances. But the available material justifies exploration and legitimates conjecture. Such matters have direct bearing on Lucilius' relationship to and attitude toward the Roman public scene.

Unresolved dispute marks discussion of Lucilian chronology. No fuel need be added to that fire here. Literary historians in antiquity located Lucilius as a contemporary of the tragic poet Accius. He is set in

7. For divergent views, see W. Krenkel, *Maia*, 20 (1968), 261–270; Raschke, *Hermes*, 115 (1987), 304–318. The article in *Maia* represents a discussion by three authors; subsequent citations will be to the author whose views are discussed.

8. B. Zucchelli's acute and intelligent discussion, *L'indipendenza di Lucilio* (Istituto di lingua e letteratura latina, Università di Parma, 1977), 81–141, points out the flaws in the *communis opinio* but offers little as a positive reevaluation. Gold, *Literary Patronage in Greece and Rome*, 51, rightly recognizes Lucilius' independence, although her very brief treatment allows no space for argument or demonstration.

9. It is important also to be alert to the fact that attitudes and opinions voiced in the fragments need not be Lucilius' own. Assertions may belong to characters or interlocutors in the satires and may even, so far as we know, be refuted by passages no longer extant. That caveat is assumed in all that follows. The expression of views in the fragments shows only that Lucilius had a purpose in presenting them—not that he held them. The distinction matters less in the case of negative characterizations of individuals. Whether or not Lucilius placed them in the mouths of interlocutors, he chose to include them, and thus to leave a desired impression.

that company by Aulus Gellius and by Velleius Paterculus, drawing directly or indirectly on the researches of Nepos and Varro.[10] Accius, as is known, was born in 170, his *floruit* placed by Jerome in 139, and he lived long enough to be heard in person by Cicero, hence to about 85.[11] Those dates provide an approximate chronological setting. And identifiable events to which Lucilius alludes fall almost entirely within the last third of the second century.

It may be prudent to seek no greater precision. Jerome provides ostensible exactitude—only to create insuperable difficulty. His chronicle gives a birthdate for the poet in 148 and his death in 102, duly specifying a lifespan of forty-six years.[12] The evidence has internal consistency but external implausibility. Nothing stands against the date of death.[13] Problems arise at the other end of the spectrum. Velleius records Lucilius' service as eques in Scipio Aemilianus' Numantine campaign of 134—a most unlikely place for a fourteen-year-old.[14] Horace asserts that the poems provide a vivid tableau of the entire life of the *senex*. Although the term is flexible, *senectus* is hardly appropriate for a man who died at forty-six.[15] Nor is it easy to believe that the satirist who enjoyed a close and even playful relationship with Scipio Aemilianus was forty years his junior.[16]

Alternative solutions have been proposed, none of them fully satisfactory. Jerome may have confused the consuls of 148 with those of 180: both years saw a Postumius Albinus and a Calpurnius Piso in office, and the earlier date would accord better with the facts of Lucilius' life.[17]

---

10. Gellius, 17.21.49: *et Pacuvio iam sene Accius clariorque tunc in poematis eorum obtrectandis Lucilius fuit*; Vell. Pat. 2.9.3–4.

11. Birthdate: Jerome, *Chron.* Ol.160.2; acquaintance with Cicero: Cic. *Brutus*, 107; cf. Val. Max. 3.7.11.

12. Jerome, *Chron.* Ol. 158.2, 169.4: *in anno aetatis* XLVI.

13. Cicero's references to Lucilius in the *De oratore*, with dramatic date of 91, imply that he is already deceased; 1.72, 2.25, 3.171.

14. Vell. Pat. 2.9.4: *sub P. Africano Numantino bello eques militaverat.*

15. Horace, *Sat.* 2.1.30–34: *ut omnis votiva pateat veluti descripta tabella vita senis.* On the meaning of *senex*, see the conflicting assessments of Krenkel, *ANRW*, I.2 (1972), 1250–1257; and J. Christes, *ANRW*, I.2 (1972), 1192–1195.

16. Schol. ad Horace, *Sat.* 2.1.71.

17. The suggestion derives from M. Haupt, in L. Müller, *NJbb*, 107 (1873), 72, and has been adopted by many; e.g. Marx, *Lucil. carm. rel.*, xxiii; B. Floch, *WS*, 38 (1916), 158–165; Kappelmacher, *RE*, 13.2 (1927), 1617–1618; Terzaghi, *Lucilio*, 79–85; I. Mariotti, *Maia*, 20 (1968), 254–256; Krenkel, *ANRW*, I.2 (1972), 1240–1259; F. Charpin, *Lucilius: Satires* (Paris, 1978–79), I, 7–8. G. d'Anna, *RendIstLomb*, 89–90 (1956), 334–342, attempts to explain Jerome's error by conjecturing that he used Nepos as a source and further conjecturing that he misinterpreted that source.

That answer is attractive but contains its own difficulties. The conjecture posits both confusion and calculation on Jerome's part: he found the consuls of 180 in his source, took them to be the consuls of 148, and then reckoned Lucilius' years from date of death as forty-six. That reconstruction ill suits Jerome's usual passive methodology.[18] A middle ground has also found favor: that Jerome erred in copying the numeral from his source and that his XLVI be emended to LXVI yielding a birthdate of 168.[19] The conjecture is unverifiable and probably unhelpful. It invites a game of emendation which does little to bolster confidence in the conclusions. Recent work has not advanced matters toward a consensus.[20]

The quest has generated needless debate. Caution precludes adoption of a particular date for the satirist's birth, but the main issues are unaffected. Lucilius' mature years encompassed the final third—and

18. See R. Helm, *Philol.*, Suppl. 21 (1929), II, 24–27; Christes, *Der frühe Lucilius* (Heidelberg, 1971), 12–13. Other arguments brought against the date of 180 by Cichorius, *Unt. zu Luc.*, 7–14, are weak and unconvincing. The idea that Lucilius would be too old to serve in Numantia at the age of forty-seven puts too strict an interpretation upon Velleius' *militaverat*. When Ennius accompanied Fulvius Nobilior on his Aetolian campaign at the age of fifty, Cicero could also describe his action as *militaverat*; *Brutus*, 79. So, rightly, Mariotti, *Maia*, 20 (1968), 254–256. Lucilius went to Spain amidst Scipio's entourage of *amici*; cf. Appian, *Iber.* 84. Cichorius points further to the incongruity of erotic verses penned by a poet in his sixties, an argument adapted by Rudd, *Themes in Roman Satire*, 45–46, who considers such verses embarrassing as revelations by sexagenarians. That argument will not persuade many.

19. So H. A. J. Munro, *JPhilol*, 8 (1879), 201–225, and, independently, Cichorius, *Unt. zu Luc.*, 13–14; followed, e.g., by Helm, *Philol.*, Suppl. 21 (1929), II, 27; Coffey, *Roman Satire*, 35.

20. Krenkel, *ANRW*, I.2 (1972), 1240–1259, offers a number of arguments, old and new, for the date of 180, but none of them definitive or compelling. Macrobius' reference to Lucilius as contemporary of C. Titius who spoke for the *lex Fannia* of 161 (*Sat.* 3.16.13–14) is inconclusive: Titius could have delivered his speech at a much later date when the law was under attack; cf. Cichorius, *Unt. zu Luc.*, 264–267. Nor should Vell.Pat. 2.9.4 be taken to point a contrast between the *iuvenes* Jugurtha and Marius at the time of the Numantine War, on the one hand, and the older Lucilius, on the other. The passage, in fact, alludes only to the skills learned by the young Marius and Jugurtha in the same camp, which they later employed against each other in opposite camps. No contrast with Lucilius is intended; so rightly Christes, *ANRW*, I.2 (1972), 1192. Christes himself offers some acute remarks in defense of Jerome's text and the birthdate of 148, but fails to get around Horace's testimony on Lucilius as *senex*; *Der frühe Lucilius*, 12–17. F. Della Corte, *Maia*, 20 (1968), 256–258, by contrast, presses the term too hard and opts for a date of 198! Christes offers a recent summary of arguments, with bibliography, in J. Adamietz, ed., *Die römische Satire* (Darmstadt, 1986), 61–67; he now prefers a compromise date of 158—for which there is no evidence.

perhaps somewhat more—of the second century. The satires addressed events and personalities prominent in that period and gained celebrity for their author.[21]

Lucilius' family itself held some prominence in Rome: though not in the front rank, it had sufficient means and connections to give access to public careers. The poet himself did not choose that path, but other members of the clan did reach magisterial office and attain senatorial status.

Three branches of the Lucilian gens appear in the Republic: the Hirri, the Balbi, and the Rufi. Representatives of the latter two occur in the lifetime of the satirist, but there is no hint of an association in the evidence.[22] The Lucilii Hirri, however, provide a more promising avenue of investigation. The house of the poet affiliated itself with a family of high political importance in the next generation. Cn. Pompeius Strabo, the powerful and controversial consul of 89, married Lucilia, who subsequently became mother of Pompeius Magnus. The satirist, as it appears, was uncle of Lucilia and thus great-uncle of Pompey the Great.[23] Lucilia came of senatorial stock, and her father was evidently a brother of the poet, thus attesting to the senatorial status of the clan.[24] The Lucilii Hirri could boast that status. Epigraphical evi-

---

21. So Vell. Pat. 2.9.4: *celebre et Lucilii nomen fuit, qui sub P. Africano Numantino bello eques militaverat.* The passage is often taken as meaning that Lucilius did not begin to write until after the Numantine War. In fact, it indicates only that he acquired fame in that period. Cf. Floch, *WS*, 38 (1916), 160–161.

22. Nothing is known of the *monetalis* Lucilius Rufus, placed in 101 by M. Crawford, *Roman Republican Coinage*, I, 327, no. 324. A Lucilius Balbus was senator in 162, as was his son Q. Lucilius Balbus in 76; Cic., *De Nat. Deor.* 2.11, 2.14–15; cf. *De Orat.* 3.78. The cognomen of M'. Lucilius M. f. Pom., who appears on the *s.c. de agro Pergameno*, probably of 101, is unknown; Sherk, *Roman Documents*, 63–73, no. 12. On the date, see H. B. Mattingly, *AJP*, 93 (1972), 412–423. Cichorius, *Unt. zu Luc.*, 2–6, has no warrant for making him the poet's brother. The idea is rightly rejected by Kappelmacher, *WS*, 31 (1909), 82–89, although still followed by some, e.g., Coffey, *Roman Satire*, 35–36. A reference to Lucilius' brother may be in Lucilius, 427,M = 455,W = 431,K.

23. The evidence is confused and by no means univocal on this point. Vell. Pat. 2.29.2 provides the information that Pompey's mother was a Lucilia. The scholia on Horace variously give Lucilius as grandfather, uncle, or great-uncle of Pompey; Schol. ad Horace, *Sat.* 2.1.29: *Magni Pompei avus*; Schol. ad Horace, *Sat.* 2.1.75: *avunculus* or *maior avunculus*; Porphyrio, ad Horace, *Sat.* 2.1.75: *avunculum maiorem Pompei.* Cf. Della Corte, *Maia*, 20 (1968), 257–258.

24. Vell.Pat. 2.29.2: *Fuit hic* [Pompeius Magnus] *genitus matre Lucilia stirpis senatoriae.* Porphyrio, ad Horace, *Sat.* 2.1.75, asserts that Pompey's grandmother was a sister of Lucilius, thus explaining the relationship between the poet and the general: *etenim avia Pompei Lucilii soror fuerat.* A. B. West, *AJP*, 49 (1928), 240–252, combines the testimony,

dence reveals a Hirrus, legate and propraetor of M. Antonius in his eastern campaign of 102/1.[25] A descendant of that individual, C. Lucilius Hirrus, tribune in 53, came to notice as a staunch and consistent supporter of Pompey the Great.[26] The tribune could claim substantial wealth, and great estates in Bruttium were included in his property.[27] The estates may indeed have been inherited from the poet himself.[28] The data do not allow for definitive reconstruction or confidence on matters of detail, but certain conclusions seem safe enough. The poet belonged to a family that had acquired senatorial rank, secured links with major political figures, and possessed the means to play a role on the public scene.

C. Lucilius stemmed from the Latin town of Suessa Aurunca, near the border of Latium and Campania.[29] That place of origin has led some to reckon the satirist as a Latin rather than a *civis Romanus*.[30] The conclusion can be unequivocally rejected. Horace declares himself *infra Lucili censum*, a remark hardly possible if Lucilius was not even on the citizen registry.[31] The poet's clan, as we have seen, enjoyed senatorial status, and he was himself described in one source as *nobilis*—an inaccurate designation but suggestive of his distinction.[32] A birthplace in Latium by no means determined citizenship. Romans dwelled in Latium, and many influential Latin families had obtained the franchise. The man whom Cicero characterized as *perurbanus* was surely no stranger to the city.[33]

having the poet's sister marry Pompey's grandfather and another Lucilia marry his father. So also Krenkel, *Lucilius*, 18–19; Christes, *ANRW*, I.2 (1972), 1196; Charpin, *Lucilius*, 9; Raschke, *Hermes*, 115 (1987), 300. It is surely easier to believe that the scholiast got the generation wrong and posited a sister of Lucilius to account for his status as *avunculus maior*.

25. *ILLRP*, 342. West, *AJP*, 49 (1928), 242–246, proposes another praetorian Hirrus, father of the legate, on the basis of Varro, *De Re Rust.* 2.5.5. But that hopelessly corrupt passage does not bear much weight.

26. Cic. *Ad Fam.* 8.4.3; *Ad Q. Frat.* 3.6.4; *Ad Att.* 8.11A; Caes. *BC*, 1.15, 3.82.4–5; Plut. *Pomp.* 54.3.

27. Varro, *De Re Rust.* 2.1.2, 3.17.3; Pliny, *NH*, 9.171.

28. Cf. Cic. *De Orat.* 2.284, and the suggestive observations of Cichorius, *Unt. zu Luc.*, 23–24; idem, *Römische Studien* (Stuttgart, 1922), 67–70. Accepted by L. R. Taylor, *The Voting Districts of the Roman Republic* (Rome, 1960), 227.

29. Juvenal, 1.20 and schol. ad loc.

30. Marx, *Luc. carm. rel.*, I, xviii; E. H. Warmington, *Remains of Early Latin* (Cambridge, Mass., 1938), III, ix. Still accepted by Drury, *Cambridge Hist. of Class. Lit.*, II, 829.

31. Horace, *Sat.* 2.1.74–75.

32. Schol. ad Horace, *Sat.* 2.1.29: *fuit enim valde nobilis Lucilius*; cf. Vell.Pat. 2.29.2.

33. The arguments of Cichorius, *Unt. zu Luc.*, 14–22, some stronger than others, long ago established Lucilius' Roman credentials.

Lucilius had the option, but eschewed the senatorial *cursus*. He remained technically an eques, his standing high within that influential *ordo*. He held equestrian rank on service in the Spanish campaign of Scipio Aemilianus.[34] But he scorned the profession of a *publicanus*, let alone a *scripturarius*. He would not exchange landed property for the occupation of collecting state revenues.[35] Lucilius evidently belonged to the class of absentee landlords, possessing extensive holdings and substantial wealth.[36] An anecdote preserved by Cicero reveals that the satirist even came under criticism by senators who charged that he allowed his flocks to graze on *ager publicus*.[37] Extant verses contain frequent references to pasture animals, race horses, beasts of burden, overseers, laborers, and slaves on agricultural estates.[38] Location of the lands goes unspecified. Hints in the poems might suggest Apulia, Bruttium, the area of Naples, Sicily, and Sardinia, a far-flung proprietorship, but we can hardly presume that all allude to the poet's possessions. It is preferable to avoid guesswork on particulars.[39] Lucilius, by any reckoning, was a man of considerable means. He used as private residence in the city a home once built to order for the royal hostage Antiochus IV of Syria.[40] The satirist plainly had a place in Rome's upper echelons. His

34. Vell. Pat. 2.9.4: *Numantino bello eques militaverat.*

35. Lucilius, 671–672,M = 650–651,W = 656–657,K: *publicanus vero ut Asiae fiam, ut scripturarius pro Lucilio, id ego nolo, et uno hoc non muto omnia.* Cf. 675,M = 647,W = 653,K: *mihi quidem non persuadetur publicis mutem meos*—if one adopts the reading *publicis* rather than *pulices*; see Cichorius, *Unt. zu Luc.*, 75. For a different view, see K. F. Smith, *AJP*, 22 (1901), 44–50. Christes gives a good discussion in *Der frühe Lucilius*, 34–35. Note also 667,M = 655,W = 650,K: *denique adeo male me accipiunt decimae et proveniunt male,* evidently a reference to tithes and tithe collections—and Lucilius' aversion to them. On Lucilius as eques, see the succinct discussion of C. Nicolet, *L'ordre équestre a l'époque républicaine (312–43 av. J.C.)* (Paris, 1974), II, 926–929.

36. Cf. Schol. ad Horace, *Sat.* 2.1.75: *et nobilis et dives fuit.*

37. Cic. *De Orat.* 2.284. Lucilius is not there explicitly identified as the poet, but the context of the dialogue makes that identification almost inevitable; cf. Cic. *De Orat.* 2.253; Mariotti, *Maia*, 20 (1968), 258–261.

38. Lucilius, 105–106,M = 133–134,W = 113–114,K; 313–316,M = 343–346,W = 318–321,K; 506–513,M = 511–517,W = 511–518,K; 579–581,M = 623–625,W = 581–583,K; 1041–1044,M = 1041–1044,W = 985–988,K; 1109,M = 154,W = 1120,K; 1246,M = 1253,W = 1263,K.

39. The speculation stems from Cichorius' bold conjectures, *Unt. zu Luc.*, 22–29, based on Cic. *De Fin.* 1.7; Lucilius, 254–256,M = 287–289,W =253–255,K; 525–526,M = 547–548,W = 526–527,K; 594,M = 635,W = 596,K; 1109,M = 154,W = 1120,K; 1124,M = 142,W = 1138,K. Often repeated by subsequent scholars; e.g., Krenkel, *Lucilius*, 21; Christes, *ANRW*, I.2 (1972), 1198; Coffey, *Roman Satire*, 36; Raschke, *Hermes*, 115 (1987), 300–301. But none of the passages makes direct reference to the poet's proprietorship.

40. Asconius, 13, Clark.

abstention from a senatorial career doubtless represents deliberate decision. Lucilius could enjoy the combination of internal connections and external detachment—a useful mix for satire.

Lucilius had close personal connection with the leading political and military figure of mid–second century Rome: P. Cornelius Scipio Aemilianus. To what extent that association affected his politics or his art remains to be determined. The conventional view that Lucilius held a brief for the Scipionic faction needs reconsideration.

The origins of the relationship escape research.[41] Lucilius' presence in the Numantine campaign of 134 and 133 under Scipio's command is the first sign of collaboration. The poet no doubt counted in the cohort of *amici* who voluntarily followed Scipio to Spain.[42] That experience does not itself signal special distinction, but relations evidently ripened into a friendship of genuine warmth. Horace noted that the satirist enjoyed the company of Aemilianus and his bosom companion C. Laelius with some regularity, sharing their meals and even engaging in frolicsome play.[43] The scholiast on that passage adds a delectable detail: Laelius once came upon Lucilius chasing Scipio around the dinner table brandishing a rolled-up napkin.[44]

The easy informality is clear. Poet and statesman could let their hair down in each other's company. The evidence betokens a relationship in which difference of status played little role. It possesses the flavor more of equality than of patronage and clientage. What reason is there to believe that the literature of the satirist served the interests of the politician?

The poems themselves would not appear to support that proposition. It has sometimes been believed that Lucilius dedicated one book of satires to Scipio Aemilianus, but the belief rests on emendation and reconstruction, not on solid textual ground. Some difficult lines in book 27 appear to offer up the poet's verses to the Roman people: *rem populi salute et fictis*

---

41. Cichorius, *Unt. zu Luc.*, 54–56, speculates that Scipio's property in the general neighborhood of the poet's home town connected the two families.

42. Vell. Pat. 2.9.4; cf. Appian, *Iber.* 84: φίλων ἴλην.

43. Horace, *Sat.* 2.1.71–74: *nugari cum illo et discincti ludere, donec decoqueretur holus, soliti.*

44. Schol. ad Horace, *Sat.* 2.1.7: *Scipio Africanus fertur intra domum tam civilis fuisse et carus Lucilio, ut quodam tempore Laelius circa lectos triclinii fugienti supervenerit, cum eum Lucilius obtorta mappa quasi feriturus sequeretur.* Cf. Cic. *De Orat.* 2.22 on the boyish behavior of Scipio and Laelius when out in the countryside.

versibus Lucilius / quibus potest, inpertit. A suggested change to *te Popli* could make the dedicant P. Scipio. The suggestion, however, lacks any basis.[45] Nor is there greater warrant for imagining that Lucilius presented his work nervously and respectfully to Scipio for approval.[46] The poet, in fact, asserted explicitly that he wrote for others than the very learned and would not submit his works to the judgment of such men as Scipio and Rutilius Rufus.[47] The sentiments may be gently ironic, a subtle mockery surely not to be taken literally.[48] Whether ironic or literal, however, the verses bely any notion that Lucilius sought Scipionic endorsement for his poems.

The poet served in the entourage of Scipio at Numantia, and the satires contain a number of allusions to Spain and the Spanish campaigns. It does not follow, however, that Lucilius aimed to celebrate the military exploits of his commander. Certain fragments may evoke the circumstances in which Aemilianus found himself when taking charge of undisciplined and self-indulgent troops in Spain. The commander, as reported by historical sources, took them vigorously in hand, restored order and military readiness, and cracked down hard on laxity in the camp.[49] Possible glances at those circumstances have been detected in Lucilius' book 11, where fragments mention lingering in the bath or washbasins, superfluous medical and dental instruments, and expulsion of malodorous individuals from the camp.[50] But the conjectures are

45. Lucilius, 688–689,M = 791–792,W = 735–736,K. The conjecture is Marx's, *Luc. carm. rel.*, II, 250–251. Thoroughly refuted by Cichorius, *Unt. zu Luc.*, 143–144; but still presented as a possibility by Krenkel, *Lucilius*, 417. See further Charpin, *Lucilius*, II, 301–302.

46. Lucilius, 1009–1011,M = 1062, 1065, 1092,W = 1073, 1088, 1108,K. The suggestion comes from Marx, *Luc. carm. rel.*, II, 325–326. Similarly, Kappelmacher, *RE*, 13.2 (1927), 1632; Terzaghi, *Lucilio*, 215–218. Cichorius, *Unt. zu Luc.*, 181–192, rejects the idea, but his own conjecture, that Lucilius turned to C. Sempronius Tuditanus as patron after Scipio's death, has no foundation. Christes, *Der frühe Lucilius*, 168–173, revives the notion of Scipio as patron, reckoning this as evidence that Lucilius was much younger than his friend. Cf. Zucchelli, *L'indipendenza di Lucilio*, 123. More probably, the lines reflect a literary rivalry; cf. J. G. Griffith, *Hermes*, 98 (1970), 71.

47. Cic. *De Fin.* 1.7: *Scipio vero et Rutilius multo etiam magis; quorum ille iudicium reformidans Tarentinis ait se et Consentinis et Siculis scribere.*

48. Cf. Christes, *Der frühe Lucilius*, 90–93.

49. Appian, *Iber.* 85; Livy, *Per.* 57; Plut. *Apophth. Scip. Min.* 16. Other evidence collected in Astin, *Scipio Aemilianus*, 136, 259–263.

50. Lucilius, 398–404,M = 429–435,W = 401–407,K. So interpreted by most commentators; e.g., Marx, *Luc. carm. rel.*, II, 150–152; Cichorius, *Unt. zu Luc.*, 303–305; Terzaghi, *Lucilio*, 408–409; Krenkel, *Lucilius*, I, 256; Charpin, *Lucilius*, II, 206–209; Raschke, *Hermes*, 115 (1987), 307.

hazardous and unpersuasive. A number of reasons undermine confidence: the name Scipio does not appear in those fragments; it is by no means clear that the fragments belong together; and even if they do refer to conditions in the Numantine camp, Lucilius may be aiming his barbs at the foibles of the soldiery rather than pointing to the virtues of their commander.[51] His métier was not that of celebratory poet. The genre he chose would be ill suited for that role. Lucilius' verses may, in fact, include an explicit disclaimer of intent or ability along those lines. Fragments of book 25 contain an exhortation that the writer trumpet the campaign of Popilius and hymn the deeds of Scipio, to win praise and gain.[52] The verses evoke a literary convention: a summons to compose epic poetry followed by a *recusatio*. A parallel text occurs in Horace, with direct reference to Lucilius. The satirist is urged to intone the accomplishments of Augustus, for the task will bring ample reward, but Horace declines on grounds of incapacity to sing of battlefield triumphs and defeats.[53] Lucilius may well have offered his own *recusatio*, disparaging his powers to reach an epic plane.[54] The self-mockery is suggestive and revealing. Lucilius did not compose poetry to extol the achievements of a military hero.

A bond between the two men does find voice in the poems. Lucilius designates Aemilianus as *Cornelius Publius noster* and even as *Scipiadas magnus*.[55] He quotes Scipio directly for a bon mot.[56] And he alludes with poignancy, so it seems, to Scipio's death.[57]

---

51. Note, for example, that criticism of undue indulgence in the bath seems hardly consistent with expulsion of the unwashed and foul-smelling from the camp. Nor is it at all clear that Scipio is meant when Lucilius refers to *praetor noster*, not the most obvious designation for the consul and proconsul. But see Festus, 267, L.

52. Lucilius, 620,M = 713,W = 690,K: *hunc laborem sumas, laudem qui tibi ac fructum ferat*; 621,M = 714,W = 689,K: *percrepa pugnam Popili, facta Corneli cane*.

53. Horace, *Sat.* 2.1.10–15. Reference to Lucilius comes in the immediately following lines.

54. Lucilius, 622,M = 691,W = 679,K: *ego si, qui sum et quo folliculo nunc sum idutus, non queo.* Cf. Marx, *Luc. carm. rel.*, II, 230; Terzaghi, *Lucilio*, 118–123; Christes, *Der frühe Lucilius*, 72–77; Charpin, *Lucilius*, II, 278; Raschke, *Hermes*, 115 (1987), 308–310. Cichorius, *Unt. zu Luc.*, 109–127, less plausibly, has Lucilius himself address the exhortation to a young historian. That Lucilius did engage a historian in dialogue is suggested by 617,M = 689,W = 674,K; cf. 612,M =700,W = 672,K. But this need bear no relation to the passages under discussion. Christes, *Der frühe Lucilius*, 26–27, 133–134, even doubts that a historian is meant, and identifies the interlocutor as Accius. The doubts are echoed by Charpin, *Lucilius*, II, 276–277.

55. Lucilius, 1138,M = 254,W = 1155,K; 394,M = 424,W = 412,K. Lucilius' lines on military exploits, 1079–1087,M = 1008–1015,W = 1059–1067,K, have been taken as

None of this, however, implies a deferential relationship. The easy familiarity that Horace attests between poet and statesman can be found in the satires as well. Lucilius (or a Lucilian character) even twitted Scipio for his affected Latin pronunciation, chiding him for know-it-all airs.[58] That is very far from deference. On another occasion the poet, while referring to *Cornelius Publius noster Scipiadas*, also makes mention of a male lover and sodomite. The passage is corrupt and unintelligible, but the juxtaposition is intriguing.[59] Lucilius also remarks upon those "who disdained you as arrogant." That is an enticing but frustrating line. One cannot be sure that Scipio is the referent. Nor is it clear whether Lucilius' target is the arrogant individual or his disdainful critics.[60] If Scipio is the man, however, Lucilius evidently did not shrink from reminding readers of his reputation for *superbia*.

The satirist and the statesman enjoyed a relationship of mutual respect. Lucilius felt free to engage in impudent banter, irreverent criticism, and even a boyish romp. Differences in social status or political authority played no apparent role in the affiliation. The poet spoke his mind, unhampered by a patron's plan.

At a time when Rome's political leadership prided itself upon cultivated tastes in the realms of art and literature and utilized them to express national qualities, aristocrats who fell short of the ideals became more embarrassing—and more vulnerable. For them the shafts of the satirist were in readiness. Lucilius delivered himself of sharp thrusts

---

reference to Scipio; so, most recently, Christes, in *Die römische Satire*, 103. The conclusion is unwarranted.

56. Lucilius, 1280,M = 1135,W = 1297,K.

57. Lucilius, 1093,M = 1005,W = 1028,K: *insperato abiit; quem una angina sustulit hora.* That this is a reference to Scipio's death was plausibly argued by Cichorius, *Unt. zu Luc.*, 212–213; so also Terzaghi, *Lucilio*, 252–253; Raschke, *JRS*, 69 (1979), 88; Christes, in *Die römische Satire*, 101; cf. Schol. Bob. 118, Stangl.

58. Lucilius, 963–964,M = 983–984,W = 971–972,K: *quo facetior videare et scire plus quam ceteri, 'pertisum' hominem, non 'pertaesum' dicere humanum genus*; cf. W. Richter, *Gymnasium*, 69 (1962), 304–305.

59. Lucilius, 1138–1142,M = 254–258,W = 1155–1159,K: *Cornelius Publius noster / Scipiadas dicto tempus quae intorquet in ipsum / oti et deliciis luci effictae atque cinaedo, et / sectatori adeo ipse suo, quo rectius dicas* [Krenkel's text]. On this fragment, see the discussion of Rudd, *Phoenix*, 15 (1961), 90–96.

60. Lucilius, 1098,M = 1006,W = 1109,K: *quotque adeo fuerint, qui te temsere superbum.* Cichorius, *Unt. zu Luc.*, 213, takes for granted that Scipio is meant and, on the basis of the *adeo*, argues that Lucilius defends his friend's reputation against hostile critics. So also Zucchelli, *L'indipendenza di Lucilio*, 122. The interpretation is by no means obvious.

against prominent public figures in middle and later second-century Rome.

L. Cornelius Lentulus Lupus, consul in 156, stands out in the roster of victims. That formidable aristocrat had once been convicted of extortion, circa 154, but shook off the setback and went on to the highest distinctions in the state, the censorship in 147 and appointment as *princeps senatus* in 131.[61] Lucilius, however, held him in the fiercest contempt.

Horace made reference to the notorious defamatory verses that Lucilius leveled at Lupus.[62] And Persius named Lupus as one of those on whom the satirist broke his jawbone.[63] Fragments of the satires, though not always easy to interpret, bear more direct witness. Lucilius represents Lentulus as ruthless and unforgiving in his judicial decisions, a hanging judge.[64] He catalogs him, and others, with the perjured and the polluted.[65] And indeed a separate satire or perhaps the whole of book 1 of the *Satires* was devoted to a council of the gods deliberating on degeneracy in Rome and contemplating judgment on the character and fate of L. Lentulus Lupus.[66] Extant fragments include references to foolish frolics among common dancers, a repulsive face suggesting venom, disease, and death, the characteristics of a vulture, and a hideous demise whether through gluttony or gangrene.[67]

---

61. On the prosecution, see Val. Max. 6.9.10; cf. Festus, 360,L; Gruen, *Roman Politics*, 11. For his naming as *princeps senatus*, see Schol. ad Horace, *Sat.* 2.1.67; Broughton, *Magistrates of the Roman Republic*, I, 500–501.

62. Horace, *Sat.* 2.1.67.

63. Persius, 1.114.

64. Lucilius, 784–790,M = 805–811,W = 789–795,K.

65. Lucilius, 1312–1313,M = 1138–1141,W = 1329–1330,K.

66. Lactantius, *Div. Inst.* 4.3.12: *concilium deorum*; Servius, *Ad Aen.* 10.104: *et agere primo de interitu Lupi cuiusdam ducis in re publica, postea sententias dicere.* As to whether this made up a single satire or a whole book, see J. Michelfeit, *Hermes*, 93 (1965), 123–125.

67. Dancing: Lucilius, 32,M = 33,W = 30,K; face: 44,M = 37,W = 38,K; vulture: 46,M = 38,W = 39,K; gluttony: 54,M = 46,W = 55,K; gangrene: 53,M = 52,W = 7,K. We have little context for any of these lines, and no certainty that all refer to Lupus, but the collectivity is telling. For various interpretations, see Marx, *Luc. carm. rel.*, II, 18, 22, 23, 27–28; Terzaghi, *Lucilio*, 268, 277–279; Krenkel, *Lucilius*, I, 107, 115, 121, 125. The date of the *concilium deorum* is often debated but not at issue here. It must have been composed after Lupus' death, but the nearly universal assumption that it appeared shortly after the death is not compelling. Cichorius, *Unt. zu Luc.*, 77–83, put it in 123 on highly speculative grounds. The death of Lupus probably came two or three years earlier; Marx, *Luc. carm. rel.*, I, xxxv–xl; W. A. Baehrens, *Hermes*, 54 (1919), 80–86; Michelfeit, *Hermes*, 93 (1965), 125–128; Raschke, *JRS*, 69 (1979), 79. The satire may have come any time after ca. 126.

The antipathy for Lentulus is clear enough. Does it have a political basis? So runs the standard reasoning: Scipio Aemilianus was rival of Lentulus; hence, Lucilius' attacks represented the Scipionic viewpoint.[68] The thesis is flimsy and circular. It rests almost exclusively on the fragments of Lucilius himself, buttressed by no direct testimony whatever on the attitudes of Scipio. An indirect argument has seen service. Lentulus attained the honorific post of *princeps senatus*, evidently named to that distinction by the censors of 131.[69] In that year, only one other patrician former censor who could have been considered for that honor was alive: P. Scipio Aemilianus. So perhaps Scipio took affront at the censors' appointment of Lentulus and passed his indignation on to Lucilius.[70] The idea lacks substance or evidence. Lentulus held seniority over Scipio both in his consular and in his censorial year. That would suffice to justify the nomination. Nor is there anything to suggest that Scipio took it amiss.[71] Lucilius could well have had his own reasons for finding Lupus distasteful: rapacity, gluttony, judicial severity, or violation of oaths. The fragments alone suggest a number of possibilities.[72] The gap between aristocratic pronouncements and Lupus' life-style was large.

Lucilius took on even bigger game. His satiric darts found their mark in one of Rome's most preeminent families, the house of the Caecilii Metelli. Nor did he shrink from even the mightiest figure in that clan, Q. Metellus Macedonicus, victor in the Fourth Macedonian War, *consularis*, *censorius*, and father of four sons whom he lived to see in high office at Rome. Macedonicus delivered a celebrated speech as censor in 131, urging the necessity of more marriages in order to swell the

---

68. So, e.g., Astin, *Scipio Aemilianus*, 92; Gruen, *Roman Politics*, 64; Charpin, *Lucilius*, I, 86–87.

69. Schol. ad Horace, *Sat.* 2.1.67; Broughton, *Magistrates of the Roman Republic*, I, 500–501.

70. Cichorius, *Unt. zu Luc.*, 58; Robinson, *CJ*, 49 (1953), 32; Gruen, *Roman Politics*, 64; Coffey, *Roman Satire*, 48. Queried but not challenged by Raschke, *JRS*, 69 (1979), 79.

71. Cf. Livy, 27.11.10: *Cornelius morem traditum a patribus sequendum aiebat ut qui primus censor ex iis qui viverent fuisset, cum principem legerent.* To be sure, Ap. Claudius Pulcher was named *princeps senatus* in 136, despite the availability of more senior figures; Broughton, *Magistrates of the Roman Republic*, I, 486. But Claudius was censor in office during that year, and appointment as *princeps senatus* by one's censorial colleague was not unusual; cf. T. Mommsen, *Römische Forschungen* (Berlin, 1864), I, 93–94. That alternative was unavailable in 131, for both censors were plebeian. On all this, see the shrewd and convincing comments of Zucchelli, *L'indipendenza di Lucilio*, 102–103.

72. So, rightly, Zucchelli, *L'indipendenza di Lucilio*, 105–107.

population. In his view, compulsion should be applied to ensure the desired demographic results.[73] A fragment of the oration discloses the cynical reasoning: wives bring only *molestia*, but since men cannot live without them anyway, it is better to consider the enduring benefit of posterity than the temporary pleasures of the moment.[74]

The speech and the reasoning supplied perfect material for satire. Lucilius parodied the concept of mandatory marriages in book 26 of his collection. Macedonicus' speech *de prole augenda* is almost certainly the object of the mockery. Lucilius adapts the censor's language to his own purposes: men themselves, not *natura*, bring on their own *molestia* by entering into marriage and producing children.[75] The precise structure and course of the satire are no longer recoverable.[76] Modern commentators reconstruct a dialogue between a spokesman for Metellus' measure and Lucilius as cynic and sharp critic. The poet, so it is sometimes asserted, attacked not only the concept of compulsion but the very institution of marriage, and his strictures are reckoned as attestation of a deep-felt misogyny.[77] That interpretation misses the point. The wit of Lucilius delivers irony and mockery, a spoof of the Metellan proposal, but not necessarily an ideological position. The extant passages borrow from comedy, play with comic language, and allude to the stereotypical themes of female cupidity, marital infidelity, wifely scheming, and husbandly efforts to maintain solvency. Lucilius even compares the desire for procreation to the acts of a lunatic. Some of this material shows off the satirist at his best. But one can hardly take it as serious social philosophy.[78]

73. Livy, *Per.* 59.

74. Gellius, 1.6.2.

75. Gellius, 1.6.2 [Macedonicus' speech]: *si sine uxore vivere possemus, Quirites, omnes ea molestia careremus; set quoniam ita natura tradidit*, etc.; Lucilius, 678–679, M = 644–645, W = 634–635, K: *Homines ipsi hanc sibi molestiam ultro atque aerumnam offerunt; / ducunt uxores, producunt quibus haec faciant liberos.* K. Heldmann, *Hermes,* 107 (1979), 339–344, suggests that Lucilius put these lines in the mouth of Jupiter as response to Metellus.

76. It may have been introduced by an encounter between two interlocutors, one of whom had just attended gladiatorial games sponsored by Metellus; Lucilius, 676–677, M = 636–637, W = 631–632, K. See Marx, *Luc. carm. rel.*, II, 246–247; Cichorius, *Unt. zu Luc.*, 137–142; Christes, *Der frühe Lucilius*, 53–54.

77. Cf. Cichorius, *Unt. zu Luc.*, 133–137; M. Galdi, *Athenaeum*, o.s. 8 (1920), 77–91; Terzaghi, *Lucilio*, 146–151; Christes, *Der frühe Lucilius*, 53–60.

78. Note, e.g., the language of Lucilius, 682–683, M = 640–641, W = 639–640, K: *depoclassere aliqua sperans me ac deargentassere, / decalauticare, eburno speculo despeculassere.* Allusion to procreation as symptomatic of madness surely derives from comedy as well; Lucilius, 686, M = 646, W = 643, K: *quapropter deliro et cupidi officium fungor liberum.* The

Exposure of Metellus Macedonicus to ridicule, however, stands out clearly enough. Nor is he the only Metellus derided in the satires. Lucilius scores a hit against a certain Caecilius recently elected as *praetor urbanus*. No urbane praetor he, says Lucilius: take care lest Caecilius become a *praetor rusticus*. The poet mocks his rural accent and peasant demeanor.[79] That remark almost certainly belongs together with lines that speak of a *praetor designatus* with the features of a farm animal.[80] The individual involved can be plausibly identified with C. Metellus Caprarius, son of Macedonicus. His cognomen ("goatman") evokes rusticity and invites derision. Scipio Aemilianus had tossed off a scornful quip at him at Numantia: if Caprarius' mother had had a fifth son, he would have been an ass.[81]

The satirist, it is plain, indulged himself by making sport of the Metelli. Did politics inspire those lampoons? A scholiast on Horace's *Satires* offers an intriguing comment: Lucilius launched attacks on Metellus Macedonicus in order to please Scipio.[82] That is the sole ancient attestation of Scipionic influence in the intent of the poet, and the passage has been reckoned as unassailable.[83] Is it so? Did Lucilius strike a blow at the Metelli in order to earn credit with Scipio?

The scholiast's authority does not easily withstand scrutiny. Inves-

---

passages identifiable as belonging to this satire are 678–686,M = 638–646,W = 633–643,K. Cichorius, *Römische Studien*, 73–75, argues that Cic. *Tusc. Disp.* 2.36 contains another fragment of this satire. Many scholars persist in seeing a sober and serious advocate in these lines. See works cited in previous note, and the commentaries of Marx, *Luc. carm. rel.*, II, 247–249; Krenkel, *Lucilius*, II, 365–369; Charpin, *Lucilius*, II, 286–290. But note that the subject was treated again later—and hardly with sobriety—in one of Varro's Menippean satires, περὶ γεγαμηκότων; see J.-P. Cèbe, *Varron: Satires ménippées* (Rome, 1980), 5, 759–774, fr. 166–168.

79. Lucilius, 1130,M = 232,W = 1146,K: *Cecilius pretor ne rusticus fiat.*

80. Lucilius, 210–211,M = 233–234,W = 212–213,K: *ne designati rostrum praetoris pedesque / spectes.*

81. Cic.*De Orat.* 2.267: *si quintum pareret mater eius, asinum fuisse parituram.* The joke probably alludes both to Caprarius' intellect and to his cognomen. The identification is generally acknowledged; Marx, *Luc. carm. rel.*, II, 86–87; Cichorius, *Unt. zu Luc.*, 277–279; Terzaghi, *Lucilio*, 14–15; Krenkel, *Lucilius*, I, 181; II, 611; Charpin, *Lucilius*, I, 264. Coffey, *Roman Satire*, 222, n. 80, without argument, suggests M. Metellus, the consul of 115. Still one other member of the family may have been lampooned by Lucilius. Note Lucilius, 801,M = 850,W = 754,K: *varicosus Vatax*—perhaps a reference to C. Servilius Vatia, son-in-law of Macedonicus; Cic. *De Domo*, 123; Cichorius, *Unt. zu Luc.*, 154–157; F. Münzer, *NJbb*, 23 (1909), 193–194.

82. Schol. ad Horace, *Sat.* 2.1.72: *Lucilius eum in gratiam Scipionis carpsit.*

83. Cf. Marx, *Luc. carm. rel.*, I, xxxii: "scholiasta certe hoc loco doctissimus"; Raschke, *JRS*, 69 (1979), 83: "We have no reason to question this."

tigation needs to begin with the lines of Horace on which he offered comment. Those lines lend small comfort to the interpretation provided. Horace responds to the warning that indulgence in satire could lead to retaliation. The Augustan writer points to Lucilius, pioneer in the genre, who stripped the covering from those who cloaked internal rot with external glitter: were Laelius and Scipio offended by the wit or did they lament the damage inflicted upon Metellus and Lupus by the satirist's biting verses?[84] The implication seems clear. Scipio did not take offense—though he might have been expected to. That expectation is hardly consonant with the idea that he encouraged or welcomed the poet's assault on his political rivals.[85] The scholiast misconstrued the meaning and muddled the commentary. Among other matters, he confused Aemilianus with Africanus, bringing into his remarks an anecdote belonging to the latter and using it unintelligibly to elucidate Lucilius' purpose.[86]

Even if the poet were inclined to promote Scipionic interests in this regard, he would have found the task no easy one. Relations between Aemilianus and Macedonicus were ambiguous and double-edged. There had been friendship between the two men until politics divided them[87]—just when or why escapes investigation. Political estrangement had occurred by 138 when Metellus came to the defense of L. Cotta, under prosecution by Scipio himself.[88] Conflict persisted or revived after the death of Tiberius Gracchus. Cicero remarks that Gracchus' tribunate and his fate divided Rome into warring factions, with those critical of and hostile to Scipio led first by P. Crassus and Ap. Claudius, later by P. Scaevola and Metellus Macedonicus.[89] But Cicero makes a point of emphasizing that political dissension between Scipio and Metellus did not lead to personal animosity: the public disputes

84. Horace, *Sat.* 2.1.67–68: *ingenio offensi aut laeso doluere Metello famosisque Lupo cooperto versibus?*

85. So, rightly, Terzaghi, *Lucilio*, 3–4. There is no suggestion of irony in these words, as Zucchelli properly points out, *L'indipendenza di Lucilio*, 96–98.

86. Schol. ad Horace, *Sat.* 2.1.72: *Scipio ait: hi sunt, quos Hannibali eripui; patere ergo, inquit, nos liberos esse. Ob quod et alia Lucilius eum in gratiam Scipionis carpsit.* See the persuasive discussion by Zucchelli, *L'indipendenza di Lucilio*, 98–99.

87. Cic. *De Amicit.* 77 [Laelius speaking]: *propter dissensionem autem, quae erat in re publica, alienatus est a collega nostro Metello.*

88. Cic. *Brutus*, 81. Other evidence on the trial, with discussion and bibliography, in Gruen, *Roman Politics*, 36–38.

89. Cic. *De Rep.* 1.31.

were conducted without private rancor.[90] Indeed, after Aemilianus' death in 129, Metellus mourned his passing and instructed his four sons to act as pallbearers at the funeral.[91] Political opposition evidently left the *amicitia* unimpaired.[92]

In short, Lucilius' ridicule of Metellus would seem to have little in common with the attitudes of Scipio. Insofar as it gave personal affront to Metellus, this would hardly gratify the victim's *amicus* Scipio Aemilianus—as Horace's lines implicitly acknowledge.[93] As for political differences, there is nothing to suggest that they centered upon Metellus' views on marriage and procreation.[94] The speech *de prole augenda* drew Lucilius' fire on its own account. State-enforced propagation had an inherent absurdity that would appeal to the satirist, and the fatuous oration of Macedonicus was ripe for burlesque. Neither politics nor ideology need be invoked to account for Lucilius' lampoon.[95] The verses condemned condescension and ridiculed empty rhetoric.

Lucilius freely jibed at the mighty. Later satirists noted his fierce combativeness. Persius has him carve up the city and break his teeth on Lupus and Mucius.[96] The attacks on Mucius evidently gained notoriety.

90. Cic. *De Amicit.* 77: *egit graviter ac moderate et offensione animi non acerba; De Off.* 1.87: *fuit inter P. Africanum et Q. Metellum sine acerbitate dissensio.*

91. Val. Max. 4.1.12; cf. Pliny, *NH*, 7.144; Plut. *Apophth. Caec. Met.* 3.

92. Val. Max. 4.1.12, to be sure, does speak of bitter disputes and contention that led to serious *inimicitiae*, but his portrait seems embroidered to dramatize Metellus' actions at the funeral of Scipio; cf. Zucchelli, *L'indipendenza di Lucilio*, 100. Astin, *Scipio Aemilianus*, 311–313, oddly gives greater weight to Valerius Maximus here than to the Ciceronian testimony, although he elsewhere concedes that the account is "plainly embellished and unreliable" (244, n. 2). For P. A. Brunt, *PCPS*, 11 (1965), 12–13, the two men expressed public courtesies but mantained covert animosity. P. B. Pellizer, *RivStorAnt*, 4 (1974), 69–88, denies that there was ever any friendship between Scipio and Macedonicus—but she fails to explain Cic. *De Amicit.* 77.

93. The scholiast himself evidently recognized the problem that his own confused interpretation created; Schol. ad Horace, *Sat.* 2.1.72: *Lucilius eum in gratiam Scipionis carpsit, quamvis amicum ipsius.*

94. Coffey, *Roman Satire*, 47–48, implausibly suggests that Scipio found Metellus' position galling because his own marriage was loveless and childless. The statement of Astin, *Scipio Aemilianus*, 237, that Metellus' speech probably "grated upon the ears of Scipio" has nothing to support it. Scipio, in fact, spoke during his own censorship against undue advantage obtained by fathers from adoptive sons; Gellius, 5.19.15–16. That stance would be quite consistent with Macedonicus' position.

95. Even Zucchelli, who exposes the flimsiness of the political interpretation, repeats conventional wisdom about Lucilius' "misogyny"; *L'indipendenza di Lucilio*, 104–105.

96. Persius, 1.114.

Juvenal too takes note of the man as victim of Lucilius' jeers.[97] Who was Mucius?

Majority opinion identifies him with P. Mucius Scaevola, eminent jurist, consul in 133, and *pontifex maximus*. Why? Because P. Scaevola is named by Cicero as guiding the opposition to Scipio Aemilianus. Hence, by extension, Lucilius took up the Scipionic cause and aimed invective at his friend's antagonist.[98] That form of reasoning, as already demonstrated, has little to recommend it. No Lucilian fragment mentions P. Scaevola. But another Mucius qualifies unequivocally as the individual in question: Q. Mucius Scaevola, consul in 117, and principal figure in book 2 of the *Satires*. Persius' comment about Lucilius' cracking his teeth on Lupus and Mucius is apt. The easy and obvious conclusion is that Persius refers to books 1 and 2 of the *Satires*, Lupus as target in the first, Mucius in the second.[99]

Pursuit of the matter can pay dividends. Book 2 (or the bulk of it) is devoted to the trial of Q. Scaevola, charged *de repetundis* in 119 by T. Albucius. The case offered stimulus to the satirist, who had a field day with both protagonists. Accusations slung about at the hearing—at least as conveyed by Lucilius—covered a colorful array of offenses. Prosecutor or hostile witnesses charged Scaevola with assault as well as theft, gave dramatic descriptions of physical attacks, detailed objects of plunder that seemed earmarked for courtesans, offered obscene and graphic allegations of homosexual behavior, imputed acts of extravagant gluttony, and slandered the accused as a foul bandit. Extant fragments can give only a taste of Lucilius' rendition and of the comic possibilities presented by the trial. They apparently included even an effort to fabricate evidence of fatal assault by use of a phony corpse.[100] Some or all of this vilification was directed at Q. Mucius, but the defendant had repartee of his own. Scaevola mocked his accuser for

---

97. Juvenal, 1.154: *quid refert, dictis ignoscat Mucius an non?*

98. Cic. *De Rep.* 1.31: *senatus alteram partem dissidentem a vobis auctore Metello et P. Mucio.* For this identification, see Cichorius, *Unt. zu Luc.*, 57; Münzer, *NJbb*, 23 (1909), 191; Terzaghi, *Lucilio*, 6; Krenkel, *Lucilius*, I, 22; and even Zucchelli, *L'indipendenza di Lucilio*, 111.

99. The reference is taken for granted by Marx, *Luc. carm. rel.*, I, xlv; also Charpin, *Lucilius*, I, 102.

100. Assault: Lucilius, 57–58, M = 54–55, W = 71–72, K; theft and plunder: 67–68, M = 58–60, W = 61–63, K; obscene allegations: 72–74, M = 61–63, W = 69–70, K; gluttony: 75, 78–80, M = 67–70, W = 64–67, K; insults: 56, M = 57, W = 60, K; phony corpse: 60–61, M = 73–74, W = 81–82, K. H. B. Mattingly, *Philologus*, 131 (1987), 76–77, implausibly questions the ascription of this satire to book 2.

fatuous Hellenic affectation, reminding Albucius of a humiliating episode that goaded him into retaliation.[101]

It would be pointless and misguided to speculate whether Lucilius'
poem took the part of defendant or prosecutor. Lucilius found the
situation tailor-made for parody and wit. The trading of insults between
the Epicurean Albucius and the Stoic Scaevola provided rich material
for the satirist's purpose. In view of the torrent of abuse the accuser
aimed at Scaevola, it is not surprising that Cicero should infer Lucilius'
irritation with the defendant.[102] Or that Persius and Juvenal should see
Mucius as under verbal assault by the poet. Albucius, the pompous
philhellene, however, surely came off no better. What emerges clearly is
Lucilius' unimpeded pasquinades of politicians. Albucius was no more
than a middle-level figure, a man who reached the praetorship late in his
career and then suffered political condemnation, retiring into exile at
Athens.[103] But Scaevola carried real weight; Cicero had extensively
praised him not only for jurisprudential expertise but for command of
every realm of knowledge. He had been elected early to an augurate that
he held throughout his life, was consul in 117, and remained an influential senatorial spokesman to the end of his long career in the 80s.[104] That
Lucilius felt no restraint in retailing the most scurrilous calumnies
against him is noteworthy. Q. Scaevola was a son-in-law and special
favorite of C. Laelius, the most intimate associate of Scipio Aemilianus.[105] His attraction to Stoicism brought him under the tutelage of
Panaetius and associated him with other intellectuals and public figures
on good terms with Scipio.[106] As is plain, Lucilius did not select his
targets by political faction.[107] The pretentiousness of those who cultivated Greek philosophy and then descended into puerile polemic laid
them open to satiric assault.

---

101. Lucilius, 88–94,M = 87–93,W = 89–95,K. For discussion of these and other
fragments of book 2, see Marx, *Luc. carm. rel.*, II, 29–44; Cichorius, *Unt. zu Luc.*, 237–
251; Terzaghi, *Lucilio*, 280–289; Krenkel, *Lucilius*, I, 126–139; Charpin, *Lucilio*, I,
101–106, 212–227. On the trial, see Gruen, *Roman Politics*, 114–116; R. A. Bauman,
Lawyers in Roman Republican Politics (Munich, 1983), 321–329.

102. Cic. *De Orat.* 1.72: *Lucilius . . . homo tibi subiratus.*

103. Cic. *Pro Scauro*, 40; *In Pis.* 92; *Div. in Caec.* 63; *De Off.* 2.50; *Tusc. Disp.* 5.108;
Gruen, *TAPA*, 95 (1964), 99–110.

104. A full but controversial analysis, with references and bibliography, is in Bauman,
Lawyers, 312–340.

105. Cic. *De Orat.* 1.35, 1.58, 2.22, 3.45; *De Rep.* 1.18; *Brutus*, 3, 26 ,101.

106. Cic. *De Orat.* 1.43, 1.75; Athenaeus, 6.274.

107. It begs the question, of course, to take Lucilius' attacks as evidence for Scaevola's
break with the Scipionic faction, as in Gruen, *Roman Politics*, 114.

The poet found a healthy number of candidates for satire in the upper registers of the Roman nobility. Association with particular individuals or groups seems quite irrelevant to Lucilius' purpose. He could, in fact, take on two generations at a shot. He labeled L. Aurelius Cotta, consul 144, a corrupt trickster, swift to take bribes but slow to pay debts, and castigated his son, probably the consul of 119, for obesity.[108] And a similar double blow landed upon the Opimii. Lucilius scored a hit against the elder Q. Opimius, consul in 154, a man both decorative and indecorous, and he simultaneously slurred the son, L. Opimius, consul 121, as *Jugurthinus*—a snide comment on his implication in the Jugurthine scandal.[109] The satirist further alluded to an exchange of insults between the elder Opimius and a certain Decius, each seeking to outdo the other with allegations of effeminacy. The same or another Decius, as tribune in 120, laid accusation against the younger Opimius, only to suffer prosecution in the following year. Lucilius certainly held no brief for either man: he included an apparently scornful verbal dismissal of Decius by Scipio Aemilianus.[110]

Still other prominent personages fell under the satirist's fire. He lumped together L. Tubulus, Lupus, and Carbo as vile perjurers.[111] The lambasting of Lupus has already received treatment. The Tubulus in question can only be L. Hostilius Tubulus, who disgraced himself as praetor in 142, charged with and convicted of corruption as presiding

---

108. Lucilius, 413–415,M = 440–442,W = 415–417,K: *Lucius Cotta senex, crassi pater huius, Paceni, / magnus fuit trico nummarius, solvere nulli / lentus.* For the identifications, see Cichorius, *Unt. zu Luc.*, 308–310; *Römische Studien*, 77–79; Terzaghi, *Lucilio*, 384–385. On Cotta's indebtedness, see further Val. Max. 6.5.4. Scipio clashed at least twice with the man, once denying him a provincial command and once accusing him *de repetundis*; Val. Max. 6.4.2; Cic. *Div. in Caec.* 69; *Pro Mur.* 58. It does not follow that Lucilius took his cue from Scipio.

109. Lucilius, 418–420,M = 450–452,W = 422–424,K: *Quintus Opimius ille, Jugurtini pater huius, / et formosus homo fuit et famosus, utrumque / primo adulescens; posterius dat rectius sese.* On L. Opimius and the Jugurthine affair, see Sallust, *Iug.* 13, 20.1; Cic. *Brutus*, 128; *Pro Planc.* 70; *Pro Sest.* 140; Vell. Pat. 2.7.3.

110. On Decius and Q. Opimius, see Lucilius, 421,M = 453,W = 425,K [Cic. *De Orat.* 2.277]; cf. Cic. *De Orat.* 2.253; Livy, *Oxyr. Per.* 48; Val. Max. 6.1.10; Münzer, *Klio*, 5 (1905), 135–139; Cichorius, *Unt. zu Luc.*, 310–312; E. Badian, *JRS*, 46 (1956), 91–92. On the tribune P. Decius Subulo's accusation of L. Opimius and the subsequent trial of Decius, see references and discussion in Gruen, *Roman Politics*, 102–105, 109–111. Scipio's remarks: Lucilius, 1280,M = 1135,W = 1297,K.

111. Lucilius, 1312–1313,M = 1138–1141,W = 1328–1330,K: *Tubulus si Lucius umquam / si Lupus aut Carbo aut Neptuni filius putasset / esse deos, tam periurus, tam impurus fuisset?*

judge in the homicide tribunal.[112] But more than one Carbo qualifies
for vilification. Three brothers, in fact, suffered obloquy and ruin in the
decade of the 110s. C. Papirius Carbo, consul in 120, had been a backer
of the Gracchi, then deserted his compatriots, underwent judicial condemnation, and committed suicide in 119. A similar fate was in store for
Cn. Carbo, consul in 113, who lost a disastrous battle against the
Cimbri, faced prosecution, and probably also took his own life. The
third, M. Carbo, whose career goes unrecorded, followed his brothers
as convicted felon, a man described as *fur magnus.* Any one of them—or
perhaps all three—could have been suitably stigmatized by Lucilius.[113]

Would-be heroes of the Spanish wars also incurred disapproval in the
poet's verses. The fragments are scanty and lack adequate context for
precise reconstruction, but allusions to unsuccessful generals present a
pattern that transcends innocent reporting. A celebrated line presses the
poet to sound off about the battle of Popillius and to sing of the exploits
of Cornelius. The contrast is patent between the ignominious defeat of
M. Popillius Laenas, consul 139, at the hands of the Numantines in 138
and the eventual success of Scipio in the Numantine War. The object
may be less to honor Scipio than to recall Popillius' reverse.[114] For
Lucilius certainly recalls other reverses. He strikes with scorn at the
campaign of M. Aemilius Lepidus Porcina, consul 137, whose siege of
Palantia in Hispania Citerior ended in failure, heavy losses, and retreat,
calling him "a certain bald-headed military incompetent in the Palantine
campaign."[115] There may be allusion also to the most notorious and

112. Cic. *De Fin.* 2.54, 4.77; *De Nat. Deor.* 1.74; cf. *Ad Att.* 12.5b.3; Asconius, 23,
Clark; Gellius, 2.7.20. Discussion in Gruen, *Roman Politics,* 29–31.

113. On the trials and their outcomes, see Cic. *De Orat.* 1.40, 3.74; *Brutus,* 103, 159;
Ad Fam. 9.21.3; Val. Max. 3.7.6, 6.5.6; Tac. *Dial.* 34; Apuleius, *Apol.* 66; cf. Gruen,
Roman Politics, 107–110, 131–132. Lucilius' target is customarily identified with C.
Carbo on the grounds that he was an *inimicus* and alleged assassin of Scipio; Livy, *Per.* 59;
Vell. Pat. 2.4.4; Cic. *Ad Q. Frat.* 2.3.3; *Ad Fam.* 9.21.3; *De Orat.* 2.170; Marx, *Luc. carm.
rel.,* II, 419–420; Cichorius, *Unt. zu Luc.,* 347; Terzaghi, *Lucilio,* 17; Coffey, *Roman
Satire,* 48; Zucchelli, *L'indipendenza di Lucilio,* 112–113; Rudd, *Themes in Roman Satire,*
50. The reasoning is not decisive.

114. Lucilius, 621, M = 714, W = 689, K: *percrepa pugnam Popili, facta Corneli cane.* On
Popillius' defeat, see Livy, *Per.* 55; Appian, *Iber.* 79. The verb *percrepare* definitely has a
negative connotation; see Terzaghi, *Lucilio,* 106, n. 1. Cichorius, *Unt. zu Luc.,* 31–32,
unconvincingly takes the passage as evidence for Lucilius' service in Spain under Popillius.

115. Lucilius, 972, M = 1123, W = 1025, K: *calvus Palantino quidam vir non bonus bello.*
On the siege of Palantia, see Appian, *Iber.* 80–82; Livy, *Per.* 56; Orosius, 5.5.13; Obseq.
25. Cf. Cichorius, *Unt. zu Luc.,* 36. Whether *calvus* refers specifically to Lepidus cannot
be ascertained.

humiliating episode connected with the Spanish wars: the decision to deliver C. Hostilius Mancinus, consul 137, naked and bound, to the Spaniards after a devastating defeat and a degrading treaty. A line of Lucilius makes tantalizing reference to a man fettered with hempen bonds.[116] And even small fry obtain mention. A certain quaestor in Spain is said to skulk in shadows and shun the light.[117]

The satirist cast his net widely. He caught a certain C. Cassius, cutpurse and thief, given the mock name of Cephalo—perhaps "big-head." That may be a spoof on Cassius Sabaco, an associate of Marius, allegedly his compatriot in electoral bribery, who was expelled from the senate by the censors of 115.[118] He also branded another secondary political figure, Ti. Claudius Asellus, tribune in 140, as *improbus*. Asellus, whose profligacy got him demoted from equestrian status to that of the *aerarii* during Scipio's censorship, returned to prosecute Scipio, denouncing the *infelicitas* of his *lustrum*. That wasted effort is specifically recorded in Lucilius' verses.[119]

The poet's judgments were his own. Nothing requires or suggests that he followed a line determined by others. It is easy enough to find instances in which Lucilius' satires victimized men otherwise known to be foes or rivals of Scipio Aemilianus: Q. Metellus Macedonicus, L. Cotta, Ti. Claudius Asellus. But the verses carried equally devastating denunciation of at least one man with close connections to Scipio: Q. Scaevola. And the large majority of Lucilius' targets have no attested link to or antagonism toward the party of the Scipiones: L. Lentulus Lupus, T. Albucius, the Opimii, L. Tubulus, Carbo, M. Popillius

116. Lucilius, 1324–1325,M = 1218–1219,W = 1340–1341,K. The suggestion that this refers to Mancinus comes from Cichorius, *Unt. zu Luc.*, 37–39. On the Mancinus affair, see now Rosenstein, *CA*, 5 (1986), 230–252.

117. Lucilius, 467–468,M = 499–500,W = 472–473,K: *Publius Pavus Tubitanus mihi quaestor Hibera / in terra fuit, lucifugus, nebulo, id genus sane.* The name is more probably Tuditanus, but the man is unknown. Cf. Cichorius, *Unt. zu Luc.*, 317–319; idem, *Römische Studien*, 80–81; Charpin, *Lucilius: Satires*, II, 233.

118. Lucilius, 422–424,M = 445–447,W = 419–421,K: *Cassius Gaius hic operarius, quem Cephalonem / dicimus; sectorem furemque hunc Tullius Quintus / iudex heredem facit, et damnati alii omnes.* On Cassius Sabaco, see Plut. *Mar.* 5.3–4. The identification was proposed by Cichorius, *Unt. zu Luc.*, 313–315; cf. Terzaghi, *Lucilio*, 385–386. Charpin, *Lucilius: Satires*, II, 212–214, discusses the passage.

119. Lucilius, 394–395,M = 424–425,W = 412–413,K: *Scipiadae magno improbus obiciebat Asellus / lustrum illo censore malum infelixque fuisse.* On the clashes between Scipio and Asellus, see Cic. *De Orat.* 2.268; Gellius, 2.20.5–6, 3.4.1, 6.11.9; Festus, 362, L. See P. Fraccaro, *Studi Storici*, 5 (1912), 375–382; Astin, *Scipio Aemilianus*, 175–177; Gruen, *Roman Politics*, 29, 31; Charpin, *Lucilius: Satires*, II, 209–210.

Laenas, and M. Lepidus Porcina. If the satirist's opinions occasionally coincided with those of Aemilianus, that was happenstance rather than design. Inquiry into Lucilius' political affiliations follows the wrong path and diverts understanding. His works had their own rationale and their own objectives.

Reference to contemporary personages occurs repeatedly through the satires. Lucilius cast aspersions on *censorii, consulares,* senators of every rank, and public figures of every stripe. The license accorded to the writer stands out strikingly and undeniably.[120] It deserves remark. An ancient provision of the Twelve Tables forbade the chanting or composition of any song that damaged the reputation or brought disgrace upon another—upon pain of capital penalty.[121] We have no recorded instance in which such a penalty was applied, and there will have been few indeed. But the praetors eventually turned their attention to defamation. An *edictum de convicio* was issued in the third or second century, declaring that public insults delivered *adversus bonos mores* were actionable.[122] That formulation gave latitude and allowed for broad interpretation. A more sweeping edict followed some time later. The praetor announced a prohibition against anything done or said that aimed at the *infamia* of anyone, making it subject to an *actio iniuriarum.* Even here, however, the praetor was not bound to give redress, and the determination of what constituted *infamia* was highly subjective.[123]

The issue had entered the realm of civil law, and actions for libel are not unknown. The dramatist Accius brought suit against an actor who had defamed him on stage and gained a favorable verdict from the presiding *iudex.* Lucilius himself took similar action against one who had libeled him in a theatrical performance, but he failed to persuade the presiding officer, and the defendant went unpunished.[124] Lucilius' own satires make reference to slanderous remarks—whether about himself

---

120. Cf. Cic. *Ad Fam.* 12.16.3: *deinde qui magis hoc Lucilio licuerit adsumere libertatis quam nobis? . . . in quos tanta libertate verborum incurreret.*

121. Cic. *De Rep.* 4.12 = Augustine, *CD,* 2.9: *XII Tabulae cum perpaucas res capite sanxissent, in his hanc quoque sanciendam putaverunt: si quis occentavisset sive carmen condidisset, quod infamiam faceret flagitiumve alteri.* On the meaning of *occentavisset,* see D. Daube, *Cambridge Law Journal,* 7 (1939), 45–46; R. E. Smith, *CQ,* 45 (1951), 169.

122. O. Lenel, *Das Edictum perpetuum*[3] (Leipzig, 1927), 400.

123. *Digest,* 47.10.15.25–28. Cf. Daube, *Atti Congr. Int. di Diritto Romano,* 3 (1951), 413–418; J. Plescia, *Labeo,* 23 (1977), 273–282. On the whole question, see A. D. Manfredini, *La diffamazione verbale nel diritto romano* (Milan, 1979), passim.

124. *Ad Herenn.* 1.14.24, 2.3.19.

or someone else.[125] Character slurs and calumnies seem common in Roman intellectual society.

The remarkable fact remains: Lucilius' verses, no matter how scurrilous and offensive, never, in our evidence, got him into legal or political difficulties. How to explain it? That he served as mouthpiece for a senatorial faction and relied on the protection of *principes* clearly will not do. Nor does it suffice to point to his wealth and equestrian status; they would not give him immunity from prosecution or retaliation. To argue that recourse at law was available to those libeled on stage but not the victims of satiric verses puts the matter on too narrow a legal front and lacks direct support in the texts. The possibility that Lucilius withheld his fire until his targets were dead, thus escaping censure, can be ruled out. At least some of his shafts struck live targets: the Metelli, Q. Scaevola, Aurelius Cotta, L. Opimius. One can claim that Lucilius' satires were meant for private readings and limited circulation, thus evading public scrutiny. But the range of subjects treated, the rich diversity of targets, and the sweeping examination of contemporary life suggest more than a narrow coterie of readers. Other answers seem more promising. The vagueness and uncertainties in the praetorian edicts could have discouraged actions at law. And Roman aristocrats may well have preferred to ignore the slights of a poet rather than dignify them with reprisals.[126] But a larger conclusion can perhaps be drawn: Roman society respected the independence of writers. Lucilius established the satire as a legitimate medium of social and political commentary, with free rein for criticism of contemporaries and sardonic review of the public scene. Artistic license reflects the sophistication and maturity of Rome's intellectual and political communities.

Political turmoil and social upheaval convulsed the later years of the second century B.C. The dramatic proposals of the Gracchi divided the citizenry and released unprecedented passions. Reform efforts and resistance raised the temperature of conflict. Hopes were aroused and disappointed. Domestic violence poisoned the atmosphere. The senate was branded an obstacle, reformers labeled popular demagogues. Battles in the courts and over the courts increased in number. Unpopular

125. Lucilius, 1015–1016, M = 1085–1086, W = 1090–1091, K. These are customarily taken as alluding to slurs against Lucilius; e.g., Terzaghi, *Lucilio*, 222–223; Krenkel, *Lucilius*, II, 583–584.
126. A variety of possibilities, plausible and implausible, are canvassed by Rudd, *Themes in Roman Satire*, 42–44.

foreign policy produced recriminations and intensified animosities. Relations between Roman citizens and Italian allies suffered strains and approached the breaking point. An unusually volatile public scene characterized the generation of the Gracchi and the heyday of Marius. In the midst of all this, the cultivated posturing of the elite must have seemed especially incongruous and comically archaic.

The times proved ripe for the invention of satire. Lucilius' themes arose directly from contemporary circumstances, and his works repeatedly advert to current affairs. The absence of extended text, of course, precludes confident reconstruction. The residue survives in fragments that lack context and often frustrate inquiry. And a reminder needs to be reissued. Assertions and judgments expressed in the extant verses represent the sentiments of the speaker, not necessarily the versifier. But exposure of the sentiments alone brings contemporary discourse to the fore. Lucilius' remarks allude with frequency to personalities, episodes, issues, and controversies of his age. Events of that turbulent time provided a laboratory for the production of satire.

Did the satirist write with a partisan bias? The inference seems logical, but as noted earlier, scholars have reached strikingly divergent conclusions. Some consider Lucilius a supporter of Gracchan causes, others a traditionalist resistant to political and social change.[127] The approach itself may be at fault. The satires served not to advance partisan aims but to expose and castigate the foibles of contemporary society.

Lucilius' dark and jaundiced view hit *populus* and *patres* alike. A preserved fragment of some length makes the point with unusual force. Commons and senators hurl themselves about the Forum from dawn to dusk—all devoted to the same pursuit: to practice deceit and devise plots against one another, as if all were enemies of all.[128] That is savage denunciation, and it encompasses both citizenry and leadership. There is no sign here of political leanings, just a plague on all houses. The era promoted cynicism.

Nobiles came in for harsh judgment. A Lucilian speaker flayed them for villainy, licentiousness, and prodigality.[129] They reckon their *nobilitas* as allowing transgression with impunity and easy rebuff of their

---

127. Lucilius as *popularis*: Krenkel, *Maia*, 20 (1968), 261–270. Lucilius as conservative: Raschke, *Hermes*, 115 (1987), 304–318.

128. Lucilius, 1228–1234,M = 1145–1151,W = 1252–1258,K: *ut si hostes sint omnibus omnes*. Lucilius here speaks in his own voice, as indicated by Lactantius, *Inst.* 5.9.20.

129. Lucilius, 257,M = 269,W = 261,K: *nequitia occupat hoc, petulantia, prodigitasque.*

enemies.[130] In this context, a reference to exclusivity fits appropriately: resistance to encroachment on property and opposition to intermarriage.[131] The lines have the distinct flavor of late second-century politics, featured by sharp attacks upon the narrowness and incompetence of the nobility at the time of the Jugurthine War.[132] It does not, of course, follow that Lucilius shared the sentiments of his speaker, but he faithfully reflected the political parlance of his age.

Criticism of the senate surfaces more than once. A fragment challenges the *ordo* to expose the crimes it had committed against itself.[133] That body, so another fragment reports, gave dispensation from the laws to an aedile whose election had been marred by irregularities.[134] A jibe at senatorial procedure may lurk in the line that notes a certain senator whose foot must carry his voice. The *pedarii* made their opinions known only by formal division; they were never called upon to express *sententiae*.[135] More serious is an attack on the *lex Calpurnia*, branded a savage law.[136] That is presumably the *lex Calpurnia repetundarum* of 149, which first installed a standing court to try senators and former magistrates accused of exacting oppressive payments from provincials or dependents of Roman authority. Denunciation of that law was probably placed in the mouth of a threatened or convicted member of the nobility.[137] Lucilius here perhaps reminded readers of misdeeds by magistrates—and their indignation when caught.

130. Lucilius, 258–259,M = 270–271,W = 258–259,K: *peccare impune rati sunt / posse et nobilitate facul propellere iniquos.*

131. Lucilius, 260,M = 272,W = 260,K: *[in] suam enim [hos] invadere [rem] atque innubere censent.*

132. Cf. Sallust, *Iug.* 85 [speech of Marius]. Cichorius, *Unt. zu Luc.*, 283–286, suggests that the speaker may be C. Memmius, the *popularis* tribune of 111. So also Terzaghi, *Lucilio*, 346–347.

133. Lucilius, 690,M = 772–773,W = 745–746,K: *proferat / ergo iamiam vester ordo scelera quae in se admiserit.* Interpretation of the fragment is disputed; see Cichorius, *Unt. zu Luc.*, 146–149; Terzaghi, *Lucilio*, 154–155; Krenkel, *Lucilius*, II, 421; Charpin, *Lucilius*, II, 305–306; Raschke, *Hermes*, 105 (1987), 311–312.

134. Lucilius, 48,M = 47,W = 34,K: *per saturam aedilem factum qui legibus solvat.* The senate is almost certainly the subject here; cf. Livy, *Per.* 50. Just what *per saturam* means is unfathomable. Marx, *Luc. carm. rel.*, II, 230–24, usefully adduces the speech of T. Annius Luscus in 133; Festus, 416, L: *imperium quod plebes per saturam dederat, id abrogatum est.* See, further, Cichorius, *Unt. zu Luc.*, 234–236; Charpin, *Lucilius*, I, 198–199.

135. Lucilius, 1102,M = 1134,W = 1113,K: *agi pes, vocem mittere coepit*; cf. Gellius, 3.18.9.

136. Lucilius, 573–574,M = 607–608,W = 574–575,K: *Calpurni saevam legem Pisonis reprendi, / eduxique animam in primoribus ⟨oribus⟩ naris.*

137. The suggestion of Mattingly, *Philologus*, 131 (1987), 79–81, that the speaker was Q. Granius, is highly implausible.

The satirist, however, can also employ his medium to embarrass those who courted the favor of the populace. A snide remark castigates the man who is the darling of the *vulgus*.[138] Lucilius or one of his speakers depicts a demagogue, shouting and wailing from the Rostra, rushing back and forth like a *servus currens*, and yelling at top voice to his audience.[139] The parody punctures the histrionics of orators who resort to crowd-pleasing devices. C. Gracchus, it is reported, was the first to pace about on the Rostra, pulling his toga off his shoulder as he did.[140] Lucilius' lines plainly allude to that demeanor—or to analogous antics by imitators. Gaius' elder brother was more sedate in delivery, but his proposals engendered equally violent reaction. He was accused even of seeking a crown and aiming at monarchy.[141] Charges of kingly ambitions became increasingly frequent in the late Republic, as may perhaps be hinted in a Lucilian fragment: Granius hated haughty kings.[142] A related passage reinforces the conjecture. The speaker points to a man who runs risks for his interest and his *regnum*.[143] One need not assume that Ti. Gracchus himself is the object here. Nothing suggests that Lucilius held a brief either for or against the Gracchi.[144] The satirist simply captures current phraseology in the form of political invective.

As he reflects contempt for senatorial behavior, so he casts obloquy upon decisions made by the people in sovereign assembly. Indeed Lucilius inveighed against all thirty-five voting tribes, so a source informs us.[145] Two fragments derive from that assault, one a reference to the Papiria as first tribe, the other to the Oufentina coming from Priver-

---

138. Lucilius, 461,M = 483,W = 459,K: *dilectum video studiose vulgus habere.*

139. Lucilius, 261–262,M = 273–274,W = 262–263,K: *haec, inquam, rudet ex rostris atque heiulitabit / concursans veluti ancarius clareque quiritans.* On ancarius, see Charpin, *Lucilius*, I, 274.

140. Plut. *Ti. Gracch.* 2.2.

141. Plut. *Ti. Gracch.* 19.2.

142. Lucilius, 1181–1182,M = 609–610,W = 1201–1202,K: *Granius autem / non contemnere se et reges odisse superbos.*

143. Lucilius, 694,M = 774,W = 740,K: *quod si observas hominem, qui pro commodo et regno audeat.*

144. For the idea that this passage refers to Ti. Gracchus, see Krenkel, *Lucilius*, I, 419; Raschke, *Hermes*, 115 (1987), 312–313. It is indeed commonly held, but without sound reason, that Lucilius' line about a man who died with no bestowal of honor, no tears by an heir, and no funeral alludes to Tiberius as well; 691,M = 790,W = 738,K: see Cichorius, *Unt. zu Luc.*, 145–146; Terzaghi, *Lucilio*, 91; Krenkel, *Lucilius*, II, 417–419; Zucchelli, *L'indipendenza di Lucilio*, 120; Christes, in *Die römische Satire*, 87; Raschke, 312–313.

145. Schol. ad Pers. 1.114: *tribus omnes xxxv laceravit ex quibus urbs tota constat.* Cf. Horace, *Sat.* 2.1.69: *primores populi arripuit populumque tributim.*

num.[146] Since the Papirian tribe does not come first in the official sequence, Lucilius doubtless calls attention to a specific gathering of the *comitia tributa* in which the first tribe was selected by lot. Just which gathering this was eludes discovery.[147] But the poet plainly brings contemporary events under scrutiny. And he makes particular play with legislative decisions of the assembly. One such decision is characterized as legislation whereby people stand outside the law.[148] What meaning does that phrase bear? The term *exlex* can have two very different connotations: either "without protection of the laws" or "lawless". Choice of the former produces a theory that Lucilius deplored passage of the *lex Junia Penni* in 126, which expelled aliens from the city. Choice of the latter, by contrast, fosters the conclusion that Lucilius attacked the measures of Ti. Gracchus' tribunate which placed the *populus* outside the reach of law.[149] Decision is unnecessary. What matters is that Lucilius excoriated acts of the assembly, pointed to particulars, and employed satire as commentary on the public scene.

Nor does Lucilius spare the electoral functions of the assembly—and the susceptibility to untoward influence. Two fragments, not always correctly interpreted, hint at corruption in the process. He stigmatizes the evil of gold, which so vehemently presses its claims upon our ears: *nequam aurum est; auris quovis vehementius ambit.* Ancient commentators offered two interpretations: Lucilius referred either to heavy golden earrings or, in general, to cupidity for wealth. Neither catches the force of *ambit*. The term, it can be surmised, here carries its meaning of "electoral canvassing." And the association with *aurum* has obvious implications for the vulnerability of voters: "It solicits our attention more ardently than anything else."[150] That rendering is buttressed by

146. Lucilius, 1259–1260,M = 1132–1133,W = 1275, 1278,K.

147. Cichorius, *Unt. zu Luc.*, 335–338, proposes the meeting in 134 when the tribes denied Scipio Aemilianus the command against Aristonicus and awarded it instead to P. Crassus Mucianus; Cic. *Phil.* 11.18. One could as well think of the tribal assembly that deposed Octavius in 133 or the confusion and dispute over the electoral assembly when Tiberius sought a second tribunate; Appian, *BC*, 1.12, 1.14; Plut. *Ti. Gracch.* 12.18. But there is little point in speculating.

148. Lucilius, 1088,M = 1017,W = 1054,K: *accipiunt leges, populus quibus legibus exlex.*

149. For the former, Cichorius, *Unt. zu Luc.*, 211–212; followed by most; e.g., Terzaghi, *Lucilio*, 254; Krenkel, *Lucilius*, II, 567; Zucchelli, *L'indipendenza di Lucilio*, 85–86. For the latter, with a valuable philological discussion, see Raschke, *JRS*, 69 (1979), 83–86; idem, *Hermes*, 115 (1987), 313–316; accepted by Christes, in *Die römische Satire*, 70.

150. Lucilius, 1220,M = 1193,W = 1244,K. Terzaghi, *Lucilio*, 393, and Krenkel, *Lucilius*, II, 659, consider only the two ancient explanations, Terzaghi opting for the former, Krenkel for the latter. Warmington, *Remains*, III, 391, has it right. The context of the fragment suggests that Lucilius was speaking *in propria persona*.

the second fragment. Lucilius again pairs *aurum* and *ambitio*: they are now mock standards for *virtus*. The remark makes best sense as reference to electoral campaigning dependent on financial favors.[151] So Lucilius' strictures fell as heavily upon the *plebs* as upon the *principes*. This is not a matter of political ideology. Lucilius held up to scorn the character of public institutions—and their manipulation. His satire on the council of the gods parodies a meeting of the Roman senate; his lampoon of the Albucius-Scaevola trial ridicules aristocratic rivalries as played out in the courts; and his thrusts against the popular assembly duly caricature the influence of wealth upon the decisions of the people. All was grist to the satirist's mill.

Comments on contemporary events recur, even though we can rarely pinpoint the events with confidence. An extant fragment alludes to the plight of *socii*: "How much value would they place upon you, *socii*, since they can show mercy [but do not do so]?"[152] The context is opaque and the meaning hardly less so. But the verse surely has bearing on strained relations between Romans and allies in the aftermath of Ti. Gracchus' agrarian law and the failure to extend citizenship rights which followed the withdrawal of Fulvius Flaccus' measure in 125. The stance of the satirist cannot be fathomed.[153] But he was attuned to the economic and political tensions that divided the inhabitants of the Italian countryside.

Another matter of high currency called forth satire: the practice of grain distribution. C. Gracchus broke new ground in sponsoring a *lex frumentaria* in 123 under which the government sold grain at a low rate in monthly allocations.[154] The measure stirred controversy and criticism. L. Piso, who resisted the bill vigorously but in vain, stood in line to claim his share of the allotment, thus to mock and discredit the

---

151. Lucilius, 1119–1120,M = 1194–1195,W = 1127–1128,K: *aurum atque ambitio specimen virtutis, utrique est. / Tantum habeas, tantum ipse sies tantique habearis.* Cf. Terzaghi, *Lucilio*, 393. Cichorius, *Unt. zu Luc.*, 333–334, misses the electoral allusion and interprets the *utrique* as reference to rivalry between the consuls of 144 for the Spanish command.

152. Lucilius, 1089,M = 1018,W = 1055,K: *quanti vos faciant socii quom parcere possint.*

153. Cichorius, *Unt. zu Luc.*, 208–210, wrongly gives the context as the revolt of Fregellae; so also Zucchelli, *L'indipendenza di Lucilio*, 113. The Fregellans were Latins, not *socii*. Raschke supposes that Lucilius refers to Scipio's efforts on behalf of Italian landowners who suffered from the Gracchan distributions; *JRS*, 69 (1979), 86–87; *Hermes*, 105 (1987), 316–317. Both Cichorius and Raschke operate on the assumption that Lucilius expressed Scipionic attitudes and policy. On Italian complaints regarding land distribution, see Cic. *De Rep.* 1.31, 3.41; Appian, *BC*, 1.19; Schol. Bob. 118, Stangl. On Flaccus' bill and its failure, see Appian, *BC*, 1.21, 1.34; Val. Max. 9.5.1.

154. Appian, *BC*, 1.21; Plut. *C. Gracch.* 5.2; Vell. Pat. 2.6.3; Livy, *Per.* 60; Schol. Bob. 135, Stangl.

institution.[155] The mockery may have found its way into Lucilius' verses as well. They include mention of a *frumentarius* equipped with measure and shovel. Whether the term designates distributor, recipient, or merchant, the Gracchan grain transactions are here at issue.[156] The satirist's position, as usual, is unrevealed. If some lines held the practice up to scorn, others noted the plight of the hungry and the public pressures to address the problem. Lucilius registers a complaint that grain runs low and the *plebs* can obtain no bread.[157] That passage evidently alludes to a shortage and points up the precariousness of those living at the margins. Similar implications emerge elsewhere. Lucilius supplies a repartee between benefactor and recipient over the quality or quantity of food distributions, both bread and meat, perhaps at a public festival.[158] Lament over the poor quality of food occurs in another passage. The speaker is willing to pay any price rather than resort to the gruel and dog food supplied "from the hand of Mago." The line, as it seems, attests to grain shortage, high market prices, and dependence on inferior imports from North Africa.[159] The poet is not to be confused with political reformer, but his verses evoke the conflicts and tensions of Roman society in the aftermath of the Gracchi.

Other isolated remarks lack discernible setting and defy conjecture. So, as example, a verse stigmatizes those who transport unregistered goods, thereby to evade payment of *portorium*—our one reference to that problem in this period.[160] The defrauding of the state treasury for private gain doubtless received increased impetus from stepped-up commercial activity in the generation after conclusion of the Achaean,

---

155. Cic. *Tusc. Disp.* 3.48; Schol. Bob. 96, Stangl.

156. Lucilius, 322–323,M = 350–351,W = 325–326,K: *frumentarius est; modium hic secum atque rutellum una adfert.* Cichorius, *Unt. zu Luc.*, 292–296, acutely points to the Piso anecdote—though it does not follow that Lucilius refers to that particular episode. What *frumentarius* means in this period remains uncertain; but note Plautus, *Pseud.* 188–191—with the connotation of grain dealer.

157. Lucilius, 200,M = 214,W = 194,K.

158. Lucilius, 474–475,M = 485–486,W = 478–479,K. Interpretation is difficult and certainty impossible. See Cichorius, *Unt. zu Luc.*, 325–327; Charpin, *Lucilius*, II, 227–228.

159. Lucilius, 711,M = 768,W = 701,K: *quanti vellet quam canicas ac pultem e Magonis manu* (Marx's text). Mago is a conventional Punic name, and also the name of a Carthaginian who composed an agricultural treatise translated into Latin by decree of the senate; Cic. *De Orat.* 1.249; Varro, *De Re Rust.* 1.1.10; Columella, 1.1.13; Pliny, *NH*, 18.22. See Warmington, *Remains*, III, 247.

160. Lucilius, 722–723,M = 753–754,W = 729–730,K: *Facit idem quod illi qui inscriptum e portu exportant clanculum / ne portorium dent.*

Punic, and Spanish wars. Comparable disregard for regulations and obligations gains voice in a fragment protesting that "no one here honors claims and sworn deposits"—perhaps an echo of disputes over land acquisition and allocation.[161] Notice of a soldier's lengthy service in Spain—around eighteen years—may allude to discontent in the rank and file or resistance to the levy.[162] Finally, there is an intriguing but baffling fragment: "one to whom the whole *populus*, even if in sworn alliance, would scarcely be equal."[163] It will be prudent to avoid speculation on the person to whom Lucilius refers. But the fragment gives reminder that power and influence wielded by the prominent had become more conspicuous and more confrontational in the last generation of the second century.

The intervention of government in underwriting the sustenance of the needy did not terminate private benefactions or relations between the mighty and their dependents. Obligations of *patroni* toward *clientes* continued, manifested in part by occasional or regular food distributions. But increased state involvement after the Gracchan reforms created competition and complications, adding to the strains that vexed late Republican society. It is not surprising that Lucilius' satires dwell at some length on food and banquets, surplus and allocation, delicacies and humble fare.

Private favors remained a fundamental prop of the social system. Indeed they may have increased in quantity and frequency at a time when public measures gave alternatives—and when political figures reaped the harvest of popular policies. Lucilius saw developments with a cynical eye. A speaker berates his addressee for feeding twenty, thirty, or even a hundred moochers at his home.[164] The hyperbole underscores the length to which traditional patrons were pushed in order to maintain prestige and standing. Another fragment depicts what is evidently a wealthy but pressured patron who calculates his resources in order to determine how much he can afford to give away and to offer.[165] New

---

161. Lucilius, 1219,M = 1144,W = 1243,K: *nemo hic vindicias neque sacramenta veretur.* Cf. Terzaghi, *Lucilio,* 347–348; Krenkel, *Lucilius,* II, 657.

162. Lucilius, 490–491,M = 509–510,W = 488–489,K. For objections to the levy in the mid–second century, see Appian, *Iber.* 49; Polyb. 35.4; Cic. *De Leg.* 3.20; Livy, *Per.* 48, 55; *Oxyr. Per.* 54–55.

163. Lucilius, 1147,M = 1153,W = 1164,K: *cui si coniuret populus vix totus satis sit.*

164. Lucilius, 718,M = 760,W = 693,K: *viginti domi an triginta an centum cibicidas alas.*

165. Lucilius, 1050,M = 1052,W = 999,K: *quid dare, quid sumti facere ac praebere potisset.*

opportunities stimulated the greed of parasites for tangible benefits.[166] In this context perhaps comes the passage noted earlier: a bantering exchange between benefactor and beneficiary over the character and amount of food supplied.[167]

Competition for clients spilled over to rivalry in lavish feasts. Lucilius' lines repeatedly advert to gourmet dishes, funds squandered on exotic fare, high-priced table delicacies, and scenes of banqueting.[168] Ostentation and wastefulness, of course, provoked criticism. Private donatives had public implications, both for the solidarity of the aristocracy and for the values they espoused. A Lucilian speaker offers a radical solution: first abolish all banquets and all eating societies.[169] That Lucilius speaks with this voice would be a hazardous assumption.[170] The moralistic posturing recalls Cato the Elder, fierce and outspoken foe of wasteful luxuries. And Cato, in fact, is mentioned in another Lucilian fragment: "was old Cato not himself aware of what he provoked?"[171] That phraseology implies a less than enthusiastic judgment on the pronouncements and policies of Cato. The satirist, it appears, took a dim view both of the ostentatious habits of the elite and of the hypocrisy of their posturing critics.

The state response to conspicuous consumption was a series of sumptuary laws. The number of such measures began to swell in the mid-second century, a sign of concern about the social and political effects of excessive private expenditure. Their proliferation, however, may have been in inverse proportion to their effectiveness, thus supplying more grist for the satirist's mill. A *senatus consultum* of 161 placed limits on outlays, type of wine, and silverware employed by *principes* for dinner parties hosted at the the Megalesian Games.[172] Much more far-reaching

---

166. Lucilius, 717, M = 762, W = 692, K: *sic amici quaerunt animum, rem parasiti ac ditias.*

167. Lucilius, 474–475, M = 485–486, W = 478–479, K.

168. E.g., Lucilius, 308–311, 440–446, 569, 751–752, 769–770, 1131, 1151, 1155–1155a, 1174–1176, 1238–1240, M = 205–207, 336–339, 465–471, 595–597, 601–604, 815–818, 1226–1227, W = 309–313, 448–454, 569, 769–770, 757–758, 1172–1173, 1133–1135, 1147, 1168, 1193–1195, 1287, K.

169. Lucilius, 438–439, M = 472, W = 455, K: *tollantur primum dominia atque sodalicia omnia.*

170. As assumed, e.g., by Charpin, *Lucilius*, II, 220–22.

171. Lucilius, 478–479, M = 487–488, W = 480–481, K: *num vetus ille Cato . . . lacessisse . . . conscius non erat ipse sibi.* It would be best to forgo suggestions to fill the lacunae.

172. Gellius, 2.24.2. See Sauerwein, *Die leges sumptuariae*, 76–79, who, however, implausibly sees the measure as representing the upper classes' desire to set an example for the lower.

was a consular law of that same year, the *lex Fannia,* which in various clauses regulated expenditures at the *ludi plebei* and the Saturnalia in detail, restricted domestic outlays on other days, and specified maximum payments for grocery items on annual household budgets.[173] Even this was evidently inadequate. Eighteen years later the *lex Didia* extended the scope of its predecessors to cover all Italy, rather than just the city of Rome, and to impose penalties not only on profligate hosts but on their invited guests.[174] Further modifications came in still another sumptuary measure, the *lex Licinia,* passed at some time in the late second century because earlier legislation had already lost force through obsolescence. The new bill repeated most of the provisions of the *lex Fannia,* adding a few clauses on disbursements for certain days, the free use of agricultural products, and the maximum weights for dried meat and fish.[175] Nor did this suffice. There followed yet another *lex sumptuaria* in 115, sponsored by the consul M. Aemilius Scaurus, accompanied by censorial measures. The new law addressed itself not to limits on expenditures but to the regulation of specified foods, especially rare and costly delicacies.[176] An inference from all this legislation seems inescapable: public relations counted for more than implementation. The aristocracy officially set its face against ostentatious luxury by individuals—but lacked the means and the will to control it.[177]

The fruitless reduplication and deficient enforcement left ample scope for mockery. The poet Laevius had some choice words for the *lex Licinia* in his collection of playful erotic verses.[178] And Lucilius, for whom food as a social and political instrument was a major theme, would not

173. Gellius, 2.24.3–6; Macrobius, 3.17.3–5; Athenaeus, 6.274 c–d; Pliny, *NH,* 10.139; cf. Macrobius, 3.13.13, 3.16.14; Sauerwein, *Die leges sumptuariae,* 79–89.

174. Macrobius, 3.17.6.

175. Macrobius, 3.17.7–10; Gellius, 2.24.7–10; cf. 15.8.1. Sauerwein, *Die leges sumptuariae,* 94–104, proposes P. Crassus Mucianus as author of the bill in a putative praetorship of 134, thus to deflate in advance the proposals of Ti. Gracchus. The suggestion is a most unlikely one. Not only was Mucianus a supporter of Gracchus, but the short span of time since the *lex Didia* would make Macrobius' statement about obsolescence a most peculiar one. Discrepancies between Macrobius and Gellius on maximum allowable expenses are irrelevant for our purposes.

176. Pliny, *NH,* 8.223, 36.4; Gellius, 2.24.12; *Vir. Ill.* 72.5; cf. Macrobius 3.17.13— wrongly ascribed to M. Aemilius Lepidus in 78. A good discussion by Sauerwein, *Die leges sumptuariae,* 120–127.

177. One *lex sumptuaria* was actually repealed on the initiative of a tribune M. Duronius—who was then expelled from the senate for his pains; Val. Max. 2.9.5.

178. Laevius, fr. 23 (W. Morel and C. Buechner, *Fragmenta poetarum Latinorum epicorum et lyricorum²* [Leipzig, 1982]) = Gellius, 2.24.8–9.

miss the ironies inherent in *leges sumptuariae*. Several fragments take swipes at the laws, noting the regular evasion of their requirements and the hypocrisy of the moralizers. One of Lucilius' speakers puts the matter quite bluntly: "let us evade the *lex Licinia*."[179] The circumvention of that law was doubtless commonplace. Another line of the satirist delivers a slap at the *lex Licinia*, one of whose clauses—a survival from the *lex Fannia*—set one hundred *asses* as the ceiling for expenditures on designated days. Lucilius refers scornfully to "the hundred-*as* dinner."[180] A similar remark is directed at the *lex Fannia*: "the miserable hundred-*as* of Fannius."[181] And Lucilius mentions still one other sumptuary law—or a facsimile thereof. The irreverent poet Valerius Valentinus lampooned a law on banquets to which he applied the invented name *lex Tappula*.[182] Lucilius knew the poem and added his own jibe: "the well-fed revelers just laugh at the *lex Tappula*," thereby delivering a slight both to the self-indulgent and to the meaningless and unenforceable law.[183] Whether *lex Tappula* is an otherwise unknown measure or a joke name ascribed to one of the recorded *leges* matters little. It may indeed be neither. Valerius Valentinus perhaps parodied the whole institution of sumptuary laws in the guise of a fictitious and ludicrous measure.[184] Lucilius appropriately fastened upon it. For the satirist who derided private opulence and public fatuousness, the *lex Tappula* was a suitable *reductio ad absurdum*.

Did Lucilius associate luxury and self-indulgence with the legacy of Hellas? The insidious effects of Greek practices upon Roman morality and patriotic virtues would admirably suit satire. And Lucilius' targets

179. Lucilius, 1200,M = 599,W = 1223,K: *legem vitemus Licini.*
180. Lucilius, 1353,M = 600,W = 1370,K: *centenaria cena.*
181. Lucilius, 1172,M = 1241,W = 1192,K: *Fanni centussis misellus*; cf. 1153–1154,M = 1242–1243,W = 1170,K.
182. Festus, 550, L.
183. Lucilius, 1307,M = 1239,W = 1323,K: *Tappulam rident legem conter . . . opimi.* The corrupt text leaves precise translation uncertain, but the general meaning is clear enough. Cichorius, *Unt. zu Luc.*, 342–343, took *opimi* as a reference to L. Opimius; accepted without argument by Terzaghi, *Lucilio*, 16; Sauerwein, *Die leges sumptuariae*, 116. The interpretation is possible but unnecessary and unsupported.
184. Valentinus' penchant for irreverent verses got him into trouble later; Val. Max. 8.1.8. A comic inscription, partially preserved, offers *Tappula* in the prescript and includes Tapponis f. Tappo among other mock names—perhaps inspired by Valentinus' poem. For discussions, see A. von Premerstein, *Hermes*, 39 (1904), 336–342; Cichorius, *Unt. zu Luc.*, 341–345; Sauerwein, *Die leges sumptuariae*, 115–120; and now the imaginative but highly speculative suggestions of C. Konrad, *ZPE*, 48 (1982), 219–234.

range widely among the dissolute and the extravagant. Yet the fragments offer no suggestion of anti-Greek bias.

The fact is remarkable, yet rarely remarked upon. The poet, to be
sure, refers to imported clothing from the East and elaborate coverlets
that now made their appearance in Roman households. The togas and
tunics, however, receive the brand of "Lydian workmanship"—a label
emblematic of eastern elegance, not a Greek product.[185] Lucilius trains
his fire on Hellenic affectations, rather than on Hellenism. The distinction bears notice. He takes some glee, as observed earlier, in having
Scaevola ridicule Albucius' philhellenic demeanor.[186] Among other
things, he debunks Albucius' obsession with the arrangement of words,
like the placement of tiles in a mosaic floor, a superficial game instead of
substantive understanding of language.[187] Albucius emerges as a pompous philhellene with only surface acquaintance with the culture. Nor
did Scaevola escape this form of criticism. The exchange of abuse
between the Epicurean Albucius and the Stoic Scaevola surely discloses
Lucilius' own disdain for Romans who have a smattering of philosophy
and a heavy dose of pretentiousness. The puncturing of pretension continues. A Lucilian character mocks those who employ Greek phrases
when perfectly good Latin words will do.[188] Lucilius inserts verses that
parade some of the commonplaces of Greek philosophy: the praise of a
Stoic sage, the conflation of body and spirit, the fundamental elements
of matter.[189] These too may convey irony if put in the mouths of the
pompous or the self-important.

To deflate would-be Hellenes, however, is not to disparage Hellenism. Lucilius, in fact, had broad and extensive exposure to Greek
intellectual traditions. He makes liberal use of Greek words, both to
comic effect and as part of his normal vocabulary.[190] He quotes, alludes
to, or is clearly familiar with a range of Hellenic authors, including

185. Lucilius, 12,M = 12,W = 14,K: *praetextae ac tunicae: Lydorum opus sordidum omne.*
Cf. Athenaeus, 12.526. On the coverlets, Lucilius, 13,M = 13,W = 15,K. See Charpin,
Lucilius, I, 196–197. One need not follow Cichorius, *Unt. zu Luc.,* 228–229, in the
assumption that Lucilius alludes to the acquisition of Pergamum and its treasures.

186. Lucilius, 88–94,M = 87–93,W = 89–95,K.

187. Lucilius, 84–85,M = 84–85,W = 74–75,K. Charpin, *Lucilius,* I, 220–221, provides a good discussion.

188. Lucilius, 15–17,M = 14–16,W = 16–18,K.

189. Lucilius, 1225–1226,M = 1189–1190,W = 1249–1250,K; 635–636,M = 676–
677,W = 660–661,K; 784–790,M = 805–811,W = 769–774,K.

190. See I. Mariotti, *Studi Luciliani* (Florence, 1960), 50–81; Rudd, *The Satires of
Horace* (Cambridge, 1966), 111–117; idem, *Themes in Roman Satire,* 165–167, 226.

Homer, Archilochus, Euripides, Plato, Xenophon, and the dramatists of New Comedy.[191] And he had more than a smattering of Greek philosophy. The eminent Academic Clitomachus composed a volume he addressed to Lucilius. That dedication may or may not suggest that the poet had an extended sojourn in Athens and imbibed philosophic precepts from the masters.[192] But it lends weight to his passing references to contemporary thinkers such as Carneades and to the teachings of Socrates and his pupils.[193] He alludes to Epicurus' atomism and to philosophical debates in the circles of the Academy.[194] And he can spoof Stoics.[195] The observations go beyond mere flippant asides. Lucilius' acquaintance with the Greek world, whether at first hand or indirectly, also emerges from remarks on the institution of the ephebate, references to the gymnasium, and appreciation of an artistic masterpiece by Apelles.[196] The satirist was a man of cultivation and no denigrator of things Greek. In that sense, he offers revealing insight into the intellectual scene of late second-century Rome. The culture of Hellas had gained respectability; it was not only imitated but acknowledged. Lucilius was inventor of a new genre that later writers identified as singularly Roman, owing nothing to Greek models.[197] He employed the genre, however, not to disparage Hellenic culture but to fracture the follies of

191. It does not follow that Lucilius adapted Greek models for his own genre of satire. See now the cogent remarks on Lucilius and Archilochus by D. Mankin, *AJP*, 108 (1987), 405–408, with bibliography.

192. So Cichorius, *Unt. zu Luc.*, 40–48; Christes, in *Die römische Satire*, 62. On Clitomachus' volume for Lucilius, see Cic. *Acad.* 2.102.

193. Lucilius, 31, 709–710, 742, M = 35, 788–789, 835, W = 51, 716–718, 800, K; cf. 834, M = 956, W = 839, K. Familiarity with Carneades may have come through Clitomachus; Cic. *Acad.* 2.137.

194. Lucilius, 753–756, M = 820–823, W = 771–774, K. See the reconstruction by Marx, *Luc. carm. rel.*, II, 269–270; cf. Terzaghi, *Lucilio*, 171–173; Charpin, *Lucilius*, II, 324–326.

195. Lucilius, 1225–1226, M = 1189–1190, W = 1249–1250, K. Cf. 515–516, M = 507–508, W = 500–501, K. Lucilius' own attitudes are on show here; Porphyrio, ad Horace, *Sat.* 1.3.124: *qui tamen poeta non simpliciter hoc, sed per derisum Stoicorum dicit.*

196. Ephebate: Lucilius, 321, 752, M = 349, 816, W = 324, 770, K; gymnasium: 641, 804, M = 688, 972, W = 670, 921, K; Apelles: 828–829, M = 954–955, W = 816–817, K.

197. Horace, *Sat.* 1.10.46–49, 1.10.64–67, 2.1.62–63; Quintilian, 10.1.93. There was, of course, an earlier form of *satura*, i.e., a literary medley or miscellany, associated with the works of Ennius and Pacuvius, but Lucilius was clearly reckoned as inventor of the genre that we call "satire"—whatever he called it; see Diomedes, in Kiel, *Grammatici latini* (Leipzig, 1855–80), I, 485, probably from Varro. A valuable discussion of the whole issue is in C. A. Van Rooy, *Studies in Classical Satire and Related Literary Theory* (Leiden, 1965), 30–89, 117–123.

its inept adherents. Lucilian fragments decry mannered affectation—but not the real thing.

Lucilius addressed morals and manners on a different front. His origins were equestrian—but rural rather than bourgeois. The wealth of the family rested on landed holdings, not commercial success. Indeed business transactions and avarice for gain generally come in for sharp strictures. Lucilius—or a Lucilian character—warns against all commercial deals and small profits that are insecure.[198] He speaks of theft in the market, of damaged merchandise praised and sold for well above its value, and of disrespect for legal claims and oaths.[199] An allusion to "hired legions" probably refers not to salaried soldiery but to the mercenary greed of those multitudes who attach themselves to the rich and powerful.[200]

The satirist plays conventional moralist. One interlocutor attacks another with charges of going like a fool to dance amid the deviants. The accusation has overtones of effeminacy and debauchery—comparable to contemporary remarks ascribed to Scipio Aemilianus.[201] A still more bitter denunciation is leveled at "beardless hermaphrodites and bearded gigolos."[202] One line laments the absence of shame and the triumph of excess.[203] Lucilius resorts further to the clichés of nostalgia. A speaker bursts out with a cry that bemoans the cares of mankind and the vanity that marks human affairs.[204] Another looks with regret upon lost opportunities.[205] And still another laments that progress has been

---

198. Lucilius, 318,M = 341–342,W = 315–316,K: *verum et mercaturae omnes et quaesti-culi isti intuti.*

199. Theft: Lucilius, 1118,M = 1169,W = 1126,K; damaged merchandise: 1282–1283,M = 1170–1171,W = 1298–1299,K; claims and oaths: 1219,M = 1144,W = 1243,K.

200. Lucilius, 10,M = 10,W = 36,K: *et mercedimerae legiones.* See Cichorius, *Unt. zu Luc.,* 236–237; contra: Terzaghi, *Lucilio,* 266; Charpin, *Lucilius,* I, 195.

201. Lucilius, 32,M = 33,W = 30,K: *stulte saltatum te inter venisse cinaedos.* For Scipio's statement, see Macrobius, 3.14.7: *eunt, inquam, in ludum saltatorium inter cinaedos, virgines puerique ingenui.*

202. Lucilius, 1058,M = 1048,W = 994,K: *inberbi androgyni, barbati moechocinaedi.* Note also a reference to *scelerosi*; Lucilius, 37–39,M = 39–41,W = 41–43,K. The meaning of the lines is obscure and debated; cf. Cichorius, *Unt. zu Luc.,* 225–226; Terzaghi, *Lucilio,* 275; Charpin, *Lucilius,* I, 210–211.

203. Lucilius, 1048–1049,M = 1046–1047,W = 991–992,K.

204. Lucilius, 9,M = 2,W = 2,K: *o curas hominum! o quantum est in rebus inane!*

205. Lucilius, 26,M = 19,W = 9,K: *vellem cumprimis, fieri si forte potisset.*

turned back and that all things are falling into rack and ruin.[206] The poet then strikes a positive note. He advises a friend on the definition of virtue: fair dealing in business transactions; knowledge of the right, useful, and honorable; awareness of the proper means and ends for ambition; defense of the good and hostility to the wicked.[207] The statements add up to nothing insightful or profound. Rather, they form a collection of platitudes. To assess such bromides as serious preaching misses the mark. The more likely interpretation is parody.

Lucilius posed as moralist. He may also have posed as embattled critic. The fragments are full of allusions to attacks and retaliation by or against Lucilius. They deliver the impression of a quarrelsome malcontent repeatedly embroiled in controversy. How far does that represent reality? Horace was convinced. In his view Lucilius spilled out his secrets in his writings, as if to trusted colleagues, thus exposing his life like an open book.[208] He stigmatized malefactors and felons with abandon, and he stripped the cover off those who were fair on the outside and foul within.[209] The image of Lucilius as feuding and contentious still prevails among moderns.[210]

Extant testimony from his own pen can lead to that conclusion. Lucilius' verses attest to a quarrel or quarrels with insults and slanders hurled back and forth, dissemination of verbal attacks, hounding, and even the intent to institute legal proceedings.[211] The pyrotechnics are

206. Lucilius, 1197,M = 1188,W = 1219,K: *intereunt, labuntur, eunt rursum omnia vorsum.*

207. Lucilius, 1326–1338,M = 1196–1208,W = 1342–1354, K. Raschke, *Latomus,* 49 (1990), 352–369, rightly shows that the verses do not reflect Stoic philosophy but convey the language of Roman public life. Her hypothesis that the addressee Albinus is A. Postumius Albinus, the man savaged by Cato and Polybius as an excessive and offensive philhellene, and that the passage attacks contemporary moral decline is, however, altogether speculative—and takes Lucilius rather too seriously as a genuine moralist.

208. Horace, *Sat.* 2.1.30–34: *ille velut fidis arcana sodalibus olim / credebat libris . . . ut omnis / votiva pateat veluti descripta tabella vita senis.* The remark by Horace, though ostensibly positive, may have negative undertones; cf. W. S. Anderson, *Essays on Roman Satire* (Princeton, N.J., 1982), 30–32. On Horace's attitude to Lucilius generally, see Anderson, 13–41.

209. Horace, *Sat.* 1.4.3–6, 2.1.62–65: *detrahere et pellem, nitidus qua quisque per ora / cederet, introrsus turpis.*

210. See, e.g., U. Knoche, *Roman Satire* (Bloomington, Ind., 1975), 43–44; Coffey, *Roman Satire,* 41–42; Rudd, *Themes in Roman Satire,* 5–8.

211. Lucilius, 920–921,M = 863–864,W = 840–841,K: *quapropter certum est facere contra ac persequi / et nomen deferre hominis.* On the bickering and verbal polemics, see Lucilius, 1014–1023,M = 1079–1087,W = 1069–1070, 1077, 1090–1091, 1098–1101, 1107,K.

generally ascribed to a literary dispute or a personal altercation.[212] On such an interpretation, other verses of the satirist constitute defense, reaction, and reprisal. He defies his foe by disparaging his assaults.[213] He promises retaliation in kind, only fiercer still.[214] Or in a different mood, he disdains requital, expressing deep confidence in the superiority of his own accomplishments.[215] So, at least, the lines have been understood.[216]

Greater caution would be advisable. The fragments rarely allow for confidence about the persons or circumstances involved. Use of the first person is too often taken as autobiographical—a hasty and imprudent conclusion. On few occasions can we be certain that Lucilius speaks in his own voice. Elaborate reconstructions of the poet's conflicts are best left aside. Indeed, hints survive suggesting that they ought not to be taken too seriously. When Lucilius once chooses to supply his own name, he does so with tongue in cheek: "We heard that you invited your friends today, together with that scoundrel Lucilius."[217] A personal reference very likely occurs also in the statement of an interlocutor who seems less than somber: "Now, Gaius, since you abuse and berate us in turn."[218] In the same spirit and perhaps the same context, Lucilius offers a suitable comment: "All are handsome and affluent in your eyes, only I am a scoundrel: so be it."[219] And one other line has similar resonance: "You too, go ahead and insult poor old me."[220] The accumulation casts doubt on the idea that Lucilius engaged in a grave struggle or a heated contest with his career on the line. The poet who mocked moral preaching could also mock intellectual feuds—including his own.

Comparable caution needs to be applied elsewhere. Pronouncements

---

212. Cf. Cichorius, *Unt. zu Luc.*, 193–202; Terzaghi, *Lucilio*, 222–227; Richter, *Gymnasium*, 69 (1962), 305–306.

213. Lucilius, 704–705,M = 766–767,W = 723–724,K; 1037–1038,M = 1088–1089,W = 1093–1094,K.

214. Lucilius, 1095–1096,M = 1000–1001,W = 1057–1058,K; cf. 1030,M = 1070,W =1103,K.

215. Lucilius, 97–98,M = 94–95,W = 98–99,K; 448,M = 475,W=447,K; 1030,M = 1009,W = 1102,K; 1012–1013,M = 1090–1091,W = 1084–1085,K.

216. See, most recently, Rudd, *Themes in Roman Satire*, 6–8.

217. Lucilius, 821–822,M = 929–930,W = 892–893,K: *amicos hodie cum improbo illo audivimus / Lucilio advocasse.*

218. Lucilius, 1035,M = 1075,W = 1089,K: *nunc, Gai, quoniam incilans nos laedis vicissim.*

219. Lucilius, 1026,M = 1077,W = 1095,K: *omnes formonsi, fortes tibi, ego inprobus; esto.* Cf. 1224,M = 1174,W = 1248,K.

220. Lucilius, 914,M = 865,W = 821,K: *insulta miserum tu quoque in me.*

extracted from the fragments seldom justify conclusions about the poet's viewpoint. The opinions may be introduced only to get shot down, or to expose the fatuity of the speaker. This caveat holds, for example, for the patriotic lines on Rome's tenacity and resolution in the field: the nation knows no disgrace through defeat by barbarians, whether a Viriathus or a Hannibal; battles were often lost, but never a war.[221] The stirring sentiments need not come from the poet's heart. One can detect convention and commonplace, perhaps subjected to irony.[222] Similar possibilities attach to the occasional pieces of sage advice that surface in the satires. They include the admonition neither to praise nor to grumble about a man; exhortations to treat life seriously rather than as a game, to prefer an active to a sedate existence, and to seek the approbation of the few and the wise; and the recommendation not to rely too much on any individual's talent.[223] The pieces form no obvious pattern, nor should they be assembled as part of a coherent philosophy. Multiple voices speak in the lines of Lucilius. They can serve to expose banality and deflate pomposity. Or they can ridicule the ignorant who harbor religious fears and foster foolish superstitions.[224] Lucilius chose to satirize, not to sermonize.

The polyphony of the poet seldom yields to personal revelation. When it does, Lucilius speaks out with some force. He pledges his well-being and his verses, composed with zeal and earnestness, to the interests of the people.[225] And he declares vehemently that he scorns mundane professions and will not change himself for all the world.[226] The stout defiance seems characteristic. Lucilius' self-assertiveness best defines the man.

The intended audience might give insight into the satirist's objectives

---

221. Lucilius, 613–616,M = 708–711,W = 683–686,K.

222. Cf. the similar phraseology in Livy, 9.18.8. Christes, *Der frühe Lucilius*, 83–84, rather too confidently, rejects the possibility of parody, but he sees the lines as part of a Lucilian *recusatio*—in which case irony can hardly be excluded. Others discuss the verses in terms of a supposed dialogue between poet and young historian; Cichorius, *Unt. zu Luc.*, 109–111, 120–127; Terzaghi, *Lucilio*, 119–123.

223. Lucilius, 426,M = 454,W = 397,K; 457–463, M = 489–494,W = 460–465,K; 1010,M = 1062,W = 1073,K.

224. Lucilius, 484–489,M = 524–529,W = 490–495,K.

225. Lucilius, 688–689,M = 791–792,W = 735–736,K: *rem populi, salute et fictis versibus Lucilius / quibus potest, inpertit, totumque hoc studiose et sedulo.*

226. Lucilius, 671–672,M = 650–651,W = 656–657,K.

and expectations. Lucilius supplies some intriguing remarks about his desired readership. A corrupt but not unintelligible passage in Pliny cites the poet on his preferences: "I write for neither the most nor the least learned; I want a Junius Congus, not a Manius or a Persius to read these lines."[227] A similar statement or part of the same is quoted by Cicero, who reports Lucilius' view that he wished to be read by neither the least nor the most literate, for the first would understand nothing and the second perhaps more than himself: "I don't care to have Persius read me, but I do want Laelius Decumus."[228] Still one other passage bears notice in this connection, not a fragment but a reference. Cicero asserts that he will not restrict his readership as Lucilius did: "Would that that Persius were still around! In fact, Scipio and Rutilius would be even more desirable. In fear of their judgment, Lucilius says that he writes for Tarentines, Consentines, and Sicilians."[229] What is to be made of this curious combination of comments?

Lucilius ostensibly seeks to escape the verdict of the erudite. The personages named appear to suit that category. Cicero characterizes Persius as "the most learned of our people."[230] Behind "Manius" may lurk M'. Manilius, consul in 149, a skilled and respected jurist.[231] Scipio, of course, is Aemilianus, and Rutilius is P. Rutilius Rufus, consul in 105, a noted student of Stoicism.[232] Such were the formidable critics to whose scrutiny Lucilius trembled to submit his verses. Two other individuals are singled out as welcome readers: Laelius Decumus and Junius Congus. Of the first, perhaps to be read as Decimus Laelius, we know nothing.[233] Junius Congus, however, was a distinguished jurist

227. Lucilius, 595–596,M = 632–634,W = 591–593,K: *nec doctissimis [nec scribo indoctis nimis]; Manium / Persium[ve] haec legere nolo, Iunium Congum volo.* The forgoing is Marx's text—not without its problems. For other suggestions, see Cichorius, *Unt. zu Luc.*, 104–109; Baehrens, *Hermes*, 54 (1919), 75–79. The text derives from Pliny, *NH*, praef. 7.

228. Lucilius, 592–593,M = 635,W = 594,K: *Persium non curo legere, Laelium Decumum volo* = Cic. *De Orat.* 2.25.

229. Cic. *De Fin.* 1.3.7: *nec vero ut noster Lucilius recusabo quominus omnes mea legant. Utinam esset ille Persius! Scipio vero et Rutilius multo etiam magis; quorum ille iudicium reformidans Tarentinis ait se et Consentinis et Siculis scribere.*

230. Cic. *De Orat.* 2.25; cf. *Brutus*, 99.

231. Cf. Cic. *De Orat.* 3.133; *De Rep.* 1.18; *Brutus*, 108; Gellius, 17.7.3; *Digest*, 1.2.2.39. The identification was made by Marx, *Luc. carm. rel.*, II, 222.

232. Cic. *Brutus*, 114; *De Off.* 3.10; Vell. Pat. 2.13.2; Athenaeus, 6.274.

233. The attempt of Cichorius, *Unt. zu Luc.*, 106–108, to see C. Laelius here, and to distinguish Laelius from Decumus is ingenious but unconvincing. See Baehrens, *Hermes*, 54 (1919), 76–77.

and historian—or rather became one. At the time he was still a young man, perhaps a coeval of Lucilius.[234] So the satirist, it has been inferred, offered his verses not to the established intellectual leadership but to young contemporaries.[235] He avoided both the most learned critics and the unlettered ones, preferring a moderate cross section of public opinion and even a provincial readership, as illustrated by Tarentines, Consentines, and Sicilians.[236] Or to put the matter in a different way, he aimed his satires at men of common sense and *ingenium*, those who preferred peasant shrewdness to doctrine, the concrete to the abstract, a middle road between rigid adherence to traditional values and a succumbing to the refinements of Hellenism.[237] On that analysis, the individuals Lucilius singled out as desired readers, as well as the designated audience outside Rome, exemplify the receptive constituency for satire, the *crassi* to whose judgment Lucilius submits his work.[238]

The whole matter needs reconsideration; it presents another instance in which Lucilius has received perhaps too solemn a treatment. Ought one really to take his statements as the outline for an agenda or a serious delineation of his constituency? The mention of Scipio and Rutilius should alert us right away. That Lucilius would quail before their judgment strains belief. We have already seen the easy familiarity between the poet and Scipio Aemilianus. Since Lucilius could even poke fun at Scipio's Latin pronunciation, he would hardly shrink in awe from

234. Cic. *De Orat.* 1.256; Pliny, *NH*, 33.35; *Digest*, 11.13.1 pr.; Lydus, *De Mag.* 1.24. On his age, see Cic. *Pro Planc.* 58; Schol. Bob. 163, Stangl; Cichorius, *Unt. zu Luc.*, 121–127.

235. So Christes, *Der frühe Lucilius*, 88–90. He neglected to notice, however, that Rutilius Rufus, one of the critics whom Lucilius supposedly shunned, would have been about the same age as Junius Congus.

236. Terzaghi, *Lucilio*, 104–106.

237. See the extensive and evocative analysis of A. Pennacini, *Atti Accad Torino*, 100 (1965–66), 293–360; followed by Zucchelli, *L'indipendenza di Lucilio*, 92–95.

238. See Lucilius, 386–387, M = 417–418, W = 389–390, K: *horum est iudicium, crassis, ut dixi, scribimus ante; / hoc est quid sumam, quid non, in quoque locemus.* A positive connotation for *crassus* may be found also in Horace, *Sat.* 2.2.3. The meaning of the passage, however, is much disputed. Marx emended *crassis* to *crisis*, thus as synonym of *iudicium* rather than description of those exercising judgment. He is followed in the editions of Warmington, Krenkel, and Charpin. Cichorius, *Unt. zu Luc.*, 299–300, preferred *Crassis* to *crassis*, thus "I write for men like Crassus"—a most implausible conjecture. The text as printed herein was adopted by Pennacini, *Atti Accad Torino*, 100 (1965–66), 311, but it too depends on emendation, that of F. Leo, *Ausgewählte kleine Schriften*, I (Rome, 1960), 235–236: *dixi, scribimus* for *descripsimus*. There is no solid ground anywhere.

his censure.[239] The satirist was evidently a close contemporary of Rutilius, an *adulescens* in 138.[240] So, Rutilius was no formidable figure to
intimidate the writer. The mysterious "Manius" remains unknown, his
identification as the jurist M'. Manilius attractive but unverifiable. And
Cicero's characterization of Persius as "most learned of our people"
seems oddly discordant and excessive for a man otherwise almost un-
heard of.[241] The "serious" interpretation begins to unravel. And when
one turns to the Tarentines, Consentines, and Sicilians as the intended
recipients of Lucilius' verses, the irony is hard to miss. These are
constituents who might not even read Latin![242] It will not do to reckon
this as feigned modesty, a form of *captatio benevolentiae*.[243] Lucilius
could have produced more suitable names for that purpose, and if this
was false humility, it was carried to such extremes as to be ineffectual—
uncharacteristic of the satirist. Cicero may have read the lines right: he
introduces Lucilius with the epithet *perurbanus*.[244] The poet's wit infuses
the lines. They may perhaps parody a form of *recusatio*. Lucilius, it can
be suggested, represented mediocrities as fearsome critics and un-
knowns as welcome readers, pretended alarm at censure by friends and
offered his compositions to those unfamiliar with the language. As
elsewhere, the satirist aimed not at sober reflection but at a laugh.

The personality of Lucilius remains concealed in the rubble of surviving fragments. Scholars have recreated a variety of individuals in the
guise of Lucilius: spokesman for the Scipionic circle, political partisan,
popular champion, defender of tradition, moral reformer, quarrelsome
combatant, or pioneer in bringing literature to the notice of a wider
audience.

239. Lucilius, 963–964, M = 983–984, W = 971–972, K.
240. Cic. *Brutus*, 85.
241. Cic. *De Orat.* 2.25: *hic fuit enim ut noramus omnium fere nostrorum hominum doctissimus*. Beyond this, we know only that Persius composed a speech for C. Fannius, the
consul of 122, to be delivered against C. Gracchus on the subject of Latins and allies; Cic.
Brutus, 99.
242. The irony here has been noted; e.g., by Cichorius, *Unt. zu Luc.*, 28; Christes,
Der frühe Lucilius, 92; Coffey, *Roman Satire*, 41; Rudd, *Themes in Roman Satire*, 118. But
its implications have not been drawn out. Rudd's view, for instance, that this shows
Lucilius not to be a thoroughgoing elitist misses the point. And even those who detect
the irony in mention of the non-Romans take the references to Persius, Manius, Laelius,
and Congus at face value.
243. As does Charpin, *Lucilius*, II, 273.
244. Cic. *De Orat.* 2.25.

Close scrutiny of his verses calls forth a different image. Lucilius emerges as beholden to no person, faction, or political philosophy. He mocked friends and adversaries alike, lampooned public figures, and parodied public actions. His satires attacked pomposity, incompetence, and villainy. He denounced both *nobiles* and *populus*, and he exposed the defects of current policies ranging from grain distributions to sumptuary laws. His reproaches of contemporary morality aim less at reform of morals than at derision of the moral reformers. Lucilius was satirist rather than preacher or pundit, a contentious critic who could laugh at his own quarrels and even taunt his own readership. He offered a rare blend of engagement and detachment. And he consistently guarded his fierce independence.

Investigation of the poems pays dividends well beyond the personality of the poet. The satires not only give access to contemporary debates on morals and politics, legislative disputes, aristocratic competition, and the intensification of political invective. They also disclose the license with which writers could attack prominent personages and timely issues, and they illuminate the artist's relationship both to Hellenic tradition and to Roman society. Lucilian poetry provides a peculiar but precious entrance into the social and cultural world of late second-century Rome.

Still another dimension, however, has received emphasis here. The nobility, as these chapters have argued, had succeeded in absorbing into the mainstream of Roman culture the traditions, literature, and art of Hellas, and had employed them to draw out the distinctive features of Roman values. That process, successful as it was, also had some unattractive consequences. It gave rise to pretentiousness, condescension, and hypocrisy. The turbulent age of the Gracchi, which rent the social fabric, cast a harsh light on those characteristics. Lucilius entered the scene at an opportune time. The vantage point of the cynical and independent thinker who was of but not in the ruling class offers an insightful reaction to the cultural campaigns of the elite. Their stewardship of the intellectual and artistic heritage of Greece proved to be a mixed blessing. It elevated their self-esteem and sharpened a sense of national identity. But in an era of social and political upheaval, national pride became perceived as oligarchic arrogance. The custodians of culture could not escape the withering glare of C. Lucilius. The search for intellectual respectability spawned a new genre that exposed the foibles of the intelligentsia itself. The cultivated elite defined its nation's distinctiveness through the literary and visual arts—only to become the victim of its own creation. The cultural crusade had come full circle. The appropriation of the Hellenic legacy and the flaunting of Roman supremacy helped to create a new cultural artifact, which, in a kind of delicious irony, was turned against the purveyors of culture themselves, transforming them for posterity into the skewered subjects of satire.

BIBLIOGRAPHY

Abel, K. "Die kulturelle Mission des Panaitios." *Antike und Abendland* 17 (1971), 119–43.

Adriani, A. "Ritratti dell' egitto greco-romano." *MdI* 77 (1970), 72–109.

Alföldi, A. *Early Rome and the Latins*. Ann Arbor, Mich., 1965.

———. *Die trojanischen Urahnen der Römer*. Basel, 1957.

Alfonsi, L. "Catone il Censore e l'umanesimo romano." *PP* 9 (1954), 161–176.

Altheim, F. *A History of Roman Religion*. London, 1938.

Ampolo, C. "Lavinium and Rome." *CR* 102 (1988), 117–120.

Anderson, W. S. *Essays on Roman Satire*. Princeton, N. J., 1982.

André, J.-M. *L'otium dans la vie morale et intellectuelle romaine*. Paris, 1966.

Andreae, B. *Das Alexandermosaik aus Pompeji*. Recklinghausen, 1977.

Armstrong, D., and J. J. Walsh. "SIG³ 593: The Letter of Flamininus to Chyretiae." *CP* 81 (1986), 32–46.

Asheri, D. *Fra Ellenismo e Iranismo*. Bologna, 1983.

———. *Saggi di letteratura e storiografia antiche*. Como, 1983.

Astin, A. E. *Cato the Censor*. Oxford, 1978.

———. "The Censorship of the Roman Republic: Frequency and Regularity." *Historia* 31 (1982), 174–187.

———. *Politics and Policies in the Roman Republic*. Belfast, 1968.

———. *Scipio Aemilianus*. Oxford, 1967.

Badian, E. "Ennius and His Friends." *FondHardt* 17 (1972), 151–199.

———. "P. Decius P. f. Subulo: An Orator of the Time of the Gracchi." *JRS* 46 (1956), 91–96.

———. *Titus Quinctius Flamininus: Philhellenism and Realpolitik*. Cincinnati, 1970.

Baehrens, W. A. "Literarhistorische Beiträge." *Hermes* 54 (1919), 75–86.

Balsdon, J. P. V. D. *Romans and Aliens*. London, 1979.

———. "T. Quinctius Flamininus." *Phoenix* 21 (1967), 177–190.

Balty, J. C. "Portrait et société au 1er siècle avant notre ère." *Wiss. Zeitschr. der Humboldt-Universität zu Berlin* 31 (1982), 139–142.

——. "La statue de bronze de T. Quinctius Flamininus *ad Apollinis in circo.*" *MEFRA* 90 (1978), 669–686.

Barchiesi, M. *Nevio epico*. Padua, 1962.

Barsby, J. *Plautus: Bacchides*. Warminster, Eng., 1986.

Bauman, R. A. *Lawyers in Roman Republican Politics*. Munich, 1983.

Beare, W. "Contaminatio." *CR* 9 (1959), 7–11.

——. "The Life of Terence." *Hermathena* 59 (1942), 20–29.

——. *The Roman Stage*³. London, 1965.

Becatti, G. *Arte e gusto negli scrittori latini*. Florence, 1951.

——. "Attikà-Saggio sulla scultura attica dell'ellenismo." *RivIstArch* 7 (1940), 7–116.

Bérard, J. *La colonisation grecque de l'Italie méridionale et de la Sicile*². Paris, 1957.

Berger, E. "Ein Vorläufer Pompejus' des Grossen in Basel." *Eikones: Studien zum griechischen und römischen Bildnis*. Antike Kunst 12 (1980), 64–75.

Berve, H. "Lustrum." *RE* 13:2 (1927), 2046–2048.

Besançon, A. *Les adversaires de l'hellénisme à Rome pendant la période républicaine*. Paris, 1910.

Bianchi Bandinelli, R. *Roma: L'arte romana nel centro del potere*. Milan, 1969.

Bickermann, E. J. "Origines Gentium." *CP* 47 (1952), 65–81.

——. "Rom und Lampsakos." *Philologus* 87 (1932), 277–299.

Bieber, M. "The Development of Portraiture on Roman Republican Coins." *ANRW* I.4 (1973), 871–898.

——. *The History of the Greek and Roman Theater*². Princeton, N.J., 1961.

——. *The Sculpture of the Hellenistic Age*². New York, 1961.

Bitto, I. "Venus Erycina e Mens." *ArchStorMessinese* 28 (1977), 121–133.

Boethius, A. "On the Ancestral Masks of the Romans." *Acta Archaeologica* 13 (1942), 226–235.

Boethius, A., and J. B. Ward-Perkins. *Etruscan and Roman Architecture*. London, 1970.

Bömer, F. *Rom und Troia*. Baden-Baden, 1951.

Bonamente, M. "Leggi suntuarie e loro motivazioni." In *Tra Grecia e Roma*, 67–92. Rome, 1980.

Bonner, S. F. *Education in Ancient Rome*. London, 1977.

Borda, M. *La scuola di Pasiteles*. Bari, 1953.

Bordenache Battaglia, G. *Le ciste prenestine, I.1: Corpus*. Rome, 1979.

Boscherini, S. *Lingua e scienza greca nel "De agri cultura" di Catone*. Rome, 1970.

Boyancé, P. "La connaissance du grec à Rome." *REL* 34 (1956), 111–131.

——. *Études sur la religion romaine*. Rome, 1972.

——. "Les origines de la légende troyenne de Rome." *REA* 45 (1943), 275–290.

Boyd, M. J. "The Porticoes of Metellus and Octavia and Their Two Temples." *PBSR* 21 (1953), 152–159.

Braccesi, L. *Alessandro e i Romani*. Bologna, 1975.

Breckenridge, J. D. *Likeness: A Conceptual History of Ancient Portraiture.* Evanston, Ill., 1968.

——. "Origins of Roman Republican Portraiture: Relations with the Hellenistic World." *ANRW* I.4 (1973), 826–854.

Bremmer, J. N., and N. M. Horsfall, eds. *Roman Myth and Mythography.* London, 1987.

Brink, C. O. *Horace on Poetry: Epistles, Book II.* Cambridge, 1982.

Briquel, D. *Les Pélasges en Italie.* Paris, 1984.

Briscoe, J. *A Commentary on Livy, Books XXXIV–XXXVII.* Oxford, 1981.

——. "Eastern Policy and Senatorial Politics, 168–146 B.C." *Historia* 18 (1969), 49–70.

——. "Q. Marcius Philippus and *Nova Sapientia.*" *JRS* 54 (1964), 66–77.

Brothers, A. J. *Terence: The Self-Tormentor.* Warminster, Eng., 1988.

Broughton, T. R. S. *The Magistrates of the Roman Republic,* I, II. Cleveland, Ohio, 1951, 1952.

Brown, R. M. *A Study of the Scipionic Circle.* Scottdale, Pa., 1934.

Brunt, P. A. "*Amicitia* in the Late Roman Republic." *PCPS* 11 (1965), 1–20.

——. *Italian Manpower, 225 B.C.–A.D. 14.* Oxford, 1971.

Buchheit, V. *Vergil über die Sendung Roms.* Heidelberg, 1963.

Budde, L. "Das römische Historienrelief, I." *ANRW* I.4 (1973), 800–804.

Buschor, E. *Das hellenistische Bildnis.* Munich, 1949.

Calabi Limentani, I. "I fornices di Stertinio e di Scipione nel racconto di Livio." *ContrIstStorAnt* 8 (1982), 123–135.

——. *Studi sulla società romana: Il lavoro artistico.* Milan, 1958.

Calcani, G. *Cavalieri di bronzo.* Rome, 1989.

Calcioni, F. "Aineias." *LIMC* I.1 (1981), 381–396.

Callier, F. "La *libertas* et les valeurs politiques dans le théâtre de Térence." *IXe Congrès Int. de l'Assoc. Budé* 1 (1973), 412–423.

Carcopino, J. *Les secrets de la correspondance de Cicéron.* Paris, 1947.

Carney, T. F. *A Biography of C. Marius*[2]. Chicago, 1970.

——. *P. Terenti Afri Hecyra.* Pretoria, 1963.

Cassola, F. *I gruppi politici romani nel III secolo a.C.* Trieste, 1962.

Castagnoli, F. *Lavinium, I: Topografia generale, fonti, e storia delle ricerche.* Rome, 1972.

——. *Lavinium, II: Le Tredici Are.* Rome, 1975.

——. "La leggenda di Enea nel Lazio." *Studi Romani* 30 (1982), 1–15.

——. "Il problema dell'Ara di Domizio Enobarbo." *Arti Figurative* 1 (1945), 181–196.

Catling, A. W. "Archaeology in Greece, 1988–89." *AR* 35 (1988–89), 3–116.

Cèbe, J.-P. "Le niveau culturel du public plautinien." *REL* 38 (1960), 101–106.

——. *Varron: Satires ménippées.* Rome, 1980.

Chalmers, W. R. "Plautus and His Audience." In *Roman Drama,* edited by T. A. Dorey and D. R. Dudley, 39–41. New York, 1965.

Charpin, F. *Lucilius: Satires.* Paris, 1978–79.

Chassignet, M. *Caton: Les Origines*. Paris, 1986.

Christes, J. *Der frühe Lucilius*. Heidelberg, 1971.

——. "Lucilius." In *Die römische Satire*, edited by J. Adamietz, 57–122. Darmstadt, 1986.

——. "Lucilius. Ein Bericht über die Forschung seit F. Marx." *ANRW* I.2 (1972), 1182–1239.

Cichorius, C. *Römische Studien*. Stuttgart, 1922.

——. *Untersuchungen zu Lucilius*. Berlin, 1908.

Cicu, L. "L'originalità del teatro di Terenzio alla luce della nuova estetica e della politica del circolo scipionico." *Sandalion* I (1978), 73–121.

Classen, C. J. "Zur Herkunft der Sage von Romulus und Remus." *Historia* 12 (1963), 447–457.

Clemente, G. "Le leggi sul lusso e la società romana tra III e II secolo a.C." In *Società romana e produzione schiavistica*, III, edited by A. Giardina and A. Schiavone, 1–14. Bari, 1981.

Coarelli, F. "L' 'ara di Domizio Enobarbo' e la cultura artistica in Roma nel II secolo a.C." *DialArch* 2 (1968), 302–368.

——. *Caratteri dell' ellenismo nelle urne etrusche*. Florence, 1977.

——. "Classe dirigente romana e arti figurative." *DialArch* 4–5 (1970–71), 241–265.

——. "Il commercio delle opere d'arte in età tardo-reppublicana." *DialArch* (1983–84), 43–69.

——. "Polycles." *Studi Miscellanei* 15 (1969–70), 77–89.

——. "Public Building in Rome between the Second Punic War and Sulla." *PBSR* 45 (1977), 1–23.

——. "Le tyrannoctone du Capitole et la mort de Tibérius Gracchus." *MEFRA* 81 (1969), 137–160.

Coffey, M. *Roman Satire*. London, 1976.

Colin, G. *Rome et la Grèce*. Paris, 1905.

Collart, J. *Varron, grammarien latin*. Paris, 1954.

Cornell, T. J. "Aeneas and the Twins: The Development of the Roman Foundation Legend." *PCPS* 201 (1975), 1–32.

——. "Aeneas' Arrival in Italy." *LCM* 2 (1977), 77–83.

——. "The Conquest of Italy." In *Cambridge Ancient History*², vol. VII.2, 351–419. Cambridge, 1989.

Crawford, M. H. *Coinage and Money under the Roman Republic*. Berkeley, Calif., 1985.

——. "Greek Intellectuals and the Roman Aristocracy in the First Century B.C." In *Imperialism in the Ancient World*, edited by P. D. A. Garnsey and C. R. Whittaker, 193–207. Cambridge, 1978.

——. *Roman Republican Coinage*. Cambridge, 1974.

Crowther, N. B. "Greek Games in Republican Rome." *AntCl* 52 (1983), 268–273.

Cugusi, P. *Epistolographi latini minores, I*. Turin, 1970.

——. *Evoluzione e forme dell' epistolografia latina*. Rome, 1983.

——. "Studi sull'epistolografia latina, I: L'età preciceroniana." *AnnUnivCagliari* 33.1 (1970), 46–54.

D'Anna, G. "Contributo alla cronologia dei poeti latini arcaici IV: Cornelio Nepote, Velleio Patercolo, e la cronologia luciliana." *RendIstLomb* 89–90 (1956), 334–342.

———. *Problemi di letteratura latina arcaica.* Rome, 1976.

Daube, D. *Aspects of Roman Law.* Edinburgh, 1969.

———. "Ne quid infamandi causa fiat: The Roman law of defamation." *Atti Congr. Int. di Diritto Romano* 3 (1951), 411–450.

———. "*Nocere* and *Noxa.*" *Cambridge Law Journal* 7 (1939), 23–55.

Daux, G. "Chronique des fouilles en 1958." *BCH* 83 (1959), 567–793.

Della Corte, F. "L'ambasceria di Cratete a Roma." *RivFilol* 12 (1934), 388–389.

———. *Catone Censore*[2]. Florence, 1969.

———. "Catone Maggiore e i *Libri ad Marcum Filium.*" *RivFilol* 69 (1941), 81–96.

Della Corte, F., I. Mariotti , and W. Krenkel. "L'età di Lucilio." *Maia* 20 (1968), 254–270.

Develin, R. *The Practice of Politics at Rome, 366–167 B.C.* Brussels, 1985.

Diels, H. *Sibyllinische Blätter.* Berlin, 1890.

Drerup, H. *Ägyptische Bildnisköpfe griechischer und römischer Zeit.* Münster, 1950.

———. "Totenmaske und Ahnenbild bei den Römern." *MdI* 87 (1980), 81–129.

Drury, M. "Publius Terentius Afer." In *The Cambridge History of Classical Literature, II: Latin Literature,* edited by E. J. Kenney and W. V. Clausen, 814–820. Cambridge, 1982.

Dubuisson, M. *Le latin de Polybe: Les implications historiques d'un cas de bilinguisme.* Paris, 1985.

———. "Le latin est-il une langue barbare?" *Ktema* 9 (1984), 55–68.

———. "Les *opici*: Osques, occidentaux ou barbares?" *Latomus* 42 (1983), 522–545.

———. "Problèmes du bilinguisme romain." *LEC* 49 (1981), 27–45.

———. "*Utraque Lingua.*" *AntCl* 50 (1981), 274–286.

———. "Y a-t-il une politique linguistique romaine?" *Ktema* 7 (1982), 187–210.

Duckworth, G. E. *The Nature of Roman Comedy.* Princeton, N. J., 1952.

Dumézil, G. *Archaic Roman Religion.* Chicago, 1970.

Dupont, F. *Le théâtre latin.* Paris, 1988.

Durante, M. "Ἄγριον ἠδὲ Λατῖνον." *PP* 6 (1951), 216–217.

Dury-Moyaers, G. *Énée et Lavinium.* Brussels, 1981.

Earl, D. C. "Terence and Roman Politics." *Historia* 11 (1962), 469–485.

Eckstein, A. M. *Senate and General: Individual Decision Making and Roman Foreign Relations, 264–194 B.C.* Berkeley, Calif., 1987.

Ehlers, W. "Die Gründungsprodigien von Lavinium und Alba Longa." *MH* 6 (1949), 166–175.

Errington, R. M. "Aspects of Roman Acculturation in the East under the Republic." In *Alte Geschichte und Wissenschaftsgeschichte: Festschrift für K. Christ,* edited by P. Kneissel, 140–157. Darmstadt, 1988.

Felten, F. "Römische Machthaber und hellenistische Herrscher." *JOAI* 56 (1985), 110–154.

Ferrary, J.-L. "Le discours de Philus et la philosophie de Carnéade." *REL* 55 (1977), 128–156.

——. *Philhellénisme et impérialisme.* Paris, 1988.

Ferrero, L. "Su alcuni riflessi del patronato nella letteratura romana del III secolo a.C." *Mondo Classico* 11 (1941), 205–231.

Floch, B. "Das Geburtsjahr des Lucilius." *WS* 38 (1916), 158–165.

Flores, E. *Letteratura latina e ideologia del III–II a.C.* Naples, 1974.

Forehand, W. E. *Terence.* Boston, 1985.

Forsythe, G. "Some Notes on the History of Cassius Hemina." *Phoenix* 44 (1990), 326–344.

Fraccaro, P. "Studi sull' età dei Gracchi." *Studi Storici* 5 (1912), 317–448.

Frank, T. *Roman Imperialism.* New York, 1914.

——. "Terence's Contribution to Plot-Construction." *AJP* 49 (1928), 309–322.

Fraser, P. *Ptolemaic Alexandria.* Oxford, 1972.

Frenz, H. G. *Römische Grabreliefs in Mittel- und Süditalien.* Rome, 1985.

Freyburger, G. "Fides et potestas, πίστις et ἐπιτροπή." *Ktema* 7 (1982), 177–185.

Frézouls, E. "Aspects de l'histoire architecturale du théâtre romain." *ANRW* 2.12.1 (1982), 343–441.

——. "La construction du *theatrum lapideum* et son contexte politique." In *Théâtre et spectacles dans l'antiquité,* 193–214. Actes du colloque de Strasbourg, 1981.

Frier, B. *Libri Annales Pontificum Maximorum: The Origins of the Annalistic Tradition.* Rome, 1979.

Fuchs, W. "Die Bildgeschichte der Flucht des Aeneas." *ANRW* I.4 (1973), 615–632.

Gabba, E. "Considerazioni sulla tradizione letteraria sulle origini della Repubblica." *FondHardt* 13 (1966), 135–174.

——. *Dionysius and the History of Archaic Rome.* Berkeley, Calif., 1991.

——. *Miscellenea di studi alessandrini in memoria di A. Rostagni.* Turin, 1963.

——. *Republican Rome: The Army and the Allies.* Berkeley, Calif., 1976.

——. "Storici greci dell'impero romano da Augusto ai Severi." *RSI* 71 (1959), 361–381.

——. "Storiografia greca e imperialismo romano (III–I sec. a.C.)." *RSI* 86 (1974), 625–642.

——. "Sulla valorizzazione politica della leggenda delle origini troiane di Roma fra III e II secolo a.C." In *I canali della propaganda nel mondo antico, ContrIstStorAnt,* edited by M. Sordi, 84–101. Milan, 1976.

Gagé, J. *Apollon romain.* Paris, 1955.

Galdi, M. "La donna nei frammenti di Lucilio." *Athenaeum* o.s. 8 (1920), 77–91.

Galinsky, G. K. *Aeneas, Sicily, and Rome.* Princeton, N.J., 1969.

——. "The 'Tomb of Aeneas' at Lavinium." *Vergilius* 20 (1974), 2–11.

——. "Troiae qui primus ab oris. . . ." *Latomus* 28 (1969), 3–18.

Galsterer, H. *Herrschaft und Verwaltung im republikanischen Italien.* Munich, 1976.

Garbarino, G. *Roma e la filosofia greca dalle origini alla fine del II sec. a.C.* Turin, 1973.

Garbrah, K. A. "Terence and Scipio: An Echo of Terence in the Oratorical Fragments of Sc. Aemilianus?" *Athenaeum* 59 (1981), 188–191.

Garton, C. *Personal Aspects of the Roman Theater.* Toronto, 1972.

Gazda, E. K. "Etruscan Influence in the Funerary Reliefs of Late Republican Rome: A Study of Roman Vernacular Portraiture." *ANRW* I.4 (1973), 855–870.

Gelzer, M. "Porcius." *RE* 31 (1953), 108–145.
——. "Römische Politik bei Fabius Pictor." *Hermes* 68 (1933), 129–166.
Gentili, B. *Theatrical Performances in the Ancient World: Hellenistic and Early Roman Theater.* Amsterdam, 1979.
Gerosa, M. *La prima enciclopedia romana. I "libri ad Marcum filium" di Catone Censore.* Pavia, 1910.
Gestri, L. "Studi terenziani." *StudItalFilolClass* 13 (1936), 61–105.
——. "Terentiana." *StudItalFilolClass* 20 (1943), 3–58.
Gilula, D. "The First Realistic Roles in European Theatre: Terence's Prologues." *QuadUrb* 33 (1989), 95–106.
——. "Greek Drama in Rome: Some Aspects of Cultural Transposition." In *The Play Out of Context,* edited by H. Scolnicov and P. Holland, 99–109. Cambridge, 1989.
——. "How Rich Was Terence?" *SCI* 8–9 (1989), 74–78.
——. "Where Did the Audience Go?" *SCI* 4 (1978), 45–49.
——. "Who's Afraid of Rope-walkers and Gladiators? (Ter. Hec. 1–57)." *Athenaeum* 59 (1981), 29–37.
Girard, J.-L. "Minerva Capta: Entre Rome et Faleries." *REL* 67 (1989), 163–169.
Gisinger, F. "Xenagoras: Historiker." *RE* 9A.2 (1967), 1409–1416.
Giuliani, L. *Bildnis und Botschaft: Hermeneutische Untersuchungen zur Bildniskunst der römischen Republik.* Frankfurt, 1986.
Golan, D. "The Problem of the Roman Presence in the Political Consciousness of the Greeks before 229 B.C." *RivStorAnt* 1 (1971), 93–98.
Gold, B. *Literary Patronage in Greece and Rome.* Chapel Hill, N.C., 1987.
Goldberg, S. M. "Terence, Cato, and the Rhetorical Prologue." *CP* 78 (1983), 198–211.
——. *Understanding Terence.* Princeton, N.J., 1986.
Gomme, A. W., K. J. Dover, and A. Andrewes. *A Historical Commentary on Thucydides.* Oxford, 1970.
Gratwick, A. S. "Drama." In *The Cambridge History of Classical Literature,* II: *Latin Literature,* edited by E. J. Kenney and W. V. Clausen, 77–137. Cambridge, 1982.
Griffith, J. G. "The Ending of Juvenal's First Satire and Lucilius Book XXX." *Hermes* 98 (1970), 56–72.
Grimal, P. "L'ennemi de Térence, Luscius de Lanuvium." *CRAI* (1970), 281–288.
——. "Existe-t-il une 'morale' de Plaute?" *BAGB* (1975), 485–498.
——. "Le théâtre à Rome." *IXe Congrès Int. de Rome de l'Assoc. Budé,* I (1973), 249–305.
Gros, P. *Architecture et société à Rome et en Italie centro-méridionale aux deux derniers siècles de la République.* Brussels, 1978.
——. "Hermodoros et Vitruve." *MEFRA* 85 (1973), 137–161.
——. "Les premières générations d'architectes hellénistiques à Rome." In *L'Italie préromaine et la Rome républicaine: Mélanges offerts à Jacques Heurgon,* II, 387–410. Rome, 1976.
——. "Les statues de Syracuse et les 'dieux' de Tarente." *REL* 57 (1979), 85–114.
Gruen, E. S. "Greek πίστις and Roman Fides." *Athenaeum* 60 (1982), 50–68.

——. *The Hellenistic World and the Coming of Rome*. Berkeley, Calif., 1984.

——. "Politics and the Courts in 104 B.C." *TAPA* 95 (1964), 99–110.

——. *Roman Politics and the Criminal Courts, 149–78 B.C.* Cambridge, Mass., 1968.

——. "Rome and Rhodes in the Second Century B.C.: A Historiographical Inquiry." *CQ* 25 (1975), 58–81.

——. "Rome and the Seleucids in the Aftermath of Pydna." *Chiron* 6 (1976), 73–95.

——. *Studies in Greek Culture and Roman Policy*. Leiden, 1990.

Guarducci, M. "Cippo latino arcaico con dedica ad Enea." *BullComm* 76 (1956–58), 1–13.

——. "Le offerte dei conquistatori Romani ai santuari della Grecia." *RendPontAccadArch* 13 (1937), 41–58.

Gundel, H. "Porcius Licinus." *RE* 22:1 (1953), 232–233.

Haarhoff, T. J. *The Stranger at the Gate*. London, 1938.

Habel, E. "Ludi Publici." *RE*, Suppl. 5 (1931), 608–630.

Habicht, C. "Eine Liste von Hieropoioi aus dem Jahre des Archons Andreas." *AthMitt* 97 (1982), 171–184.

Haffter, H. *Römische Politik und römische Politiker*. Heidelberg, 1967.

Hafner, G. *Das Bildnis des Q. Ennius: Studien zur römischen Porträtskunst des 2. Jahrhunderts v. Chr.* Baden-Baden, 1968.

——. "Frauen- und Mädchenbilder aus Terrakotta im Museo Gregoriano Etrusco." *MdI* 72 (1965), 41–61.

——. "Männer- und Jünglingsbilder aus Terrakotta im Museo Gregoriano Etrusco." *MdI* 73–74 (1966–67), 29–52.

——. *Späthellenistische Bildnisplastik*. Berlin, 1954.

Handley, E. W. "Plautus and His Public: Some Thoughts on New Comedy in Latin." *Dioniso* 46 (1975), 117–132.

Hanson, J. A. *Roman Theater Temples*. Princeton, N.J., 1959.

Harris, W. V. *Rome in Etruria and Umbria*. Oxford, 1971.

Harrison, E. *The Athenian Agora*, I: *Portrait Sculpture*. Princeton, N.J., 1953.

Haupt, M. In L. Müller, "Zu Lucilius und Tacitus." *NJbb* 107 (1873), 365.

Haywood, R. M. *Studies on Scipio Africanus*. Baltimore, 1933.

Heldmann, K. "Zur Ehesatire des Lucilius." *Hermes* 107 (1979), 339–344.

Helm, R. "Hieronymus' Zusätze in Eusebius' Chronik und ihr Wert für die Literaturgeschichte." *Philol.* Suppl. 21, vol. II (1929), 1–98.

Heurgon, J. *Scripta varia*. Brussels, 1986.

Heuss, A. "Abschluss und Beurkundung des griechischen und römischen Staatsvertrages." *Klio* 27 (1934), 14–53, 218–257.

Hiesinger, U. W. "Portraiture in the Roman Republic." *ANRW* I.4 (1973), 805–825.

Hill, H. "Dionysius of Halicarnassus and the Origins of Rome." *JRS* 51 (1961), 88–93.

——. "Tacitus, *Annals*, XIV.21.2." *CR* 46 (1932), 152–153.

Himmelman, N. *Herrscher und Athlet: Die Bronzen von Quirinal*. Milan, 1989.

Holleaux, M. *Rome, la Grèce, et les monarchies hellénistiques au IIIe siècle avant J.-C. (273–205)*. Paris, 1935.

Hölscher, T. "Die Anfänge römischer Repräsentationskunst." *MdI* 85 (1978), 315–357.

———. "Beobachtungen zu römischen historischen Denkmälern." *ArchAnz* 94 (1979), 337–348.

———. *Griechische Historienbilder des 5. und 4. Jahrhunderts v. Chr.* Würzburg, 1973.

Horsfall, N. "The Collegium Poetarum." *BICS* 23 (1976), 79–95.

———. "Corythus: The Return of Aeneas in Virgil and His Sources." *JRS* 63 (1973), 68–79.

———. "Doctus sermones utriusque linguae." *EMC* 23 (1979), 85–95.

———. "Patronage of Art in the Roman World." *Prudentia* 20 (1988), 9–28.

———. "Some Problems in the Aeneas Legend." *CQ* 29 (1979), 372–390.

———. "Stesichorus at Bovillae?" *JHS* 99 (1979), 26–48.

Hough, J. N. "The Use of Greek Words by Plautus." *AJP* 55 (1934), 346–364.

Howard, S. "A Veristic Portrait of Late Hellenism: Notes on a Culminating Transformation in Hellenistic Sculpture." *CSCA* 3 (1970), 97–113.

Hunter, R. L. *The New Comedy of Greece and Rome.* Cambridge, 1985.

Ireland, S. *Terence: The Mother in Law.* Warminster, Eng., 1990.

Jackson, D. "Verism and the Ancestral Portrait." *Greece and Rome* 34 (1987), 32–47.

Jacoby, F. *Apollodors Chronik.* Berlin, 1902.

Jax, K. "Gestalten des Widerstandes gegen den griechischen Kultureinfluss in Rom." *Serta Philologica Aenipontana* 7–8 (1962), 289–310.

Jocelyn, H. D. "Homo sum: Humani nil a me alienum puto." *Antichthon* 7 (1973), 14–46.

Johansen, F. S. "The Portraits in Marble of G. Julius Caesar: A Review." In *Ancient Portraits in the J. Paul Getty Museum, I.* Occasional Papers on Antiquities, 4, edited by A. A. Houghton, M. True, and J. Frel, 17–40. Malibu, Calif., 1987.

Jordan, H. *M. Catonis praeter librum de re rustica quae extant.* Leipzig, 1860.

Jory, E. J. "Associations of Actors in Rome." *Hermes* 98 (1970), 223–253.

———. "Dominus Gregis?" *CP* 61 (1966), 102–105.

———. "Continuity and Change in the Roman Theater." *Studies in Honour of T. B. L. Webster.* Bristol, 1986.

Josifovic, S. "Lykophron." *RE,* Suppl. 11 (1968), 888–930.

Jucker, H. *Vom Verhältnis der Römer zur bildenden Kunst der Griechen.* Frankfurt, 1950.

Kähler, H. *Der Fries vom Reiterdenkmal des Aemilius Paullus in Delphi.* Berlin, 1965.

———. *Rom und seine Will: Erläuterungen.* Munich, 1960.

———. *Seethiasos und Census: Die Reliefs aus dem Palazzo Santa Croce in Rom.* Berlin, 1966.

Kaimio, J. *The Romans and the Greek Language.* Helsinki, 1979.

Kammer, U. "Untersuchungen zu Ciceros Bild von Cato Censorinus." Diss., Frankfort, 1964.

Kappelmacher, A. "Beiträge zur Lebensgeschichte des Dichters Lucilius." *WS* 31 (1909), 82–96.

———. "C. Lucilius 4." *RE* 13.2 (1927), 1617–1637.

Kaschnitz von Weinberg, G. *Ausgewählte Schriften,* II. Berlin, 1965.

Kenney, E. J., and W. V. Clausen, eds. *The Cambridge History of Classical Literature*, II: Latin Literature. Cambridge, 1982.

Keramopoullou, A. D. "'Ανάθημα [Κορω]νέων έν Θήβαις." *Arch Delt* 13 (1930–31), 105–118.

Kiel, H. *Grammatici latini*, 7 vols. Leipzig, 1855–80.

Kienast, D. *Cato der Zensor*. Heidelberg, 1954.

———. "Rom und die Venus vom Eryx." *Hermes* 93 (1965), 478–489.

Kierdorf, W. "Catos 'Origines' und die Anfänge der römischen Geschichtsschreibung." *Chiron* 10 (1980), 205–224.

Kindermann, H. *Das Theaterpublikum der Antike*. Salzburg, 1979.

Kleiner, D. E. E. *Roman Group Portraiture*. New York, 1977.

Klingner, F. "Cato Censorius und die Krisis des römischen Volkes." *Die Antike* 10 (1934), 239–263 = *Römische Geisteswelt*[5], 34–65. Munich, 1965.

Klose, D. *Die Didaskalien und Prologe des Terenz*. Bamberg, 1966.

Knoche, U. *Roman Satire*. Bloomington, Ind., 1975.

Koeppel, G. "The Grand Pictorial Tradition of Roman Historical Representations during the Early Empire." *ANRW* 2.12.1 (1982), 507–535.

———. "Official State Reliefs of the City of Rome in the Imperial Age: A Bibliography." *ANRW* 2.12.1 (1982), 477–506.

Konrad, C. "*Quaestiones Tappulae*." *ZPE* 48 (1982), 219–234.

Konstan, D. *Roman Comedy*. Ithaca, N.Y., 1983.

Krenkel, W. *Lucilius: Satiren*. Leiden, 1970.

———. "Zur Biographie des Lucilius." *ANRW* 1.2 (1972), 1250–1257.

Krenkel, W., F. Della Corte, and I. Mariotti. "L'età di Lucilio." *Maia* 20 (1968), 254–270.

Künzl, E. *Der römische Triumph*. Munich, 1988.

Kuttner, A. "Some New Grounds for Narrative: Marcus Antonius' Base ('the Altar of Domitius Ahenobarbus') and Other Republican Biographies." In *Narrative and Event in Ancient Art*, edited by P. Holliday. Cambridge, forthcoming.

Lahusen, G. *Untersuchungen zur Ehrenstatue in Rom*. Rome, 1983.

———. "Zur Funktion und Rezeption des römischen Ahnenbildes." *MdI* 92 (1985), 261–289.

Lana, I. "Terenzio e il movimento filellenico in Roma." *RivFilol* 75 (1947), 44–80.

La Rocca, E. "Fabio o Fannio: L'affresco medio-repubblicano dell'Esquilino come riflesso dell'arte 'rappresentiva' e come espressione di mobilità sociale." In *Ricerche di pittura ellenistica*, 169–191. Rome, 1985.

Latte, K. *Römische Religionsgeschichte*. Munich, 1960.

Lattimore, S. *The Marine Thiasos in Greek Sculpture*. Los Angeles, 1976.

Le Bonniec, H. *Le culte de Céres à Rome*. Paris, 1958.

Leeman, A. D. "L'hyperbole et l'ironie chez les Romains en tant que mécanismes de défense et d'assimilation a l'égard de la culture grecque." In *Hommages à Robert Schilling*, edited by H. Zehnacker and G. Hentz, 347–356. Paris, 1983.

Leeman, A. D., and H. Pinkster. *M. Tullius Cicero: De Oratore, Libri III*. Heidelberg, 1981.

Lenaghan, J. O. *A Commentary on Cicero's Oration "De Haruspicum Responso."* The Hague, 1969.

Lenel, O. *Das Edictum Perpetuum*[3]. Leipzig, 1927.

Leo, F. *Ausgewählte kleine Schriften, I.* Rome, 1960.

Letta, C. "L'Italia dei mores Romani nelle *Origines* di Catone." *Athenaeum* 62 (1984), 3–30 and 416–439.

Léveque, P. "Lycophronica." *REA* 57 (1955), 36–56.

Levine, L. W. *High Brow/Low Brow.* Cambridge, Mass., 1988.

Linderski, J. "The Aediles and the Didascaliae." *AHB* 1 (1987), 83–88.

Lindsay, W. M. "Terence and Scipio." *CQ* 22 (1928), 119.

Ling, R. "Hellenistic Civilization." In *Cambridge Ancient History*[2], Plates to vol. VII.1, 91–206. Cambridge, 1984.

Lippold, A. *Consules.* Bonn, 1963.

Macchiaroli, G., ed. "Lazio arcaico e mondo greco." *PP* 32 (1977), 1–460, and *PP* 36 (1981), 1–432.

MacKendrick, P. "Demetrius of Phalerum, Cato, and the *Adelphoe.*" *RivFilol* 82 (1954), 18–35.

McLeod, W. "The 'Epic Canon' of the Borgia Table: Hellenistic Lore or Roman Fraud?" *TAPA* 115 (1985), 153–165.

MacMullen, R. "Hellenizing the Romans (2nd Century B.C.)." *Historia* 40 (1991), 419–438.

Magie, D. *Roman Rule in Asia Minor.* Princeton, N.J., 1950.

Manfredini, A. D. *La diffamazione verbale nel diritto romano.* Milan, 1979.

Manganaro, G. "Una biblioteca storica nel ginnasio di Tauromenion e il P. Oxy. 1241." *PP* 29 (1974), 389–409.

Mankin, D. "Lucilius and Archilochus: Fragment 698 (Marx)." *AJP* 108 (1987), 405–408.

Manni, E. "Sulle più antiche relazioni fra Roma e il mondo ellenistico." *PP* 11 (1956), 179–190.

Marabini-Moevs, M. T. "Le Muse di Ambracia." *Bolletino d'Arte* 66.12 (1981), 1–58.

Marcadé, J. *Au musée de Delos.* Paris, 1969.

———. *Receuil de signatures de sculpteurs grecs.* Paris, 1957.

Mariotti, I. *Studi Luciliani.* Florence, 1960.

Mariotti, I., F. Della Corte, and W. Krenkel. "L'età di Lucilio." *Maia* 20 (1968), 254–270.

Marmorale, E. V. *Cato Maior*[2]. Bari, 1949.

———. *Naevius poeta.* Florence, 1953.

Marshall, B. A. *A Historical Commentary on Asconius.* Columbia, Mo., 1985.

Marti, H. "Terenz, 1909–1959." *Lustrum* 8 (1963), 6–101.

Martin, P. M. "Énée chez Denys d'Halicarnasse: Problèmes de généalogie." *MEFRA* 101 (1989), 113–142.

Martin, R. H. *Terence: Adelphoe.* Cambridge, 1976.

Martina, M. "Aedes Herculis Musarum." *DialArch* (1981), 49–68.

———. "I censori del 258 a.C." *QuadStor* 12 (1980), 143–170.

———. " 'Grassatores' e 'Carmentarii.' " *Labeo* 26 (1980), 155–175.

———. "Terenzio e i nobiles: Sul prologo dell' *Eunuchus.*" *QuadStor* 17 (1983), 161–167.

Marx, F. *Lucilii carminum reliquiae*. Leipzig, 1904.

Mattingly, H. B. "The Chronology of Terence." *RivCultClassMed* 5 (1963), 12–61.

———. "The Date of the *Senatus Consultum de Agro Pergameno*." *AJP* 93 (1972), 412–423.

———. "A New Look at the Lex Repetundarum Bembina." *Philologus* 131 (1987), 71–81.

———. "The Terentian Didascaliae." *Athenaeum* 37 (1959), 148–173.

Mazzarino, A. *Introduzione al "De agri cultura" di Catone*. Rome, 1952.

Mazzarino, S. *Il pensiero storico classico I²*. Bari, 1973.

———. *Il pensiero storico classico II²*. Bari, 1974.

Mele, A. "Il pitagorismo e le popolazioni anelleniche d'Italia." *AION* 3 (1981), 61–96.

Meyer, H. *Kunst und Geschichte*. Munich, 1983.

Meyer, R. D. *Literarische Fiktion und historischer Gehalt in Ciceros "De Oratore."* Stuttgart, 1970.

Michalowski, K. *Delos XIII: Les portraits hellénistiques et romaines*. Paris, 1932.

Michelfeit, J. "Zum Aufbau des ersten Buches des Lucilius." *Hermes* 93 (1965), 113–128.

Mingazzini, P. "Scopas Minore." *Arti figurative* 2 (1946), 137–148.

Mitchell, R. E. "Roman Coins as Historical Evidence: The Trojan Legends of Rome." *Illinois Classical Studies* 1 (1976), 65–85.

Molisani, G. "Lucius Cornelius Quinti Catuli architectus." *RendAccadLinc* 26 (1971), 41–49.

Momigliano, A. *Alien Wisdom*. Cambridge, 1975.

———. *The Classical Foundations of Modern Historiography*. Berkeley, Calif., 1990.

———. "J. Perret. *Les Origines de la légende troyenne de Rome*." *JRS* 35 (1945), 99–104.

———. *Secondo contributo alla storia degli studi classici*. Rome, 1960.

———. *Settimo contributo alla storia degli studi classici e del mondo antico*. Rome, 1984.

———. "Terra Marique." *JRS* 32 (1942), 53–64.

———. *Terzo contributo alla storia degli studi classici e del mondo antico*. Rome, 1966.

Mommsen, T. *Römische Forschungen*. Berlin, 1864.

———. *Römisches Staatsrecht*. Leipzig, 1887.

Montella, C. "Il *fidus interpres* nella prassi della traduzione orale." *AION* 4 (1982), 197–212.

Morel, W., and C. Ruechner. *Fragmenta poetarum Latinarum epicorum et lyricorum²*. Leipzig, 1982.

Moretti, L. "Chio e la lupa capitolina." *RivFilol* 108 (1980), 33–54.

———. "Le *Origines* di Catone, Timeo ed Eratostene." *RivFilol* 80 (1952), 289–302.

Morgan, M. G. "The Perils of Schematism: Polybius, Antiochus Epiphanes, and the 'Day of Eleusis.'" *Historia* 39 (1990), 37–76.

———. "Politics, Religion, and the Games in Rome, 200–150 B.C." *Philologus* 134 (1990), 14–36.

———. "The Portico of Metellus: A Reconsideration." *Hermes* 99 (1971), 480–505.

Moyaers, G. "Énée et Lavinium à la lumière des découvertes archéologiques récentes." *RevBelge* 55 (1977), 21–50.

Munro, H. A. J. "Another Word on Lucilius." *JPhilol* 8 (1879), 201–225.

Münzer, F. "Anmerkungen zur neuen Livius-Epitome." *Klio* 5 (1905), 135–139.

——. "L. Mummius." *RE* 16.1 (1933), 1195–1206.

——. "Lucilius und seine Zeitgenossen nach den neuesten Untersuchungen." *NJbb* 23 (1909), 180–195.

Münzer, F., and C. Cichorius. "L. Cincius Alimentus." *RE* 3.2 (1899), 2556–2557.

Musti, D. *Gli Etruschi e Roma*. Rome, 1981.

——. "Polibio e la storiografia romana arcaica." *FondHardt* 20 (1974), 103–143.

——. *Polibio e l'imperialismo romano*. Naples, 1978.

Nash, E. *Pictorial Dictionary of Ancient Rome*. London, 1961–62.

Nenci, G. "Graecia capta ferum victorem cepit." *AnnPisa* 8 (1978), 1007–1023.

Nicolet, C. *L'ordre équestre a l'époque républicaine (312–43 av. J.-C.)*. Paris, 1974.

——. "Polybe et les institutions romaines." *FondHardt* 20 (1974), 209–258.

——. *The World of the Citizen in Republican Rome*. Berkeley, Calif., 1980.

Noack, F. "Die erste Aeneis Vergils." *Hermes* 27 (1892), 407–445.

Nodelman, S. "How to Read a Roman Portrait." *Art in America* 63 (1975), 27–33.

——. "The Portrait of Brutus the Tyrannicide." *Ancient Portraits in the J. Paul Getty Museum, I*. Occasional Papers on Antiquities, 4, edited by A. A. Houghton, M. True, and J. Frel, 41–86. Malibu, Calif., 1981.

Ogilvie, R. M. *A Commentary on Livy, Books 1–5*. Oxford, 1965.

——. "The Fragments of Cato." *CR* 88 (1974), 64–65.

——. "Lustrum Condere." *JRS* 51 (1961), 31–39.

Oost, S. I. *Roman Policy in Epirus and Acarnania in the Age of the Roman Conquest of Greece*. Dallas, 1954.

Opelt, I. "La coscienza linguistica dei Romani." *Atene e Roma* 14.2–3 (1969), 21–37.

——. "Roma = Ῥώμη und Rom als Idee." *Philologus* 109 (1965), 47–56.

Padberg, F. "Cicero und Cato Censorius. Ein Beitrag zu Ciceros Bildungsgang." Diss., Münster, 1933.

Palmer, R. E. A. *Roman Religion and Roman Empire*. Philadelphia, 1974.

Pape, M. *Griechische Kunstwerke aus Kriegsbeute und ihre öffentliche Aufstellung in Rom*. Hamburg, 1975.

Paul, G. M. *A Historical Commentary on Sallust's "Bellum Jugurthinum."* Trowbridge, Eng., 1984.

Pearson, L. *The Greek Historians of the West: Timaeus and His Predecessors*. Atlanta, 1987.

——. "Myth and Archaeologia in Italy and Sicily—Timaeus and His Predecessors." *YCS* 24 (1975), 171–195.

Pellizer, P. B. "I rapporti politici fra Scipione Emiliano e Metello Macedonico." *RivStorAnt* 4 (1974), 69–88.

Pennacini, A. "Docti e crassi nella poetica di Lucilio." *AttiAccadTorino* 100 (1965–66), 293–360.

Pensabene, P. "Auguratorium e tempio della Magna Mater." *Archeologia Laziale* 2 (1979), 67–74.

Perelli, L. *Il teatro rivoluzionario di Terenzio*. Florence, 1973.

Perna, R. *L'originalità di Plauto*. Bari, 1955.

Perret, J. "Athènes et les légendes troyennes d'Occident." In *L'Italie préromaine et la Rome républicaine: Mélanges offerts à Jacques Heurgon*, II, 791–803. Rome, 1976.

———. *Les origines de la légende troyenne de Rome (231–81)*. Paris, 1942.

———. "Rome et les Troyens." *REL* 49 (1971), 39–52.

Petrochilos, N. *Roman Attitudes to the Greeks*. Athens, 1974.

Philipp, H., and W. Koenigs. "Zu den Basen des L. Mummius in Olympia." *AthMitt* 94 (1979), 193–216.

———. "Zu einer Gewichtsbüste aus dem Kerameikos." *AthMitt* 94 (1979), 137–159.

Phillips, E. D. "Odysseus in Italy." *JHS* 73 (1953), 53–67.

Pietilä-Castrén, L. *Magnificentia Publica: The Victory Monuments of the Roman Generals in the Era of the Punic Wars*. Helsinki, 1987.

———. "New Men and the Greek War Booty in the 2nd Century B.C." *Arctos* 16 (1982), 121–143.

———. "Some Aspects of the Life of Lucius Mummius Achaicus." *Arctos* 12 (1978), 115–123.

Plescia, J. "The Development of *Iniuria*." *Labeo* 23 (1977), 271–289.

Pollitt, J. J. *Art in the Hellenistic Age*. Cambridge, 1986.

———. "The Impact of Greek Art on Rome." *TAPA* 108 (1978), 155–174.

Posani, M. R. "Le didascalie delle comedie di Terenzio e la cronologia." *AttiAccad d'Italia* 7 (1942), 247–280.

———. "Osservazioni su alcuni passi dei prologhi Terenziani." *StudItalFilolClass* 37 (1965), 85–113.

Poucet, J. "Albe dans la tradition et l'histoire des origines de Rome." In *Hommages à Josef Veremans*, edited by F. Decreus and C. Deroux, 238–258. Brussels, 1986.

———. "La diffusion de la légende d'Énée en Italie Centrale et ses rapports avec celle de Romulus." *LEC* 57 (1989), 227–254.

———. "Énée et Lavinium. A propos d'un livre récent." *RevBelge* 61 (1983), 144–159.

———. "Le Latium protohistorique et archaique." *AntCl* 48 (1979), 177–220.

———. *Les origines de Rome*. Brussels, 1985.

Poulsen, F. "Die Römer der republikanischen Zeit und ihre Stellung zur Kunst." *Die Antike* 13 (1937), 125–150.

Préaux, J. "Caton et l'*Ars poetica*." *Latomus* 25 (1966), 710–725.

Prestianni Giallombardo, A. M. "Lucio Mummio, Zeus e Filippo II." *AnnPisa* 12 (1982), 513–532.

Ramage, E. S., D. L. Sigsbee, and S. C. Fredericks. *Roman Satirists and Their Satire*. Park Ridge, N.J., 1974.

Raschke, W. J. "*Arma pro amico*—Lucilian Satire at the Crisis of the Roman Republic." *Hermes* 115 (1987), 299–318.

———. "The Chronology of the Early Books of Lucilius." *JRS* 69 (1979), 78–89.

———. "The Virtue of Lucilius." *Latomus* 49 (1990), 352–369.

Rawson, E. "Architecture and Sculpture: The Activities of the Cossutii." *PBSR* 43 (1975), 36–47.

———. *Intellectual Life in the Late Roman Republic*. London, 1985.

———. "Roman Tradition and the Greek World." In *Cambridge Ancient History*², VIII, 422–476. Cambridge, 1989.

Richard, J.-C. "Ennemis ou alliés? Les troyens et les aborigènes dans les *Origines* de Caton." In *Hommages à Robert Schilling*, edited by H. Zehnacker and G. Hentz, 403–412. Paris, 1983.

Richter, G. M. A. "The Origin of Verism in Roman Portraits." *JRS* 45 (1955), 39–46.

———. *Three Critical Periods in Greek Sculpture*. Oxford, 1951.

Richter, W. "Staat, Gesellschaft, und Dichtung in Rom im 3. und 2. Jahrhundert v. Chr." *Gymnasium* 69 (1962), 286–310.

———. "Who Made the Roman Portrait Statues—Greeks or Romans?" *Proc. Amer. Philos. Soc.* 95 (1951), 184–208.

Ridgway, B. S. *Roman Copies of Greek Sculpture: The Problem of the Originals*. Ann Arbor, Mich., 1984.

Rigsby, K. J. "Phocians in Sicily: Thucydides 6.2." *CQ* 37 (1987), 332–335.

Rizzo, F. P. *Studi ellenistico-romani*. Palermo, 1974.

Robinson, L. A. "The Personal Abuse in Lucilius' *Satires*." *CJ* 49 (1953), 31–35.

Rosenstein, N. "*Imperatores Victi*: The Case of C. Hostilius Mancinus." *CA* 5 (1986), 230–252.

Rossi, O. "De Catone Graecarum litterarum oppugnatore, Latinitatis acerrimo defensore." *Athenaeum* o.s. 10 (1922), 259–273.

Rubensohn, O. "Parische Künstler." *JdI* 50 (1935), 49–69.

Rudd, N. "Horace's Encounter with the Bore." *Phoenix* 15 (1961), 90–96.

———. *The Satires of Horace*. Cambridge, 1966.

———. *Themes in Roman Satire*. London, 1986.

Rumpf, A. "Die Entstehung des römischen Theaters." *MdI* 3 (1950), 40–50.

Sadurska, A. *Les Tables Iliaques*. Warsaw, 1964.

Salmon, E. T. "The *Coloniae Maritimae*." *Athenaeum* 41 (1963), 3–38.

———. *The Making of Roman Italy*. London, 1982.

———. *Samnium and the Samnites*. Cambridge, 1967.

Sandbach, F. H. "How Terence's *Hecyra* Failed." *CQ* 32 (1982), 134–135.

Sauerwein, I. *Die leges sumptuariae als römische Massnahme gegen den Sittenverfall*. Hamburg, 1970.

Saunders, C. "The Nature of Rome's Early Appraisal of Greek Culture." *CP* 39 (1944), 209–217.

———. "The Site of Dramatic Performances at Rome in the Times of Plautus and Terence." *TAPA* 44 (1913), 87–97.

Schauenberg, K. "Aeneas und Rom." *Gymnasium* 67 (1960), 176–191.

Schefold, K. *Der Alexander-Sarkophag*. Berlin, 1968.

Schilling, R. *La religion romaine de Vénus*. Paris, 1954.

Schlag, U. "Livius' Vorlage für den Bericht über die Megalesien im Jahre 194 v. Chr." *Historia* 17 (1968), 509–512.

Schmid, B. "Studien zu griechischen Ktesissagen." Diss., Freiburg, Switzerland, 1947.

Schmidt, P. L. "Catos *Epistula ad M. filium* und die Anfänge der römischen Briefliteratur." *Hermes* 100 (1972), 568–576.

Schmitt, H. H. *Rom und Rhodos*. Munich, 1957.

———. *Untersuchungen zur Geschichte Antiochos' des Grossen und seiner Zeit.* Wiesbaden, 1964.

Schröder, W. A. *M. Porcius Cato: Das erste Buch der "Origines."* Meisenheim am Glan, 1971.

Schur, W. "Griechische Traditionen von der Gründung Roms." *Klio* 17 (1921), 137–152.

Schweitzer, B. *Die Bildniskunst der römischen Republik.* Weimar, 1948.

Scullard, H. H. *Roman Politics, 220–150 B.C.*². Oxford, 1973.

Segal, E., and C. Moulton. "*Contortor Legum*: The Hero of the *Phormio.*" *RhM* 121 (1978), 276–288.

Shatzman, I. *Senatorial Wealth and Roman Politics.* Brussels, 1975.

Sherk, R. K. *Roman Documents from the Greek East.* Baltimore, 1969.

Shipp, G. B. "Greek in Plautus." *WS* 66 (1953), 105–112.

Skutsch, O. *The Annals of Quintus Ennius.* Oxford, 1985.

Smith, K. F. "*Mutare Pulices*: A Comment on Lucilius, Non. 351, M." *AJP* 22 (1901), 44–50.

Smith, P. M. "Aineiadai as Patrons of *Iliad* XX and the Homeric *Hymn to Aphrodite.*" *HSCP* 85 (1981), 17–58.

Smith, R. E. "The Aristocratic Epoch in Latin Literature." In *Essays in Roman Culture: The Todd Memorial Lectures,* edited by A. J. Dunston, 187–223. Toronto, 1976.

———. "Cato Censorius." *Greece and Rome* 9 (1940), 150–165.

———. "The Law of Libel at Rome." *CQ* 45 (1951), 169–179.

Smith, R. R. R. "Greeks, Foreigners, and Roman Republican Portraits." *JRS* 71 (1981), 24–38.

———. *Hellenistic Royal Portraits.* Oxford, 1988.

Solin, H. *Beiträge zum Kenntnis der griechischen Personennamen in Rom.* Helsinki, 1971.

Solmsen, F. "Aeneas Founded Rome with Odysseus." *HSCP* 90 (1986), 93–110.

Sommella, P. "Das Heroon des Aeneas und die Topographie des antiken Lavinium." *Gymnasium* 81 (1974), 283–297.

———. "Heroon di Enea a Lavinium: Recenti scavi a Pratica di Mare." *RendPontAcc* 44 (1971–72), 47–74.

Sordi, M. *I canali della propaganda nel mondo antico. ContrIstStorAnt.* Milan, 1976.

Stefani, E. "Gualdo Tadino: Scoperta fortuita di un sepolcro e di una fornace sopra l'acropoli di 'Tadinum.'" *NotSc* 11 (1935), 167–173.

Steingräber, S. "Zum Phänomen der etruskisch-italischen Votivköpfe." *MdI* 87 (1980), 215–253.

Stewart, A. *Attika: Studies in Athenian Sculpture of the Hellenistic Age.* London, 1979.

———. *Greek Sculpture.* New Haven, Conn., 1990.

———. "Hellenistic Art and the Coming of Rome." In *Hellenistic Art in the Walters Art Gallery,* edited by E. D. Reeder, 35–44. Baltimore, 1988.

Strasburger, H. "Der *Scipionenkreis.*" *Hermes* 94 (1966), 60–72.

———. "Zur Sage von der Gründung Roms." *SitzHeid* (1968), 1–43.

Strong, D. E. *Roman Art²*. London, 1988.

Suohlati, J. *The Roman Censors: A Study on Social Structure*. Helsinki, 1963.

Tamm, B. "Le temple des Muses à Rome." *Opuscula Romana* 3 (1961), 157–167.

Taylor, L. R. "The Opportunities for Dramatic Performances in the Time of Plautus and Terence." *TAPA* 68 (1937), 284–304.

———. *Roman Voting Assemblies*. Ann Arbor, Mich., 1966.

———. *The Voting Districts of the Roman Republic*. Rome, 1960.

Terzaghi, N. *Lucilio*. Turin, 1934.

Till, R. "Die Anerkennung literarischen Schaffens in Rom." *Neue Jahrbücher* 115 (1940), 161–174.

Timpe, D. "Le Origini di Catone e la storiografia latina." *MemAccadPatav* 83 (1970–71), 1–33.

Toohey, P. "Politics, Prejudice, and Trojan Genealogies: Varro, Hyginus, and Horace." *Arethusa* 17 (1984), 5–28.

Torelli, M. "Il donario di M. Fulvio nell' area di S. Omobono." *Studi di Topografia Romana* 5 (1968), 71–75.

———. *Lavinio e Roma*. Rome, 1984.

———. *Typology and Structure of Roman Historical Reliefs*. Ann Arbor, Mich., 1982.

Touchais, G. "Chroniques des fouilles et découvertes archéologiques en Grèce en 1985." *BCH* 110 (1986), 671–761.

Toynbee, J. M. C. *Roman Historical Portraits*. London, 1978.

———. *Some Notes on Artists in the Roman World*. Brussels, 1951.

Van Rooy, C. A. *Studies in Classical Satire and Related Literary Theory*. Leiden, 1965.

Van Sickle, J. "The Elogia of the Cornelii Scipiones and the Origin of Epigram at Rome." *AJP* 108 (1987), 41–55.

Versnel, H. *Triumphus*. Leiden, 1970.

Vessberg, O. *Studien zur Kunstgeschichte der römischen Republik*. Lund, 1941.

Veyne, P. *Bread and Circuses: Historical Sociology and Political Pluralism*. London, 1990.

Viereck, P. *Sermo graecus*. Göttingen, 1888.

Vollenweider, M.-L. *Die Porträtgemmen der römischen Republik*. Mainz, 1974.

———. *Die Steinschneiderkunst und ihre Künstler in spätrepublikanischer und augusteischer Zeit*. Baden-Baden, 1966.

Von Bothmer, B. *Egyptian Sculpture of the Late Period, 700 B.C.–A.D. 100*. Brooklyn, N.Y., 1960.

Von Domaszewski, A. "Die Triumphstrasse auf dem Marsfelde." *Arch. v. Religionswiss.* 12 (1909), 67–82.

Von Graeve, V. *Der Alexandersarkophag von Sidon und seine Werkstatt*. Istambuler Forschungen, 28. Berlin, 1970.

Von Premerstein, A. "Lex Tappula." *Hermes* 39 (1904), 327–347.

Von Ungern-Sternberg, J. "Die Einführung spezieller Sitze für die Senatoren bei den Spielen (194 v. Chr.)." *Chiron* 5 (1975), 157–163.

Walbank, F. W. *A Historical Commentary on Polybius*, II, III. Oxford, 1967, 1979.

———. "Timaeus' Views on the Past." *SCI* 10 (1989–90), 41–54.

Wallace, R. W. "Hellenization and Roman Society in the Late 4th Century B.C.: A

Methodological Critique." In *Staat und Staatlichkeit in der frühen römischen Republik*, edited by W. Eder, 278–291. Stuttgart, 1990.

Wallace-Hadrill, A. "Greek Knowledge, Roman Power." *CP* 83 (1988), 224–233.

———. "Roman Arches and Greek Honours: The Language of Power at Rome." *PCPS* 36 (1990), 143–181.

Warde Fowler, W. *The Religious Experience of the Roman People.* London, 1911.

Wardman, A. *Rome's Debt to Greece.* London, 1976.

Warmington, E. H. *Remains of Early Latin.* Cambridge, Mass., 1938.

Waurick, G. "Kunstraub der Römer: Untersuchungen zu seinen Anfängen anhand der Inschriften." *JbRGZ* 22 (1975), 1–46.

Weber, E. "Die trojanische Abstammung der Römer als politisches Argument." *WS* 85 (1972), 213–225.

Weber, H. "Sur l'art du portrait à l'époque hellénistique tardive en Grèce et en Italie." *Ktema* 1 (1976), 113–127.

Weinstock, S. "Penates." *RE* 19.1 (1937), 428–440.

———. "Two Archaic Inscriptions from Latium." *JRS* 50 (1960), 112–118.

Werner, R. *Der Beginn der römischen Republik.* Munich, 1963.

West, A. B. "Lucilian Genealogy." *AJP* 49 (1928), 240–252.

West, M. L. *Hesiod: Theogony.* Oxford, 1966.

West, S. "Lycophron Italicised." *JHS* 104 (1984), 127–151.

———. "Notes on the Text of Lycophron." *CQ* 33 (1983), 114–135.

Wikander, O. "Caius Hostilius Mancinus and the *Foedus Numantinum.*" *Opuscula Romana* 11 (1976), 85–104.

Wikén, E. *Die Kunde der Hellenen von dem Lande und den Völkern der Apenninenhalbinsel bis 300 v. Chr.* Lund, 1937.

Williams, G. "Phases in Political Patronage of Literature in Rome." In *Literary and Artistic Patronage in Ancient Rome*, edited by B. Gold, 28–49. Austin, Tex., 1982.

Wiseman, T. P. "The Circus Flaminius." *PBSR* 42 (1974), 3–26.

———. "Literary Genealogies in Late-Republican Rome." *Greece and Rome* 21 (1974), 153–164.

———. "Roman Legend and Oral Tradition." *JRS* 79 (1989), 129–137.

———. *Roman Studies, Literary and Historical.* Liverpool, 1987.

Wissowa, G. *Religion und Kultus der Römer.* Munich, 1902.

Woodford, S., and M. Loudon. "Two Trojan Themes: The Iconography of Ajax Carrying the Body of Achilles and of Aeneas Carrying Anchises in Black Figure Vase Painting." *AJA* 84 (1980), 25–40.

Wright, F. W. *Cicero and the Theater.* Smith College Class. Stud., 11. Northampton, Mass., 1931.

Wright, J. *Dancing in Chains: The Stylistic Unity of the Commoedia Palliata.* Rome, 1974.

Zadoks-Josephus Jitta, A. *Ancestral Portraiture in Rome and the Art of the Last Century of the Republic.* Amsterdam, 1932.

Zanker, P. "Grabreliefs römischer Freigelassener." *JdI* 90 (1975), 267–315.

———. *The Power of Images in the Age of Augustus.* Ann Arbor, Mich., 1988.

———. "Zur Bildnisrepräsentation führender Männer in mittelitalischen und campanischen Städten zur Zeit der späten Republik und der julisch-claudischen Kaiser." In *Les "bourgeoisies" municipales italiennes aux IIe et Ier siècles av. J.C.*, Coll. Intern. Inst. Franc. de Naples, 251–266. Paris, 1983.

——."Zur Rezeption des hellenistischen Individualporträts in Rom und in den italischen Städten." In *Hellenismus in Mittelitalien II*, edited by P. Zanker, 581–619. Göttingen, 1976.

Zetzel, J. E. G. "Cicero and the Scipionic Circle." *HSCP* 76 (1972), 173–179.

Zevi, F. "L'identificazione del tempio di Marte *in circo* e altre osservazioni." In *L'Italie préromaine et la Rome républicaine: Mélanges offerts à Jacques Heurgon*, II, 1047–1066. Rome, 1976.

——. "Note sulla leggenda di Enea in Italia." In *Gli Etruschi e Roma*, edited by G. Colonna et al., 145–158. Rome, 1981.

Ziegler, K. "Lykophron." *RE* 13.2 (1927), 2316–2381.

Ziolkowski, A. "Mummius' Temple of Hercules Victor and the Round Temple on the Tiber." *Phoenix* 42 (1988), 309–333.

Zucchelli, B. *L'indipendenza di Lucilio.* Istituto di lingua e letteratura latina, Università di Parma, 1977.

INDEX

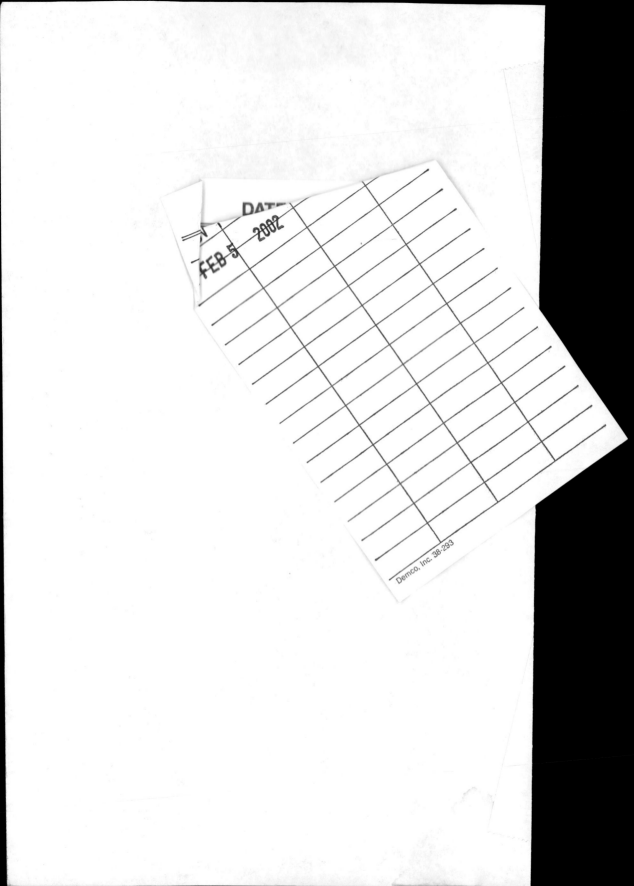

DATE

FEB 5   2002

Demco, Inc. 38-293